Bluetooth™
Connect Without Cables
Second Edition

Jennifer Bray
Charles F Sturman

Prentice Hall PTR
Upper Saddle River,
www.phptr.com

3-066106-6

90000

0 661066

Library of Congress Cataloging-in-Publication Data

Bray, Jennifer.
  Bluetooth 1.1: connect without cables/Jennifer Bray, Charles Sturman.—2nd ed.
    p.cm.
  Includes bibliographical references and index.
  ISBN 0-13-066106-6
    1. Bluetooth technology. 2. Telecommunication—Equipment and supplies. 3. Computer
network protocols. I. Sturman, Charles F. II. Title.

TK5103.3 .B72 2002
004.6'2—dc21   2001054573

Publisher: Bernard Goodwin
Editorial Assistant: Michelle Vincenti
Marketing Manager: Dan DePasquale
International Product Manager: Mike Vaccaro
Manufacturing Manager: Alexis Heydt-Long
Cover Design: Talar Agasyan-Boorujy
Cover Design Director: Jerry Votta
Cover Photograph: Charles F Sturman
Compositor/Production Services: Pine Tree Composition, Inc.

© 2002, 2001 by Prentice Hall PTR
Prentice-Hall, Inc.
Upper Saddle River, NJ 07458

BLUETOOTH is a trademark owned by Bluetooth SIG, Inc., USA.

All products or services mentioned in this book are the trademarks or service marks of their respective companies or organizations.

Some material in Chapter 10 © ETSI 1999, TS 101 369 v3 is the property of ETSI. Further use, modification, redistribution is strictly prohibited and must be the subject of another Copyright Authorisation. The above-mentioned standard may be obtained from the ETSI Publication Office, publications@etsi.fr, Tel: +33 (0)4 92 94 42 41 or downloaded from the website at http://www.etsi.org/eds/eds.htm

Printed in the United States of America
10 9 8 7 6 5 4 3 2 1

ISBN 0-13-066106-6

Pearson Education Ltd., *London*
Pearson Education Australia Pty, Limited, *Sydney*
Pearson Education Singapore, Pte. Ltd,
Pearson Education North Asia Ltd. *Hong Kong*
Pearson Education Canada, Ltd., *Toronto*
Pearson Educación de Mexico, S.A. de C.V.
Pearson Education—Japan, *Tokyo*
Pearson Education Malaysia, Pte. Ltd.

This book is dedicated to my mother Beryl,
who taught me to aim high and would now be so proud.

Charles

Contents

Protocol Stack Part 1—The Bluetooth Module

2   Antennas   25

3   Radio   32

4   Baseband   41

Protocol Stack Part 2—The Bluetooth Host

Protocol Stack Part 3—Cross Layer Functions

Applications—The Bluetooth Profiles

19   Foundation Profiles

20   Draft Post – Foundation Profiles   388

Test and Qualification

Bluetooth in Context

Foreword to the Second Edition

It is often said that a single radio transceiver is uninteresting; two transceivers that exchange useful information become interesting. BLUETOOTH™ wireless technology promises to make the world a very, very interesting place.

The vision of a world where you can Connect Without Cables that Jenny and Charles described in their original edition is now becoming a reality. Early products began to show up on store shelves soon after the publication of their book. Part of the process of creating a new technology is developing these early products to validate the thousands and thousands of work days put into making it a reality. Many things must be confirmed when a new technology is rolled out.

There was a confirmation that the very talented pool of BLUETOOTH wireless technology engineers got almost everything right with version 1.0. As could be expected, there were some things that seemed OK on paper that did not work optimally when translated into hardware and software. A few things were omitted; there were some instances of vagueness in the text of the original specification; and there were a few outright errors. These deficiencies manifested themselves in interoperability problems. Version 1.1 was published in early 2001 to address those issues.

As I implied above, Jenny and Charles' original work predated the current version of the BLUETOOTH specifications. Although much of their previous writing was still vital and valid, it was important to update their work. Updating they have done—and more. There is an added section on the new application profiles that are being developed.

These profiles are becoming available for companies to create new and exciting products. Many of these new developments are being introduced to the general public for the first time with this text.

In addition to the technology being refined, so has the organization behind it. Since the original publication of this book the Bluetooth Special Interest Group—often referred to as the SIG—has undergone significant changes. The SIG started out as a loose confederation of companies with the idea of creating a low-cost, easy-to-use method of eliminating wire between personal devices. It is now an independent corporation with many, many member companies.

Participation by this expanded membership in Working Groups, Study Groups, Expert Groups, and oversight committees is invaluable. I encourage the readers of this book to consider joining—and becoming active in—Bluetooth SIG, Inc. I look for the membership to make even more important contributions in the future.

Member companies help to define the expansion and evolution of Bluetooth wireless technology. The SIG has established a set of rules and procedures that ensure the products created today will continue to work with the products created in the future. The technology the authors describe here is the baseline for all future BLUETOOTH work.

In describing the baseline technology, Jenny and Charles move from overview to technical details in a seamless transition. Establishing context and moving to descriptions of a sophisticated protocol stack is not easy. Doing it in a clear, concise, and easy to use fashion is next to impossible. These two authors have done just that.

Tom Siep
General Manager
Bluetooth SIG, Inc.

Garland, Texas
November 2001

Foreword to the First Edition

Many people have envisioned wireless devices effortlessly communicating with one another. In this panacea, devices of all types begin to correspond just by coming within proximity of each other. Imagine one device fulfilling the needs of another, and ultimately serving the needs of mankind. Although Bluetooth wireless technology began as a simple, "get rid of the cables" concept, it has come to embody the hopes and dreams of many visionaries who feel that this may be the technology that will allow us to fulfill at least a portion of these dreams.

Bluetooth: Connect Without Cables is an important book. Indeed, there is a very good chance it will become required reading for anyone who is considering the use of Bluetooth wireless technology in their designs or is looking to gain a complete understanding of this technology.

As we have learned from the past, the simpler a device is for its user, the more complex it is to its designer. Since Bluetooth wireless technology is targeted at non-technical consumers, it must be "transparent to the user," both practically and literally. This is a daunting task for a designer, but even more daunting was the task of the individuals that drafted the Bluetooth specification. Although they did a good job at defining the specifications, understanding these in their raw form can be confusing and time consuming.

It's at this point that *Bluetooth: Connect Without Cables* takes over. This book provides a clear and concise interpretation of the Bluetooth specifications, which are provided in a step by step tutorial format. In addition to quickly gaining an understanding of the technology and its capabilities, the authors provide additional insights, which will assist in resolving issues that are hinted at in the specification, but certainly not discussed. In fact, the authors have endeavored to touch on every aspect of Bluetooth, from the specification and its shortcomings to enhancements that may be required, implementation concepts and issues, health concerns, competing and associated technologies, the match between technology push and market pull, and a discussion on accounting management issues.

Bluetooth: Connect Without Cables provides a complete tutorial of the technology, beginning with the antenna, through the protocol stack and its interfaces, to the applications and user interfaces that drive them. At each level, you will be presented with an easy to understand discussion in which the authors provide invaluable insight. Discussions include: timing requirements, differences between specification recommendations and actual implementations, as well as workarounds to their shortcomings, and suggested methods for selecting various options provided in the specification.

The authors have not only provided suggestions for improvements to the specification, such as increasing the length of the preamble, but have also openly shared their expertise. As an example, the authors have devoted an entire chapter to the utilization of a Device and Security Manager module. This level of insight is normally held in reserve and can only be obtained after spending enormous amounts of money in research or through the utilization of customized consulting firms.

To aid in the usability of this book, the authors have included extensive graphics and numerous examples. In addition, they have broken each main segment of the technology into its own chapter. An extremely comprehensive glossary is found in the back of the book.

By the time you complete your reading, you will have a full understanding of Bluetooth wireless technology, including how HCI commands are used, what people are doing about things that have been removed from earlier versions of the specification, when to use different modes, and the issues you may run into when implementing this robust technology.

Joe Mendolia
Computer Access Technology Corporation

Preface to the Second Edition

A year later, and another version of the Bluetooth specification released, the Bluetooth World has moved on far enough to justify a second edition of this book. Whilst updating for version 1.1 we've also taken the opportunity to correct a few errors that crept into the first edition, thanks to Don Felton, Bill Saltzstein, Klaus Mehle, Steve Singer, Simon Morris, and everyone else who provided us with errata.

Each section of the book has been updated with information on version 1.1 of the Bluetooth specification. Many of the changes have just been clarifications, but here and there functionality has been altered and improved. Where 1.0b and 1.1 are different we have identified the changes, and where relevant included notes on backwards compatibility.

For those of you who want a summary of the changes there is an appendix with details on the critical errata which led to version 1.1. This appendix tells you in one place what is different, and why it was altered.

Of course as the specification progresses, so does the rest of the community of Bluetooth users. In the past year many new products and components have qualified, and the qualification program itself has matured. Real products have come on the market, and we're starting to see Bluetooth technology in use for real. To reflect those developments you'll find the section on Bluetooth in Context has changed.

We've reached version 1.1, but still more progress is being made in many Bluetooth SIG working groups to bring out a new generation of profiles, and to enhance the core Bluetooth specification. As we were updating the book for version 1.1 some draft profiles were put on public release. These profiles open up new applications for Bluetooth devices, so to cover them we've added a whole new section to the book called "Applications—The Bluetooth Profiles". The draft profiles may change slightly before being formally adopted, and more new profiles are due for public release soon. Watch the book's companion web site http://www.phptr.com/bluetooth/bray/index.html for more details: we'll publish these after information is made available in public.

Preface to the First Edition

This book came about from a conversation in the Hotel Mercure bar in Brussels, Belgium. We had just finished the first day of client training in our Bluetooth solution, and hadn't said a single word about our implementation yet! Why? Well, Bluetooth was so new that nobody knew much about it, there were no textbooks, no courses, nothing but a thick specification document and a few white papers. So before we could begin to explain the fine details of what we'd done, we had to spend a day explaining the Bluetooth specification. After the first beer, we thought somebody ought to write a book about Bluetooth; after the second beer, we thought we should do it; after the last beer, we had a contents page.

Why the title? Well, "Connect Without Cables" is basically what Bluetooth started out doing. It's a short range wireless communication system, and the word "wireless" pretty much says it all. The first applications people came up with were all about throwing away the clutter of cables that plagues modern portable devices—Bluetooth took away the cable dangling from a headset, removed the clutter of wires at the back of a PC, and let a phone talk to a PDA without needing a cable that took up more pocket space than either device. Now there are more imaginative uses than straight cable replacement, from small wireless office networks to the much hyped Personal Area Network, or PAN. But the basic functionality that Bluetooth provides is still the same: connection without cables.

During the last year or so, we have seen a Bluetooth system design evolve from abstract idea to evaluation board. Along the way, we struggled to understand the Bluetooth specification. Some parts of it don't make sense until you've read later parts, some parts don't make sense until you've tried them out, and some of the parts we started with will never make sense and have since been corrected. The specification is in a much better state than the preliminary versions we started with, but like all such things, it's still not an easy read. So this book aims to provide people working with Bluetooth an easier introduction than the one we had.

A new version of the Bluetooth specification (version 1.1) is due to be published during the 4th quarter of 2000. In order to keep this text consistent, we only consider the existing version 1.0B specification except for one or two proposed corrections for v1.1, which are especially worth mentioning here. Although these are mostly minor improvements and clarifications to the existing 1.0B specification, it is important for the reader to keep abreast of any revisions particularly since there may well be other refinements before the major evolution which Bluetooth 2.0 will represent. To facilitate this, there is a companion Website to accompany *Bluetooth: Connect Without Cables* where we will place any errata and useful updates to the text as Bluetooth evolves.

Acknowledgments

Writing a book such as this while holding down a "day job" is not a trivial exercise, and there are a number of people whose help and assistance have made it possible. First and foremost, we would like to thank Heather and Don for all their support and understanding; putting up with late nights, lost weekends, and sheets of paper strewn around the house!

We would also like to thank:

TTP Communications for allowing us to write the book, and everyone in the "Toothbrush" team for their hard work without which this book would not have been possible.

Bernard, Lisa, and the staff at Prentice Hall for bearing with us in our first foray into the publishing world, and Patty at Pine Tree Composition for being so helpful with revisions.

Larry Taylor, for originally explaining what a WLAN is!

Mike Witherspoon of Personal Development Alliance for sowing the seeds of the can-do attitude in the first place.

Tina and Steve for the cooked breakfasts one very long bank holiday weekend.

Thanks are also due to:

gigaAnt (*www.gigaAnt.com*), Alcatel Microelectonics (*www.alcatel.com*), 3Com (*www.3com.com*), TTP Communications (*www.ttpcom.com*), and Ericsson (*www.ericsson.com*) for providing photographic material and technical information. Antenova (*www.antenova.com*) for providing a photograph of their ceramic antenna; Hewlett-Packard (*www.hp.com*) for providing a photograph of their Deskjet 995 printer; Logitech for providing a photograph of their cordless mouse; Parrot (*www.say-parrot.com*) for providing a photograph of their CK3000 handsfree car kit; and CSR (*www.csr.com*) for providing a photograph of their BlueCore chip.

Introduction

Bluetooth is set to be the fastest growing technology since the Internet or the cellular phone, with forecasts of 200M devices shipped in 2001 and a total component market of $1 billion in the same year. Incredible, especially considering that the specification providing this worldwide industry standard only saw its first public outing in mid 1998. Although Bluetooth represents a very simple proposition, obviating the need for connectivity via physical wires, this is itself the powerful added value of Bluetooth. Connectivity becomes simple, seamless, and intuitive. However, like many things, in order to deliver an apparently simple and transparent function to the user requires complexity and much work behind the scenes.

The Bluetooth system is both complex and full-featured, with many components and layers of abstraction. As hinted at already, many people are likely to come into contact with Bluetooth from various angles: technology development, from commercial exploitation, or as users, and this book is intended to provide something for each of these different groups. The text is written to allow the reader to obtain the level of information required. As such, it should appeal to everyone, from application developers looking to understand what their applications must interface to, to systems designers wishing to evaluate how and what Bluetooth can add to their products, to managers and marketers wishing to obtain an overview of the Bluetooth space.

We start out with an overview of Bluetooth, which summarises many of the areas covered later on in detail. The overview can be read as an introduction to the topics which follow, or as a standalone introduction to Bluetooth for the reader who requires much less detail. The book then goes on to explain the technical operation of the Bluetooth system in detail, where it is intended to be a much easier read and a more accessible text than any formal specification could ever be.

We work our way up the protocol stack from antennas and radios to host applications, and also look at the wider implications of how one might set about using or designing in Bluetooth technology. The book also looks at the higher level issues of applications and host system considerations before moving on to discuss the potential market for Bluetooth technology and Bluetooth enabled products as well as other related or even competing technologies which are in existence. We then look to the future and what one might expect to see happening in the fast moving arena of wireless technology over the next few years.

To make the text easier to use as a reference and to allow readers to access the information they require, the book is split into five distinct sections as follows:

- Protocol Stack Part 1—The Bluetooth Module
  These chapters describe the lower parts of the system from the radio up to the host interface.
- Protocol Stack Part 2—The Bluetooth Host
  Higher parts of the system which would typically exist on or in a host system that is "Bluetooth Enabled" are described in these chapters.
- Protocol Stack Part 3—Cross Layer Functions
  This part covers aspects and functions of Bluetooth that cross over the boundaries between different layers in the stack.
- Test and Qualification
  Production testing and conformance or type approval are explained in this section.
- Bluetooth in Context
  This section addresses product implementation and commercial issues, including an analysis of the Bluetooth market potential and time frame.

Jargon and acronyms can often be barriers to understanding material which would otherwise be straightforward, and so we have explained terms as we use them in the text. To allow the text to be used as a reference, however, we have also provided a full glossary of acronyms and terms. We hope this will prove useful, not just when reading this book, but also when reading other material on Bluetooth.

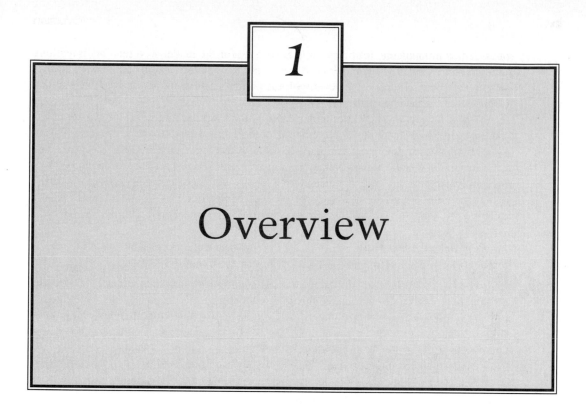

Overview

Bluetooth has been the subject of much hype and media attention over the last couple of years. As various manufacturers prepare to launch products using Bluetooth technology, an unsuspecting public is about to be catapulted into the next stage of the information technology revolution.

Bluetooth is a low cost, low power, short range radio technology, originally developed as a cable replacement to connect devices such as mobile phone handsets, headsets, and portable computers. This in itself sounds relatively innocuous; however, by enabling standardised wireless communications between any electrical devices, Bluetooth has created the notion of a Personal Area Network (PAN), a kind of close range wireless network that looks set to revolutionise the way people interact with the information technology landscape around them.

No longer do people need to connect, plug into, install, enable, or configure anything to anything else. Through a ubiquitous standardised communications subsystem, devices will communicate seamlessly. One does not need to know where one's cellular phone is, or even if it is switched on. As soon as the Web browser appears on the mobile computer screen, a link is established with the phone the Internet Service Provider is connected to, and the user is surfing the Web.

The Bluetooth specification is an open, global specification defining the complete system from the radio right up to the application level. The protocol stack is usually implemented partly in hardware and partly as software running on a microprocessor, with different implementations partitioning the functionality between hardware and software in different ways.

1.1   BLUETOOTH'S ORIGINS

Version 1.0 of the Bluetooth specification came out in 1999, but Bluetooth started five years earlier, in 1994, when Ericsson Mobile Communications began a study to examine alternatives to the cables that linked its mobile phones with accessories. The study looked at using radio links. Radio isn't directional, and it doesn't need line of sight, so it has obvious advantages over the infra-red links previously used between handsets and devices. There were many requirements for the study, including handling both speech and data, so that it could connect phones to both headsets and computing devices.

Out of this study was born the specification for Bluetooth wireless technology. The specification is named after Harald Blatand (Blatand is Danish for Bluetooth), Harald was a tenth-century Danish Viking king who united and controlled Denmark and Norway. The name was adopted because Bluetooth wireless technology is expected to unify the telecommunications and computing industries.

1.2   THE BLUETOOTH SIG

The Bluetooth Special Interest Group (SIG) is a group of companies working together to promote and define the Bluetooth specification. The Bluetooth SIG was founded in February 1998 by the following group of core promoters:

- Ericsson Mobile Communications AB.
- Intel Corp.
- IBM Corp.
- Toshiba Corp.
- Nokia Mobile Phones.

In May 1998, the core promoters publicly announced the global SIG and invited other companies to join the SIG as Bluetooth adopters in return for a commitment to support the Bluetooth specification. The core promoters published version 1.0 of the Bluetooth specification in July 1999, on the Bluetooth Web site, http://www.bluetooth.com. In December 1999, the Bluetooth core promoters group enlarged with the addition of four more major companies:

- Microsoft.
- Lucent.
- 3COM.
- Motorola.

1.2.1   Joining the Bluetooth SIG

Any incorporated company willing to sign the Bluetooth SIG membership agreement can join the SIG as a Bluetooth adopter company. To join the SIG, companies simply fill in a form on the Bluetooth Web site, www.bluetooth.com. This form commits SIG members to contributing any key technologies which are needed to implement Bluetooth.

   This commitment to share technology means that Bluetooth SIG member companies who put their products through Bluetooth qualification are granted a free license to build products using the Bluetooth wireless technology. The license is important because there are patents required to implement Bluetooth; companies that do not sign the Bluetooth adopter's agreement will not be entitled to use the technology. This offer proved so attractive that by April 2000, the SIG membership had grown to 1,790 members.

   In addition to getting a free license to patents needed to implement Bluetooth wireless technology, Bluetooth SIG members also have permission to use the Bluetooth brand. There are restrictions on the use of the brand, and these are set out in the Bluetooth brand book. The trademark may only be used on products which prove they are correctly following the Bluetooth specification by completing the Bluetooth qualification program (a testing process).

   To get the Bluetooth figure mark and instructions on how to use it, companies sign the Bluetooth trademark agreement, also available on www.bluetooth.com. Questions on the Bluetooth trademark can be emailed to brand.manager@Bluetooth.com.

1.2.2   Bluetooth SIG Organisation

At the head of the Bluetooth SIG is the program management board. This board oversees the operations of a number of other groups as shown in Figure 1–1.

   The main work of defining the specification is done by the technical working groups. Adopter companies can apply to become associate members of the SIG; they may then apply to join working groups and hence contribute directly to the forming of Bluetooth specifications.

   Sitting on the technical working groups is quite time-consuming, and so many companies with valid comments on the specification do not have the resources to sit on the working groups. These companies can pass comments via email to the writers of the standard and can also participate in an online discussion forum on the Bluetooth Web site.

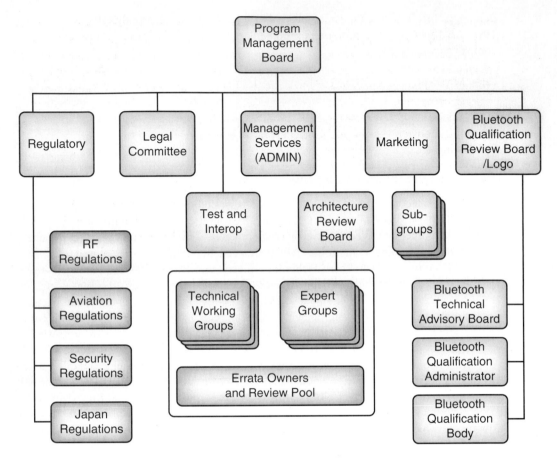

Figure 1–1   Organisation of the Bluetooth SIG.

1.3   AIMS

Why should a group with such diverse interests as the Bluetooth promoters cooperate? Basically, because it's good for their businesses. The members of the Bluetooth promoters group all stand to gain something from mobile devices communicating better, whether by selling devices that have enhanced functionality or by selling the extra software that people will need once they can more easily access information on the move.

The reasons for making the Bluetooth specification freely available to anyone who cares to sign an adopter's agreement are basically the same. The Bluetooth promoters group has made Bluetooth an open specification, rather than keeping it restricted and proprietary, because consumers are more likely to adopt a technology which can be bought from many manufacturers than one which is just limited to a select few. Wide acceptance among consumers is likely to lead to a larger overall market for Bluetooth devices. So the promoters will gain from more companies becoming involved in the Bluetooth SIG.

The aim of the Bluetooth specification is basically to sell more of the core promoters' products. This will happen because Bluetooth will make their products more useful by improving communications between them. Before the advent of Bluetooth, telecommunications and computing devices were usually connected by cables, which were easily broken or lost. Cables are also awkward to carry around. The Bluetooth specification aimed to ease communication between mobile devices by providing a cable replacement.

Being a cable replacement technology imposes several requirements. If Bluetooth technology is to replace cables, it can't be much more expensive than a cable or nobody will buy it. At the time of writing, a data cable for a cellular mobile phone was about $10. Allocate half the cost of the cable to each end of the link and it's obvious that for a cable replacement technology to be attractive on purely financial grounds, each unit should cost no more than $5. So, the two ends of the link should cost the same as the cable they replace.

Because Bluetooth technology is designed for mobile devices, it must be able to run on batteries. So, it must be very low power, and should run on low voltages. It must also be lightweight and small enough not to intrude on the design of compact mobile devices such as cellular phones, headsets, and PDAs.

It must be as easy and convenient to use as plugging in a cable, and it must be as reliable as the cable it replaces. Because it is a wireless technology, to be reliable, Bluetooth must also be resilient. Reliability means it works overall; resilience means that it can cope with errors.

So, Bluetooth aims to be widely available, inexpensive, convenient, easy to use, reliable, small, and low power. If Bluetooth achieves all these goals, it will be incredibly good for the businesses involved with it.

1.4   THE PROTOCOL STACK

A key feature of the Bluetooth specification is that it aims to allow devices from lots of different manufacturers to work with one another. To this end, Bluetooth does not just define a radio system, it also defines a software stack to enable applications to find other Bluetooth devices in the area, discover what services they can offer, and use those services.

The Bluetooth stack is defined as a series of layers, though there are some features which cross several layers.

Every block in Figure 1–2 corresponds to a chapter in the core Bluetooth specification. The core specification also has three chapters on test and qualification:

- Bluetooth Test Mode.
- Bluetooth Compliance Requirements.
- Test Control Interface.

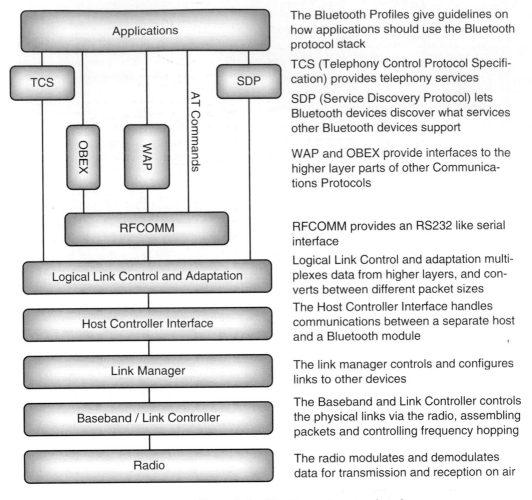

The Bluetooth Profiles give guidelines on how applications should use the Bluetooth protocol stack

TCS (Telephony Control Protocol Specification) provides telephony services

SDP (Service Discovery Protocol) lets Bluetooth devices discover what services other Bluetooth devices support

WAP and OBEX provide interfaces to the higher layer parts of other Communications Protocols

RFCOMM provides an RS232 like serial interface

Logical Link Control and adaptation multiplexes data from higher layers, and converts between different packet sizes

The Host Controller Interface handles communications between a separate host and a Bluetooth module

The link manager controls and configures links to other devices

The Baseband and Link Controller controls the physical links via the radio, assembling packets and controlling frequency hopping

The radio modulates and demodulates data for transmission and reception on air

Figure 1–2   The Bluetooth protocol stack.

The Bluetooth specification encompasses more than just the core specification. There are also profiles which give details of how applications should use the Bluetooth protocol stack, and a brand book which explains how the Bluetooth brand should be used.

1.4.1   The OSI Reference Model

Figure 1–3 shows the familiar Open Systems Interconnect (OSI) standard reference model for communications protocol stacks. Although Bluetooth does not exactly match the model, it is a useful exercise to relate the different parts of the Bluetooth stack to the vari-

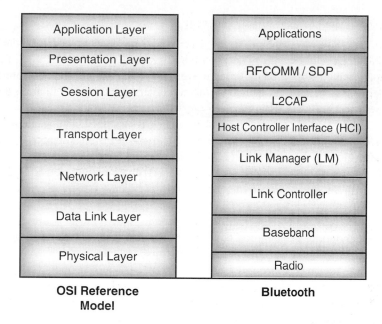

Figure 1–3 OSI reference model and Bluetooth.

ous parts of the model. Since the reference model is an ideal, well-partitioned stack, the comparison serves to highlight the division of responsibility in the Bluetooth stack.

The Physical Layer is responsible for the electrical interface to the communications media, including modulation and channel coding. It thus covers the radio and part of the baseband.

The Data Link Layer is responsible for transmission, framing, and error control over a particular link, and as such, overlaps the link controller task and the control end of the baseband, including error checking and correction.

From now on, it gets a little less clear. The Network Layer is responsible for data transfer across the network, independent of the media and specific topology of the network. This encompasses the higher end of the link controller, setting up and maintaining multiple links, and also covering most of the Link Manager (LM) task. The Transport Layer is responsible for the reliability and multiplexing of data transfer across the network to the level provided by the application, and thus overlaps at the high end of the LM and covers the Host Controller Interface (HCI), which provides the actual data transport mechanisms.

The Session Layer provides the management and data flow control services, which are covered by L2CAP and the lower ends of RFCOMM/SDP. The Presentation Layer provides a common representation for Application Layer data by adding service structure to the units of data, which is the main task of RFCOMM/SDP. Finally, the Application Layer is responsible for managing communications between host applications.

1.4.2   The Physical Layer

Bluetooth devices operate at 2.4 GHz in the globally available, licence-free ISM band. This band is reserved for general use by Industrial, Scientific, and Medical (ISM) applications, which obey a basic set of power and spectral emission and interference specifications. This means that Bluetooth has to be very robust, as there are a great many existing users and polluters of this shared spectrum.

The operating band is divided into 1 MHz-spaced channels, each signalling data at 1 Megasymbol per second so as to obtain the maximum available channel bandwidth. With the chosen modulation scheme of GFSK (Gaussian Frequency Shift Keying), this equates to 1 Mb/s. Using GFSK, a binary 1 gives rise to a positive frequency deviation from the nominal carrier frequency, while a binary 0 gives rise to a negative frequency deviation.

After each packet, both devices retune their radio to a different frequency, effectively hopping from radio channel to radio channel (FHSS—frequency hopping spread spectrum). In this way, Bluetooth devices use the whole of the available ISM band and if a transmission is compromised by interference on one channel, the retransmission will always be on a different (hopefully clear) channel. Each Bluetooth time slot lasts 625 microseconds, and, generally, devices hop once per packet, which will be every slot, every 3 slots, or every 5 slots.

Designed for low-powered portable applications, the radio power must be minimised. Three different power classes are defined, which provide operation ranges of approximately 10 m, 20 m, and 100 m; the lowest power gives up to 10 m range, the highest up to 100 m.

1.4.3   Masters, Slaves, Slots, and Frequency Hopping

If devices are to hop to new frequencies after each packet, they must all agree on the sequence of frequencies they will use. Bluetooth devices can operate in two modes: as a Master or as a Slave. It is the Master that sets the frequency hopping sequence. Slaves synchronise to the Master in time and frequency by following the Master's hopping sequence.

Every Bluetooth device has a unique Bluetooth device address and a Bluetooth clock. The baseband part of the Bluetooth specification describes an algorithm which can calculate a frequency hop sequence from a Bluetooth device address and a Bluetooth clock. When Slaves connect to a Master, they are told the Bluetooth device address and clock of the Master. They then use this to calculate the frequency hop sequence. Because all Slaves use the Master's clock and address, all are synchronised to the Master's frequency hop sequence.

In addition to controlling the frequency hop sequence, the Master controls when devices are allowed to transmit. The Master allows Slaves to transmit by allocating slots for voice traffic or data traffic. In data traffic slots, the Slaves are only allowed to transmit when replying to a transmission to them by the Master. In voice traffic slots, Slaves are required to transmit regularly in reserved slots whether or not they are replying to the Master.

Figure 1–4 Point to point and point to multipoint piconets.

The Master controls how the total available bandwidth is divided among the Slaves by deciding when and how often to communicate with each Slave. The number of time slots each device gets depends on its data transfer requirements. The system of dividing time slots among multiple devices is called Time Division Multiplexing (TDM).

1.4.4 Piconets and Scatternets

A collection of Slave devices operating together with one common Master is referred to as a piconet (see Figure 1–4). All devices on a piconet follow the frequency hopping sequence and timing of the Master.

In Figure 1–4, the piconet on the left with only one Slave illustrates a point to point connection. The piconet on the right with three Slaves talking to the Master illustrates a point to multipoint connection. The Slaves in a piconet only have links to the Master; there are no direct links between Slaves in a piconet.

The specification limits the number of Slaves in a piconet to seven, with each Slave only communicating with the shared Master. However, a larger coverage area or a greater number of network members may be realized by linking piconets into a scatternet, where some devices are members of more than one piconet (see Figure 1–5).

When a device is present in more than one piconet, it must time-share, spending a few slots on one piconet and a few slots on the other. On the left in Figure 1–5 is a

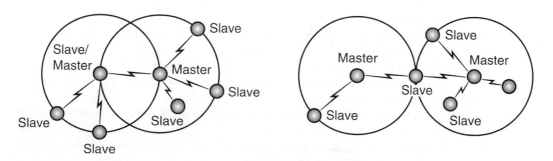

Figure 1–5 Scatternets.

scatternet where one device is a Slave in one piconet and a Master in another. On the right is a scatternet where one device is a Slave in two piconets. It is not possible to have a device which is a Master of two different piconets, since all Slaves in a piconet are synchronised to the Master's hop sequence. By definition, all devices with the same Master must be on the same piconet.

In addition to the various sources of interference mentioned already, a major source of interference for Bluetooth devices will clearly be other Bluetooth devices. Although devices sharing a piconet will be synchronised to avoid each other, other unsynchronised piconets in the area will randomly collide on the same frequency. If there is a collision on a particular channel, those packets will be lost and subsequently retransmitted, or if voice, ignored. So, the more piconets in an area, the more retransmissions will be needed, causing data rates to fall. This is like having a conversation in a noisy room: the more people talking, the noisier it gets, and you have to start repeating yourself to get the point across.

This effect will happen if there are many independent piconets in one area, and it will also happen to scatternets, since the piconets making up the scatternet do not coordinate their frequency hopping.

1.4.5   Radio Power Classes

The Bluetooth specification allows for three different types of radio powers:

- Class 1 = 100mW (20 dBm).
- Class 2 = 2.5mW (4 dBm).
- Class 3 = 1mW (0 dBm).

These power classes allow Bluetooth devices to connect at different ranges. At the time of writing, most manufacturers are producing Class 3, low power, 1 mW radios. These can communicate for a maximum of around 30 feet (10 m). However, because things like bodies and furniture absorb microwaves, reception may not be reliable at the limit of this range. So, when using 1 mW radios, a more realistic figure for reliable operation in a normal room will probably be 5 m. This provides a low cost, low power communications solution which has plenty of range for a cable replacement technology.

Obviously, higher power radios have longer ranges. The maximum range for a Class 1, 100 mW radio is about 100 metres. There is also a minimum range for a Bluetooth connection. If radios are put too close together, some receivers may saturate, so a few Bluetooth radios may be unreliable on short link lengths (under 10 cm).

A 100 m link needs a high power Class 1 device at both ends, but it is possible to create piconets with a mixture of high and low power devices at different ranges. Figure 1–6 shows a mixture of high and low power devices in different piconets occupying an area.

This figure shows piconets which overlap each other. This is possible because each Master has its own frequency hopping sequence, so two piconets are unlikely to be on the same frequency at the same time. If they do meet on the same frequency, after the next

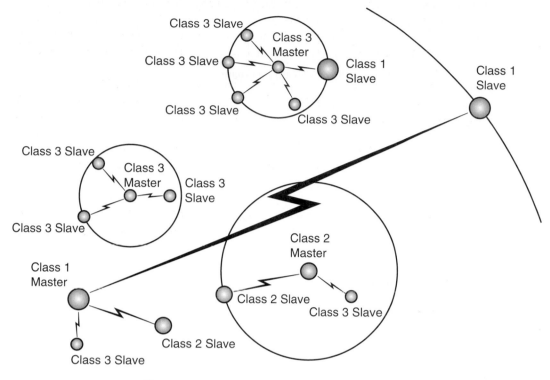

Figure 1–6 Piconets made up of different power class devices.

frequency hop they will not still be on the same frequency, so the data which may have been lost when the two piconets were on the same frequency can be resent.

1.4.6 Voice and Data Links

Bluetooth allows both time critical data communication such as that required for voice or audio, as well as high speed, time insensitive packet data communication. To carry such data, two different types of links are defined between any two devices. These are SCO (Synchronous Connection Oriented) links for voice communication and ACL (Asynchronous Connectionless) links for data communication.

ACL data packets are constructed from a 72-bit access code, a 54-bit packet header and a 16-bit CRC code, in addition to the payload data. There are a variety of packet types allowing different amounts of data to be sent. The packet which carries the largest data payload is a DH5 packet, which stretches over five slots. A DH5 packet can carry 339 bytes, or 2,712 bits of data. So, 2,858 bits are sent on air for 2,712 bits of information.

A DH5 packet uses up five slots, and the minimum length reply is one slot. Thus, the maximum baseband data rate in one direction is 723.2 kb/s. In this case, with 5-slot packets sent in one direction, the 1-slot packets sent in the other direction will only carry

57.6 kb/s, so this would be an asymmetric link with more data going in the direction using 5-slot packets. If 5-slot packets were sent in both directions, the data rate obtained would be 433.9 kb/s, quite a reduction from the 1 Mb/s data rate on air.

This overhead in both data encoding and frequency hopping is necessary mainly to provide a robust link since the ISM band is a shared resource with many devices, and indeed other communications standards and even noise sources, cohabiting in the same spectrum. In addition, to further reduce the interference problem in the spectrum, national radio regulations limit the power emission per unit time in the ISM band, making a frequency hopping scheme necessary to spread transmissions over the spectrum and over time.

The higher layers of the protocol stack also use up some of the bandwidth, so at the application level, the maximum data rate could be around 650 kb/s.

The SCO links work at 64 kb/s, and it is possible to have up to three full-duplex voice links at once or to mix voice and data. These voice channels give audio communication of a quality one would expect from a modern mobile cellular phone system such as GSM. As such, SCO links are not really suitable for delivering audio of a quality required for music listening.

One alternative to support music delivery is to use an ACL channel to carry audio. Raw CD-quality audio requires 1411.2 kb/s, but with suitable compression, such as MP3, which reduces this bit rate to around 128 kb/s, near CD-quality audio could easily be carried providing the time criticality of the audio was maintained.

1.5   SECURITY

The high speed, pseudo-random frequency hopping algorithm employed in Bluetooth makes it very difficult to listen in on a Bluetooth connection. In fact, the U.S. military considers a communications link using frequency hopping over 79 channels to be secure in itself.

For link encryption and authentication, Bluetooth uses a strong contemporary cipher algorithm available in the public domain called SAFER+, which generates 128-bit cipher keys from a 128-bit plain text input.

1.6   APPLICATIONS AND PROFILES

Looking back to Section 1.3, the Bluetooth specification aimed to produce convenient, reliable, resilient, cost effective, low power, short range voice and data communications. It has achieved all these, but what sort of applications does this enable?

At its most basic, Bluetooth wireless technology replaces a cable and untethers devices. This makes it suitable for short range connections between a variety of mobile devices such as:

- Mobile cellular phone to Public Switched Telephone Network (PSTN) through an access point.
- Mobile cellular phone to a notebook PC.

- Mobile cellular phone to a headset.
- LAN access points for laptops or palmtops.
- Notebook, palmtop, or other Internet access device to the Internet via a PSTN access point or access module.
- Communication between laptops and palmtops.

In addition to the core specification, which defines the Bluetooth wireless communications protocol, the Bluetooth specification includes a profiles document. Each profile describes how a particular application can be implemented, including which parts of the core Bluetooth protocol should be used to support the profile. Version 1.0 of the Bluetooth specification provides profiles for all of the connections listed above. The Bluetooth SIG continues to define profiles to support further applications.

1.7 USING BLUETOOTH

Bluetooth is unlike any wired network, as there is no need to physically attach a cable to the devices you are communicating with; indeed, you may not know exactly what devices you are talking to and what their capabilities are. To cope with this, Bluetooth provides inquiry and paging mechanisms and a Service Discovery Protocol (SDP).

This section examines how these mechanisms are used to allow Bluetooth devices to link up and use one another's services.

1.7.1 Discovering Bluetooth Devices

Imagine two Bluetooth enabled devices, say, a cell phone and a laptop computer. The cell phone is capable of acting as a modem using the dial up networking profile, and it periodically scans to see if anyone wants to use it.

The user of the laptop opens up an application that needs a Bluetooth dial up networking connection. To use this application, the laptop knows it needs to establish a Bluetooth link to a device supporting the dial up networking profile. The first stage in establishing such a connection is finding out what Bluetooth enabled devices are in the area, so the laptop performs an inquiry to look for devices in the neighbourhood.

To do this the laptop transmits a series of inquiry packets, and eventually the cell phone replies with a Frequency Hop Synchronisation (FHS) packet. The FHS packet contains all the information that the laptop needs to create a connection to the cell phone. It also contains the device class of the cell phone, which consists of major and minor parts. The major device class tells the laptop that it has found a phone; the minor part says that the type of phone is a cellular phone. This exchange of messages is illustrated in Figure 1–7.

In the same way, every Bluetooth-enabled device in the area that is scanning for inquiries will respond with an FHS packet, so the laptop accumulates a list of devices.

What happens next is up to the designer of the application. The laptop could present the user with a list of all the devices it has found and let the user choose what to do next; but if it did that at this stage, all it could do is tell the user about the types of devices it has found. Instead of telling the user about the devices it has found, the application could au-

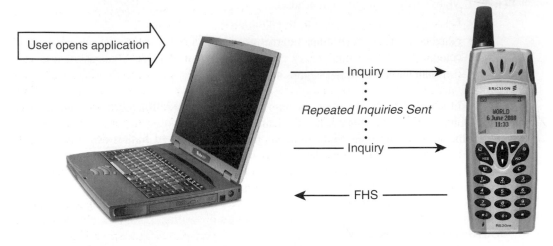

Figure 1–7   Discovering a Bluetooth device.

tomatically go on to the next stage and find out which devices in the area support the dial up networking profile.

1.7.2   Connecting to a Service Discovery Database

To find out whether a device supports a particular service, the application needs to connect to the device and use the service discovery protocol (SDP). Figure 1–8 illustrates how this is done. First the laptop pages the cellular phone, using the information it gath-

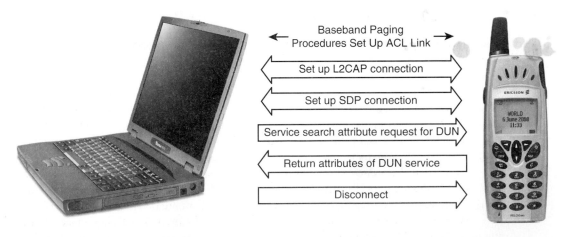

Figure 1–8   Retrieving information on services.

ered during inquiry. If the phone is scanning for pages, it responds, and an ACL baseband connection can be set up to transfer data between the two devices.

Once an ACL connection has been established, a Logical Link Control and Adaptation Protocol (L2CAP) connection can be set up across it. An L2CAP connection is used whenever data has to be transferred between Bluetooth devices. L2CAP allows many protocols and services to use one baseband ACL link. L2CAP distinguishes between different protocols and services using an ACL connection by adding a Protocol and Service Multiplexor (PSM) to every L2CAP packet. The PSM is different for every protocol or service that uses the link. Since this connection will be used for service discovery, its PSM = 0x0001, a special value that is always used for service discovery.

The laptop uses the L2CAP channel to set up a connection to the service discovery server on the cellular phone. The laptop's service discovery client can then ask the cellular phone's service discovery server to send it all the information it has relating to the dial up networking profile. The service discovery server on the cellular phone searches through its database and returns the attributes (characteristics) relating to dial up networking.

Once the service discovery information has been retrieved, the laptop may decide to shut down the connection to the cellular phone. If the laptop wants to collect service discovery information from many devices in the area, then it makes sense to shut down the links after using them, since one device can only use a limited number of links at a time, and keeping the links alive will consume battery power unnecessarily.

After the laptop has collected service discovery information from devices in the area, what happens next is again up to the application. It could display the information on all devices it has found which support the dial up networking profile and let the user decide which one to connect to. Alternatively, the application could decide for itself which device to use without bothering the user.

Either way, the service discovery information tells the laptop everything it needs to know to connect to the dial up networking service on the cellular phone.

1.7.3   Connecting to a Bluetooth Service

The process of actually making a connection is shown in Figure 1–9. The paging process which establishes a baseband ACL link is the same as was used when connecting for service discovery.

This time the link is being set up for a protocol which may have particular quality of service requirements, so the application running on the laptop may wish to configure the link to meet its requirements. This is done by the application sending its requirements to the Bluetooth module using the Host Controller Interface. Next, the module's link manager configures the link using the link management protocol.

Once the ACL connection is set up to the laptop's satisfaction, an L2CAP connection is set up. The dial up networking profile uses RFCOMM, an RS-232 emulation layer, so the L2CAP connection uses the Protocol Stack Multiplexor for RFCOMM (PSM = 0x0003).

After the L2CAP link has been set up, an RFCOMM connection can be set up across it. RFCOMM, like L2CAP, can multiplex several protocols or services across one connection. Each protocol or service is given its own channel number. The cellular

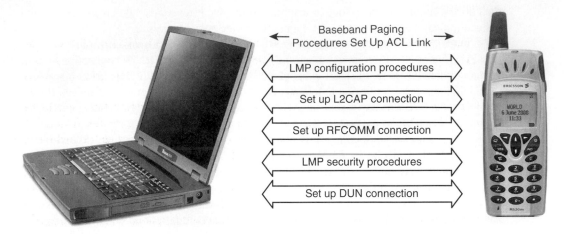

Figure 1–9   Connecting to a Dial Up Networking service.

phone's channel number for Dial Up Networking was sent to the laptop in the service discovery information, so the laptop knows which channel number it should use when setting up the RFCOMM connection.

Finally, the Dial Up Networking (DUN) connection is set up using the RFCOMM connection, and the laptop can start to use the dial up networking services of the cellular phone. Now, the laptop can use the cellular phone to make connections across the phone network without the two needing to be joined together by a data cable.

If the cellular phone is picked up and taken out of the range of the laptop, the laptop will have to repeat the procedure and find another device to connect to. Meanwhile, the cellular phone is still scanning and might be connected to another device elsewhere. The process of connecting is ad hoc and arbitrary with Bluetooth connections, possibly only lasting for a short period of time as devices move around.

1.7.4   Discoverability and Connectability Modes

It is important to realise that for a connection to be established using Bluetooth wireless technology, both ends of the link have to be willing to connect.

Some devices may be set so that they will not scan for inquiries; in this case, other devices cannot discover them, and they will effectively be invisible. Similarly, some devices may be set so that they do not perform page scans. In these cases, they can still initiate connections, but they will not hear other devices trying to connect to them.

Applications can choose whether to make devices connectable or discoverable. A connection cannot be forced on a device which is not in the correct mode to accept it.

1.8 MANAGEMENT

Some parts of the Bluetooth system have to manage the links, establishing ACL links as needed and disconnecting when they are finished with them. L2CAP could fulfill this function, but since links must also be managed at the RFCOMM and SDP levels, it makes sense to have a separate device manager.

The core specification of Bluetooth does not say how the connections should be managed, although the security white paper gives some hints. The reason for this lack of mention in the specification is that device management does not affect end-to-end inter-operation, so it is safe to leave it up to individual implementers to find their own solutions. Furthermore, the most appropriate solution is likely to be different for different devices. For instance, a headset only has to handle a single link, which is used for SDP and the headset service, so management is likely to be pretty simple, whereas a LAN access point has to juggle multiple links and balance bandwidth between them, so management of the links will be much more complex.

Bearing in mind that no single solution will be optimal for all possible devices, Figure 1–10 shows a possible protocol stack with a device and security manager that can handle establishment and configuration of the links.

The device manager interfaces to the HCI layer, SDP, RFCOMM, L2CAP, and to applications. It can provide the following facilities:

- Fault management—Detects, isolates, and corrects abnormal operation.
- Accounting management—Enables charging for use of managed objects and services.
- Configuration and name management—Controls, identifies, collects data from, and provides data to managed objects to assist in interconnection services.
- Performance management—Evaluates the behaviour of managed objects and the effectiveness of communication activities.
- Security management—Provides security management to protect managed objects and services.

Those familiar with the OSI model will recognise these facilities as those provided by OSI management.

Applications will have to register with the Bluetooth device manager to use Bluetooth links. They may then ask the device manager for connections, and request particular security and quality of service levels. If all applications go through the device manager, this allows it to create a database of higher layer protocols, applications, and services using links.

The device manager can also handle timeouts, shutting down links when they are no longer needed.

Bluetooth's management facilities do not have to be handled by a separate device management entity as described above. This function could be built into L2CAP, or into a

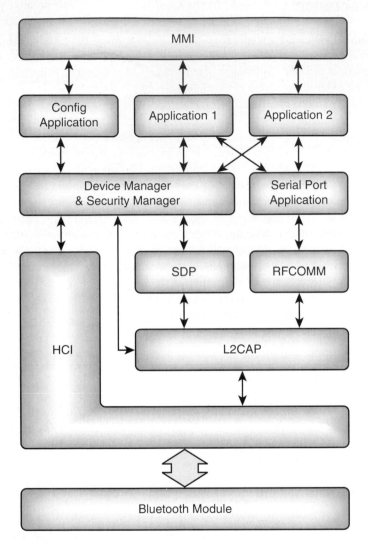

Figure 1–10 Management of the Bluetooth protocol stack.

profile application. However it is done, there must be some part of every Bluetooth implementation which handles management of the links.

1.9   TEST AND QUALIFICATION

The terms of the Bluetooth adopters agreement entitle all signatories to use the essential Intellectual Property Rights (IPR) underpinning Bluetooth free of charge. However, this entitlement for a particular product is conditional on that product passing successfully through the Bluetooth qualification program. To facilitate recognition in the marketplace of approved Bluetooth devices, qualification also entitles a product to use the Bluetooth brand. This mechanism makes it possible for the SIG to take legal proceedings against any nonconformant products which purport to offer Bluetooth functionality but fall short of the specification. The result is that the market should see only products which work reliably with all other Bluetooth products supporting the same profiles.

The requirements for qualification are split into four categories:

- Bluetooth radio link requirements.
- Bluetooth protocol requirements.
- Bluetooth profile requirements.
- Bluetooth information requirements.

In addition to the preceding, manufacturers must also ensure that the radio is tested appropriately to meet local radio emissions standards in the countries where it will be sold.

Interoperability tests must also be carried out to ensure that Bluetooth devices correctly implement the Bluetooth profiles, and can interwork with other devices implementing the same profiles. Devices can then be sold with a statement concerning which profiles they support so that it is perfectly clear to consumers which products they will work with and in what ways.

1.10   BLUETOOTH IN CONTEXT

Bluetooth does not exist in a vacuum. This section summarises some of the issues that affect Bluetooth devices which are not covered by the Bluetooth specification itself: how to implement Bluetooth, related technologies, the market for Bluetooth, health concerns, and the future of the specification.

1.10.1   Implementing the Technology

The key issue faced by implementers is that of partitioning. The hardware/software partition inside the Bluetooth subsystem trades off performance, cost, and power consumption against risk and time to market. The partition between the host system and the Bluetooth subsystem is where (usually in software) the stack is partitioned. This will either add loading to the host's processing resources or require more performance and resources in the highly cost sensitive Bluetooth subsystem. Ultimately, the demand for a full implementation as a self contained, embedded Bluetooth solution will require very careful design and optimisation to avoid creating an uncommercial product.

The quality of the "user experience" is very important for any Bluetooth product and will also require careful design and a good understanding and specification of the target application. Bluetooth is going to be a very high volume system and demand very low cost with high levels of optimisation being crucial.

1.10.2   Related Technologies and Standards

Bluetooth, like most innovations throughout history, does not have the field to itself. There are many other initiatives and standards for wired and wireless data communications, either already deployed or under development. They vary between overlapping with Bluetooth's sphere of operation, while exhibiting clear differentiators, to potential head-on competitors of Bluetooth. The two most active areas of work at the current time are the distribution of data and voice in a personal sphere of influence, the so called Personal Area Network (PAN), which appears to be Bluetooth's home ground, and the emerging demand for high speed wireless multimedia data distribution.

1.10.3   The Bluetooth Market

Most commentators agree that the Bluetooth market is going to be huge, with forecasts putting the installed base at half a billion devices by 2004, with a total market for Bluetooth components worth $2 billion in the same year. It seems that, for once, the technology push provided by Bluetooth is a good match for the market pull in terms of consumer needs and wants at this time.

There are a great many opportunities for Bluetooth-enabled products which exploit the various features of the technology to add value. However, there are many issues which are yet to be resolved. Potentially competing technologies could cause consumer confusion and at worst push Bluetooth into a niche corner. For manufacturers, the cost of the technology is paramount, and for Bluetooth to become ubiquitous, it must be built into all products, not just the high-end models.

For consumers, poor interoperability and/or poor user experience would be a major problem for Bluetooth and cause it to falter. The well-discussed "Out of Box Experience" has to be seamless and simple. The hope is that the strength of the Bluetooth brand will promote the notion of reliability and ease of use.

1.10.4   Health

Bluetooth uses frequency spectrum in the range of 2400 MHz to 2483.5 MHz. This range encompasses the natural frequency of H_2O molecular oscillation at 2450 MHz, which is also used by microwave ovens specifically to excite water molecules inside food in order to cook it.

Sharing the same frequency range as microwave ovens has led to some concerns that Bluetooth devices might *cook* their users. Some microwave radiation will be absorbed in flesh. It will be absorbed by field-induced rotation of polarized water molecules, which is converted to heat through molecular friction. Basically, the microwaves shake the water in flesh, and it heats up as it shakes. But, as the radiated output power of Bluetooth devices is incredibly low and spread in spectrum in time, experts concur that Bluetooth radiation does not pose a risk to health.

A 1 mW Bluetooth radio emits 1/1,000,000 the amount of power in a 1 KW microwave oven. Also, in a microwave oven, all the power is directed inward at the food, whereas in a Bluetooth device, the power is radiated outward, so the user only ever intercepts the smallest fraction of the radio waves which are heading in their direction.

It is interesting to compare Bluetooth devices with other popular communications devices. Bluetooth operates at 2.4 GHz and uses 1 mW (0 dBm) for most applications, with a maximum of 100 mW (20 dBm) for extended range. This means that Bluetooth signals have a penetration depth of only 1.5 cm into flesh. In comparison, cellular handsets have a power of 10 mW to 2 W peak, using 450 MHz to 2200 MHz, and exhibit a penetration depth of 2.5 cm in the middle of their range at 900 MHz. So, mobile cellular handsets give rise to a measurable heating effect of 0.1°C, compared with no measurable increase for Bluetooth devices. Although studies have shown this small heating effect, it is too low to be noticed by the user. Most of the temperature increases that mobile phone users feel when holding a handset next to their ears is caused by an insulating effect. Since the head radiates a lot of heat, if a handset blocks that radiation, then the head heats up. Getting a hot ear from a mobile phone is not necessarily a sign that you are absorbing radiation!

There has already been some controversy regarding cellular handsets and whether they have a negative impact on health. Although scientific opinion is pretty conclusive that there are no risks, to be safe, various organisations have undertaken studies and research and have laid down guidelines for exposure to radio frequencies.

The WHO, ICNIRP, and IEEE have developed Radio Frequency (RF) exposure recommendations and these guidelines have been adopted by many national authorities. In the usual way of health and safety guidelines, they incorporate large safety margins. The guidelines specify near-field[1] restrictions (referred to as SAR) between 10 MHz to 10 GHz, which devices with an output power of less than 1.6 mW are incapable of exceeding. So, all low power Bluetooth devices will fall within these restrictions. Higher power Bluetooth devices may need to be tested for SAR limits, and this will be done as part of radio regulatory testing.

The guidelines also specify a standard for total RF exposure. This is given as a power density of 10 W/m^2. This level of spectral density would require an unrealistic number of Bluetooth devices to operate continuously in a very small space, which would actually not be possible due to the limited spectrum in the ISM band.

Several expert panels formed from organisations such as WHO, ICNIRP, EC, and the Royal Society of Canada have debated the topic of health in the context of existing higher power cellular technology in recent years. They have all concluded that there is no credible or convincing evidence that RF exposure from wireless devices operating within accepted exposure limits causes adverse human health effects. They did, however, recommend additional research to clarify some areas and fill gaps in existing knowledge.

In conclusion, experts agree that Bluetooth devices are too low in power to have any negative health consequences. Even the higher power devices are an order of magnitude lower in power than existing cellular devices, which, based on existing research and official guidelines, have already been proven to be safe.

---

[1]Near field are those radio waves found close to an emitting device.

1.10.5   The Future

The Bluetooth SIG has a series of working groups continuing the development of the Bluetooth specification in three key areas: correction and clarification of the version 1.1 specification, development of further profiles, and evolution of the core specification for enhanced performance. The core specification will evolve from version 1.1 to include various improvements affecting different parts of the system; Radio, Baseband, and Protocol software.

The mechanism for adopter companies to propose more profiles will facilitate optimised Bluetooth implementations for specific applications. Future versions of the specification are expected to provide higher data rates for Bluetooth (between 2 and 10 Mb/s) and to provide the multimedia distribution facilities which are becoming a key requirement for the future of information technology. Other work is underway to improve on the overall feature set of the 1.1 specification in areas such as quality of service and link handover between devices in a way that is similar to that which occurs in mobile cellular phone networks.

1.11   SUMMARY

The Bluetooth core promoters group has produced a specification for short range, low cost wireless communications. This is the Bluetooth core specification. The complete Bluetooth specification also includes profiles which detail how applications should use the Bluetooth protocol stack, and a brand book which covers how the Bluetooth brand should be presented.

The Bluetooth specification not only covers how to set up short range wireless links, but also describes the Bluetooth qualification process. By putting their products through this process, companies that join the Bluetooth SIG can get a free license to use the Bluetooth wireless technology and Bluetooth brand.

Bluetooth wireless technology allows up to eight devices to connect together in a communicating group called a piconet. The maximum speed of a link in a piconet is 723.2 kb/s at the baseband layer (the data rate seen at the Application Layer will be lower due to the intervening layers of the protocol stack using some of the bandwidth). Different piconets can be linked into scatternets, but the data rate between scatternets will be lower than the rate possible within a single piconet.

PART I

PROTOCOL STACK: THE BLUETOOTH MODULE

2

Antennas

The antenna transmits and receives the radio waves which Bluetooth wireless technology uses to communicate, so it is a crucial part of any Bluetooth implementation. At their crudest, 2.4 GHz antennas can be simple lengths of wire, but for the best performance and to fit well with a product's form factor, more sophisticated antenna designs are required.

When choosing and positioning antennas, the surrounding environment has to be taken into account, as this can have marked effects on antenna performance.

2.1 RADIATION PATTERN

Antenna radiation patterns are usually plotted in two dimensions: azimuth and elevation. The azimuth pattern is the pattern of radiation looking down on the antenna from above. The elevation pattern is the pattern of radiation looking at the antenna from the side.

A dipole antenna radiates in a torus (a doughnut shape). Figure 2–1 shows the radiation patterns this gives. At the left is the azimuth pattern; the radiation is a perfect circle with the same strength in all directions. At the right is the elevation pattern; at the sides of the antenna, the radiation is strong, dropping away to nothing above and below the antenna.

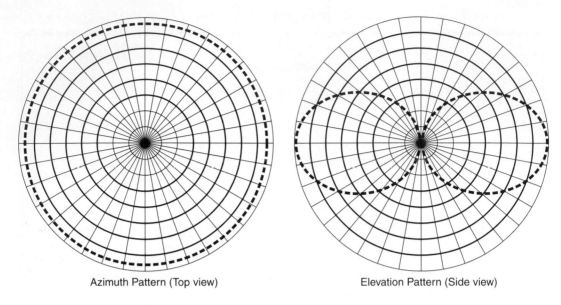

Azimuth Pattern (Top view)   Elevation Pattern (Side view)

Figure 2–1   Azimuth and elevation patterns for a dipole antenna.

The radiation pattern of an antenna is useful in designing Bluetooth products because it tells you what the signal strength will look like from different angles to the product. In the example of a dipole aerial given above, the antenna works best if it is at 90 degrees to the path leading to the device it is communicating with. So if devices are spaced out horizontally, dipoles work best if they are kept vertical. On the other hand, there is still good signal strength at up to a 45 degree angle, so the product could be held at an angle and the aerial would still work; or, products could be spaced out with say a laptop on a desk and a cellular phone under the desk, and there would still be a good chance of the two devices getting a good enough signal to connect.

Some antennas have very directional radiation patterns, and others are closer to isotropic (a spherical pattern the same in every direction). The ability of an antenna to concentrate radiation in a particular direction is known as its directive gain.

The desired pattern will vary according to the type of product an antenna is being built into. LAN access points may wish to cover a room and have directional coverage which can be targeted into the room. This is possible for a LAN Access Point, as its antenna can be aimed when it is installed. Conversely, handheld devices such as cellular phones generally need to transmit and receive over a wide range of angles, so you definitely do not want strongly directive gain patterns. When choosing an antenna for a product, the desired radiation pattern suitable for its usage and positioning should be taken into account.

Finally, the orientation of the electromagnetic waves may be taken into account. This is known as the polarisation. Polarisation has linear and circular elements. For the best performance, transmit and receive antennas are matched for polarisation. This is unlikely to be practical with Bluetooth systems, as such a wide variety of devices will be operating at such a wide variety of angles. A combination of antenna radiation patterns and polarisation effects could lead to devices performing better when held at different angles. Ideally the user should not be aware of these effects, and Bluetooth should appear to be a completely directionless system.

2.2 GAINS AND LOSSES

The gain of an antenna is the ratio of power in to power out. Usually antenna gain is measured in dBi; this is gain relative to an isotropic antenna (an antenna which radiates the same in all directions in a perfect sphere and has a gain of one, so power out = power in).

Severe losses can occur if the feed between the radio and the antenna is not well matched, as the signal will be reflected back down the feeder. Further losses are experienced in the antenna itself, and then there are material losses due to the signal being absorbed in the propagation medium.

In the case of microwave transmissions, water is a strong absorber, so signals which have to pass through flesh (mostly water) will suffer high material losses. Losses will also occur through furniture, and metals will block the signal.

Figure 2–2 illustrates the losses in getting a signal from the radio transmitter through to the receive antenna.

Of course, the material losses in the propagation path will include the casing of the Bluetooth module. Products such as laptop computers are typically manufactured with

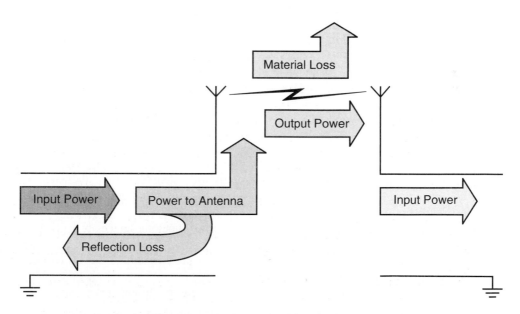

Figure 2–2 Losses in transmitting through an antenna.

metal screening around the internal components. The metal screen is designed to contain radio signals, so a Bluetooth antenna could not be placed inside such a screen. This is the reason why Bluetooth PCMCIA cards have bulges protruding outside the laptop; these contain the antenna.

Most plastics do not absorb significantly in the ISM band, so plastic casings should not cause significant material losses for Bluetooth systems.

2.3   TYPES OF ANTENNAS

The most popular antenna types for Bluetooth devices are dipole, flat panel, and microstrip. Other antenna types are possible in the ISM band, such as multiple element dipoles, Yagis, parabolic dishes, and slotted antennas. However, the more complex antennas are less likely to have uses in Bluetooth systems. This is because of cost, form factor, or because their radiation patterns are strongly directional, which tends not to suit Bluetooth applications.

2.3.1   Dipole Antennas

Dipole antennas are cylinders, with the signal usually feeding in from the bottom. Very simple dipole antennas are often made out of short sections of coaxial cable for development purposes.

As the elevation patterns in Figure 2–1 showed, a dipole antenna transmits best from the side of the antenna. Usually it is fed from the base of the antenna, but it can also be fed from the centre of one side.

The length of a dipole antenna must be related to the wavelength of the signal it is carrying. Half wave and quarter wave dipoles are commonly used.

Dipole antennas are available in various form factors. Figure 2–3 illustrates the variety available with a snap in surface mounted package at the left, and a swivel antenna with SMA connector at the right. Both are half wave dipole antennas.

2.3.2   Flat Panel

Flat panel antennas are small metal patches, and are usually square or rectangular. They are strongly directional, so their radiation pattern is not ideal for handheld devices. On the other hand, they can be made very small for the ISM band and can be mounted directly onto PCBs, both of which help to reduce costs.

A popular form of flat panel antenna used in Bluetooth devices is a PIFA (Planar Inverted F Antenna). This antenna is named for its resemblance to a capital F on its side. It has a flat panel as far away from the ground as possible and is fed by two contacts which form the arms of the F (see Figure 2–4).

A PIFA antenna can also be fabricated as a microstrip antenna using tracks on a Printed Circuit Board, or PCB (see next section).

Figure 2–3   Two types of dipole antenna package (pictures supplied by Giga-Ant).

2.3.3 Microstrip

Microstrip antennas are simply patterns on PCBs. The fact that tracks on a PCB can be made into a useful antenna illustrates the care that designers must take in product design if they are not to inadvertently produce radiating components where they don't want them!

The radio module of the Ericsson Bluetooth Developer's Kit comes with a microstrip antenna, which is implemented as a printed pattern on a small PCB.

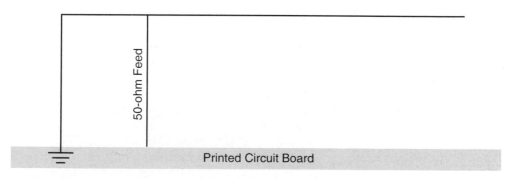

Figure 2–4   PIFA antenna structure.

Figure 2–5   High efficiency ceramic antenna (courtesy of Antenova).

2.4   CERAMIC ANTENNAS

Ceramic antennas can take advantage of phyiscal properties of specialised ceramic materials, such as high permittivity, to produce miniaturised antennas.

Recent developments in ceramic antenna technology are adding functionality and improving performance of antennas. For instance, it is now possible to construct a ceramic antenna which is highly efficient and can be made both directional and steerable (see Figure 2–5). Many antennas are highly affected by their surroundings and perform poorly when placed close to one another, these new antennas experience less proximity effects.

2.5   ON-CHIP ANTENNAS

For the ultimate in integration, an on-chip antenna is a possibility. At the time of writing, at least one supplier has announced a Bluetooth baseband and radio chip with an on board antenna (see Figure 2–6). The antenna is implemented as a four armed, spiral microstrip

Figure 2–6   Bluetooth chip with on-chip antenna (courtesy of Alcatel Micro Electronics).

on the top surface of the Bluetooth chip's ceramic package. An RF filter is also printed on the top of the package to improve the characteristics of the device's transceiver.

The cost and space savings of such antennas are obvious; however, because the radio signal is blocked by the chip beneath it, the on chip antenna can only radiate in a hemisphere on one side of the chip.

This might be seen as an advantage for some products such as headsets, where health concerns have been expressed. Users may be able to put up with the inconvenience of only being able to connect to devices on one side of their body for the sake of the assurance that radiation levels will be reduced yet further below the already low levels of Bluetooth. However, there are some products which will require more complete coverage; therefore, even a device with an on board antenna will typically provide for the alternative of connecting an external antenna.

2.6 ANTENNA PLACEMENT

The characteristics of an antenna are strongly affected by the surrounding ground planes. Shielding from casings and components also affects antenna radiation patterns, and of course, the feed to the antenna affects reflection losses. The combination of these factors means that for optimum radio performance, it is crucial to take the antenna into account when designing PCBs for microwave devices.

2.7 SUMMARY

Handheld Bluetooth devices require antennas which radiate in a pattern as close to a sphere as possible, so that they can connect in any direction, at any angle. For devices such as LAN access points, a more directional antenna could be beneficial so that coverage could be restricted to a single room.

Different antenna types will radiate in different patterns, so the type of product may affect the antenna choice. The available space and the cost of different types of antennas will also affect the choice of antenna for a product.

Surrounding components and casings can affect the performance of an antenna as well. In particular, the feed and proximity of ground planes can affect an antenna's characteristics.

Thus, the positioning and characteristics of the antenna must be considered when designing Bluetooth products.

3

Radio

3.1 INTRODUCTION

Bluetooth devices operate in the globally available, unlicensed ISM band situated at 2.4 GHz. This band is reserved for general use by Industrial, Scientific, and Medical (ISM) applications, which obey a basic set of power and spectral emission and interference specifications such as defined by the ETSI ETS 300-328 in Europe or the FCC CFR47 Part 15 in the United States. Although globally available, the ISM band has restrictions in some geographical locations. The SIG is actively lobbying regulatory bodies to harmonise these regulations worldwide and to date has had success with Japan and Spain and positive reactions from France. The situation at the time of publication is described in Table 3–1 and France is due to release the full ISM band in 2003. We will refer to the majority situation in this text.

The ISM band is occupied by a plethora of other RF emitters, ranging from wireless applications such as short range proprietary techniques (car security, cordless headphones, etc.) and standardised WLAN (Wireless Local Area Networking) applications (IEEE 802.11) to random noise generators such as microwave ovens and sodium vapour street lamps, which contribute significantly to the noise floor. As a result, the 2.4 GHz band is not a terribly stable or reliable medium. However, the band's worldwide availability ensures widespread acceptance of Bluetooth. To cope with the hostile environment presented by the ISM band, Bluetooth specifically employs several techniques: frequency hopping, adaptive power control, and short data packets.

Table 3–1   ISM Band Availability by Geographical Location

Geographic Area	ISM Band (GHz)	Lower Guard Band	Upper Guard Band	Available Channels
France	2.4465–2.4835	7.5 MHz	7.5 MHz	23
Rest of World (including United States, Japan, and Europe)	2.4000–2.4835	2 MHz	3.5 MHz	79

3.2   FREQUENCY HOPPING

Originally invented by the Austrian born actress Hedy Lamarr during World War II, the mechanism of frequency hopping has been used to great effect both as a means for secure communication and robust communication. Both attributes of the technique are important for Bluetooth. It is always possible for a radio channel to become temporarily blocked by an interference source, and as described above, this is quite likely in the busy ISM band. Although Bluetooth provides a retransmission scheme for lost data packets, it is altogether more efficient and robust to retransmit the data on a new channel, which is unlikely to also be blocked. Indeed, the algorithm employed to calculate the hop sequence ensures maximum distance between adjacent hop channels in the sequence. Also several active Bluetooth piconets may be within range of each other; with each piconet hopping independently with a pseudo random sequence based on each piconet's identity/access code, collisions will be minimised. This is important as all Bluetooth devices only have 79 channels in which to operate. In an office or public environment, the number of active devices can very quickly reach this limit, and a low correlation between noncommunicating pairs is essential.

3.3   MODULATION

The operating band of 83.5 MHz is divided into 1 MHz spaced channels, each signalling data at 1 M symbols per second so as to obtain the maximum available channel bandwidth. With the chosen modulation scheme of GFSK (Gaussian Frequency Shift Keying), this equates to 1 Mb/s. A binary 1 gives rise to a positive frequency deviation from the nominal carrier frequency, while a binary 0 gives rise to a negative frequency deviation.

To obtain the most efficient use of bandwidth while still maintaining acceptable error probability, the digital bit stream is modulated using GFSK with a BT product of 0.5 and a modulation index of between 0.28 and 0.35. The BT product is the product of adjacent signal frequency separation[1] (0.5MHz) and symbol duration (1 μs). 0.5 corresponds to the minimum carrier separation to ensure orthogon

---

[1]The separation between modulation alphabet members or channel separation between m

correlation) between signals in adjacent channels. The modulation index represents the strength of the peak frequency deviation (fd) and can be expressed as 2fdT, where T is the symbol duration. This translates to a frequency deviation range of 140 KHz to 175 KHz. The Bluetooth specification gives 115 KHz as an absolute minimum deviation.

GFSK employs a Gaussian filter to smooth the frequency transitions so that the modulated carrier frequency changes smoothly with a Gaussian shaped envelope. This maintains continuous phase of the carrier frequency and reduces the emitted spectral side-lobes, allowing better spectral efficiency and less intersymbol interference. The Gaussian filter acts on the transmit bit stream and may be implemented in the radio as an analog filter, carried out in the digital part of the baseband using a FIR filter implemented as a Linear Feedback Shift Register (LFSR), or as part of a modulation lookup table.

3.4   SYMBOL TIMING

The Bluetooth specification demands a symbol timing accuracy of ± 20 ppm. This means that the clock which is driving the baseband symbol processing logic must be accurate over all operating conditions and its operating life to this figure. With modern quartz crystal technology, this is not terribly demanding, and indeed, due to the easy availability of accurate 13 MHz references for GSM cellular phone applications, does not impose a large cost burden on a Bluetooth enabled product.

The result of this requirement is that over the longest transmitted packet—DH5—the worst case error in the phase of the last symbol as determined by the worst case receiver oscillator will be:

$$\frac{40}{1000000} \times 2870 \ \mu s \ = \ 0.12 \ \mu s$$

which is less than one-eighth of a symbol period. During the next reception, the symbol timing will be resynchronised. For this reason, very simple timing recovery schemes are possible for Bluetooth without necessarily needing to continuously track the on-air data burst.

3.5   POWER EMISSION AND CONTROL

FCC regulations permit transmit power up to 0 dBm in the ISM band without spread spectrum operation. For high power emissions, a spread spectrum scheme must be adopted. Through the use of frequency hopping, Bluetooth is able to operate at up to 20 dBm, allowing a range of up to 100 m.

Three power classes are defined in the Bluetooth specification (see Table 3–2). Power Class 3 is the most common scheme adopted by manufacturers and of course is the lowest power consumption option. Power Class 1 has a mandatory requirement for power control, while classes 2 or 3 make this optional. Although, for minimum power consumption, power control is always preferable.

Table 3–2   Transmit Power Classes

Power Class	Output Power (Max)	Minimum Output at Max Setting	Power Control
1	100 mW (20 dBm)	1 mW (0 dBm)	Mandatory: +4 dBm to 20 dBm Optional: -30 dBm to 4 dBm
2	2.5 mW (4 dBm)	0.25 mW (-6 dBm)	Optional: -30 dBm to 4 dBm
3	1 mW (0 dBm)	–	Optional: -30 dBm to 4 dBm

Power control operates by a receiver monitoring the Received Signal Strength Indication (RSSI) and sending LMP control commands back to the transmitter, asking for their transmit power to be reduced if the RSSI value is higher than that strictly necessary to maintain a satisfactory link. Should the RSSI value drop too low, then the receiver may request the power to be increased. The specification requires power to be controlled in steps of 2 dB to 8 dB, while RSSI measurements must be accurate to ± 4 dB at -60 dBm, with a minimum range of operation of 20 ± 6 dB, starting at -60 dB.

3.6   RADIO PERFORMANCE PARAMETERS

The Bluetooth specification gives minimum performance parameters for the RF system. However, care must be taken because several of the parameters are only acceptable on paper and in particular do not address the real-world scenarios in which Bluetooth is to be employed. It is for this reason that many commercial Bluetooth RF devices significantly exceed the specified performance.

Bluetooth is specified to operate with a maximum Bit Error Rate (BER) of 0.1%. This gives a figure for receiver sensitivity of -70 dBm as described in the Bluetooth specification. In practice, receivers often exceed this by 10 or more dBm.

The specification does not give figures for synthesiser settling time. However, due to the high bandwidth of processing operations in the lower layers of the protocol stack, synthesiser settling time is a key performance parameter of any system. Figure 3–1 illustrates the timing of operations during any Rx / Tx transaction. The lower layer's protocol processor must first decide what state to put the baseband link controller into and program various associated data into the baseband. The baseband is then able to calculate the appropriate frequency hop channel number and program the synthesiser. This must of course occur long enough before the expected start of the data burst to allow the synthesiser to settle. This imposes a practical limit on the synthesiser settle time of around 180 μs, and indeed many radios have settle times much lower, between 130 μs to 170 μs. The lower the settling time, the fewer are the performance requirements placed on the protocol processor.

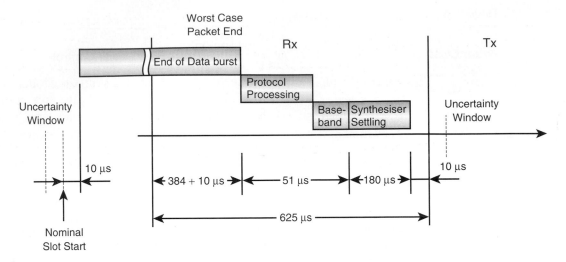

Figure 3–1   System timing requirements.

3.7   SIMPLE RF ARCHITECTURE

There are various alternative radio system architectures such as zero IF or direct conversion, heterodyne or single bit modulation, multi-bit IQ sample modulation using lookup tables, and even direct transmit modulation onto the transmit synthesiser. However, in this section, we consider a simple single bit modulation heterodyne radio as an illustration of the various components that constitute a typical Bluetooth RF system. The block diagram in Figure 3–2 shows such a typical radio system. The control signals (TxOn, PaOn, VcOn, RxOn) are timing strobes derived from an intra slot time base by comparing against preset time values, together with a receive / transmit selection signal (Rx/nTx), which indicates whether to receive or transmit in the current slot.

Data is clocked into the transmit path bit-serially (TxData) under control of the baseband transmit clock (TxClk) derived directly from the timebase. On receive, data is clocked into the baseband from the radio (RxData) under control of the receive clock (RxClk). RxClk may be provided either by the radio or it can be derived within the baseband. In either case, a clock recovery circuit is required. As explained previously, this does not need to be a complicated mechanism due to the relatively high tolerance on the symbol clock of ± 20 ppm. A form of digital Phase Locked Loop (PLL) is typically used.

The Bluetooth channel number (ChanNo) must be provided by the baseband to the RF channel synthesiser, which produces the exact carrier frequency to use in the IF mixer. The channel frequency required is 2402 + ChanNo MHz.

Turning on the various sections in the radio is controlled by the timebase. A number of timebase values referenced to the start of a slot are preset within the baseband and these control signals to the RF system, which power up or down various sections of the radio during receive or transmit operations. Typically, the following signals are used: VcoOn, TxOn, PaOn, and RxOn to enable the synthesiser, transmit path, power amp, and receive path, respectively.

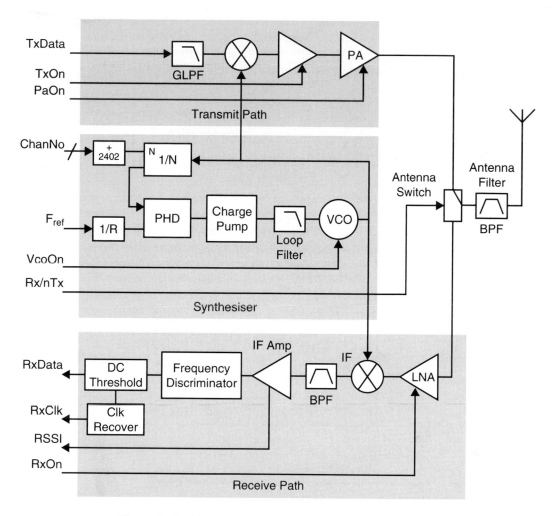

Figure 3–2   Simple radio system with direct connection to the baseband.

3.7.1   Channel Number Selection

Frequency selection is communicated to the RF device by simply passing the frequency hopping generated channel number. To support reduced hop schemes in different countries, an offset may need to be added to the frequency hop channel as shown in Table 3–1.

3.7.2   Receive Clock and Data Recovery

The function of clock recovery is to retrieve a valid clock signal with which to validate the received data. Due to the relatively tight symbol timing tolerance described above, which results in only one-eighth of a symbol error at the end of a maximal (5 slot) length packet, Bluetooth clock recovery does not necessarily need to be active across the entire packet. Practical experience shows that the optimum mechanism employed for clock recovery is really dependent on the radio architecture used. Two variants of clock recovery are in common use for Bluetooth systems. The first type attempts to recover the clock based on knowledge of the expected preamble sequence of four bits plus the first synchword bit, while the second is a more common technique in systems such as DECT, where a simple digital PLL-type circuit detects edges in the incoming data stream, adjusting the phase of the recovered clock to track the data edges with an overall hysteresis to manage glitches and wide symbols. This is sometimes referred to as an "early-late" synchroniser.

In both cases, the important and reliable component of the data to recover the clock from is the 5 bit preamble sequence (including the first bit of the synchword). However, most radios will lose the first one, two, or even three symbols due to slew in the analog receive path and DC thresholding circuit. The result of this is that only one or two symbols are available for clock recovery, and experience shows that really four or five are required as a minimum. Moving in to the synchword and using some of these bits is the usual answer, and indeed, the early-late synchroniser does this automatically. However, using more than one or two synchword bits starts to eat into the correlation threshold uncertainty and will reduce overall link sensitivity. DECT by comparison uses a preamble sequence of 16 bits.

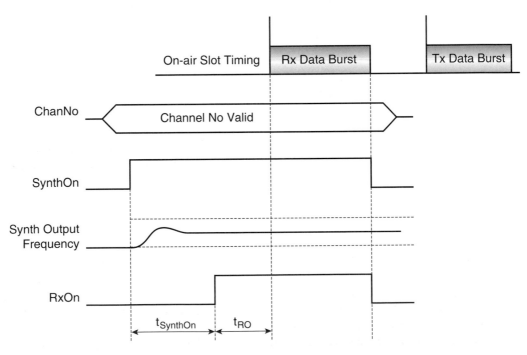

Figure 3–3   Receive slot timing.

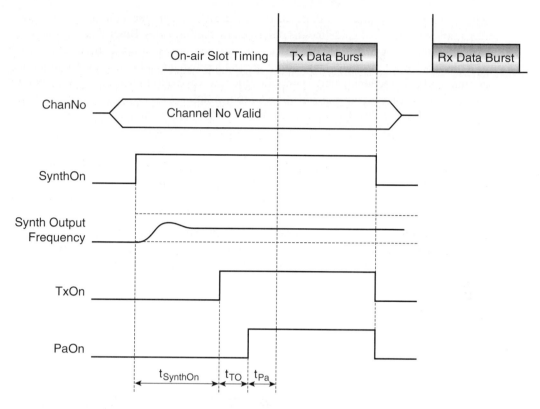

Figure 3–4   Transmit slot timing.

3.8   RF SYSTEM TIMING

The timing diagrams in Figures 3–3 and 3–4 illustrate the relative timing of the various control signals on the radio. Specific values of these will appear in manufacturers' data sheets.

3.9   BLUE RF

An initiative was started by several companies in mid 1999 to standardise the interface between baseband and radio around a minimal number of signals and control so as to minimise device pin count and provide for interchangeability of parts and second-sourcing opportunities. Many radio device manufacturers have signed up to join the BlueRF consortium, but the original goal of one standard interface for Bluetooth radio chips has not been realised. Today, the BlueRF specification is no longer maintained and promoted and each manufacturer has made their own implementation of the specification. However, what has resulted is a form of de-facto standardisation, where the vast majority of interfaces fall within a set of guidelines as described by the following BlueRF summary.

Essentially, two different modes of operation are provided for: bidirectional, which provides the lowest pin count but requires control logic in the radio to sequence on-air operation, and unidirectional, which simplifies the radio and allows it to be completely controlled by the baseband but demands a higher pin count.

In addition to this, there are three receive modes which alter the partition between RF and the baseband device for Rx. These are defined as follows:

- RxMode1—The radio only contains the demodulator and the baseband contains the DC thresholding and data extraction (including the correlator) circuitry.
- RxMode2—The radio contains the demodulator and DC thesholding circuitry, and the baseband contains the data extraction circuitry.
- RxMode3—The radio contains all three functions.

In each case, the pin count is reduced at the expense of a more complex radio design.

3.10 SUMMARY

Bluetooth devices operate at 2.4 GHz in the globally available, license-free ISM band. Although widely available, the use of this band by many other systems and the pollution of it by other sources such as microwave ovens make this a rather hostile environment. Bluetooth employs a fast frequency hopping scheme to counteract this, together with error protection and correction.

The specification of the radio requirements has been relaxed as far as possible to facilitate low cost and low power design. The modulation used is simply GFSK with one symbol per bit, providing a gross bit rate of 1 Mb/s from a channel bandwidth of 1 MHz. By specifying tight constraints on symbol timing and drift rate, the task of recovering the received data stream is also simplified.

In spite of this, there are some key design issues to be addressed in making such a low cost system reliable and robust, and some close attention must be given to system design. Other parts of the Bluetooth specification itself impose some constraints on the radio system and these must also be accounted for.

To facilitate the reuse and interoperability of radio parts with different baseband devices, an initiative named BlueRF has been launched to standardise the Bluetooth radio interface and this has been somewhat successful.

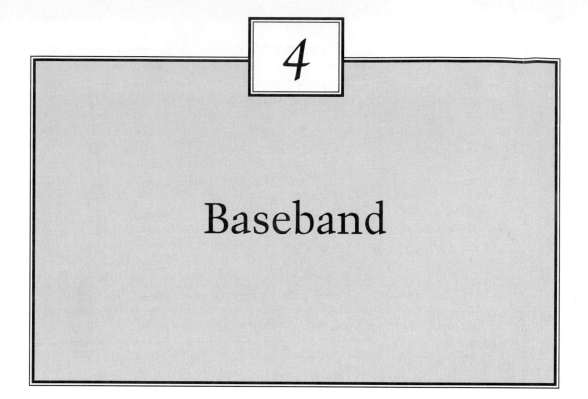

4

Baseband

4.1 INTRODUCTION

We begin this chapter by making some clear distinctions between the terms "Link Controller" and "Baseband" (see Figure 4–1). The Bluetooth specification uses these terms somewhat ambiguously, and a clear distinction will provide a useful handle on which to hang some later concepts.

The Link Controller (LC) is responsible for carrying out link level operations over several data packet durations in response to higher level commands from the Link Manager (LM). The local and remote LC entities will manage the packet by packet process of establishing the link once commanded by LM and will maintain the link once established. The OSI Physical (PHY) layer is represented by the radio and the baseband. The radio interfaces between the on-air channel medium and the digital baseband, which formats data supplied by the LC for robust and reliable transmission over the channel and retrieves data from the channel for passing up the stack. The baseband is responsible for channel coding and decoding and low level timing control and management of the link within the domain of a single data packet transfer.

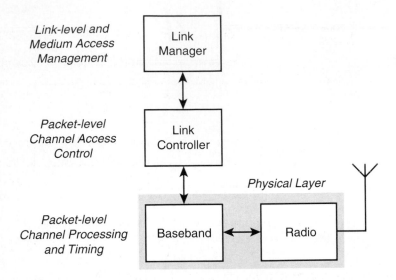

Figure 4–1 Link control and the baseband.

4.2 BLUETOOTH DEVICE ADDRESS

Each Bluetooth device has a 48 bit IEEE MAC address known as the Bluetooth Device Address (BD_ADDR). This is used as a seed in some of the serial bit processing operations, and in particular for the derivation of the access code. The MAC address is split into Non-significant Address Part (NAP), Upper Address Part (UAP), and Lower Address Part (LAP) as follows:

- BD_Addr[47:32] –   NAP[15:0]
  Used to initialise the encryption engine stream LFSR.
- BD_Addr[31:24] –   UAP[7:0]
  Used to initialise the HEC and CRC calculations and for frequency hopping.
- BD_Addr[23:0] –   LAP[23:0]
  Used by sync word generation and frequency hopping.

4.3 MASTERS, SLAVES, AND PICONETS

Bluetooth is a Time Division Multiplexed (TDM)[1] system, where the basic unit of operation is a slot of 625 μs duration. In connection (i.e., transferring data), all transmit or receive operations occur in 1, 3, or 5 slots (a packet). In preconnection operation (i.e., the

---

[1]Strictly speaking, it is also Frequency Division Multiplexed (FDM) as well due to the use of frequency hopping. However, this is not used to increase a link's capacity, but rather to increase robustness and reuse of the same spectrum.

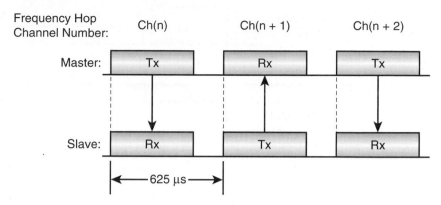

Figure 4–2   Slot timing for single-slot packets.

inquiry, paging, or scanning operation which precedes a connection), transmit and receive can sometimes occur in half slots. The packets are joined together in transmit and receive pairs. In connection, a packet pair can be 2, 4, 6, 8, or 10 slots long.

Each Bluetooth device may be either a Master or a Slave at any one time, though not simultaneously. These two roles are defined as follows:

Master—The device which initiates an exchange of data.

Slave—The device which responds to the Master.

In addition, when communicating, Slave devices will utilise the timing of their Master and hop in synchronisation. With reference to Figure 4–2, the Master first transmits to the Slave device. This occurs with both devices tuned to radio channel Ch(n) 625 µs later, the two devices retune their radios, or "Hop" to Ch(n+1), and now the Slave is not only allowed to transmit, but indeed must respond whether it successfully understood the last packet or not. Following the Master's reception slot, the Slave will now once again listen for a message. However, the Master may choose to transmit to someone else, or not transmit at all. The Slave will not transmit again until the Master again transmits to it.

Each device will hop once per packet. This is a fundamental part of the Bluetooth system and provides the following features:

• Security—Since the hopping is to a defined pseudo random sequence based on the device address of the Master.
• Reliability—Since if a particular radio interferer causes a packet to be lost on Ch(n), it is unlikely to be such a strong interferer on Ch(n+m), where n+m is guaranteed to be a significant distance from n due to the pseudo random hopping algorithm.

Bluetooth defines data packets which are 1, 3, or 5 slots long, and Figure 4–3 shows how the timing changes slightly for these multi-slot packets. Using a longer length packet allows higher data rates at the cost of reliability. Enough bursts of errors or interference to

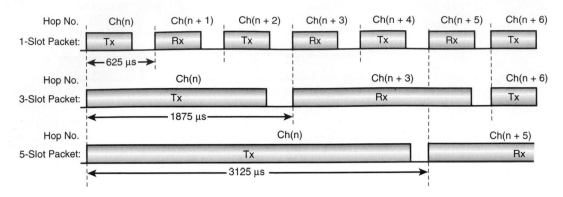

Figure 4–3   Slot timing for multi-slot packets.

cause a packet to be rejected are more likely to occur during one single long packet on the same channel than in every single one of a number of shorter packets on different channels.

All packets have the same header and control data overhead, and so multi-slot packets are more data efficient. Also, since it is impractical to hop during a single packet due to the long radio settling time, the maximum amount of time is used for data transfer.

So, a Master is in control, deciding what—if anything—to transmit (1, 3, or 5 slot packet) and when to transmit it. The Slaves sit quietly, listening at the expected time, and any Slave hearing a packet with its own address receives the packet and responds to it.

Bluetooth would be a useful technology if all it did was facilitate point to point communication; however, it is much, much more than this. In fact, Bluetooth creates a kind of miniature Local Area Network (LAN); of course there is yet another Bluetooth buzz-word for this: "piconet".

A piconet is an arbitrary collection of Bluetooth-enabled devices which are physically close enough to be able to communicate and are exchanging information in a regular way. A piconet is formed by a device configured as a Master, who "owns" the piconet, and between one and seven devices that always act as Slaves to this Master. All Slaves adopt the timing of the Master and will respond to any messages that include the Master's "Access Code" (derived from the Master's device address).

Figure 4–4 illustrates the topology of a point to point link between Master and Slave, together with a typical piconet. The third diagram shows something slightly different. Here, we have a Master with three Slaves, but the Master is itself a Slave belonging to another Master device. This is the so called "Scatternet." Since Bluetooth has a limit of seven Slaves in a piconet, it may be desirable to link piconets together to form either wider physical coverage areas or just to link together more than eight devices. We will discuss the exact mechanism for this later, but essentially this is achieved by the Master device switching roles on a TDM basis between Master in its own piconet and Slave in the other Master's piconet. This is illustrated in the diagram by the M/S label.

As mobile devices move around, they can easily move out of range and lose contact with the piconet. Each link has a supervision timeout, which ensures that such links are closed down.

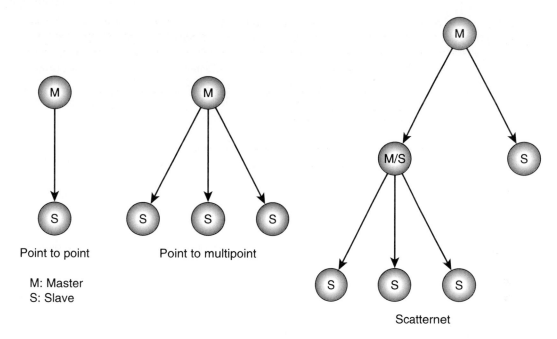

Figure 4–4   Piconets and scatternets.

This ability of devices to move around makes a Bluetooth piconet very different from a traditional wired network. Because it is much more dynamic, network participants can be changing constantly. This makes the normal network administrator function far too cumbersome for administration functions such as network configuration and adding new members. It is for this reason that such networks are referred to as "ad-hoc" networks. The Bluetooth Link Controller has specific operations which can detect new devices in range and can easily form links to them.

4.4   SYSTEM TIMING

Before we look at the actual structure of the various Bluetooth packets and how a device addresses messages to specific other devices, it is useful to focus a little more on system timing and to understand the concept of the Bluetooth clock.

Like many communications protocols, Bluetooth synchronises most operations to a real time clock or time of day counter. This ensures that we can, for example, synchronise Tx-Rx data exchanges between devices, differentiate between lost and re-sent packets, and generate a predictable and reproducible pseudo random sequence of frequency hop channel numbers. The Bluetooth clock is a 28 bit count which is reset to 0 at power up and free-runs thereafter, incrementing every half slot, or 312.5 µs. It wraps approximately once per day. Every device has its own "Native" free-running counter that controls the timing and operation of that device. The native clock is referred to as CLKN.

If a device is operating as a Master it controls the piconet, and so it uses CLKN as its internal reference timing. If a device is operating as a Slave, then its timing must be exactly synchronised to that of its Master. Synchronising to the Master ensures that a Slave's Rx and Tx slots line up correctly with the Master's and that it chooses correctly matching hop channel numbers. To synchronise with the Master, a Slave must add an offset value onto its own native clock (CLKN) (see Figure 4–5). This offset derives a new clock value, CLK, which is its estimate of the Master's CLKN. This is also referred to as the "piconet clock."

There is one other clock value defined in Bluetooth: CLKE, which is derived by adding another offset to CLKN. It is used by a Master to create an estimate of the CLK in a Slave device. This is used in the specific case of establishing a connection with a Slave before the Slave has synchronised to the Master. This will be explained later when we look at establishing a connection using the paging procedures.

The lowest two bits of CLK are directly used to delimit the slots and half slots for packet transmit and receive. They also set the criteria for the choice of Tx or Rx, depending on whether the device is acting as a Master or a Slave. A Master transmission in connection always starts when $CLK[1:0] = 00$, and a Slave transmission in connection always starts when $CLK[1:0] = 10$. Figure 4–6 shows how $CLK[27:0]$ is driven from the 1 µs symbol timing and how the lower parts of the clock, $CLK[12:0]$, control the most important Bluetooth time periods.

Figures 4–7 and 4–8 illustrate the use of $CLK[1:0]$ and introduce the "Uncertainty window," which accommodates any variation in the system timing between two communicating devices. The receiver in the Slave will be enabled some time earlier than we would expect the Master's transmission to begin, and in the event of no transmission from the Master, the Slave's radio will be turned off only after a timeout delay. This straddling of the "ideal" Rx start point allows timing drift to be accommodated and the Slave to resynchronise each time it receives. All devices perform a correlation against the first part of the packet; the "synchronisation word" so as to realign their timing

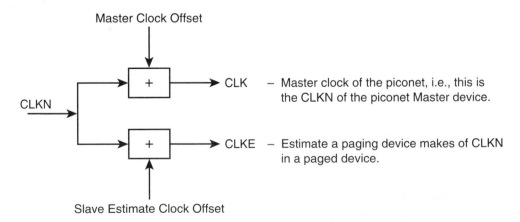

Figure 4–5   Conceptual Bluetooth CLK offset application.

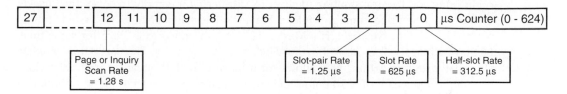

Figure 4–6   The Bluetooth clock.

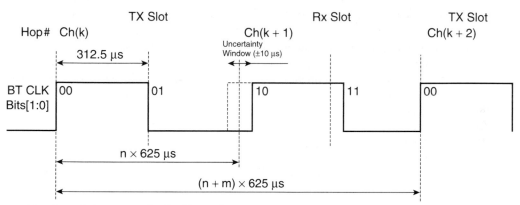

n: Number of slots occupied by Tx packet.
m: Number of slots occupied by Rx packet.

Figure 4–7   Tx - Rx cycle of transceiver in normal Master mode.

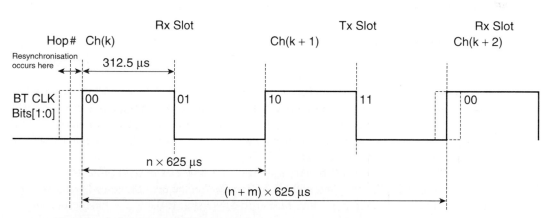

n: Number of slots occupied by Rx packet.
m: Number of slots occupied by Tx packet.

Figure 4–8   Rx - Tx cycle of transceiver in normal Slave mode.

to the start of the transmitting device. A Master will simply receive this packet on the resynchronised timing, while a Slave will actually change its system timing to match that of the Master's. If a Master has not transmitted to a Slave for some time, the Slave will resynchronise within this window. In a connection, the uncertainty window is normally set to ± 10 μs. This allows for a Slave to be left alone for up to 800 slots, assuming a worst case of ± 20 ppm accuracy on each of the Master's and Slave's timing references.

4.5   PHYSICAL LINKS: SCO AND ACL

A link is established between a device acting as Master and a device acting as Slave. Once a link has been set up, there are two basic types of data packets that may be exchanged with one very important distinction between the two—each is characterised by the two following link types:

- Asynchronous Connection-Less (ACL).
- Synchronous Connection Oriented (SCO).

4.5.1   ACL

An ACL link exists between a Master and a Slave as soon as a connection has been established. A Master may have a number of ACL links to a number of different Slaves at any one time, but only one link can exist between any two devices. As described above, the Master does not always transmit to the same Slave in a regular fashion. Thus the ACL link provides a packet-switched connection where data is exchanged sporadically as and when data is available from higher up the stack. The choice of which Slave to transmit to and receive from is up to the Master on a slot by slot basis, and so both asynchronous and isochronous (time bounded) services are possible. Most ACL packets facilitate error checking and retransmission to assure data integrity.

ACL links carry data to and from either the L2CAP or LMP layers. All user data is sent through L2CAP and passed to the baseband as L2CAP packets. Configuration and control of the links is carried out by the two opposing LM entities, and the associated command and control data is passed to the baseband as LMP packets. We will discuss this further in the section on logical links. Data is carried in DH (Data High rate) packets and DM (Data Medium rate) packets; the medium rate packets carry less data, but provide extra error protection.

A Slave may only respond with an ACL packet in the next Slave-to-Master slot if it has been addressed in the preceding Master-to-Slave slot. If the Slave fails to decode the Slave address in the packet header, it does not know for sure whether it was addressed or not and so is not allowed to respond.

Broadcast packets are ACL packets that are not addressed to a specific Slave and so are received by every Slave.

4.5.2   SCO

A SCO link is quite different and provides a symmetric link between Master and Slave with reserved channel bandwidth and regular periodic exchange of data in the form of reserved slots. Thus, the SCO link provides a circuit-switched connection where data is regularly exchanged, and as such it is intended for use with time-bounded information such as audio.

A Master can support up to three SCO links to the same Slave or to different Slaves. A Slave can support up to three SCO links from the same Master. Due to the time-bounded nature of SCO data, SCO packets are never retransmitted.

The Master will transmit SCO packets to the Slave at regular intervals, defined by the parameter T_{SCO}. This is referred to as the "SCO interval" and is counted in slots. The Slave is always allowed to respond with a SCO packet in the reserved response slot, unless it correctly decoded the packet header and discovered that it had not been addressed as expected. If the packet was incorrectly decoded due to errors, then the Slave may still respond as the slot is reserved. Indeed, in normal operation, the Master is not allowed to transmit elsewhere in the reserved slot. An exception is a broadcast LMP message, which would take precedence over the SCO link.

A SCO link is set up by a Link Manager (LM) command from the Master to the Slave. This message will contain timing parameters to specify the reserved slots such as the SCO interval, T_{SCO}, and the starting offset, D_{SCO}. To avoid offsets being introduced by clock wrap-arounds, an initialisation flag in the setup command indicates which one of two initialisation procedures to use. The SCO link then commences as follows:

$$\text{Master } CLK[27] = 0: \text{ Initialisation 1}$$
$$CLK[27:1]\,\text{mod}\ T_{SCO} = D_{SCO}$$
$$\text{Master } \overline{CLK[27]} = 1: \text{ Initialisation 2}$$
$$(\overline{CLK[27]}, CLK[26:1])\ \text{mod}\ T_{SCO} = D_{SCO}$$

From now on, SCO data will be exchanged every T_{SCO} slots.

A device must schedule any ACL traffic around reserved SCO slots so as to preserve the integrity of the SCO link. The one exception to this are Link Management control packets, which are allowed to override the SCO link since there must be a way to shut down SCO links in the event all bandwidth is reserved.

4.6   BLUETOOTH PACKET STRUCTURE

This section introduces the different types of packets that are used for communicating over interdevice ACL and SCO links. We break down the packets into their constituent parts such as access code, packet header, payload header, and payload.

Every packet consists of an access code, a header, and a payload as illustrated in Figure 4–9. The access code is used to detect the presence of a packet and to address the packet to a specific device. For example, Slaves detect the presence of a packet by matching the access code against their stored copy of the Master's access code. The header con-

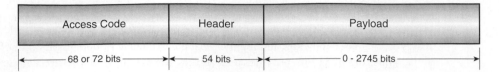

Figure 4–9 Bluetooth packet structure.

tains all the control information associated with the packet and the link, such as the address of the Slave for which the packet is intended. Finally, the payload contains the actual message information if this is a higher layer protocol message such as might be sent from L2CAP or LM, or the data if this is actually data being passed down the stack.

4.6.1 Access Code

During a connection when a link is active, the access code (see Figure 4–10) identifies the packet as being from or to a specific Master, as it is formed from the Master's Bluetooth device address. In other modes of operation, a special device address may be used, for example, in inquiry to produce the Inquiry Access Code (IAC).

The first part of the access code is a 4 bit preamble which is used to detect the edges of the received data. The preamble is a fixed sequence of either 0 1 0 1 or 1 0 1 0, depending on the value of the first bit of the synchronisation word[2] (sync word) so as to form a known 5 bit sequence. This gives the DC thresholding and clock recovery circuitry only 5 μs to create a reliable clock signal with which to sample and clock in the remainder of

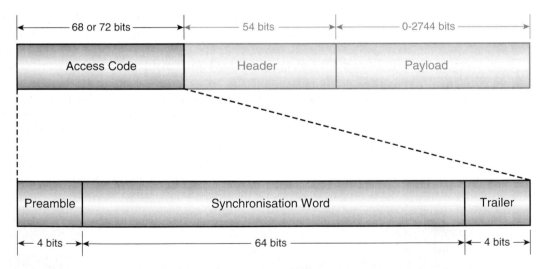

Figure 4–10 Bluetooth access code structure.

[2]The preamble is 0101 for a sync word which starts with a 0, and 1010 otherwise. The trailer is 1010 for a sync word which ends with a 0, and 0101 otherwise.

the data. If a payload is following on, then the last part of the access code is a four bit trailer, and, similar to the preamble, this may be used to perform more accurate DC thresholding and clock recovery. However, by this stage, the radio must already be settled to get good access code matching performance in a real-world environment.

The synchronisation word (see Figure 4–11) is formed from the 24 bit Lower Address Part (LAP) of the Bluetooth device address using an algorithm defined in the Bluetooth specification. First, the algorithm appends a predefined 6 bit sequence known as a Barker sequence to the LAP to improve the autocorrelation properties of the sync word. This is then XOR'd with bits 34 to 63 of a full length, 64 bit PN sequence P[63:0]. The resulting 30 bit sequence is then encoded with a (64, 30) BCH (Bose-Chaudhuri-Hocquenghem) block code to yield a 34 bit parity word. The remaining bits, 0 to 33 of the PN sequence, are then XOR'd with the 34 bit BCH parity word to derive the final coded parity word. The second XOR'ing stage removes the cyclic properties of the block code from the result.

A more complete derivation is given in the specification. However, the significant point is that the 34 bit BCH parity word is the key element of the sync word and exhibits very high auto-correlation and very low co-correlation properties. Thus, when a device is correlating against its expected sync word, it will find a strong peak exactly where the reference sync word and received sync word line up. Other nonmatching sync words will feature no such peak and indeed will have a low average, much less than 50% of the maximum 34 possible. The remainder of the sync word is constructed from the actual LAP and Barker sequence used to generate the parity word and, as such, is less useful—the LAP in particular. Two devices' LAPs may differ in only one bit; the two parity words, however, will be quite different, while the remainder of the sync words will be very similar.

It is a topic of debate in the industry that some of the space occupied by including the whole LAP may have been put to better use as an extended preamble to ease the DC thresholding and clock recovery problems in the radio. Oversampling the access code can mitigate this problem by allowing clock recovery to extend into the access code region.

The receiving device continually shifts data into a correlator which does a complete 64 point correlation against the reference or expected sync word. A match indicates that this packet is intended for the receiving device, and it will continue to receive the packet header; otherwise, after the uncertainty window has passed, the radio can be shut down to conserve power. In this way, a Slave will only receive packets which are transmitted by its Master within the Master's own piconet. If two piconets are close by, each set of Slaves will only receive packets on its own piconet, which has that piconet's sync word. The point in time at which the correlator match occurs is crucial, as this is when the Master is exactly 68 μs into its slot. This allows the Slave to readjust its own subslot timing to match up with the Master to within 1 μs. Similarly, a Master will only receive from its own Slaves.

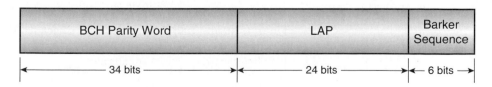

Figure 4–11   Synchronisation word structure.

4.6.1.1 Access Code Types. There are four distinct access codes, which might be in use at any one time, as follows:

- Channel Access Code (CAC)—The CAC is derived from the Master's LAP and is used by all devices in that piconet during the exchange of data over a live connection.
- Device Access Code (DAC)—The DAC is derived from a specific device's LAP. It is used when paging a specific device and by that device in Page Scan while listening for paging messages to itself.
- General Inquiry Access Code (GIAC)—The GIAC is used by all devices during the inquiry procedures, as no prior knowledge of anyone's LAP will exist. The GIAC is fixed in the specification as 0x9E8B33.
- Dedicated Inquiry Access Code (DIAC)—There is a range of DIACs reserved by the specification for carrying out inquiry procedures between a specific set of devices only, i.e., printers or cellular handsets. These use LAPs in the range 0x9E8B00 – 0x9E8B3F. There have not been any definitions of specific DIACs for specific classes of devices as yet, and so the Generic Access Profile (GAP) specification indicates that only the Limited Inquiry Access Code (LIAC) should be used. This is the only currently defined DIAC and is based on the LAP 0x9E8B00. Two devices may use the LIAC on a temporary basis only where user intervention has caused them to attempt to discover and be discovered by each other.

4.6.2 Packet Header

The packet header in Figure 4–12 contains control information associated with the packet. In total, the header contains 18 bits of information, which are protected by a Forward Error Correction (FEC) code of 1/3. This encoding replicates the data three times so that

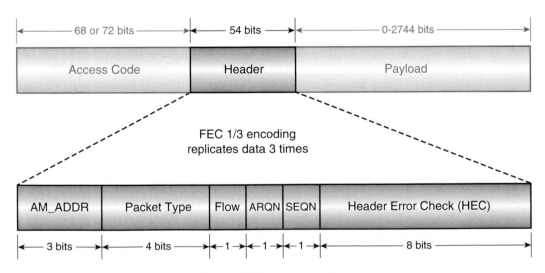

Figure 4–12 Packet header structure.

each bit occupies 3 μs, or 3 bit periods on air. The resulting header is then 54 μs in length. This high level of redundancy and coding overhead is employed because each field is crucial to the correct operation of the link control protocol and thus the link. A CRC field is included to allow the entire packet to be ignored and the link status maintained should any of the contents become corrupted.

AM_ADDR.   During the paging process, the Master will assign an Active Member ADDRess (AM_ADDR) to the Slave. This will then form the connection handle used to address all communications to the Slave and for the Master to differentiate between responses from different Slaves. The 3 bit field is sufficient for seven Slaves. An AM_ADDR of zero corresponds to a broadcast packet from the Master to be received by all of its Slaves. The FHS is an exception in that it is not a broadcast packet but can carry an AM_ADDR of zero. This is because no AM_ADDR has been assigned at the instant the FHS packet is first transmitted.

Packet Type.   The packet type defines which type of traffic is carried by this packet (SCO, ACL, NULL or POLL), the type of error correction used for the payload, and how many slots the payload will last for.

Flow.   This flag is asserted by a device when it is unable to receive any more data due to its receive buffer not being emptied.

ARQN and SEQN.   The ARQN flag is asserted by a device to indicate that the previous reception was successful following validation of the CRC (ACKnowledge or ACK-condition). If, however, the ARQN was lost due to failure of the returned header, then the original sender of the data will assume a Negative-AcKnowledge (NAK) condition and retransmit the first packet again. Each time a new packet is sent, the SEQN (Sequence) flag is toggled. However, in this case, because the packet is resent, the SEQN flag will stay the same and the recipient will see two identical packets where the SEQN flag has not changed. It will then ignore the second and all subsequent packets until the SEQN flag changes. Even if the link is very bad, an ACK will eventually get through and the sequence will move on.

Header Error Check (HEC).   The HEC field is simply a CRC function performed on the header represented in octal notation by the generator polynomial 647. It is initialised with either the Master or Slave UAP or DCI, depending on the packet. (DCI is a Default Check Initialisation and is all zeroes.) The HEC allows a recipient to ignore the remainder of a packet following failure of the HEC.

4.6.3 ACL Payload

The payload field of all ACL packets (Figure 4–13) is split into three parts; the payload header, the payload data itself, and the Cyclic Redundancy Check (CRC) field.

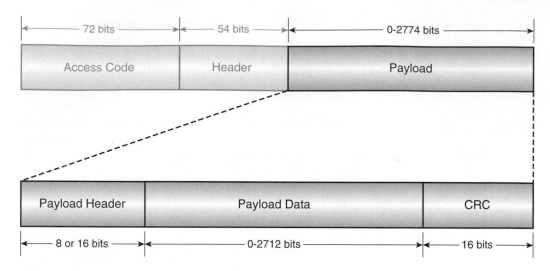

Figure 4–13   ACL payload structure.

4.6.4   ACL Payload Header

The payload header field contains the following logical link control information (see Figure 4–14):

- The L_CH (Logical Channel) field—Indicates whether this payload is the start or continuation of an L2CAP message (since L2CAP messages may last several ACL packets) or an LMP message (which is carried only in single-slot ACL packets).

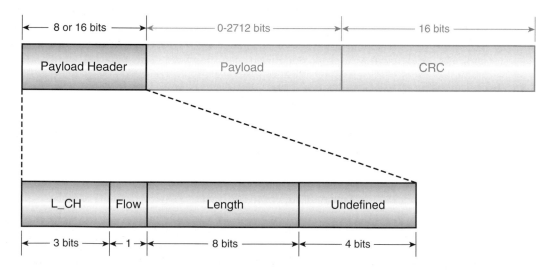

Figure 4–14   ACL payload header structure.

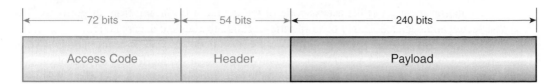

Figure 4–15   SCO packet structure.

- The flow flag—Controls data transfer at the L2CAP level.
- The length field—Details the length in bytes of the payload data itself.

4.6.5   SCO Packet Structure

SCO packets (Figure 4–15) share the same access code and header as ACL packets, though the flow, ARQ, and SEQ fields are redundant since flow control and retransmission do not apply to SCO links. A CRC field is also absent. The size of the payload is fixed at 30 bytes (240 bits), with a source data size of 10, 20, or 30 bytes, depending on the packet type which selects the FEC ratio to use (1/3, 2/3, or none).

4.6.6   Mixed SCO / ACL Packet Structure

A special case of SCO is the DV packet in Figure 4–16, which, like SCO packets, must be sent at regular intervals. The voice field is only large enough to send 10 byte, HV1-style data which is not FEC-protected. Similar to normal SCO packets, the voice field can not be retransmitted. However, the data field is protected with 2/3 FEC coding, a CRC field, and the usual flow, ARQ, and SEQ flags. Retransmission of the data field is possible, and this will occur alongside the ongoing SCO transmission in the voice field.

The data payload field will carry up to 9 bytes (72 bits) of data, and as such, the data field is closest to a DM1 packet in nature, although it is almost half the bandwidth. The pad field at the end of the packet is appended, as required, to the source data to ensure it is a multiple of 10 bits prior to FEC encoding.

4.6.7   Special Packets—ID, NULL, POLL, and FHS

The ID packet consists only of the access code and is used during "preconnection" operation, where a link has not yet been established and the relative timings between devices may be unrelated. The ID packet is a highly robust signalling mechanism, since the only

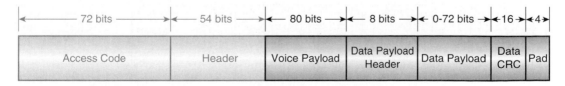

Figure 4–16   DV packet structure.

information it carries is the access code of the device it is coming from or going to. It is detected and decoded simply by correlating against the desired access code.

The NULL packet consists only of the access code and packet header and is used to pass acknowledgment (ARQ) or flow control back to a device following reception of a packet. The NULL packet itself does not require acknowledgement.

This typically occurs during a link when the recipient of a data transfer has nothing to send in return. It must, however, still acknowledge the packet it has received. Indeed, on initial establishment of a link between two devices but in the absence of any data to transfer, the Slave sends NULL packets.

The POLL packet has the same structure as the NULL packet, but whereas the NULL packet does not have to be acknowledged, the POLL packet must be acknowledged whether or not the recipient has any data of its own to return. However, the POLL packet does not itself affect the acknowledgement or retransmission control scheme governed by ARQ and SEQ. The typical use of POLL is by a Master to check the presence of Slaves in a piconet, which must then respond if they are present.

The Frequency Hop Synchronisation (FHS) packet in Figure 4–17 is sent by an inquiry scanning device to an inquirer during the inquiry procedure, by a Master to a Slave during the page procedure and by a device taking over as Master when Master and Slave devices switch roles. In all cases, the FHS packet provides all the information required by the recipient to address the sender in terms of timing, and thus frequency hop channel synchronisation and correct device access code. The contents of the FHS packet are as follows:

The BCH parity word field contains the key part of the sync word, and, together with the LAP and relevant Barker sequence, it will form the Device Access Code of the sender. Note, some Bluetooth devices always require the BCH parity word, even though it is possible to calculate the correct BCH word to use on-the-fly from the relevant LAP (and some devices do this).

The LAP, UAP, and NAP are the complete 48 bit device address of the sender and are used for different purposes in packet coding and hopping calculation.

SR and SP specify the page Scan Repetition and Scan Period times, respectively, while the page mode field indicates which page mode is used by the sender by default.

The class field indicates which device class the sender belongs to, such as printer, PDA, cellular handset, etc.

The AM_ADDR field indicates the AM_ADDR to be used by the recipient if being sent by a Master during paging or Master/Slave switch, or it must be zero if being returned by an inquiry scanning device.

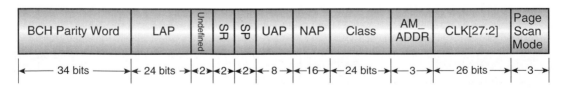

Figure 4–17 FHS payload format.

The CLK field is the native Bluetooth clock of the sender to a slot-pair accuracy, that is CLK[27:2]. This allows the recipient to synchronise its complete clock by calculating the relevant offset and applying this to the native clock. The lower order bits and sub-slot, (i.e., µs) synchronisation is obtained by the action of the correlator matching against the Master's DAC (or in the case of a Master/Slave switch, a separate message is sent giving the synchronisation information for the low order bits).

4.7   PACKET TYPES AND PACKET CONSTRUCTION

Table 4–1 lists all the different packet types and their particular characteristics.

The Segment column splits the different packets into special control packets: single-slot data, 3 slot data, and 5 slot data, respectively. The different ACL packet types trade off more or less FEC coding and shorter or longer packets for lower data throughput with more robustness versus higher data throughput with less robustness. Greater protec-

Table 4–1   Packet Type Summary

Segment	Type Code	No. of Slots	SCO Link	ACL Link	Payload Header (bytes)	User Payload (bytes)	FEC	CRC
-	-	1/2	ID		0	0	No	No
1	0000	1	NULL	NULL	No	No	No	No
	0001	1	POLL	POLL	No	No	No	No
	0010	1	FHS	FHS	No	18	2/3	No
	0011	1	DM1	DM1	1	0-17	2/3	Yes
2	0100	1	*Undefined*	DH1	1	0-27	No	Yes
	0101	1	HV1	*Undefined*	No	10	1/3	No
	0110	1	HV2	*Undefined*	No	20	2/3	No
	0111	1	HV3	*Undefined*	No	30	No	No
	1000	1	DV[3]	*Undefined*	1	10 0-9	2/3	Yes
	1001	1	*Undefined*	AUX1	1	0-29	No	No
3	1010	3	*Undefined*	DM3	2	0-121	2/3	Yes
	1011	3	*Undefined*	DH3	2	0-183	No	Yes
	1100	3	*Undefined*	*Undefined*	-	-	-	-
	1101	3	*Undefined*	*Undefined*	-	-	-	-
4	1110	5	*Undefined*	DM5	2	0-224	2/3	Yes
	1111	5	*Undefined*	DH5	2	0-339	No	Yes

[3]The grey boxes indicate parameters with respect to the ACL element of a DV packet; the remainder are applicable to the SCO element. DV packets are thought of as belonging to the SCO family.

tion against errors is at the expense of data redundancy, while long packets (i.e., Dx3 / Dx5) are more susceptible to an irrecoverable number of burst errors during the longer on-air packet time.

The different SCO packet types simply use increasing error correction to add redundancy and thus robustness. Bluetooth coded audio does not require the data bandwidth which a multi-slot packet would provide.

It is the responsibility of the Link Manager (LM) to monitor the quality and reliability of the link and decide what packet types are appropriate at any given time. Some devices will not support all the packet types, and so at link setup time, some negotiation is often necessary.

Symmetric throughput is obtained by using the same packet types in both directions. However, many applications have asymmetric bandwidth requirements. In general, a link may pass different length packets in one direction, to those passed in the other direction. Indeed, the maximum data throughput of 723.2 kb/s can be achieved with 5 slot packets in one direction and single-slot packets in the reverse direction at 57.6 kb/s. This compares with the maximum symmetric rate of 433.9 kb/s using DH5 packets in both directions.

4.8 LOGICAL CHANNELS

The specification defines five logical information channels which are carried over the physical SCO and ACL links. Although not commonly referred to, they are important in differentiating between the content of the various packets being passed and the information they carry. The channels are as follows:

LC (Link Control)—This is carried via the packet header and consists of the ARQ, SEQ, and associated control data. As described previously, this data is crucial to maintaining and controlling the link.

LM (Link Manager)—This is carried via a dedicated ACL payload and contains LM control data being exchanged between the two LM entities. Typically carried by DM-type packets, the LM channel is indicated by the L_CH = 11 code. Note that the DM1 packet is common to SCO and ACL links. This is to allow LMP messages to be carried over an active SCO link.

UA / UI (User Asynchronous) or User-Isochronous data)—This is carried via the ACL payload and contains L2CAP user data. Fragmentation is handled by the appropriate value of L_CH; 10 for start packets and 01 for continuation packets. Isochronous, though outside the scope of the baseband, will be correctly transported provided that it is timed correctly by entities higher up the stack.

US (User-Synchronous data)—Transparent Synchronous data is carried via SCO channel payloads.

4.9 CHANNEL CODING AND BITSTREAM PROCESSING

Figure 4–18 describes the baseband data flow and how channel coding fits into the overall picture. Since each coding function is carried out on all or part of the data bitstream as it passes through the baseband, we shall also refer to this as bitstream processing.

Coding of data before transmission through a carrier medium or channel is important to protect the data against an imperfect channel. Since Bluetooth is only designed to work over a line-of-sight link and the data rates are relatively modest for the signalling bandwidth, the necessary coding is not too complex. The coding applied to the data bitstream in Bluetooth consists of the following elements:

CRC (Cyclic Redundancy Check) and **Header Error Check (HEC)** A CRC is performed on all packet headers and on ACL payload data to validate the integrity of the received data. FEC processing has a limited scope for correction and even detection of errors, while a CRC will flag any errors in the data. The 8 bit HEC is calculated over the packet header before applying FEC. The 16 bit CRC is calculated over the payload header and payload. In both cases, the LFSRs are initialised with an appropriate device UAP to provide more dependence on correct addressing to increase robustness to errors.

Encryption The details of encryption are covered separately in the section on security and encryption. The cipher stream, which is sourced by the encryption engine, is simply exclusive OR'd into the bitstream data path.

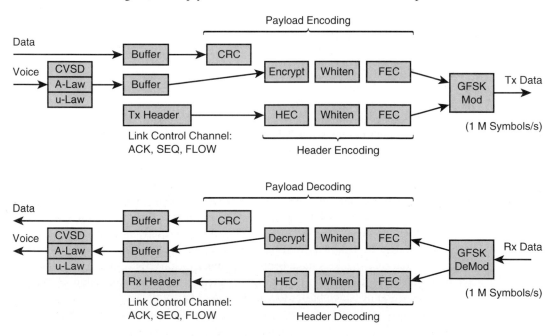

Figure 4–18 Baseband data flow.

Whitening or **bit randomisation** Whitening involves mixing a pseudo-random bit sequence with the data bitstream to randomise the data. This greatly reduces the possibility of long sequences of zeros or ones, or put another way, DC bias. This would cause certain radio architectures (especially those that directly drive Tx data onto the VCO) to drift off channel. It also gives rise to better performance from the receive chain in a radio due to the avoidance of offsets which might otherwise build up.

FEC (Forward Error Correction) By adding extra "parity" bits created from the input data, a number of bit errors in the data may be detected and corrected. There are three FEC options selected by virtue of the packet type: non, 1/3, and 2/3. The strongest, 1/3 encoding, involves simply repeating each bit three times and is decoded by carrying out a majority function on the receive side. This is sufficient to detect two in every three bits input and to correct one in every three. The packet header uses 1/3 encoding, as the link information contained therein is the most critical part of the packet. 2/3 FEC is a (15, 10) shortened Hamming code typically implemented as an LFSR. For every 10 bits of data which pass through, the LFSR is "open circuited" (i.e., the taps removed) and the contents of the five registers are shifted out to form a 5 bit parity value. Thus, for every 10 bits input, 15 bits are output. This protection is sufficient to detect 2 bits in the 10 bit input and to correct 1 in every 10. Padding after the CRC is required to ensure the input data is a multiple of 10 bits in length.

Whitening and the HEC are applied to all packets with at least a header. FEC and CRC are only applied depending on the packet type, as shown in Table 4–1, and FEC may be traded off against link bandwidth as we have already discussed.

The ordering of bitstream processes is important. Considering the transmit path shown in Figure 4–18, first the CRC or HEC is attached to provide validation of the raw data. Then, the whitening is applied to randomise the data. Finally, the FEC is performed. The use of whitening before FEC maintains the performance of the FEC process where there is a long sequence of zeros or ones, which is quite likely in user data payloads.

SCO data is encoded or decoded by one of the three audio coding schemes and bypasses the CRC stage in both directions, since retransmission of SCO is not possible. The Tx / Rx buffers shown are to allow transmit data to be written and receive data to be read while the bitstream is processing live data. Each link will require its own transmit buffer since any previously transmitted ACL packet may have to be retransmitted much later after several other ACL packets have been transmitted on different links. Thus, the next packet may not be sent, it being replaced in sequence by a retransmission of the old packet. This selection of which buffer to send is under control of the ARQ scheme.

As an illustration of the application of FEC, Table 4–2 lists the complete composition of the FHS packet as transmitted on-air with 2/3 FEC. Note, the order of transmission is Least Significant Bit (LSB) first.

Table 4–2   FHS Packet Composition

Bit Position		Contents	No. of Bits
Start	**End**		
0	3	Preamble	4
4	67	Access Code	64
68	71	Trailer	4
72	125	Packet Header	54
126	135	Parity(9:0)	10
136	140	————FEC Check Word————	5
141	150	Parity(19:10)	10
151	155	————FEC Check Word————	5
156	165	Parity(29:20)	10
166	170	————FEC Check Word————	5
171	180	[LAP(5:0), Parity(33:30)]	10
181	185	————FEC Check Word————	5
186	195	LAP(15:6)	10
196	200	————FEC Check Word————	5
201	210	[Undefined(1:0), LAP(23:16)]	10
211	215	————FEC Check Word————	5
216	225	[UAP(5:0), SP(1:0), SR(1:0)]	10
226	230	————FEC Check Word————	5
231	240	[NAP(7:0), UAP(7:6)]	10
241	245	————FEC Check Word————	5
246	255	[Class(1:0), NAP(15:8)]	10
256	260	————FEC Check Word————	5
261	270	Class(11-2)	10
271	275	————FEC Check Word————	5
276	285	Class(21-12)	10
286	290	————FEC Check Word————	5
291	300	[Clk(6:2), AM_ADDR(2:0), Class(23-22)]	10
301	305	————FEC Check Word————	5
306	315	Clk(16:7)	10
316	320	————FEC Check Word————	5
321	330	Clk(26:17)	10
331	335	————FEC Check Word————	5
336	345	[CRC(5:0), PSMODE(2:0), CLK(27)]	10
346	350	————FEC Check Word————	5
351	360	CRC(15:6)	10
361	365	————FEC Check Word————	5
		Total:	**366**

4.10   TIMEBASE SYNCHRONISATION AND RECEIVE CORRELATION

Now that we have discussed the operation of the overall system timing and have looked at the structure of the various packets, it is useful to understand how a Bluetooth device maintains timebase synchronisation by periodically correlating against the sync word. This is shown in Figure 4–19. Nominally, the window of accuracy expected within Bluetooth is ± 10 μs or 20 symbols, which as described above requires resynchronisation at least every 800 slots. However, in other circumstances, such as inquiry scan or returning from park mode, this window may be larger.

Correlation is carried out against the stored sync word of 64 bits and so the correlator must first shift in the full number of 64 receive bits. This process is started half the uncertainty window before the beginning of the slot. A 64 point correlation is then carried out and compared with a threshold value. Each successive receive bit is shifted in and the correlation repeated until a number (equal to the uncertainty window) of correlations have been made or the threshold value is breached. If the threshold is breached, the access code has been matched; if, on the other hand, the end point is reached, then the correlation has "timed out" and no valid access code was found.

At the point where the correlator matches, two operations must occur:

- An event is signalled to the receive state machine to commence reception.
- A measure of the subslot symbol accurate timing offset between the two devices is made and the complete clock offset updated appropriately to maintain CLK.

The match point is the point at which the last bit of the Master's transmitted sync word has been received. Either the next bit in 1μs time (68 bit access code) or the fifth bit in 5μs time (72 bit access code) will be the start of the packet header. The timing offset between transmitter and recipient is measured at this point. If TMatch is the time in sym-

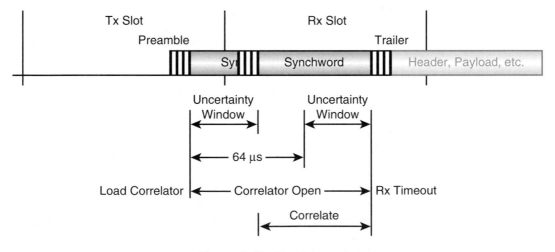

Figure 4–19   Receive correlator timing.

bol ticks from the start of the recipient's receive slot to the correlator match point as taken from the current value of the timebase, the offset is TMatch less the sync word length (64) and less the preamble length (4), or TMatch - 68.

The updated CLK and subslot count are applied immediately, and so the following reception of header and payload will be correctly synchronised. If the device is a Slave, then it updates its offsets so as to align with the Master. However, if the device is a Master, each subsequent slot pair will involve a different Slave, each using the Master's timing. So, although the Master maintains an offset of zero in each case, it must resynchronise its receive process to find the correct start of data following the correlator match.

4.11   FREQUENCY HOPPING

Frequency hopping really is at the heart of Bluetooth, and we will see in the next chapter how it forms a fundamental part of the protocol. The hop channel selection function itself is a straightforward mapping algorithm which follows a different sequence depending on the link control state (i.e., inquiry, paging, etc.). It selects a particular sequence depending on parts of the supplied BD address (LAP and UAP). It then indexes through that sequence using the supplied Bluetooth CLK value. Due to the restrictions on channel allocation described in the radio chapter, the algorithm may be truncated to work with only 23 channels in some countries, rather than the usual 79.

The stream of channel numbers generated is passed to the RF subsystem, where they are programmed into the channel synthesiser.

For each of the 79 channels and 23 hop modes of operation, there are four sequences defined as listed below. The following descriptions are specific to 79 channel hop operation and selection is based on the LC state.

(i) Page or Inquiry

This is a fast sequence driven by the half slot clock using 32 equally distributed hops over the full range for transmit. The transmit sequence is split into two "trains"—A and B. The A train contains the 16 frequencies on either side of and nearest to the expected[4] page or inquiry scan frequency that the scanning device is listening on. The B train contains the next 16 split on either side of the A train. The result is the sequence that follows:

$$f(k-8)...f(k)...f(k+7), f(k+8)...f(k+15), f(k-16)...f(k-9)$$

where f(k) is the expected channel as defined by CLKE during page. During inquiry, since no estimate exists, the sequence is driven by CLKN of the inquirer and we just start at a random point in the sequence. The correct BD address (or inquiry LAP / UAP) is of course important to provide both units with the same sequence. Over time, the order within the trains is shifted to avoid any constant mismatch.

[4]For inquiry there is no expected inquiry scan frequency.

After two half-slot transmits, the device listens on two half slots, but on frequencies corresponding to two successive page / inquiry response sequence frequencies that would follow from the two page / inquiry frequencies used for transmit. The algorithm is effectively a superset of that used for the response calculation to facilitate this "frequency handshaking" operation.

(ii) Page Response or Inquiry Response

During a response state, the CLKE (page response) or CLKN (inquiry response) input to the selection algorithm is frozen[5] at its value when the scanning device correlator fires signalling reception of the ID packet. This ensures that once channel coincidence has been found, it is not lost. The first response is made at the same frequency, but each subsequent transmission is at the next in the page / inquiry sequence, obtained simply by incrementing a counter offset "N" once per slot pair in page response or after each FHS reply in inquiry response.

(iii) Page Scan or Inquiry Scan

This is a very slow sequence, that uses the same BD address inputs as the page / inquiry scheme and thus follows the same sequence but is driven by CLKN bits 15 to 12 and thus hops at 1.28s.

(iv) Connection

Channel hops are produced at a rate of one per slot, except during multislot packets. There is no hop during a multislot packet, although the sequence continues unhindered after the packet. The sequence involves all 79 (or 23) hop frequencies spread equally, but with the maximum distance between each, with the longest possible time interval between repeats. Repeat patterns are not exhibited over a short time period.

4.12 SUMMARY

The baseband is responsible for channel coding and decoding and low level control of the timing and management of the link within the domain of a single data packet transfer. It adds addressing and link control fields to the raw payload data and provides error detection and correction.

Devices exist in two basic modes of operation, either Slave or Master, and communicate between each other in miniature networks known as piconets, which consist of a number of Slaves controlled by a Master. The data links which exist between devices are classified into SCO for time bounded data such as audio and ACL for packet based data.

A number of different packet types exist, and these offer a tradeoff between reliability and data bandwidth.

Bluetooth ensures that devices maintain time synchronisation by repeatedly resynchronising to the Master's transmissions. Since the frequency hopping algorithm is based on the device clock, this also ensures that frequency hopping is in step.

---

[5]Bluetooth V1.1 does not freeze the CLKN input to the selection algorithm as it is pointless.

5

The Link Controller

5.1 INTRODUCTION

This chapter continues on from where the baseband chapter left off, looking at how the link control layer configures and controls the link and packet-oriented baseband. The link control layer carries out higher level operations such as inquiry and paging and manages multiple links with different devices and even different piconets.

5.2 LINK CONTROL PROTOCOL

The link control protocol is carried in the LC Channel as defined in the previous chapter, and is responsible for the mechanics of maintaining a link once it has been set up. Before moving onto looking at the overall link control state machine, we will first consider the Acknowledgement/Request (ARQ) scheme used for retransmission of corrupted data, as this forms a key part of the overall picture.

In every packet header, the ARQN flag will indicate the status of the previously received packet. ARQN = 1 (ACK) means the packet has been received and correctly decoded. ARQN = 0 (NAK) means that the previous receive failed.

A NAK occurs under the following conditions:

- A Slave fails to detect an access code and no receive occurs—Although mentioned in the specification, this is not actually possible as a Slave may only respond when it knows it has been transmitted to.
- A Master fails to detect an access code and no receive occurs—The Slave's response to a Master transmission has been lost.
- An access code is detected and the HEC fails—If the HEC has failed, we do not know who the packet was addressed to. In a piconet, all Slaves will potentially respond with NAK, except they are not allowed to respond unless they successfully decode and match the AM_ADDR. As for the first point, this is also not possible.
- An access code is detected and the CRC fails—This is the usual reason for a retransmit condition during connection.

Each time a new packet with a CRC is transmitted, the SEQN flag is toggled, whereas for a retransmitted packet, the SEQN flag will remain the same as the previous value. This allows a receiver to tell the difference between a packet which has been retransmitted because the receiver NAK'd the previous packet and a packet which has been retransmitted because the transmitter failed to receive the receiver's ACK flag correctly. In essence, if a packet is received correctly, but the SEQN flag is the same as the previously received SEQN flag on that link, then the packet is ignored. However, an ACK is returned subsequently so that the remote device will eventually stop retransmitting.

The Link Manager (LM) may request the Link Controller (LC) to flush its transmit buffer. Typically, this will occur after a timeout following a repeated retransmission attempt. If the payload is flushed, the SEQN flag will be unaffected, since an ACK is still required. If the ACK arrives just prior to transmission of the new packet following the flush, then the SEQN flag will be toggled in the normal way. Otherwise, the SEQN will remain as before and we will now be awaiting an ACK for what is now a new payload. This facilitates the transmission of isochronous data (see the section on logical channels).

In certain circumstances, the ARQN / SEQN state on receive and transmit is maintained as unaffected across several slots and executed much later. Packets where the access code and HEC check out, but the AM_ADDR is not that of the recipient or reception of any packet other than a Dx (DH, DM, or DV), do not affect the ARQN and SEQN flags. They are also unaffected during Hold or Sniff modes.

The ARQN and SEQN flags are initialised by the first packet exchange following setup of a link. The initial ARQN = NAK from both Slave and Master and both SEQNs are initialised to 1.

5.2.1 Broadcast

A Master may send data to all Slaves participating in the piconet simultaneously. The Master does this by sending any packet where the AM_ADDR field is set to zero (the broadcast address). All Slaves that successfully decode this "broadcast" packet will act on it. Since the broadcast is directed at more than one device, the ARQ scheme described above is not applicable.

The alternative used is to always retransmit broadcasts a specified number of times. The ARQN flag is unused; however, the SEQN flag is used to identify the retransmitted packets. A broadcast message lasting several packets is segmented into a number of Bluetooth packets, where each is retransmitted "N_{BC}" times in succession.

Broadcast L2CAP packets will be fragmented into multiple baseband packets, with each one transmitted N_{BC} times. Each new broadcast packet in a sequence is identified by toggling SEQN. However, the specification specifies that the sequence is reset to 1 at the start of each broadcast L2CAP or LMP packet. LMP packets fit into a single baseband packet, so if a series of LMP messages are sent, the SEQN flag will remain at 1. So there is no way of filtering out repeat LMP transmissions. Similarly, if an L2CAP packet is segmented into an odd number of baseband packets, the SEQN flag will be set to 1 for the transmissions of the end fragment of the L2CAP packet and will be forced to remain at 1 for the start of the next L2CAP packet. So the SEQN bit cannot be used to distinguish between the final fragment of the first packet and the start of the next packet. L2CAP cannot filter these packets either, and so they will be sent further up the stack, causing higher layers to receive multiple packet fragments. Indeed, the L2CAP part of the specification specifies that the use of baseband broadcast packets is prohibited if reliability is required. A somewhat telling statement!

A simple way to remedy the situation would be to make broadcast sequencing behave the same way as for any other packet. The SEQN sequence would continue from one sequence of broadcast packets to the next, instead of being reset to 1 at every LMP or L2CAP start packet. For single packet messages, SEQN would toggle on each one and any successive identical values would truly identify a retransmission, with the receive being aborted in the usual way.

This would require a change to the specification and many existing Bluetooth products. Therefore, it is unlikely to occur for the existing 1.1 specification. However, this is one of a number of issues that are worthy of consideration as the specification evolves past 1.1.

5.3 LINK CONTROLLER STATES

At any one time, a Bluetooth device is in one of a number of different states. The "major" link control states are first defined below, before a detailed examination of how a device moves from one state to another and carries out higher level operations such as connection establishment under the control of the application via the stack and LM.

5.3.1 Standby

In the standby state, the device is inactive, no data is being transferred, and the radio is not switched on. Thus, the device is unable to detect any access codes. This state is used normally to enable low power operation.

5.3.2 Inquiry

Inquiry is the process whereby a device will attempt to discover all the Bluetooth enabled devices in its local area. The baseband end of the Service Discovery Protocol (SDP), it allows a device to compile a list of devices which it may wish to connect with at a later time. During the inquiry procedure, the inquired upon devices will supply FHS packets to the inquirer. The FHS packets allow the inquirer to build a table of the essential information required to make a connection, such as CLKN, which controls the on-air timing, and frequency hop sequence, BD_ADDR, which controls the frequency hop sequence and forms part of the access code, and the BCH parity word, which also forms part of the access code.

5.3.3 Inquiry Scan

Inquiry scan is the other half of the inquiry procedure. Although scanning is optional and up to the application, most devices will periodically enter inquiry scan state to make themselves available to inquiring devices. They listen for an extended time (this is necessary, as they have no knowledge of the timing or frequency hop behaviour of any inquiring devices) for the inquiry packet using the fixed General or Dedicated Inquiry Access Codes (GIAC, DIAC). When they receive a valid inquiry message, they enter the *inquiry response* substate and respond with the FHS information as described above. The inquiry and inquiry scan states utilise a special hopping sequence (fast for inquiry and slow for inquiry scan), which is designed to reduce the amount of time before a frequency match occurs.

5.3.4 Page

To establish a connection, the device which is to become Master is instructed by the application to carry out the paging procedure. The Master first enters the page state, where it will transmit paging messages directed at the intended "Slave" device (using the access code and timing information gained from the previous inquiry procedure). The Slave acknowledges the paging message and the Master enters the **master response** substate and responds with its FHS packet.

5.3.5 Page Scan

As for inquiry scan, a device will typically enter page scan periodically to allow paging devices to establish a connection with it. Once a device in page scan state has successfully received a paging packet, it will enter the **Slave response** substate where it acknowledges the packet and awaits the FHS. On reception of the FHS, it updates its own CLK timing and sync word / access code reference before entering the connection state. Again, like the inquiry procedure, the paging procedure uses a special hopping sequence (fast for page and slow for page scan), which is designed to reduce the amount of time before a frequency match occurs.

It is possible to carry out the paging procedure with no prior inquiry if the device address is already known, as may be the case with a dedicated laptop/cellular phone arrangement, for example. The paging device is able to address the intended Slave, but because no CLKE (estimate of the Slave's clock) is available, the procedure will take much longer. In theory, the maximum length of time is 10s.

5.3.6   Connection – Active

On entry to the connection state, the Slave switches to the Master's CLK (by applying the relevant offset to its own CLKN) and thus moves on to the Master's frequency hop and timing sequence. The Master transmits a POLL packet to verify that the link has been successfully set up. The Slave must then respond with any type of packet, typically a NULL. Both ARQN flags are set for NAK, but the next transmission by the Master will start the ARQ, SEQ sequencing for real. If the connection fails to establish in this way, then after suitable timeouts, both devices revert to page and page scan, respectively and the whole process may restart.

Although a Slave may not actually be addressed for many slots, it stays synchronised to the Master during a connection by correlating against the Master's access code— referred to as the Channel Access Code (CAC)—in each packet the Master transmits, even if it is not destined for that Slave. The Master must therefore keep transmitting periodically, even if there is no data to send. It will use NULL packets for this purpose if necessary.

Once a Slave has triggered on the CAC and received the packet header, it will often find that the AM address does not match its own and must then abort the remainder of the reception. Since the packet type field in the header will tell it how many slots the packet will last for, it may use this information to enter Low Power Sleep mode for the duration of the Master's transmission.

During connection state, various data exchanges and logical channels are possible. However, from time to time, any device in connection state may move into a low power substate as described below.

5.3.7   Connection – Hold

In Hold mode, a device ceases to support ACL traffic for a defined period of time to free up bandwidth for other operations such as scanning, paging, inquiry, or Low Power Sleep. The device does, however, maintain its AM address. After the hold time has expired, the device synchronises to the CAC and begins to listen for traffic again.

5.3.8   Connection – Sniff

In Sniff mode, a Slave device is given a predefined slot time and periodicity to listen for traffic. The Slave will listen at slot number D_{sniff} every T_{sniff} slots for a timeout period of N_{sniff} slots. On reception of a packet during this time, it will continue to listen until packets with its AM address stop and the timeout period ceases. It then waits for the next sniff period.

5.3.9   Connection – Park

In Park mode, a Slave gives up its AM address and listens for traffic only occasionally. For the most part, the device is able to enter Low Power Sleep mode. The device only needs to wake up at a defined "Beacon" instant to synchronise to the CAC before returning to low power mode again. In this way, the Slave is able to stay synchronised to the Master even though it is running from a far less accurate Low Power Oscillator (LPO).

5.4   LINK CONTROLLER OPERATION

The familiar Bluetooth device state diagram appears in Figure 5–1. This diagram apparently shows routes going from standby, through inquiry, to connection. In fact, there is no such direct route. To establish a connection, one must go through paging or page scanning. The diagram is intended to show that the inquiry state can be entered either from

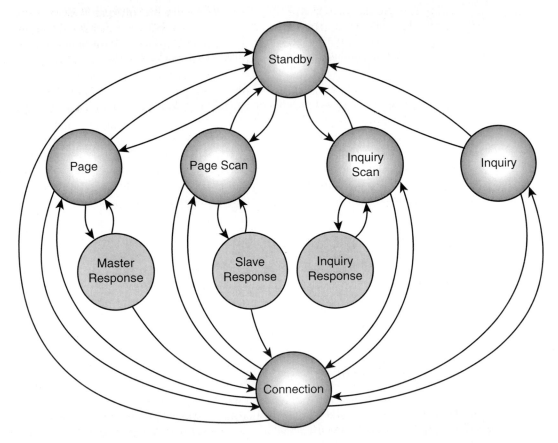

Figure 5–1   Link controller state diagram.

standby or from connection. It does not show the routes through the states to establish connections.

A simpler view of the major routes through the state diagram is illustrated in Figure 5–2. This gives a clear and simple picture of how a single link is established from scratch. However, in practice, the state transitions can be much more complex. For example, a Master in connection state already occupied with regular SCO traffic may carry out periodic inquiry operations to look for new would-be Slaves, paging operations to add new Slaves to the piconet, and even inquiry or page scans in case other would-be Masters are looking to add it as a switched Master / Slave to their piconets to create a scatternet!

In fact, a device in a fully active scatternet situation may switch from almost any of the major states to another as it moves between connection, link setup, inquiry, and power-saving operations. It is very important to realise that the apparently simple state machine shown in Figure 5–1 effectively represents only the state of one link between two devices at any one time. As another link is established, another instantiation of the state machine is made. Thus, a Master may be in connection with one Slave while simultaneously inquiring, paging, and scanning several other devices. Indeed, since inquiry or paging may last several seconds, the Master will effectively be moving directly from connection to inquiry, to scan, to page, and back to connection as it works around the set of devices it is interacting with. In essence, the one state controller entity requires a set of contexts for each of its active interactions or links. This is also true for the LC protocol, ARQN, SEQN, and retransmit packets. Early Bluetooth implementations placed much of this control in hardware and found this to be a very difficult juggling act. One of the key challenges for Bluetooth designers is getting the partitioning between hardware and software right. This area of state control and link context management is at the sharp end of the partitioning problem. We examine this in more detail in the implementation chapter.

The diagram in Figure 5–2 illustrates the state transitions and packet exchanges which occur while a pair of devices moves from standby into connection through a simplified view of the inquiry and paging procedures. We now look in more detail at the exact message exchange sequence and timing related to inquiry and paging.

5.4.1 Device Discovery and Inquiry

Due to the ad-hoc nature of a Bluetooth network, where highly mobile devices may come into and go out of range of other communicating devices, the network topology and membership can be constantly changing. The Bluetooth specification provides a mechanism for device discovery, which is what the Service Discovery Protocol (SDP) is built upon. The LC uses inquiry and inquiry scan states to manage the process of device discovery in the devices wishing to discover and be discovered, respectively.

Figure 5–3 shows the messages exchanged between two devices during inquiry and inquiry scan. The inquiring device is asking "Is anybody out there?" while the scanning device is constantly listening in case anybody inquires.

The inquiring device calls out by transmitting ID packets containing an Inquiry Access Code (IAC) as described in the section on access codes in the baseband chapter. Usually, the General Inquiry Access Code (GIAC) is used, which is common between all

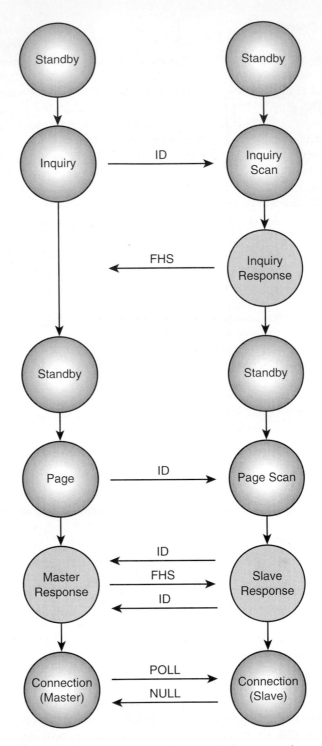

Figure 5–2 State transition from standby into connection.

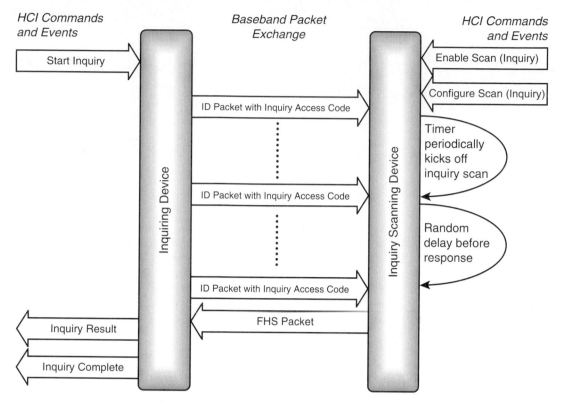

HCI Commands and Events

Baseband Packet Exchange

HCI Commands and Events

Start Inquiry

Enable Scan (Inquiry)

Configure Scan (Inquiry)

ID Packet with Inquiry Access Code

Inquiring Device

Inquiry Scanning Device

Timer periodically kicks off inquiry scan

ID Packet with Inquiry Access Code

Random delay before response

ID Packet with Inquiry Access Code

FHS Packet

Inquiry Result

Inquiry Complete

Figure 5–3 Message sequence chart for inquiry and inquiry scan.

devices performing inquiry procedures. However, devices can use a Dedicated Inquiry Access Code (DIAC). The concept of a Dedicated Inquiry Access Code was originally provided to allow only certain classes of devices to be enquired upon, but the only DIAC defined to date is the Limited Inquiry Access Code (LIAC). The LIAC is designed to be used by a pair of devices for a short period of time. This would be by Application Level selection on both devices and provide a quick way of discovering a "known" device.

To conserve power and fit in with other link activity in which a device may be engaged, inquiry will only happen if specifically requested by the higher layer control protocols. Likewise, the device will normally be set to only perform inquiry scan periodically over a short window. The chapter on the host controller interface gives more detail on how this is done.

When an inquiry scanning device hears an inquiry, it could respond immediately, but this could result in several scanning devices responding together the moment an inquiry was sent. The responses would interfere with one another, so the inquirer would not receive any of them. To stop this from happening, a random back-off period is used. When a scanning device first hears an inquiry, instead of responding immediately, it waits

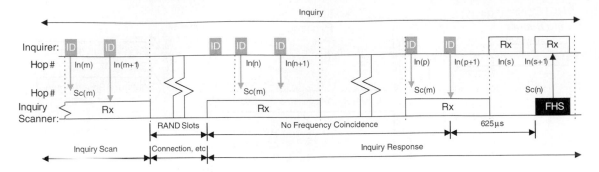

Figure 5–4   Inquiry procedure timing.

for a random period, and then re-enters the scanning state, listening once more for another ID. This time, if it hears the inquiry, it will reply with the FHS packet. In this way, several devices can respond to an inquirer, but their responses will be spaced out randomly and will not interfere. Clearly, the inquirer must keep inquiring for longer than the range of the random period.

Figure 5–4 shows in detail how an inquiring device transmits twice per slot on successive hop channels (fast hopping), trying to "catch" a device performing inquiry scan which hops at the scan rate of only once every 2,048 slots, or 1.28s. The inquirer transmits using the inquiry hop sequence and listens in both halves of the slot on the associated response hop sequence. See the section on frequency hopping in Chapter 4, "Baseband."

Once the inquiry scanning device successfully receives an ID packet, it waits for the random back-off period (RAND), between 0 and 1,023 slots, or up to 640 ms to avoid collisions. After the RAND period, the inquiry scanning device enters inquiry response and on the next reception of an ID packet, responds with the FHS packet 625 μs later, providing the inquirer with the required information. Both devices hop between two different points in the sequence depending on their own values of CLKN(1), which is 0 for the inquiry device on transmit and the scanning device on receive. Thus Sc(m) = In(p+1) in Figure 5–4. The response is then made in the next slot where CLKN(1) is 1, and so Sc(n) = In(s + 1), where m and n and p and s differ only by the effect of the respective CLKN(1). The scanning device then re-enters inquiry scan state on the next channel in the inquiry scan hop sequence and waits for another ID packet.

Because the inquirer always listens on the response hop channel corresponding to the previous inquiry transmission, when the inquiry scanning device returns an FHS packet, it is ready to receive it. However, because there is no defined relationship between the two CLKNs, this is not an exact process and that is why repeat attempts are made. The inquiry procedure timing is as it is exactly to maximise the "chance" of coinciding.

If the inquirer receives the FHS packet in the first half of its receive slot, it cannot receive a response from another Slave in the second half of the slot because it does not have time to hop to the second frequency after receiving the FHS packet. Similarly, if the FHS packet comes in the second half of the receive slot, the inquiring device will miss the

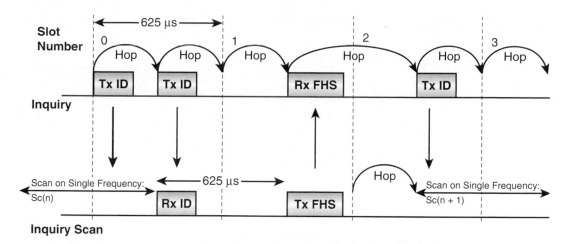

Figure 5–5 Hopping during inquiry response.

transmission of the first ID packet in the following transmit slot (this is shown in Figure 5–5).

As the inquiring device hops twice per slot while the inquiry scanning device listens on a single frequency, the time taken for an inquiry to be received is reduced to half the time which would be taken if the inquiring device hopped at the normal rate of once per slot. Such rapid frequency hopping is only possible because ID packets are very short.

If the inquiry scanning device does not receive the first or second ID packets during the scan timeout period, then it will leave inquiry scan and return to standby or connection as appropriate. The inquiry state lasts either as long as required to collate the desired number of responses, or until a timeout set by the host elapses. In an error-free environment, the worst case is around 10 s to guarantee frequency coincidence with all devices in the inquiry hop sequence. If the inquiring device has active SCO links, then the period must increase to take account of the lost time due to the regular SCO activity. See the section on SCO links.

It is permissible to avoid Inquiry altogether if the address of the device to connect to is known. Paging may be entered directly, although it may take longer to establish a link, as without the CLKE estimate, the paging hop sequence is not predictable. This may be appropriate, for example, where a very low cost mobile phone and headset combination had a minimal Man Machine Interface (MMI) and their respective addresses were factory preset to tie them together.

5.4.2 Connection Establishment and Paging

We have already seen in the previous chapter that the Bluetooth system is based around the notion of links between a Master device and a Slave device. To establish such a link, one device must initiate the connection by addressing a request directly to the other device saying: "Will you connect with me?" This is referred to as paging. The other device

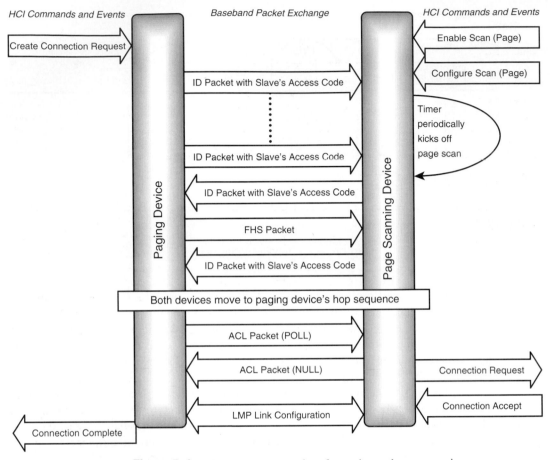

Figure 5–6   Message sequence chart for paging and page scanning.

must likewise be listening for such a request, and this is referred to as page scanning. At the conclusion of the paging process, the pager becomes the Master and the page scanner becomes the Slave, though this may subsequently change due to a Master / Slave switch.

Figure 5–6 shows the messages exchanged between two devices during the connection establishment process using the mandatory paging procedure. One optional paging procedure is defined, although others may be added in the future. We describe the mandatory scheme in detail here, but look briefly at the optional scheme later.

The create connection command causes a device to enter paging mode, where it sends out a series of paging packets (ID packets based on the paged device's address). Meanwhile, the page scanning device is configured to carry out periodic page scans of a specified duration, and at a specified interval. The scanning device starts a timer and kicks off a periodic scan when the timer elapses. (This is the same mechanism used to configure periodic inquiry scans and is also described in Chapter 8 on the Host Controller Interface.) The pager transmits ID packets with the page scanner's address. If the page scanner

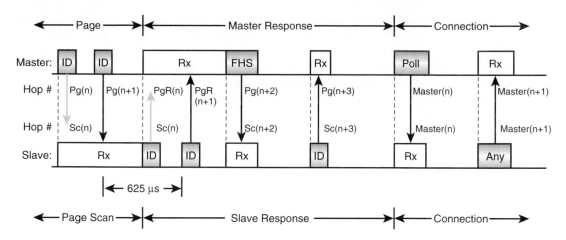

Figure 5–7 Page procedure timing.

is scanning during this time, it will trigger and receive the ID packet, replying with another ID, again using its own address. Unlike inquiry, there is only one device with that ID, so only one device can reply and there is no need for any random back-off delay. The pager receives the page scanner's ID packet and, following this handshake, knows that the page scanner is ready to receive the pager's FHS packet, which it then transmits. The page scanner acknowledges the FHS packet by replying with another ID. Now the page scanner can extract the necessary parameters from the FHS packet (Bluetooth CLK, AM_ADDR, etc.) to use in the new connection. Using these parameters, the page scanner is able to calculate the pager's hop sequence. It can stop using the special paging hop sequence and move instead to the connection hop sequence with the pager as Master of the connection. As both devices now move into the connection state, the pager becomes the Master and the page scanner becomes the Slave.

After both devices have moved to the new hop sequence, the Master sends a POLL packet to check that the frequency hop sequence switch has happened correctly. The Slave must then respond with any ACL packet (typically a NULL, as there is unlikely to be any data to send at that specific time). Following this link test and first ACL packet exchange, various LMP link configuration packets are exchanged. At this point, Master and Slave can agree to swap roles in a "Master/Slave switch" if required.

Figure 5–7 shows in detail the packet exchange and timing between a pager and page scanner during the mandatory paging procedure.

The Master[1] transmits IDs on a sequence of hop channels which straddle the predicted channel of the Slave[1] based on the estimate (CLKE) of the Slave's CLKN at a fast

---

[1]We have adopted the terms "Master" and "Slave" here in place of "pager" and "page scanner," since as the Bluetooth specification describes paging procedures in terms of Master and Slave. Thus, the response substates are Master response and Slave response. This is a little confusing, however, as a Master in an existing piconet might be the page scanner in another *new* piconet.

rate, twice per slot. This is necessary, as CLKE may be inaccurate or even nonexistent where an inquiry has not previously been carried out. The 32 channel hop sequence is split into 16 surrounding the predicted channel and a further 16 split either side of these. The inner set, or "Train A," is tried first, and then the more distant set, "Train B". This aims to give the fastest response possible if an accurate CLKE is available, while guaranteeing success eventually in the worst case scenario. As with inquiry, the paging device hops twice per slot to maximise the chance of hitting the page scanner's frequency. The scanner hops over the same channels, but at a rate of only once per 2,048 slots, or 1.28s. This ensures that they will eventually coincide, providing the respective timeout periods are sufficient.

In the diagram, "Pg" refers to the page hop channels and "Sc" to the page scan hop channels. "PgR" indicates the page hop channel, which is used for the Master response and is linked to the page hop channel during which the ID was successfully received by the Slave. Once the scanning device has received the ID packet, it freezes the hop clock and starts to hop in sequence with the paging device. It does this using the page response hop sequence discussed in the previous chapter.

When the Master receives the ID, it transmits the FHS packet at the beginning of its next slot, to allow the Slave to synchronise its slot reference. The Slave must therefore open its correlator 312.5 μs after the ID is sent and keep it open for at least 625 μs, as the FHS could be due in either 312.5, or 625 μs time. Following reception of the FHS packet, the Slave responds with an ID. Up to this point, both devices are using the Slave's DAC, the Slave's timing (Slave: CLKN, Master: CLKE), and a paging hop sequence derived from the Slave's LAP. The next transmission is from the Master using the CAC and its own CLKN, which the Slave receives as it has now switched to the Master's CAC and CLK and both devices are in connection state. The devices now exchange POLL and NULL packets to verify the link. If the POLL packet is not received or acknowledged within a timeout period, then both devices will return to page and page scan states, respectively.

5.4.3   Optional Paging Scheme

In version 1.0b of the Bluetooth specification, one optional paging scheme was defined; others may be added to later versions of the specification. The current optional scheme operates as follows: The paging device transmits for eight slots in both odd and even slots, then inverts the ID packet and transmits again. In the tenth slot, it listens for the Slave's response. Whereas the normal ID packets will generate a positive signal from the scanning device's correlator, the inverted packet will generate a negative signal. By checking the sign of the correlator's output signal, the scanning device can detect when the ID packet is inverted and work out when to send its response.

By transmitting for nine slots out of ten, rather than the mandatory scheme's five slots out of ten, the page scanner has more of a chance of detecting the pager's transmission. This allows the page scan window to be reduced, but at the expense of a more complex train configuration. Because optional paging is a recent addition to the specification, it is not well supported currently.

5.5 PICONET OPERATION

In a piconet, the Master will transmit to and receive from each of the Slaves, which are allocated an AM address and are active at that time. If there is nothing to send, the Master may either omit that Slave or transmit a NULL packet. If a SCO link is in operation, then that Slave must be communicated with regularly according to the SCO repetition rate, T_{sco} (see Chapter 6). As was mentioned above, the LC protocol and

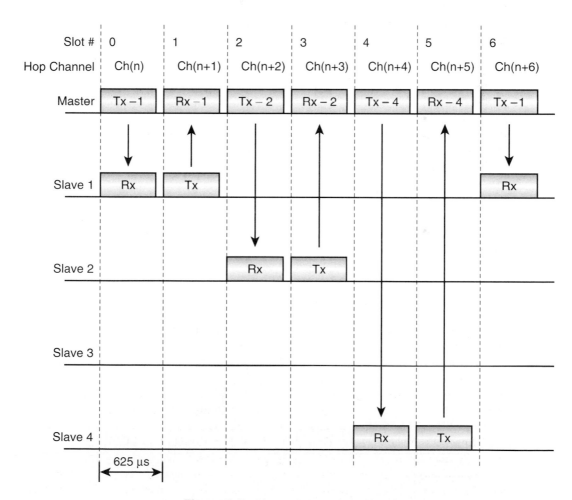

Figure 5–8 Piconet in operation with ACL traffic.

retransmission sequence information must be maintained across all other links ready for the next communication.

5.5.1   ACL Links

Figure 5–8 shows how a Master is able to communicate with several Slaves in sequence. The Master always transmits on even slots and the Slave replies on odd-numbered slots. The diagram shows ACL traffic where the Master only transmits data when there is something to send. Slave 3 is "missed out", as there is nothing to send to it at this time. This illustrates the point that a Slave may only transmit if it has been transmitted to, as the Master is able to immediately move on to communicate with Slave 4.

5.5.2   SCO Links

Figure 5–9 shows a Master transmitting to two Slaves, where slots 4 and 5 have been reserved for a SCO link with Slave 2. The other slots are not reserved for SCO, and so the Master can choose which device to transmit ACL traffic to, if at all. Unless the Master is sending LMP traffic to control the Slave 2 link, it must send SCO traffic to Slave 2 in slot 4. Because the SCO slots are reserved, the SCO Slave may reply in the reserved Slot 5 whether or not it detected a packet addressed to itself from the Master.

SCO slots may be spaced to use every slot pair, every second slot pair, or every third slot pair. The spacing of the SCO slots is negotiated when the SCO link is set up, and thereafter those slots are reserved until the SCO link is torn down again. Because the

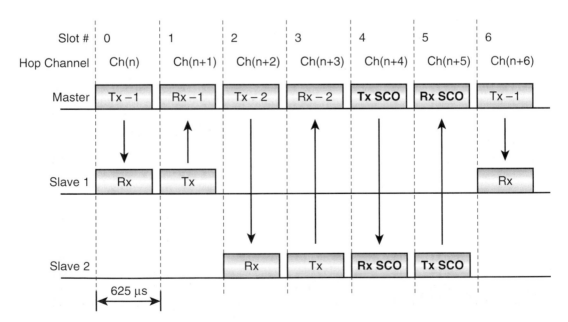

Figure 5–9   Piconet in operation with SCO traffic.

widest spacing for SCO slots is every third slot pair, the maximum number of SCO links which can be supported in a piconet is three. More details on SCO link configuration can be found in Chapter 6.

5.5.3 SCO Links during Inquiry, Paging, and Scanning

As they use reserved capacity, SCO links will continue through inquiry, paging, inquiry scan, and page scan, greatly reducing the opportunity to discover neighboring devices and connect to them.

Figure 5–10 illustrates a SCO slot interrupting inquiry scan to show why SCO reduces the chances of the inquiry succeeding. The diagram shows the timing of the device carrying out the inquiry scan. It must receive an ID packet and respond 625 μs later with an FHS packet. However, it must also regularly receive and transmit SCO packets.

The diagram shows the last moment when an ID packet can arrive and still be responded to before the radio begins to hop onto the frequency for the SCO slot. Any packet arriving after the ID packet shown cannot be responded to without interfering with the reserved SCO slot, thus violating the specification. Not only are the two slots for SCO lost, but also the 625 μs wait for the FHS response, the length of the FHS packet itself, and the time taken for the radio to hop and settle to the required SCO channel frequency. This is because any ID packet received after the one shown in the diagram must be ignored, since the FHS cannot be sent in the time left before the SCO packet must start. In total, the inquiry scan time lost is 2241 μs + the radio settle time, which could add up to another 200 μs. This is made up as follows:

- Two slots for the SCO.
- One slot for the wait to transmit the FHS packet.

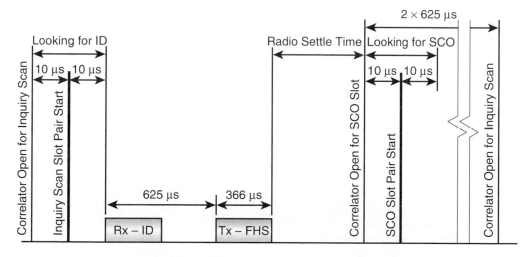

Figure 5–10 Timing of SCO slots during inquiry scan.

- 366 μs FHS packet duration.
- Radio channel synthesiser settle time.

This means that around 60% of the scanning time is lost when a SCO link is present in every third slot pair. If two SCO links are present, using up two slot pairs in three, then over 90% of the scanning time is lost.

The specification recognises that SCO links will interfere with inquiry and suggests that the number of repetitions of the inquiry should be doubled if one slot pair in three is in use by SCO, and trebled if two slots in three are in use by SCO. It also recommends increasing the scan window from the default 11.25 ms in the absence of SCO to 36 ms with one slot pair in three used for SCO and 54 ms for two slot pairs in three used for SCO. However, to make the scanning process reliable, it is preferable to hold the SCO links.

Similar conditions apply in page scanning, except that the longer sequence of packets exchanged during connection setup means that SCO links interfere with paging and page scanning even more than they interfere with inquiry and inquiry scanning.

5.6 SCATTERNET OPERATION

A scatternet comprises two (or theoretically more) piconets, where at least one device is active in both. Switching between the piconets requires keeping track of two timebases, as each piconet is synchronised to a different Master's CLKN. A device which is active in two piconets must maintain and select between two piconet clocks, CLK_1 and CLK_2, and two access codes, CAC_1 and CAC_2.

The switch in timebases will require guard time to synchronise to the new timebase, as the piconet's timings will be asynchronous to each other. In the worst case, they could be a whole slot pair out of sync. This puts a severe limit on how many piconets can be linked together if any meaningful degree of traffic is to be supported on each. SCO makes this especially difficult, as it uses reserved slots. Indeed, only one SCO link using HV3 packets may be active; even then, this only allows one other piconet to be visited in the four slots between the HV3 packets scheduled every six slots. Of the four intervening slots, two are used as guard slots and two are available for traffic in the other piconet.

In Figure 5–11 the top line shows the Master of piconet 1. The middle line shows one of its Slaves, which is also the Master of a second piconet 2; the bottom line shows the Slave on piconet 2. Master 1 transmits to and receives from its Slave in slots 0 and 1. Slave 1 then moves timing onto its own piconet in order to act as Master 2 and transmit to its own Slave. However, due to the difference in timing between the two piconets, it doesn't have time to retune its radio and transmit, so it waits during slots 2 and 3 before successfully transmitting and receiving in slots 4 and 5. Slave 1/Master 2 may then return immediately to piconet 1 ready for slot 0 again.

Because of the necessity for guard slots created by this difference in slot timings, a device which is present on two piconets will never provide the maximum data bandwidth it would have were it only on one piconet.

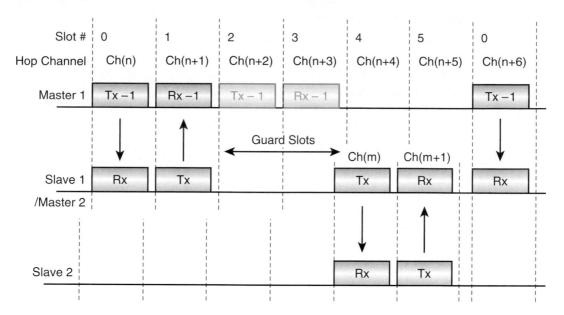

Figure 5–11   Scatternet timing.

When a device is busy on another piconet, it can no longer be contacted by its Master and must therefore warn the Master of the periods when it will be away, so that the Master doesn't think it has lost communication with the Slave altogether. This may be done if the Slave negotiates entry into a low power mode with the Master. In low power modes a device is allowed to switch off for some of the time. (For more information on low power modes please refer to Chapter 17, Low Power Operation.) For a device which will regularly communicate on two piconets, sniff mode is probably the most useful since it allows a device to reduce communication to a regular agreed periodic slot sequence. Of course, in this case, the device is not going to sleep, it is in fact busy talking to someone else.

5.6.1   SCO Links and Scatternets

As the widest spacing for SCO slots is every third slot pair, it is not possible for a device to have SCO links in two piconets at once. First of all, the SCO links would need to be synchronised so they were chosen to fit in the time a device could be present on each piconet, yet the Master chooses the timing of the reserved slots, not the Slave, so a Slave cannot force this synchronisation. Second, if the slots happened to fit so that the Slave could switch piconets, and the links were in the right place not to coincide, over time the two piconet clocks would drift until eventually the two SCO links overlapped.

Figure 5–12 shows a SCO link on piconet 1 in slots 0 and 1, while the SCO link for piconet 2 is currently spread across the slots numbered 3 to 5 in piconet 1. At this instant, the SCO slots in the two piconets do not overlap, but as the clocks of the two piconets' Masters drift, the two SCO links will move until they overlap one another.

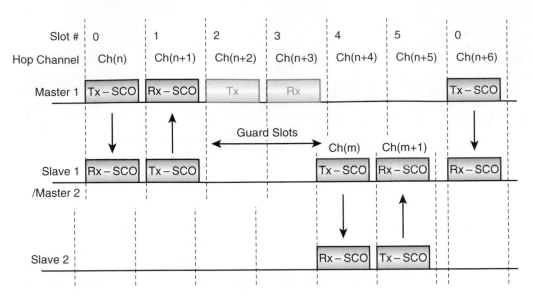

Figure 5–12 SCO links in a scatternet.

5.7 MASTER / SLAVE ROLE SWITCHING

Bluetooth allows any device to request a switch in roles with respect to another device it is communicating with. For example, a Master in an existing piconet might allow itself to be paged and connected to a new device and then switch between Slave/Master (temporarily imposed by the paging procedure) and Master/Slave to integrate the new Slave into its piconet. This is accomplished with a Master/Slave switch and is particularly useful in situations where a connection has just been established by a device which normally wishes to be a Slave, such as where a mobile computing device enters a piconet controlled by a LAN access point.

The mechanism essentially involves the Slave sending the difference between its clock and the master's clock in an LMP message, then asking for a switch and, if accepted, sending an FHS packet to the Master. The Master takes on a CLK offset to match the Slave's CLKN, while the Slave switches to using its own CLKN, and each device swaps access codes.

5.7.1 Messaging

Figure 5–13 shows the sequence of messages exchanged when a Slave becomes a Master by initiating a Master / Slave switch. The Master side can also request the role switch. The LMP_switch_req message also gives the instant when the switch will happen.

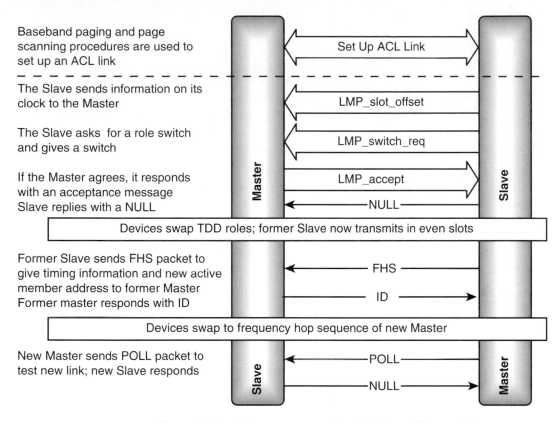

Baseband paging and page scanning procedures are used to set up an ACL link

The Slave sends information on its clock to the Master

The Slave asks for a role switch and gives a switch

If the Master agrees, it responds with an acceptance message
Slave replies with a NULL

Former Slave sends FHS packet to give timing information and new active member address to former Master
Former master responds with ID

New Master sends POLL packet to test new link; new Slave responds

Figure 5–13   Message sequence chart for Master / Slave switch.

The Slave gives the Master detailed information on its clock, so that the Master can move onto the Slave's timing. An LMP_slot_offset message is used by the Slave to pass this information to the Master.

Figure 5–14 illustrates how the slot offset is derived. The Slave knows the timing of its own native clock, and, because it is synchronised to the master, it also knows the timing of the Master's clock. The Slave works out the instant when a transmit slot starts in the current piconet, then works out how many microseconds it would have to wait for a transmit slot in the piconet timing where it is Master. This value is sent to the current Master of the piconet, along with the BD_ADDR of the Slave which will become Master after the switch.

In version 1.1 of the Bluetooth core specification, the baseband also describes a mechanism by which a Slave which is becoming a master can acquire any other Slaves which belonged to the former Master. The new Master sends an LMP_slot_offset message to tell the Slave the new timing it should use, the Master then sends an FHS, the slave responds with an ID, and both devices move onto the new Master's hop sequence. The procedure is similar to a Master and Slave's swapping roles, except that the TDD switch is not needed as the Slave is already on the correct TDD timing.

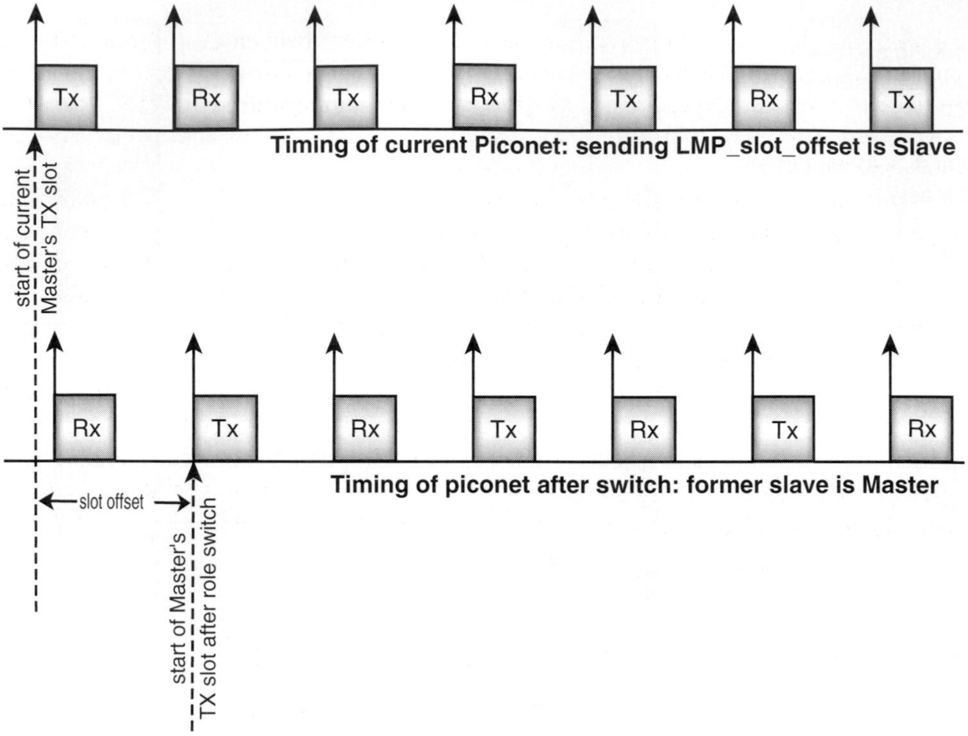

Figure 5–14   Timing for LMP_slot_offset message.

LMP does not provide any messages to tell the new Master the active member addresses of the old Slaves or to pass on information about Slaves in Hold, Park, or Sniff modes. For the new Master to attempt to acquire the Slaves of the old Master, it has to poll all seven active member addresses using the old Master's hop sequence and timings and see if any respond.

It is worth noting that the Host Controller interface does not provide commands to control the acquisition of Slaves from a former Master after a role switch.

In practice, the acquisition of Slaves from a Master is unlikely to be a problem, as the main use for a Master/Slave switch is to allow a device to join a piconet quickly by paging, then hand control of piconet back to the former Master of the piconet.

5.7.2   Uniting Scatternets with Role Switch

The devices linking a scatternet are present on more than one piconet and have to time share, spending a few slots on one piconet and a few slots on the other. Each device has its own independent clock, and when devices join a piconet, they track the timing of the piconet's Master by keeping track of the offset between their clock and the Master's clock. This means that when devices are present on more than one piconet, they will have to track two sets of timings. When switching between timings, there will be some slots which cannot be used (for a fuller description of scatternet timings and how to manage them, refer to Chapter 18).

Sometimes it is desirable to have a device join a piconet as a Master as shown in Figure 5–15. Consider a LAN Access Point (LAP). It does not know which devices in the area wish to connect, and it would be wasteful of its resources to constantly poll devices to try to connect to them. Instead, it periodically page scans, and any devices wishing to connect page it. This means that connecting devices become Masters of a small piconet containing just themselves and the LAN access point.

If the situation were left like this, the LAN access point would lose control. It must be the Master of its links so that it can control the allocation of bandwidth to the devices connected to it. So, the LAN access point requests a Master / Slave switch as it accepts the connection. The new joiner accepts the switch, and the LAN access point is restored to working in a piconet rather than a scatternet, as shown in Figure 5–15.

Step 1
Piconet with Master and several Slaves.

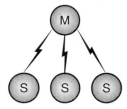

Step 2
The piconet's Master page scans,
allowing a new device to connect as its Master.

The piconet's Master is now also a Slave;
a Scatternet has been established.

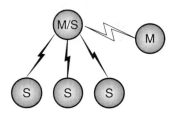

Step 3
Master Slave switch on the new link.
The scatternet is united into a piconet.

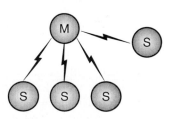

Figure 5–15 Forming a scatternet and uniting it into a piconet.

5.8   LOW-POWER OPERATION

During Standby, Park, Hold, Sniff, or even between an active transmit or receive operation,[2] a device may enter low-power operation, where any protocol or bit processing elements (hardware or software) may be turned off. All system clocks may be disabled, and the device may enter a very low power consumption mode of operation. Certain static data must be maintained, such as LC protocol state and buffer contents, and the only dynamic information which must be maintained is the native clock counter, CLKN. To conserve power, this may be clocked with a much lower power, and therefore less accurate 32 KHz oscillator ($\div 10 = 3.2$ kHz). The tolerance specified in the standard on the Low Power Oscillator (LPO) is $\pm$ 250 ppm.

An accuracy of 250 ppm gives rise to a worst case slippage of 1 slot every 2.5 s. This is why regular resynchronisation is important and is explained further in the later section on low-power operation. By way of illustration, the maximum duration for which a device is allowed to remain inactive in Sniff or Hold mode, or between synchronising beacon instants in Park mode, is 40.9 s. This equates to 65,440 slots, which requires an uncertainty window of $\pm$ 17 slots.

It is worth noting that 32 kHz crystals are not at present commonplace, unlike the 32.768 kHz crystals commonly used in wristwatches and the like. The tolerance of a quartz crystal does not allow "pulling" over such a large distance, and so we must wait for the commercial success of Bluetooth to create a large demand for 32 kHz parts to force the price of such components down.

5.9   BASEBAND / LINK CONTROLLER ARCHITECTURAL OVERVIEW

In this short section, we will tie together the material in both the previous chapter and this chapter to examine the overall architecture of a typical Link Controller / Baseband system.

Figure 5–16 shows a possible baseband/Link Controller system. The data path is either SCO (via a direct PCM interface, through HCI) processed by the audio CODEC subsystem, or ACL via HCI. The data is buffered, so it may be read out at system speed subsequently following reception or stored awaiting transmission. Typically, double buffering is used to ease the scheduling of these operations. Indeed, double buffering on transmit is almost essential for a multi-link device where retransmissions must be anticipated.

The data path has already been discussed; it encodes or decodes data bursts during Tx or Rx, respectively. The Rx correlator effectively "sniffs" the received data and, when enabled, will search for the required access code. The sync word generator supplies a valid sync word derived from the appropriate LAP to the radio interface and the correlator

---

[2]When another device's packet header transmission has been received, indicating a multi-slot packet but with a different AM address, and thus is not directed at the present device.

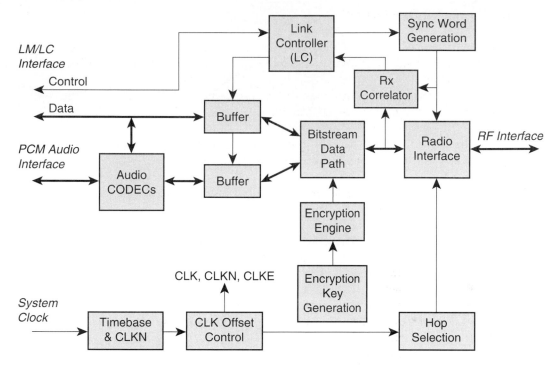

Figure 5–16 Baseband / LC architecture.

as appropriate. The timebase produces a native clock: CLKN from the appropriate system reference clock, which must therefore be accurate to ± 20 ppm. An offset control function then maintains and applies the necessary offsets to produce CLKN, CLK, and CLKE as required.

The hop selection function combines the required CLK and BD address parts to produce the channel number and feeds these to the radio interface. Finally, the encryption key generator produces and stores keys, which are then loaded up by the key stream generator and processed at symbol rate to produce a cipher stream for use by the bitstream data path.

The heart of the system is the Link Controller entity, which controls and sequences the above functions and operations. This typically consists of two main state machines, one for receive and one for transmit. Simplistic examples of these (neglecting aux packets) are shown in Figure 5–17 and Figure 5–18.

The Tx start trigger from the timebase occurs when the CLK counter increments to CLK[1:0] = 00, 01, 10, or 11, depending on whether the device is configured as a Master on whole-slot or half-slot operation or a Slave on whole-slot or half-slot operation, respectively. The Rx start trigger is the correlator match event and of course requires that the radio and correlator have been enabled appropriately some time before the beginning of the uncertainty window. As the diagram shows, the ARQ and SEQ processing is car-

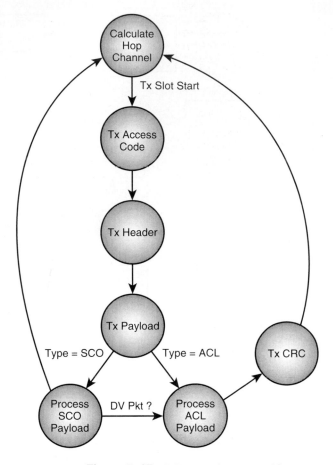

Figure 5–17   LC transmit state machine.

ried out during the receive process and the appropriate values stored, ready for the subsequent transmit operation.

5.10 SUMMARY

The link control layer is responsible for managing device discoverability, establishing connections, and once connected, maintaining the various on-air links. It does this through a set of state machines, which drive the baseband through the following stages to establish links:

- Host requests an inquiry.
- Inquiry is sent using the inquiry hopping sequence.

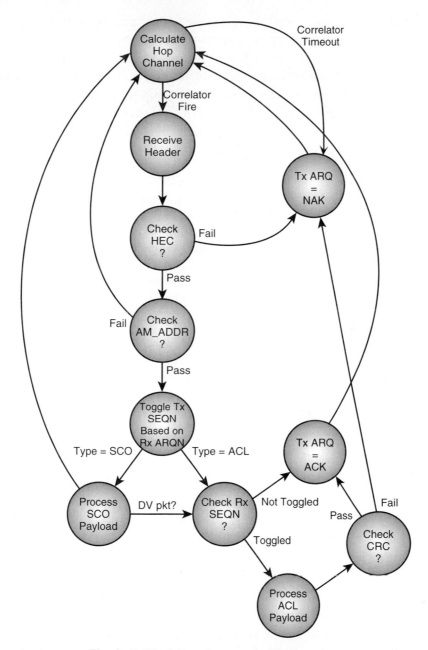

Figure 5–18 LC receive state machine.

- Inquiry scanning devices respond to the inquiry scan with FHS packets which contain all the information needed to connect with them.
- The contents of the FHS packets are passed back to the host.
- The host requests connection to one of the devices that responded to the inquiry.
- Paging is used to initiate a connection with the selected device.
- If the selected device is page scanning, it responds to the page.
- If the page scanning device accepts the connection, it will begin hopping using the Master's frequency hopping sequence and timing.

The control of links rests with the local device. Although the Master governs when devices may transmit once connected, it is up to a device to allow itself to be connected with. If a device does not make itself discoverable by inquiry scanning, it cannot be found. If it does not make itself connectable by page scanning, it cannot be linked with, and once in a connection, it is free to disconnect without warning at any time.

Once a baseband link is established, the Master and Slave can exchange roles, so that Slave becomes Master and Master becomes Slave.

The baseband links are used to carry link management traffic, voice traffic (on SCO links), and data traffic (on ACL links).

Mechanisms are also included to support multiple piconets and the exchange of Master and Slave roles between communicating devices, together with several low power periodic operating modes.

The Link Control and Baseband work very closely together, and careful consideration must be given to the overall system design and partitioning for an optimal solution.

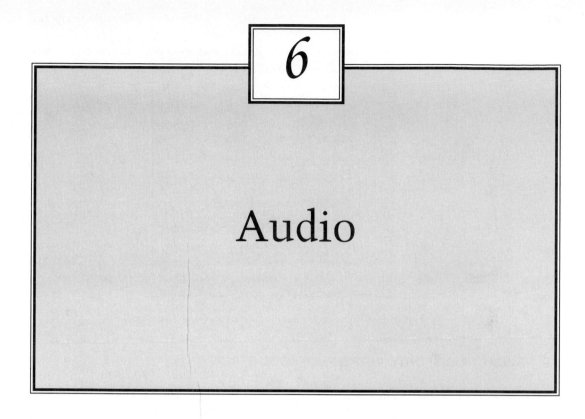

6

Audio

6.1 INTRODUCTION

A major application for Bluetooth is as a carrier of audio information. Indeed, we have already seen that up to three full-duplex audio channels are provided for in the standard. This functionality allows us to build devices such as wireless headsets, microphones, and headphones using Bluetooth for all manner of consumer products such as cellular phones, call centre switchboards, or even personal music playback. The audio quality provided by Bluetooth is the same as one would expect from a cellular telephone (not surprising since Bluetooth uses the same audio data format as the GSM system).

Audio data is carried via Synchronous Connection-Oriented (SCO) channels and through the use of several coding schemes. Different trade-offs of quality and robustness are available.

This chapter explains how this capability is provided, how to control it, and what limitations exist. We begin at the bottom of the protocol stack by explaining the physical interfacing and coding operations involved, and work our way up the stack looking at how the audio subsystem of a Bluetooth device is configured and controlled. We conclude by examining the level of performance and quality one can expect from Bluetooth so as to allow us to make qualitative judgements on the suitability of Bluetooth audio transmission and reception for a given application.

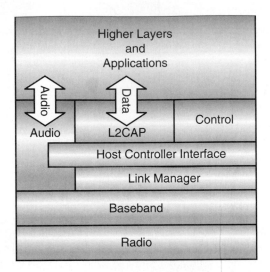

Figure 6–1   Position of audio in the Bluetooth protocol stack.

6.2   AUDIO TRANSPORTS IN THE PROTOCOL STACK

The standard specifies that audio should be carried on SCO channels, while data is carried on ACL channels. Version 1.0b of the standard only defines profiles and transport mechanisms for SCO via HCI in the same way as for ACL; see Figure 6–1.

However, packets crossing the HCI are flow controlled and are subject to variable latency due to the microcontroller executing the HCI and LM tasks. These interruptions in the audio path can lead to SCO packet loss or a requirement for expensive buffering in the baseband. To avoid such complications, many implementers use a direct PCM route[1] to interface the audio CODECs directly to a serial digital PCM stream at 8kHz.

6.3   QUALITY AND BANDWIDTH

The correct way to evaluate audio quality is to use subjective techniques, especially because the various compression schemes in current use exploit the way that the human ear interprets the audio signal. However, a simple way to evaluate the audio quality delivered by a Bluetooth SCO link is to compare the un-coded audio bandwidth and sampling size with that of other audio systems, as shown in Table 6–1. Note how the data rate reduces as more or stronger compression or coding is used.

Clearly, a Bluetooth SCO link can not encode and carry raw CD quality sound. However, with suitable compression, such as MP3 (MPEG Layer 3 Audio) it would be

---

[1]The direct PCM route was originally presented as an HCI transport mechanism in the Bluetooth white papers, which were a precursor to the specification. However, the PCM transport did not make it into either the 1.0b or present 1.1 specifications, although there is some mention of it in the baseband part of the standard.

Table 6–1   Comparison of Audio Data Rates

System	Quality or Audio Bandwidth	Data Rate (kb/s)
Audio CD	Stereo 16 bit, 22 kHz	1411.2
MP3 Encoded Audio	Stereo Near-CD Quality	128
POTS Telephone or ISDN audio channel	Mono 13 bit, 4 kHz	64 (A-law or μ-law compressed)
Bluetooth SCO channel	Mono 13 bit, 4 kHz	64 (A-law, μ-law compressed or CVSD encoded)
GSM Audio	Mono 13 bit, 4 kHz	22.8 (RELP or CELP encoded)

technically feasible to use an ACL channel[2] for high quality audio, although version 1.1 of the specification does not define a profile for such a device.

The level of audio quality provided by a SCO link is approximately equivalent to that of a GSM cellular telephone audio channel. Not surprising considering the origins of the Bluetooth standard.

6.4   SCO LINKS

When SCO link is established via the initial ACL link setup and subsequent SCO link negotiation, the packets are exchanged on air as shown in Figure 6–2, where D_{SCO} and T_{SCO} are the start offset and repeat period respectively, as defined in Chapter 4. One, two, or three channels are possible, however, in each case, the bandwidth of each channel is always 64 kb/s. This can be shown as follows:

On each channel, new packets comprising n bits are sent and received once every T_{SCO} slots. Thus, the number of bits passed in each direction per second is:

$$n \times \frac{1}{T_{SCO}} \times \frac{2}{1250 \ \mu s} = 64,000 \ \text{bits/second}$$

where $T_{SCO} = 6$ and $n = 240$ for an HV3 packet. For more protected SCO packets, where less source data is carried, T_{SCO} must be reduced to maintain the source bandwidth. For an HV2 packet (FEC = 2/3), $T_{SCO} = 4$, $n = 160$, and for an HV1 packet (FEC = 1/3), $T_{SCO} = 2$, $n = 80$.

This places a basic requirement on the audio to be carried by Bluetooth and is a fundamental reason for the need to use audio coding techniques, since 64 kb/s does not provide satisfactory audio quality for typical Bluetooth applications. By comparison, the raw,

---

[2]The maximum asymmetric data rate for a Bluetooth ACL link is 723.2 kb/s, which would comfortably carry MP3-coded audio. However, the coded audio data rate must be sustained.

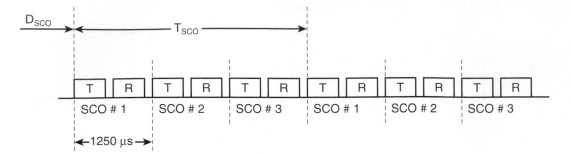

Figure 6–2   SCO channel timing.

linear PCM audio bandwidth of a GSM cellular phone before speech transcoding is 104 kb/s. The other fundamental reason for using any audio coding is to increase robustness to noise and on-air error sources.

6.5   AUDIO CODECs

Bluetooth specifies three different audio coding techniques: Log PCM coding using either A-law or μ-law and CVSD (Continuous Variable Slope Delta modulation). The 64-ksamples/s source signal must be band limited to 4kHz to prevent aliasing in the encoder.

6.5.1   Log PCM

Log PCM coding is used in a whole manner of existing devices such as fixed-line telephone handsets and the PSTN (Public Switched Telephone Network). Log coding compresses the input data via a logarithmic transfer function so as to represent the more accurate (higher bit width) data with a less accurate (lower bit width) output value. However, the logarithmic transfer function ensures that the effect of the compression gives rise to a minimal decrease in quality as perceived by the human ear.

The specification of the exact characteristics are defined by the International Telecommunications Union (ITU-T), recommendation G.711, which provides conversion tables to and from linear PCM and log PCM for both A-law and μ-law compression. These tables are based on an approximation of the logarithmic function by a series of linear segments.

The input to the log PCM encoders is up to 3 channels of 13 bit (for A-law) or 14 bit (for μ-law) linear PCM at 8kHz, while the output is up to 3 channels of 8 bit encoded data at 8kHz.

6.5.2   CVSD

CVSD is a more complex technique than log coding, which exploits the strong correlation between adjacent audio samples by quantising the difference in amplitude between the two samples as opposed to the entire sample amplitude. This requires fewer quantisation

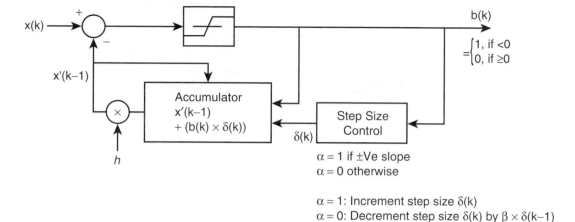

Figure 6–3   CVSD encoder block diagram.

steps for the same signal quality, and consequently lower bandwidth. Generally referred to as DPCM (Differential PCM), this approach can be modified to reduce the required bandwidth even further by making the quantisation step adaptive, so-called ADPCM (Adaptive DPCM). This technique represents low-amplitude signals with acceptable accuracy without sacrificing performance on large-amplitude signals.

In essence, CVSD is ADPCM with delta modulation, where only two levels are used to represent the differential in amplitude or delta. Because a single binary digit is used to represent each sample, the sample rate and bit rate are equal, and as a consequence, the signal quality (SNR) is directly related to the sample rate. By transmitting the delta signal as a sequence of single bits on air, CVSD is much more robust to random bit errors in the channel than the log PCM techniques described above.

The use of a 64-kb/s CVSD CODEC provides toll quality speech, which is acceptable for most Bluetooth applications. Indeed, due to its encoded nature and low bandwidth but acceptable quality, CVSD has often been used in military communications systems since it was first proposed by Greefkes and Riemens in 1970.[3]

6.5.2.1   CVSD Operation.   The CVSD encoder and decoders are shown in Figures 6–3 and 6–4, respectively.

The step size is crucial to the performance of any delta modulation scheme. If small, tracking of slowly changing, low amplitude signals is good at the expense of poor tracking of fast, abruptly changing signals. When the step size is such that the CODEC is unable to keep up with the input signal, a phenomenon called slope overload occurs (see Figure 6–5).

Increasing the step size will reduce the problem of slope overload at the expense of increased noise due to the resulting large grained quantisation steps. Ultimately, low am-

[3]J.A. Greenfkes and K. Riemens, "Code Modulation with Digitally Controlled Companding for Speech Transmission," Philips Technical Review, pp. 335–353, 1970.

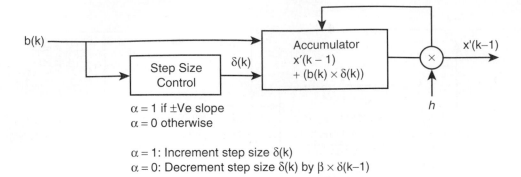

Figure 6–4 CVSD decoder block diagram.

plitude signals are not quantised accurately enough and they appear as an alternating one-zero pattern. Since an alternating one-zero bit pattern has a mean value of zero, the decoded output signal will integrate to zero and the signal will be lost. By adjusting the quantisation step size, CVSD makes a compromise between these two extremes.

The step size, $\delta(k)$, increases whenever a certain proportion of the previous bits are the same. In other words, if the input slope is seen to be going in the same direction relative to the CVSD approximation, then the step size is increased to catch up with it. This is accomplished by increasing the step size if the previous four bits are identical, that is, if the input has been consistently ahead of (greater or smaller than) the CVSD approximation for four consecutive bits.

The syllabic companding parameter, α, determines when to increase the step size (when the last four input bits are the same) or allow it to decay (when not). The step size decay time, β, is related to the length of a speech syllable. Although a human speech syllable is around 100ms in duration, pitch changes are around 10ms in duration. Bluetooth specifies a β which corresponds to 16ms.

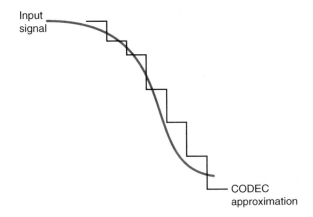

Figure 6–5 CVSD slope overload.

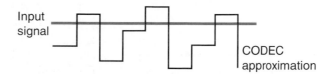

Figure 6–6 Effect of large decay factor.

The accumulator decay factor, h, determines how quickly the output of the CVSD decoder returns to zero in the absence of a strongly changing input. Bluetooth specifies an h which causes the output to decay to zero on the order of 0.5ms. The specification is rather vague on the reasoning behind the choice of such a large value for the accumulator decay h. As illustrated in Figure 6–6, the large decay factor means it can require several positive steps to recover from a single negative step. Indeed, positive steps are lessened by the decay, while negative steps are enhanced. This follows since the step parameter δ only operates when $x(k) < x^1(k-1)$ and $b(k) = 1$.

Bluetooth specifies 0.1% raw BER from the radio under various test conditions. Since audio data is not retransmitted and may not use FEC, this BER of 0.1% will be evident at the input to the CVSD decoder. Simulation shows that a BER of 0.1% does not significantly degrade the quality of the CVSD decoder output. A BER of 1% is quite noticeable, while a BER of around 5% and above causes the output to become unintelligible.

Bluetooth specifies the sample input and output to the CVSD CODEC as 16 bit signed.

6.5.2.2 Sample Rate Conversion (Interpolation and Decimation). Clearly, the processing frequency for log PCM and CVSD are not the same; Log PCM processes 13 or 14 bit samples and 8 bit symbols at 8kHz, while CVSD process 16 bit samples and single-bit symbols at 64kHz. It is possible to simply configure the PCM interface of the audio subsystem to operate at either 8kHz or 64kHz as appropriate and indeed with only analog / digital converters connected to the CODECs, this is acceptable. However, the extra information represented by the 16 bit samples at 64kHz are redundant and merely a side effect of the CVSD process. Furthermore, the effective data rate is far too high to make it sensible to pass on to another device as it is, particularly if the audio is to be routed via HCI. Therefore, it is necessary to interpolate and decimate so as to reduce the 64kHz sample data rate to the same 8kHz rate as that required for the log PCM CODECs.

This up sampling to 64kHz and down conversion to 8kHz must not introduce any significant noise above 4kHz. The simplest way to achieve this is by using a low-pass FIR filter with a sufficient number of taps. The baseband input data is interpolated from 8kHz up to 64kHz by the filter, which is clocked at 64kHz. For down-conversion, only every eighth output is used, but again filtering is required. The resulting data stream should exhibit negligible difference in power spectral density with respect to the input signal.

6.6 AUDIO SUBSYSTEM

Figure 6–7 shows a block diagram of a typical Bluetooth audio subsystem. As described, the log PCM encoding and decoding functions share a common path to and from the PCM

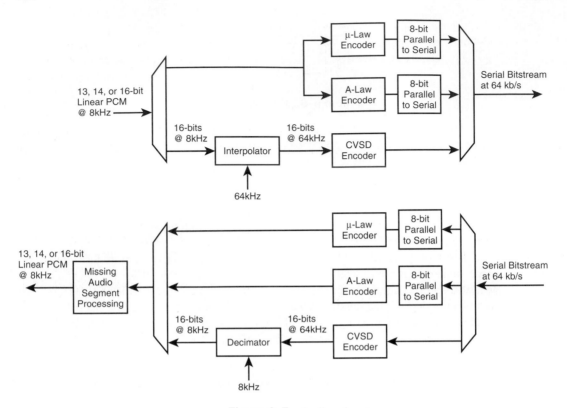

Figure 6–7 Audio subsystem.

data at 8kHz; the CVSD CODEC, however, requires interpolation and decimation. Each of the blocks shown has already been discussed, except for one labeled "Missing Audio Segment Processing."

6.6.1 Error Handling (Missing Audio Segment Processing)

Although some SCO packets are protected by FEC, none of the audio traffic is protected by a CRC and re-transmission is of course not possible due to the time-bounded nature of SCO data. Further, although much has been made of the robustness of CVSD to random bit errors, it is always possible that sufficient errors will occur so as to render a packet unusable. Although errors will not be detected in the packet payload, it is quite likely that the access code may be rejected or that the HEC will fail. In such situations, there will not be a valid audio packet for the CODECs to decode and so a mechanism for filling in or masking the missing data is required. The simplest technique is to repeat the decode of the previous packet again. A more sophisticated approach (and probably the acceptable minimum) is to dither the subsequent "repeat" packets with a random white noise to reduce the possibility of an audible tone due to the discontinuity clicks between packet repeats. If a new packet is not received after a predetermined time, it may also be necessary to fade the audio level to avoid the repetition becoming audible.

Since CVSD is a differential scheme, the decoder output depends on many previous symbols (unlike log PCM). When data is lost, the information about the current status of the accumulator and the step size is also lost. There are various ways to restart the algorithm when a new packet arrives. The simplest way is to reset the step size and accumulator to their initial values upon receipt of a new packet. The algorithm recovers itself quickly, and even for multiple missing bursts, the effect on sound quality is small.

6.7 AUDIO DATA FORMATS AND HCI

HCI uses the command HCI_Write_Voice_Setting to configure the audio subsystem and HCI_Read_Voice_Setting to read back the configuration status. The voice setting parameters apply equally to all audio channels and specify the baseband format for audio samples together with the chosen on-air coded format. Table 6–2 summarises the various parameters which comprise the two byte Voice_Setting commands and their meaning.

The specification of the HCI voice settings shows clearly that not only can the on-air coding format be chosen from CVSD, A-law, and μ-law, but so too can the sample input / output data be chosen from three options: linear PCM, μ-law log PCM, and A-law log PCM. This avoids the need to decode in the host and re-encode in the Bluetooth device if the host device already handles audio data in a log PCM encoded form—as is the case in much PSTN equipment.

This choice of input formats leads to another complication in the audio subsystem, which is the requirement to be able to convert from A-law and μ-law into μ-law and A-law, or even CVSD where the chosen input format is not linear PCM. Although the ITU-T G711 recommendations provide conversion tables for A to μ-law and μ to A-law, due to the need to support CVSD, it is arguably more elegant to simply utilise the existing CODECs to return the data to linear PCM before re-encoding it appropriately.

Table 6–2 HCI Voice Setting Parameters

Name	Bits	Description	
Baseband Coding	0:1	00: Linear 10: A-law	01: μ-law 11: Reserved
Baseband Data Format	2:3	00: 1's Complement 10: Sign-Magnitude	01: 2's Complement 11: Reserved
Baseband Sample Size	4	0: 8 bit *—Only when using linear PCM*	1: 16 bit
PCM Bit Offset	5:7	Offset in bit positions of sample from MSB of input word (0–7) *—Only when using linear PCM*	
Air Coding Format	8:9	00: CVSD 10: A-Law	01: μ-law 11: Reserved
Reserved	10:15	Reserved	

The choice of 8 or 16 bit sample size only applies to linear PCM since log coded data will always be 8 bits wide. When the sample data is 13 or 14 bits wide for log coding, the PCM bit offset parameter defines the displacement of the sample word within a 16 bit field.

6.8   IMPLEMENTATION

To implement an audio processing subsystem for Bluetooth, the subsystem above must be replicated for a maximum of three channels, either physically or temporally, and interfaced to a PCM data stream.

The higher layers of the standard describe HCI based SCO, where audio passes through the HCI via the protocol stack. The HCI route for audio is suitable where audio data is received directly by the HCI via a microcontroller interface, as may be the case with PC sourced audio. However, early Bluetooth white papers also described PCM based SCO—a transport route for audio PCM source data directly into and out of the CODEC subsystem via a dedicated PCM port. In the version 1.1 specification, this transport interface was not defined. However, it was hinted at in the baseband section, and indeed, has been implemented by the majority of Bluetooth component designers and manufacturers. The direct route to the CODECs is suitable for applications where digital audio is available directly, such as in cellular telephone, headset, or microphone applications.

6.8.1   Interfacing to Host Device Audio Levels

The specification again refers to the ITU-T G711 recommendations on audio levels and frequency response.

6.9   SUMMARY

Audio is a fundamental component of the Bluetooth specification, which is capable of supporting up to 3 full duplex audio channels simultaneously. These SCO channels use pre-reserved slots to maintain temporal consistency of the audio carried on them. Because Bluetooth is a wireless protocol data, it may be corrupted in transmission by random interference. To compensate for this Bluetooth uses a delta modulation technique called CVSD. For higher quality over a good link Bluetooth also provides A-law and μ-law log PCM capability.

There are two routes for audio to pass through a Bluetooth system: to and from the HCI as data in HCI packets and via direct PCM connection to the baseband CODECs. The HCI route has some deficiencies in carrying audio data, such as HCI flow control holding up audio data in a system carrying mixed voice and data. The direct PCM route is not well specified in the Bluetooth specification, but is very common in commercial implementations.

The audio capabilities of Bluetooth are very suitable for "toll quality" voice applications such as between cellular mobile phone handsets and associated headsets. However, for higher quality audio applications such as hi-fi music, a far better alternative would be to send compressed audio using Bluetooth ACL data links.

7

The Link Manager

The host drives a Bluetooth device through Host Controller Interface (HCI) commands, but it is the Link Manager (LM) that translates those commands into operations at the baseband level, managing the following operations.

- Attaching Slaves to a piconet and allocating their active member addresses.
- Breaking connections to detach Slaves from a piconet.
- Configuring the link including controlling Master/Slave switches (where both devices must simultaneously change roles).
- Establishing ACL (data) and SCO (voice) links.
- Putting connections into low-power modes: Hold, Sniff, and Park.
- Controlling test modes.

A Bluetooth Link Manager communicates with Link Managers on other Bluetooth devices using the Link Management Protocol (LMP).

The Bluetooth specification merely defines the LMP messages exchanged between Link managers; it does not go into any details as to how the protocol's instructions are carried out. However, given the content of the messages, one can draw sensible conclusions about what the Link manager does: It controls piconet management (establishes and destructs links), link configuration, and security functions.

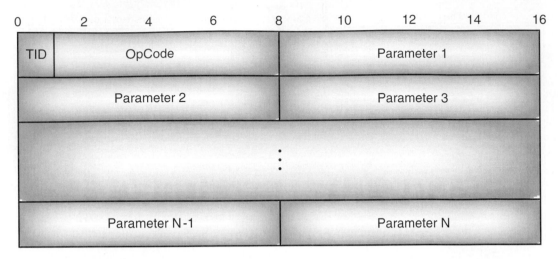

Figure 7–1   LMP PDU payload body.

Some LMP messages require responses, others do not. If a Link Manager receives a message which is disallowed on a link and the message requires a response, then it responds with an LMP_not_accepted message using a reason code of "PDU not allowed", otherwise the PDU should be ignored.

7.1   LMP PROTOCOL DATA UNITS (PDUs)

Link Managers communicate with their peers on other devices using the Link Management Protocol. This defines a set of messages which are passed between Link Managers.

Every LMP message (see Figure 7–1) begins with a single bit transaction identifier (TID), which is 0 if a Master initiated the transaction and 1 if a Slave initiated the transaction. A transaction can extend across several LMP exchanges, for instance all the exchanges required to set up pairing, including mutual authentication after link key creation form a single transaction, so all use the transaction ID from the first LMP_in_rand.

The transaction ID is followed by a 7 bit Operation Code (OpCode), which identifies the type of LMP message being sent. The OpCode is followed by the message's parameters, each of which occupies an integral number of bytes (except for unpark messages, which are not byte-aligned to make them as short as possible).

7.2   THE LINK MANAGEMENT CHANNEL

LMP PDUs are passed as single slot packets on the link management logical channel, (see section 4.8 for more details on Logical Channels). This channel is identified by setting the logical channel field in the packet header to 11.

The Link Manager sends its messages to the Link Controller for transmission. The Link Controller only guarantees to communicate on a link once every T_{poll} slots, so there may be a significant time lag between the Link Manager sending a message to the Link Controller and the message being transmitted on air. The Link Manager has to be aware of this potential for delayed transmission, as it can affect the timing of transactions such as master slave switch, and starting hold mode.

Because flow control is intended to stop L2CAP data packets from being transferred, it is not used for LMP, so the flow bit on LMP PDU packets is always left as 0 by the transmitting device. In any case, its value doesn't matter. As for LMP packets, the flow bit is ignored by the receiving device!

Now that we have seen how LMP PDUs can be sent and received by the lower layers, let's look in more detail about what can be accomplished by sending LMP messages.

7.3   LINK SETUP

The Link Manager is responsible for setting up and managing the baseband connections that link Bluetooth devices. The Link Manager establishes ACL links by controlling the baseband; then LMP messages can be used to establish a SCO (voice) link across an existing ACL connection.

The Link Manager maintains data on Slaves to which it has allocated an Active Member Address (AM_Addr).

Figure 7–2 shows the messages involved in setting up an ACL connection. The Link Controller layer must establish a link between devices before LMP messages can be exchanged.

In between the Link Controller setting up a connection and the Link Manager sending the LMP_host_connection_req, optionally a limited set of messages can be sent. For version 1.1 of the Bluetooth specification these optional messages are:

- LMP_clkoffset_req.
- LMP_name_req.
- LMP_detach.
- LMP__version_req.

The first three of these messages can be used to temporarily connect to a device, retrieve its name and clock offset, and then detach before the host is informed of the link. The clock offset message is a useful part of this sequence because it allows a Master to speed up paging the next time it makes a connection by predicting where on its hopping sequence a potential Slave will be scanning.

The LMP_version_req is provided because some details of LMP messages and timeouts change between versions, so it is useful to find out as soon as possible which version of Link Manager is at the remote end of a connection.

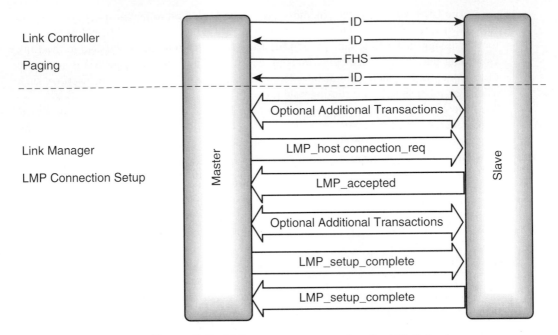

Figure 7–2   LMP message sequence chart for ACL link setup.

LMP has a 30-second timout between a message being sent and its response being received. If this timeout is exceeded, the link is assumed to be dead. Before version 1.1 there were problems with the initial setup of a link because there was no timer running before LMP traffic started. This meant that if a Link Manager did not start correctly, there was no way to detect this and shut down the link. Version 1.1 solved this problem by specifying that the 30-second LMP response timeout should apply to the time between a Link control level connection being established and the LMP_host_connection_req being sent.

The LMP_setup_complete message is generated independantly by both Master and Slave when each is satisfied with the state of the link. This means that it is not obvious how the LMP_response_timeout should be applied to the LMP_setup_complete message, but a timeout is needed as there must be a way to shut down a link if the remote Link Manager never sends the LMP_setup_complete message. Version 1.1 specified that the LMP_setup_complete message should be sent before the LMP response timeout from the previous transaction has timed out. This means that if a series of transactions are carried out before sending LMP_setup_complete, then each transaction must start before the LMP_response_timeout of the previous transaction has expired.

Another possible source of confusion in the LMP_setup_complete message is the transaction ID. Because each Link Manager decides independantly when to send the message, each LMP_setup_complete counts as a separate transaction and carries its own transaction identifier. This was not obvious in version 1.0B of the Bluetooth specification, so version 1.1 specified explicitly that when the Master sends the LMP_setup_complete message it sets the transaction ID to 0, and when the Slave sends the message it sets the transaction ID to1.

Once an ACL link has been established, either the Master or Slave can request a SCO link setup across the ACL link. Both Master and Slave use an LMP SCO request to initiate a SCO connection setup as shown in Figure 7–3.

When the Master requests a SCO link, it sends an LMP_SCO_req containing the parameters for the link. SCO link parameters are:

- SCO handle.
- Timing control flags (used to request a timing change on an established link).
- D_{SCO}—The SCO dedf2delay which indicates when the first SCO slot will happen.
- T_{SCO}—The SCO interval which separates SCO slots.
- SCO packet type to use: HV1, HV2, HV3, DV.
- Air mode coding: μ-law, A-law, CVSD.

The Slave simply replies with LMP_accepted (or LMP_not_accepted).

A Master may have SCO links to several Slaves at once. Once a Master has set up one SCO link, it has limited freedom to assign other slots. Therefore, it makes sense to let Masters choose the timing parameters for SCO links. Typically, a Master will manage links to many Slaves, so the Master chooses connection handles. If a Slave chose a handle, it might pick one that the Master was already using on another link. So, when a Slave sends an LMP_SCO request, the timing parameters are not valid, and the handle is invalid and left at 0. If the Master is willing to set up a SCO link, it replies with

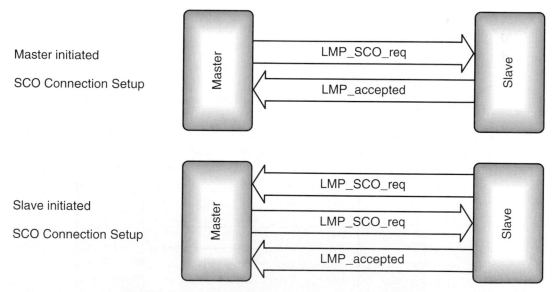

Figure 7–3   LMP message sequence charts for SCO connection setup.

an LMP_SCO_req with valid parameters, and the Slave acknowledges with LMP_ accepted, just as if the Master had initiated the transaction. (Of course, if the Master is not willing to set up a SCO link, it can reply to the Slave's request with LMP_not_ accepted.)

7.4 LMP LINK SHUTDOWN

Any time that a Master or a Slave wishes to shut down a Bluetooth link, it sends an LMP_detach command as shown in Figure 7–4. A reason for the detach is included in the command; possible reasons are:

- User ended connection.
- Low resources.
- About to power off.

When a Slave has been detached from a piconet, the Master can reuse the slave's active member address (AM_ADDR) to identify a new slave. If a slave did not detach correctly, there could be problems with two slaves trying to respond to the same AM_ADDR. Thus there is a detach procedure used by the Link Manager initiating the detach to ensure that a slave is fully detached before its address is reused:

- The LM initiating the detach finishes sending the current ACL packet with L2CAP data.
- The LM initiating the detach stops sending L2CAP data (obviously it makes no sense to send data to a device which is being detached!).
- The LM initiating the detach queues an LMP_detach for transmission and starts a timer of $6*T_{poll}$ slots (T_{poll} is the poll interval for the connection).
- If the $6*T_{poll}$ timer expires before a baseband acknowledgement of the LMP_detach is received, the link is dropped and a link supervision timeout is started. If a baseband acknowledgement is received, a timer of $3*T_{poll}$ slots is started.
- When the second timer (link supervision or $3*T_{poll}$) expires, then the AM_ADDR can be reused.

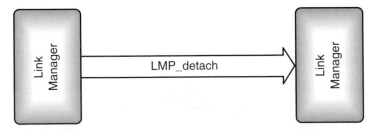

Figure 7–4   LMP message sequence chart for LMP_detach.

A timer is also used on the receiving side: If a Master receives an LMP_detach message, it starts a timer of $6*T_{poll}$ slots; if a Slave receives an LMP_detach message, it starts a timer of $3*T_{poll}$ slots. When this timer expires, the link can be dropped and the AM_ADDR from the link can be reused.

If the LMP_detach message is lost due to interference or devices moving out of range, then a link supervision timeout will occur and eventually the link will be detached anyway.

7.5 ROLE CHANGE

Normally, the device which pages becomes the Master of a piconet, and the device which page scans becomes the Slave. The Slave can only transmit in reply to a transmission from the Master (except for reserved SCO slots). The Master also sets packet sizes, SCO intervals, and timing. All this means that the Master controls the bandwidth available to the Slave.

In some cases, the roles in which Master and Slave find themselves are not appropriate. They could shut down the link and set it up again with the former Slave paging and the former Master page scanning, but this is quite a time-consuming procedure, and of course, during the time the link is being re-established, no data can be transferred. To avoid this waste of time, LMP provides a means for the Master and Slave to switch roles (see Figure 7–5).

The device wishing to initiate a role change simply sends an LMP_switch_req. In version 1.1 a switch instant parameter was added to the LMP_switch_req to specify ex-

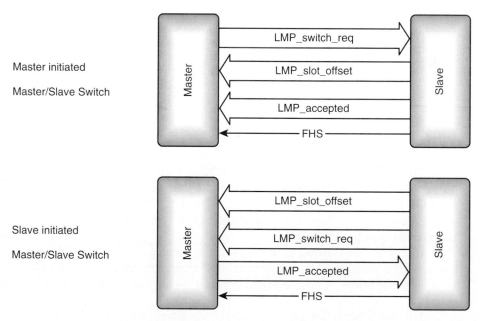

Figure 7–5   LMP message sequence chart for role change.

actly when the Master/Slave switch should happen (in previous versions of the Bluetooth specification the message has no parameters.) Some implementations cannot react quickly to switch requests. To ensure that enough time is allowed, the switch instant must be $2*T_{poll}$ or 32 slots after the switch request (whichever is greater).

If the Master sends the LMP_switch_req, the Slave responds with an LMP _slot_offset message. If the Slave initiated the switch by sending the LMP_switch_req, then it follows up by sending an LMP_slot_offset.

The LMP_slot_offset message contains a BD_ADDR and a slot offset. The BD_ADDR is the address of the Slave which is going to become Master after the switch. The slot offset is worked out by calculating the value in microseconds of the start of a TX slot if the Slave were Master of a piconet, then the value in microseconds of the start of the current Master's transmit slot is subtracted. If the result is greater than 1250, a modulo 1250 operation is used to make the value between 0 and 1249. So if the time a transmit slot starts on the current piconet is TXstart$_{slave's\ clock}$, and the time a transmit slot would start if the slave were master is TXstart$_{master's\ clock}$, the the offset is given by the equation:

$$\text{offset} = (\text{TXstart}_{slave's\ clock} - \text{TXstart}_{master's\ clock}) \bmod 250$$

During the Master/Slave switch, an FHS packet is used to synchronise the two devices. The 1.25 ms accuracy of an FHS packet is not sufficient to allow the two devices to synchronise, so the device which starts as Slave uses an LMP_slot_offset message to send the difference between its clock and the other device's clock. If the Slave requests the switch, it sends this message before the LMP_switch_req. If the Master requests the switch, the Slave sends LMP_slot_offset before the LMP_accepted message.

If the role change is accepted, the Slave must take over as Master. This means that the Master must synchronise to the Slave's Bluetooth clock. Whichever side initiates the switch, the Slave sends the Master an FHS packet to enable the Master to synchronise to its clock. After the FHS packet has been acknowledged, both devices switch to the new timing.

It is important to note that Bluetooth version 1.0 does not define a mechanism for a Master with many Slaves to pass information from one Slave's FHS packet on to its other Slaves. This means that a Slave cannot acquire the Master's other Slaves.

Figure 7–6 shows what happens to a Master with three Slaves when it accepts a Master/Slave switch from one Slave. The Master's single piconet splits into two piconets, joined in a scatternet by the former Master. The former Master (device A in Figure 7–6) now has a dual role as Master of the Slaves which have not switched role and Slave of the other device which switched roles.

If device A in Figure 7–6 did not support scatternets or did not have sufficient resources to be present on two piconets, it could choose to either refuse the Master/Slave switch or disconnect Slaves D and C, which it would not be able to support after the switch.

For more information on Master/Slave switch procedures, see Chapter 5.

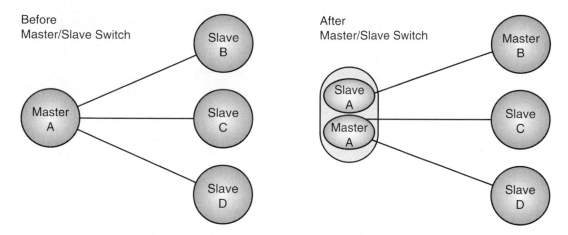

Figure 7–6   Piconet configuration before and after Master/Slave switch.

7.6   CONTROL OF MULTI-SLOT PACKETS

When a link is first set up, it uses single-slot packets by default. Multi-slot packets make more efficient use of bandwidth, but there are circumstances in which they shouldn't be used:

- On noisy links, multi-slot packets are more likely to be corrupted by a burst of interference.
- SCO links may not leave sufficient space between their slots for multi-slot packets.

Prior to version 1.1 because Masters often had links to several Slaves, it was the Master which usually had the tightest constraints on available slots, so the Master chose the packet types used on a link. The procedure was as follows:

The Master imposed a maximum packet size on the Slave by sending an LMP_max_slot command (see Figure 7–7). The Slave could not refuse, so there was no need for an LMP_accepted reply (the baseband acknowledgement scheme ensured that the LMP message is reliably transmitted). If the Slave wished to change the maximum packet size, it sent the Master an LMP_max_slot_req. If the Master was willing to allow the Slave to use this packet size, it replied with an LMP_accepted; otherwise, it sent an LMP_not_accepted and the Slave had to stick to the previous maximum packet size.

The system of allowing the Master to dictate packet sizes caused problems for Slaves which could not handle multi-slot packets (for example because they had tight time constraints imposed by scatternet operation), so version 1.1 changed the procedures to allow slaves to take a greater part in negotiation of packet types. The default for any new connection is now set to single slot packets only (this includes connections formed by Slaves returning from park mode, or connections formed after a Master/Slave switch). A device can signal that it wants to receive a different set of packet types by sending an LMP_max_slot message. If it wants permission to transmit multi-slot packets, it sends an

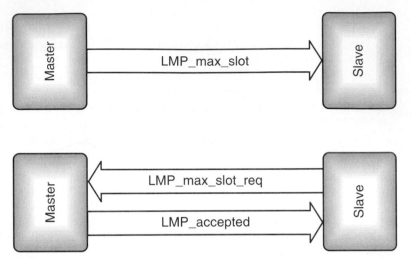

Figure 7–7   LMP message sequence chart for control of multi-slot packets.

LMP_max_slot_req. If it receives an LMP_accepted in reply, it may then transmit multi-slot packets; if it receives an LMP_not_accpted in reply, it is restricted to the packet types already negotiated.

7.7   SECURITY

The Bluetooth baseband includes an encryption key generation and cipher engine. For encryption and decryption, this engine must be configured and controlled by higher layers, and that control must be synchronised at both ends of the Bluetooth link. LMP provides the mechanism for negotiating encryption modes and coordinating encryption keys used by devices at either end of the link. For details of LMP's security procedures, see Chapter 15.

7.8   LOW-POWER MODES

LMP supports control of low-power connection modes. In these modes, a Slave and Master remain synchronised, but can save power by leaving the connection dormant for defined periods. These modes and how LMP controls them are covered in detail in Chapter 16.

7.9   POWER CONTROL

The transmit power emitted by the radio should be kept to a minimum to extend battery life, as well as to minimise interference.

Battery life will be radically affected by the power used by the radio, as it is likely to be the main power drain in the system. As many Bluetooth devices will be part of small, portable devices, they will be powered by batteries, so keeping power low to extend battery life is an important capability.

If Bluetooth piconets operate close to each other, their radio transmissions will tend to interfere. The lower the power, the less interference there will be with adjacent piconets, so using minimal power allows more piconets to exist in a given space.

Minimal power is important, but how does a Bluetooth device know what the minimum level is? Only the receiving device knows whether reception is good enough for power to be reduced, so Bluetooth allows the receiving device to request changes in the transmit power.

As Figure 7–8 shows, a device wishing to change power levels at the far end of the link simply sends an LMP_incr_power_req to increase power or an LMP_decr_power_req to decrease power. There is no need for an LMP_accepted response to these requests, because if the request is not received, the requesting device will detect that the power is still at the wrong value and reissue the request.

There are limits to the radio power allowed for Bluetooth devices, so eventually there comes a point where the power cannot be increased any more, no matter how bad reception is. Similarly, a radio can only have its power reduced by a limited amount before reducing power more turns it off. To avoid a device repeatedly making requests that the far end can't satisfy, the LMP provides reply messages to tell a device requesting an increase in power when the power cannot be changed as requested. Figure 7–9 shows these messages. LMP_max_power is returned if a device requests an increase in power when power is at maximum; LMP_min_power is returned if a device requests a decrease in power when power is at minimum.

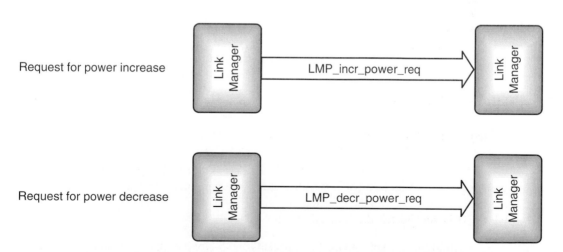

Figure 7–8 LMP message sequence charts for successfully changing power levels.

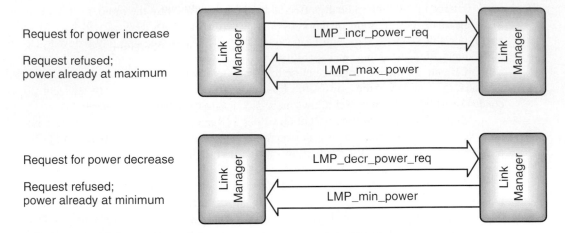

Request for power increase

Request refused;
power already at maximum

Request for power decrease

Request refused;
power already at minimum

Figure 7–9   LMP message sequence charts for failing to change power levels.

7.10   QUALITY OF SERVICE

LMP supports messages to configure the quality of service on a connection. It also supports messages which can set a channel to automatically change packet types according to
the channel quality. So, data can be transferred at a higher rate when the channel quality is
good, but a lower rate with more error protection can be used if the channel quality deteriorates. These messages are covered in detail in Chapter 17.

7.11   INFORMATION MESSAGES

LMP provides a variety of messages to request information from the far end of the link.
Some of the messages are used to retrieve information requested by a device's host, and
some are to retrieve information needed by the Link Manager itself.

7.12   SUPPORTED FEATURES

Some of the features of the Bluetooth standard are optional. The LMP_features_req message is used to inquire about which features are supported, and the LMP_features_res
message responds with the information.
     For version 1.0, the optional features are:

- Multi-slot packets—both 3-slot packets and 5-slot packets are optional.
- Encryption.

- Low-power modes—Hold, Park, and Sniff are all optional.
- RSSI—this is useful to higher layers, but support is optional.
- Power control for low-power radios—power control is mandatory for radios over 1 mW (0 dBm).
- Channel-quality-driven data rate changes.
- SCO links and where SCO is supported—HV2 and HV3 packets are optional.
- Voice coding schemes—CVSD, log μ-law, and log A-law.
- Optional paging schemes.
- Timing accuracy message.
- Master/Slave switch and slot offset messages (a slot offset message is needed to switch roles).

Version 1.1 added some extra fields to the end of the features parameter:

- Transparent SCO data—this indicates whether data can be sent unchanged through a SCO channel, for instance, to transmit synchronous data bypassing the SCO codecs.
- Flow control lag the total amount of L2CAP data that can be sent following the receipt of a valid payload header with the payload header flow bit set to 0.

When the baseband receives an ACL packet with the flow bit set to zero, it should stop transmitting L2CAP data. However, in some implementations processing delays mean that some L2CAP data is sent after the zero flow bit has been received; this delay in implementing flow control is called flow control lag. For maximum efficiency, it is useful to know what the flow control lag at the other end of a link is. That way, a flow bit can be set to 0 when there are still enough buffers left to accommodate data sent during the flow control lag period. The flow control lag field allows this information to be passed. It is a 3-bit field and the unit for flow lag is 256 bytes (so, for example, 0b010 gives a flow lag of 512 bytes).

The supported features information can be used within the Link Manager; for example, if it knows the remote device does not support 5-slot packets, it can avoid wasting time trying to configure the connection for that type of packet. The information can also be passed to higher layers of the protocol stack through the HCI command HCI_Read_Remote_Supported_Features, so that the upper layers can also avoid wasting time trying to use unsupported features.

7.13 LMP VERSION

The LMP_version_req is used to request version information from a Bluetooth device. The version information is returned in an LMP_version_res message.

Early versions of the Bluetooth standard used a different OpCode to identify the LMP_version_req, so developers cannot rely on this command to get version information on devices using LMP versions before release 0.8. This problem is confined to a few early releases of development kits and will not affect any consumer products. Any developer who suspects he or she may have an early version development kit can retrieve version information using the HCI command Read_Local_Version_Information. Many suppliers of development kits will be able to supply software to upgrade devices to later versions.

The version information which is supplied in the LMP_version_res is as follows:

- VersNr—The version of LMP supported.
- CompId—A company ID for the company which created the Link Manager implementation.
- SubVersNr—The developing company's version number for the Link Manager implementation.

The version information can help track problems with LMP implementations, and can also be used to allow workarounds when connecting to implementations with known problems. Future versions of LMP will add new features, so the Bluetooth version number will be useful to identify, as a supplement to the LMP_features_req, the capabilities of an LMP implementation.

7.14   NAME REQUEST

Every Bluetooth device has a user-friendly name which can be up to 248 bytes long. LMP provides the LMP_name_req message to request a user-friendly name and the LMP_name_res message to respond with the name.

All LMP messages are carried in DM1 packets, and the data payload in a DM1 packet is only 17 bytes. One byte is used to identify the LMP message, so this only leaves 16 bytes, not enough to carry a 248 byte name!

LMP solves this problem by using a series of messages to pass fragments of the user-friendly name. The LMP_name_req message has an offset parameter which identifies the first byte of the fragment it is requesting, and the LMP_name_res message has the same offset parameter. It is possible that the fragment of name requested might not completely fill the LMP_name_res message, so there is also a parameter in the response to give the length of the name fragment. With a byte used for the name offset and a byte used for the length of the name fragment, this leaves 14 bytes to carry the name fragment itself.

For example, if a host has a name "My Bluetooth Device," the sequence of messages in Figure 7–10 is used to retrieve the name. In the first LMP_name_req, the name offset is 0, so the first 14 bytes of the name are retrieved. The requesting device keeps adding 14 to the offset until it has retrieved the whole name. In this case, the name fits

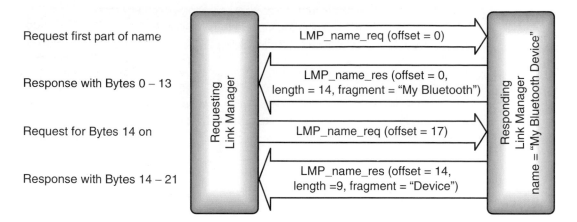

Figure 7–10 LMP message sequence chart for passing a user friendly name.

into two responses, the second response has length 9 because a NULL byte (0x00) terminates the name.

In the example above, it is obvious that the second response has the last part of the name because the name fragment doesn't fill the whole message. If the last part of the name filled the whole response message, the requesting device would send out another request with an offset that was past the end of the name. In this case, the responding link manager simply sends back an LMP_not_accepted with an error reason "Invalid LMP Parameters".

7.15 TEST MODE

Test modes are useful both for certification of Bluetooth devices by testing authorities and for a manufacturer's production line testing of devices. LMP provides the LMP_test_activate message to put devices into a special test mode. Once a device is in a test mode, LMP_test_control messages can be used to start specific tests. Further details of LMP's test control mechanism are given in Chapter 20.

7.16 SUMMARY

Figure 7–11 summarises LMP operations. As you can see, there are many alternative paths through this diagram. The simplest route after the LC has finished with paging and page response is to just exchange messages to confirm connection setup is complete.

More complex routes can involve changing roles of Master and Slave, either after paging but before connection setup is complete or at any time thereafter. Similarly, the security procedure's authentication, pairing, and encryption can be passed through on the way to connection setup-complete, or they can be visited at any time afterwards.

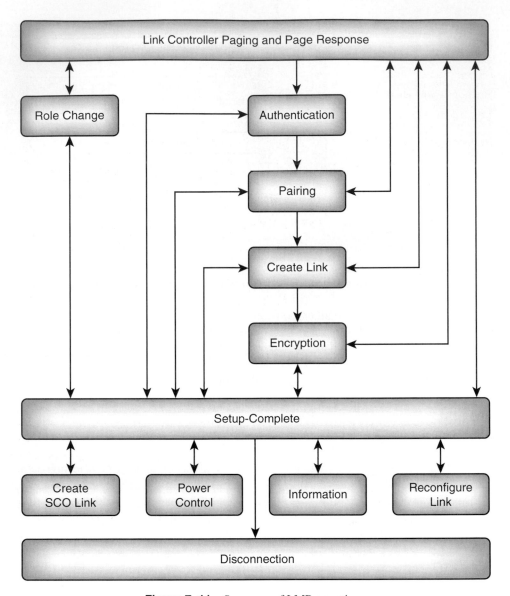

Figure 7–11 Summary of LMP operations.

Once the connection has been set up, it can have up to three SCO connections created across it, or its mode can be changed either to a low power mode or test mode. The link can also be reconfigured at any time, including at mode changes, quality of service changes, packet type changes, and power level changes. Finally, information about an active link can be retrieved at any time.

When the connection is no longer required, LMP can cause disconnection.

8

The Host Controller Interface

Some Bluetooth systems will have the baseband and Link Manager on one processor with higher layers such as L2CAP, SDP, RFCOMM, and applications running on a separate host processor. A Bluetooth PCMCIA card for a PC could be implemented like this with the Link Manager and baseband in the PCMCIA card, and the higher layers on the PC's processor.

In systems where the higher layers are run on a host device's processor and lower layers on a Bluetooth device, an interface is needed between the higher and lower layers. The Bluetooth standard defines the Host Controller Interface (HCI). By making this a standard interface, it is possible to mix and match higher and lower layers, so, for instance, one set of higher layer software on a PC could run with PCMCIA cards from different manufacturers.

A device such as a Bluetooth card for a PC may use the HCI to separate upper and lower layers for many reasons:

- Hosts such as PCs have spare capacity to handle the higher layers, allowing the Bluetooth device to have less memory and a less powerful processor or DSP, thus reducing its cost.
- The host device can sleep and be awoken by an incoming Bluetooth connection.
- The HCI interface is useful for test and type approval of Bluetooth devices.

Figure 8–1 shows how the Bluetooth Protocol stack may be split into two parts linked by the Host Controller Interface.

Why not move the whole stack onto a host's processor? This could be done, but Bluetooth's slot timing means that the host would have to be able to respond within microseconds to interrupts from the Bluetooth radio. Although hosts may have spare MIPS, most would not be able to guarantee that the processor would be available when it is needed. Therefore, it makes sense to keep the lower time critical layers on a separate processor, which can guarantee a fast response.

Standardising the Host Controller Interface allows drivers to be written which can be used with a variety of Bluetooth modules from different manufacturers. It also provides a standard test interface which can be used to exercise the radio and lower portions of the Bluetooth stack.

It is possible to have Bluetooth systems where all layers of the protocol stack run on one processor; a headset is an example of such a system. Headsets need to be small, inexpensive, light, and low power. Running the whole Bluetooth stack on one processor fits in well with these requirements. These single-processor devices still need to support an HCI for test purposes, however.

In this chapter and throughout this book, all HCI commands and events are prefixed with "HCI_." In the standard this is not done, but it is done here because in the diagrams which show several layers of the protocol stack interacting, the prefix makes it easier to identify the HCI layer. This chapter covers many of Bluetooth HCI commands, but ex-

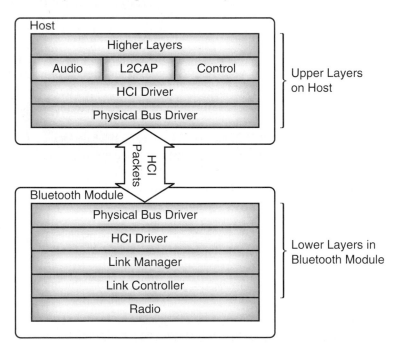

Figure 8–1   Position of the Host Controller Interface in the Bluetooth protocol stack.

cludes those covered in the chapters on security, low-power modes, quality of service, and testing (see Chapters 15, 16, 17 and 19).

8.1 HCI PACKET TYPES

The Bluetooth standard for the Host Controller interface (HCI) defines the following:

- Command packets used by the host to control the module.
- Event packets used by the module to inform the host of changes in the lower layers.
- Data packets to pass voice and data between host and module.
- Transport layers which can carry HCI packets.

Figure 8–2 shows the directions the HCI packets flow.

8.1.1 HCI Commands

HCI commands are used by the host to control the Bluetooth module and to monitor its status. Commands are transferred using HCI command packets.

The HCI command packet structure is shown in Figure 8–3. It begins with a 2 byte OpCode identifying the type of the command. The first byte of the OpCode is the OpCode Group Field (OGF), which identifies a group of commands. The second byte holds the OpCode Command Field (OCF) and identifies a command within the group.

The OpCode is followed by a single byte field giving the length of the following parameters in bytes. The parameters themselves come next, and each occupies an integral number of bytes. Note that since the parameters are not all single bytes, the parameter total length need not necessarily give the total number of parameters.

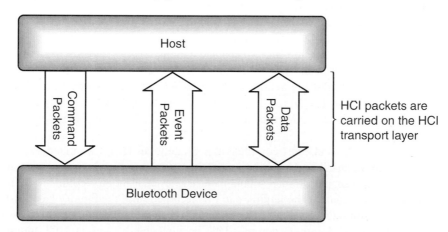

Figure 8–2   The three types of HCI packets.

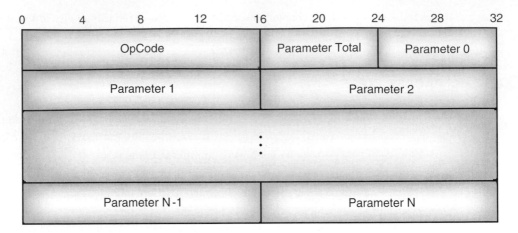

Figure 8–3   HCI command packet.

If a command can complete immediately, an HCI_Command_Complete event is returned immediately to indicate that the command has been dealt with. One exception to this use of HCI_Command_Complete is when it is a reply to an HCI_Reset command. After a full reset, the module can't tell whether it has reset because it was just powered on, or whether it has reset because it received an HCI_Reset command. This means that it would be impossible for the HCI_Command_Complete to be sent after the reset (when the command has really completed), so instead, an HCI_Command_Complete is sent to tell the host that the command has been received and will be acted upon.

Between version 1.0b and 1.1 there was a change in the specification of the HCI_reset command: In version 1.0b it reset the HCI transport layer, so that for instance a USB implementation of HCI would re-enumerate after an HCI_reset. In version 1.1 the specification was changed so that LM and layers below are rest, but the HCI transport layer remains unaffected. Also in version 1.1 the host is allowed to send commands as soon as it has received the HCI_Command_Complete event associated with the reset, so any implementations which will be unable to handle further commands whilst processing the reset should delay the HCI_Command_Complete until they are ready to handle further commands from the host. This change makes implementation easier for host programmers, as they don't have to cope with the HCI transport layer restarting, but it makes implementation more difficult for the lower layers as they must implement the rest in software (a full hardware reset would reset the HCI transport later along with the rest of the stack).

If a command can't complete immediately, an HCI_Command_Status event is returned immediately, and another event is returned later when the command has completed. An example of such a command is the HCI_Inquiry command, which starts an inquiry. The result of the inquiry can't be returned until the inquiry has finished, and this will take some time, so an HCI_Command_Status is returned immediately to acknowledge that the HCI_Inquiry command has been received. Later, an HCI_Inquiry_Complete event is returned.

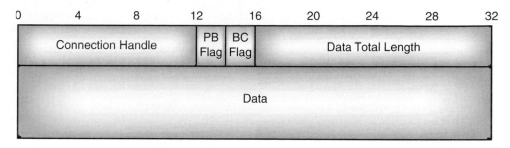

Figure 8–4   HCI ACL data packet.

8.1.2   HCI Data Packets

HCI data packets are used to pass both data (ACL) and voice (SCO) information across the HCI. Different packets are used for ACL and SCO data.

Figure 8–4 shows the HCI data packet used to transfer ACL data. The fields in this packet are as follows:

- The connection handle identifies the ACL connection for the data.
- The Packet Boundary (PB) flag identifies whether the packet data carries the start of a higher layer L2CAP packet, or is a continuing fragment of an L2CAP packet.
- The Broadcast (BC) flag identifies point to point data from broadcast data and discriminates between point to point, active broadcast (for active Slaves) and piconet broadcast (for active and parked Slaves, hence must be sent in beacon slots). Note that sniffing slaves are not guaranteed to receive either type of broadcast.
- Data total length gives the length of data in bytes.

The data total length field is 2 bytes, so the maximum theoretical size of data an HCI packet could carry is 65,535 bytes. However, many Bluetooth modules will not have buffers large enough to receive this size packet. An HCI command, HCI_Host_Buffer _Size, can be used to limit the maximum size of ACL data packet which can be transferred, but every Bluetooth module and host are required to support packets with a data length of up to 255 bytes.

Figure 8–5 shows the HCI packet used to transfer SCO (audio) data. Its structure is very similar to the ACL packet with a few differences:

- There are no PB or BC flags; their places are reserved.
- The data total length field is only 1 byte, restricting the data field to 255 bytes.

The reason for the smaller length field is that the SCO link is intended for two-way audio; if too much data is passed in one packet, it increases the time lag between the ends of the SCO link.

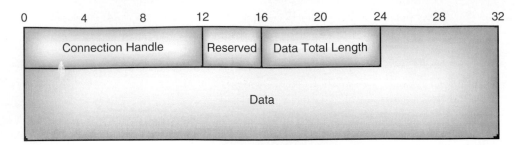

Figure 8–5 HCI SCO data packet.

8.1.3 HCI Event Packets

The format of HCI event packets is similar to HCI command packets, as shown in Figure 8–6. They carry an event code identifying the event. This performs a similar function to the OpCode field, which identifies HCI commands. Like the command packet, there is a field giving the total length of the parameters, followed by a list of parameters.

The HCI_Set_Event_Mask command is used to tell the Bluetooth module which events it wishes to know about. This command can switch on or off any events except the HCI_Command_Complete event, the HCI_Command_Status event, and the HCI_Number_Of_Completed_Packets event. These three events cannot be switched off because they are needed for flow control (see section 8.3, Flow Control).

HCI_Set_Event_Filter command is also used to disable reporting of events, but rather than simply switching events on and off, it uses event filters to specify which modules the host is interested in for inquiries and connections.

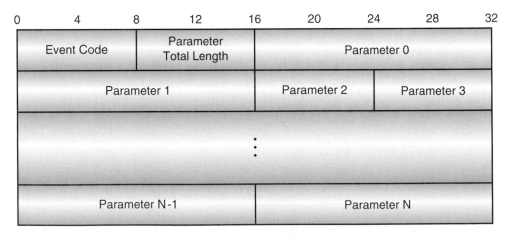

Figure 8–6 Structure of an HCI event packet.

The Inquiry_Result_Filter command allows the host to choose whether to see inquiry events from any module, from only a specified device classes, or from only a specified device.

The Connection_Setup_Filter command allows the host to make the same choices for connections: the host may choose to connect to any device, to devices with a specific device classes, or to a specified device.

8.2 THE HCI TRANSPORT LAYER

A transport layer is needed to get HCI packets from the host to the Bluetooth module. Bluetooth defines three transport layers:

- USB—Universal Serial Bus.
- RS-232—a serial interface with error correction.
- UART—Universal Asynchronous Receiver Transmitter, a serial interface without error correction.

8.2.1 USB Framing

USB maps the different types of HCI packets onto the USB standard's different logical endpoints:

- HCI commands—USB control endpoint.
- HCI ACL data—USB bulk endpoint.
- HCI SCO data—USB isochronous endpoint.
- HCI events—USB interrupt endpoint.

A bulk endpoint is used for ACL data for two reasons: first, it allows many 64-byte USB packets to be transferred in each millisecond long USB frame, so it is fast enough for ACL data; second, because it has the ability to detect and correct errors, so it assures that the data arrives uncorrupted.

The isochronous endpoint transfers SCO data directly into the host's SCO FIFO buffers. If the FIFO buffers are full, the new SCO data simply overwrites the stale data. In accordance with the USB specification, the isochronous endpoint should be set up with an interval of 1 ms. There is no error correction across this endpoint, so SCO data may be corrupted.

The interrupt endpoint is used for events. Using a 1 ms interval ensures that events are transferred promptly across the USB interface.

To allow the correct USB driver to load, a USB class code has been assigned to Bluetooth devices specifying class, subclass, and protocol codes as follows:

- bbDeviceClass = 0xE0 (wireless controller).
- bbDeviceSubClass = 0x01 (RF controller).
- bbDeviceProtocol = 0x01 (Bluetooth programming).

Bluetooth is intended to be a low-power protocol for battery-operated devices. A USB host controller will check memory to see if it has to do anything every millisecond. This can adversely affect power saving on hosts. For example, a notebook processor with an active USB Bluetooth module will not be able to drop into the C3 low-power state. This will cause significantly shorter battery life. More information on USB is available from http://www.usb.org.

8.2.2 Serial Transport Layers

RS-232 and UART are both serial links. They both include framing to identify the packet type as follows:

- 0x01—HCI command packet.
- 0x02—HCI ACL data packet.
- 0x03—HCI SCO data packet.
- 0x04—HCI event packet.

UARTs are not expected to cope with errors or have to negotiate link configuration, but the RS-232 protocol needs to cope with these, so RS-232 also provides:

- 0x05—error message packet.
- 0x06—negotiation packet.

On the UART transport layer, the packet indicator identifying the packet type is sent immediately before the packet. The HCI packet's length field can be used to work out the boundaries of the packets, and hence when to expect the next packet indicator.

The UART transport layer uses null-modem connections as shown in Figure 8–7. Transmit data (TXD) is connected to receive data (RXD), and Clear To Send (CTS) is connected to Ready To Send (RTS).

On UART interfaces, it is possible for the UART's buffers to run out of space, so RTS/CTS flow control is used to flow control the UART interface. CTS set to 1 stops the other end from sending; CTS set to 0 gives permission to send. Bluetooth defines a 3 ms delay between setting RTS to 1 and data flow stopping, so this time lag should be taken into account when setting RTS.

RS232 links are subject to errors, so they are slightly more complex than UART links. The same single byte packet type indicators are used, but a single byte sequence number is added to allow retransmissions to be identified. The sequence number is incremented on every packet except for retransmissions, so if it stays unchanged, the receiving side knows the packet is a retransmission.

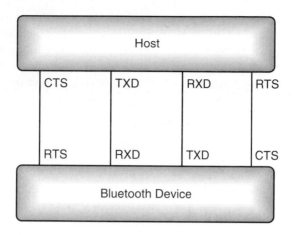

Figure 8–7   Connections for HCI UART transport layer.

Figure 8–8 shows the structure of HCI packets used on RS232 links.
The Bluetooth HCI transport layer initialises with a set of default parameters:

- Baud rate = 9600 bps.
- No parity.
- 8 data bits.
- 1 stop bit.
- Protocol mode = 0×13 (HDLC like framing, with COBS/CCITT-CRC).

The host and Bluetooth module should begin by negotiating agreed parameters for these variables and also the value for T_{detect}, the time to stop sending after CTS is set. These values can also be renegotiated later if required. The negotiation packets are used to negotiate these values.

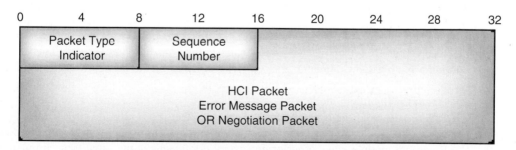

Figure 8–8   RS-232 HCI packet frame.

COBS/CCITT-CRC delimits frames with $0 \times 7E$, and immediately before the final delimiter includes a CRC to allow error checks. When the receiving end detects an error, it sends an error packet back. This identifies the sequence number of the packet with the error, and the type of the error (chosen from: FIFO overrun, parity error, framing error, CRC error, missing sequence number, or missing retransmission packet). The transmitting end can then retransmit the packet with the error.

8.3 FLOW CONTROL

Some HCI transport interfaces offer data rates much larger than the data rate across the Bluetooth radio and air interfaces, so a host can pass data down faster than it can be transmitted out of the module. The Bluetooth module could simply buffer the data until it is ready to transmit, but for modules such as Bluetooth PC cards, the host will have far more memory available than the Bluetooth module (just adding more memory is not a sensible solution as it would make the module far more expensive). So if a Bluetooth module can't transmit data fast enough and doesn't have space to store it, what's the solution?

One possibility would be to slow down the HCI transport interface, but that would slow down commands as well as data, and besides, the data rate on air is variable according to interference and the capabilities of the device at the far end of the Bluetooth link. So, a mechanism is needed to slow down data transport across the HCI only when the Bluetooth module's buffers are overloaded and to allow the HCI transport layer to run at full speed the rest of the time. Bluetooth solves this problem by providing flow control of the HCI.

8.3.1 Command Flow Control

Each time a command is sent to the Bluetooth module, the module responds with a HCI_Command_Complete or HCI_Command_Status. HCI_Command_Complete is used if the command can be executed immediately, otherwise HCI_Command_Status is used and HCI_Command_Complete is sent when the command has completed (see Figure 8–9).

When the system is first switched on, the host may only send one command until it has received an HCI_Command_Complete or HCI_Command_Status event. These events contain a Num_HCI_Command_packets field, which tells the host how many command packets the Bluetooth module can buffer. The host may then send that many command packets to the Bluetooth module.

For instance, if the Num_HCI_Command_packets parameter is 3, then the host can send 3 commands to the Bluetooth module without waiting for a response. Even though the Bluetooth module may be buffering several commands at the same time, it must deal with them in the order in which they were sent.

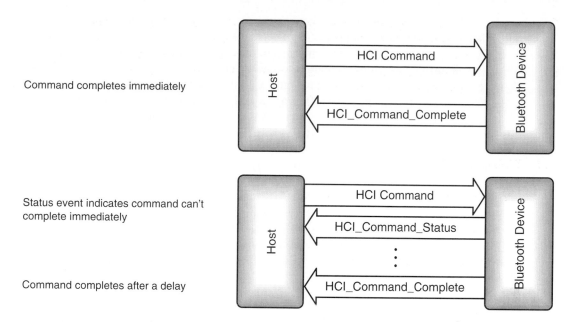

Command completes immediately

Status event indicates command can't complete immediately

Command completes after a delay

Figure 8–9   Message sequence charts for HCI command flow control.

8.3.2   Flow Controlling Data from the Host

A different mechanism is used for flow controlling data across the HCI interface. The HCI_Read_Buffer_Size command is used to find out how much buffer space the Bluetooth module has. The Bluetooth module replies with the numbers of SCO and ACL packets it can buffer, and the maximum size of HCI SCO data and HCI ACL data packets.

Typically, a module will not buffer much SCO data because SCO data should pass regularly through the protocol stack with as little latency as possible. ACL data is usually more bursty in nature, so modules can buffer ACL data without adversely affecting the application.

Once the host knows how many SCO and ACL packets the Bluetooth module can buffer, it can send up to that number of packets across the HCI to the Bluetooth module. Once the host has sent enough packets to fill up the module's buffers, it must wait for the module to tell it that more space is available.

A Bluetooth module tells its host that it has buffers free for more data packets by sending the HCI_Number_Of_Completed_Packets event. This event tells the host how many HCI data packets have been removed from the module's buffers since the last HCI_Number_Of_Completed_Packets event was sent. The packets may be cleared from the module's buffers either because they have been transmitted or because they have been flushed.

The parameters in the HCI_Number_Of_Completed_Packets event include a list of connection handles and a number of completed packets for each handle, so that if several connections are in use, the host is informed of the activity on each connection separately.

It is up to each implementation to decide how often the HCI_Number_of_Completed_Packets event is sent. At the extreme, it could be sent after each packet transmitted, or the module could wait until its buffers are completely empty before sending the event.

SCO data's synchronous nature means that every time a SCO slot becomes available, either a SCO packet is sent or discarded. This means that the module telling the host the number of completed packets on a SCO channel is really a waste of time; the host could just figure out the numbers for itself. Because of this, Bluetooth provides an HCI_Write_SCO_Flow_Control_Enable command, which stops the Bluetooth module from sending any information on SCO channels in the HCI_Number_of_Completed_Packets events (the HCI_Read_SCO_Flow_Control_Enable can be used to find out how SCO flow control reporting has been set). Note that the command does not actually have any effect on the flow of data across the baseband SCO channels; it only affects whether the host is informed when SCO data buffers are available.

8.3.3 Flow Controlling Data from the Bluetooth Module

Usually there will be no problem with the host accepting data as fast as the Bluetooth module can send it. However, some hosts with limited processing capacity such as mobile phone handsets may not be able to accept data at full rate, and may need to flow control the Bluetooth module. Flow control of the Bluetooth module is switched on with the command HCI_Set_Host_Controller_To_Host_Flow_Control.

The HCI_Host_Buffer_Size command is then used to notify the module of the host's buffering capabilities. It contains the numbers of SCO and ACL packets the host can buffer, and the maximum size of HCI SCO data and HCI ACL data packets.

The host uses the HCI_Host_Number_Of_Completed_Packets command to tell the Bluetooth module how many buffers it has freed on each connection. This command may be sent at any time and is not affected by the usual flow control mechanisms.

When connections are closed, all untransmitted packets are flushed. Since both the host and Bluetooth module know that this happens, the flushed packets are not mentioned in the next HCI_Number_Of_Completed_Packets events.

8.4 CONFIGURING MODULES

HCI provides configuration commands to set up the characteristics of the local module. Since these commands don't involve the Bluetooth link, they return immediately with an HCI_Command_Complete event.

8.4.1 Version and Features Information

Before a module can be used at all, it is crucial to know its capabilities and which version of the standard it supports. The HCI_Read_Local_Version_Information returns:

- A status byte—zero if the command succeeded, no zero for errors.
- HCI version.
- HCI revision.
- LMP version.
- Manufacturer name.
- LMP sub-version.

In versions before 0.7, the parameters were different:

- HCI version.
- HCI revision.
- LMP version.
- LMP revision.

How does the host get version information when the version information command changes between versions? It is possible to figure out whether the parameters are from pre or post version 0.7 as the earlier version has a shorter parameter list. So when interpreting this command, the parameter total length field should be taken into account (see Figure 8–6). The only version 0.7 devices available were development kits, and these can be upgraded to later versions; so in practice, encountering version 0.7 parameters is unlikely to cause problems for commercial Bluetooth products.

The HCI_Read_Remote_Version_Information mirrors the HCI_Read_Local_Version_Information, but returns the information on a connected device. The device is specified by a connection handle.

8.4.2 Local and Remote Name Request

Every Bluetooth device has a friendly name which is a UTF-8 encoded string up to 248 bytes long. (If the name is less than 248 bytes long, it is terminated with a NULL 0x00.) The HCI_Read_Local_Name command can be used to find out the friendly name of the local module. To change the local module's friendly name, use the HCI_Change_Local_Name command. Friendly names are transmitted starting with the first byte of the name. This is contrary to the usual rule of sending multi byte parameters in little Endian Format (least-significant byte first).

The HCI_Remote_Name_Request is used to request the friendly name of a remote device. This command can be used even if there is no current connection to the device, in which case, the device first establishes a connection, then uses the LMP_name_req to get the name of the remote device. So that the device can establish a connection, the parameters required are passed in the HCI_Remote_Name_Request. These are the BD_ADDR, Page_Scan_Repetition_Mode, Page_Scan_Mode, and Clock_Offset.

It may take some time to establish a connection and get the remote device's name, so when the module receives the HCI_Remote_Name_Request, it acknowledges it with an HCI_Command_Status event. Once the remote name has been obtained, the module sends an HCI_Remote_Name_Request_Complete event containing a status field indicating success or a reason for failure, the BD_ADDR of the device, and its friendly name. The most common reason for failure in the status field is likely to be maximum number of connections, which indicates that there are insufficient resources to establish a connection to the remote device.

8.4.3   Class of Device

An example of a command which generates an immediate HCI_Command_Complete event is shown in Figure 8–10. The host sends an HCI_Read_Class_Of_Device request so that it can find out the setting of the device type which is passed in the FHS packets used to respond to inquiries. The Bluetooth module will immediately generate an HCI_Command_Complete event. This event's parameters contain the device class information requested by the host.

For a device such as a handset, which has the Bluetooth module built in, the class of device is unlikely to change. However, one could have a Bluetooth PCMCIA card which could be inserted into a laptop or handheld PC. In this case, the device type would need to be written to the card using the HCI_Write_Class_Of_Device command. Like the HCI_Read_Class_Of_Device, this command returns immediately with an HCI_Command_Complete.

The class of device must be set up before a device can interact with other Bluetooth devices. This is because the class of device is written into the FHS packet, which is used in inquiry and paging procedures.

8.4.4   Voice Settings

Chapter 6 covered the three different CODECs Bluetooth provides (A-law, μ-law, and CVSD). The HCI_Write_Voice_Setting command allows both the input coding format and the air coding format to be set. It also allows the host to choose 1's complement or 2's complement input data format. As well as the three on air formats, the input format can be

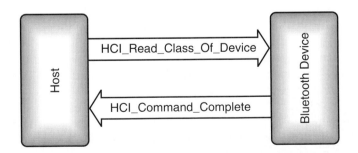

Figure 8–10   Message sequence chart for HCI_Read_Class_Of_Device.

linear PCM; in this case, the sample size can be chosen to be 8 or 16 bits. It is possible to align the samples within an HCI packet so that the MSB of the voice sample is not the MSB of the payload; in this case, HCI_Write_Voice_Setting can be used to specify which bit of the HCI payload holds the MSB of the voice sample.

While HCI_Write_Voice_Settings can be used to specify both the baseband input format and the on air format of voice, in practice it is most likely that a device would be expected to convert only from linear PCM.

Because it is unlikely that all Bluetooth devices would need to convert between any pair of formats, many Bluetooth devices will not support all conversions which are specified. In these cases, an "unsupported feature or parameter value" error would be returned in the HCI_Command_Complete event.

The voice settings of a Bluetooth module may be checked by the host at any time using the HCI_Read_Voice_Setting command.

8.4.5 Supported Features

Bluetooth includes many optional features. Obviously, it is important for a host to know the capabilities of the Bluetooth module it is using and the device at the other end of the link, so Bluetooth provides commands to read the supported features of both the local module and remote device.

HCI_Read_Local_Supported_Features gets the features for the local module, and HCI_Read_Remote_Supported_Features retrieves the features for a remote device specified by its connection handle.

The features which are optionally supported are:

- Multi-slot data packets—Single slot is mandatory, 3 slot and 5 slot are optional.
- Encryption and authentication support.
- Master/Slave switch and slot offset (to do a Master/Slave switch, a Slave device must be able to report the difference in slot offset between the Master's timing and its own).
- Timing accuracy—Information on the long-term drift and jitter of both the remote and local devices' clocks can help to set scan windows efficiently for Hold, Park, and Sniff modes, but providing timing information is optional; without it, the worst case timing is assumed.
- Low power modes—Hold, Park, and Sniff mode.
- SCO (voice) channel—If SCO is supported, then HV1 packets must be supported.
- HV2 and HV3 packets on SCO channels.
- Different voice CODECs—A-law, μ-law, and CVSD.
- Optional paging schemes.
- Power control and RSSI (Received Signal Strength Indication).

8.4.6   Country Code

In France, part of the ISM (Industrial, Scientific, and Medical) band used by Bluetooth is reserved for military use, so the frequency range is different from the range used by the rest of the world. In other words, French devices use a more limited frequency range than the rest of the world.

The country code identifies whether the module is using the full frequency range or the limited French range. In early versions of the standard, there were also different frequency ranges for Spain and Japan.

The country code cannot be set in the version 1.0B standard; it can only be read using the command HCI_Read_Country_Code. Up to version 0.8 of the Bluetooth standard, the country code could be written by the host as well as read; then, the HCI_Write_Country _Code command vanished without explanation in version 0.9 of the specification. Some manufacturers have chosen to implement the HCI_Write_Country_Code as a proprietary extension to the HCI command set, but as it is a proprietary extension, there is no standard OpCode to identify it.

8.4.7   HCI_Read_BD_ADDR

The Bluetooth device address cannot be set because each device is manufactured with its own unique address. If it were possible to alter it, then two devices could end up with the same address. Although the address can't be written, it can be read. This information is useful, as it might be manually entered into a remote device's applications to enable them to contact the local device by paging its Bluetooth device address. The HCI_Read_BD_ADDR command allows a host to retrieve the Bluetooth device address from a module.

8.5   INQUIRING: DISCOVERING OTHER BLUETOOTH DEVICES

Chapter 4 explained how the baseband can use an inquiry to discover other Bluetooth devices in the neighbourhood. All aspects of the inquiry process can be controlled through the HCI.

8.5.1   Initiating an Inquiry

The HCI_Inquiry command is used to initiate an inquiry. It has three parameters:

- Inquiry LAP—The inquiry access code to be used.
- Inquiry Length—The total length of the inquiry (in units of 1.28 s).
- Num_responses—The number of inquiry results to wait for. Zero does not mean no responses: It has a special reserved meaning and signifies that the number of responses should be ignored so that the inquiry only terminates when the inquiry length is reached.

8.5.2   Handling Inquiry Responses

Inquiry responses received are reported to the host in an HCI_Inquiry_Result event (unless they have been filtered out using the HCI_Set_Event_Filter command). Each HCI_Inquiry_Result event carries information needed to connect the responding device:

- Number of inquiry responses covered in the event packet.
- Bluetooth addresses of responding device(s), which are used to page device(s).
- Page scan repetition mode—There are three modes: R0 is continuous page scanning, R1 page scans at least every 1.28 s, and R2 scans at least every 2.56 s.
- Page scan period mode—A device which is configured to use an optional page scanning scheme will use mandatory page scanning for a while after responding to an inquiry. The length of time it uses mandatory page scanning is governed by the page scan period mode.
- Page scan mode—This says whether a device is using optional page scan modes, which is useful if the inquiring device later decides to page the responding device (if the inquiring device wants to page immediately, it can use mandatory paging, because devices perform a mandatory page scan for a period after an inquiry response).
- Class of responding device(s)—This information can be useful to applications deciding whether to connect to a responding device.
- Clock offset—Bluetooth clock bits 16:2 of responding device(s). This can be used to estimate the clock of the device when paging, potentially speeding up connection.

An inquiring device may not be interested in every device in the area, and in environments where many Bluetooth devices are present, receiving information about all of them could be a nuisance. For example, on devices such as cellular phone handsets, the limited size of display screens might mean that interesting results can't be seen without scrolling past loads of devices the user didn't want to know about. To provide the host with some control over the results it sees, the HCI_Set_Event_Filter command can be used to set an inquiry result filter, which means that some devices will not be reported in HCI_Inquiry_Result events. Inquiry results can be filtered out using three criteria:

- Report only new devices not seen before.
- Report only devices with a specific device type.
- Report only the device with a specified Bluetooth device address.

Of course this filtering could be done at the Application Level instead, but module-level filtering results in the Bluetooth device not using the limited bandwidth of the HCI to report information that's not going to be used.

8.5.3 Stopping an Inquiry

An inquiry will stop when Num_responses devices have responded to the inquiry, or when inquiry length time has passed, whichever happens first. Figure 8–11 shows the two ways in which an inquiry can successfully complete. In the top message sequence chart, an inquiry is started using the General Inquiry Access Code (GIAC), looking for a maximum of two devices and using a 3*1.28s timeout. The Bluetooth device transmits a stream of ID packets containing the GIAC. Two devices respond. Each response generates an HCI_Inquiry_Result, and after the second response, the HCI_Inquiry_Complete event is generated. In the lower message sequence chart, no responses are returned, so the inquiry times out, and the HCI_Inquiry_Complete event indicates that no responses have been received.

If the host decides to stop the inquiry early, it can do this with an HCI_Inquiry_Cancel command. Whether an inquiry completes on its own or is stopped because of an HCI_Inquiry_Cancel, an HCI_Inquiry_Complete event will be generated when it finishes. The HCI_Inquiry_Complete event contains a field giving the total number of devices which responded during the inquiry and a status field saying whether the inquiry completed successfully. The status field could contain an error code if the parame-

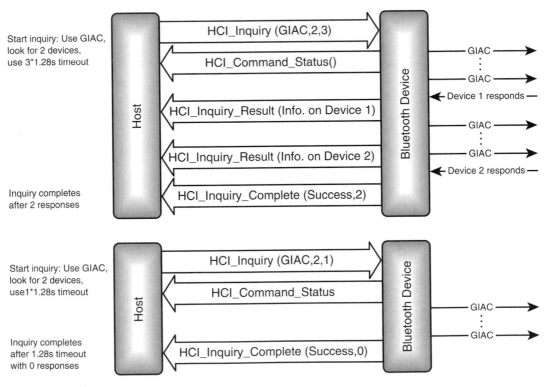

Figure 8–11   Message sequence charts for inquiries completing.

ters used in the HCI_Inquiry request were invalid, if the module ran out of memory while collecting responses, or if there was a hardware failure during the inquiry.

8.5.4   Timing of Inquiries

Often, a host will want to keep inquiring for other Bluetooth devices in the area so that it is continuously updated with a picture of the Bluetooth neighbourhood. Continuously inquiring would drain batteries on a Bluetooth device, plus using the limited hop sequence of inquiry for long periods would violate radio regulations in some countries. The solution is to periodically perform short inquiries. The host could do this by periodically requesting the Bluetooth module to perform an inquiry, but the HCI offers an alternative where the Bluetooth module is put into a periodic inquiry mode. In this mode it will automatically perform inquiries. A host puts a Bluetooth module into the periodic inquiry mode using the HCI_Periodic_Inquiry_Mode command, and the mode is left using the HCI_Exit_Periodic_Inquiry_Mode command.

If inquiries were always performed at the same interval, it would be possible for an inquiring device and a scanning device to miss one another every time, so the periodic inquiry mode is not really periodic. Instead, inquiries are started at random intervals with the maximum and minimum intervals being specified in the HCI_Periodic_Inquiry_Mode command. These intervals are specified in multiples of 1.28 s. The HCI_Periodic_Inquiry_Mode command also includes all the parameters used in the HCI_Inquiry_Command: LAP, Inquiry_Length, and Num_Responses.

8.6   INQUIRY SCAN: BECOMING DISCOVERABLE

A Bluetooth device allows other devices to discover it by conducting inquiry scans. (For more details on inquiry scanning, see Chapter 4.) A device which is conducting inquiry scans is said to be in discoverable mode. Devices in discoverable mode are able to respond to inquiring devices, thus allowing those devices to find out information about the discoverable device.

8.6.1   General and Limited Inquiry Access Codes

When a Bluetooth device conducts an inquiry, it sends out ID packets containing an Inquiry Access Code (IAC). Usually the General Inquiry Access Code (GIAC) will be used, but optionally a Limited Inquiry Access Code (LIAC) can be used for a short period of time. For instance, a group of users might agree to set their devices to use the LIAC to make their devices easier to discover in an environment with many Bluetooth devices.

An inquiry scanning device uses a correlator to listen for the Inquiry Access Code. Bluetooth devices can be built with multiple correlators so that they can scan for both Inquiry Access Codes simultaneously, although most devices will only have one correlator and will only be able to listen for one Inquiry Access Code at a time. A host can use the command HCI_Read_Number_Of_Supported_IAC to find out how many access codes a module can listen for simultaneously. Since version 1.0 of the Bluetooth standard only defines two possible Inquiry Access Codes, the number supported should be 1 or 2.

A host can find out which access codes a module is set to Inquiry Scan for using the command HCI_Read_Current_IAC_LAP. If the desired Inquiry Access Codes are not being used, the command HCI_Write_Current_IAC_LAP can be used to change Inquiry Access Codes.

8.6.2 Timing of Inquiry Scans

What's the best strategy for a device wanting to be discovered by another? A device wanting to be discovered could conduct an inquiry scan until it has responded to an inquiry, then do a mandatory page scan. If that doesn't result in a connection, it can go back into inquiry scan. At first thought, this seems like an excellent scheme; it means the device is spending as much time as possible in the inquiry scan state, so it's maximising the chances of being discovered by an inquiring device, while dropping into page scan after responding to an inquiry still allows other devices to connect with it.

There are two problems with this idea of continuous inquiry scanning:

- Many Bluetooth devices will be battery-powered, and switching on the radio receiver uses far more power than leaving it idle, so continuous scanning could drain a device's batteries.
- Some devices will want to conduct scans while connected so that they can connect to more devices. Continuous scanning would cause their existing connections to time out.

The solution is to scan in short bursts. The Generic Access Profile (GAP) recommends that a device should only scan for a 10.625 ms window. Of course, if a device is just scanning for a short period of time, it may miss an inquiry, so the Generic Access Profile recommends that inquiries last for 10.24 s, and devices in discoverable mode have a maximum interval of 2.56 s between starting one inquiry scan and starting the next. This means that while a device is conducting an inquiry, discoverable devices in the neighbourhood will conduct several inquiry scans, so they have a good chance of being discovered.

The host uses the command HCI_Write_Inquiry_Scan_Activity to set the interval between starting one scan and starting the next. The same command is also used to set the window of how long each scan lasts. If this command has never been sent to a device, the default interval between starting scans will be 1.28 s and the default window will be 11.25 ms. Naturally, the inquiry scan window must be less than or equal to the interval between starting inquiry scans. If the interval and window are set to be equal, the device will scan continuously. Normally, this would only be done for non-battery-powered devices that do not have any established connections. A host can use the HCI_Read_Inquiry_Scan_Activity command to check the settings of inquiry scan activity.

Even though a device is only scanning in short bursts, this would still cause extra drain on its batteries if it was idle or interfere with traffic if it was in connection. So, most devices will only scan occasionally. This means that it is important for scans to last long enough to give a good chance of being discovered by inquiring devices. The Generic Access Profile recommends that an inquiry last 10.24 s; it also recommends that devices remain discoverable for three times as long, at least 30.72 s. Inquiry scanning lasting three times as long as inquiry means that there is a good chance of inquiring devices in the area discovering inquiry scanning devices.

Figure 8–12 shows the timings the Generic Access Profile recommends for inquiry and inquiry scan. Although the figure is not drawn to scale, it still shows how during its time in discoverable mode, a device will repeatedly scan for short windows, whereas an inquiring device will occasionally conduct an inquiry over a relatively long window.

8.6.3   Enabling Inquiry Scan

Scanning is enabled using the HCI_Write_Scan_Enable command. The command HCI_Read_Scan_Enable may be used at any time to check whether scanning is enabled. This command returns the status of both inquiry scanning and page scanning.

Figure 8–13 shows the message sequence chart for both inquiry and inquiry scan. When the inquiry scan has been enabled, the inquiry scanning module replies with HCI_Command_Status to confirm that it has received the command. After that, the inquiry scanning module can respond to any inquiries it sees, but it will not inform the host that it has responded. However, it may initiate a page scan after responding to an inquiry, and if that page scan results

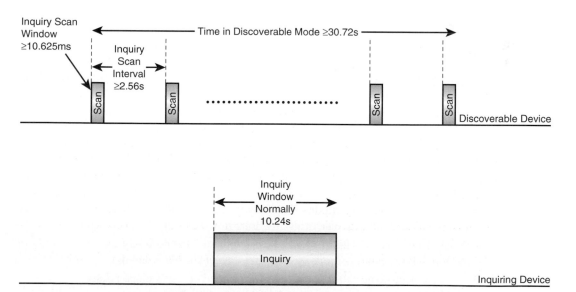

Figure 8–12   Recommended timings for inquiry and inquiry scan.

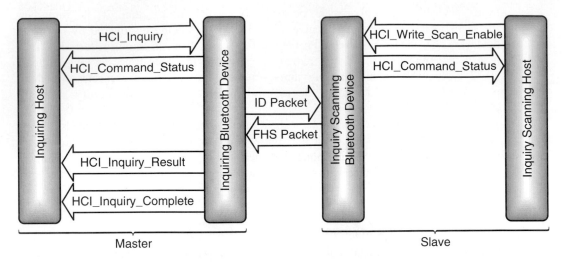

Figure 8–13   HCI message sequence chart for inquiry and inquiry scan.

in it being paged, it will send an HCI_Connection_Request event to its host (for more details of how page scans may be conducted after inquiry responses, see section 8.8.2).

8.7 PAGING: INITIATING CONNECTIONS

A Bluetooth device connects to other devices by paging them, sending their Bluetooth address in an ID packet (for more details on paging, see Chapter 4).

The host uses an HCI_Create_Connection command to begin paging. This command contains all the information that the module needs to establish a connection. Its parameters are:

- BD_ADDR—The address of the device to connect with; this is sent in the paging ID packets.
- Packet_Type—The set of packet types which may be used on the connection (this sets the initial types, which can be changed later using HCI_Change_Connection_Packet_Type).
- Page_Scan_Repetition_Mode—This gives the interval between successive page scans starting, and hence governs how long it is likely to take to connect.
- Page_Scan_Mode—This specifies whether the device normally uses mandatory or optional page scanning mode (see section 8.8.2.1 for more details).
- Clock_Offset—The estimated offset of the paged device's clock relative to the local clock.n

- Allow_Role_Switch—This tells the device whether to accept a Master/Slave switch during establishment of a connection (see Chapter 7 for more details on Master/Slave switch).

If the device being paged recently replied to an inquiry scan, then Page_Scan _Mode, Page_Scan_Repetition_Mode, and Clock_Offset information will have been returned in the FHS packet used for the inquiry response. However, it is possible to connect to a device just by entering its Bluetooth device address at the user interface. In this case, these three items of information may be missing. It would be possible to require the user to enter the information, or to conduct an inquiry to discover the extra information, but either option would slow down the process of connecting. It makes more sense to just set unknown parameters to default values. The Bluetooth standard does not specify defaults, but looking at what each parameter does, it is possible to work out some values which could be used:

- Page_Scan_Repetition_Mode—This parameter governs the time between successive page scans starting. It is best to assume the worst case: mode R2, time between successive page scans starting at 2.56 s.
- Page_Scan_Mode—Begin by assuming the device uses mandatory scanning; most devices will use this. If no connection is established, try again with this parameter set to optional page scanning.
- Clock_Offset—If the device was not found in a recent inquiry, this information is irrelevant, and the value may as well be set to zero.

Paging is started with an HCI_Create_Connection; it either finishes when a connection is established or when a Page Timeout elapses. The timeout value can be set using the HCI_Write_Page_Timeout command, and checked with the HCI_Read_Page_Timeout command.

An HCI_read_clock_offset command allows the host to read the clock offset between the remote device on a connection handle and the local clock. The result is received in an HCI_read_clock_offset_complete_event. The clock offset decides the phase in the page scan sequence on which a device is listening at any moment, so if the information could be passed to another device, it could be used to facilitate handover of Bluetooth Slaves from one Master to another. Of course, the hosts handing over would need some data link to exchange the slot offset information—for instance, LAN access points could ecxhange the information across the LAN backbone.

8.8 PAGE SCAN: RECEIVING CONNECTIONS

A Bluetooth device allows other devices to connect to it by entering page scan mode (for more details on page scanning, see Chapter 4). A device which is page scanning listens for its own ID in packets sent from a paging device. If it sees its own ID, it will respond and the two devices set up a new connection.

8.8.1   Timing of Page Scans

Section 8.6.2 dealt with inquiry scans and explained that continuous inquiry scanning would waste power and bandwidth. The same arguments apply to page scanning, so page scans are conducted in short bursts, and commands are provided to set the timing parameters of the page scanning bursts.

HCI_Write_Page_Scan_Activity sets the interval between the start of successive page scans and the length of the window over which a device page scans. This command is very similar to the command HCI_Write_Inquiry_Scan_Activity described in Section 8.6.2. To check the value of the page scan activity parameters, the host can use the HCI_Read_Page_Scan_Activity command at any time.

Changing the page scan interval could change the page Scan Repetition mode. The page Scan Repetition mode (SR) is a rough measure of the interval between consecutive page scans ($T_{page scan}$). There are three modes defined: R0 continous scanning, R1 $T_{page scan}$ ≤ 1.28s, and R2 $T_{page scan}$ ≤ 2.56s.

If a module notices that the page scan repetition mode of a remote device has changed, it notifies its host using an HCI_Page_Scan_Repetition_Mode event. Since the page SR mode is only passed between devices in the SR field of an FHS packet, only an inquiring module would notice the change in the scan repetition mode. The module could simply send an HCI_Inquiry_Result event with the new page scan repetition mode in it, but it might be configured so that it cannot send multiple HCI_Inquiry_Result events for the same device, making this an impractical solution. The HCI_Page_Scan_Repetition_ Mode event allows the Bluetooth module to let the host know of the change without needing another HCI_Inquiry_Result event.

8.8.2   Enabling Page Scan

Page scanning is enabled using the same command used to enable inquiry scanning, the HCI_Write_Scan_Enable command.

One odd feature of the scan settings is that if HCI_Write_Scan_Enable is set so that inquiry scanning is enabled but page scanning is disabled, after responding to an inquiry, a Bluetooth device can still enter a page scan. At first thought, this may seem nonsensical. Why conduct a page scan if page scanning has been disabled? On the other hand, consider: What's the point of responding to an inquiry and announcing your presence if you won't let other devices connect to you? Sensibly, the writers of the Bluetooth specification reasoned that nobody would want to respond to inquiries but not allow devices to connect. They could have just not allowed Bluetooth devices to have inquiry scanning enabled when page scanning was disabled, but instead they provided a special mechanism to allow Bluetooth devices to save battery power by having devices with these settings only page scanning just after they responded to an inquiry. This way, they can receive connections, but they don't waste battery power or bandwidth by doing page scans when there are no other devices in the area that know their address.

Table 8–1 summarises the behaviour of a device according to its scan settings.

The HCI_Read_Scan_Enable command may be used at any time to check whether scanning is enabled. This command returns the status of both inquiry scanning and page scanning.

8.8.2.1 Accepting a Connection. If a page scan is successful, eventually an ID packet will be received with the page scanning device's Bluetooth device address in it. It is possible that the module has been set to automatically accept connections using the HCI_Set_Event_Filter command. In this case, the host would not know the connection was there until it was completely set up. However, if the host has not set the module to automatically accept connections, the module will announce to its host that it has been paged by sending the host an HCI_Connection_Request event. The host will reply with an HCI_Accept_Connection_Request or HCI_Reject_Connection_ Request.

If the host does not reply for some reason, then the connection needs to be rejected. How long is it reasonable to wait for the host's reply? There is no absolute answer, as some systems ought to respond faster than others. For example, if the host is a PC which may have to be booted before it can decide whether to accept the connection, then a very long timeout is needed. If the host is always on, then a faster timeout would be appropriate. To cope with the different timeouts which different hosts require, Bluetooth's HCI standard provides an HCI_Write_Connection_Accept_Timeout command. This allows the host to set the time a module will wait for the response to the HCI_Connection_Request message. The timeout's default value is 5 s, but it may be set to values between 0.625 ms and 29 s. The timeout is set in multiples of 0.625 ms (the time for one baseband slot). If the host has not responded when the timeout elapses, then

Table 8–1   Scan Settings

Page Scan Setting	Inquiry Scan Setting	Result
Enabled	Enabled	Periodically conduct both inquiry scans and page scans. Device can be connected to by other devices whether or not they already know its Bluetooth device address.
Enabled	Disabled	Periodically conduct page scans. Device can only be connected to by other devices which already know its Bluetooth device address.
Disabled	Enabled	Periodically conduct inquiry scans. If device responds to an inquiry, conduct a page scan. Device can normally only be connected to by devices which don't know its address and therefore first conduct an inquiry.
Disabled	Disabled	No page or inquiry scans; device can receive no new connections. If it has no established connections, it can use a power-saving mode.

the connection is rejected as if the host had sent an HCI_Reject_Connection_Request command. A host may use the HCI_Read_Connection_Accept_Timeout command at any time to check the current value of a module's Connection_Accept timeout.

If the connection is accepted by the host, then the baseband and LMP layers finish setting up the connection. Once this is done, the hosts on both sides are notified by their modules sending them an HCI_Connection_Complete event, which contains the connection_handle that is used to uniquely identify the connection. The sequence of HCI commands leading up to the connection being completed is shown in Figure 8–14.

Once the connection is finished, the host can use an HCI_Disconnect command to terminate the connection. The link to disconnect is specified using the connection handle that was passed to the host in the HCI_Connection_Complete event. A reason code is used to indicate why the disconnect is sent; for example, possible values include Authentication Failure error code, Other End Terminated Connection error codes, and Unsupported Remote Feature error code.

8.8.3 SCO Connections

Once an active ACL connection has been set up, a SCO connection can be set up across it using the HCI_Add_SCO_Connection command. The parameters for this command specify the connection handle of the ACL connection across which the SCO connection will be set up, as well as the packet type to be used on the SCO connection. This must be one of the SCO packet types: HV1, HV2, or HV3.

As for creating a SCO connection, an HCI_Command_Status event is returned immediately to acknowledge the command. When the connection has been established, an

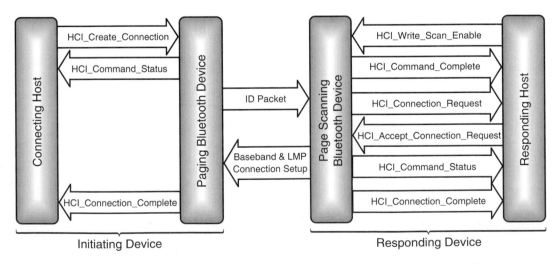

Figure 8–14 HCI message sequence chart for creating a connection.

HCI_Connection_Complete event is returned with the connection handle for the SCO connection (if the connection fails, the HCI_Connection_Complete event will still be returned, but its status field will carry the reason for failure).

8.8.4   Optional Page Scan Modes

In normal Bluetooth operation, the Master transmits in even slots and the Slaves reply in odd slots. This applies to Bluetooth's mandatory paging mode. Bluetooth also has an optional paging mode in which the Master transmits ID packets for eight slots; in the ninth slot, an inverted ID packet is sent, and the tenth slot is free for the Slave to reply (for more details see section 5.4.3).

The page scan mode can be changed with an HCI_Write_Page_Scan_Mode command. When the mode changes, an HCI_Page_Scan_Mode_Change Event is generated by the module and sent to the host. If the host wants to check the current page scan mode, it uses an HCI_Read_Page_Scan_Mode command. It is possible for a module to use more than one mode at once, in which case, all modes supported are returned in the HCI_Command_Complete event, which is used to respond to the HCI_Read_Page_Scan_Mode command.

Because the optional page scan modes are not supported by all devices, it is possible for an inquiring device which doesn't support optional page scanning to get a response from a device which is using optional page scanning. To give the inquiring device a chance to connect to the devices it discovers, all devices use the mandatory page scan mode for a short time after each inquiry response.

Every time an inquiry response is sent, the Bluetooth device starts a timer, T_mandatory_pscan. Until this timer expires, the mandatory page scanning scheme is used for all page scans.

The page scan period mode decides how long the T_mandatory_pscan timer will be. There are three possible modes:

- P0, $T_{\text{mandatory pscan}} >= 20$s.
- P1, $T_{\text{mandatory pscan}} >= 40$s.
- P2, $T_{\text{mandatory pscan}} >= 60$s.

The inquiring device can tell how long it has to page a device it discovered because the page Scan Period (SP) mode is passed in the inquiry response in the SP field of the FHS packet.

To change the page scan period mode (SP), the host simply sends a new mode using an HCI_Write_Page_Scan_Period_Mode command. To check the value, the host sends an HCI_Read_Page_Scan_Period_Mode.

8.9   SENDING AND RECEIVING DATA

When a connection is set up across HCI, a connection handle is returned to the host in the Connection_Complete event. When the host sends and receives data, this handle is used

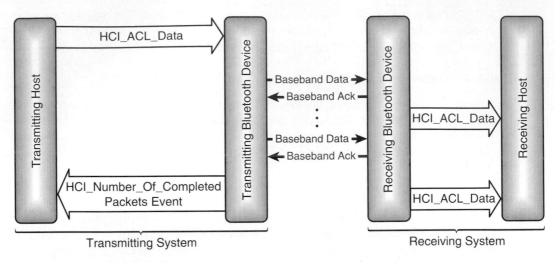

Figure 8–15 HCI message sequence chart for ACL data exchange.

in the HCI_ACL_data packet to identify the connection (see Figure 8–4 for details of the packet structure).

Figure 8–15 shows how data is exchanged. The HCI_ACL_Data packet containing the data is sent from the transmitting host to the Bluetooth module. The data from the packet is transmitted across an ACL link in a series of baseband packets. At the far end of the link, the data is passed to the receiving host in one or more HCI_ACL_Data packets. The diagram shows data passing in one direction only, but, of course, ACL links are bi-directional, so data can pass in both directions.

It is possible that the size of the payload carried in HCI_ACL_Data packets at each end of the link may be different, or the receiving module may even decide to generate one HCI_ACL_Data packet for each baseband packet it receives; as long as the order of the data is preserved, this does not matter.

8.9.1   Broadcasting Data

Systems which use connection handles usually reserve a special handle to identify a broadcast. Bluetooth does not have a reserved handle for broadcast; instead, the first time the host wants to broadcast data, it uses a handle which has not been used for a connection. When the Bluetooth module receives a packet with a connection handle which has not yet been allocated, it is allocated as the new handle for the broadcast channel.

Having the Bluetooth module allocate all point to point handles but letting the Bluetooth host allocate the broadcast handle complicates the implementation of HCI on the Bluetooth module. Usually, handles have some internal significance to the module; for instance, they may contain pointers to data structures holding channel parameters. This may mean that the Bluetooth module has to translate the host's broadcast handle to its own internal broadcast handle. If letting the host allocate broadcast handles causes such trouble for the Bluetooth module, why did Bluetooth implement broadcast handles this way? In version 1.0 of the specification, no handle was reserved for broadcast, and the specification writers had agreed not to add assigned numbers to the lower layers of the protocol stack, so having broadcast handles chosen at run time avoids an extra assigned number.

One complication of the host allocating the broadcast handle is that data sent on a new broadcast channel could overlap with an HCI_Connection_Complete event which uses the same handle. The host handles this as follows:

- Stops sending broadcast packets using the conflicting broadcast handle.
- Waits for an HCI_Number_Of_Completed_Packets event, indicating all broadcast packets sent on the conflicting handle have been sent.
- Allocates a new broadcast channel handle which doesn't conflict with point to point handles.

8.10 SWITCHING ROLES

During initial configuration of a connection, or at any time while it is in active use, devices can request to switch Master and Slave roles. A host can force this to happen with an HCI_Switch_Role command. The parameters for this command are the Bluetooth device address of the device with which the role switch is to be performed and the role which the host wants to have on the link. If the command is successful and a role change takes place, an HCI_Role_Change event will be sent to the host (this is sent instead of the HCI_Command_Complete event, which is usually sent to the host when a command finishes). The same HCI_Role_Change event is sent if a role change occurred which was initiated at the remote end of the link.

It is possible that a host may lose track of whether it is currently a Master or a Slave on a link. In this case, it may send an HCI_Role_Discovery command to its module. As a Bluetooth device can be a Master on some links and a Slave on others, this command takes a connection handle to identify the link for which the role is to be discovered.

The HCI_Write_Link_Policy_Settings command can be used to disable role switching on any link. The current policy settings for any link can be checked at any time using the HCI_Read_Link_Policy_Settings command.

8.11 POWER CONTROL

In Chapter 1, we saw how LMP could be used to control end-to-end power on a Bluetooth link. Power control uses the Receive Signal Strength Indication (RSSI), and the host can read this value using the HCI_Read_RSSI command. Since a Bluetooth device may be connected to several other devices simultaneously, and these devices may be different distances away and have different receiver qualities, the RSSI may be different on each link.

Therefore, the HCI_Read_RSSI command takes as a parameter a connection handle to identify which link's RSSI is being read.

Transmit power as well as receive strength can be read. The HCI_Read_Transmit_Power_Level command takes a connection handle parameter to specify which link's transmit power level is being read. This command can be used to read both the current transmit power level and the maximum power level the module can transmit. A type parameter is used to identify which is being requested. Power levels are returned in an HCI_Command_Complete event in units of dBm.

8.12 SUMMARY

A Bluetooth device can be made up of two parts: a host implementing the higher layers of the stack (L2CAP and above) and a module implementing the lower layers (LMP and below). The Host Controller Interface (HCI) provides a uniform interface between a Bluetooth host and its module. Because the HCI is standardised, host software can interwork with Bluetooth devices from a variety of manufacturers.

The HCI uses three packet types: commands which go from host to module, events which go from module to host, and data packets which travel in both directions. Between them, these three packet types can be used to completely control a Bluetooth module and to transfer any data required.

HCI commands allow the host to completely control a Bluetooth module, including:

- Control of links, including setting up, tearing down, and configuring links.
- Setting the link policies on whether power saving modes and role switches are allowed.
- Direct access to information on the local Bluetooth module and access to information on remote devices by triggering LMP exchanges.
- Control of many baseband features such as timeouts.
- Retrieving status information on a module.
- Invoking Bluetooth's test modes for factory testing, and for Bluetooth qualification.

The HCI includes flow control capabilities, so implementers may wish to use an alternative route to get SCO data into the baseband; otherwise, the flow control may interfere with the regular synchronous transfer of voice samples to and from the Bluetooth module.

PART 2

PROTOCOL STACK: THE BLUETOOTH HOST

9

Logical Link Control and Adaptation Protocol

Logical Link Control and Adaptation Protocol (L2CAP) takes data from higher layers of the Bluetooth stack and from applications and sends it over the lower layers of the stack. L2CAP passes packets either to the Host Controller Interface (HCI), or in a host-less system, L2CAP passes packets directly to the Link Manager (LM).

Figure 9–1 shows L2CAP's position in the Bluetooth stack for the cases with and without a Host Controller Interface. Note that L2CAP transfers data, not audio (though protocols such as voice over IP are regarded as data and would use L2CAP packets if transferred over a Bluetooth system).

L2CAP has many functions:

- Multiplexing between different higher layer protocols, allowing them to share lower layer links.
- Segmentation and reassembly to allow transfer of larger packets than lower layers support.
- Group management, providing one-way transmission to a group of other Bluetooth devices.
- Quality of service management for higher layer protocols.

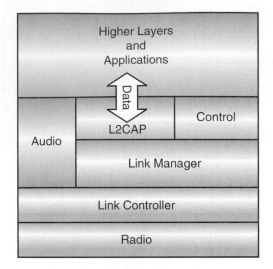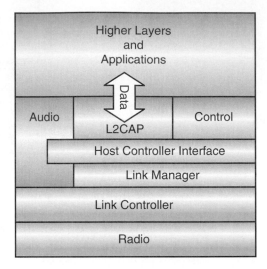

Figure 9–1   L2CAP's position in the Bluetooth protocol stack.

L2CAP relies on ACL connections to pass data reliably from end to end. A separate control function must set up the ACL connections when they are required by L2CAP and close them down when they are no longer required. L2CAP also relies upon the ACL connection's quality of service to provide the quality of service negotiated with higher layers.

9.1   MULTIPLEXING USING CHANNELS

L2CAP provides multiplexing to allow several higher layer links to pass across a single ACL connection. This allows several different user applications to share an ACL link with the higher layers of the Bluetooth stack (such as the service discovery protocol).

L2CAP uses channel numbers to label packets so that when they are received, they can be routed to the correct place. Because L2CAP entities must also communicate with one another to control channels, a special channel number is reserved for signalling packets used to control L2CAP connections. A second channel number is reserved for receiving multicast packets. A range of channel numbers are available to label L2CAP connections being used by higher layers. These channel numbers are allocated as connections are set up (see section 9.2, L2CAP Signalling).

The channel number is carried in a two byte channel identifier, which comes after the length field in every L2CAP packet as shown in Figure 9–2.

The rest of the L2CAP packet carries the data from higher layers. The packet size is variable, and the length of the data is only limited by the two byte field. This allows L2CAP to carry up to 65,535 bytes of data per packet. The large capacity of L2CAP packets allows the packet boundaries of higher layer protocols to be preserved.

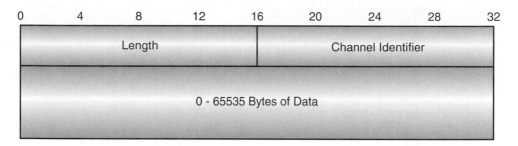

Figure 9–2 Structure of an L2CAP packet.

9.2 L2CAP SIGNALLING

The L2CAP signalling channel is allocated the channel ID 0x0001. It is used to send control information between peer L2CAP entities to handle connecting, configuring, and disconnecting L2CAP connections. Bluetooth has rules for naming the signals which follow a convention commonly used in communications protocols. These rules are illustrated in Figure 9–3.

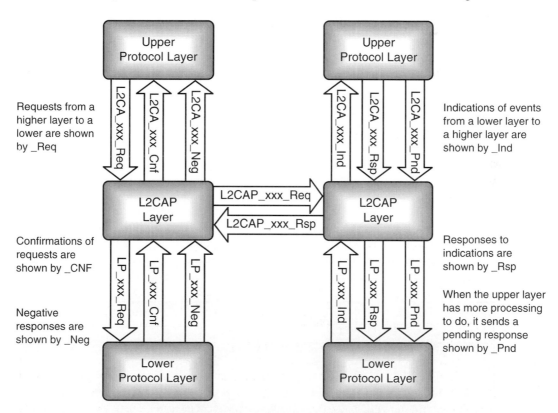

Figure 9–3 Conventions for naming L2CAP signals.

The rules for naming signals are:

- Prefix signals between peers at the same layer with the protocol's initials (e.g., L2CAP).
- Prefix signals between higher and lower layers with the lower layer's initials (e.g., L2CA).
- Suffix requests from a higher layer to a lower layer with "Req".
- Suffix confirmations of requests sent from a lower layer to an upper layer with "Cnf".
- If a response from a lower layer is negative, the suffix "Neg" may be used instead of "Cnf".
- Suffix indications of events sent from a lower layer to a higher layer with "Ind".
- Suffix responses to indications sent from a higher layer to a lower layer with "Rsp".
- If a response to an indication requires further processing, "Rsp" may be replaced with "Pnd", which is an abbreviation for pending response.

All requests from a higher layer to a lower layer must be acknowledged by a corresponding confirmation, but not all indications from a lower layer require a response or pending response.

9.2.1 L2CAP Signalling Structures

As with other layers of the Bluetooth stack, L2CAP signals use the common structure shown in Figure 9–4. The first byte has the OpCode identifying the contents of the signal. This is followed by an identifier field. Many commands may be sent in one packet, and the responses to these may return split across more than one packet, making it difficult to match up responses with original requests. To make it easier to pair up responses and requests, a new identifier is used for each request, and the identifier is copied from the request into the response.

L2CAP starts a timer when a message is sent, and if no response arrives, the message is re-sent. In this case, the original identifier is recycled, so if the command was received and it was the response that was lost, the responding device knows it should send another response, but it shouldn't execute the command twice. Apart from retransmis-

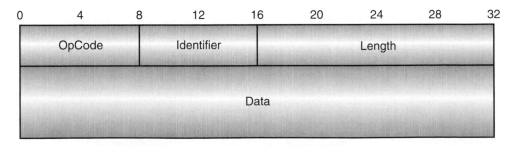

Figure 9–4   Structure of an L2CAP command.

sions of commands, the identifiers shouldn't be reused for 6 minutes; this allows 255 commands to be sent in 6 minutes (you might think the 1-byte field length for the identifier would allow 256 identifiers rather than 255, but the identifier 0x0000 is not used).

After the identifier field comes a length field; this gives the length of the data field.

Many commands can be sent within one L2CAP packet; they are simply lined up one after another as shown in Figure 9–5. Different implementations of L2CAP can support different lengths of L2CAP packets. The maximum size of packet payload supported is called the Maximum Transmission Unit, or MTU. All implementations of L2CAP are required to support a packet payload length of at least 48 bytes for signalling, so unless the MTU is known, a signalling packet's payload should be restricted to this length.

If a signalling packet is received which is longer than the MTU, it is rejected. A special reject packet is available which has a reason field giving the reason for the command being rejected. The reject packet is shown in Figure 9–6. It contains an identifier for the command being rejected. Of course, if many commands are being rejected because they are in a packet payload larger than the receiving device's MTU, the receiving device may not be able to read all the commands, so this poses a potential problem copying identifiers into reject packets. To get around this problem, if a command packet payload is received which is larger than the receiving device's MTU, all commands in the packet are rejected together using one reject packet. In this case, the identifier copied into the reject packet is the one taken from the first command in the packet.

Version 1.0 of the Bluetooth standard defines three reasons for rejecting a packet; these are:

- Command not understood—In this case, no data is returned.
- The request had an invalid connection identifier—The identifier is returned in the data field.

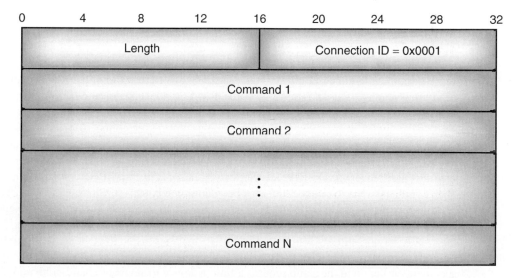

Figure 9–5 L2CAP signalling packet containing multiple commands.

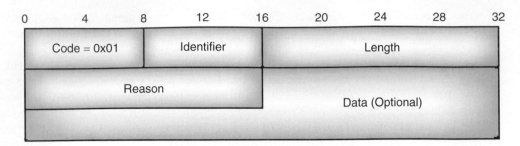

Figure 9–6 Structure of the L2CAP reject packet.

- The command packet payload was larger than the rejecting device's MTU—In this case, the correct size of MTU is returned in the data field.

The reason field is two bytes long, so there is plenty of scope for future versions of the standard to define more reject reasons.

9.3   ESTABLISHING A CONNECTION

L2CAP uses ACL links to reliably pass data without errors across the lower layers of the Bluetooth stack. Bluetooth's broadcast transmission is not reliable, so broadcast should not be used, and L2CAP implementations should use point to point ACL links.

To establish a link, the higher layer protocol will send a request to the L2CA layer to connect. If there is no existing ACL connection, this causes L2CAP to send a request to a lower layer protocol to connect. As shown in Figure 9–1, the protocol below the L2CA layer could be either HCI or LM. Figure 9–7 illustrates the case where there is an HCI layer and L2CAP uses HCI to establish an ACL connection. (In this diagram, messages in italics are implementation-dependent, but use names suggested by the Bluetooth specification. Messages not in italics have formats fully defined by the specification.)

As can be seen from Figure 9–7, the steps involved in setting up an ACL connection are quite complex. This diagram illustrates how L2CAP relies on the rest of the protocol stack to provide reliable data connections.

Messages 8 and 9 show HCI on the side accepting the connection, indicating to the L2CAP layer that it has been paged and a decision is required on whether or not to connect. In the L2CAP standard, there are no primitives defined for the lower layers to indicate that a connection request has been received. Instead there is just an LP_ConnectInd primitive, which indicates that the connection has been completely set up. One could argue that the writers of the standard intended that the baseband should be set to auto-accept connections, in which case, it would only be informed after the connection had been fully set up. In this case, only having an LP_ConnectInd primitive makes sense. However, it is possible that some implementers may want more control over the connections, as having the ability to reject them earlier on in the setup process allows a device to save both bandwidth and power.

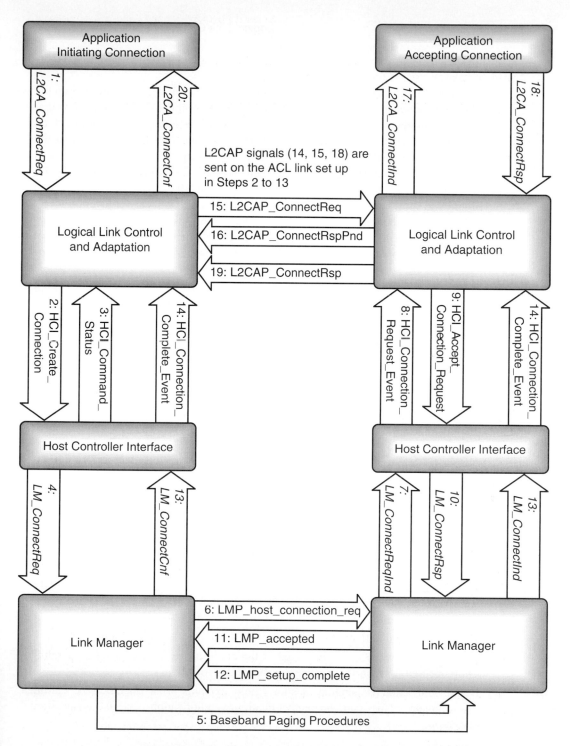

Figure 9–7 Messages for setting up an L2CAP connection over HCI.

If the device was set to auto accept connections, Messages 8 and 9 would be omitted; otherwise, it makes sense to send the message to L2CAP as shown.

Also note in the diagram the two sets of messages, 13 and 14, which are sent up the stack when the connection is complete. The L2CAP entities on both sides must know that the ACL link is in place before they can exchange L2CAP messages. In a system with an HCI, message 14, the HCI_Connection_Complete event, indicates to both sides that the ACL connection is available for exchange of L2CAP messages. The same HCI event is used on both the initiating and accepting sides, and as it is sent almost simultaneously on both sides, the two sets of messages are given the same number.

Figure 9–8 shows a general case with L2CAP connecting via a lower layer protocol. In a hostless system, the lower protocol layer could be the Link Manager. This illustrates successful establishment of a connection across the lower layers, but if the lower protocol failed to establish a connection, LP_ConnectCnfNeg messages would be sent in place of the LP_ConnectCnf.

In this diagram, the stage of accepting the connection between receiving a paging packet and configuring the connection has been left out, so, unlike the previous diagram, it is assumed that the baseband has been set up to accept connections without informing higher layers until they are complete.

Once an ACL connection is established across the lower layers, L2CAP packets can be sent across it. In Figures 9–3, 9–7, 9–8, L2CAP packets are shown being exchanged directly between peer L2CAP entities, but, of course, they are transferred across the lower layers of the stack in lower layer Protocol Data Units (PDUs). The first message sent is an L2CAP_ConnectReq (Figure 9–9). In addition to the usual OpCode, identifier, and length fields, the message carries the following parameters:

- A Protocol Service Multiplexer (PSM) value specifying the protocol using this connection.
- A source Channel ID (CID), the Channel CID allocated to the connection by the initiating device.

An L2CAP_ConnectionRsp message is sent in response to the connection request. The response contains the following parameters:

- The destination Channel ID (CID) containing the CID which will be used for the connection by the responding device. This must be stored, as it will be needed later when disconnecting.
- The source Channel ID (CID), which is copied from the L2CAP_ConnectionReq.
- A result field, which gives the status of the connection: successful setup, pending setup, refused for security reasons, or refused due to lack of resources.
- If the connection is pending, a status field explains what operation is waiting to complete. This can be authentication, authorisation, or an unspecified operation.

The structure of the L2CAP_ConnectionRsp packet is shown in Figure 9–10.

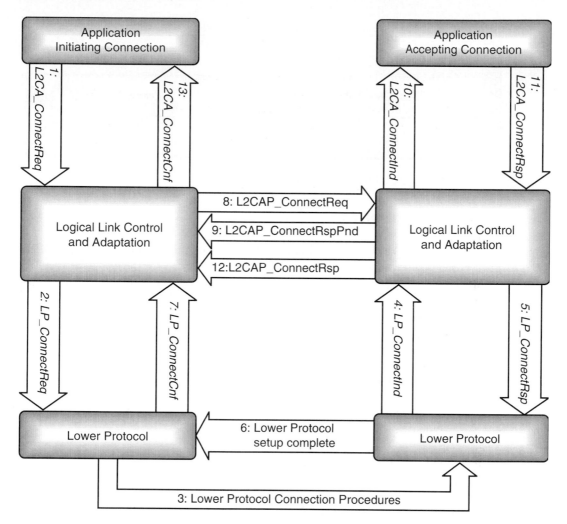

Figure 9–8   Messages for setting up an L2CAP connection over a lower protocol.

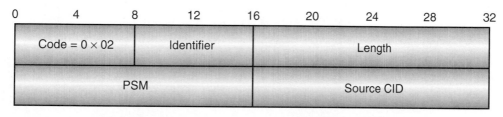

Figure 9–9   Structure of an L2CAP connection request packet.

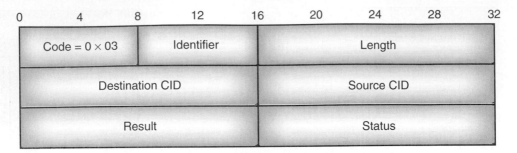

0	4	8	12	16	20	24	28	32

Code = 0 × 03	Identifier	Length	
Destination CID		Source CID	
Result		Status	

Figure 9–10   Structure of an L2CAP connection response packet.

9.4   CONFIGURING A CONNECTION

Once a connection has been established, it must be configured. The initiating L2CA begins by sending configuration requests in L2CAP_ConfigReq messages. If these are rejected, an L2CAP_ConfigNegRsp message is returned (or a command reject is sent if the request is badly formed—for instance, with an illegal channel ID), and the initiating device must try again with different parameters until its parameters for the connection are accepted with an L2CAP_ConfigRsp message.

Once the initiating device has configured the outbound channel going to the accepting device, the accepting device can configure the return channel using the same set of messages as shown in Figure 9–11.

If two devices have difficulty deciding on a mutually agreeable set of parameters, L2CAP_ConfigReg and L2CAP_ConfigNegRsp messages could be exchanged for a

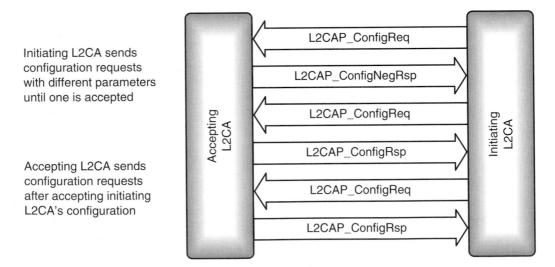

Initiating L2CA sends
configuration requests
with different parameters
until one is accepted

Accepting L2CA sends
configuration requests
after accepting initiating
L2CA's configuration

L2CAP_ConfigReq

L2CAP_ConfigNegRsp

L2CAP_ConfigReq

L2CAP_ConfigRsp

L2CAP_ConfigReq

L2CAP_ConfigRsp

Accepting L2CA

Initiating L2CA

Figure 9–11   Message sequence chart for L2CAP configuration.

very long time. When devices abandon attempts to configure the channel is up to each implementation, but the standard sets an absolute maximum time of two minutes; after that time, the devices either work with the parameters they have or close down the connection.

Parameters which can be configured are:

- Maximum Transmission Unit (MTU).
- Flush timeout.
- Quality of service.

9.4.1   Maximum Transmission Unit

The MTU specified in an L2CAP_ConfigReq message is the maximum size in bytes of packet payload a device is willing to accept. As mentioned above, if the MTU requested is larger than a device can support, it will reject the request with a reject packet containing the MTU it can handle. Then it is up to the requesting device to decide whether to accept that size MTU or abandon the connection.

9.4.2   Flush Timeout

The flush timeout gives the amount of time in milliseconds that a device will spend trying to transmit an L2CAP packet segment before it gives up. If a packet segment does not get through before the flush timeout is exceeded, the segment can't get through and the whole packet is flushed (thrown away). The flush timeout controls how many times the baseband can retransmit a packet. Since a baseband slot pair takes 1.25 ms if the flush timeout is set to 1, it is below the minimum polling interval of the baseband, so the value of 1 is taken to mean no retransmissions. The value 0xFFFF also has a special meaning: It is used when there is no timeout and the link manager keeps retransmitting the packet until link manager decides the link has been lost.

The flush timeout is applied to the channel in the same direction as the L2CAP_ConfigReq travels; that is to say, the transmitting device tells the receiving device what flush timeout it wishes to implement. If no flush timeout is specified, the default value is 0xFFFF (retransmit until the link is lost).

9.4.3   Quality of Service

The quality of service option can select best effort, or a guaranteed quality of service. Keep in mind that a wireless link subject to interference cannot guarantee quality of service, it can only configure the channel so that it does not compromise quality of service by accepting more traffic than it can handle. Values such as token rate, token bucket size, peak bandwidth, latency, and delay variation can also be negotiated.

The quality of service is applied to the channel in the same direction that the L2CAP_ConfigReq travels; that is to say, the transmitting device tells the receiving device what quality of service it wishes to implement. More details of how L2CAP handles quality of service can be found in Chapter 17.

9.5 TRANSFERRING DATA

Once the channel has been created and configured, it can be used to transfer data. How the higher layers pass data to and from the L2CA layer is implementation dependent, but the standard suggests that L2CA_DataWrite and L2CA_DataRead signals can be used as shown in Figure 9–12. An L2CAP_Data message is used to carry the data between peer L2CA entities.

If a higher layer tries to send a packet which would exceed the receiving end's MTU, then only the first MTU bytes are sent.

9.5.1 Segmentation and Reassembly

Some higher layer protocols use packet sizes larger than those which Bluetooth can handle, so L2CAP provides segmentation of higher layer packets going down the stack, and reassembles them as they pass up the stack (see Figure 9–13).

L2CAP data packets have a 4 byte header which is transmitted with the data. Naturally, the more data that can be transmitted with one header, the more efficient the system is, so L2CAP packets are very large, carrying up to 65,535 bytes of data.

The Host Controller Interface (HCI) uses smaller packets. The actual size of the packet is implementation-dependent because some embedded systems will have very little memory and won't be able to buffer large packets. However, HCI also

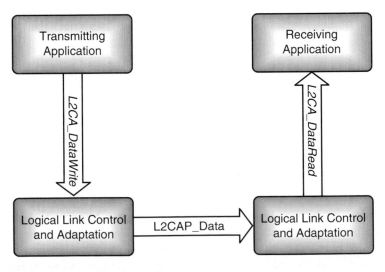

Figure 9–12   L2CAP data exchange.

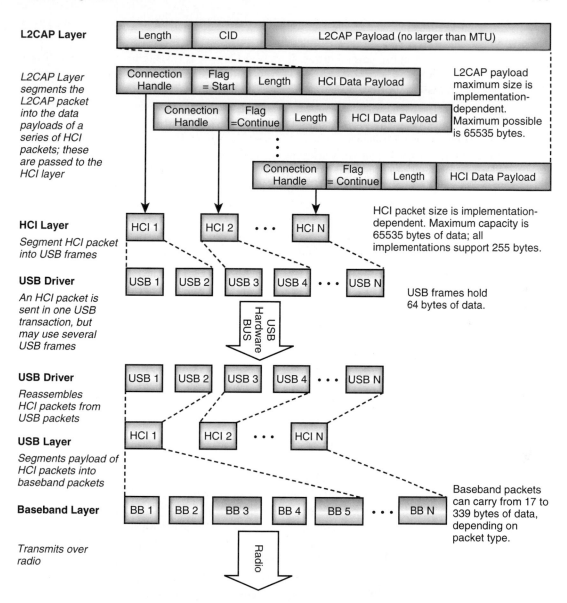

Figure 9–13 Segmentation and transport of L2CAP packets.

has headers, and if packets become too small, it would be inefficient, so the specification says that all implementations must support packets carrying up to 255 bytes of data. Because HCI packets are smaller than L2CAP packets, the L2CAP packets may have to be segmented into the data portions of several HCI packets. When the packets come to be reassembled, the L2CAP layer has to know where the start of each L2CAP packet is, so the

HCI Packet Boundary (PB) flag is used to identify which HCI packet has the start of the L2CAP packet.

The HCI can use several different transport layers. If USB (Universal Serial Bus) is used, each HCI packet is sent in one USB transaction, but a USB transaction may involve the transfer of several 64 byte USB frames. Whatever transport layer is used, the same HCI packets are reassembled on the lower side of the HCI layer as were transmitted on the upper side.

The baseband uses a variety of different packets with varying data capacities. The lower layers of the Bluetooth stack may have to pick different packet types on a slot by slot basis. For example, some slots may be reserved for communicating with Slaves in low power modes such as Sniff or Park, so a link which normally uses 5 slot packets may sometimes only have space for a single slot packet as other slots have been reserved. Because the slot sizes available may change moment by moment, only the lower layers of the stack can decide what size baseband packet to use. Therefore, there is another level of segmentation which is performed in the lower layers of the stack, where HCI packets may be split up into the payloads of several baseband packets.

It is still important that the start of L2CAP packets is recognisable, so the baseband logical channel field identifies packets which carry the start of a new L2CAP packet.

Each baseband packet may have to be retransmitted several times, but unless the link is lost altogether, the baseband will reliably transfer packets in order, and any repeats received will be filtered out (as long as broadcast is not used). So even though L2CAP packets may be split up and reassembled several times in passing through the Bluetooth protocol stack, they can always be delivered reliably and reassembled in the right order, with the start of each L2CAP packet easily identifiable.

9.6 DISCONNECTING AND TIMEOUTS

There are two ways for an L2CAP channel to be closed down: a higher layer protocol or service can request that it be closed down or it can time out.

Once data transfer has finished, the protocol or service using the channel can send an L2CA_DisconnectReq to request disconnection. The exact format of this message is implementation specific, but it should contain the ID of the channel to disconnect.

When L2CAP receives the L2CA_DisconnectReq, it causes an L2CAP_Disconnect-Req packet to be sent across the baseband link to the peer L2CAP at the other end of the channel. At the same time, L2CAP stops sending and receiving data on the channel. Any queues of data for transmission are emptied, and any data received is just discarded.

The L2CAP_DisconnectReq packet is shown in Figure 9–14. Because each L2CAP connection has a different channel ID at each end of the connection, the disconnect request contains two channel IDs: the ID for the source end of the connection can be copied from the L2CA_DisconnectReq, and the Channel ID for the destination end was passed in the connection response and stored in L2CAP when the channel was first set up.

The device receiving the L2CAP_DisconnectReq discards all data queued for transmission on that channel, since the device which sent the L2CAP_DisconnectReq is dis-

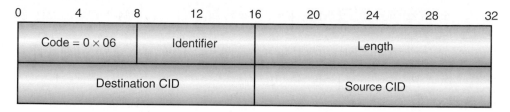

Figure 9–14   Structure of an L2CAP disconnect request packet.

carding all data it receives anyway. The device receiving the L2CAP_DisconnectReq replies with an L2CAP_disconnectRsp as shown in Figure 9–15.

When the L2CAP that sent the L2CAP_DisconnectReq receives the L2CAP_DisconnectRsp, it can inform the upper protocol layer of the result of its disconnect request. A result with the code 0x0000 is sent back to indicate success. If no response is received, 0xEEEE is sent back to indicate that the request timed out. The upper layer protocol or service can then decide whether to re-issue the request. The exchange of messages used to disconnect an L2CAP channel is shown in Figure 9–16.

In addition to channels being disconnected by the upper layers sending messages, they can also be disconnected as a result of timeouts. Every time L2CAP sends a signal, it starts a Response Timeout Expired (RTX) timer. The length of the RTX timer varies between implementations, but it must start between one second and one minute. Obviously, it doesn't make sense to retransmit a packet while the baseband is still attempting to transmit it, so the RTX timer should be set so that retransmission doesn't start until after the baseband has given up transmitting the packet. If the flush timeout is infinite so the baseband keeps trying to retransmit until the link is lost, then L2CAP should not retransmit at all.

If the timer expires before the response is received, either a duplicate message can be sent or the channel can be disconnected. If a duplicate message is sent, the RTX timeout for the duplicate is double the previous timeout. It is up to the implementers to decide how many times to retransmit, but obviously it doesn't make sense to keep trying forever if the message isn't getting through. In these cases, the baseband link has probably been lost, so if no response is received within 60 seconds, the channel should just be disconnected without sending an L2CAP_DisconnectReq.

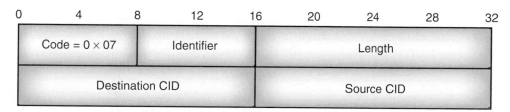

Figure 9–15   Structure of an L2CAP disconnect response packet.

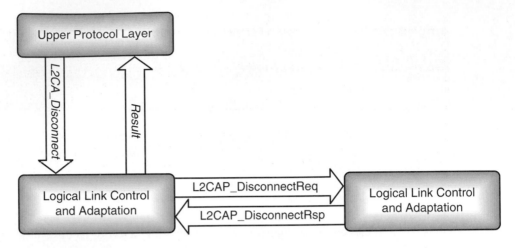

Figure 9–16 Message sequence chart for disconnecting an L2CAP channel.

There is one exception to disconnecting after 60 seconds: If the far end returns a response which indicates it has more processing to do, then an Extended Response Timeout Expired (ERTX) timer may be used instead of the RTX timer. The ERTX timer is just like the RTX timer except that where the RTX timer can take any value between one second and one minute, the ERTX timer's range is between one minute and five minutes. The ERTX timer must be within this range, but its exact value is up to the implementation.

As each signal is sent, an RTX timer is started, and this can be changed to an ERTX timer where the far end of a link returns a pending response (for example, an L2CAP_ConnectRspPending, which indicates the far end is processing a connect request). This means that there can be many RTX and ERTX timers running simultaneously.

9.7 CONNECTIONLESS DATA CHANNELS

L2CAP provides connectionless channels to connect a device to a group of one or more other devices in a single direction.

Connectionless channels cannot be configured for quality of service. This is because trying to negotiate the same quality of service with a whole group of devices could take forever, so it's only practical to use best effort (which is the default quality of service). L2CAP sends connectionless data to all devices in a group, but because connectionless channels are best effort, the data is not guaranteed to arrive.

Transmit connection IDs are set up as connectionless channels are established, but the same L2CAP channel Identifier 0x0002, is used as the receive end of all connectionless channels.

With connection oriented L2CAP traffic, a Protocol Service Multiplexer (PSM) value is associated with a particular connection ID, but this cannot be done with connectionless traffic because all connectionless traffic is received on the same connection ID

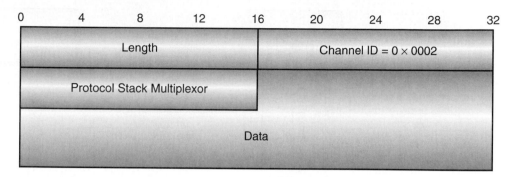

Figure 9–17   Structure of a connectionless L2CAP packet.

(0x0002). To provide a way of associating a PSM value with connectionless traffic, the PSM value is added into every connectionless L2CAP packet at the start of the payload data field as shown in Figure 9–17.

The PSM field takes up at least two bytes. The least significant bit of each byte in the PSM field is a continuation flag. If it is zero, there are more bytes to come; if it is 1, then this is the last byte of the PSM field.

Some PSM values are defined by the Bluetooth standard; these are:

- 0x0001 service discovery protocol.
- 0x0003 RFCOMM, serial port emulation.
- 0x0005 TCS-BIN, Telephony Control protocol Specification - Binary.
- 0x0007 TCS-BIN-CORDLESS.

PSM values 0x1001 upwards are available for assigning to services as L2CAP connections are established (although because of the rules for the continuation flag, not all values of PSM are legal as the least significant byte must be odd and all other bytes in a PSM must be even).

9.8   ENABLING AND DISABLING INCOMING CONNECTIONLESS TRAFFIC

It is possible that higher layer applications might only want to receive traffic addressed directly to them, so L2CAP defines messages to disable connectionless traffic.

The exact format of the message to disable connectionless traffic is implementation dependent, but the message should include a Protocol Service Multiplexer (PSM) parameter. Traffic destined for one protocol or service can be disabled by specifying its PSM value. For example, the message sequence chart at the right of Figure 9–18 shows connectionless traffic destined for RFCOMM being disabled by a message specifying the PSM

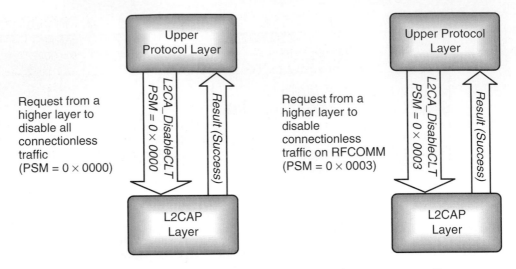

Figure 9–18   Message sequence charts for disabling connectionless traffic.

reserved for RFCOMM, which is 0x0003. The result of the L2CA_DisableCLT is simply success or fail; no reason for failure need be given.

To disable all connectionless reception, the PSM parameter is set to the invalid value 0x0000 as shown at the left of Figure 9–18. Implementations are allowed to only support blocking all connectionless reception; in this case, any attempts to block with the PSM parameter being anything other than zero would fail.

An L2CA_EnableCLT message works similarly to the L2CA_DisableCLT and enables reception of connectionless packets. It also has a PSM parameter which works the same way as the PSM parameter for L2CA_DisableCLT, with an all zero value specifying that connectionless reception should be enabled for all protocols and services.

9.9   HANDLING GROUPS

To send connectionless traffic, first an L2CAP group must be created. As with all messages between L2CAP and higher layer protocols, the exact format of the message is implementation specific, but it should include a PSM field for the protocol or service which will transmit to the group. The response carries the connection ID (CID), which will be used by the upper protocol layer to transmit to the group. The connection ID is also used to add devices to the group; this is done by sending the group's connection ID and the Bluetooth device address of the device to be added. For instance, the message sequence chart at the left of Figure 9–19 shows a group being created for RFCOMM (PSM = 0x0003). The result returns an ID of 0x0040 for the new group. The chart at the right shows a device being added to the newly created group. The parameters for the L2CA_GroupAddMember request are the connection ID and the Bluetooth device address of the device to be added; the reply is a success (0x0000) or failure (0x0001) result.

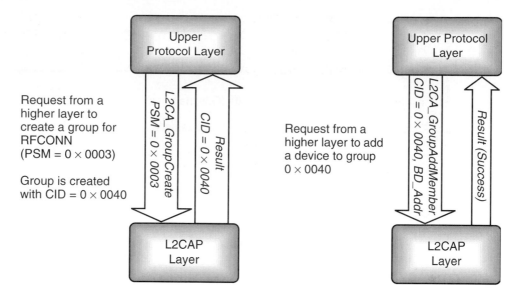

Figure 9–19 Message sequence chart for creating a connectionless group and adding a device.

An L2CA_GroupRemoveMember command is also available; this is similar to the L2CA_GroupAddMemberCommand and takes the same parameters: an ID to specify the group from which the device is to be removed and the Bluetooth device address of the device to be removed. The result is either success (0x0000) or failure (0x0001) if the specified device was not a member of the specified group.

L2CA_GroupClose may be used to close down a connectionless channel. This request takes a single parameter: the ID of the connection to be closed.

Finally, the L2CA_GroupMembership request may be used to find the Bluetooth device addresses of devices in a group. The CID of the group is passed as a parameter of L2CA_GroupMembership; the result is success (0x0000) or failure (0x0001). If success, then a list of Bluetooth device addresses is also returned in the result. The list comes after the success code.

A peculiarity of the Bluetooth standard is that while devices must be individually added to a group, when data is sent to the group, it is permissible to send it to devices which are not in the group. Perhaps this was originally specified because it would allow the baseband to broadcast L2CAP data. Whatever the original reason, the version 1.0 baseband broadcast mechanism has flaws which mean it cannot reliably be used for L2CAP data, so it is difficult to see why bandwidth should be wasted transmitting an L2CAP packet to devices not in the group it is intended for. It is unlikely that any implementation would choose to waste bandwidth in this way, but applications writers should be aware that connectionless L2CAP traffic may be sent to devices outside the group it is intended for; so where privacy is important, encryption should be used.

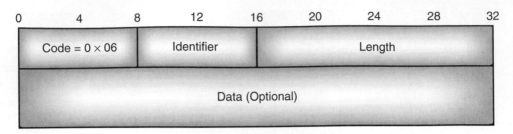

Figure 9–20   Structure of an L2CAP echo request packet.

9.10 ECHO AND PING

Echo requests ask the peer L2CAP device to send an echo response back. They can be used simply to test a link, or they can be used to pass implementation specific commands, since they include a data field as shown in Figure 9–20. Naturally, any devices using the echo request data field to extend the L2CAP command set should be careful to ensure that there is a matching implementation at the other end or their commands could have unexpected results!

The echo response packet matches the echo request in everything but the packet's code. The identifier from the echo request is copied to the echo response, as is the length field and any data (see Figure 9–21).

An upper protocol layer can initiate an L2CAP echo request and response exchange using the L2CA_Ping request. This request is implementation dependent, but it should take the following parameters:

- BD_ADDR—Bluetooth device address of device to which the L2CAP_EchoReq will be sent.
- ECHO_DATA—A pointer to the data to be sent in the L2CAP_EchoReq (this is optional).

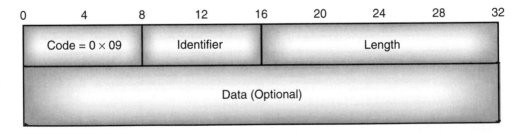

Figure 9–21   Structure of an L2CAP echo response packet.

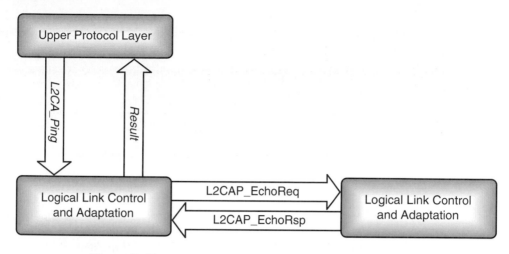

Figure 9–22   Message sequence chart for L2CAP ping and echo.

- Length—Two bytes giving the length of the ECHO_DATA (if there is no data, length = 0).

The result begins with a success (0x0000) or fail (0x0001) code. The ping fails when an echo request is sent but L2CAP times out before a response is received (refer to Figure 9–22).

9.11   GET INFORMATION

L2CAP has L2CAP_InfoReq and L2CAP_InfoRsp messages, which can be used to exchange information between peer L2CA layers.

Figure 9–23 shows that the L2CAP_InfoReq packet. The information type parameter specifies the type of information being requested. Version 1.0 of the standard only specifies one information type which can be retrieved: 0x00001 gets the value of the MTU on the connectionless channel.

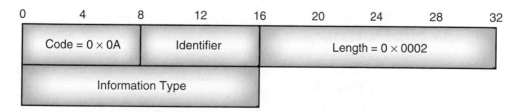

Figure 9–23   Structure of an L2CAP information request packet.

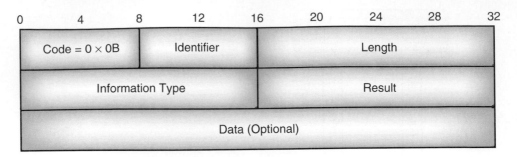

Figure 9–24   Structure of an L2CAP information response packet.

Figure 9–24 shows that the L2CAP_InfoRsp information type matches the information type sent in the request; the result is 0x0000 for success or 0x0001 for failure. If the information request was successful, the data field holds the requested information. For the connectionless MTU, this takes two bytes.

If an upper protocol layer wants to get information from L2CAP, it sends an L2CA_GetInfo request. The exact format of this request is implementation-dependent, but it should include the Bluetooth device address of the device to which the request will be sent and the information type field to identify the information being requested (for version 1.0 implementations, the information type must be 0x0001 to request the connectionless MTU).

The result of the L2CA_GetInfo request carries a result parameter, which can take the following values:

- 0x0000—Success, a response was received; this result will be followed by MTU data.
- 0x0001—The request was not supported by the local device, so there is no data.
- 0x0002—The request was not supported by the remote device, so there is no data.
- 0x0003—The request timed out before a response was received, so there is no data.

If the request was successful, a pointer to the requested data and a size field giving the length of the data are also returned. (For the connectionless MTU request; the response is two bytes long, so the length field will be 0x0002.) Figure 9–25 shows how the L2CA_GetInfo request triggers the L2CAP_InfoReq and L2CAP_InfoRsp messages between peer L2CA layers.

9.12   L2CAP STATE MACHINE

Internally, L2CAP has a state machine driven by L2CA signals from higher layers and L2CAP signals carried across lower layers. Figure 9–26 shows the L2CAP state machine for setting up a connection. At any stage, if L2CAP signals fail to appear before a Response

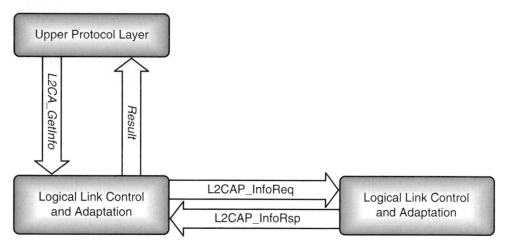

Figure 9–25   Message sequence chart for L2CA_getInfo.

Timeout (RTX), the channel will be closed. (Notice that the RTX applies only to the L2CAP signals. The standard does not specify timeouts for the L2CA signals from higher layers.)

Figure 9–26 shows how higher layers drive L2CAP, and how L2CAP peers communicate. It does not show signals going to lower protocol layers, so data transfer in the open state does not show the signals used to pass data across the lower layers. For clarity, the diagram only shows data being passed from the initiating device to the responding device, although in reality, data can go in both directions.

Notice that the device which is initiating the connection waits for signals from its higher layer application, so its higher layer application drives it through the states. In this example, the device accepting the connection waits for L2CAP signals from the device initiating the connection, and is driven through states by L2CAP signals. However, its application could also drive the L2CAP connection, for example, by either requesting to reconfigure the link or requesting disconnect.

9.13   IMPLEMENTATION-DEPENDENT ISSUES

The L2CAP specification does not include many things which are needed to implement the system. The most obvious omission is the exact format of the L2CA primitives used to communicate with higher layers and the LP primitives used to communicate with lower layers. However, there are other issues, not quite so obvious, which any implementor needs to consider. This section highlights a few of those issues.

L2CAP messages which cause L2CAP connections to be dropped are specified, but the L2CAP specification makes no mention of an LP primitive to drop the baseband link. If a Bluetooth device has been set up to keep a connection alive by passing poll packets when there is no data, then links which are not being used by L2CAP could stay up, caus-

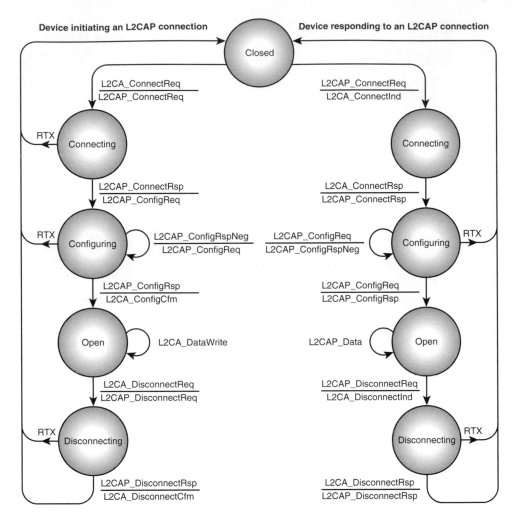

Figure 9–26   L2CAP state machine.

ing an unnecessary waste of bandwidth and unnecessary power consumption. Implementers of Bluetooth systems need to decide sensible ways for L2CAP to drop baseband links after the last L2CAP connection using a link has closed down.

There is a lower protocol message, LP_ConnectInd, which is sent to L2CAP when lower layers have finished setting up a link. This is equivalent to the HCI_Connection_Complete event, which signals to a host that a connection has been set up and configured for use. However, there is no equivalent to the HCI_Connection_Request, which signals to a host that a device has been paged and allows the host to accept or reject the connection before configuration commences. Implementers may wish to add extra primitives to allow information to be passed to L2CAP at the stage when a device has been paged but has not yet configured a connection. If they do not do this, then the device will have to be set to automatically accept connections; otherwise, connections could time out before they have been configured because there is no entity in the system accepting connection requests.

Of course, the functionality described above does not have to be handled by L2CAP. Some implementors choose to add a separate device manager which handles accepting lower layer connections for L2CAP and also handles tearing down ACL connections when L2CAP no longer needs them.

9.14 SUMMARY

L2CAP provides the facilities higher layer protocols need to communicate across a Bluetooth link. These facilities are:

- Establishing links across underlying ACL channels using L2CAP signals.
- Multiplexing between different higher layer entities by assigning each one its own connection ID.
- Providing segmentation and reassembly facilities to allow large packets to be sent across Bluetooth connections.

Higher layer applications and protocols communicate with L2CAP using implementation dependent primitives known as L2CA signals. The standard defines what these signals should do, but the exact implementation can vary from one Bluetooth system to the next.

All applications must use L2CAP to send data. It is also used by Bluetooth's higher layers such as RFCOMM and SDP, so L2CAP is a compulsory part of any Bluetooth system.

10

RFCOMM

RS-232 serial ports have nine circuits, which can be used for transferring data and signalling. RFCOMM can emulate the serial cable line settings and status of an RS-232 serial port. RFCOMM provides multiple concurrent connections by relying on L2CAP to handle multiplexing over single connections, and to provide connections to multiple devices.

RFCOMM relies on the Bluetooth baseband to provide reliable in-sequence delivery of byte streams. It does not have any ability to correct errors. Up to version 1.0b RFCOMM's flow control relied entirely on the baseband's capabilities, but in version 1.1 RFCOMM acquired a credit based flow control system which allows individual RFCOMM channels to maintain seperate flow control.

RFCOMM data rates will be limited in devices where there is a physical serial port involved (Type 2 devices). Implementations may optionally pace data on virtual serial ports (in Type 1 devices). In the absence of pacing, RFCOMM will deliver the highest possible data rate, although what the highest data rate is can be a complicated issue in the presence of multiple connections (see Chapter 18).

RFCOMM is a simple, reliable transport protocol with framing, multiplexing, and the following additional provisions:

- Modem status—RTS/ CTS, DSR/ DTR, DCD, ring.
- Remote line status—Break, overrun, parity.

- Remote port settings—Baud rate, parity, number of data bits, etc.
- Parameter negotiation (frame size).
- Optional credit based flow control.

10.1 SERIAL PORTS AND UARTs

Typically, serial port transmit and receive data lines are connected to a UART (Universal Asynchronous Receiver Transmitter). The job of the UART is to convert between the serial data sent down cables and the parallel data processing which devices use. UARTs use buffers to convert between serial and parallel data. This allows them to reduce the load on the processor. Instead of the processor having to be interrupted for every single bit that is sent down the cables, the UART transfers the bits between the cables and buffers, then the processor only has to get involved when there is a whole buffer to deal with.

The signals from a UART are connected, so they appear in the system address map. Some processors reserve a special range of addresses for I/O; other systems can map them into any part of normal memory. Because UARTs look like areas of memory to a microprocessor, it is possible to emulate a serial port in software by taking an area of memory and setting values as they would appear if they were set by a UART.

The Bluetooth RFCOMM specification talks about emulating the nine circuits of an RS-232 serial port, and specifies how a serial data stream can be emulated. But because the serial stream from an RS-232 port is viewed by the microprocessor after it has been through a UART, software dealing with serial ports is actually handling parallel data. Similarly, RFCOMM software deals with parallel data delivered by the lower layers of the Bluetooth stack.

A UART connects to some piece of hardware: wires or buffers. RFCOMM connects up to the lower layers of the software stack via L2CAP.

10.2 TYPES OF RFCOMM DEVICES

RFCOMM supports two types of devices:

- Type 1—Internal emulated serial port (or equivalent).
- Type 2—Intermediate device with physical serial port.

A protocol stack for a Type 1 RFCOMM device is shown on the left in Figure 10–1. The port emulation entity maps a system specific communication interface (API) to the RFCOMM services. This can be used to connect to legacy applications as shown, or it can be used to connect to applications specifically written for Bluetooth. A Type 1 device would usually be the end of a communication path, for example, a PC or printer.

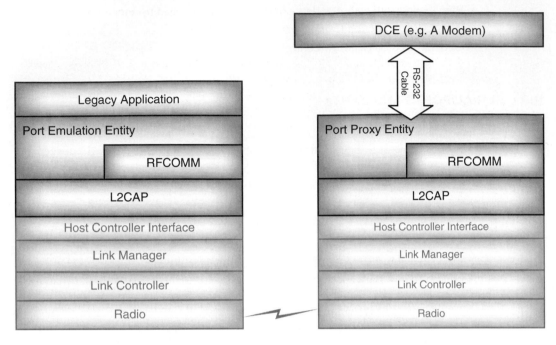

Figure 10–1   Type 1 and Type 2 RFCOMM devices.

A protocol stack for a Type 2 RFCOMM device is shown on the right in Figure 10–1. The port proxy entity relays data from RFCOMM to an external RS-232 interface linked to another device. Type 2 devices are intermediate devices which sit in the middle of a communication path. A modem is an example of a Type 2 device.

10.3   RFCOMM FRAME TYPES

RFCOMM is based on GSM TS 07.10, which is an asymmetric protocol used by GSM cellular phones to multiplex several streams of data onto one physical serial cable. RFCOMM is symmetric, and sends TS 07.10 frames over L2CAP using a subset of TS 07.10 feature frames and commands. Some of TS 07.10's features are adapted for Bluetooth.

RFCOMM communicates with frames. The RFCOMM frames become the data payload in L2CAP packets. There are five different frame types:

- SABM—Start Asynchronous Balanced Mode (startup command).
- UA—Unnumbered Acknowledgement (response when connected).
- DISC—Disconnect (disconnect command).

- DM—Disconnected Mode (response to a command when disconnected).
- UIH—Unnumbered Information with Header check.

SABM, UA, DM, and DISC are "low- level" control frames. RFCOMM uses channels, each of which has a Data Link Connection Identifier (DLCI). UIH frames on DLCI = 0 are used to send control messages. UIH frames on DLCIs ≠ 0 are used to send data.

GSM TS 07.10 also has optional UI (Unnumbered Information) frames; RFCOMM doesn't use these.

10.4   CONNECTING AND DISCONNECTING

Because RFCOMM frames are carried in the payload of L2CAP packets, an L2CAP connection must be set up before an RFCOMM connection can be set up.

RFCOMM has a reserved Protocol and Service Multiplexer (PSM) value which is used by L2CAP to identify RFCOMM traffic. The RFCOMM PSM is defined in the Bluetooth core specification as 0x0003. Any L2CAP frames received with this value in the PSM field will be sent to RFCOMM for processing.

The first frame to be sent on an RFCOMM channel is a SABM frame; this is a Start Asynchronous Balanced Mode command. If the responding device's RFCOMM is willing to connect, it goes into Asynchronous Balanced Mode (ABM) and sends back an UA frame. If the responding device's RFCOMM doesn't want to connect, it refuses the connection by sending a DM frame. Figure 10–2 shows an RFCOMM channel setup being refused in this way.

RFCOMM has a 60 s timer which is started when a command is sent. If an acknowledgement isn't received when the timer elapses, the connection will be shut down. This is different from GSM 07.10, which resends the command when the timer elapses. In the case of RFCOMM, the Bluetooth baseband provides a reliable link, so if the command wasn't acknowledged first time, it is not likely to be acknowledged a second time. For the

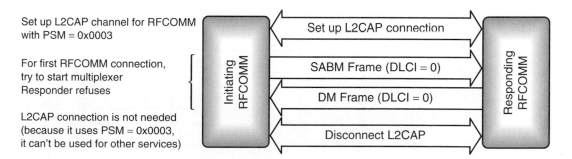

Figure 10–2   Refusing an RFCOMM connection.

SABM command, the timeout can be extended because security procedures might mean that this command takes longer to process than others. If RFCOMM ever times out and disconnects, it must send a DISC (disconnect) command frame on the same DLCI as the original SABM frame, just in case the other side has come back into range and thinks the connection is still active. Figure 10–3 shows a channel being closed down because the initiator timed out.

If the connection succeeds, the responder replies to the SABM frame with a UA (unnumbered acknowledgement) frame. This is followed by a Parameter Negotiation (PN) command from the initiator and PN response from the responder, as shown in Figure 10–4.

Once a connection with DLCI = 0 has been set up, this is available for RFCOMM signalling. To transfer data, other RFCOMM channels must be set up. Figure 10–4 shows a second RFCOMM channel being set up to transfer data. In this case, the channel requires authentication, so there is a pause for LMP authentication and encryption between the SABM command frame and the UA response frame. Once the UA frame has been received, modem status commands are exchanged to communicate the state of the control signals. Data can then be transferred immediately as shown, or there could be an exchange of PN command and response to configure the new connection's parameters.

The user data should include MSCs (Modem Status Commands), which communicate the state of serial port control signals.

To shut down an RFCOMM connection, a DISC command is sent. When the last data link has been shut down, a DISC should be sent on DLCI=0 to shut down the multiplexer. Then, whichever device shut down the multiplexer is responsible for disconnecting the L2CAP channel.

10.5   STRUCTURE OF RFCOMM FRAMES

RFCOMM borrows its frame structure from the GSM 07.10 standard. Figure 10–5 shows the frame structure for the GSM 07.10 basic option. (There is also an advanced option, which lacks the length field; RFCOMM always uses the basic option.)

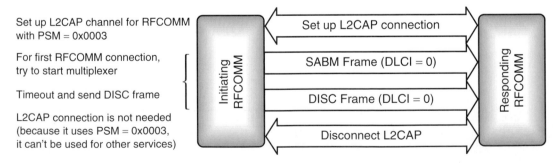

Figure 10–3   RFCOMM channel timeout.

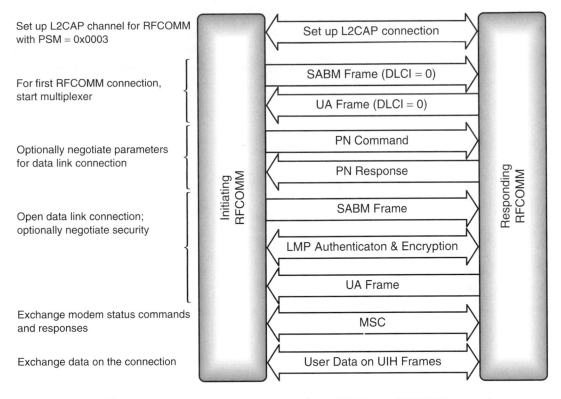

Figure 10–4 Message sequence chart for establishing an RFCOMM connection.

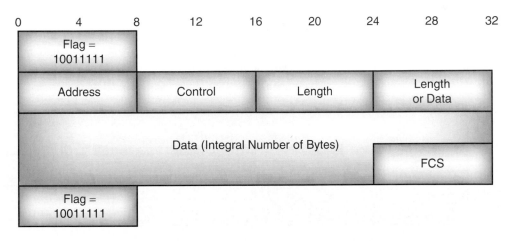

Figure 10–5 Structure of a GSM07.10 basic option frame.

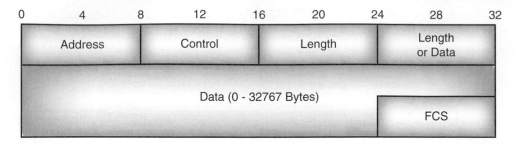

Figure 10–6   Structure of an RFCOMM frame.

Figure 10–6 shows the structure of an RFCOMM frame. This is identical to the GSM07.10 basic option frame except that RFCOMM misses out the start and end flags, and RFCOMM has to limit the number of bytes in a packet because of the limit on the size of L2CAP packets.

RFCOMM doesn't need the start and end flags because each RFCOMM frame is carried in a single L2CAP packet. There is no need to pick RFCOMM frames out of a data stream, so there is no need for flag bits to mark where the frames start and end.

Figure 10–7 shows how the RFCOMM frame structure changes when credit based flow control is in use. The length field is followed by a credit field which is used to give the remote device permission to send frames.

10.5.1   Address Field

An RFCOMM frame begins with an address field. This identifies which of the many multiplexed channels the frame belongs to. The address field is split up as shown in Figure 10–8.

The EA (Extend Address) field can be used to extend an address. If EA=0, then more address octets follow; if EA=1, then this is the last octet of the address. Since the Bluetooth specification says that server applications are assigned a server channel number in the range 1 to 30 and an RFCOMM address frame has five bits for the server channel,

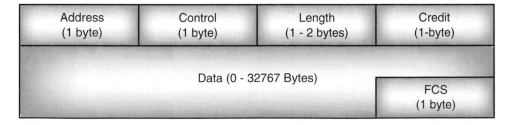

Figure 10–7   Structure of an RFCOMM frame with credit based flow control.

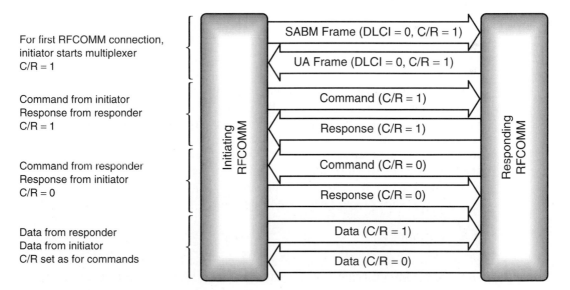

Figure 10–8 Address field.

there will never be any need to use extended addressing, so the EA bit will always be set to 1 in an RFCOMM address field.

    The C/R (Command/Response) bit says whether the frame is a command or a response. Its value depends not only on whether the frame carries a command or a response, but also on which end of the channel is sending the frame. The device which set up the connection (by sending a SABM command on DLCI 0) is called the initiator. The device which responded (by sending the UA response on DLCI 0) is called the responder. As long as the traffic follows this original pattern, the C/R bit is 1, so commands from the initiator and responses from the responder have C/R = 1. For exchanges in the opposite direction, the C/R bit is 0, so commands from the responder and responses from the initiator have C/R = 0. When sending data, the initiator sets C/R = 1 and the responder sets C/R = 0. Figure 10–9 illustrates how the C/R bit is set.

    After the C/R bit comes the Data Link Connection Identifier (DLCI). In GSM TS 0.10, this is one undivided field, but in RFCOMM, it is split up into a direction bit and a server channel number. The initiator always sets the direction bit to 1 (D=1); the responder always sets the direction bit to 0 (D=0). As with the C/R bits, who is the initiator and responder is defined by which device sent the SABM frame to start up the connection.

Figure 10–9 Settings of C/R bit in RFCOMM exchanges.

Table 10–1   Control Field Values

Control Bit Number	1	2	3	4	5	6	7	8
SABM (Set Asynchronous Balanced Mode)	1	1	1	1	P/F	1	0	0
UA (Unnumbered Acknowledgement)	1	1	0	0	P/F	1	1	0
DM (Disconnect Mode)	1	1	1	1	P/F	0	0	0
DISC (Disconnect)	1	1	0	0	P/F	0	1	1
UIH (Unnumbered Information with Header Check)	1	1	1	1	P/F	1	1	1

The server channel number has five bits; this would give it a range from 0 to 31, but 0 and 31 are reserved, so only 1 to 30 can be allocated as server channel numbers for services. Channel 0 is used for sending control information; channel 31 is reserved by TS 07.10. Bluetooth avoids using channels which are reserved by TS 07.10 to preserve compatibility with TS 07.10 applications.

The DLCI is calculated once before the data link connection is established. The RFCOMM server channel number in the responding device is used for the DLCI. Because server channel numbers 1 to 30 are available, one device can have up to 30 services using RFCOMM.

10.5.2   Control Field

Referring back to Figure 10–6, the next field in an RFCOMM frame is the control field. This is used to identify the type of the frame. Table 10–1 shows the control field values used in RFCOMM frames. (These match the values used in the corresponding GSM TS 07.10 Frames.)

P/F is the Poll/Final bit. In commands, it is called the P (Poll) bit; in responses, it is called the F (Final) bit.

A command with its P bit set to 1 is used when a response or a series of responses is wanted from the device at the far end of the link. The responding device should send back its responses with the F bit set to 1. There should only ever be one command frame with P bit set to 1 waiting for a response.

DM packets are processed regardless of the state of the P/F bit, but SABM or DISC commands and UA responses are thrown away if the P/F bit is set to zero.

10.5.3   Length Field

The length field begins with an EA bit as shown in Figure 10–10. If this is 1, then it is followed by seven bits of length, so the length field is one byte long. If the EA bit is 0, then it is followed by fifteen bits of length, so the length field is two bytes long.

The default length of an RFCOMM frame is 32 bytes; the maximum length is 32,767.

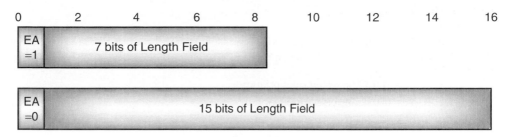

Figure 10–10   Structure of RFCOMM length fields.

10.5.4   Credit Field

The credit field only exists when the use of credit based flow control has been negotiated. An initial number of credits is granted using three bits in the parameter negotiation command. Each unit then keeps track of how many credits it has. Each time an RFCOMM frame is sent one credit is used up, each time a frame with a non-zero credit field is received, the value in the credit field is added onto the receiving units total credits.

10.5.5   Data

The data field is only present in UIH frames. There must be an integral number of bytes in the data up to 32,767. The size limit is set by the Maximum Transmission Unit (MTU) on L2CAP packets, so if a system has a smaller L2CAP MTU, the size of RFCOMM data will also be restricted.

10.5.6   Frame Check Sequence

To calculate the FCS:

Count up k, the number of bits the FCS will be calculated on. For SABM, DISC, UA, and DM frames, the frame check sequence is calculated on the address control and length fields. For UIH frames, it is calculated on the address and control fields.

Then:

(a) Calculate the remainder of x^k ($x^7 + x^6 x^5 + x^4 + x^3 + x^2 + x^1 + 1$) divided modulo 2 by the generator polynomial ($x^8 + x^2 + x + 1$).

(b) Take the contents of the frame that the FCS is calculated over before any start and stop elements have been inserted and before any other extra bits have been inserted. Multiply by x^8 and divide by the generator polynomial ($x^8 + x^2 + x + 1$).

(c) Add the results of (a) and (b) modulo 2, and take the 1's complement to get the FCS.

Because UIH frames only calculate FCS on the address and control fields, their data field is not protected by the FCS. This might be a drawback for reliable data transmission, but it does have the advantage that the FCS patterns can be precalculated for all the DLCIs that are in use. This precalculation could be done when the channel is set up.

10.6 MULTIPLEXER FRAMES

Multiplexer commands and responses are sent on DLCI = 0. They are used to control the RFCOMM link. There are seven types of commands or responses:

- PN—DLC parameter negotiation.
- Test—Checks communication link.
- FCon / FCoff—Aggregate flow control on all connections.
- MSC—Modem status, used for flow control per connection.
- RPN—Remote Port Negotiation.
- RLS—Remote Line Status.
- NSC—Non-Supported Command (response only).

The multiplexer commands and responses are carried as messages inside an RFCOMM UIH frame as shown in Figure 10–11. It is possible to send several multiplexer command messages in one RFCOMM frame or split a multiplexer command message over more than one frame.

10.6.1 PN—DLC Parameter Negotiation

The PN command is used to negotiate the parameters of a data link connection. PN commands are exchanged before a new data link connection is opened. In version1.0b this was not compulsory; in version 1.1 parameter negotiation became mandatory.

In pre-version 1.1 systems, if no PN commands are sent, default parameters will be used for the connection. This means that pre-version 1.1 systems must be able to support the default RFCOMM frame length.

A PN command is identified by the type field shown in Figure 10–12. This type field is the first information byte in the UIH frame carrying the PN command (see Figure 10–12). The EA bit is 1 because the type field occupies one byte. The C/R bit is used to indicate whether the message is a command or a response.

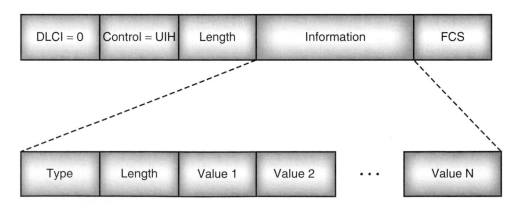

Figure 10–11 Structure of an RFCOMM multiplexer control frame.

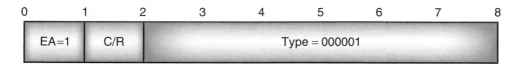

Figure 10–12   Type field for Parameter Negotiation (PN).

The length field in a PN message is always set to 8, and the value field contains 8 bytes as shown in Figure 10–13. These bytes define the parameters which will be used on a data link connection as follows:

- Six DLCI bits identify the data link connection for which parameters are being negotiated.
- Two padding bits which are always set to zero follow the DLCI; these are inserted to avoid splitting parameters across bytes.
- Four I bits give the type of frames used to carry information on the channel. In RFCOMM UIH frames indicated by the value 0b1000 are used.

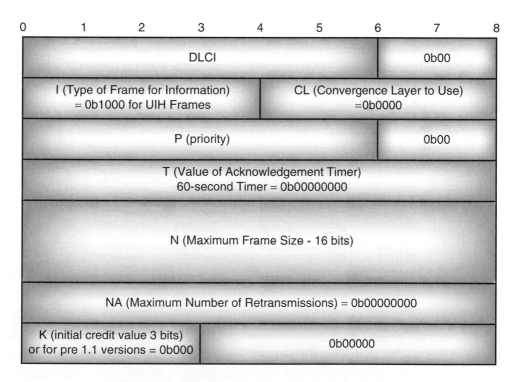

Figure 10–13   Content of value bytes in a PN message.

- Four CL bits give the convergence layer to be used. RFCOMM uses Type 1 (unstructured octet stream) = 0b0000 in versions after 1.0b this may also be set to 0x0F to enable credit based flow control.
- Six P bits assign a priority to the data link connection: 0 is the lowest priority, 63 is the highest.
- Two padding bits which are always set to zero follow the P bits; these are inserted to avoid splitting parameters across bytes.
- Eight T bits give the value of the acknowledgement timer, in GSM 07.10, this would be used to trigger a retransmit; in RFCOMM, if the timer elapses, the connection is closed down. The timer's value is not negotiable, but is fixed at 60 s. This field is set to 0 to indicate that the timer is not negotiable.
- Sixteen N bits give the maximum size of the frame.
- Eight NA bits give the maximum number of retransmissions. Because the Bluetooth baseband gives RFCOMM a reliable transport layer, RFCOMM will not retransmit, so this value is set to zero.
- Three K bits are used to indicate the initial number of credits issued to a peer; the initial credit value can range from 0 to 7. If credit based flow control is not used, the k1-k3 bits are set to zero.
- Five padding bits set to zero fill the rest of the last value field to round up the values to an integral number of bytes.

All parameters being negotiated are sent with the LSB in bit 1; this is the general rule for RFCOMM information.

It is worth noting that RFCOMM follows the conventions of the GSM 07.10 standard and numbers the bits in a frame from 1 for the least significant bit to 8 for the most significant bit. This may be confusing to people who are used to seeing the bits in a byte numbered from 0 to 7.

One device sends a PN message, and the other responds with another PN message. The response may not change the DLCI, the priority, the convergence layer, or the timer value. The response may send back a different timer value. In this case, the device which sent the first PN messages will still use the timer it proposed, but the device at the other end of the connection will use the value it sent in its message.

The response may have a smaller value for the maximum frame size, but it may not propose a larger value for this parameter.

In GSM 07.10, PN messages are optional. In RFCOMM, support of the PN message and its response are compulsory. Up to version 1.0b if default parameters are satisfactory, PN messages do not have to be sent. Version 1.1 made PN messages mandatory, even if the default parameters are satisfactory. PN messages may be exchanged until the device which sent the first message is happy with the parameters it gets sent back to it. Once it has a satisfactory set of parameters in the reply, it can go on to set up the connection.

One reason for parameter negotiaton mandatory was to enable negotiation of credit based flow control. Without mandatory parameter negotiation the responding unit could be left with no opportunity to negotiate. When not using credit based flow control,

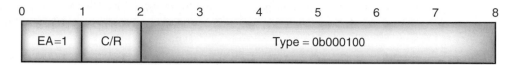

Figure 10–14   Type field for test.

RFCOMM channels used FCON and FCOFF messages for flow control on individual channels. Because Bluetooth channels are unreliable, these messages could require several retransmissions to switch off the flow of packets. This could lead to RFCOMM layer buffers overflowing and data being lost. Therefore, applications which would suffer if data buffers overflow must negotiate credit based flow control.

10.6.2   Test

The test command is used to check the RFCOMM connection. As is normal, the length byte gives the number of value bytes which follow. The number of value bytes is not fixed and is used to hold a test pattern. The remote end of the link echoes the same value bytes back.

The type field for the test command is shown in Figure 10–14. Because only a single byte is used, the EA bit is set to 1. The C/R bit is used to indicate whether the message is a command or a response.

10.6.3   FCon / FCoff—Aggregate Flow Control on All Connections

RFCOMM has a flow control mechanism which applies to all channels between two RFCOMM entities. When either RFCOMM entity can't receive RFCOMM information, it sends a Flow Control off (FCoff) command. When it is able to receive data again, it sends a Flow Control on (FCon) command.

The structure of the type field for the two flow control commands is shown in Figure 10–15. Both begin with an EA bit, which is 1 to indicate that there is only one byte in the command type. The length field in the frame carrying the command is set to zero because there is no other data in the frame. The C/R bit is used to indicate whether the message is a command or a response.

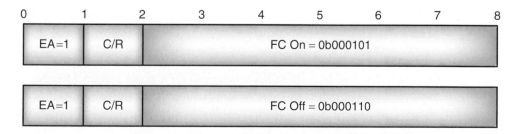

Figure 10–15   Type fields for FCon and FCoff commands.

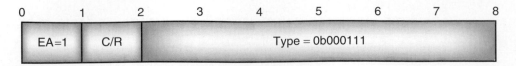

Figure 10–16   Type field for MSC command.

10.6.4   MSC—Modem Status Command

RFCOMM also has a flow control mechanism which can be applied to just one channel at a time. This is the Modem Status Command (MSC), and it is indicated by the type field shown in Figure 10–16. The EA bit is 1 because the type field occupies one byte. The C/R bit is used to indicate whether the message is a command or a response.

The command field of the MSC contains virtual V.24 control signals—that is to say, the settings that the RS 232 control wires would have if the RFCOMM data were being transferred across wires rather than across a Bluetooth connection. The signals in the command field are as follows:

- EA—Extended Address, set to 1 to indicate there is only 1 byte of command.
- FC—Flow Control bit, set to 1 when a device is unable to accept any RFCOMM frames. When the device is able to receive again, it sends another MSC with the flow control bit set to 0.
- RTC—Ready To Communicate bit, set to 1 when the device is ready to communicate.
- RTR—Ready To Receive bit, set to 0 when the device cannot receive data and 1 when it can receive data.
- IC—Incoming Call, 1 indicates an incoming call.
- DV—Data Valid, set to 1 to indicate that valid data is being sent.

These values may not seem to make sense when sent in a packet, but that is because they map onto the lines of an RS 232 interface. It might be obvious when a packet is sent that it is going to have valid data; who would bother to send a packet with invalid data? However, when dealing with physical serial port lines, such signals make more sense. A signal to say that valid data is being sent can be used to activate circuits to handle the data. The MSC command just mimics the values of the V.24 signals, which would be used on a wired RS 232 interface.

The signals from an MSC map onto RS 232 signals as follows:

- RTC maps onto DSR (Data Set Ready) and DTR (Data Terminal Ready).
- RTR maps onto RTS (Request To Send) and CTS (Clear To Send).
- IC maps onto RI (Ring Indication).
- DV maps onto DCD (Data Carrier Detect).

Figure 10–17   MSC control signal field.

Figure 10–17 shows how the signals are carried in the control field of the command.

The MSC is sent on a connection before any data is sent to establish the state of the RS 232 control signals. It should also be sent whenever the signals need to be changed.

In the MSC, the state of the signals in the device sending the command is sent. The response just carries a copy of the signals from the command.

10.6.5   RPN—Remote Port Negotiation

The Remote Port Negotiation (RPN) command is used to set communication settings at the remote end of a data link connection. If any of the communication settings need to be changed during a connection, the RPN command can be resent to change them.

The RPN type field is shown in Figure 10–18.

The EA bit is 1 because the type field occupies one byte. The C/R bit is used to indicate whether the message is a command or a response.

The length byte in an RPN command is either 1 or 8. If the length is 1, then there is a single value byte which contains the DLCI for the connection, and the message is interpreted as a request for the link's parameters. In this case, the remote end replies with the current parameters on the link. If the length byte is set to 8, then eight bytes of link parameters follow. If they are sent in a command, then they are a request to set up the link's parameters.

Figure 10–19 shows the order of values within an RPN command with length byte set to 8.

The parameter mask defines which parameters are being changed by the message. Figure 10–20 shows the position of bits in the RPN parameter mask.

In an RPN command, if a parameter mask bit is set to 1, it indicates a particular parameter that should be changed. If it is set to 0, then the parameter is not being changed and the value can be ignored.

In an RPN response, if a parameter mask bit is set to 0, then it means the proposal sent in an RLS has not been accepted. Conversely, a parameter mask bit set to 1 means

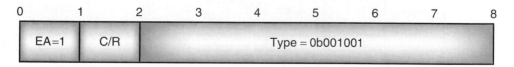

Figure 10–18   Type field for RPN.

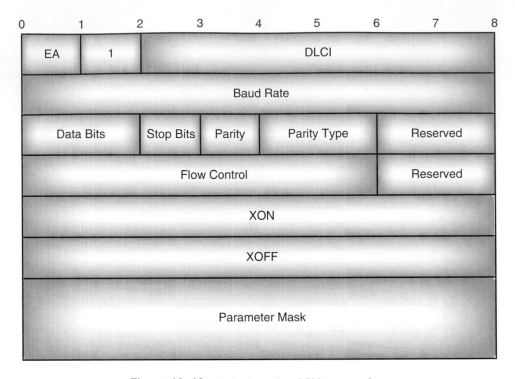

Figure 10–19   Value bytes in a RPN command.

the new value has been accepted, and the sender of the response is now using the new value.

The values of the various fields in an RLS command have the same meanings as in GSM 07.10.

10.6.6   RLS—Remote Line Status

A device sends a Remote Line Status (RLS) command when it needs to tell the other end of the link about an error.

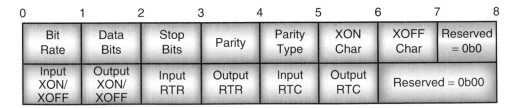

Figure 10–20   Bits in an RPN parameter mask.

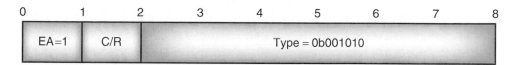

Figure 10–21 Type field for RLS.

The RLS command is identified by the type field shown in Figure 10–21. The EA bit is 1 because the type field occupies one byte. The C/R bit is used to indicate whether the message is a command or a response.

The length byte is set to 2, as there are two value bytes: the first value byte carries an EA bit, C/R bit, and the data link connection identifier common to all multiplexer command messages; the second value byte carries the error status in its first four bytes as shown in Figure 10–22.

The Line (L) status bits can signal three different errors as follows:

- 0b1100—Overrun error, a received character has overwritten a character which had not yet been read.
- 0b1010—Parity error, the parity was wrong on a received character.
- 0b1001—Framing error, a character did not end with a stop bit.

If the first line status bit is set to 0, then the RLS command is simply reporting that there are no errors on the line.

When an RLS command is received, a response is sent back with the line status copied from the command into the response.

RFCOMM implementations must recognise and respond to RLS commands, but how they deal with the line status information is up to the implementor to decide.

10.6.7 NSC—Non-Supported Command (Response Only)

The Non-Supported Command (NSC) Response is sent whenever a device receives a command it does not support.

The type field used to identify a message containing an NSC is shown in Figure 10–23. The EA bit is 1 because the type field occupies one byte. The C/R bit is used to indicate the message is a response. If the message comes from the device which initiated the connection by sending a SABM, then C/R = 0. If the message comes from the device which responded to the initial SABM, then C/R = 1.

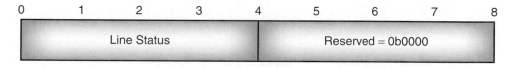

Figure 10–22 Second value byte of RLS message.

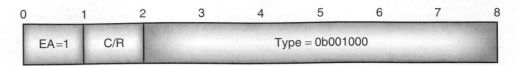

Figure 10–23   Type field for NSC response.

10.7   SERVICE RECORDS

Bluetooth devices offering services supported by RFCOMM must have an entry in their service discovery database which gives information on how to connect over RFCOMM.

RFCOMM server channel numbers are dynamic. That is to say, a service's channel number can change. Although a service's channel number doesn't change while the service is in use, it can be reallocated when the service is not in use.

The minimum information needed to connect to a service over RFCOMM is a service name (to identify the type of service) and a channel number on which to transfer data. Many services will have other additional parameters which are also needed to connect to the service. By querying SDP records, a device can find out all the information it needs to connect to a service via RFCOMM.

Table 10–2 shows a minimal service record which might be used to provide the information needed to connect to a service across RFCOMM. The ServiceClassIDList gives the name of the service. The ProtocolDescriptorList gives the supported protocols. Since RFCOMM rests on L2CAP, the L2CAP service must be present whenever RFCOMM is present. This service also has a text name which can be used to represent it on a user interface.

For more information, see Chapter 11, Table 11–1, which shows how RFCOMM information is presented for a headset application. The headset application also uses RFCOMM services to set up and control headset connections.

Table 10–2   Service Attributes Needed to Connect to an RFCOMM Service

Item	Type	Value	Attribute ID
ServicerRecordHandle	Uint32	Assigned by Server	0x0000
ServiceClassIDList			0x0001
ServiceClass0	UUID	*SERVICE NAME*	Service UUID
ProtocolDescriptorList			0x0004
Protocol0	UUID	L2CAP	0x0100
Protocol1	UUID	RFCOMM	0x0003
ProtocolSpecificParameter0	Uint8	*Server Channel #*	
ServiceName	String	*"TEXT NAME"*	0x0000 +Language Offset

10.8 SUMMARY

RFCOMM provides serial port emulation, which can be used to connect to legacy applications. It is also used for data transfer in several of the Bluetooth profiles.

RFCOMM supports two types of devices: A Type 1 device is the end of a communications path and supports an application on top of RFCOMM, and a Type 2 device is an intermediate device and has a physical RS-232 serial port on top of RFCOMM.

To set up an RFCOMM connection, an L2CAP connection must first be set up. RFCOMM frames are sent in the payload field of L2CAP packets. Once the L2CAP connection is set up, RFCOMM control frames are sent back and forth to establish a signalling channel with a Data Link Connection Identifier (DLCI) set to 0. After this is set up, subsequent channels are established for transferring data. Up to 30 data channels can be set up, so RFCOMM can theoretically support 30 different services at once. (In practice, most Bluetooth devices will not have the resources to support 30 different services.)

RFCOMM is based on the GSM 07.10 standard with a few minor differences to allow for the differences between a Bluetooth connection and a GSM cellular phone connection.

11

The Service Discovery Protocol

A Bluetooth piconet is quite different from a traditional LAN. Rather than connecting to a network, you connect straight to another device. Connections can change quickly, and in this dynamic environment, the structuring normally provided by a network manager is missing.

In a normal LAN, you find a connection to a printer, and once found, it stays in place for months, or years. Bluetooth is designed to allow you to walk into an area and find a printer without having to preconfigure settings. When you've used the printer, you can walk away and forget its details. Service Discovery Protocol (SDP) is the part of Bluetooth that allows this to happen. SDP provides the means to find a device that will print for you or to browse through the range of other services Bluetooth devices in the area can offer you.

Figure 11–1 shows SDP's position in the Bluetooth protocol stack. SDP relies on L2CAP links being established between SDP client and server. Once an L2CAP link has been established, it can be used to find out about services and how to connect to them. L2CAP does not handle connections to services itself, it merely provides information. So, to find and connect to a service offered by an SDP server, a client must go through the following steps:

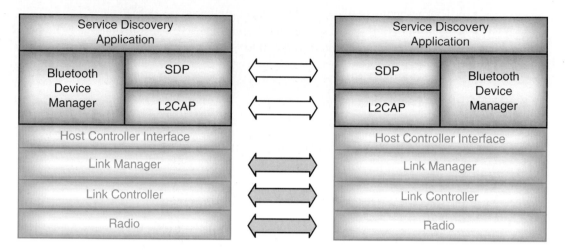

Figure 11–1   SDP's position in the Bluetooth protocol stack.

- Establish L2CAP connection to remote device using channel identified by PSM=0x0001.
- Search for specific class of service, or browse for services.
- Retrieve attributes needed to connect to the chosen service.
- Establish a *separate* (non-SDP) connection to use the service.

The L2CAP channel used for SDP can be dropped once it is no longer needed, or it may be left open if the client is likely to want to query the server's database for more SDP services.

The L2CAP Protocol and Service Multiplexer (PSM) value for SDP is defined as 0x0001. Having a known PSM means that once an ACL link has been established, the SDP client automatically knows the number to use to establish a link with the SDP server on the remote device.

Bluetooth does not define a man machine interface for service discovery; it merely defines the protocol to exchange data between a server offering services and a client wishing to use them.

11.1   SDP CLIENT/SERVER MODEL

An SDP server is any Bluetooth device which offers a service or services to other Bluetooth devices (a service is a feature usable by another device). Information about services is maintained in SDP databases. Each SDP server maintains its own database; there is no centralized database.

SDP clients use services provided by servers. To allow them to do this, servers and clients exchange information about services using service records.

- A device wanting to find out about services in the area is an SDP client.
- A device offering services is an SDP server. Devices can simultaneously be both clients (using services) and servers (offering services).

11.2 THE SDP DATABASE

The SDP database is simply a set of records describing all the services which a Bluetooth device can offer to another Bluetooth device. SDP provides the means for another device to look at these records.

11.2.1 Service Attributes

An SDP service is described by service attributes, which provide the information a client needs to use the service.

Each attribute has a 16 bit identifier and a value, as shown in Figure 11–2. Attribute values can be text strings, Boolean values, or integers.

Attributes are used to pass information on services and on the hierarchy of services available. Each attribute in the record describes a different aspect of a service. Version 1.0b of the Bluetooth standard defines twenty-eight types of attributes:

- ServiceRecordHandle—A 32 bit number uniquely identifying a service record within a server.
- ServiceClassIdList—The type of services covered by this service record.
- ServiceRecordState—A 32 bit number that is changed whenever any attribute in the record changes. This allows a client to cache information and easily check if it's up to date.
- ServiceID—A unique identifier for this instance of the service. The same service will have different ServiceID values on different servers.
- ProtocolDescriptorList—The protocols needed to use the service.
- BrowseGroupList—A list of groups used when browsing for services (see section 11.3).

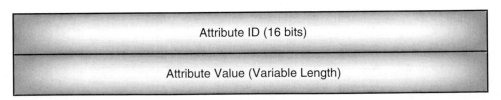

Figure 11–2   Structure of an SDP service attribute.

- LanguageBasedAttributeList—A list of languages which a service record supports. Each language listed has a language identifier, an identifier for how characters are encoded, and an attribute ID. Adding a language attribute ID to the attribute ID of a string value gives the attribute ID for retrieving the string in that language.
- ServiceInfoTimeToLive—A 32 bit integer giving an estimate of the number of seconds until the service record will next change (allows clients with cached information to poll for changes).
- ServiceAvailability—An 8 bit integer reflecting the fraction of the maximum number of clients which the service is already serving, roughly (1-(current clients/maximum clients)) *0xFF.
- BluetoothProfileDescriptorList—A list of Bluetooth profiles supported by a service.
- DocumentationURL—A URL for documentation on the service.
- ClientExecutableURL—A URL for an executable that is needed to use the service.
- IconURL—A URL for an icon that the client's user interface may use to represent the service.
- ServiceName—A string with the service's name for use by the client's user interface.
- ServiceDescription—A string describing the service, for use by the client's user interface.
- ProviderName—A string with the name of the service provider.
- VersionNumberList—A list of versions supported.
- ServiceDatabaseSet—A 32 bit integer which changes when any service record on a server changes. This allows a client to cache information and easily check if it's up to date.
- GroupId—Identifier for a group of services, used when browsing services (see section 11.3).
- RemoteAudioVolumeControl—Whether remote volume control is supported (for headsets).
- External Network—Used by the cordless telephony protocol to identify the type of telephone network the telephone is connected to. The value is one of: PSTN=1, ISDN=2, GSM=3, CDMA=4, analog cellular=5, packet-switched=6, or other=7.
- Service Version—Version number of the service, e.g., 0x0100 means version 1.00.
- Supported Data Stores List—Used by the synchronization profile.
- Supported Formats List—Used by the object push profile, a list of the formats of objects which can be pushed. The format value is a Uint8 and is one of: phonebook=1, calendar=3, notes=5, messages=6.
- Fax Class 1 Support—Used by the FAX profile; a Boolean describing whether industry-standard Class 1 FAX is supported.
- Fax Class 2.0 Support—Used by the FAX profile; a Boolean describing whether industry-standard Class 2.0 FAX is supported.

- Fax Class 2 Support—Used by the FAX profile; a Boolean describing whether manufacturer-specific Class 2 FAX is supported.
- Audio Feedback Support—Used by the dialup networking profile: a Boolean value which describes whether audio feedback is provided on an SCO channel during call setup.

Some of the attributes are specific to Bluetooth profiles. It is likely that as more Bluetooth profiles are defined, more types of attributes will be defined for them.

11.2.2   Data Elements

Attributes have values, and those values can have various types and sizes. So that a device receiving an attribute knows what type and size it is receiving, attributes are sent in data elements which begin with data element descriptors that describe the type and size of the attribute being sent.

The first byte of a data element contains the data element type descriptors; the first five bits are the data element type descriptor, and the next three bits are the data element size descriptor.

The data element type descriptor gives the type of attribute in the data element. There are nine different types numbered as follows:

- 0—The null type.
- 1—Unsigned integer.
- 2—Signed 2's complement integer.
- 3—Universally Unique Identifier (UUID).
- 4—String of text.
- 5—Boolean, true or false.
- 6—A sequence of data elements, all of which make up the data.
- 7—A sequence of data elements, one of which must be chosen, called a data sequence alternative.
- 8—Uniform Resource Locator (URL).

The data element size descriptor gives the size of the attribute in the data element. It starts off with a size index. If the size index is 0, 1, 2, 3, or 4, it gives the length of the attribute which follows:

- 0—1 byte, or 0 bytes if it's a null data element.
- 1—2 bytes.
- 2—4 bytes.
- 3—8 bytes.
- 4—16 bytes.

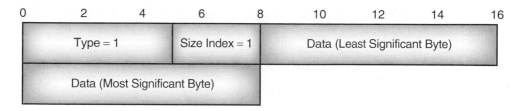

Figure 11–3 Data element containing a 16 bit integer.

If the size index is 5, 6, or 7, it is followed by the size:

- 5—Data size is in next 1 byte.
- 6—Data size is in next 2 bytes.
- 7—Data size is in next 4 bytes.

Why have such a complex system where sometimes there is a size field and sometimes there isn't? It would have been possible to forget about having to always send the size in a 32 byte field, but many attributes will fit into 1, 2, 4, 8, or 16 bytes. Thus, for these attributes, it saves a significant amount of bandwidth to just use the size index and not send a separate size field. The data element type descriptor leaves three spare bits in its byte. These three bits are just enough to use for the size index, so this index isn't using any extra bytes in the PDU. On the other hand, it's not possible to avoid sometimes sending the size information separately because attributes which are made up of sequences and attributes which are text strings can be very long, so their length can't be adequately described by the size indexes.

Examples of data elements are the easiest way to understand how the data element descriptor structures work. Figure 11–3 has an example of a data element containing a 16 bit integer. The first five bits have the type; this is 1, which indicates that the attribute is an unsigned integer. The size index is 1, which says the attribute is two bytes long. The attribute's data then follows: first the least significant byte, then the most significant byte.

Figure 11–4 has an example of a data element containing the string "Cats". The first five bits have the type; this is 4, which indicates that the attribute is a text string. The

0	2	4	6	8	10	12	14	16
Type = 4			Size Index = 5		Size = 4 Bytes			
"C"					"a"			
"t"					"s"			

Figure 11–4 Data element containing a text string.

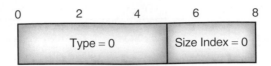

Figure 11–5 Data element containing a null.

size index is 5, which says the attribute size is in the next byte. The attribute's size in bytes is then given. Since characters are encoded one byte per character, this size is also the length of the string. The attribute's data, "Cats," then follows.

Sometimes there is no attribute data to put in a parameter, but the parameter still has to be sent. In these cases, a null data element is used. A null data element is shown in Figure 11–5; it's type is 0, indicating a null. The size index is also 0. Normally, this would mean one byte of data, but in combination with the null type, it means that there is no attribute data following.

Sometimes a parameter needs to carry several attributes. To do this, a data element sequence or data element alternative is used. Both of these allow a list of attributes to be sent. In a data element sequence, all of the attributes are to be used; in a data element alternative, only one attribute is chosen to be used.

Figure 11–6 shows an example data element sequence. This sequence contains a list of UUIDs—such a list might be sent as a ServiceSearchRequest parameter by a client trying to find out whether a server supported one of a set of services.

The first two bytes describe the sequence: the type is 6 for data element sequence. Because the sequence takes up six bytes, the size doesn't fit in the size index, so an index of 5 is used to indicate that the size comes in the next byte. The size byte gives the length in bytes of the whole sequence.

Each data element in the data element sequence has its own data element descriptors. Both elements are UUIDs, so they both have a data element type descriptor of 3. Both UUIDs are two bytes long, so both data elements have a SizeIndex of 1.

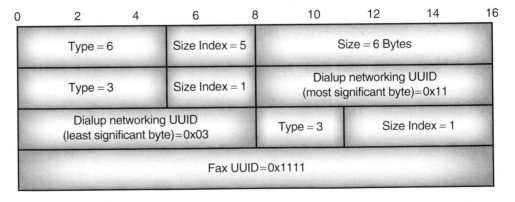

Figure 11–6 Data element containing a data element sequence.

There is no particular significance to the way the bytes are split up in the diagram; they have just been split up into two byte rows for convenience. However, the splitting up of the Dial Up Networking UUID illustrates the byte order that SDP uses with the most significant byte being sent first and least significant byte sent last.

A data sequence alternative is sent in a similar way, with one set of data element descriptors for the whole sequence, and then a data element descriptor for each data element in the sequence.

11.2.3   Service Records

Attributes are values describing a service which a server is making available to clients. A service record holds all the information a server provides to describe a service, so it is made up of a series of attributes. The class of the service defines the meanings of the attributes, so an attribute might mean something different in different service records.

Table 11–1 shows an example of the Bluetooth headset's service record, which illustrates how a service record is made up. The first part of the service record deals with the services offered by the device. The headset service is made up of two services: the headset service and the generic audio service on which the headset service is based. The service record then goes on to list the protocols that are needed to use the headset service. The headset service requires L2CAP and RFCOMM. The channel number of the RFCOMM server is needed before a device can access RFCOMM, so along with the pro-

Table 11–1   Service Records for a Bluetooth Headset

Item	Type	Value	Attribute ID
ServicerRecordHandle	Uint32	Assigned by Server	0x0000
ServiceClassIDList			0x0001
ServiceClass0	UUID	Headset	0x1108
ServiceClass1	UUID	Generic Audio	0x1203
ProtocolDescriptorList			0x0004
Protocol0	UUID	L2CAP	0x0100
Protocol1	UUID	RFCOMM	0x0003
ProtocolSpecificParameter0	Uint8	Server Channel #	
BluetoothProfileDescriptorList			0x0009
Profile0	UUID	Headset	0x1108
Parameter0	Uint16	Version 1.0	0x0100
ServiceName	String	"Headset"	0x0000 +language offset
Remote Audio Volume Control	Boolean	False	0x0302

tocol descriptor for RFCOMM, there is an extra protocol specific parameter. The client device knows how to use RFCOMM, so it knows that this protocol specific parameter is the channel number; retrieving this number allows the client to begin using RFCOMM.

Next comes a BluetoothProfileDescriptorList, which lists the profiles which the service supports. Profiles should only be listed if the device fully supports them, so it is possible for a device to have no list of profiles in any of its service records (for example, a Bluetooth development system may not support any profiles). Naturally, the headset service implements the headset profile, so the unique identifier for this profile is given, followed by a version number. The headset profile is based upon the serial port profile, and all profiles require the generic access profile. But as support of these two profiles is implicit in support of the headset profile, there is no need to explicitly list them. In fact, because the generic access profile is required for all other profiles, it has not even been assigned its own service class UUID in Bluetooth's assigned numbers, so it is not possible to list it in an SDP service record.

The record finishes with some extra attributes needed to use the headset profile: the name given by the service provider to the headset service, which defaults to "Headset", but could be changed by the service provider; and finally, an entry to inform the client that this headset does not support the optional feature allowing remote setting of headset volume by an audio gateway.

Note that one ServiceRecord may contain the ServiceName in several languages. The client adds different offsets to the AttributeID to get the attribute in different languages. The device's primary language is given the offset 0x0100, so to get the Service-Name in the primary language, the client would add 0x0100 to the base ServiceName attribute ID of 0x0000 to give 0x0100.

To find out what the language offsets are for a device, the client would request the LanguageBaseAttributeIDList, which has attribute ID = 0x0006.

11.3   BROWSING SDP RECORDS

To make it easier to find the service you want, services are arranged in a hierarchy structured as a tree which can be browsed. Clients begin by examining the root of the hierarchy, then follow the hierarchy out to the leaf nodes, where individual services are described.

It is up to each service provider to decide what services will be browsable and how the browsing hierarchy will be constructed. For example, a smart phone offering several different services to other Bluetooth devices could have the browse structure shown in Figure 11–7.

The service provider has chosen to organize the services into two groups. The audio group covers audio gateway services, which allow Bluetooth headsets to connect to cellular connections and local Bluetooth intercom connections. The organizer group includes calendar facilities, which include the ability to synchronise calendars and alarms.

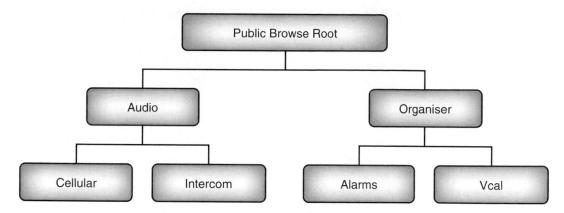

Figure 11–7 A possible SDP browsing hierarchy for a cellular phone.

An alarm facility is common to many mobile phones, but is not defined under Bluetooth, so the alarms category shows how SDP can be used to publish information about new services not defined in the Bluetooth specification. A user of the alarms service would have to know something about how it worked so that they could connect to it, but any parameters necessary to connect to this particular instance of the alarms service could be retrieved via SDP. For instance, the alarms service might provide the ability to set alarms via an RFCOMM connection, so the RFCOMM channel for connecting to the alarms service could be retrieved by querying the SDP service records for the alarms service.

11.3.1 Browse Groups and Browse Group Lists

Service classes are used to identify services. Each service class record includes a BrowseGroupList attribute. The value of the BrowseGroupList is a list of the UUIDs of all the browse groups associated with the service.

Table 11–2 shows the set of service records used for browsing the hierarchy in Figure 11–7. Each group entry lists the IDs of any groups above it and its own group ID. The services don't just list the IDs of the groups they belong to.

The top level of the browsing tree is called PublicBrowseRoot and has the UUID 0x1002 (this is the short form, the long form of this is 0x00001002-0000-1000-7007-00805F9B34FB). All browsing hierarchies have this top level. Because there is no entry above the PublicBrowseRoot, and all devices know its Group ID, there is no need to include an entry for the PublicBrowseRoot in the table.

11.4 UNIVERSALLY UNIQUE IDENTIFIERS (UUIDs)

Universally Unique Identifiers (UUIDs) are 128 bit numbers. Each record has a UUID attribute; these are used to search for a record. The Bluetooth standard specifies UUIDs for the attributes needed for the Bluetooth profiles.

Table 11–2   Service Records for a Possible SDP Browsing Hierarchy for a Cellular Phone

Service/Group Name	Service Class	Attribute Name	Attribute Value
Audio	BrowseGroupDescriptor	BrowseGroupList	PublicBrowseRoot
		GroupID	AudioID
Organiser	BrowseGroupDescriptor	BrowseGroupList	PublicBrowseRoot
		GroupID	OrganiserID
Cellular	BrowseGroupDescriptor	BrowseGroupList	AudioID
Intercom	BrowseGroupDescriptor	BrowseGroupList	AudioID
Alarms	BrowseGroupDescriptor	BrowseGroupList	OrganiserID
Vcal	BrowseGroupDescriptor	BrowseGroupList	OrganiserID

11.4.1   UUIDs Assigned by the Bluetooth Specification

The Bluetooth specification's UUIDs are likely to be used a lot, so to save bandwidth transferring them and space storing them, they can be shortened to 32 bit or 16 bit forms. This is possible because all the Bluetooth specification's UUIDs are based in the same Bluetooth base UUID: 0x00000000-0000-1000-7007-00805F9B34FB.

To compare a pair of UUIDs, they must be converted into the same format. The rules for converting UUIDs assigned by the Bluetooth specification are quite simple:

- To convert a 16 bit UUID into a 32 bit UUID, it is just zero-extended to 32 bits. For example, the 16 bit UUID 0x1265 becomes the 32 bit UUID 0x00001265.
- To convert a 16 or 32 bit UUID into a full 128 bit UUID, it is multiplied by 2^{96} and added to the Bluetooth base UUID. For example:

$0x1265*2^{96}$ + 0x00000000-0000-1000-7007-00805F9B34FB = 0x00001265-0000-1000-7007-00805F9B34FB

11.4.2   UUIDs Assigned by Manufacturers

A manufacturer defining a new service is allowed to allocate its own UUIDs. This could easily lead to clashes of IDs, so SDP uses a method of allocating UUIDs which makes them extremely unlikely to be duplicated.

A UUID is made up of the following parts:

- time_low—32 least significant bits of the timestamp (bits 0 to 31).
- time_mid—16 bits of the middle field of the timestamp (bits 32 to 47).
- time_high_and_version—A 16 bit value:
    - least significant 12 bits are the most significant 12 bits of the timestamp (bits 48-59).
    - most significant 4 bits are the version.

- clock_seq_hi_and_reserved—An 8 bit value:

  - 6 least significant bits are the 6 most significant bits of the clock sequence (bits 8 to 13).

  - 2 most significant bits are the variant (this may be set to 10).

- clock_seq_low—The low field of the clock sequence.

- node—The unique node identifier.

The unique node identifier is used to guarantee that the UUIDs allocated by one node are different from those allocated by other nodes. A 48 bit IEEE address is used for this field. As these are allocated uniquely, it provides a convenient guarantee that the node ID is unique. Usually, the address used will be the address of the host.

The timestamp is 60 bits of coordinated Universal Time Clock (UTC), which is the number of 100 nanosecond intervals since 00:00:00.00 on 15 October 1582. This may seem like an odd date to pick, but it is the date of the Gregorian reform of the Christian calendar, so it is the start of the most widely used system of dating in use today. This timestamp will not wrap around to zero until around 3400 A.D.

The clock sequence value is used because some systems will not have a real-time clock that is calibrated to a date, or for some other reason their value of the coordinated UTC goes backwards. This could lead to duplication of UUIDs. To get around this problem, the 14 bit clock sequence value is changed every time the UTC value goes backwards and every time the system reboots. Random numbers can be used to make sure the clock sequence value changes if the system can't store values across a reboot. The clock sequence value ensures that even if the same UTC value is generated twice, the UUIDs will still be different.

The variant field describes the layout of the UUID. Microsoft has reserved a variant ID of 110. Variants beginning with zero are reserved for backwards-compatibility with the Network Computing System (NCS), which originated the UUID system. The variant with MSBs 10 was used in an Internet draft and is used by the DCE 1.1 Remote Procedure Call specification. The binary value 10 is used in the Bluetooth base UUID, and it may be used in the variant field to assign UUIDs for Bluetooth SDP purposes.

The version field describes how a UUID was allocated. The time-based version described here is identified by the binary sequence 00011. There are other ways of assigning UUIDs, based on functions of names or on random numbers. Each method has its own different variant value, so they each produce a different range of UUIDs. This helps to ensure that UUIDs stay unique, whatever method was used to allocate them.

The parts of the UUID are written as a series of hexadecimal digits separated by hyphens in the following order:

UUID = time_low - time_mid - time_high_and_version - clock_seq_hi_and_
reserved - clock_seq_low - node

For storage and transferring in a data stream, the UUID is just treated as a sequence of octets.

The full rules on using and assigning UUIDs are available at: http://www.open group.org/publications/catalog/c706.htm or http://www.iso.ch/cate/d2229.html, and in the International Organization for Standardization publication ISO/IEC 11578:1996, "Information Technology—Open Systems Interconnection-Remote Procedure Call (RPC)".

11.5 SDP MESSAGES

To browse service classes or get information about a specific service, SDP clients and servers exchange messages. These messages are carried in SDP Protocol Data Units (PDUs). There are only seven types of SDP PDUs defined, and each has its own PDU ID to identify it:

- 0x01 = SDP_ErrorResponse.
- 0x02 = SDP_ServiceSearchRequest.
- 0x03 = SDP_ServiceSearchResponse.
- 0x04 = SDP_ServiceAttributeRequest.
- 0x05 = SDP_ServiceAttributeResponse.
- 0x06 = SDP_ServiceSearchAttributeRequest.
- 0x07 = SDP_ServiceSearchAttributeResponse.

The client always initiates SDP transactions with a request; the server always answers with a response as shown in Figure 11–8. (Note that some responses may be split across several packets.)

All SDP PDUs share a common structure as explained in section 11.5.1.

11.5.1 SDP Protocol Data Units

SDP uses Protocol Data Units (PDUs) with the structure shown in Figure 11–9. The first byte is an ID, identifying the message in the PDU. This is followed by two bytes of transaction ID. When a client sends an SDP request, it is given a transaction ID; the server

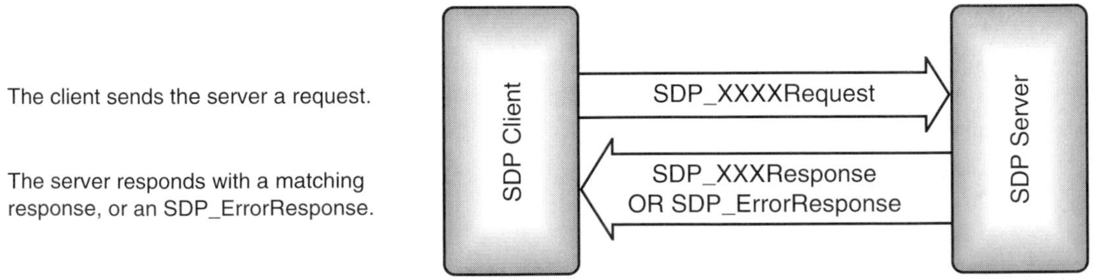

The client sends the server a request.

The server responds with a matching response, or an SDP_ErrorResponse.

SDP Client — SDP_XXXXRequest → SDP Server

SDP Client ← SDP_XXXResponse OR SDP_ErrorResponse — SDP Server

Figure 11–8 Message sequence chart for SDP request and response.

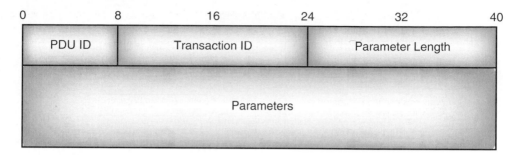

Figure 11–9   Structure of an SDP PDU.

copies that transaction ID into the response, so that if the client sends several requests, it can sort out which response goes with which request.

Except for the SDP_ErrorResponse, all SDP PDUs have a ContinuationState as their last parameter. This allows a message to be split across more than one PDU. If the message is not continued, the ContinuationState is a single byte set to zero. If the message is continued, then the first byte of the ContinuationState parameter begins with a single byte length field followed by some ContinuationInformation. The ContinuationInformation is a handle which can be used to request the rest of the message: the client simply repeats the request and copies the ContinuationState parameter from the partial response into the last parameter of the request. When the server receives the request, it uses the ContinuationInformation to identify where it split the response and continues the next response where it left off.

Figure 11–10 shows an SDP PDU with a ContinuationState parameter showing the parameter starting with a single byte of InfoLength, followed by the ContinuationInformation.

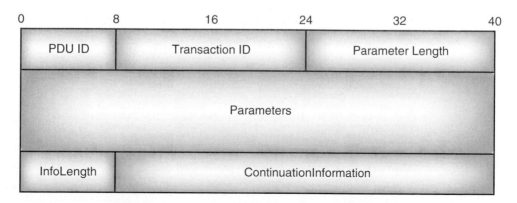

Figure 11–10   SDP PDU with ContinuationState parameter.

The client sends a search request, including a pattern for the server to match and a maximum number of records for the server's response.

If the server has the service requested, it responds with the service's handle.

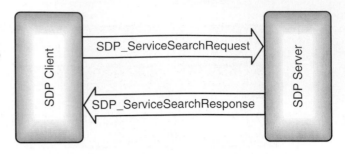

Figure 11–11   Message sequence chart for SDP service search.

11.5.2   Searching for Services

Whether a client is starting at the public browse root and searching through the hierarchy of services, or looking for a specific service, it uses an SDP_ServiceSearchRequest. This contains a ServiceSearchPattern made up of UUIDs, which the server is to look for in its database. The server responds with an SDP_ServiceSearchResponse containing information about any service records which match the ServiceSearchPattern as shown in Figure 11–11.

The ServiceSearchRequest has three parameters:

- ServiceSearchPattern, for the server to match in its database.
- MaximumServiceRecordCount, which tells the server the maximum number of records the client wants information on. For instance, if this is set to 2, a server that had six service Records matching the ServiceSearchPattern would only return information on the first two.
- ContinuationState, which tells the server whether the message had to be split across two PDUs.

The structure of an example SDP_ServiceSearchRequest is shown in Figure 11–12. It begins with the header used by all SDP PDUs:

- One byte of PDU ID—0x02 signifies that the PDU carries an SDP_Service-SearchRequest.
- Two bytes of transaction ID—This is copied into the response to the PDU, and helps the client tie the server's response with this request.
- Two bytes of parameter length—This gives the total length of all the parameters which follow.

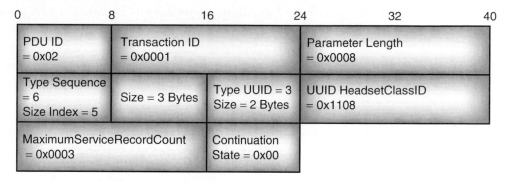

Figure 11–12   Structure of an SDP_ServiceSearchRequest.

The header is followed by the message's parameters: ServiceSearchPattern, MaximumServiceRecordCount, and ContinuationState. The ServiceSearchPattern is made up of several parts.

- Five bits of data element type descriptor = 6 = data element sequence—This tells the server that it is to expect more data elements following.
- In the same byte are three bits of data element size descriptor = 5—This tells the server that the size of the data element sequence is given by the next byte.
- One byte of data element sequence size = 3—This tells the server to expect three bytes of data element sequence before the next parameter.

In this case, the data element sequence just contains one data element, which is made up as follows:

- Five bits of data element type descriptor = 3 = UUID—This is the ID that the server must search for in its database.
- In the same byte are three bits of data element size descriptor = 1—This tells the server that the size of the data element sequence is two bytes.
- Two bytes giving the UUID to search for.

The single UUID completes the ServiceSearchPattern parameter. This is followed by the last parameter:

- Two bytes of MaximumServiceRecordCount = 0x003. There is no need for a size or type parameter, as the server receiving the PDU knows to expect two bytes of parameter here.

The PDU contains a single byte of ContinuationState.

- ContinuationState = 0—This tells the server that this message is a fresh request, not a request for a continuation of data from a previous request.

The ContinuationState is a parameter like all the others, so the parameter length includes the lengths of the ServiceSearchPattern, the MaximumServiceRecordCount, and the ContinuationState.

Note that the ServiceSearchPattern parameter can contain up to twelve UUIDs. Because its length can vary, it begins with data element type and size descriptors, giving the length of the sequence of UUIDs. In this example, there is only one UUID, and since UUIDs can vary in length, it too must begin with data element type and size descriptors to let the server know its length. The other parameters have fixed types and lengths, so they don't have to have data element type and size descriptors.

11.5.3   Responding to a Search for Services

A server receiving a valid SDP_ServiceSearchRequest replies with an SDP_Service-SearchResponse. This has four parameters:

- TotalServiceRecordCount—The total number of ServiceRecordHandles the server is sending. If the response is split into several PDUs, this is the sum of handles in all response PDUs.
- CurrentServiceRecordCount—The total number of ServiceRecordHandles in this PDU.
- ServiceRecordHandleList—A list of handles for services which match the Service-SearchRequest.
- ContinuationState—Whether the message had to be split across two PDUs.

The structure of an example SDP_ServiceSearchResponse is shown in Figure 11–13. (There is no significance to the way the structure has been drawn with different numbers of bytes on different lines; the diagram has just been broken up into rows at convenient places.) The SDP_ServiceSearchResponse begins with the header used by all SDP PDUs:

- One byte of PDU ID—0x03 signifies that the PDU carries an SDP_Service-SearchResponse.
- Two bytes of transaction ID—This is copied from the request PDU and helps the client tie this response with the correct request.
- Two bytes of parameter length—This gives the total length of all the parameters which follow.

The header is followed by the message's parameters: TotalServiceRecordCount, CurrentServiceRecordCount, ServiceRecordHandleList, and ContinuationState:

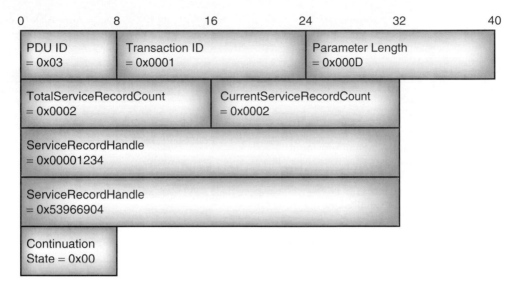

Figure 11–13   Structure of an SDP_ServiceSearchResponse.

- TotalServiceRecordCount = 2—Since the request asked for the headset service with a MaximumServiceRecordCount of 3, the client can work out that the handles for all instances of the headset service are being returned.
- CurrentServiceRecordCount = 2—This tells the client that the next parameter contains two ServiceRecordHandles. From the TotalServiceRecordCount, the client can work out that this is all the ServiceRecordHandles.
- The ServiceRecordHandleList contains a series of 32 bit ServiceRecordHandles. These are just integers which uniquely identify each service the server is offering. Because the list has to contain handles, and the handle size is fixed at 32 bits, there is no need for a data element type descriptor or a data element size descriptor, the handles can just be sent as a list of 32 bit numbers.
- Finally, one byte of ContinuationState is set to 0—This tells the server that the whole message is carried in this PDU, that is to say, there will be no continuation.

The service handles returned by this message can be used to request the SDP server for the service's attributes.

11.5.4   Requesting the Attributes of a Service

Once a client has a service's handle, it can use an SDP_ServiceAttributeRequest to retrieve the service's attributes. Figure 11–14 shows an example of such a request. It begins with the header used by all SDP PDUs:

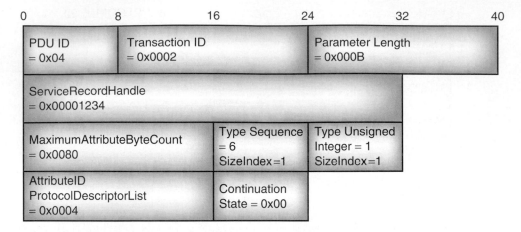

Figure 11–14   Structure of an SDP_ServiceAttributeRequest.

- One byte of PDU ID—0x04 signifies that the PDU carries an SDP_ServiceAttribute-Request.
- Two bytes of transaction ID—This is copied into the response to the PDU, and helps the client tie the server's response with this request.
- Two bytes of parameter length—This gives the total length of all the parameters which follow.

The header is followed by the message's parameters—ServiceRecordHandle, MaximumAttributeByteCount, AttributeIDList, and ContinuationState.

- The ServiceRecordHandle identifies the service for which attributes are being requested.
- The MaximumAttributeByteCount sets a limit on the number of bytes of attributes the server can respond with.
- The AttributeIDList identifies the attributes the client is requesting. Because several attributes can be requested, it is a sequence of data elements and begins with a data element descriptor identifying the parameter as a data element sequence. In this case, there is only one parameter, the AttributeID for a ProtocolDescriptorList. This is 0x0004, which is a 16 bit integer, so its data element Descriptor identifies it as an unsigned integer with a length of two bytes.
- ContinuationState is set to 0—This tells the server that this message is a fresh request, not a request for a continuation of data from a previous request.

11.5.5   Responding to a Request for the Attributes of a Service

The SDP_ServiceAttributeRequest in section 11.5.4 asked for the ProtocolDescriptorList associated with a headset service. Table 11–1 shows that a headset service record has a

ProtocolDescriptorList with two protocols: L2CAP and RFCOMM, and the RFCOMM protocol has one parameter associated with it: the server channel number used for the headset service.

Figure 11–15 shows how the headset's ProtocolDescriptorList is fitted into a SDP_ServiceAttributeResponse. The PDU begins with the header used by all SDP PDUs:

- One byte of PDU ID—0x05 signifies that the PDU carries an SDP_ServiceAttribute-Response
- Two bytes of transaction ID—This is copied from the request PDU and helps the client to tie up this response with the correct request.
- Two bytes of parameter length—This gives the total length of all the parameters which follow.

The header is followed by the message's parameters: AttributeListByteCount, AttributeList, and ContinuationState:

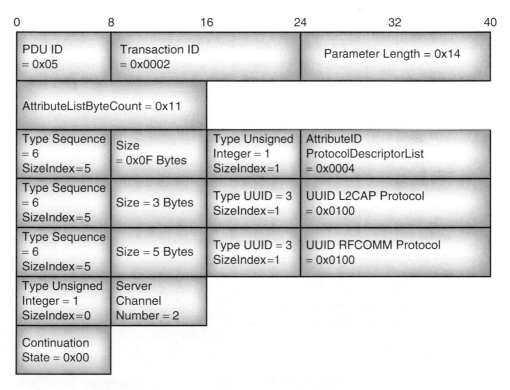

Figure 11–15 Structure of an SDP_ServiceAttributeResponse.

- AttributeListByteCount gives the total number of bytes in the AttributeList. This must be no larger than the MaximumAttributeByteCount sent in the SDP_ServiceAttributeRequest.

The AttributeList parameter is split up into several parts:

- The Attribute List begins with a data element type descriptor identifying the AttributeList as a sequence of data elements and a data element size descriptor giving the total length of the sequence of elements. Because the sequence is fifteen bytes long, it can't be described by the SizeIndex, so the SizeIndex is set to 5, indicating that the size is given in the following byte.
- The first data element in the sequence is an AttributeID, which identifies the following elements as a ProtocolDescriptorList.
- The first protocol supported is L2CAP. Because a ProtocolDescriptor can contain parameters, it is passed as a sequence of data elements, so it begins with a data element descriptor for a sequence. In the case of L2CAP, there are no parameters, so the list has a single data element which contains the UUID for the L2CAP protocol.
- The second protocol supported is RFCOMM. Again it begins with a data element descriptor for a sequence. In the case of RFCOMM, there is a parameter, so the list has two data elements: the UUID for the L2CAP protocol and the RFCOMM server channel number for the headset service.
- Finally, one byte of ContinuationState is set to 0—This tells the server that the whole message is carried in this PDU, that is to say, there will be no continuation.

11.5.6   Searching for a Service with an Attribute Request

Sections 11.5.2 and 11.5.4 described how a client searches for a service and how a client requests the attributes of a service. Sections 11.5.3 and 11.5.5 described how the server responds to those requests. Often clients wanting to connect to a service will want to find out the services available and some of their attributes. To speed up the process, SDP offers a message which combines a service search with an attribute request.

Figure 11–16 shows an example of an SDP_ServiceSearchAttributeRequest. It begins with the header used by all SDP PDUs:

- One byte of PDU ID—0x06 signifies that the PDU carries an SDP_ServiceSearchAttributeRequest.
- Two bytes of transaction ID—This is copied into the response to the PDU, and helps the client tie the server's response with this request.
- Two bytes of parameter length—This gives the total length of all the parameters which follow.

The header is followed by the message's four parameters: ServiceSearchPattern, MaximumAttributeByteCount, AttributeIDList, and ContinuationState.

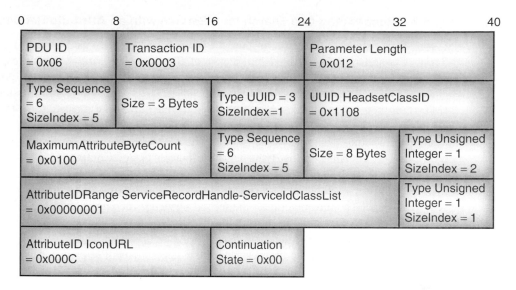

Figure 11–16 SDP_ServiceSearchAttributeRequest message.

- ServiceSearchPattern—Like the pattern in the SDP_ServiceSearchRequest, this is a sequence of patterns to search for, so it begins with the data element descriptors for a sequence. In this case, there is one element in the sequence: the UUID for the headset class. This is prefixed by its own data element descriptors giving its type (UUID) and size (2 bytes).
- MaximumAttributeByteCount—This gives the maximum number of bytes of attribute data the server is to return in response to this request. This parameter has a fixed format; it is always a 16 bit unsigned integer, so it is just sent as two bytes of data. It does not need to be sent as a data element and does not need a data element descriptor.
- AttributeIDList—Like the AttributeIDList in the SDP_ServiceSearchRequest, this is a list of attributes to retrieve from a service, except here the service is specified by the ServiceSearchPattern instead of by a handle. Since the parameter can contain a series of attributes to match, it begins with the data element descriptor for a sequence. This is followed by a series of AttributeIDs and/or AttributeIDRanges. An AttributeID is a 16 bit integer, so if the data element size descriptor has a SizeIndex=1, the data element contains two bytes and must be an AttributeID. If the data element size descriptor has a SizeIndex=2, the data element contains four bytes and must contain a pair of AttributeIDs specifying an AttributeIDRange. In the example below, the AttributeIDList contains one AttributeIDRange, which goes from ServiceRecordHandle = 0x0000 to ServiceIdClassList = 0x0001, the list also contains an IconURL attribute.
- ContinuationState is set to 0—This tells the server that this message is a fresh request, not a request for a continuation of data from a previous request.

11.5.7   Responding to a Search for a Service with an Attribute Request

Figure 11–17 shows an example of how the headset service's ServiceRecordHandle and ServiceClassIdList can be fitted into a pair of SDP_ServiceSearchAttributeResponses. The response has been split across two response packets. This may have to be done because the SDP PDU size may be larger than the L2CAP Maximum Transmission Unit (MTU), or memory limitations in an embedded device may make it easier for it to generate a series of small responses rather than one large response.

The structure is similar to the examples above, using the standard header followed by the parameters AttributeListByteCount, AttributeLists, and ContinuationState.

Note that the AttributeLists parameter is made up of a sequence of two data elements: the information retrieved for the first service and the information retrieved for the second service. (The information for the second service is incomplete because it is continued in another PDU.) This means that the AttributeLists parameter's data element descriptor gives its type as a sequence of data elements.

The information on the first service is also a data element sequence, because it also has two data elements: the Service RecordHandle and the attribute list for the first service. The ServiceRecordHandle is a 32 bit unsigned integer, but the attribute list is again a sequence of data elements; in this case, the attributes requested for that service.

So, the PDU's AttributeIDList consists of nested data elements with sequences inside sequences inside sequences until finally the attributes of services matching the search pattern are reached.

The example PDU given in Figure 11–17 has ContinuationState = 2, indicating that the PDU does not have a complete response and that there are two bytes of Continuation-Information. When the client receives the ServiceSearchAttributeResponse with a non-zero continuation state, it reads the ContinuationInformation, and to get the second part of the response, the client reissues the SDP_ServiceSearchAttributeRequest with the ContinuationState ContinuationInformation copied into the end of the PDU (see Figure 11–18).

The SDP server receives the second request with a non-zero ContinuationState and uses the ContinuationInformation to work out where it stopped sending data in the first PDU. It can then send the rest of the data in a continuation PDU. Since this is the last PDU in the sequence, it has a zero value for ContinuationState.

In the second PDU, in Figure 11–19, there is only an attribute list for one service. Since there is no list of attributes for several services, and no list of service handle followed by service attributes, there are not so many levels of nested sequence data elements. Note: for simplicity, our example response omits the IconURL, so does not match the example request.

11.5.8   Handling Errors

If an SDP server receives a request which it can't respond to correctly, it replies with an SDP_ErrorResponse. This carries two parameters: an ErrorCode and additional ErrorInfo.

In version 1.0b, the format of the ErrorInfo is not defined. It is difficult to know what to do with an undefined parameter. One possibility is to ignore it, but since some sort of Error-

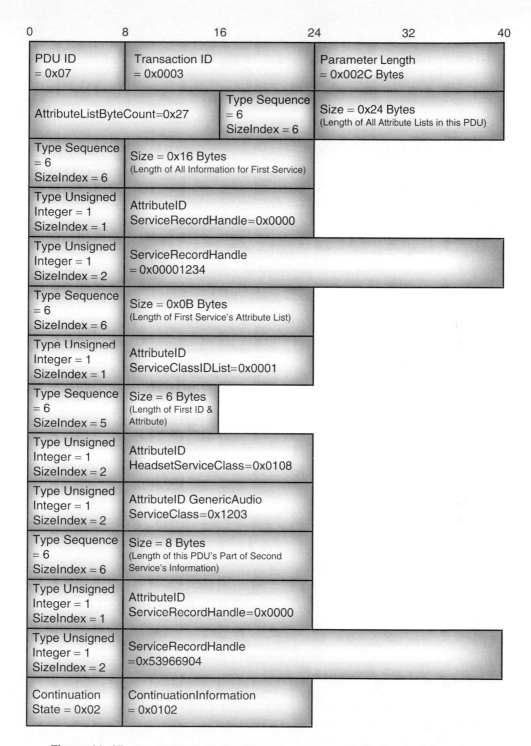

0	8	16	24	32	40

PDU ID = 0x07	Transaction ID = 0x0003	Parameter Length = 0x002C Bytes
AttributeListByteCount=0x27	Type Sequence = 6 SizeIndex = 6	Size = 0x24 Bytes (Length of All Attribute Lists in this PDU)
Type Sequence = 6 SizeIndex = 6	Size = 0x16 Bytes (Length of All Information for First Service)	
Type Unsigned Integer = 1 SizeIndex = 1	AttributeID ServiceRecordHandle=0x0000	
Type Unsigned Integer = 1 SizeIndex = 2	ServiceRecordHandle = 0x00001234	
Type Sequence = 6 SizeIndex = 6	Size = 0x0B Bytes (Length of First Service's Attribute List)	
Type Unsigned Integer = 1 SizeIndex = 1	AttributeID ServiceClassIDList=0x0001	
Type Sequence = 6 SizeIndex = 5	Size = 6 Bytes (Length of First ID & Attribute)	
Type Unsigned Integer = 1 SizeIndex = 2	AttributeID HeadsetServiceClass=0x0108	
Type Unsigned Integer = 1 SizeIndex = 2	AttributeID GenericAudio ServiceClass=0x1203	
Type Sequence = 6 SizeIndex = 6	Size = 8 Bytes (Length of this PDU's Part of Second Service's Information)	
Type Unsigned Integer = 1 SizeIndex = 1	AttributeID ServiceRecordHandle=0x0000	
Type Unsigned Integer = 1 SizeIndex = 2	ServiceRecordHandle =0x53966904	
Continuation State = 0x02	ContinuationInformation = 0x0102	

Figure 11–17 ServiceSearchAttributeResponse message with ContinuationInformation.

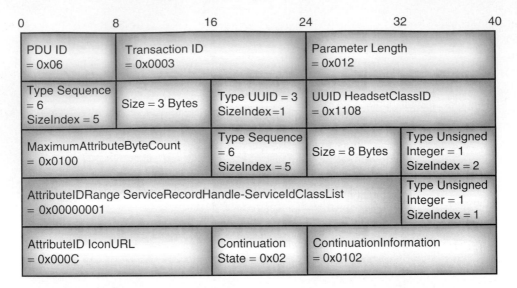

Figure 11–18 ServiceSearchAttributeRequest message with ContinuationInformation.

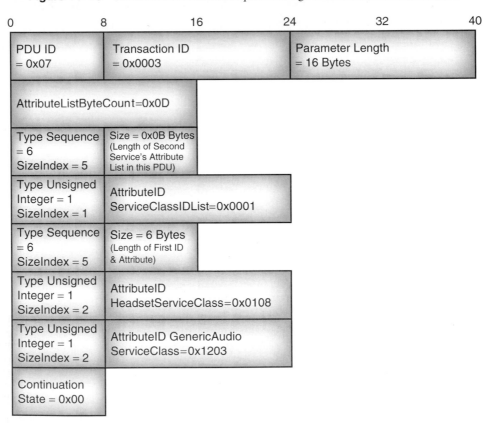

Figure 11–19 Continuation of a ServiceSearchAttributeResponse.

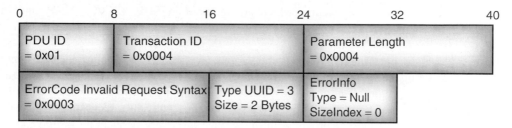

Figure 11–20   Structure of an SDP_ErrorResponse PDU.

Info parameter is specified, some implementations might regard it as an error if one isn't supplied, so perhaps a better solution is to send a null data element as illustrated in Figure 11–20.

There are six possible values specified for ErrorCode:

- 0x0001—The SDP client is using an invalid or unsupported version of SDP.
- 0x0002—The request contained an invalid ServiceRecordHandle.
- 0x0003—The syntax of the request was incorrect.
- 0x0004—The PDU size of the request was invalid.
- 0x0005—The continuation state of the request was invalid.
- 0x0006—The server has insufficient resources to respond correctly to the request.

The example shown in Figure 11–20 has ErrorCode 3, which shows that it is a response to a request with invalid syntax.

11.6   SERVICE DISCOVERY PROFILE

The service discovery profile describes how applications running on an SDP client use SDP and other features of the Bluetooth protocol stack to discover services provided by Bluetooth devices within range.

The service discovery profile provides:

- A series of service primitives which an application can use to drive service discovery.
- Example operational frameworks, which are sequences showing how an application might inquire for devices, connect to them, and use service discovery in response to a user's input.
- Message sequence charts showing the stages in setting up and using an SDP connection.
- A statement that devices supporting the SDP application profile must support pairing and authentication (though the profile does not impose particular requirements for them to be used).

- Lists of the features which are required in SDP, L2CAP, LMP, and the link
  controller.

Figure 11–21 shows how the various layers of the stack must each connect in turn
to set up an SDP session. The SDP application profile gives examples of when these connections might be set up; for instance, a client might already be connected when it begins
an SDP session, or it might only connect in response to a user requesting information.

The primitives provided in the service discovery application profile include Ser-
viceBrowse and ServiceSearch, which simply use SDP's browsing and searching capabilities. There is also an enumerateRemDec primitive, which causes an inquiry and results in

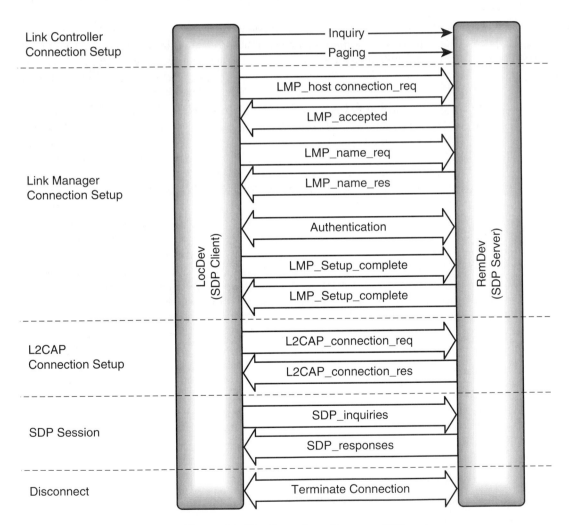

Figure 11–21   Stages in setting up an SDP session.

the application reporting the other Bluetooth devices in the neighborhood. Finally, there is a terminatePrimitive, which causes the link to a device to be torn down after the SDP application has finished with it.

11.7 SUMMARY

The Service Discovery Protocol (SDP) provides a means for an SDP client to access information about services offered by SDP servers. A server can be any Bluetooth device offering a service which can be used by another Bluetooth device, and a client can be any device wanting to use a service. So, a device could be an SDP client and server at the same time.

SDP servers maintain a database of service records. Each service record provides information that a client needs to access a service. This information may include URLs for executables, documentation, and icons associated with the service. So, a client may have to follow these URLS and retrieve information from elsewhere to be able to use the service.

To use SDP, an L2CAP channel must be established between the SDP client and server. This channel has a protocol service multiplexer reserved for SDP, so that any device can easily connect to the SDP service on another device. After the SDP information has been retrieved from the server, the client must establish a separate connection to use the service (the connection used for SDP cannot be used for anything else).

Services have Universally Unique Identifiers (UUIDs) which describe them. The services defined by the Bluetooth profiles have UUIDs assigned by the standard, but service providers can define their own services and assign their own UUIDs to those services. The UUIDs are allocated by a method that guarantees they will not be duplicated, so there is no need for a central authority or a central database to allocate the UUIDs.

A UUID can be sent in a message asking a server if it supports the service identified by the UUID. Alternatively, instead of asking for a specific service, SDP can provide a mechanism for organising services in trees, along with messages for browsing through the trees to look for a service.

SDP does not define the applications needed to drive the service discovery process, nor does it define an interface to applications; this is left up to implementers. If required, it may be used alongside other service discovery methods which provide Application Programming Interfaces (APIs) such as salutation or SLP (Service Location Protocol).

12

The Wireless Application Protocol

Wireless Application Protocol (WAP) is a wireless protocol that allows mobile devices to use data service and access the Internet. WAP can work with a variety of different wireless technologies, each of which connects at the bottom of the WAP stack as a bearer. Bluetooth simply provides another possible bearer beneath the WAP stack.

In the same way that Bluetooth has the SIG which defines standards and helps to ensure interoperability of Bluetooth devices, WAP has the WAP forum. The WAP forum brings together companies from all parts of the wireless industry to define WAP standards and to help ensure interoperability between WAP products. WAP standards can be downloaded from the WAP forum Web site at http://www.wapforum.org.

WAP supports many wireless networks: CDPD, CDMA, GSM, PDC, PHS, TDMA, FLEX, ReFLEX, iDEN, TETRA, DECT DataTAC, and Mobitex, but at the time of writing, Bluetooth has not been formally adopted as a bearer layer by the WAP forum. This does not mean that there will be no standards for interoperability between WAP-enabled Bluetooth products. The Bluetooth specification includes a section on how to interoperate with WAP, and the Bluetooth SIG is working with the WAP forum to help ensure interoperability of Bluetooth and WAP.

WAP supports a client/server architecture. The client communicates with a server (or proxy) using the WAP protocols. WAP-enabled client devices can use microbrowsers, which are specially designed Web browsers that fit onto mobile devices such as mobile cellular phone handsets. A microbrowser is designed to work with a small screen, and to use less memory than a browser running on a desktop PC. WAP supports such facilities through the Wireless Markup Language (WML). This works in similar ways to Hypertext Markup Language (HTML). HTML is used to design pages on the World Wide Web; WML pages work in a similar way to HTML pages, but are designed to cope with the smaller screen sizes typically found on today's mobile devices.

Content providers (the people who put up Internet sites) are providing WAP pages because it allows them to access a huge market of mobile customers, many of whom browse the Web at home, or at the office, but cannot access it on the move. The market for WAP services extends much further than this though, around twice as many mobile phones are sold as desktop PCs, so as more and more phones become "smart phones" with microbrowsers, many people who do not have a PC will be able to access the World Wide Web through their mobile phone.

WAP does not just work with phones. Pagers and PDAs are obvious candidates to work with WAP; in fact, any device with a screen and the ability to support a wireless connection could be turned into a WAP device.

12.1   THE WAP FORUM

The WAP forum is headed by a board of directors; below the board is the specification committee, the architecture group (a group who specifies what working groups will do), and the expert working groups themselves (see Figure 12–1). It is the expert working groups who define the details of the WAP standard. Members of the WAP forum can at-

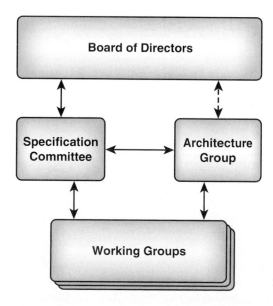

Figure 12–1   Structure of the WAP organisation.

tend these groups and participate in the definition of the WAP standard. Nonmembers can still influence the specification by submitting comments to the WAP Web site at http://www.wapforum.org.

The board of directors staffs the specification committee. The specification committee is in charge of releasing WAP specifications, and it is also in charge of their content. To aid in this work, the specification committee forms expert working groups and specification working groups.

Members of the WAP forum can attend the working groups which define the WAP specification, allowing them to participate directly in the process of writing new versions. They can also help to define the marketing messages for WAP, nominate and elect directors to the WAP forum board, and, of course, network with other companies interested in WAP.

The architecture group is staffed from the working groups. This group provides technical direction for the specification and expert working groups, including resolving issues and conflicts. The architecture group also tracks the overall architecture of WAP.

Companies apply to join the WAP forum by filling out a form. This form is available from the WAP Web site. At the time of writing, the Bluetooth SIG is free to join, but the WAP forum costs $27,500 USD for full membership and $7,500 for associate membership. Only full members may vote in the elections for the WAP board of directors.

Members who join the WAP forum agree to license the IPR (Intellectual Property Rights) essential to implementing WAP on "fair, reasonable, and non-discriminatory terms". This probably means that essential IPR for WAP will not be free. This is in contrast with the Bluetooth license, which provides SIG members with free access to essential IPR.

On the other hand, content and application developers get a royalty free IPR license. This is because widespread availability of WAP pages and WAP applications will assist the take-up of WAP.

12.2 THE WAP STACK

WAP uses a combination of Internet protocols (such as UDP) and protocols specially modified to work with mobile devices (such as WML,which is based on XML, the same standard on which HTML is based).

The WAP components used above the Bluetooth protocol stack and shown in Figure 12–2 are:

- WAE (Wireless Application Environment)—Provides a user interface, typically a microbrowser, which is a lightweight version of a Web browser.
- WSP (Wireless Session Protocol)—Supports the session between a WAP client and the WAP server.
- WTP (Wireless Transport Protocol)—Provides a reliable transport layer for WSP. If other layers below WSP provide a reliable service, there is no need for WTP. Since

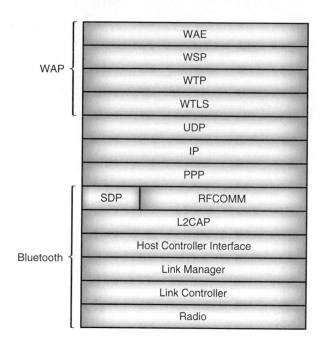

Figure 12–2 WAP on the Bluetooth protocol stack.

the Bluetooth baseband provides reliable transport, WTP could be omitted when Bluetooth is used as a bearer for WAP.

- WTLS (Wireless Transport Layer Security)—Provides security. This layer can be omitted for applications which do not require more security than the Bluetooth baseband provides.

The WAP layers are joined to Bluetooth by three Internet protocol layers, which allow datagrams to be sent across Bluetooth's RFCOMM serial port emulation layer.

- UDP (User Datagram Protocol)—Provides unreliable, connectionless datagram transport.
- IP (Internet Protocol) A protocol which supports addressing, routing, segmentation, and reassembly of packets.
- PPP (Point to point Protocol)—A client/server-based packet transport system commonly used on dial-up links to carry IP traffic.

12.3 PPP LINKS

PPP is used to carry packets from the higher IP and WAP layers across Bluetooth's RFCOMM serial port emulation layer. RFC1661 describes PPP, and RFC1662 describes how it can be carried across High Level Data Link Control (HDLC) framing systems. (RFCOMM is an HDLC framing system.)

PPP encapsulates information for transmission in RFCOMM frames as shown in Figure 12–3.

The protocol field is used to identify what sort of PPP message is being sent. The categories for protocol are:

- 0x0001 Padding protocol.
- 0xC021 Link Control Protocol (LCP).
- 0xC023 Password Authentication protocol.
- 0xC025 Link Quality Report.
- 0xC223 Challenge Handshake Authentication protocol.

The information field is used to carry the datagrams, which are transferred across a PPP link. The datagrams can be information from UDP and above, or they can be encapsulated PPP control packets. For instance, a single PPP link control protocol packet can be transferred in the information field.

The information field can be missing. PPP has a Maximum Receive Unit (MRU); the padding field can be used to round up the length of the packet to the MRU, but it is not compulsory to use padding.

12.3.1   PPP Link Control Protocol

The Link Control Protocol (LCP) configures and controls PPP links. A single LCP packet is encapsulated in the information field of a PPP frame. The structure of an LCP packet is shown in Figure 12–4.

The code field is a single byte, and identifies the type of LCP packet. The possible types are:

- 0x01 Configure-Request—Used to send options for use on a link.
- 0x02 Configure-Ack—Acknowledges Configure-Request if options are acceptable.
- 0x03 Configure-Nak—Replies to Configure-Request if some options not acceptable; the Configure-Nak specifies new options.
- 0x04 Configure-Reject—Replies to a Configure-Request if options are unrecognisable, or if the responder does not wish to negotiate the options.
- 0x05 Terminate-Request—Used to request shut down of a PPP link.

Protocol Field (8 or 16 Bits)	Information (0 or More Bits)	Padding (Optional)

Figure 12–3   Structure of PPP encapsulation.

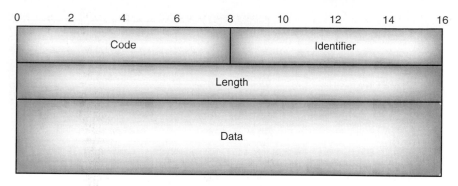

Figure 12–4   Structure of a PPP LCP packet.

- 0x06 Terminate-Ack—Acknowledges that the link is to be shut down.
- 0x07 Code-Reject—Used to reject a PPP LCP packet with an unrecognised code.
- 0x08 Protocol-Reject—Used to reject a PPP packet with an unrecognised protocol field.
- 0x09 Echo-Request—Requests an Echo-Reply to test the link.
- 0x0A Echo-Reply—Responds to an Echo-Request.
- 0x0B Discard-Request—These packets are discarded on reception; they are provided for debug and test purposes.

The identifier field is a single byte used to match up requests and replies. Response packets carry an identifier value copied from the request packet they are answering.

The length field is two bytes, which gives the total length of the LCP packet, including code, identifier length, and data fields.

To set up a PPP link first, an RFCOMM connection is established (see Figure 12–5). Then each side sends LCP packets for link test and configuration. Parameters which can be configured are:

- Maximum-Receive-Unit—The maximum length of a PPP information field; defaults to 1500 bytes.
- Authentication-Protocol—The protocol for authentication; either password authentication protocol or challenge handshake authentication protocol can be used.
- Quality-Protocol—Whether a quality monitoring protocol will be used to determine whether the link is dropping packets (this should not be needed on Bluetooth as the baseband links are reliable).
- Magic-Number—Random number used to detect looped back links.
- Protocol-Field-Compression—Can be used to select different lengths of protocol field in PPP packets.

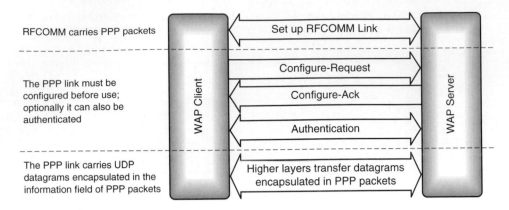

Figure 12–5   Message sequence chart for setting up a PPP link.

- Address-and-Control-Field-Compression—Used to negotiate compression of the address and control fields of the data link layer.

After configuration, packets can then be sent across the link, which configures the higher layer protocols that are using the link (IP and WAP protocol layers).

12.3.2   PPP States

PPP links have various states. LCP messages and authorisation messages move the links between the states. Figure 12–6 shows the states of a PPP link.

The link begins in the dead state. Exchange of configuration messages is carried out in the establish state, which opens the link.

Authentication is not mandatory, but if it is being done, it is the next phase. If it succeeds or if there is no authentication, the PPP link goes to the network state, where data is

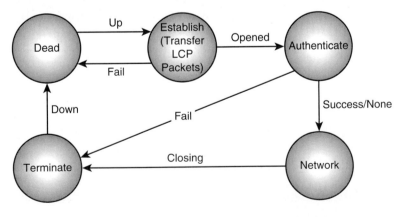

Figure 12–6   State transition diagram for a PPP link.

transferred. If authentication fails, the link is taken straight to a terminate state, which shuts it down. The link also goes through the terminate state when the link is being shut down.

12.4 WAP CLIENTS AND SERVERS

WAP uses a client/server architecture. Typically a WAP client will be a mobile device with lower bandwidth links than one would find on wired devices such as networked PCs. Because of their low bandwidth links, WAP content is communicated in a compact encoded format.

WAP supports Wireless Markup Language (WML), which is similar to the Hypertext Markup Language (HTML) that is used to encode Web pages. Both WML and HTML are derived from a set of rules for producing markup languages called XML. The two have so many elements in common that it is possible to produce a Web page that could be read by both a WML browser and an HTML browser. However, WML has been designed to suit the capabilities of mobile devices with limited screen sizes.

WAP clients can talk to WAP servers which hold WML pages in plain text format. When a WAP client requests a page from a WAP server, it is put through a content encoder, then sent to the WAP client in the compact encoded format. The encoding converts the page into a series of tokens, which provide a shorter representation than the human-readable text form of the page.

In addition to Wireless Markup Language (WML), the WAP standard defines a format for simple bitmap images, called WBMP (Wireless Bitmap), and a scripting language which can be used to run programs on a WAP client called WMLscript. WMLscript is comparable to JavaScript and allows WAP pages to initiate actions on the device displaying them.

Figure 12–7 shows a closed system where the WAP client can only see one WAP server. This is typically found in high security situations such as banking. However, most WAP clients will wish to retrieve files from servers on the Internet. Devices called gateways are used to access files from Internet servers. Figure 12–8 shows a WAP client accessing files from a WAP server, which is also a WAP gateway.

When the WAP client requests a file which is on the WAP gateway/server, the request is routed up the WAP stack to the user agent. This takes the request for a URL, realises that it refers to a local file, and routes it as a file request to the local file store.

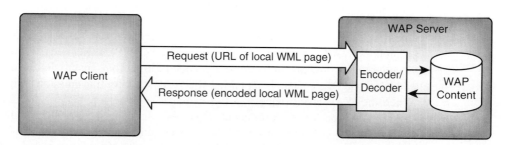

Figure 12–7   Retrieving WAP content from a WAP server.

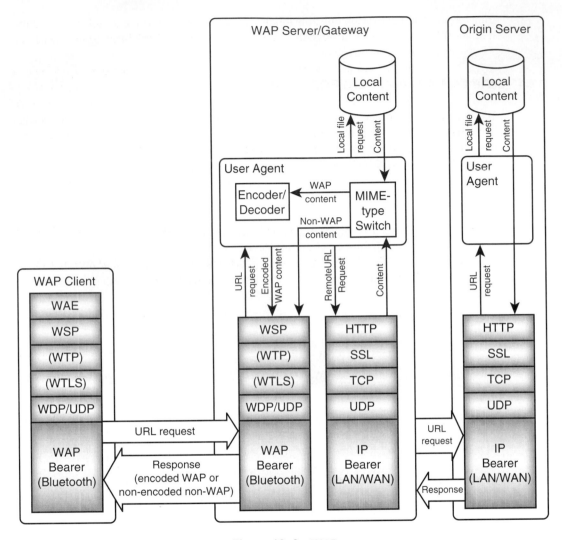

Figure 12–8 WAP gateway.

The file store returns its content, which the user agent directs to a MIME type switch. If the content is WAP content (WML, WMLScript, WBMP), then it is sent to the encoder/decoder to be converted into compact encoded format for transmission on air. From the encoder/decoder, the content is sent down the WAP stack for transmission to the client.

When the WAP client requests a file which is on a remote server, the request is routed up the WAP stack to the user agent. This takes the request for a URL, realises that it refers to a remote URL, and performs DNS (Domain Name Server) resolution. DNS resolution involves taking the URL, which is made up of a file location and a domain name, and resolving the domain name to an Internet address.

For example, <http://www.Bluetooth.com> resolves to the Internet address 192.36.140.2, which is the address of a server. The file part of the location can be routed to this server via the WAP server's/gateway's IP stack.

The origin server, which has the URL, routes the request to its user agent, which retrieves the content from its file store and sends the reply back down the origin server's IP stack. The content is passed up the WAP server's/gateway's IP stack, and into the MIME type switch. If it is WAP content, it will be encoded for transmission to the WAP client in compact format. If it is nonWAP content, it cannot be tokenized by the encoder/decoder so it will have to be transmitted in its raw format. Either way, the content is transmitted down the WAP server's/gateway's stack to be sent to the WAP client.

The gateway is performing two services:

- It is receiving on an IP stack and transmitting on a WAP stack with Bluetooth as its bearer layer.
- It is encoding WAP content into a compact format for transmission, whether this is local WAP content or WAP content received from remote servers.

12.5 SUSPEND AND RESUME

WAP provides suspend and resume facilities, which might be used to halt a WAP session temporarily if a WAP client with a Bluetooth bearer layer moved out of range of its server. However, implementers should be aware that not all versions of WAP can suspend cleanly when the bearer layer fails.

The Bluetooth specification also suggests that clients with multiple protocol stacks (such as GSM handsets with Bluetooth capabilities) could connect to WAP servers via more than one stack. If such a device connected over Bluetooth, it could retrieve the information necessary to connect to the server via another WAP bearer, then if the client lost its Bluetooth bearer, it could resume the session using the alternate bearer. Again, implementers should be aware that not all versions of WAP may support this functionality, so it may be necessary for the WAP application to completely shut down the WAP session and restart it on the alternate bearer.

12.5.1 Server Push

Most communications protocols rely on client pull, that is to say, the client requests data from the server. WAP supports server push, where the server initiates transactions actively, sending out data to all clients in an area. There are many applications for server push—for example, database updates can be pushed out from a desktop to a PDA, or advertisements could be pushed out from a shop to passing Bluetooth devices with WAP clients.

Of course, once you're considering server push, there are huge security implications. Without security, a WAP server could push code for execution onto your device—it could pull off your confidential information, or it could instruct your Bluetooth enabled phone to run up a huge bill calling a high rate off-shore sex line! To avoid this, the Bluetooth bearer layer uses encryption and authentication, so some authenticating PIN number must be entered into the WAP client and server before they can communicate.

Version 1.0b of the Bluetooth specification references WAP version 1.0. At this level of the standard, the server push facilities were not fully defined throughout the WAP stack. Version 1.3 of WAP introduced the WAP push architecture with support throughout the WAP stack, so work remains to be done before Bluetooth devices can fully take advantage of server push.

12.6   SERVICE DISCOVERY

A WAP client using Bluetooth as a WAP bearer layer which wants to connect to a WAP server first has to find the server. It could be preconfigured with the Bluetooth device address of a WAP server in range, or it could find it by conducting an inquiry, then use service discovery to find a WAP server.

Even if the WAP client has been preconfigured with the Bluetooth device address of the WAP client, it will still need to use SDP to find the RFCOMM server number the WAP client has allocated to WAP services. The WAP server's service discovery record will also identify whether the server is a proxy (used to access files on other devices), an origin server (provides its own files), or both. A home URL, the page to begin browsing at, is provided. A service name, for instance "train timetable information," is provided. A set of parameters needed to connect to the WAP service are given; these are the port numbers allocated to the various layers of the WAP stack.

Once the service discovery information has been retrieved, an L2CAP link for RFCOMM is established, and a WSP session is set up over this link. Finally, URLs can be requested by WAE across WSP.

Figure 12–9 shows the process of establishing a link between WAP client and server. If the link was established to retrieve information directly from the local WAP server, the first URL requested would be the home URL of the WAP server. The home URL is passed from server to client in the WAP server's service record.

12.7   WAP INTEROPERABILITY

Just as the Bluetooth SIG arranges for Bluetooth qualification testing, the WAP forum has compliance specifications and test suites.

12.8   USING WAP

WAP implementations supporting server push allow smart servers to announce themselves to passersby. The owner of a WAP-enabled PDA could walk into a waiting room,

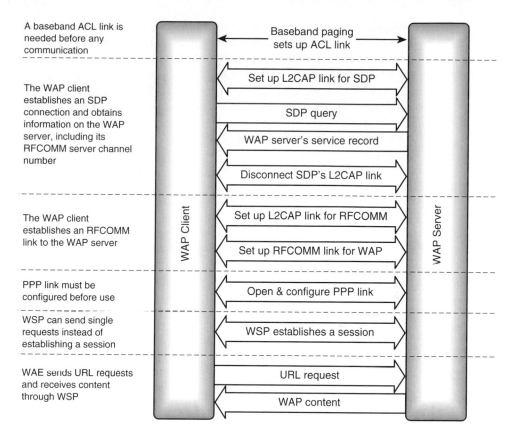

A baseband ACL link is needed before any communication

Baseband paging sets up ACL link

The WAP client establishes an SDP connection and obtains information on the WAP server, including its RFCOMM server channel number

Set up L2CAP link for SDP

SDP query

WAP server's service record

Disconnect SDP's L2CAP link

The WAP client establishes an RFCOMM link to the WAP server

Set up L2CAP link for RFCOMM

Set up RFCOMM link for WAP

PPP link must be configured before use

Open & configure PPP link

WSP can send single requests instead of establishing a session

WSP establishes a session

WAE sends URL requests and receives content through WSP

URL request

WAP content

WAP Client

WAP Server

Figure 12–9   Establishing a WSP session and retrieving WAP content.

get out the PDA to check appointments, and have a message from a LAN access point pop up, offering to connect to timetable information. Clicking on yes, up pops a page with hypertext links guiding around arrivals and departures. Of course, if all this information isn't wanted, there is always the option of making a Bluetooth device nondiscoverable so it doesn't answer inquiries from the local WAP servers, and they don't know it's there. Or to still allow connection to other devices, applications can be set to refuse contacts from WAP servers that haven't been preauthorised.

Another use for server push is setting up personal devices to automatically synchronise with one another. For example, when a user's WAP-enabled phone gets within Bluetooth range of the same user's WAP-enabled PC, it automatically initiates a link, transferring its up-to-date phone book information. Once the user has installed and configured the applications, it all happens automatically without further intervention.

The combination of Bluetooth wireless technology and WAP data transfer technology provides the potential for local data transfer in new environments. There are many cases where local short range information transfer is useful, and the limited range of Bluetooth links can be an asset, ensuring that the information transferred is relevant to the environment. For example, tourist information from a local WAP kiosk could be automatically tailored to the location of the user, whereas tourist information transferred from a more remote server might not be so relevant.

12.9 SUMMARY

WAP (Wireless Application Protocol) is defined and promoted by the WAP forum, which organisations may join for an annual fee.

WAP provides a protocol stack similar to the IP (Internet Protocol) stack, but it is tailored for the needs of mobile devices. It caters to the limited display size and resolution typically found on mobile devices by providing special formats for Web pages which suit their capabilities. It also provides for the low bandwidth of mobile devices by defining a method for WAP content to be compressed before it is transferred across a wireless link.

The WAP stack can be used to transfer files which do not have WAP content, but when nonWAP content is transferred, it cannot be compressed.

Version 1.3 of WAP supports server push, which allows a WAP server to initiate a transfer of information to a device.

WAP can use Bluetooth as a bearer layer in the same way as it can use GSM, CDMA, and other wireless services. The WAP stack is joined to the Bluetooth stack using UDP, IP, and PPP.

13

OBEX and IrDA

OBEX (Object Exchange) is a binary protocol designed to allow a variety of devices to exchange data simply and spontaneously. Spontaneity is important for Bluetooth, where short duration ad-hoc connections can be set up.

OBEX has a client/server architecture, and allows a client to push data to a server or pull data from a server. For example, a PDA might pull a file from a laptop, or a phone synchronising an address book might push it to a PDA.

The Infrared Data Association (IrDA) is a non profit organisation which created the IrDA standards that specify how to connect and transfer data across infrared links. OBEX is an IrDA specification. The IrDA has similarities to the Bluetooth SIG in that both have an international membership, and both create and promote communication specifications. More details on IrDA can be found at http://www.irda.org. The IrDA specifications can be downloaded from this site.

IrDA and Bluetooth both support short range, ad-hoc links. IrDA supports higher data rates than Bluetooth, and also has higher layers in the stack than Bluetooth (see Chapter 26 for more details on how IrDA compares with Bluetooth). The similarities between the two communications protocols' lower layers mean that IrDA's OBEX protocol is ideally suited to transferring objects between Bluetooth devices. This is one reason why the Bluetooth core promoters decided to adopt OBEX from IrDA. Another reason is that adopting existing standards means there is a larger base of available support for the standard, and of course, adopting an existing working standard is less work and lower risk than "reinventing the wheel."

The OBEX definition includes:

- An object model to represent data objects. This gives information about objects, and provides a standard format for transferring objects
- A session protocol for transferring requests and responses between devices

The OBEX definition can be downloaded from the Infrared Data Association's Web site. In addition to the parts above, it also includes an application framework, examples of OBEX exchanges, details of how to implement OBEX with other IrDA specifications, and test guidelines.

13.1 OBEX IN THE BLUETOOTH STACK

Figure 13–1 shows the IrDA DATA stack (there is also an IrDA standard for control) and the Bluetooth protocol stack with OBEX. The two stacks have many parallels:

- IrLAP provides reliable, ordered transfer of data and device discovery, as does the LC in Bluetooth.
- IrLMP multiplexes many channels from the higher layers onto lower layer channels, as does L2CAP (although in the case of Bluetooth, this can support multiple ACL links, whereas IrDA supports a single physical link).

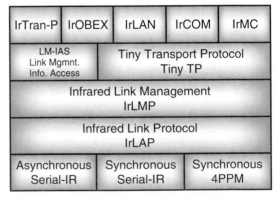

Figure 13–1   Bluetooth and IrDA DATA protocol stacks.

- Tiny TP can provide flow control, segmentation, and reassembly; Bluetooth has flow control in HCI and segmentation and reassembly in L2CAP.
- IrCOMM provides serial and parallel port emulation; RFCOMM does not provide parallel port emulation, but it does provide serial port emulation.

Bluetooth's OBEX is the same as IrOBEX (OBEX is just short for IrOBEX). OBEX provides object exchange services similar to hypertext transfer protocol (htttp), allowing arbitrary data objects to be exchanged between devices.

In the IrDA DATA protocol stack, OBEX can use IrCOM and Tiny TP. The Bluetooth specification does not require these elements of the IrDA DATA stack, but allows for implementations which support them. It is left up to implementers to decide whether to implement these layers.

13.1.1 OBEX over RFCOMM

The Bluetooth specification defines a series of rules for how Bluetooth devices handle OBEX over RFCOMM:

- Bluetooth devices supporting OBEX over RFCOMM must be able to act as either clients or servers.
- If a Bluetooth device runs multiple OBEX servers at once, then each must have its own RFCOMM server channel.
- OBEX applications running as servers must register their service record in the service discovery database. This service record will include an RFCOMM channel number for the OBEX server. The format of OBEX service records is specified in the Bluetooth profiles.

OBEX packets are carried in RFCOMM frames. The data part of an RFCOMM frame is just an undifferentiated byte stream, so the receiving OBEX implementation must sort this byte stream into packets. This should not be difficult because all OBEX packets include a length field, which can be used to figure out where one packet finishes and the next one starts.

13.1.2 OBEX over TCP/IP

Bluetooth specification 1.0 and 1.1 does not specify how to map TCP/IP over Bluetooth links; however, it does give some rules for mapping OBEX over TCP/IP.

- Bluetooth devices supporting OBEX over TCP/IP must be able to act as either clients or servers.
- The server must use port number 650 or a value above 1023. Port number 650 is the recommended setting.
- The client will initialise a socket with a port number above 1023.

- OBEX applications running as servers must register their service record in the service discovery database. The format of OBEX service records is specified in the Bluetooth profiles.

When an OBEX server using TCP/IP starts up, it should initialise its TCP port and register with the service discovery database. When an OBEX client using TCP/IP starts up, it discovers the server's SDP information, initialises a socket (with a number higher than 1023), and establishes a connection to the OBEX server's host. The client then sends an OBEX connect request to the server as described in Section 13.3.3.

To disconnect, the client sends the disconnect request and closes the TCP port.

13.2 OBJECT MODEL

Applications which are going to exchange data need to agree on a standard way of representing it. The object model fills this need by defining a series of headers which can hold data objects and information about them.

Each header carries a piece of information about the object, or in the case of body headers, it can carry the object itself. Figure 13–2 shows the structure of a header: it begins with a single-byte Header ID (HI), which says what information is in the rest of the header and how it is formatted. This is followed by the header value, which is a byte or more of information.

Bits 7 and 8 of the Header ID describe the format of the data in the header value. The choice of formats is:

- 0b00—Two bytes of length followed by a null-terminated Unicode text string (length is an unsigned integer; it covers the header ID and the whole of the header value, including the length bytes and the two bytes of null terminator).
- 0b01—Two bytes of length followed by a byte sequence (length is an unsigned integer sent high byte first; it covers the header ID and the whole of the header value).
- 0b10—A single byte value.
- 0b11—A four byte value, sent high byte first.

Objects do not have to use headers. If two applications know exactly what data they are going to exchange, then headers might not be needed. However, they are available for applications which want to use them.

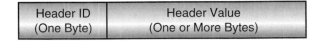

Figure 13–2   An OBEX header.

The type of the header is carried in bits 1 to 6 of the header ID. There are sixteen types of headers defined in version 1.2 of OBEX:

- 0xC0 Count—The number of objects to be sent; a four byte integer.
- 0x01 Name—An object's name; for example, this could be a filename. A name header of length three is used as an empty name header.
- 0x42 Type—The type of an object, sent as null terminated ASCIII text, preferably using IANA registered media types (see http://www.isi.edu/I-notes/iana/assigne ments/media-types). The default type is binary.
- 0xC3 Length—A four byte value giving the length of the object in bytes. For objects over 4Gb, an http content-length header is used instead.
- 0x44 Time—An ISO 8601 version date and timestamp.
- 0xC4 Time—A four-byte date and timestamp. This is for backwards compatibility with applications released before ISO 8601 date and timestamps were used.
- 0x05 Description—A null terminated Unicode text string describing the object.
- 0x46 Target—The name of the service the object is being sent to. OBEX provides a series of well-known target header values. If new target values are defined, they should use Universally Unique Identifiers, or UUIDs (see Chapter 11).
- 0x47 HTTP—An HTTP version 1.x header, including the terminating CRLF.
- 0x48 Body—A part of the object body (could be sent many times for one object where an object is "chunked," or sent in a series of body headers).
- 0x49 End of Body—Identifies the final part (or chunk) of an object body.
- 0x4A Who—The peer OBEX application the object is being sent to, typically a 128 bit UUID of a service which has accepted an OBEX connection.
- 0xCB Connection ID—This is used when multiplexing OBEX connections to identify which particular connection this object is being sent on. When used, this must be the first header sent.
- 0x4C Application Parameters—Information relating to application requests and responses.
- 0x4D Authentication Challenge—An authentication digest-challenge.
- 0x4E Authentication Response—An authentication digest-response.
- 0x4F Object Class—The OBEX object class of the object.

Connection IDs and targets both identify the destination of the headers. Since they fulfill the same purpose, one or the other is used; they are never both used together.

Application parameters, authentication challenges, and authentication responses use an extra layer of structure to carry information. They send triplets of tag, length, and value. The tag and length fields are each one byte, and the value can be up to 255 bytes long. The tag values identify the parameters being passed and are defined by the applications or protocol layers which will use the values. This means that tag values do not have the same meaning to other applications or protocols.

Because each of the headers has its own Header ID, they can be sent in any order, and they will still be interpreted correctly. The connection ID is an exception to this rule, since it says which one of several multiplexed connections the object is being sent on. It must be the first header, so the system knows where to direct the rest of the headers.

In addition to the list above, the range from 0x30 to 0x3F has been reserved for user defined header IDs. Of course these should be used with care, as different systems will interpret them differently; however, the user defined headers provide complete freedom for application developers to transfer data types which are not covered by the standard OBEX headers.

13.3 SESSION PROTOCOL

The OBEX session protocol describes how two OBEX clients and servers can communicate by exchanging request and response messages. The client sends requests and the server sends responses.

13.3.1 Request and Response Packets

Requests are sent as packets. The structure of a request packet is shown in Figure 13–3. Each packet starts with a single byte OpCode which identifies the type of request in the packet. This is followed by a two byte packet length sent high byte first. Finally, the request has one or more headers (as described in Section 13.2).

Because of the two byte length field, the maximum length of a packet is 65535 bytes, and the packet length on a particular connection may be negotiated to a shorter value. This means that large requests may not fit in one packet, so it is possible to split a request across several packets. If a request is split across several packets, the most significant bit of the OpCode is used as a continuation flag. The most-significant bit of the OpCode is set to 1 for the last packet in the request, and set to 0 for all other packets in the request.

Responses have a similar structure to requests as shown in Figure 13–4. A one byte code identifies the type of the response, and again there is a two byte length field. Responses can be split into several packets, with one response packet being sent for every request packet received.

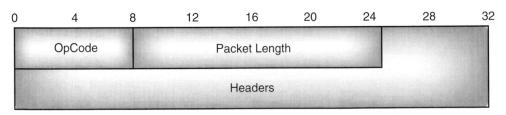

Figure 13–3 Structure of an OBEX request packet.

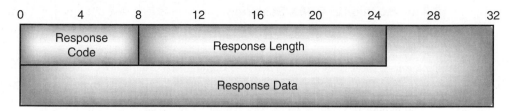

Figure 13–4   Structure of an OBEX response packet.

The response code has an http status code in the seven least significant bits. The most significant bit of the response code is called the final bit and is always set to 1; this lets the client know that it can send another request packet.

The response data can include headers and objects, or other application-specific data. It is possible for a response to carry no data at all; in this case, the response code carries all the information needed to interpret the response, and the length field is set to 3.

When the client sends a request packet with part of a request which will be continued in other packets, the server will usually reply with a "continue" response code (0x10). When the client sends a request packet with the final part of a request, the server will usually reply with a "success" response code (0xA0). The OBEX protocol specification defines a series of other response codes which can be used by the server to indicate various actions and errors.

13.3.2   OBEX Operations

OBEX defines six different operations; these (with their OpCodes) are:

- 0x80 Connect—Used to set up an OBEX connection.
- 0x81 Disconnect—Used to close down an OBEX connection.
- 0x02 Put—Used to send an object.
- 0x03 Get—Used to request an object.
- 0x85 SetPath—Used to set the directory on the receiving side, which information is sent to.
- 0xFF Abort—Used to terminate an operation before it would normally finish. This can only be used with operations which are split across several packets.

In addition, a range of OpCodes are reserved from (0x10 to 0x1F) for user defined operations. As always with user defined elements, care should be taken as these could be misinterpreted by some devices. Versions 1.0 and 1.1 of the Bluetooth specification say that user defined OpCodes will not necessarily be adopted when OBEX is used over Bluetooth.

13.3.3   Setting Up OBEX Sessions

Before a Bluetooth device can start an OBEX session, it must know the correct RFCOMM channel to use. The OBEX client sends SDP requests to the server to find out information on the OBEX server. The OBEX client then establishes an RFCOMM channel to the OBEX server using the channel number given in the OBEX server's service record.

Next, an OBEX session is started by the client sending a connect request. The connect request contains the parameters for the session. The server accepts the request by sending a response with response code = success. Any other response rejects the connection.

The session will remain in place until it is deliberately disconnected by the client, or until some sort of failure causes it to be shut down; for example, if one device goes out of range and the underlying ACL link times out.

Figure 13–5 illustrates the various stages in a client setting up an OBEX session over a Bluetooth link.

The structure of the connect request is shown in Figure 13–6. It begins with the OpCode and packet length common to all OBEX requests.

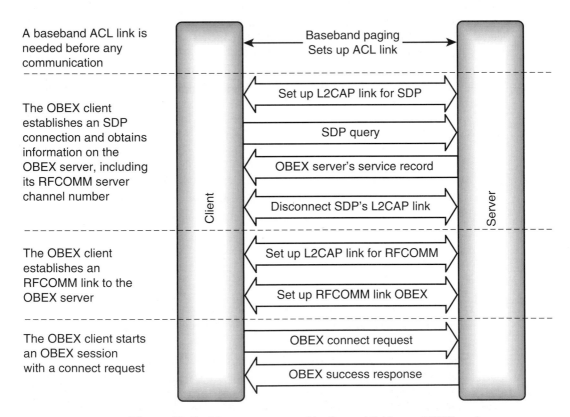

Figure 13–5   Message sequence chart for establishing an OBEX session.

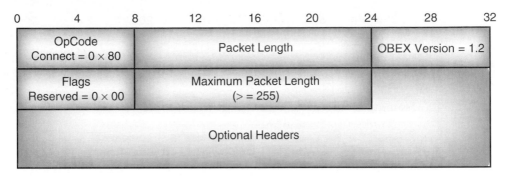

Figure 13–6   Structure of an OBEX connect request.

The third byte of the connect request gives the version of OBEX which the client proposes to use for the session. The Bluetooth version 1.0 and 1.1 specifications reference version 1.2 of OBEX, so Bluetooth devices should be capable of handling this version of OBEX, and this should be the default type for a connect message. The version number is encoded with the major version (1) in the four most significant bits and the minor version (.2) in the four least significant bits. So, version 1.2 is represented as 0x12.

In version 1.2 of OBEX, the flag bits in a request are all reserved; they should be set to 0 by the client and ignored by the server.

The maximum OBEX packet length a client can receive can be used to restrict the length of packets to a value less than the maximum defined by OBEX (OBEX's maximum packet length is limited by the two-byte packet length field to 65535). The maximum packet length should never be set to less than 255 bytes, otherwise requests and responses which have to be sent in a single packet might not fit.

Optionally, other headers can be sent in the connect request packet, but the connect request is not allowed to be split across more than one packet, so this may limit the headers which can be sent.

Count and length headers may be used to indicate how much data will be sent during the session. Target or who headers may be used to indicate where to send the data. Description headers may be used to describe the connecting device or service.

A server is allowed to discard headers which it does not understand; in particular, it may not understand user defined headers. Because all headers have a standard format for their format and length, devices should be able to interpret enough of any header to figure out how long it is so that it can be cleanly discarded without affecting other headers in the packet.

The structure of the response to a successful connect request is shown in Figure 13–7. Any response code other than success (0xA0) means that the request has not succeeded. The response code and packet length follow the common format used by all OBEX packets. The version number is encoded in the same way as in the connect request, and should also indicate version 1.2 for OBEX on Bluetooth 1.0 and 1.1 implementations.

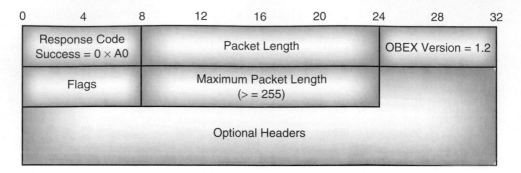

Figure 13–7 Structure of an OBEX connect response.

Bit 0 of the flag field is used to indicate that multiple OBEX connections can be handled. The rest of the response flags are reserved and should be set to 0 by the sending server and ignored by the receiving client.

The maximum packet length limits the size of the packet the server is willing to accept; this is not necessarily the same as the length the client was willing to accept.

The optional headers can include a description header, which describes the device or service handling the connection. If the connect fails, the optional headers can include a description header, which gives more information on why it failed.

It is possible to use OBEX commands to transfer objects even if a connect request has not been sent, although if this is done, there is no guarantee that opposite ends of the link are using compatible settings. If default values are being used, a maximum packet length of 255 bytes should be assumed since all implementations should be able to handle these size packets.

13.3.4   Closing Down OBEX Sessions

A client can shut down an OBEX session with a disconnect request as shown in Figure 13–8. If a disconnect message is sent, it contains the usual OpCode and packet length, and optionally can contain more headers describing why the link is being shut down.

A disconnect message cannot be refused, so the server should always respond with a packet containing the response code "success."

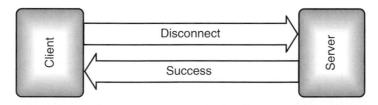

Figure 13–8   Message sequence chart for closing down an OBEX session.

The Bluetooth core specification says that a disconnect message should be sent to close down an OBEX session. However, a session can also be shut down just by closing down the underlying links. This may happen if a device moves out of range, so all Bluetooth implementations must be able to terminate OBEX sessions if underlying links are shut down.

13.3.5   Transferring Objects from Client to Server

A put request is used to send an object from a client to a server. Usually, the put request will include name and length headers, as well as a body header for the data.

For a small object, a put request may fit into one packet. Figure 13–9 shows a message sequence chart where this is the case. The client sets the final bit to indicate that this is the last packet in the request, and sends the put request, including the object, in an end of body header. The server replies with a response containing the response code "success" to indicate that it has accepted the object.

Objects such as files may not fit in one request packet. In this case, the client will send a series of put request packets as shown in Figure 13–10. All the put request packets except the final one will have a chunk of the object sent in a body header. The final packet puts the last chunk of the object in an end of body header. The final flag in all the put requests except for the last one is set to 0 to indicate that there is more of the request to come. The last packet in the put request is set to 1 to indicate that it is the end of the put request.

The server responds to put requests which do not have the final flag set with continue responses. When the server receives a put request with the final flag set, it responds with success (assuming there have been no errors in the transfer). All response packets have the final flag set to 1, regardless of whether they are responses to put requests which will be continued or to the final put request.

The put request can use any OBEX headers to describe the object being sent to the server. These should come before the body headers so that the server knows what sort of object it is using before it gets the object (although it is only mandatory for name and type headers to precede the body, an awkward implementer could choose to send other headers after the body).

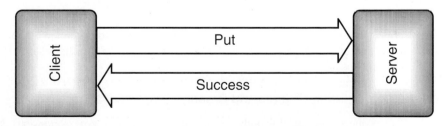

Figure 13–9   Message sequence chart for transferring a small object from client to server.

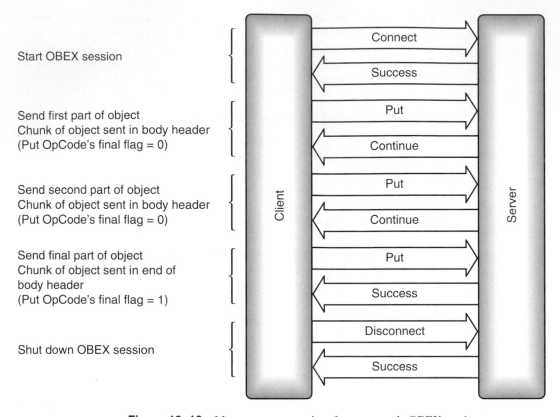

Start OBEX session

Send first part of object
Chunk of object sent in body header
(Put OpCode's final flag = 0)

Send second part of object
Chunk of object sent in body header
(Put OpCode's final flag = 0)

Send final part of object
Chunk of object sent in end of
body header
(Put OpCode's final flag = 1)

Shut down OBEX session

Connect
Success
Put
Continue
Put
Continue
Put
Success
Disconnect
Success

Client

Server

Figure 13–10   Message sequence chart for an example OBEX session.

The client can use target and type headers to suggest what the server should do with the object being sent, but it is entirely up to the server whether it chooses to obey those suggestions.

The server can use a setpath operation to suggest a directory into which objects will be transferred. This is particularly useful if a whole hierarchy of files and folders is being transferred. Setpath can be used to create a directory, then put places objects in the directory. However, again the server could choose not to follow the directions. For instance, it is common for all received objects to be placed in a directory labeled "incoming." In systems which do this, if a client specified the directory /etc/bin, the result would be to put files in incoming/etc/bin.

13.3.6   Deleting Objects and Creating Empty Objects

A put request without any body or end of body headers puts a non-existent object on the server. If an object with the specified name exists in the current working directory, then that object is deleted. Devices are not required to support delete operations.

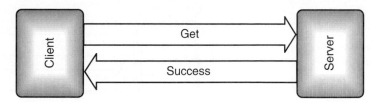

Figure 13–11　Message sequence chart for transferring a small object from server to client.

A put request with an empty end of body header creates an empty object; for instance, this might be used to create an empty file.

13.3.7　Transferring Objects from Server to Client

The get operation is used to request an object from the server. A get request begins with the OpCode (0x03) and two bytes of packet length. Then there are optionally a series of headers giving information about the object to get. Usually, a name header would be included to specify which object to get; however, it is possible that some applications may only ever get one object, in which case, as long as both sides know this, there is no need to specify a name.

As Figure 13–11 shows, the server replies with the return code "success" if it accepts the get. If the object is small enough to fit in a single OBEX packet, the server also sends the requested object in an end of body header in the response packet.

As for get requests, it is possible that the requested object will not fit into a single OBEX packet. In this case, the server sends a continue response with part of the object in a body header. The client keeps sending get requests until it receives a success response, indicating that it has the final part of the object as shown in Figure 13–12.

Note that the final flag in every response is set to 1. Unless the client continues to send get requests, the transaction will finish.

It is possible to get default objects of certain types; for example, a default business card or a default Web page. In this case, the full details of the object would not have to be specified in the get request's headers.

13.4　SUMMARY

OBEX (Object Exchange) is a protocol for transferring data objects between devices that Bluetooth has adopted from the Infrared Data Association (IrDA) specifications.

OBEX defines a session protocol which is used to send requests from a client to a server. The server replies with responses. Both requests and responses are sent in packets.

Response has first part of object
Chunk of object sent in body header
(Put Response code's final flag = 1)

Response has second part of object
Chunk of object sent in body header
(Put OpCode's final flag = 1)

Response has final part of object
Chunk of object sent in end of
body header
(Put OpCode's final flag = 1)

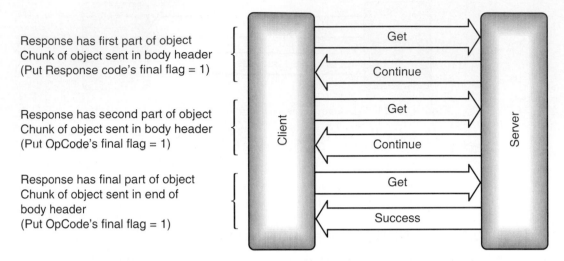

Figure 13–12   Message sequence chart for getting a large object from server to client.

OBEX packets can contain various headers which describe data, and body headers which contain chunks of data.

OBEX can specify a particular service or protocol which receives data objects, and can also specify a directory in which objects such as files should be placed. Although it is up to the device receiving files where to put them, it is not forced to follow the path suggestions of the sending device. For example, if a sender asks for a file to go in the Windows directory, the receiving device could choose to put the file in a directory called incoming\Windows. This allows a user to "quarantine" files in an area where they can be checked before they are put into use.

The Bluetooth specification references version 1.2 of the OBEX specification, which was written in March 1999.

14

The Telephony Control Protocol

Bluetooth's Telephony Control protocol Specification (TCS) defines how telephone calls should be sent across a Bluetooth link. It gives guidelines for the signalling needed to set up both point to point, and point to multipoint calls. It also provides a way to send DTMF tones across a Bluetooth link. TCS is adapted from ITU-T Recommendation Q.931. Bluetooth also defines a subset of TCS called "lean TCS".

The acronym used for telephony control does not fit in with the convention used in the rest of the Bluetooth stack. The Link Manager Protocol specification is abbreviated to LMP, the Logical Link Control and Adaptation Protocol specification is abbreviated to L2CAP, but the Telephony Control protocol Specification is abbreviated to TCS. The reason for not following the convention of the rest of Bluetooth is that the acronym TCP is so widely used for the Internet task control protocol that reusing the same acronym would be certain to cause confusion.

Figure 14–1 shows how TCS fits into the rest of the Bluetooth protocol stack. A hostless system is shown so there is no Host Controller Interface (HCI) layer. If TCS were implemented on a system with HCI, then the HCI layer would sit below L2CAP and above the baseband and Link Manager.

Telephony control relies upon the presence of a speech synchronisation and control system which can be used to set up speech paths through the baseband using SCO links.

Telephony control is split up into four parts:

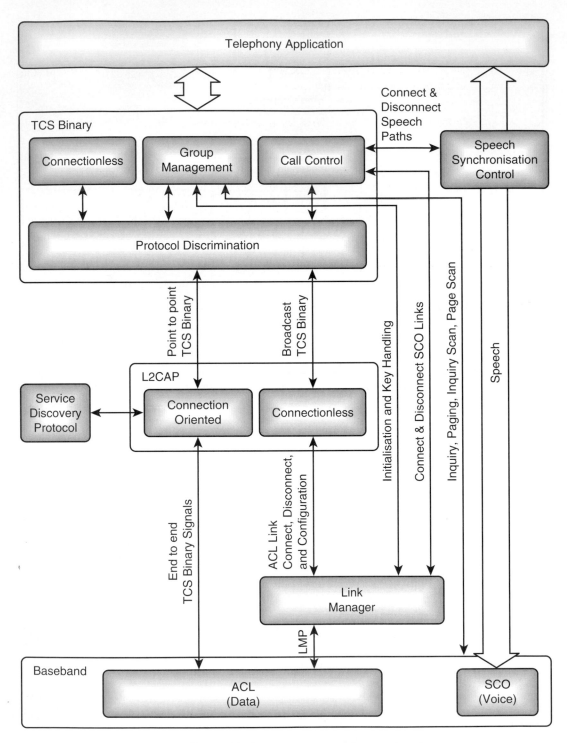

Figure 14–1 Telephony control protocol stack.

- Call control—Handles connection and disconnection.
- Group management—Handles groups of devices; this part manages inquiry, paging, and scanning, as well as security.
- Connectionless—Handles broadcast information.
- Protocol discrimination—Handles directing messages between the other parts of TCS and L2CAP.

TCS is driven by a telephony application which provides the user interface, and provides the source of voice or data transferred across the connections set up by TCS.

The specification for TCS suggests that multiple calls could be handled by running multiple instances of TCS, each with its own L2CAP channel identifier. The assigned numbers part of the Bluetooth core specification allocates L2CAP protocol service multiplexer numbers for TCS-BIN and for TCS-BIN cordless. The mechanism by which more instances could be identified has not been defined.

14.1 TCS SIGNALLING

TCS signalling messages are carried in the payload of L2CAP packets. TCS adapts the format used by Q.931, as not all of the information is required. For comparison, Figure 14–2 shows the original Q.931 structure and Figure 14–3 shows the structure used in TCS. Q.931 has extra length fields and also has a call reference value (a handle used to connect a call with a local application which registered the call and which will handle cancellation of the call).

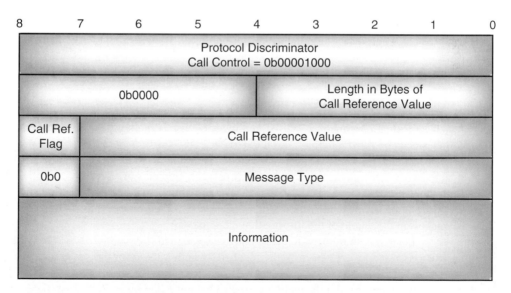

Figure 14–2 Structure of a Q.931 signalling message.

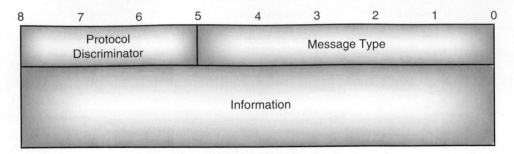

Figure 14–3   Structure of a TCS signalling message.

Note that in Figure 14–2, and elsewhere in this chapter, the least significant bit is on the right. This is the opposite of the convention used in other chapters, but follows the form used in the Q.931 standard and in the TCS part of the Bluetooth specification. Q.931 and TCS use a different convention for bit ordering from most Bluetooth protocols, so care should be taken when interpreting messages that the Endianness is correct.

The three bits of the protocol discriminator field are used to distinguish between Call Control (CC) messages and other TCS messages. It has three possible values:

- 0b000—Call Control (CC) signalling.
- 0b001—Group Management (GM) signalling.
- 0b010—Connectionless (CL) signalling.

The five bits of message type are used to identify which message is being sent. The message types can be divided up into groups: call establishment, call clearing, miscellaneous, group management, and connectionless. The following sections examine the groups of signals and describe how they are used.

14.1.1   Information Elements

The information part of a TCS signalling message is made up of information elements. These can be fixed length or variable length.

Figure 14–4 shows the two types of fixed length information elements: single byte and two byte elements. Fixed length information elements always have a single bit flag in bit 8 of the first byte, which is set to 1. The remaining seven bits of the first byte carry an information element identifier. For a single byte, fixed length information element, this makes up the whole of the information element.

Double byte information elements have the identifier followed by a byte of content. It is possible to work out from the identifier whether the information element will be one or two bytes.

Variable length information elements have the flag bit set to 0. Just like fixed length information elements, they begin with seven bits of information element identifier, which

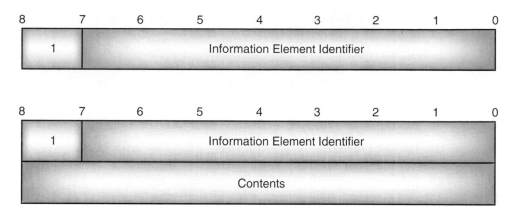

Figure 14–4   Fixed length information elements.

is followed by a single byte length field giving the length of the rest of the information in bytes, and finally the content follows in the rest of the information element. A variable length information element is illustrated in Figure 14–5.

It is possible to have a variable length information element with a length of 0; this is interpreted as if it were absent from the message. Only optional information elements can be sent with the length set to 0.

Most TCS messages have an optional company specific information element. (In fact, only the five messages dealing with DTMF tone generation don't have an optional company specific information element.) This allows designers to add their own extensions to TCS, but of course, care should be taken when using these because all devices must be able to interoperate with devices which don't support added in company specific features. The company specific information element includes a company identifier. This is needed so that one company's commands aren't confused with another's. Company

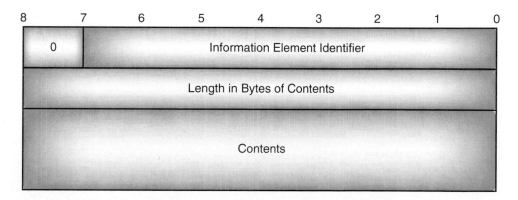

Figure 14–5   Variable length information element.

identifiers have been allocated for the original promoters group: Ericsson, Nokia Mobile Phones, Intel Corporation, IBM Corporation, and Toshiba Corporation; all other values are reserved. This means that unless more numbers are allocated in future versions of the specification, other companies should not add proprietary extensions to the specification (if they do, they risk these extensions being misinterpreted by other devices, and causing unpredicted effects).

14.2   CALL ESTABLISHMENT SIGNALLING

Call establishment messages (with their type values) are:

- 0b00101—SETUP.
- 0b00110—SETUP ACKNOWLEDGE.
- 0b01010—INFORMATION.
- 0b00100—PROGRESS.
- 0b00000—ALERTING.
- 0b00001—CALL PROCEEDING.
- 0b00010—CONNECT.
- 0b00011—CONNECT ACKNOWLEDGE.

TCS calls can be set up using signalling on a point to point channel or a point to multipoint channel. Point to point would be used when it is known exactly which device the call is intended for. Point to multipoint could be used when a variety of devices might answer the call. For example, a home telephony system might want to send a call alert to every phone in range, whichever phone answers first then takes the call.

Figure 14–6 shows the simpler connection scenario where a call is routed to one known device. First an L2CAP channel is established to the device, then a call request is

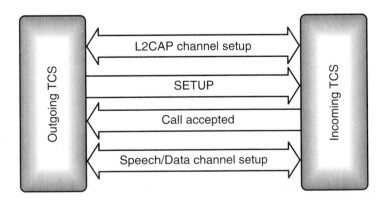

Figure 14–6 Connecting a point to point call.

Call request signal sent to all
devices by broadcast

Device accepting call sets up
point to point L2CAP channel

Call accepts signal sent on
point to point L2CAP channel

Speech or data channel
established

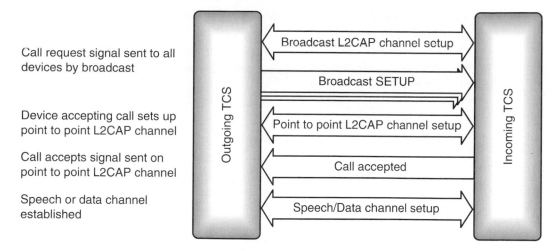

Figure 14–7   Connecting a point to multipoint call.

sent on the L2CAP channel. If the call is accepted, then a speech or data channel is set up between the two devices.

Setting up a call via the broadcast channel is shown in Figure 14–7. It is a little more complex than setting up a point to point call. The signal must be broadcast on the beacon channel. The beacon channel reaches Slaves which are parked, as well as active Slaves. (The broadcast signal may not reach Slaves in Park or Sniff mode.) Only the Master of a piconet may broadcast on the beacon channel, so only the Master may broadcast a call request.

Slaves wishing to accept the call request may not have an active TCS L2CAP signalling channel available. If they do not, then they must set up an L2CAP channel using the Protocol and Service Multiplexer (PSM) number reserved for TCS, which is 0x0005. This will be a point to point link. Once this link has been established, then the device can accept the call on it, and both devices can go on to establish a link for voice or data traffic.

It is possible when a SETUP message is broadcast that several devices will be willing to accept the call, so several devices will answer. For example, a home telephony system could have several handsets all capable of answering incoming phone calls on the same home phone number. TCS only supports point to point calls, so the connection can only be made to one device. The connection will be made to the first device which answers; any other devices which answered the SETUP message but were not assigned the call are sent RELEASE messages to let them know they will not receive a connection.

14.2.1   SETUP Message

The SETUP message carries all the information needed to establish a data or voice connection for a call:

- Call class—Identifies a call as an external call, internal call, service call, or emergency call.
- Sending complete—Sent when the called party number is complete.
- Bearer capability—Gives information on the required capabilities for the link to be used as a TCS bearer channel.
- Signal—Information about whether tones and alerts a handset can generate are switched on or off.
- Calling party number—The number which originated the call.
- Called party information number digits—The number the call is directed to.
- Company specific—This information element can be used to add vendor specific information to any message.

Only the call class is mandatory. The call class is external call for a call connected to a third party on an external network, for example, GSM, ISDN, or PSTN. The call class is internal call for an intercom call, that is to say, a call between two members of a Wireless User Group (see Section 14.5 for more on wireless user groups). The call class is service call for a call which is just used to transfer configuration information. An emergency call is a special class of external call; it has its own call class because emergency calls are often handled differently from normal calls. For example, emergency calls are not charged to the user, and on GSM networks, the SIM card which authorises network access is not needed for emergency calls.

The bearer capability describes the type of link which is needed for the call. It includes the link type (SCO for voice or ACL for data), the packet type (HV1, HV2, HV3, or DV), the voice coding (CVSD, PCM A-law, or PCM μ-law), and the quality of service parameters for the link. If there is no bearer information, then the link type defaults to a SCO link using CVSD coding and HV3 packets.

In Q.931 as in TCS, the signal information element says whether tones and alerts are on or off. Q.931 has values for setting ring, intercept, network congestion, confirm, answer, call waiting, off-hook warning, preemption, and various alerting tones. Bluetooth versions 1.0 and 1.1 have just three possible values: external call, internal call, and call back. TCS has a very limited set of tones compared with the range the Q.931 standard supports, presumably the reasoning behind this is that limiting the range of tones generated will make implementing TCS tone generation simpler. However, it is also possible that this part of the TCS specification needs more work, because it is unclear from the values how a tone is switched on and off. In Q.931, the signal information element has different values when switching a tone on and off, whereas TCS only has one value for each of external call, internal call, and call back.

14.2.2   Message Sequences for Establishing a Call

The SETUP message is the first message sent when establishing a call. In lean TCS, it only has to carry a call class to say whether the call is internal, external, service, or emergency.

If lean TCS is not being used and the SETUP message doesn't have a sending complete information element, the called party number might be incomplete. If an incoming side isn't using lean TCS and suspects the called party number is incomplete, then it has to try to get some more information. It does this by sending a SETUP acknowledgement message.

The outgoing (calling) side responds with one or more INFORMATION messages. When the incoming side gets a message with a sending complete information element or otherwise works out that it has the whole of the called number, then it sends a CALL PROCEEDING message to the outgoing side, to let that side know that it is processing the call.

Next, the incoming side starts alerting its user; typically this would involve sounding a ring tone or tune to let the user know a call is coming in. The incoming side sends an ALERTING message to let the outgoing side know that the user is being alerted.

When the user accepts the call (usually by pressing a button), the incoming side tells the outgoing side by sending a CONNECT message. The outgoing side replies with a CONNECT accept message and the call begins. The call setup messages are shown in Figure 14–8.

The SETUP message may carry all the information needed to connect, in which case, the SETUP ACKNOWLEDGE and INFORMATION messages are not needed.

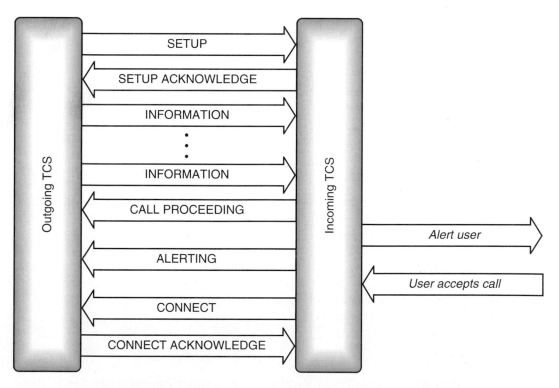

Figure 14–8   Message sequence chart for TCS connection with optional messages.

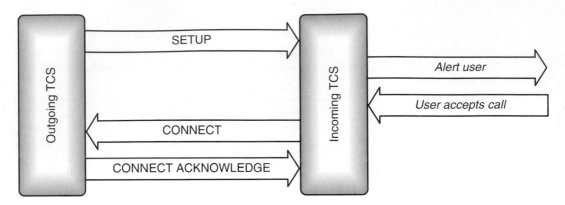

Figure 14–9   Lean TCS message sequence chart for TCS connection.

Also, the incoming side can omit either of the CALL PROCEEDING and ALERTING messages.

Figure 14–9 shows a minimal set of messages to establish a connection. This minimal set would be implemented by a device using lean TCS.

If a SCO link is being used as the bearer for the call, then the SCO link initialisation is started before the CONNECT message is sent. The audio path is connected to the SCO link when the CONNECT or CONNECT ACKNOWLEDGE message is received.

14.2.3   Timeouts

What happens if the call isn't picked up? Even a normal PSTN phone will not ring forever; eventually the network will decide that nobody is going to answer the call and will disconnect. With Bluetooth devices setting up calls over TCS, there may be no network involved, so the devices have to decide for themselves when to give up trying to connect a call.

To do this, the outgoing device starts a 20 s timer, T303, when it sends the SETUP message. If there is no response to the setup message by the time T303 expires, then the outgoing side gives up on the call. What it does depends upon whether the SETUP message was broadcast or sent to one device.

- If the SETUP message was broadcast, the outgoing side just gives up on the call.
- If the SETUP message was sent point to point to one device, then a RELEASE COMPLETE message is sent to the same device.

The release complete message has a parameter which specifies why the call was released. In this case, the parameter is set to 102, which means "recovery on timer expiry".

Similarly, a series of other timeouts are used throughout call establishment. These are illustrated in Figure 14–10. There is no timeout defined on the incoming side during

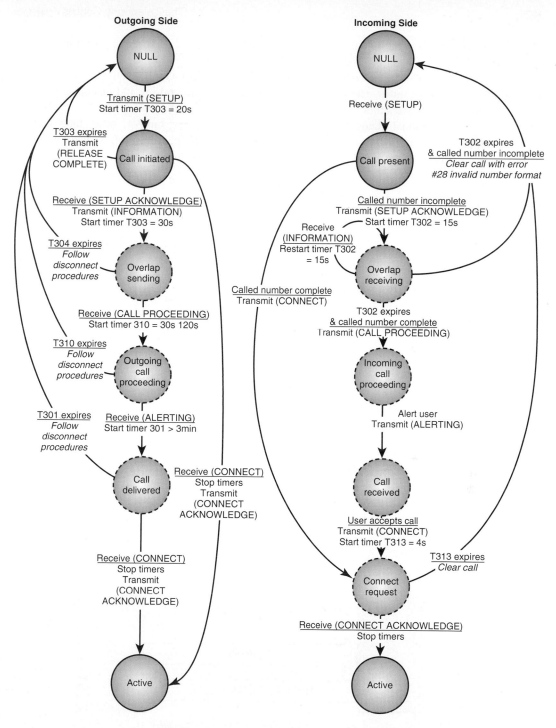

Outgoing Side

NULL

Transmit (SETUP)
Start timer T303 = 20s

T303 expires
Transmit
(RELEASE
COMPLETE)

Call initiated

Receive (SETUP ACKNOWLEDGE)
Transmit (INFORMATION)
Start timer T303 = 30s

T304 expires
Follow
disconnect
procedures

Overlap
sending

Receive (CALL PROCEEDING)
Start timer 310 = 30s 120s

T310 expires
Follow
disconnect
procedures

Outgoing
call
proceeding

T301 expires
Follow
disconnect
procedures

Receive (ALERTING)
Start timer 301 > 3min

Call
delivered

Receive (CONNECT)
Stop timers
Transmit
(CONNECT
ACKNOWLEDGE)

Receive (CONNECT)
Stop timers
Transmit
(CONNECT
ACKNOWLEDGE)

Active

Incoming Side

NULL

Receive (SETUP)

T302 expires
& called number incomplete
*Clear call with error
#28 invalid number format*

Call present

Called number incomplete
Transmit (SETUP ACKNOWLEDGE)
Start timer T302 = 15s

Receive
(INFORMATION)
Restart timer T302
= 15s

Overlap
receiving

Called number complete
Transmit (CONNECT)

T302 expires
& called number complete
Transmit (CALL PROCEEDING)

Incoming
call
proceeding

Alert user
Transmit (ALERTING)

Call
received

User accepts call
Transmit (CONNECT)
Start timer T313 = 4s

T313 expires
Clear call

Connect
request

Receive (CONNECT ACKNOWLEDGE)
Stop timers

Active

Figure 14–10   States involved in call establishment.

the period when the user is being alerted. The assumption is that the application will implement its own timeout and either accept or reject the call.

For lean TCS, the outgoing (left) side of the diagram would just have null, call initiated, and active states. The incoming (right) side of the diagram would just have null, call present, and active states.

The optional states are shown with dashed outlines; any of these states can be skipped. For clarity, Figure 14–10 does not show all the possible state transitions when some of the optional states are skipped.

14.3   CALL CLEARING SIGNALLING

The disconnect procedure uses three call clearing messages:

- 0b00111—DISCONNECT.
- 0b01000—RELEASE.
- 0b01001—RELEASE COMPLETE.

Either the incoming or outgoing side can start a disconnect by disconnecting from the bearer channel and sending a DISCONNECT message. The side receiving the disconnect message also disconnects from the bearer channel and sends a RELEASE message and goes to the null state. When the side which initiated the disconnect receives a RELEASE COMPLETE message, it too goes to the null state. The message exchange to disconnect is shown in Figure 14–11.

The side which transmits the DISCONNECT starts a 30 s timer, T305, when it sends the DISCONNECT message. If this expires it sends a RELEASE message.

Whenever a RELEASE message is sent, a 4 s timer, T308, is started. If the timer expires before a RELEASE COMPLETE is received, the side which sent the RELEASE returns to the null state. This applies whether the RELEASE was sent because a DISCONNECT was received, or because T305 timed out.

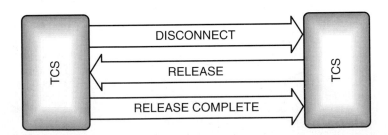

Figure 14–11   Message sequence chart for call clearing.

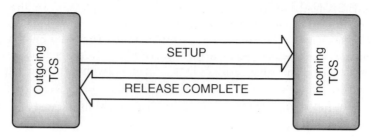

Figure 14–12   Message sequence chart for rejecting a call.

The outgoing side can send in band tones while the call is being cleared. If it wants to do this, it tells the other side by sending the progress indicator message "#8 in-band information or appropriate pattern is now available" in the DISCONNECT signal.

A call can also be cleared by the incoming side rejecting a SETUP message by responding with a RELEASE COMPLETE message, as shown in Figure 14–12.

When a SETUP signal is sent on the broadcast channel, it is possible that more than one device will respond. The outgoing side sends a release message to any device which sends a SETUP ACKNOWLEDGE, CALL PROCEEDING, ALERTING, or CONNECT and which hasn't been selected for the connection. These messages are sent on the L2CAP channel the device responded on. The messages for call clearing are shown in Figure 14–13.

Because a call is only assigned to one device, it is not possible for multiple devices to join in on a call at the same time. This means that TCS is limited to point to point links; it does not support conference calls among Bluetooth devices in a WUG.

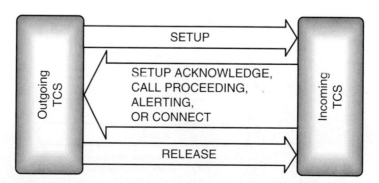

Figure 14–13   Message sequence chart for clearing a call to a multipoint device.

14.4   DTMF SIGNALLING

TCS messages can be used to control DTMF (Dual Tone Multiple Frequency) tone generation. DTMF tones are pairs of tones sounded together which are used to send numbers down a phone line. The messages in this category (with their type values) are:

- 0b10000: Start DTMF—Starts a DTMF tone at the far end of a link.
- 0b10001: Start DTMF acknowledge—Confirms that the tone is being sounded.
- 0b10010: Start DTMF reject—Refuses a start DTMF message.
- 0b10011: Stop DTMF—Stops a DTMF tone at the far end of the link.
- 0b10100: Stop DTMF acknowledge—Confirms that the tone has been stopped.

DTMF tones can only be sent while a call is in the active state.

To get a device to generate DTMF tones, it is sent a start DTMF message. The side receiving the message can either reject it with a start DTMF reject message, or begin generating a tone and respond with a start DTMF acknowledge message.

To stop a DTMF tone, a stop DTMF message is sent. This message cannot be rejected, so the DTMF tone generation is always stopped and a stop DTMF acknowledge reply sent.

14.4.1   Register Recall

In register recall, a register in a mobile phone handset is seized by an incoming call so that a value can be entered into the register, or so that some action in the handset can be triggered.

To do this in TCS, an INFORMATION message is sent with a keypad facility information element set to 0x16 = register recall. Once the INFORMATION message has been sent, numbers can be sent as DTMF tones using the DTMF tone control messages as shown in Figure 14–14. In this way, the far end of the link can control a phone handset as if its keypad buttons were being pressed.

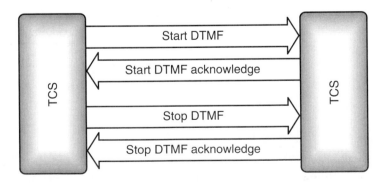

Figure 14–14   Message sequence chart for DTMF tone generation.

14.5   WIRELESS USER GROUP (WUG) SIGNALLING

A Wireless User Group (WUG) is a collection of Bluetooth devices which support TCS. When devices in a WUG are joined in a piconet, the Master of the piconet is also the Master of the WUG. WUG functions are provided by the Group Management (GM) part of TCS (see Figure 14–15).

The Master of a piconet communicates with every device in the piconet, but the Slaves only communicate directly with the Master. So, it makes sense for the Master to act as a co-ordinator for the WUG by gathering information and distributing it to the Slaves.

The Master coordinates the WUG by telling the members of the WUG which other devices are in the same WUG. The Master also coordinates authentication by telling all the members the parameters they should use for authentication and encryption. Because the Master distributes authentication and encryption information, once a Slave has paired with the WUG Master, it can use the same parameters for any WUG member without pairing again. This means that establishing secure links within a WUG is faster because the pairing step can be skipped.

The GM messages (with their type values) are:

- 0b00110—ACCESS RIGHTS REQUEST.
- 0b00111—ACCESS RIGHTS ACCEPT.
- 0b01000—ACCESS RIGHTS REJECT.
- 0b00000—INFO SUGGEST.

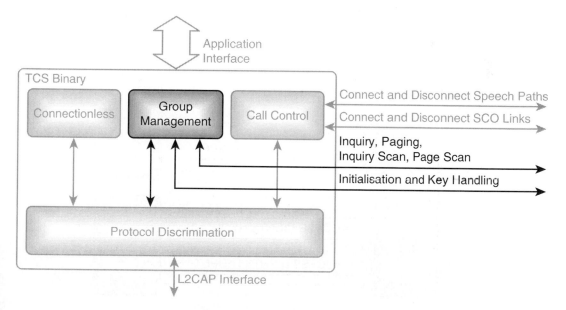

Figure 14–15   TCS group management.

- 0b00001—INFO ACCEPT.
- 0b00010—LISTEN REQUEST.
- 0b00100—LISTEN SUGGEST.
- 0b00011—LISTEN ACCEPT.
- 0b00101—LISTEN REJECT.

ACCESS RIGHTS messages are used when devices join a WUG. INFO messages are used to distribute information needed to connect between WUG members. LISTEN messages are used by WUG members to connect directly to one another, bypassing the WUG Master.

14.5.1   Joining a WUG

For a device to join a WUG as an active member, it must first join the piconet where the Master is the WUG Master. The device joining can stop there and just use the TCS services of the WUG Master, or it can ask for full access rights to the WUG.

To ask for access rights to the WUG, the new device sends an ACCESS RIGHTS REQUEST message to the WUG Master. As shown in Figure 14–16, the Master can choose to accept or reject the new joiner. Every WUG member is given access to security information on all WUG members, so it is important that the WUG Master does not accept the access rights request if it does not trust the joining device.

14.5.2   Configuration Distribution

Unlike normal networks, Bluetooth piconets can frequently change their configuration as devices move in and out of range. This means that the members of a WUG which are visible to the Master can keep changing. The Master needs to be able to tell all the members of the WUG when a WUG member disappears or a new member appears.

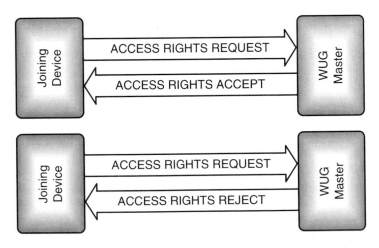

Figure 14–16   Message sequence charts for obtaining access rights.

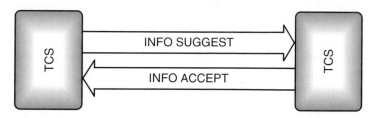

Figure 14–17   Message sequence chart for configuration distribution.

To do this, the Master sends information to all the WUG members it can see using an INFO SUGGEST message. The WUG member replies with an INFO ACCEPT message (Figure 14–17). There is no message for refusing the INFO SUGGEST message, but the WUG members are not forced to store and use the information it contains.

The INFO SUGGEST message carries a configuration data information element. This begins with the standard fields for a variable length information element: the information element identifier (0b00000001), followed by the length of the contents in bytes. Next, the configuration information for each active member of the WUG is listed, starting with the lowest numbered WUG member. The information given is:

- Two bytes of internal number, encoded in IA5 characters.
- Six bytes of Bluetooth address.
- Sixteen bytes of link key for using on the outgoing channel to the WUG member.

Every time the configuration of the WUG changes, all information needed to contact every active member of the WUG is sent.

It may seem insecure to send all the link keys every time the WUG configuration changes, but because all communications within a WUG are encrypted, they are always transmitted in encrypted form. To keep the configuration information as secure as possible, the Master does not broadcast it, instead the Master transmits the INFO SUGGEST message separately to each device on a point to point channel using that device's link key.

Handing over every single device's link keys to any new WUG member means that member has access to all the services provided by every other WUG member. This is the reason why the WUG Master is allowed to refuse a new member sending an ACCESS REQUEST to join the WUG.

14.5.3   Fast Intermember Access

There would be no point in handing out information on the link keys of WUG members if they could only communicate through the Master, so not surprisingly, WUGs have facilities for links to be set up directly between members.

A WUG member which wants to talk directly to another WUG member sends a LISTEN REQUEST message to the WUG Master. This message carries the number of the

WUG member the sender wants to connect with. The Master forwards a LISTEN SUGGEST message to the WUG member identified by the number in the LISTEN REQUEST message.

The LISTEN SUGGEST message has at most two information elements: one identifying the type of the message and an optional element for company specific information. This means that the WUG member receiving the LISTEN SUGGEST knows another device wants to establish a link with it, but has no idea who the other device is.

If the device receiving the LISTEN SUGGEST is willing to link directly with another WUG member, it replies with a LISTEN ACCEPT containing its clock offset, and the Master forwards this to the device which requested the link.

The message sequences for accepting a LISTEN REQUEST are shown in Figure 14–18.

The clock offset in the LISTEN ACCEPT message has to be an offset from the WUG Master's clock since this is the clock that all WUG members are synchronised with, and it is their only common point of reference.

The device sending the LISTEN ACCEPT message starts a 2 s timer, T405, and begins page scanning immediately after sending the message. The device which sent the original LISTEN REQUEST receives the LISTEN ACCEPT and immediately uses the clock offset information to start paging the device it wants to connect with.

Setting up a connection between two WUG members in this way is faster than normal paging and page scanning for two reasons. First, the devices can guarantee that their paging and page scanning will be in phase; they don't have a delay while they wait for a page and page scan to coincide. Second, because the paging device knows the clock offset of the page scanning device, it can predict what frequency it will be scanning on, so it can hop onto that frequency faster than if it were just probing randomly.

It is possible that the LISTEN SUGGEST will be rejected. The two possible sequences for a LISTEN SUGGEST being rejected are shown in Figure 14–19.

The top chart shows the Master rejecting the message. This can happen for three reasons. First, it can occur when the WUG member uses a called party number which doesn't match any of the devices in the WUG. In this case, the Master replies with a LISTEN REJECT message containing the error code "#1 unallocated (unassigned) number". Second,

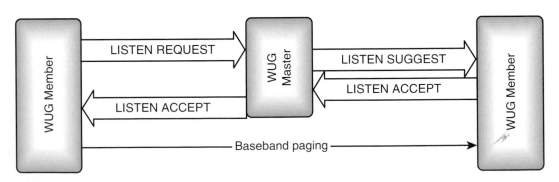

Figure 14–18   Message sequence chart for fast intermember access.

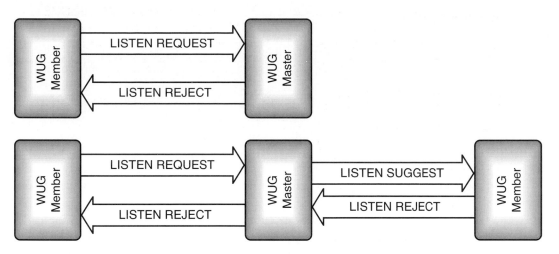

Figure 14–19 Message sequence charts for rejecting fast intermember access.

the Master can reject when the called number is valid but the device isn't answering (probably because it moved out of the range of the Master). In this case, the Master replies with a LISTEN REJECT message containing the error code "#20, Subscriber absent". The third possible reason for rejecting is when the called party number belongs to a WUG member which is already involved in an external call via the WUG Master. In this case, the Master replies with a LISTEN REJECT message containing the error code "#17, User busy".

The lower chart shows the second WUG member rejecting the connection. The user is only allowed to reject the call if it is already involved in an internal call within the WUG. In this case, the call is rejected with a LISTEN REJECT message containing the error code "#17, User busy".

14.6 CONNECTIONLESS SIGNALLING

There is just one connectionless message:

- 0b00000—CL INFO.

The CL INFO message can carry audio control information and vendor specific information. It does not apply to a specific channel.

The audio control information element can be used to increase or decrease volume and microphone gain.

When TCS signalling messages are sent on the connectionless (broadcast) channel, the Master must switch from using the usual semi-permanent link keys to using K_{Master}, the broadcast link keys. For more details on security on the broadcast link, see Chapter 15.

14.7   TCS CALL STATES

TCS uses the user side of Q.931, however this is still quite complex, so a subset of Q.931 states has been defined called "lean TCS". Figure 14–20 shows the state transition diagram for lean TCS.

There are five general states which can apply to both incoming and outgoing sides:

- Null—No call is present.
- Active—A call has been allocated to a particular device, and channels have been set up.
- Disconnect Request—A request to disconnect has been sent, but no response has been received.
- Disconnect Indication—The network (outgoing) side has disconnected, so the incoming side has been invited to disconnect.
- Release request.

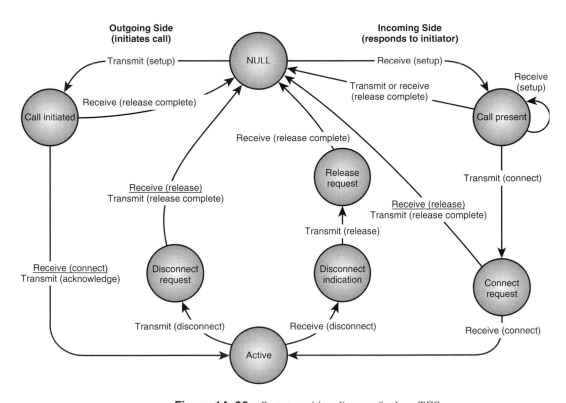

Figure 14–20   State transition diagram for lean TCS.

The outgoing side can also be in the call initiated state. The incoming side can also be in the call present or connect request state.

TCS allows for the implementation of more states to cover the complete Q.931, but only the lean TCS states are mandatory. Lean TCS has been defined because many hand-held Bluetooth devices will have limited computing resources, so lean TCS allows a simpler implementation, saving on memory and processing.

14.8 SUMMARY

TCS provides call control signalling to establish voice and data calls between Bluetooth devices. These can be used to direct calls from an external network to other Bluetooth devices. For instance, a cellular phone could receive a call and use TCS to redirect the call to a laptop, allowing the laptop to be used as a hands-free phone.

TCS signals are sent on an L2CAP channel with a Protocol and Service Multiplexor (PSM) reserved for TCS. A separate bearer channel is established to carry the call; this can be a SCO channel or an ACL channel. Once TCS calls have been established, DTMF tones can be sent on the TCS signalling channel.

TCS can be used to join devices in a Wireless User Group (WUG). A piconet Master acts as the WUG Master and handles pairing to all devices which join the WUG. The WUG Master distributes information on WUG members throughout the WUG. Devices in a WUG can request connections directly to one another, allowing calls to be set up faster than if they were not in the WUG.

TCS does not define handover of calls from one device to another, and does not provide a mechanism for groups of devices to enter into conference calls; only point to point links are supported.

PART 3

CROSS LAYER FUNCTIONS

15

Encryption and Security

Cable based communication is inherently secure. However, since anyone could potentially listen into a wireless transmission, security is a key issue for wireless communications systems.

Security is dealt with at many levels in the Bluetooth specification:

- The baseband specification details the SAFER+ algorithms used for security procedures.
- The Link Manager specification covers link level procedures for configuring security.
- The HCI specification details how a host controls security and how security-related events are reported by a Bluetooth module to its host.
- The Generic Access Profile covers security modes and user-level procedures for use in all products implementing Bluetooth profiles.
- There is also a Bluetooth SIG white paper on the security architecture, which suggests a framework for implementing security and gives examples of how services might use security.

The Bluetooth specification uses a variant of the SAFER+ cipher to authenticate devices (to ensure they are who they claim to be). Designed by Cylink Corporation as a candidate for the U.S. Advanced Encryption Standard (AES), it has since been released into the public domain.

The encryption engine must be initialised with a random number. After initialisation, the encryption engine needs four inputs:

- A number to be encrypted or decrypted (this is the data being passed between devices).
- The Master's Bluetooth device address.
- The Master's Bluetooth slot clock (clock bits 26-1; bit 0, which measures half slots, isn't used).
- A secret key which is shared by both devices.

All devices in a piconet know the Master's Bluetooth device address and slot clock. The secret key used for encryption varies. Sometimes a device wants to verify that it shares a secret key with another device that claims to share the key. The verifier can't just ask the claimant to transmit the key because anybody could eavesdrop on it. Instead, the verifier sends a random number and gets the claimant to encrypt the number using the secret key and return the encrypted version. The verifier can encrypt the random number using the secret key, and compare its result with the claimant's result. If they match, then both sides must have had the same secret key. This exchange of messages is shown in Figure 15–1.

The full exchange of messages to authenticate a device is slightly more complicated than this, as both devices' encryption engines must first have been initialised with the same random number.

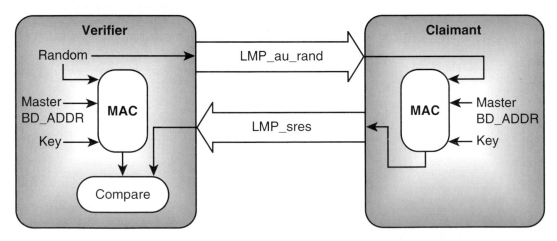

Figure 15–1   Authentication using the Bluetooth encryption engine.

15.1 KEY GENERATION AND THE ENCRYPTION ENGINE

The cipher algorithm adopted by the Bluetooth SIG for authentication and encryption is a variant of a strong contemporary algorithm available in the public domain. SAFER+ (Secure And Fast Encryption Routine) is the latest in a family of 64 bit block ciphers developed by the Swiss Federal Institute of Technology and Cylink Corporation in the United States since 1993. SAFER+ generates 128 bit cipher keys from a 128 bit plaintext input.

In 1998, SAFER+ was submitted as a candidate successor to the Data Encryption Standard (DES)—referred to as the Advanced Encryption Standard (AES)—in the United States.

During the AES candidate testing phase in 1999, SAFER+ was found by the U.S. National Institute of Standards and Technology (NIST) to have a good security margin with only some minor security gaps. In fact, these do not affect the 128 bit version of the algorithm used in Bluetooth anyway. However, it was not accepted into the second round due to its relatively slow speed when compared with the other candidates, especially for 32 and 64 bit microprocessor-based implementations.

More details on the SAFER+ algorithm are available in[1] or on the NIST Web site at *http://www.nist.gov/aes.*

In Bluetooth, the plaintext is provided by a combination of a predefined device PIN number or a unit key and random number. The resulting key is then loaded together with the BD address, Master clock bits, and another 128 bit random number into a bank of Linear Feedback Shift Registers (LFSRs). The output of these LFSRs is combined by a Finite State Machine (FSM) called the "Summation Combiner" to produce a cipher stream which is then exclusive-OR'd (XOR'd) with either the transmit or receive data streams as required.

The LFSR block and Summation Combiner are together referred to as the "Encryption Engine" and this process as the "E0" algorithm. This is the part that actually encrypts or decrypts the data bitstream, while the key generator is the part that uses the SAFER+ algorithm to generate the keys used by E0.

The diagram in Figure 15–2 illustrates the functional structure of the authentication and encryption procedures. During initialisation, a device specific PIN number is used to generate a 128 bit key using the BD_ADDR of the claimant and a random number shared by the claimant and verifier. The authentication procedure ensures that both units are using the same 128 bit key, and therefore that the same PIN number was entered into both units. This key (K_{init}) is used to create a new 128 bit key, shared between two units (K_{combo}) by the key generator which includes the current key, a new random number from each unit, and each unit's BD_ADDR. This new key is a link key and is used with the BD_ADDR and the results of the authenticate routine to produce an encryption key K_c. This encryption key may be shortened to K'_c due to national security export restrictions in some countries. The encryption key is then used with the Bluetooth clock value and the BD_ADDR to initialise the Encryption Engine, which produces the cipher stream. This cipher stream is then used to both cipher and decipher the bitstream data.

---

[1]Prof. J.L. Massey, Prof. G.H. Khachatrian, Dr. M.K. Kuregian, *SAFER+ Candidate Algorithm for AES—Submission Document,* Cylink Corp, June 1998.

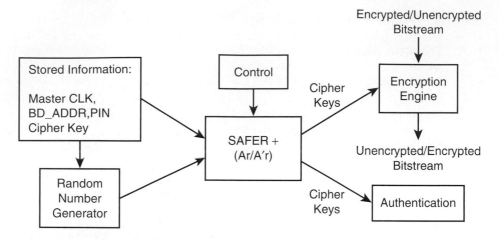

Figure 15–2   Encryption and authentication block diagram.

There are three main operations that need to be performed:

- Random number generation—This may be carried out in hardware or software.
- Key generation—Based on the SAFER + algorithm, this is a slow process, typically involving hardware and software elements. Since key generation is not performed frequently and then only during the lengthy LMP negotiation procedures, it is not time critical.
- Encryption—Engine initialisation and cipher stream generation use precalculated encryption keys and address/clock information, but the stream generation occurs in real time and is thus typically implemented in hardware.

15.1.1   Encryption Keys

There are a number of different keys used in Bluetooth, and these can be divided into three main types: link keys, sub-keys, and the resulting encryption keys. Each key is generated using one of a set of five different "E" algorithms, and with the exception of E0, they are all based on the SAFER+ algorithm.

15.1.1.1   Link Key: K.   Link keys are used as authentication keys between Bluetooth devices and to generate encryption keys. There are various types of link keys, each is generated in a different way. Link keys are 128 bit numbers generated using "E" implementations of the SAFER+ algorithm. They are used for all security transactions. Link keys can be either semipermanent (used for many sessions) or temporary (used during a current session only). Whenever a new link key is generated, it is verified by mutial authentication.

15.1.1.2   Master Key: K_{master}.   This type of key is for point to multipoint communications and may replace for a time the current link key. This key is generated using an E_{22} implementation of the SAFER+ algorithm and is temporary.

15.1.1.3   Unit Key: e.g., K_A.   This semipermanent key is generated in every single unit often only once during factory setup. While it is unlikely, the unit key might be changed at any time.

15.1.1.4   Combination Key: K_{AB}.   Changing the unit key is undesirable since in some systems, many units may wish to use the same unit key as link key. A combination key is dependent on two units; each unit produces and sends a random number to the other. A new 128 bit combination key is derived using SAFER+ for each new combination. A combination key replace is often used to replace the unit key for a period and while they are generated in a different way, they are functionally indistinguishable. A combination key is often created toward the end of unit pairing.

15.1.1.5   Initialisation Key: K_{init}.   The 128 bit initialisation key is a link key used for a single session and is created each time the unit is initialised. The initialisation key is only used when no combination keys or unit keys have been exchanged yet. The key is generated using an E_{22} implementation of SAFER+ and uses the PIN number. An initialisation key is often created toward the beginning of unit pairing.

15.1.1.6   Encryption Key: K_c.   This key is derived from the current link key, but may be shortened due to national security export restrictions in some countries. The full-length key is derived with the E_3 SAFER+ algorithm. The Encryption Engine, E0, uses this key to produce the cipher stream.

15.1.2   The E Algorithms

E0—Cipher stream generation / Encryption Engine.

E0 creates and applies the cipher stream to the bitstream data.

First the block of LFSRs is loaded with the BD address, Master clock bits, and 128 bit random number in an appropriate order. The outputs of these LFSRs are combined by a Finite State Machine (FSM) called the "Summation Combiner" to produce a cipher stream. This is then exclusive-OR'd (XOR'd) with either the transmit or receive data streams as required. The Bluetooth clock, CLK[26:1], is of course incremented on each slot and since E0 is reinitialised at the start of each new packet, a new cipher stream will be created for each packet.

- E1—Authentication. Here, both Ar and A'r are used to encrypt and validate the E2-generated keys used in the authentication process.
- E2—Authentication key generation. E2 creates the keys which are to be used by the E1 authentication algorithm. Two modes of operation are used depending on the key to be generated:
  - E21—Uses a 48 bit BD address to create unit keys and combination keys.
  - E22—Uses a user-supplied PIN to create initialisation keys and the master key
- E3—Encryption key generation. E3 is the algorithm that generates the ciphering key, K_c, used by E0. E3 is based on A'r, the modified SAFER+ algorithm.

All SAFER+ based algorithms—that is E1, E2x, and E3—take a 128 bit input and return a 128 bit key. However, to comply with certain national security export restrictions, E0 includes a key length reduction mechanism, which ensures that the LFSRs are loaded with a key of the permissible effective length.

15.1.3   Key Generation and SAFER+

The original SAFER+ algorithm uses a fixed block size of 128 bits, with key lengths of 128, 192, or 256 bits. For Bluetooth, the key length is between 1 and 16 octets, so a Bluetooth key is between 8 and 128 bits. If a key length shorter than 128 bits has been selected, then the key length used for encryption is reduced by a modulo operation. The reduced key is encoded with a block code; this is done to more uniformly distribute the starting states of the encryption sequence.

The SAFER+ algorithm processes the 128 bit input as 16 octets. The algorithm is broken down into 8 rounds, where all 16 octets are processed bit serially in parallel.

For each round, two sub-keys are combined with the new input data. One sub-key is applied to the input data, while the other is applied to the data after the substitution stage. In both cases, the sub-key elements are added both bitwise and octetwise. After the last round, a seventeenth sub-key is also applied, this time to the result data. Each of the sub-keys is created from the input word according to a schedule, which is dictated by the "Bias Words". This serves to randomise the sub-keys produced.

Each round consists of two "substitution" functions: one that implements an exponential function and one that implements a logarithmic function. These introduce the desired nonlinearity.

An Invertible Linear Transform (ILT) is then imposed in the form of a Pseudo Hadamard Transformation (PHT), followed by an Armenian Shuffle (AS) bitwise interleaving function. These two operations are carried out three times with a final PHT phase at the end. The PHT function consists of multiple accumulates and bit shifting operations.

The seventeen sub-keys are generated from the 128 bit input to the algorithm. The Sub-Key Generation (SKG) process involves creating a parity word, rotating each of the octet bits, and rotating the octets. The result is then added mod256 to a precalculated bias word.

The block diagram in Figure 15–3 depicts the basic structure of the algorithm. Look-up tables are shown for the log, exponent, and bias functions, which is the most likely implementation, though the actual function could of course be used if appropriate.

15.1.3.1   Ar and A'r.   The SAFER+ algorithm is referred to as Ar in the Bluetooth standard. However, as such, it is only used as part of the authentication procedure. The A'r algorithm is used at least once in almost all key generation procedures and is a modified version of the SAFER+ algorithm where the input to Round 1 is fed back into the algorithm during Round 3. This makes A'r noninvertible and of course unsuitable for use as an encryption algorithm.

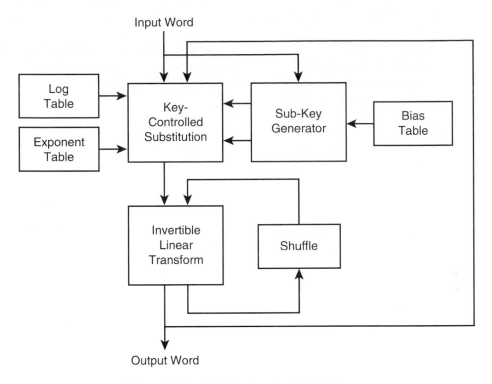

Figure 15–3   SAFER+ functional block diagram.

15.1.3.2   Advantages of SAFER+ and Associated Implementation Issues.   In cryptographic terms, SAFER+ is a relatively simple algorithm, yet it provides a high level of security. Its designers claim that it has no weak keys, is robust against both linear and differential cryptanalyses, and its transparency (that is, its use of only well defined mathematical functions) makes it clear that there are no so-called "trap doors" allowing third party deciphering. The minor security gaps mentioned above were uncovered using differential cryptanalysis and affect the 192 and 256 bit versions of SAFER+. The 128 bit version as used in Bluetooth diffuses the full key into the algorithm very quickly and so is robust to such attacks. In addition, regular link key changes will further prevent the viability of a cryptoanalysis attack.

Its regular structure and byte orientation make the algorithm suitable for implementation in silicon and small footprint microprocessors (i.e., 8 bit), while also being highly optimisable for modern high performance DSPs or 32 bit microprocessors. A silicon implementation of the SAFER+ algorithm can compute a 128 bit key in less than 100 μs when clocked at 20 MHz.

The following sections explain how the SAFER+ encryption engine can be used to support a variety of security features.

15.2   SECRET KEYS AND PINS

To use encryption, Master and Slave **must** share the same secret key. This secret key is **never** transmitted on air. The secret key could be built in by manufacturers (a fixed key), or it could be derived from a Personal Identification Number (PIN) entered through a user interface (a variable key).

An example of a device which could sensibly use fixed keys is a headset for a cellular phone. These could be sold with fixed keys, so that they would not need a costly and bulky user interface to enter security information. To ensure that both ends of the link share the same keys, the user could enter the headset's information into a cellular handset (these already have an interface suitable for entering numbers, so, unlike the headset, a facility to enter PINs would not add to the cost of the device).

An example of an application where PINs might need to be altered frequently is a hotel or conference center offering Bluetooth LAN access points. When a guest checked in, he or she could be given a PIN number which would allow use of encryption on data sent to the LAN access points.

If a device is to have variable PINs, then naturally the user interface must support entering new PINs. So for devices with an HCI, it is the host (which owns the user interface) that determines whether the PIN is fixed or variable. The HCI_Write_PIN_Type command is used by the host to tell the Bluetooth device whether the PIN is fixed or variable. (The HCI_Read_PIN_Type command can be used to check whether the lower layers believe a fixed or variable PIN is in use.)

When a Bluetooth device needs to query the host for a PIN, it can send the event HCI_PIN_Code_Request_Event. If the host can supply a PIN, it replies with the command HCI_PIN_Code_Request_Reply, which contains the PIN in its parameter list. If the host has no PIN to supply, it responds with the command HCI_PIN_Code_Negative_Request_Reply, which will cause attempts at using security features to fail.

15.2.1   The Bluetooth Passkey

The Generic Access Profile defines the terms used by a Bluetooth device's user interface. HCI and LMP use the term "PIN," but the Generic Access Profile requires the user interface to use the term "Bluetooth passkey".

The PIN used by the baseband can be up to 128 bits (16 bytes). PINs can be entered as decimal digits, or optionally they may be entered as alphanumeric characters. Unicode UTF-8 coding is used to transform the characters into digits.

Because some devices which allow PINs to be entered will not support alphanumeric entry, devices sold with fixed PINs should be sold with a note of the PIN given as decimal digits.

The Logical Link Control and Adaptation Layer (L2CA) needs to be aware that entering PINs through a user interface may take some time. L2CA has a timeout on a response (RTX). The RTX timer's value is implementation dependent, but it is initially set between 1 and 60 seconds. If the timer elapses while waiting for PIN entry, the timed out request will be resent with the timeout doubled. This continues until the requester decides to abandon configuration. To avoid this timing out, a device which knows it will take some time should send a connection pending response to its peer. This indicates that some processing is happening which may take some time and causes an Extended Response Timer (ERTX) to be started in place of the RTX timer, thus giving sufficient time for the PIN to be entered. ERTX is again implementation dependent, but its value is initially between 1 minute and 5 minutes, so it allows much more time for the user to enter a PIN.

15.3 PAIRING AND BONDING

The Generic Access Profile calls two devices that know they share a link key **bonded**. The procedures involved in creating a relationship based on a common link key is called bonding.

Bonding involves creating a link specifically for the purpose of creating and exchanging a common link key. During bonding, the link managers create and exchange a link key then verify it by mutial authentication. The Link Level procedures of link key generation and authentication as shown in Figure 15–4 are collectively called **pairing**.

Bonding may involve higher layer initialisation procedures as well as link level pairing. At the User Interface Level, the term "Bluetooth bonding" is used to refer collectively to bonding and pairing procedures.

15.3.1   Authentication

Authentication is the process by which devices verify that they share a link key.

Mutual authentication takes place when link keys are generated; authentication can also be controlled using HCI commands. The process of authentication itself uses a series of messages to be exchanged using Link Management Protocol.

Authentication can be triggered via HCI commands at any time; it does not have to happen at link setup. For instance, a new application which requires security might start using an existing link. This would trigger authentication.

Authentication would usually take place as a prelude to setting up encryption on a link, but authentication can be done independently of encryption. It is conceivable that a device might want to use authentication to check if it is communicating with the correct device, even if it had chosen not to encrypt traffic on the link.

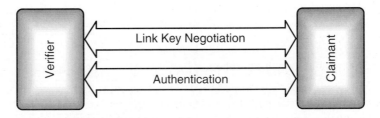

Figure 15–4   LMP procedures involved in pairing.

For devices with an HCI, authentication can be requested with the command HCI_Authentication_Requested. When authentication completes, the HCI_Authentication_Complete event is sent from the device to the host. This contains a status field, which either indicates success or failure. Possible reasons for failure are:

- The connection being authenticated doesn't exist.
- Authentication failed.
- Authentication isn't a supported feature on the Bluetooth device.
- The command is not allowed (for example, when authentication has been disabled).

Authentication can also fail if the claimant does not have a link key to authenticate with. In this case the claimant responds to the LMP_au_rand with LMP_not_accepted.

As a side effect of a successful authentication procedure, a parameter called the Authenticated Ciphering Offset (ACO) is calculated and then used to generate the ciphering keys, which are then used to encrypt data. If a Master and a Slave initiated authentication together, they could end up with two different ACOs, so they would not be capable of decrypting one another's encrypted data. To keep this from happening, version 1.1 introduced a new rule that link managers must reply to any outstanding LMP_au_rand authentication request signals with LMP_sres secure response signals before sending their own LMP_au_rand authentication request signals. It is still possible for LMP_au_rand messages to cross, however. If this happens and the Master receives a reponse to its own LMP_au_rand, it is allowed to respond with LMP_not_accepted with the error code "LMP Error Transaction Collision". In this way, Link Managers should be capable of ensuring that only one authentication is in progress at any time, thus also avoiding mismatching ACOs.

Authentication can be enabled or disabled via the HCI using the command HCI_Write_Authentication_Enable. HCI_Read_Authentication_Enable can be used to check whether authentication is enabled or disabled. Authentication cannot be enabled on a per-connection basis; it is either enabled or disabled on all connections at once.

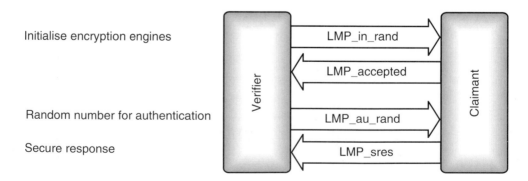

Figure 15–5   LMP message sequence chart for authentication.

Before authentication can take place, both devices must initialise their encryption engines with the same number, this process is shown in Figure 15–5. An LMP_in_rand message is sent carrying the random number; both sides then use the to initialise their encryption engines.

Next the verifier sends an LMP_au_rand message containing the random number to be authenticated by the claimant. The claimant encrypts this number using its link key, and then returns the encrypted number in a secure response message, LMP_sres. The verifier encrypts the random number from LMP_au_rand with its link key and compares it with the encrypted version in LMP_sres. Thus the verifier can decide whether both sides share the same link key without the link key ever being transmitted on air.

15.3.2 Unit Keys

Every Bluetooth device that supports security has a unit key. The unit creates the unit key using its random number generator on first startup; thereafter, the unit key normally does not change. The unit key is used when generating link keys for secure communications.

If a Bluetooth device is sold or otherwise changes hands, the new owner might want to change the unit key. For devices with an HCI, this is simply done by sending the HCI_Create_New_Unit_Key command. If the old key is in use, the old key carries on being used for existing links. So for maximum security, old link keys should be deleted when a new unit key is created. The host does not need to know the unit key, so there are no messages for a host to read or write the unit key.

15.3.3 Link Key Generation

Once Master and Slave know that they share a secret key, they could use that key for encrypting traffic. But if data with a pattern is sent, then it is possible to eventually crack the link key. Therefore for maximum security, the link key should be changed regularly. So a mechanism is needed to create link keys to use for data encryption. Obviously a key that was just transmitted on the air would not be very secure, so keys are disguised by exclusive ORing them with a key generated from the random number in the LMP_au_rand message previously sent and the PIN.

To get a shared key, each unit sends a key in an LMP_unit_key or LMP_comb_key message as shown in Figure 15–6. The rules for choosing a key are:

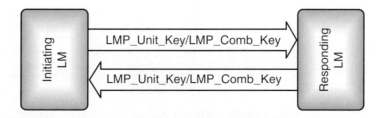

Figure 15–6 LMP message sequence chart for link key generation.

- If both devices send a LMP_unit_key, the Master's unit key is used.
- If one device sends a LMP_unit_key and one sends a LMP_comb_key, the unit key is used.
- If both devices send a LMP_comb_key, then a combination key formed from two keys is used.

So a link key can be a unit key chosen by one unit only, or a combination key made of elements from both units. Since it is possible that either device's unit keys may have been compromised, the combination key is more secure and is recommended.

After generation of the link key, both devices mutually authenticate one another by exchanging LMP_au_rand and LMP_sres messages. First the initiating LM sends LMP_au_rand and the responding LM sends LMP_sres, then the responding LM sends LMP_au_rand and the initiating LM sends LMP_sres.

An example of a set of LMP messages used to initialise encryption, generate combination keys, and authenticate are shown in Figure 15–7. It is worth noting that the messages exchanged during this process changed between version 1.0b and version 1.1: in

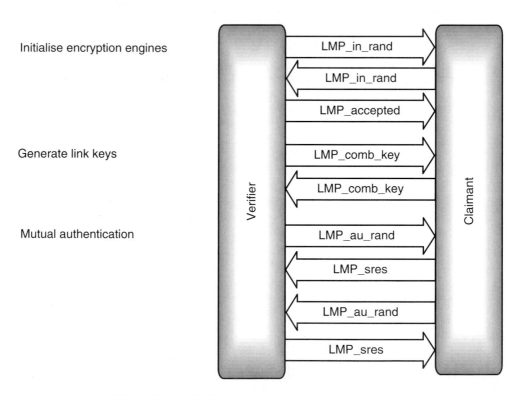

Figure 15–7   LMP message sequence chart for authentication.

version 1.0b authentication took place after the generation of initialisation keys, as well as after generation of link keys. Authenticating twice slowed down the process and did not increase security, so the duplicate authentication was removed from version 1.1 of the Bluetooth specification.

15.3.4 Changing Link Keys

If the host decides for some reason that the current link key may have been compromised, it can create a new link key using the HCI command HCI_Change_Connection_ Link_Key. Because each connection uses a different link key, this command has a connectionHandle parameter to identify the connection on which the link key is to be changed. It may take some time for a new link key to be negotiated, so the Bluetooth module replies to this command with an HCI_Command_Status event.

The sequence of LMP messages used to change the link key is shown in Figure 15–8. It is exactly the same as the messages used to negotiate the key in the first place. If the key is a unit key, it cannot be changed at the LMP level, so when a new combination key is sent, it will be rejected with an LMP_not_accepted message.

Once the new link key has been generated, an HCI_Link_Key_Notification event and HCI_Change_Connection_Link_Key_Complete event are sent to the host. Both devices also conduct mutual authentication after changing the link keys.

15.3.5 Changing to Temporary Link Keys

If broadcast information is to be encrypted, a temporary link key must be used. A temporary key is needed because when a device receives a packet, it must decrypt it immediately so that it can respond to any errors in the packet. A Slave device does not know until

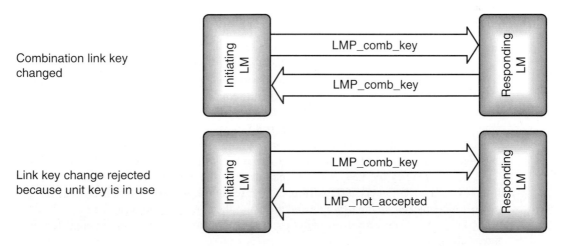

Figure 15–8 Message sequence charts for changing a link key.

it receives a packet whether it is broadcast or point to point, and so does not have time to switch between a broadcast key and a link key. Since there is no time to switch keys, the device must use the same key for broadcast and point to point links.

Because broadcasts are sent to every device in the piconet, the same broadcast link key must be used by all devices on the piconet. This means that devices which previously had individual link keys and could not read one another's packets are now all using the same key, so security is compromised. Furthermore, the link key must be usable by all devices, so it must use the shortest key length of any of the devices in the piconet. Obviously if security has to be compromised in this way to implement broadcast encryption, the links should return to using their normal link keys as soon as broadcast encryption is switched off again; therefore, the link key used for broadcast is a temporary key.

Because only the Master can broadcast, it is the Master that creates the temporary link key. An HCI_Master_Link_Key command can be used by the host to force a Master to create and use a temporary link key. This command has a Key_Flag parameter which is used to specify the type of link key being created. Because some link management level negotiation must take place before the keys are in use, the module responds immediately with an HCI_Command_status event, and only sends an HCI_Master_Link_Key_Complete event when all LMP negotiations have taken place and the new key is in use. Both devices conduct mutual authentiocation to verify the new link key.

The temporary link key will only be valid for the current session, so every time a new encrypted broadcast session is started, a new temporary link key will need to be created (and mutual authentication is conducted to verify the key). Because the temporary link key is only used for a short period, temporary link keys cannot be changed (in version 1.0b any keys could be changed, but in practice temporary link keys never needed to be changed, version 1.1 removed the ability to change temporary link keys).

To create a temporary link key, the Master first creates a 128 bit master key, K_{master}. The Master creates this key by combining two 128 bit random numbers using the SAFER+ Encryption Engine. This Encryption Engine is used instead of using a random number directly in case the Master's random number generator is not very good. By combining two random numbers in this way, an extra degree of randomness is introduced, making it much more difficult for a snooping device to guess the master key.

Having created the master key, the Master creates another random number and sends it to the Slave in an LMP_temp_rand message. Both Master and Slave then use the SAFER+ Encryption Engine to combine the random number and the current link key to create an overlay. The Master adds this overlay modulo-2 to the master key and sends the result in LMP_temp_key as shown in Figure 15–9.

Because the Slave calculates the same overlay, it can extract the master key. Thus, as soon as it receives LMP_temp_key, it extracts the master key, mutual authentication takes place to verify the key, and it is then used as the current link key. Every time the link key is changed, encryption is stopped and restarted to ensure that all devices on the piconet have picked up the new key and are using the correct parameters.

The master key carries on being used until the end of the session, or until the link key is changed again.

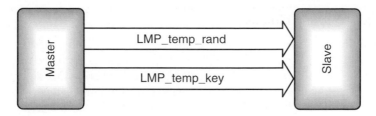

Figure 15–9   Message sequence chart for changing to a temporary link key.

15.3.6   Reverting to Semipermanent Link Keys

The semipermanent link keys are just the normal link keys used for point to point communications. For some devices, such as headsets, there may be no facility to enter new keys. For these devices the term "semipermanent" may be misleading, as the key used for point to point communications is permanently stored. For other devices the key may occasionally be changed and the term "semipermanent" is more accurate. The same HCI_Master_Link_Key command that was used to switch to a temporary key is used to switch back to a semipermanent key. Only the Key_Flag parameter is changed to specify that the key is reverting back to the semipermanent link key which was in use before the temporary link key.

Because the semipermanent link key is the link key which was in use before, both devices already know the key. This means that there is no need to send the key, so the LMP_use_semi_permanent_key message has no parameters. The Slave cannot refuse a request to return to using the semipermanent link key, so it simply acknowledges receipt of the message with LMP_accepted as shown in Figure 15–10.

As for all other link key changes, when the piconet reverts to using the semipermanent link key, encryption must be stopped and restarted. The device which sent LMP_use_semi_permanent_key initiates authentication once encryption is back on to verify the new link key (arguably this check is redundant as it could tell the key was correct by successful decryption of data).

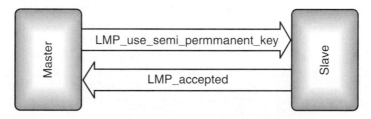

Figure 15–10   Message sequence chart for changing to a semipermanent link key.

15.3.7 Storing Link Keys

In the procedure described above, a link key was created by negotiation. Link keys can also be set up by simply writing via the HCI, or the keys from one session can be read by the host, stored, and then written back later. Remembering link keys from previous sessions can obviously save the time involved in negotiation and get an encrypted link running faster. Many hosts have nonvolatile memory available, so having the host store data between sessions saves adding cost to the Bluetooth device. Another advantage of the host remembering keys is that if the host is something like a laptop with Bluetooth PCMCIA card, changing cards will not cause keys to change. Also, if the card is removed, security keys cannot be read from it. Keys stored on the host can be protected by passwords and so are potentially more secure than keys stored in a removable Bluetooth device.

Every time a new link key is generated, an HCI_Link_Key_Notification event is sent to the host. The parameters of this message are the new link key and the Bluetooth Device Address (BD_ADDR) of the device at the other end of the connection.

When the module wants to retrieve a link key from the host, it sends an HCI_Link_Key_Request event. This event has a single parameter: the Bluetooth Device Address of the device at the other end of the ACL link for which the link key is required. If the host can supply the link key, it is sent back in an HCI_Link_Key_Request_Reply command; if for some reason the host can't supply a link key, it responds instead with a HCI_Link_Key_Request_Negative_Reply command.

The Bluetooth module does not remember link keys when power cycled. Since it tells the host every time a new link key is generated, the host should know all the link keys in use, but it is possible that a Bluetooth module which has its own power source may be connected to a new host, then the host would not know the keys in the module.

The host is provided with a HCI_Read_Stored_Link_Key command to retrieve link keys from the module. The module responds with the HCI_Return_Link_Keys event; this event has three parameters:

- Num_Keys—The number of link keys being requested.
- BD_ADDR[i]—An array of Num_Keys Bluetooth Device Addresses.
- Link_Key[i]—An array of link keys which match the Bluetooth Device Addresses.

The command HCI_Read_Stored_Link_Key can be used to read the key for a particular link, or to read all link keys. HCI_Write_Stored_Link_Key is used to store a key for a given link (the link is specified by the Bluetooth Device Address of the device at the other end of the link). A device may only be able to store a limited number of keys, so HCI_Delete_Stored_Link_Key can be used to remove link keys from storage.

15.3.8 General and Dedicated Bonding

Bonding involves setting up a link for the purpose of exchanging link keys, and possibly other security information. Because the device which initiates bonding is the device which sets up the connection by paging, when bonding, it is always the paging device which initiates authentication procedures.

The Generic Access Profile divides bonding into two procedures: general bonding and dedicated bonding. Dedicated bonding happens when devices only create and exchange a link key. As soon as Link Level authentication procedures have completed, the channel is released before the higher layers connect. General bonding may involve exchange of data by higher layers to initialise their security parameters.

Link keys for bonded devices are stored by a Bluetooth device so that it does not have to create new link keys every time it connects. Since bonding involves creating a new link key, any old link key for the device being bonded with is deleted before bonding is performed. On devices with an HCI, the host can force deletion of a link key using the HCI_Delete_Stored_Link_Key command.

Because bonding involves pairing, the paged device must be in pairable mode before bonding can take place.

Figure 15–11 shows dedicated bonding. Note that there is no connection made above link manager level.

As Figure 15–12 shows, general bonding involves all the same steps as dedicated bonding, but in addition, an L2CAP channel is set up, and, depending on the application requiring security, higher layer channels may also be set up. Once such channels are set up, security information from higher layers may be passed across the channel. After higher layers are configured, the connection is torn down again.

Once two devices are bonded, they share a link key and can connect using that link key without having to go through pairing procedures again.

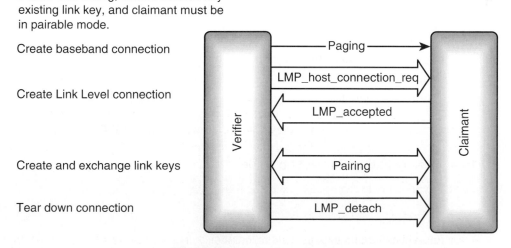

Figure 15–11 Dedicated bonding.

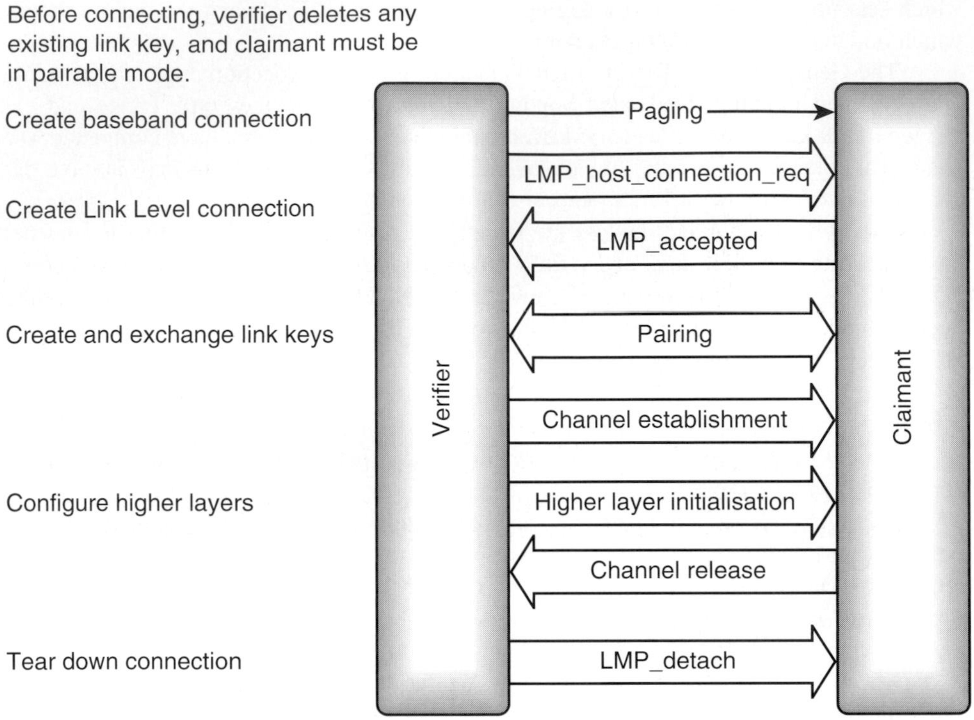

Before connecting, verifier deletes any existing link key, and claimant must be in pairable mode.

Create baseband connection

Create Link Level connection

Create and exchange link keys

Configure higher layers

Tear down connection

Paging

LMP_host_connection_req

LMP_accepted

Pairing

Channel establishment

Higher layer initialisation

Channel release

LMP_detach

Verifier

Claimant

Figure 15–12 General bonding.

15.4 STARTING ENCRYPTION

Once two Bluetooth devices have undergone authentication and agreed on a link key, there are three more steps before encrypted traffic can be exchanged:

- Negotiating encryption mode.
- Negotiating key size.
- Starting encryption.

The messages exchanged to start encryption are shown in Figure 15–13.

15.4.1 Negotiating Encryption Mode

The encryption mode can be any one of the following:

- No encryption.
- Encrypt both point to point and broadcast packets.
- Only encrypt point to point packets.

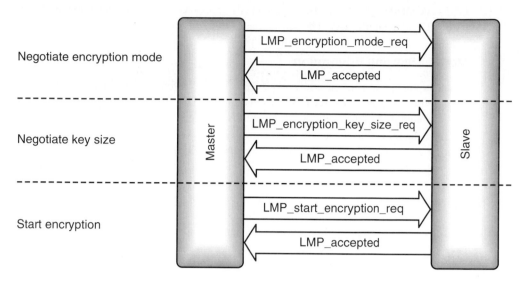

Figure 15–13   LMP message sequence chart for starting encryption.

On devices with an HCI, the encryption mode can be set using an HCI_Write_Encryption_Mode command and can be checked at any time using the HCI_Read_Encryption_Mode command.

The Link Manager uses an LMP_encryption_mode_req to request that the desired encryption mode be used on the channel. If the encryption mode is accepted, LMP_accepted is sent back; if it is not, LMP_not_accepted is sent, and the Master is free to try again, requesting a different encryption mode.

The encryption modecan be changed by resending the LMP_encryption_mode_req. Data transmission must be stopped when encryption mode changes; otherwise, data could be sent when the encryption mode is indeterminate, which would lead to data being corrupted or lost. To avoid this, data transmission is stopped before any encryption change. Version 1.0b of the specification said that data traffic had to be temporarily stopped, but there was some disagreement among implementers as to when to stop it: Should it stop immediately, at the end of an ACL packet, or at the end of an L2CAP packet? Version 1.1 of the specification clarified that data transmission should stop at the end of the current ACL packet with L2CAP data.

15.4.2   Negotiating Key Size

The United States has regulations governing the export of devices capable of using strong encryption schemes for encrypting data. To comply with these regulations, it is possible to manufacture a Bluetooth device which will not use the full 128 bit keys for encrypting data. Before encryption can be switched on, both units must agree on a key length to use. The Master begins by requesting the maximum key length it can use. If it is within the capabilities of the Slave, an

LMP_accepted is returned; otherwise, an LMP_not_accepted is returned and the Master must try again with a shorter key. The Master keeps trying until it gets an LMP_accepted.

15.4.3 Starting Encryption

Once an encryption mode and key size has been chosen for the link, encryption can be switched on and off. The HCI_Set_Connection_Encryption command uses an ACL connection handle to identify the device which is having encryption switched on or off. When the link manager has finished negotiating encryption on the link, an HCI_Encryption_ Change event is sent back to the host. No traffic should be sent on the ACL link while encryption is being enabled or disabled, as the link will be occupied with LMP traffic.

The final step is to send an LMP_start_encryption_req. Once the LMP_accepted reply has been received, encrypted data can be exchanged on the ACL link.

This section has described the Master driving encryption mode, but it is also possible for the Slave to send the messages to authenticate, pair, negotiate modes, and switch encryption on and off. We have also described a sequence where each message is exchanged in sequence at link setup, but it is equally possible for authentication to proceed at any time, and for link keys to be changed at any time, or indeed link keys from a previous encryption session could be stored and used.

15.4.4 Stopping Encryption

Since encryption does nor slow down traffic on a link usually once encryption has been started there is no need to stop it. However there may be a need to change encryption parameters after encryption has been started, and this cannot be done whilst encryption is active. Before making changes which affect encryption—for example, changing link keys—encryption is stopped, it is then restarted after the change.

In version 1.0b, the master could stop encryption with an LMP_stop _encryption_mode_req, but there was no clearly defined way for the slave to stop encryption. Version 1.1 specified that any unit wanting to stop encryption could send an LMP_encryption_mode_req with the encryption-mode parameter set to no encryption (zero). If the other device responds with LMP_accepted, the Master sends an LMP_stop _encryption_req message to stop encryption.

After any changes are made, encryption can be restarted using the same LMP_encryption_mode_req which was used to initially start encryption.

15.5 SECURITY MODES

The Generic Access Profile defines three security modes:

- Security Mode 1 is nonsecure—Devices in Security Mode 1 will never initiate any security procedure. Supporting authentication is optional for devices which only support Security Mode 1.

- Security Mode 2 gives Service Level-enforced security—The channel or service using an L2CAP connection decides whether or not security is required. So until an L2CAP channel has been established, a device in Security Mode 2 will not initiate any security procedures. Once an L2CAP channel has been established, the device then decides whether or not it needs authorisation, authentication, and encryption, and goes through appropriate security procedures.

- Security Mode 3 is Link Level-enforced security—A device in Security Mode 3 initiates security procedures before it sends an LMP_setup_complete message. If security measures fail the device, the connection will not be set up. It is possible to set up devices supporting Security Mode 3 so that they will only connect with pre-paired devices. In this case, they would reject an LMP_host_connection_req from any other devices (they would reply with an LMP_not_accepted message).

In addition to these specific security modes, the other modes of a Bluetooth device may be used to increase security. For maximum protection of data, a device can be set in nonconnectable mode when it is not in use. In this mode, the device will not respond to paging, so other devices cannot connect with it.

Nondiscoverable mode can be used to stop a device from responding to inquiries. If this is used, then only devices which already know the device's Bluetooth Device Address can connect to it.

15.6   SECURITY ARCHITECTURE

The Bluetooth security white paper defines a security architecture which may be used to implement Mode 2 Service Level-enforced security on Bluetooth devices. Because the implementation of security at Service Level does not affect interoperability, the white paper is purely advisory and is not a Bluetooth specification.

15.6.1   Security Levels

In addition to the authentication procedures defined in the Bluetooth specification, the security white paper introduces the concept of an authorised or trusted device. An authorised device has been specifically marked in a server's database as having access to a service.

Devices and services can be divided into different security levels. The security white paper splits devices into three categories and two trust levels:

- Trusted devices—Paired or bonded devices which are marked in a database as trusted, and can be given unrestricted access to all services.

- Known untrusted devices—Devices which have been paired or bonded, but are not marked in a database as trusted; access to services may be restricted.

- Unknown devices—No security information is stored, the device is untrusted, and access to services may be restricted.

It would also be possible to implement different levels of trust for services as well as devices. For example, reading and writing to a calendar could be defined as different services. Read access to the calendar might be restricted to a range of devices known to belong to co-workers who had an interest in seeing appointments. Write access to the calendar might be restricted to a smaller set of devices belonging to the owner of the calendar.

The security white paper suggests that the security requirements for authorisation, authentication, and encryption of services could be set separately. This gives three security levels for services:

- Open services—Any device may access these; there are no security requirements.
- Authentication-only services—Any device which can go through authentication may access these (authentication proves it shares a secret key with the service provider).
- Authentication and authorisation services—Only trusted devices may access these (trusted devices are recorded as trusted in the server's database as well as having a secret key).

Each service should have its security level set independently, so a device having access to one service does not imply that it has access to others. It should be possible to define a default level of security which will apply to all services, unless they are specifically set to a different level.

15.6.2 The Security Manager

The existence of trusted devices and of different levels of authorisation for different services imposes a requirement for databases to hold device and service information.

Different protocols will wish to access the information in these databases according to the profile being implemented; for instance:

- L2CAP will enforce security for cordless telephony.
- RFCOMM will enforce security for dialup networking.
- OBEX will use its own security policy for file transfer and synchronisation.

To allow uniform access to the databases by all layers, a security manager handles security transactions with the various layers. All exchange of information with the security databases goes through the security manager as illustrated in Figure 15–14.

Applications and protocols wishing to use security features register with the security manager. The security manager stores security information in the security databases on behalf of the rest of the system. Security policies are enforced by exchanging queries with the security manager:

- Applications query to find out whether a particular device is allowed to access a service.

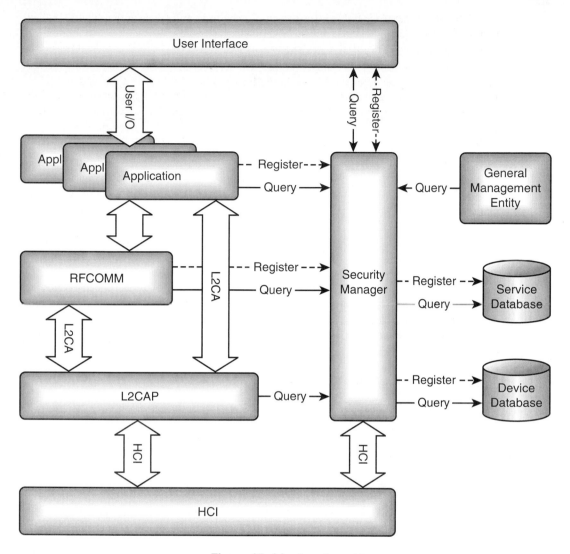

Figure 15–14   Security architecture.

- HCI queries to find out whether to apply authentication and/or encryption to a connection.
- The user interface is queried by the security manager to get PINs.
- The user interface is queried by the security manager to authorise new devices.
- Protocol layers query the security manager with access requests.

The device database holds information on whether devices are authenticated and authorised. The service database holds information on whether authorisation, authentication, and encryption are required for access to a service.

The security white paper suggests that if a service has not registered with the service database, then the default settings should be:

- Incoming connection—Requires authorisation and authentication.
- Outgoing connection—Requires authentication.

As the security white paper is not a part of the Bluetooth specification, there is no requirement to implement security in the way suggested by the white paper. However, designers implementing security in Bluetooth devices should consider the white paper's recommendations.

15.6.3 Setting up Security on New Connections

Because it is the service that decides the level of security to be enforced, security cannot be enforced when an ACL (data) connection is first set up. Instead, security is enforced only when access is requested to a protocol or service which requires security. The protocol or service requests access from the security manager. The security manager looks up the service or protocol in the service database to see what level of security to impose. Then it looks up the connecting device in the device database to see whether it meets the requirements of the service. If necessary, the security manager enforces authentication and/or encryption, and sends any necessary queries for PINs or authorisation to the user interface. Access is then granted or refused, and if access was granted, the service can be used.

It is possible that some services may use a connection without encryption, then another service will begin using the service which requires encryption. Encryption will be set up for the service which requires it, but other than a short pause in traffic while LMP messages are exchanged, this will not be apparent to the other services.

Other than the link management messages required to configure security, there is no impact on bandwidth. The same number of bits are sent on air for an encrypted link as are sent on an unencrypted link.

15.7   SUMMARY

Bluetooth has powerful security features with the SAFER+ encryption engine using up to 128 bit keys.

At the Link Level, it is possible to authenticate a device: This verifies that a pair of devices share a secret key derived from a Bluetooth passkey, also known as a Personal Identification Number (PIN). The Bluetooth passkey is either entered in a user interface, or, for devices such as headsets which do not have a user interface, it can be built in by the manufacturer.

After authentication, devices can create shared link keys which can be used to encrypt traffic on a link. The combination of authentication and creating link keys is called pairing. At the Application Level, pairing, possibly accompanied by exchange of higher level security information, is called bonding.

Authentication may be repeated after pairing, in which case the link key is used as the shared secret key.

Three modes of security can be implemented: Mode 1 is not secure, Mode 2 has security imposed at the request of applications and services, and Mode 3 has security imposed when any new connection is established.

A Bluetooth security white paper suggests an architecture for implementing security in the higher layers of a Bluetooth protocol stack. This is based on Mode 2 security. In addition to being authenticated by the link management procedures, the security architecture introduces the idea of devices being authorised by a user to use particular services. The security architecture suggests implementing this through a pair of databases: one holds information on which devices are authenticated and/or authorised, and the other holds information on whether services require authentication, authorisation, and/or encryption. Services and protocols register with a central security manager, which handles access to the databases. After registration, the central security manager grants permissions to use services.

Security is essential to many applications which will use Bluetooth links, but hiding the complexity of Bluetooth security from the user is essential if Bluetooth devices are to be easy to use. Through the security architecture, it is possible to implement security at a variety of levels with minimal intervention from the user.

16

Low-Power Operation

Many Bluetooth devices will be battery powered. Because a Bluetooth radio can use up to 30 mA when receiving, it is important that it be used as little as possible to save battery power. Bluetooth provides low-power modes of operation to minimise nonessential operation and conserve power.

It can take several seconds to set up an ACL link, so once one has been established, devices which are likely to have more data to transfer don't want to lose it and have to go through the delay of setting it up again. For instance, if a headset is connected to a cellular phone, it is vital that the headset can pick up a call quickly before the caller decides that nobody's listening and hangs up. But in between calls there are long periods when no data needs to be transferred, and leaving the handset and headset fully connected would run down their batteries.

The need to keep connections going for fast response conflicts with the need to maximise battery life. The Bluetooth specification solves this dilemma by providing low-power modes. These allow devices to keep connections, but switch off receivers for as long as possible. There are three low-power modes:

- Hold—Allows devices to be inactive for a single short period.
- Sniff—Allows devices to be inactive except for periodic sniff slots.
- Park—Similar to Sniff, except parked devices give up their active member address.

The radio is the biggest power drain on a Bluetooth device, but the Voltage Controlled Oscillator (VCO) that drives the Bluetooth clock is another power hungry component which can be switched off. For devices with requirements for maximum power saving, the Bluetooth specification provides the means to switch to a less accurate lower power oscillator (LPO) when the accuracy of the normal oscillator is not needed.

16.1 CONTROLLING LOW-POWER MODES

A host can check the link policy settings on a module by sending the HCI_Read_Link_Policy_Settings command. Because link policy can be different on each ACL connection, the command takes a Connection_Handle parameter to specify which connection's link policy is being read. This handle must belong to an ACL (data) connection, not a SCO (voice) connection. The Connection_Handle and the link policy for that handle are returned in an HCI_Connection_Complete event.

The HCI_Write_Link_Policy_Settings command can be used by a host to control power saving settings on a Bluetooth module. The settings are configured on a per connection basis, so the command takes a Connection_Handle parameter as well as link policy settings. Because power saving can only be used on ACL (data) connections, the Connection_Handle parameter must be the handle of an ACL connection. This command can be used to independently disable or enable each of the low-power modes (the same command is also used to control whether or not Master Slave switch is enabled or disabled).

16.2 HOLD MODE

Hold mode is used to stop ACL traffic for a specified period of time. It does not affect SCO traffic. An example of when Hold mode might be used is if a device wanted to perform an inquiry, page, or scan operation. These operations take up all the ACL slots for a known length of time, so the link may as well be held, allowing the device at the other end to switch off its receiver.

A hold message does not order a device to switch off its receiver during ACL slots; it is left entirely up to the held device to decide what to do in the free slots.

16.2.1 Requesting Hold Mode

Both Master and Slave can force or request Hold mode. A connection enters Hold mode because of a request from the local host, because a link manager at the remote end of a connection requested it to hold, or because the local link manager autonomously decided to put the connection in Hold mode.

A device may have several active connections, either because it is a Master with several Slaves, or because it is active on more than one piconet. A complete device enters Hold mode when all of its connections are in Hold mode.

The HCI_Hold_Mode command is used by the host to ask a module's Link Manager to put a specific connection into Hold mode. This command takes three parameters:

- Connection_Handle—Identifies the connection to be put into Hold mode. The connection handle must belong to an ACL (data) connection; SCO (voice) connections cannot be held.
- Hold_Mode_Max_Interval—The longest time the connection should be held.
- Hold_Mode_Min_Interval—The shortest time the connection should be held.

The Bluetooth module will take some time to process this command, as negotiation between link managers is needed to put a device into Hold mode. So the module acknowledges the HCI_Hold_Mode command with an HCI_Command_Status event, then when Hold mode is finally entered, the module sends its host an HCI_Mode_Change event. The host sets minimum and maximum values for time in Hold mode, so it does not know the actual time which was negotiated. The HCI_Mode_Change event tells the host what value was negotiated for the hold time.

If the module has more than one active connection, this command only affects one connection; the other connections are still active. If the module only has one active connection, then the command stops all ACL traffic.

By default, a Bluetooth device in Hold mode maintains its current power state; however, a host can set the activities a module can perform during Hold mode, enabling it to save power. This is done with the HCI_Write_Hold_Mode_Activity command. Possible settings are:

- Maintain the current power state (this is the default).
- Suspend page scan.
- Suspend inquiry scan.
- Suspend periodic inquiries.

When all of a device's connections are in Hold mode, these settings provide an opportunity for power saving. If a module is set to not do page scan, inquiry scan, and periodic inquiries, then it can enter a low-power state for the period during which it will be held.

A host can check the settings for Hold mode activity on its module by sending the HCI_Read_Hold_Mode_Activity command.

16.2.2   LMP Negotiations for Hold Mode

The Bluetooth devices at either end of the connection have to agree on the time for which the connection will be held. The Link Manager handles negotiating timing of Hold mode between devices.

An LMP_hold_req message is used to request Hold mode. It includes parameters for the hold time (length of hold) and hold instant (when to start). When one side requests Hold mode, the other side has three choices: it can accept the hold request with an LMP_accepted, reject it with LMP_not_accepted, or return the request with a different

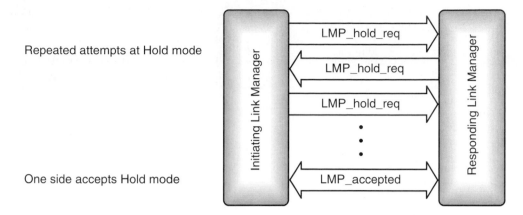

Figure 16–1   LMP message sequence chart for requesting Hold mode.

hold time. LMP_hold_req messages can be sent back and forth until one side sends an LMP_accepted or LMP_not_accepted, as shown in Figure 16–1.

In version 1.0b of the specification LMP_hold and LMP_hold_req messages did not have the hold instant parameter, this could cause problems. For example, a Master could ask a Slave to hold, and the Slave would send a response that then got lost. The Master would then continue trying to hold the Slave, while the Slave was inactive. If the link supervision timeout didn't elapse, the Master would still be trying to hold the Slave when it came back out of Hold mode, so the Slave would exit Hold mode only to go straight back in again. Obviously, this sort of thing can waste a lot of bandwidth, so the hold instant parameter was added to specify exactly when the hold should happen. That way, if the link controller sends a stale LMP_hold message, the receiving device can see that the message is out-of-date because the hold instant will be in the past. To give the message a chance to work its way through from one link manager to the other, the hold instant must be set to at least 6*Tpoll slots in the future.

Hold mode is forced with an LMP_hold from the Master. The Master can only force Hold mode if the Slave has previously accepted a request for Hold mode. The Hold mode time in the LMP_hold message can be no longer than a hold time the Slave has previously accepted in a LMP_hold_req. The Slave cannot force Hold mode, it may only request the Master to hold.

If a Slave wishes to request Hold mode, it sends an LMP_hold to the Master, this message specifies the hold time (length of hold), and the hold instant (when to start). The Master echoes the LMP_hold back to the Slave as shown in Figure 16–2.

While a Slave is in Hold mode, its clock free-runs and drifts out of synchronisation with the Master. So when it returns from Hold mode, it must open its correlators over a wider uncertainty window. Bluetooth clocks are allowed $10\mu S$ jitter, meaning that at any time, the slot start can be $10\mu S$ too soon or too late (this is the reason for the +/- $10\mu S$ window normally used for reception). In addition, the clock can drift by up to 250ppm. So device going into Hold mode, it has a default uncertainty window of +/- $10\mu S$. After a 1s hold time, its own clock can have drifted by 250 microseconds, and the clock at the other

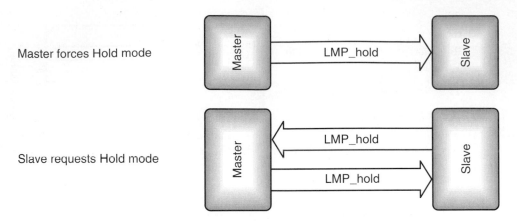

Figure 16–2   LMP message sequence chart for forcing Hold mode.

end could have drifted in the other direction by 250 microseconds. So the device returning from hold must add 500 microseconds to its uncertainty giving a window of +/- 510µs.

Some Bluetooth devices will have more accurate clocks than the worst case the standard permits. A device always knows its own clock accuracy, but if it can find out the accuracy at the other end of the link too, then it can minimise the scan window for a given hold time. The LMP_timing_accuracy_req message can be used to request the accuracy of the clock at the opposite end of the link; an LMP_timing_res message responds with the clock's accuracy, as shown in Figure 16–3.

Bluetooth devices don't have to support the LMP_timing_accuracy_req message. If they don't, they respond to an LMP_timing_accuracy_req message with LMP_not_accepted containing an error code of LMP_unsupported_feature, and the requesting device has to assume that it is dealing with worst case timings.

16.3 SNIFF MODE

Sniff mode is used to reduce traffic to periodic sniff slots. This mode can be used to save power on low data rate links. For example, consider the case of a PDA which needs to re-

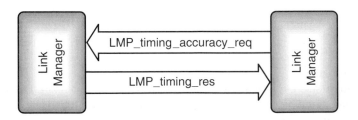

Figure 16–3   Message sequencing chart for requesting timing accuracy.

ceive email from a data-enabled mobile phone. Normally, there would be no traffic on such a link, but when there is traffic, the PDA needs to be ready quickly. Sniff mode can be used to allow the PDA to reduce the slots in which it has to listen, but to react fast when traffic appears.

16.3.1   Sniff Mode Timing

A device in Sniff mode only wakes up periodically in prearranged sniff slots. The Master and Slave must negotiate the timing of the first sniff slot (D_{sniff}) and the interval at which further sniff slots follow (T_{sniff}). They also negotiate the window in which the sniffing Slave will listen for transmissions ($N_{sniff\ attempt}$) and the sniff timeout.

The sniffing Slave listens for traffic during the sniff slots determined by the sniff attempt parameter (coloured dark grey in Figure 16–4). If no message addressed to the sniffing Slave is received, the sniffing Slave ceases listening for packets. If a message with the sniffing Slave's active member address is received, it continues listening for further sniff timeout slots after the sniff slot.

In the example of a PDA wanting to receive email from a mobile phone given above, the mobile would be the Master and the PDA the sniffing Slave. The mobile could use the sniff slots to send a command to unsniff the PDA; after the email had been sent, the mobile could then force the PDA back into Sniff mode.

Alternatively, the sniff timeout could be set to a value large enough to transmit as much data as the phone needs to send. An extreme case would be setting the sniff timeout large enough to keep the sniffing Slave listening throughout the sniff interval. In this way, once a packet had been sent to the Slave in the sniff slot, it would automatically keep listening throughout the transmission.

Because Bluetooth's radio links are unreliable, the sniff attempt window should be wide enough to give the Master a chance to retry transmissions to the sniffing Slave if necessary. (The size of the broadcast window might be a good size to pick for this, as the broadcast window is set to give enough retries to give a reasonable guarantee of reception.)

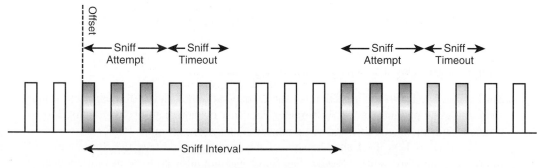

Figure 16–4   Timing of Sniff mode slots.

16.3.2 Requesting Sniff Mode

A device enters Sniff mode because of a request from its own host, or because a link manager at the remote end of a connection requested or forced it to enter Sniff mode. (Masters can force Slaves into Sniff mode; Slaves can only request that they enter Sniff mode, and must get the Master's consent.)

The HCI_Sniff_Mode command is used by the host to ask a module's link manager to put a specific connection into Sniff mode. This command takes five parameters:

- Connection Handle—Identifies the connection to be put into Sniff mode. Only ACL connections can be put into Sniff mode, so this must not be an SCO connection handle.
- Sniff _Max_Interval—The maximum time between sniff periods.
- Sniff _Min_Interval—The minimum time between sniff periods.
- Sniff_Attempt—Time at the end of a sniff interval during which a Slave listens for transmissions.
- Sniff_Timeout—If a Slave receives during the sniff attempt time, it keeps listening until the sniff timeout time elapses.

In version 1.1 of the Bluetooth specification the Sniff Attempt and sniff timeout parameters are expressed as the number of receive slots. In version 1.0b they were specified as slots, some implementors counted transmit and receive slots, some just counted receive slots, so by explicitly specifying receive slots version 1.1 has cleared up an ambiguity which led to some 1.0b implementations having timeouts twice as long as others. This change has helped to make sniff mode more interoperable in version 1.1.

The Bluetooth module will take some time to process this command, as negotiation between link managers is needed to put a device into Sniff mode. So the module acknowledges the HCI_Sniff_Mode command with an HCI_Command_Status event, then when Sniff mode is finally entered, the module sends its host an HCI_Mode_Change event. The host sets minimum and maximum values for the sniff interval, so it does not know the actual sniff interval which was negotiated. The HCI_Mode_Change event tells the host what value was negotiated for the sniff interval.

If a host wishes to end Sniff mode for a connection on its module, it simply sends the HCI_Exit_Sniff_Mode command. This command only needs one parameter: the connection handle of the connection to be removed from Sniff mode.

16.3.3 LMP Negotiation for Sniff Mode

Sniff mode applies to a connection, so the devices at either end of the connection must share the same parameters for Sniff mode. The Link management protocol is used to coordinate Sniff mode at either end of a connection as shown in Figure 16–5.

In version 1.0b the Link Manager of the Master could force the Slave into Sniff mode using an LMP_sniff message. The Slave was not allowed to refuse the request, so did not need to reply with an LMP_accepted. This feature was removed in version 1.1 be-

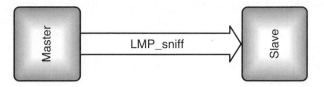

Figure 16–5 LMP message sequence chart for Master-forced Sniff mode (preversion 1.1 only).

cause many implementations could not support all possible combinations of sniff parameters. In particular many implementations had problems staying synchronised if there were long periods of inactivity between sniff slots (that is to say large values of T_{sniff}). If the Master forces Sniff mode, it has no way to know if the Slave can support the parameters it has supplied, so it may force parameters that the Slave cannot handle. To solve this problem the forced sniff feature was removed from version 1.1 of the Bluetooth specification, so Sniff mode must always be negotiated. Because the option of negotiating Sniff mode is still available, there is no real loss in functionality by removing the LMP_sniff message, so it is a good idea to avoid forcing Sniff mode even when using implementations before version 1.1.

Negotiation of Sniff mode is similar to negotiation of Hold mode. An LMP_sniff_req message is used to request Sniff mode. When one side requests Sniff mode, the other side has three choices: it can accept the sniff request with an LMP_accepted, reject it with LMP_not_accepted, or return the request with different timing parameters. LMP_sniff_req messages can be sent back and forth until one side agrees to Sniff mode by sending an LMP_accepted as shown in Figure 16–6 or terminates the transaction by sending LMP_not_accepted.

Versions 1.0 and 1.1 of the Bluetooth specification specify that a sniffing Slave shall listen to packets with its own active member address. This would imply that it is not

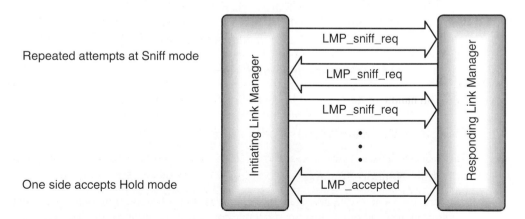

Figure 16–6 LMP message sequence chart for negotiation of Sniff mode.

possible to send broadcast packets to sniffing Slaves, so to send a piconet broadcast to every Slave on a piconet, each sniffing Slave would have to receive the broadcast message as a unicast message.

16.3.4 Data Transfer in Sniff Mode

In version 1.0b of the Bluetooth specification ARQN numbers, which are used to acknowledge data transfer, were frozen throughout Hold and Sniff modes. In Hold mode no data can be transferred, so the ARQN field is never used, and specifying it as frozen has no effect, but data can be transferred in Sniff mode and freezing ARQN numbers stopped the usual acknowledgement procedure from working. Without effective acknowledgements, data transfer during Sniff mode was unreliable in version 1.0b. Version 1.1 solved this problem by making Sniff mode acknowledgements operate in the same way as active mode, so in version 1.1 Sniff mode has the ability to transfer data reliably.

16.4 PARK MODE

A device which has parked gives up its active member address and ceases to be an active member of the piconet. As long as it is parked, it cannot transmit, and, as it has no active member address, it cannot be addressed directly by the Master. However, it wakes up periodically and listens for broadcasts, so these can be used to unpark it, bringing it back to active life.

A device in Park mode only wakes periodically to listen for transmissions from the Master at prearranged beacon instants. A beacon instant marks the start of a beacon train, with each train having a series of beacon slots during which the Master can transmit to parked Slaves.

16.4.1 Beacon Instant

The Master transmits to parked Slaves using a periodic beacon, which begins at a beacon instant. The Master tells the Slaves when the first beacon instant will be using two parameters: D_B, which gives the timing of the first beacon slot, and the timing control flags, which are used to avoid uncertainties in timing caused by clock wraparound.

16.4.2 Beacon Retransmissions

Parked Slaves do not respond immediately to the Master's transmissions in the beacon train, so there is no acknowledgment mechanism to tell the Master that its transmission has been received. Therefore, the Master needs to retransmit its messages several times to increase the chances of the packet being received. The number of retransmissions is given by N_B.

16.4.3 Beacon Spacing

Figure 16–7 shows the arrangement of slots within a beacon train. The beacon slots are coloured grey; all other slots are available for transmission of traffic. The spacing of beacon slots within a train is given by Δ_B. In the example, $\Delta_B = 2$, so every second slot within

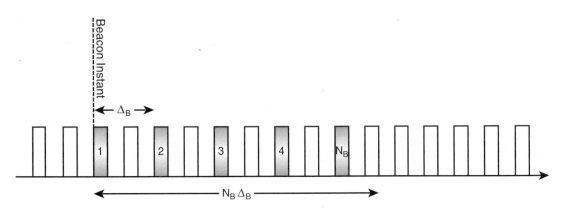

Figure 16–7   Slots within a beacon train.

the train is a beacon slot. Spacing out the slots within a beacon train in this way can be used to allow the Master the regularly spaced slots needed to maintain SCO links to other Slaves while transmitting the beacon train. After the first beacon slot, beacons are transmitted periodically at a spacing of T_B.

The parked Slaves use the beacons to resynchronise to the Master's timing. Therefore, the parked Slaves need some sort of transmission in the beacon slot. If there is nothing else to send the Master sends a NULL packet (which carries no data) to allow the Slaves to synchronise.

16.4.4   Access Windows

The Master can command the Slaves to unpark in the beacon slots, but a mechanism for Slaves to transmit a request for unparking is also required. The opportunity for parked Slaves to request unparking is provided by a series of access windows which come after the beacon train. The length of the beacon train is given by $N_B \Delta_B$. A series of access windows come after the beacon train. The start of the first access window comes D_{access} after the beacon instant. Usually the access windows come straight after the beacon train, so $D_{access} = N_B \Delta_B$.

A series of M_{access} access windows come after the beacon train. As Figure 16–8 shows, the access windows start D_{access} after the beacon instant. Each window is the same width, and that width is given by T_{access}.

Within an access window, the Master broadcasts transmitting on even slots as usual. Normally Slaves cannot respond to broadcasts, but in the access windows, this is changed. Each Slave in turn is allocated a half slot in the Slave to Master slots. Figure 16–9 shows an access window for a Master with four parked Slaves. The Slave to Master half slots are allocated to each Slave in turn according to their access request addresses. So in the first Slave to Master slot of the access window, the two parked Slaves with access request addresses 1 and 2 can respond. If the Master does not broadcast, the parked Slaves are not allowed to respond, and must wait for the next access slot. For example, if the Master has SCO links, some Slaves' access request slots will be used by the SCO packets.

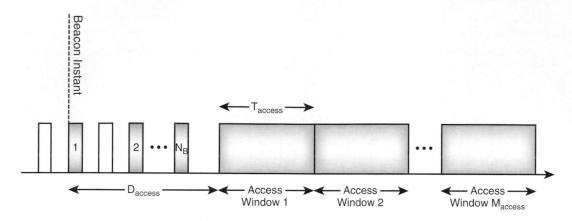

Figure 16–8 Access windows for Slave-initiated unparking.

After the Slave has sent an access request, it listens for the Master broadcasting an unpark message with the parked Slave's Bluetooth device address or parked member address (the parked member address was allocated to the Slave when it was parked and gave up its active member address).

16.4.5 Sleeping through Beacon Slots

A parked Slave can sleep for longer times by sleeping through some beacon trains. The park message carries a parameter telling a Slave the count of beacon trains to wake up at, N_{Bsleep}, and a parameter, D_{Bsleep}, identifying the first train to wake in. The maximum interval between beacon trains is just under 41 seconds. Theoretically, the Slave could wake after

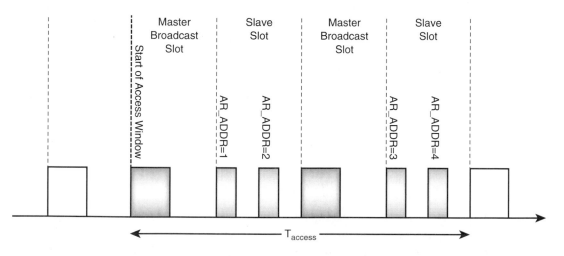

Figure 16–9 Structure of an access window.

255 beacon trains, but parked Slaves can use an inaccurate low power oscillator, which means they slowly drift away from the Master's timing. With the maximum gap between beacon trains and sleeping through the maximum number of slots, a Slave would have over 29 hours between waking up! By this time, it would have hopelessly lost synchronisation with the Master, so parked Slaves should obviously not be set to wake so infrequently.

To ensure that parked Slaves do not totally lose synchronisation with the Master, the Master should unpark and repark them occasionally. This is the only way that the Master can be sure that they are still synchronised.

16.4.6   Requesting Park and Unpark

Both Master and Slave can request that a connection be parked. For systems with an HCI, a host can request its module's LM to park a specific connection using the HCI_Park_Mode command. This command has three parameters:

- Connection_Handle—Identifies the connection to be parked. Only ACL connections can be parked, so this must not be a SCO connection handle.
- Beacon_Max_Interval—The maximum interval between beacon slots.
- Beacon_Min_Interval—The minimum interval between beacon slots.

The Bluetooth module will take some time to process this command, as negotiation between link managers is needed to put a device into Park mode. So the module acknowledges the HCI_Park_Mode command with an HCI_Command_Status event, then when the connection is finally parked, the module sends its host an HCI_Mode_Change event. The host sets minimum and maximum values for beacon interval, so it does not know the actual interval which was negotiated. The HCI_Mode_Change event tells the host what value was negotiated for the beacon interval.

If a host wishes to end Park mode for a connection on its module, it simply sends the HCI_Exit_Park_Mode command. This command only needs one parameter: the connection handle of the connection to be removed from Park mode.

16.4.7   LMP_park_req Message

The LMP_park_req message shown in Figure 16–10 carries more parameters than any other LMP message. The parameters in the park message are as follows:

- Timing control flags—Used to avoid uncertainties in timing caused by clock wrap around.
- D_B—Timing of the first beacon slot.
- T_B—Interval between beacon trains.
- N_B—Number of beacon slots within one beacon train.
- Δ_B—Spacing of beacon slots in the beacon train.
- PM_ADDR—Parked member address; identifies the Slave when it is unparked by the Master.

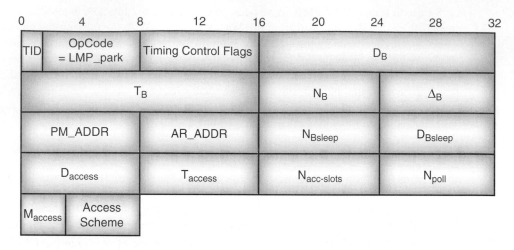

Figure 16–10 The LMP_park_req message.

- AR_ADDR—Access request address used when the Slave requests unparking.
- N_{Bsleep}—Number of beacon train at which Slave wakes (it sleeps for N_{Bsleep}-1 beacon trains).
- D_{Bsleep}—Timing of first beacon train at which the Slave wakes.
- D_{access}—Time from beacon instant to first access slot.
- T_{access}—Width of access window.
- $N_{acc\text{-}slots}$—Number of Slave to Master access slots.
- N_{poll}—Number of slots after access window a Slave listens after requesting unpark.
- M_{access}—Number of repetitions of the access window.
- Access scheme—Slave access techniques supported (only polling is defined!).

The LMP_park_req message is used to park a Slave as shown in Figure 16–11. There are two ways that a Slave can be parked:

- The Master requests a Slave to enter Park mode.
- The Slave requests to be put into Park mode.

In version 1.0b there was also an LMP_park message which the Master could use to force a Slave into Park mode. Slaves may not be able to support all possible park parameters, so this message was removed so that the Slave always gets a chance to negotiate Park mode parameters.

To put a Slave into Park mode a Master sends an LMP_park_req message. If the Slave accepts the request, it replies with an LMP_accepted as shown in Figure 16–11; if it rejects the request, it responds with an LMP_not_accepted as shown in Figure 16–12.

Figure 16–11   LMP message sequence chart for when a Master requests a
Slave to enter Park mode and Slave accepts.

If there is no interference, the Slave sends a packet in its response slot and the
packet's acknowledge flag bit tells the Master that the LMP_park_req message had been
received. However, the Slave's response could get lost due to interference on air. This
leaves the Master unsure whether the slave has seen the LMP_park_req message, so it resends. If the Slave parked immediately, the Master would keep resending until the link
timed out. To avoid this the Slave starts a timer of $6 * T_{poll}$ when it sends the LMP_ac-
cepted, and parks when it receives a baseband level acknowledgement of the LMP_ac-
cepted, or when the timer expires (whichever happens sooner). This keeps the Slave
active for long enough for the LMP_park_req and LMP_accepted to be exchanged even
in the prescence of some interference.

A Slave requests to be put into Park mode by sending an LMP_park_req as shown
in Figure 16–13. The Master can reply with an LMP_not_accepted, or with an
LMP_park_req in which case parking proceeds as if the Master requested it (in version
1.0b the Master can reply with LMP_park; this is kept for backwards compatibility). The
timing parameters in the Slave's LMP_park_req message are suggestions, and the
PM_ADDR and AR_ADDR are ignored entirely: the Master decides the park parameters.

Once the Master has parked Slaves, it can broadcast LMP_unpark messages or data
to them in beacon slots. If a Master has more data than will fit in the beacon slots, it can
broadcast an LMP_set_broadcast_scan_window message, which tells the parked Slaves to
keep listening for an extra window after the beacon slots.

If the Master will regularly have more or less data to send to the Slaves, it can send
an LMP_modify_beacon message to change the beacon parameters. Parameters which
can be changed by the LMP_modify_beacon message are:

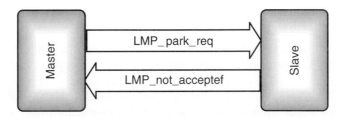

Figure 16–12   LMP message sequence chart for when a Master requests Park mode
and Slave does not accept.

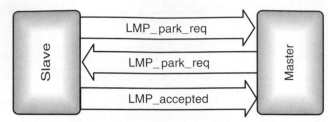

Figure 16–13 LMP message sequence chart for when a Slave requests to enter Park mode.

- D_B—Timing of the first beacon slot.
- T_B—Interval between beacon trains.
- N_B—Number of beacon slots within one beacon train.
- Δ_B—Spacing of beacon slots in the beacon train.
- D_{access}—Time from beacon instant to first access slot.
- T_{access}—Width of access window.
- $N_{acc\text{-}slots}$—Number of Slave to Master access slots.
- N_{poll}—Number of slots after access window a Slave listens after requesting Unpark mode.
- M_{access}—Number of repetitions of the access window.
- Access scheme—Slave access techniques supported (only polling is defined!).

In version 1.0b there was a potential problem if a Master sent an LMP_park_req and the Slave's LMP_accepted response got lost, for example, due to interference. In this situation the Master would keep on trying to park the Slave, but the Slave would never reply again because it was already parked. Eventually the link supervision timeout would elapse and the Master would mark the Slave as disconnected, but the Slave could wait forever for an umpark message which would never come!

The Master could of course assume that it had missed the LMP_accepted and assume the Slave was parked, but this just causes problems if the LMP_park_req message was lost. In that case the Master might reuse an active member address from a Slave it thinks is parked, when the Slave is really still active. This leads to two Slaves sharing one active member address.

Version 1.1 of the Bluetooth specification mitigated this problem by adding some timers as follows:

- The Slave attempts to send the LMP_accepted message until it gets a baseband acknowledgement or until 6*Tpoll slots have passed, whichever is sooner.
- The Master is not allowed to reuse the parked Slave's AM_ADDR until 6*Tpoll slots after it has received LMP_accepted.

- If the Master doesn't receive LMP_accepted, then the Slave is detached when the link supervision timeout happens.

These procedures aren't perfect, it is still possible for a Slave's LMP_accepted message to not get through, so the Slave parks and the Master detaches it. However, because the Slave sends the LMP_accepted for up to 6*Tpoll slots, there is a good chance of the message getting through. It seems that there is no perfect way to guarantee to park a Slave using messages across an unreliable radio link. These procedures are at least a lot more reliable than the 1.0b procedures for parking.

16.4.8   LMP_unpark Message

When Slaves are parked, they give up the Active Member Address (AM_ADDR) and are assigned a Parked Member Address (PM_ADDR). To return a parked Slave to active mode, the Master must send that Slave a new AM_ADDR to use.

Because a parked Slave has no AM_ADDR, it is addressed by its Bluetooth Device Address (BD_ADDR) or by its PM_ADDR. There are two different unpark messages according to which type of address is being used to unpark Slaves: LMP_unpark_PM_ADDR_req and LMP_unpark_BD_ADDR_req. (It is worth noting that the LMP_unpark message changed slightly for version 1.1 of the core Bluetooth specification. In version 1.0b the LMP_unpark_PM_ADDR_req message had 4 bits allocated for the Active Member Address, when in fact the address is only 3 bits long. This caused confusion because manufacturers were unsure where to place the address in the 4 bit field. This caused some interoperability problems which were solved in verson 1.1 by making the field 3 bits long.

Two Slaves can be unparked with a single message simply by placing both their addresses in one unpark message. As Figure 16–14 shows, the sequence of messages and actions is the same whether the parked Slaves are addressed using their PM_ADDRs or BD_ADDRs.

First, an unpark message is sent. This message is broadcast by the Master in a beacon slot. It contains the addresses of the Slaves the Master wishes to unpark (BD_ADDR or PM_ADDR); the message also assigns a new AM_ADDR for each Slave to be unparked.

When the Slaves receive the unpark message, they return to active mode instead of going to sleep as parked Slaves would. To check that the Slaves have received the unpark message, the Master must poll each Slave in turn. Each Slave responds with an LMP_accepted message when it receives the poll.

As the Master is establishing a new active connection, the same timeout is used for unparking Slaves as is used for setting up new connections (newconnectionTO). The Master may continue polling the Slaves until the timeout expires. If the Master does not receive an LMP_accepted, it must assume the unpark failed and wait until the next beacon before trying again to unpark Slaves which did not respond.

16.4.9   Timing Accuracy

When a Slave device returns from Hold mode, it has not received any transmissions for a while, so its clock will have drifted out of synchronisation with the Master's clock. Nor-

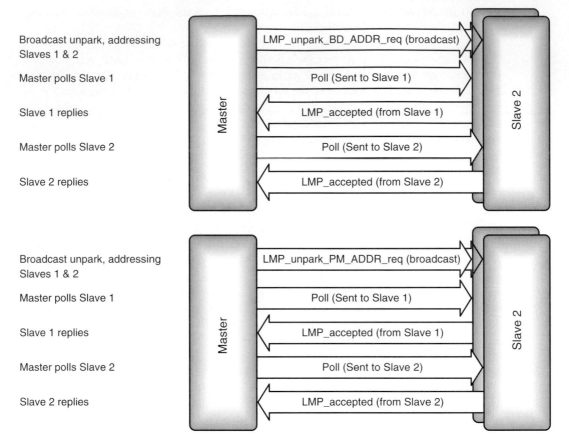

Figure 16–14   LMP message sequence charts for when a Master requests Unpark mode.

mally, a Slave predicts the start of the next transmission from the Master, and opens its correlator for a period of 10 μS on either side of the expected start. On returning from Hold mode, because it can't accurately predict the start of the Master's transmission, a Slave must open its correlator across a wider scan window than normal.

Figure 16–15 shows the difference between the slot timing of an active device and a device returning from Hold mode. The shaded blocks at the top of the diagram show the correlator opening for 10 μS on either side of the estimated start of the receive slot. If the device is a Slave, it recalibrates its estimate of the start of the slot according to when it actually begins to receive.

The shaded blocks at the bottom of the diagram show the correlator opening on return from Hold mode. The device has not received any packets from the Master during Hold mode, so its estimate of the slot timing has not been corrected for a while.

The device can work out how wide to open the correlators by looking at the accuracy of its own clock and the accuracy of the clock at the other end of the connection. If

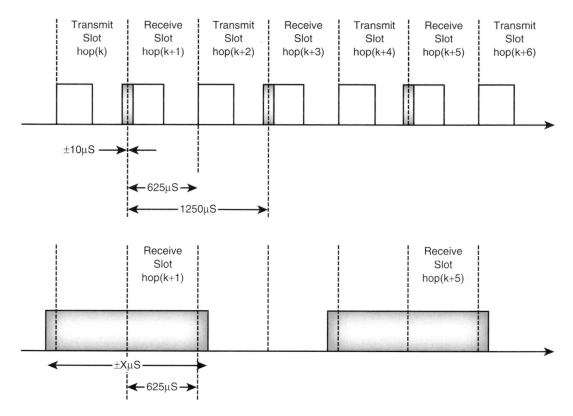

Figure 16–15   Widening correlation window on return from Hold mode.

the accuracy is unknown, the worst case accuracy is used as a default. The worst case allowed by the Bluetooth specification is a clock with jitter of ±10 µS and drift of 250 ppm. This worst case is for a low-power oscillator (see section 16.5); most active devices will perform much better than this.

The accuracy of the clock at the other end of the connection can be retrieved with an LMP_timing_accuracy_req. The remote link manager responds with a LMP_timing_accuracy_res message, which includes parameters for drift and jitter.

Once the device has predicted the width of the uncertainty window, it opens its correlators over the wider window. This may lead to the correlator being opened over more than a slot, as is the case in Figure 16–15. The device continues opening its correlators for the calculated uncertainty window centered on its predicted timing until it receives a packet, or its link supervision timeout elapses.

When slots are missed because the correlator is open over more than a slot, the hop frequency used is the frequency for the receive slot the correlator is centred upon.

Parked and sniffing devices also have to open their correlators wider than usual, because like devices returning from Hold mode, they have not received transmissions from a Master for a while, so their estimate of the beginning of the receive slot will be less accurate.

16.5 LOW-POWER OSCILLATOR

While a device is not receiving because it is in standby (unconnected) Hold or Park mode, it is allowed to save power by switching off the reference crystal oscillator which drives the Bluetooth clock. Some system is still needed to drive the clock, so instead of the reference oscillator, a low-power oscillator is used.

The reference crystal oscillator has an accuracy of ± 20 ppm; the low-power oscillator (LPO) has a far more relaxed requirement for accuracy at only ±250 ppm. It is the low-power oscillator's accuracy that sets the default of 250 ppm, which devices must assume when calculating the uncertainty in their prediction of slot boundaries.

16.6 SUMMARY

Many Bluetooth devices will be operated by batteries, so it is important that they do not use more power than necessary.

Some Bluetooth devices such as headsets connected to cellular mobile phones need to respond fast to signals, so ideally they should stay connected all the time to avoid the delay of setting up a connection extending their response time. However, being constantly connected would mean using the radio a lot and would drain the device's batteries. Bluetooth provides three low-power modes which extend battery life by reducing activity on a connection. These modes are called Park, Hold, and Sniff.

Park mode provides the greatest opportunities for power saving. The device only wakes up in periodic beacon slots, where it listens for unpark transmissions from the Master. If it is not unparked, it goes back to sleep, switching off its receiver. A special unpark message is used to restore the device to normal activity. Devices which are parked give up their active member addresses, so the unpark messages either use a special parked member address, which is assigned to devices when they are parked, or they can use the device's Bluetooth Device Address (BD_ADDR). Because a parked device gives up its active member address, one Master can have more than seven devices in Park mode at once (it is the size of the active member address which limits a Master to having a maximum of seven active Slaves).

In Sniff mode, the device wakes up periodically and listens for transmissions, but no special unpark messages are needed to communicate with it. Devices in Sniff mode keep their active member address. Typically, sniffing devices will be active more often than parked devices.

Park and Sniff modes both involve putting devices into a state where they wake up periodically. Conversely, Hold mode just puts a connection in a low-power state for a single period. Connections to Slaves might usefully be put into Hold mode while a Master performs an inquiry or a page, as the Master knows in advance that it will not be able to service the connections for a while.

Many layers of the Bluetooth protocol stack are involved in low-power modes: the baseband/link controller layer alters correlator properties, as after periods of inactivity, the device may lose synchronisation and need to listen for transmissions over a wider window than usual. The link controller layer is also involved with state machines for timing the low-power modes. The link manager provides a variety of messages to configure and negotiate the low-power modes between ends of a connection. HCI provides a set of commands which may be used by a host to configure and control the power-saving capabilities of a module. L2CAP must be aware of low-power modes for its quality of service commitments.

The detailed operation of the power-saving modes can be complex to understand, but for the user of a Bluetooth device, that complexity will be invisible. Properly configured, a Bluetooth device will perform power saving, and the only visibility to the user will be an extended battery life.

17

Quality of Service

Simple Bluetooth devices will have one application or protocol using a single link. Different applications and protocols will place different demands on the link. For example, a file transfer wants to move data reliably and as fast as possible; it doesn't matter if the link is bursty (sometimes fast, sometimes slower when there are errors on the link and packets have to be retransmitted). On the other hand, an application transferring compressed video or audio streams may want a link that is not bursty and may be able to miss a few packets as long as the delay on the link is not too high.

In devices where there are many links operating at once, the bandwidth allocated to each link must be decided. Many applications or protocols will want high bandwidth, but some applications will never require high data rates; for instance, many remote controls will never transfer more than a few bytes a second.

The Bluetooth specification provides Quality Of Service (QOS) configuration to allow the properties of links to be configured according to the requirements of higher layer applications or protocols. The properties which can be configured are:

- The type of QOS—Whether the link guarantees its settings, will just make an attempt at achieving them, or possibly offer no service at all.
- Token rate—The rate at which data may be sent on a link.

- Token rate bucket size—This is a measure of how much storage will be available in the stack for data. Bursty links will most likely need more storage than links which flow evenly.
- Peak bandwidth—The maximum rate that back to back packets can be sent—that is to say, packets all dedicated to one link with no other links getting to transfer in between them.
- Latency—The delay between data being ready to send and being sent out over the radio for the first time.
- Delay variation—The spread between the maximum and minimum delay across a link.

Figure 17–1 shows how messages throughout the Bluetooth protocol stack are used to control QOS. Messages configuring and setting up QOS flow vertically up and down the layers of the stack, but there is also horizontal messaging when peer entities on different devices negotiate QOS. Both the link manager (LM), and the Logical Link Control and Adaptation Layer (L2CA) are involved in peer to peer negotiations to configure QOS for a link.

The L2CA uses the Logical Link Control and Adaptation Protocol (L2CAP) to request a particular QOS on a link. The L2CA at the far end of the link tries to achieve the requested QOS by asking its local link manager. On systems with an HCI, L2CA communicates with LM via HCI as shown in Figure 17–1.

The link manager configures and controls the baseband links. So it is LM which actually implements QOS policies. LM has various means to try to meet the QOS which L2CA requests.

To ensure that data is removed from its transmission buffers fast enough to satisfy the token rate LM has guaranteed on a connection, LM guarantees a polling interval, that is to say a maximum gap between subsequent transmissions on a link. If the packet type on a connection changes, the amount of data transferred in each packet will change, so the polling interval may also change.

Under some circumstances, the polling interval will not change even if packet types change. This is because the poll interval is the maximum time between transmissions from the Master to a particular Slave. The gap between transmissions affects the latency (delay) on a connection, as well as the bandwidth available to a Slave. So if increasing the poll interval would take latency beyond what has been guaranteed, then the poll interval won't be changed.

The link manager can also affect the overall behaviour of the system according to the QOS settings it has accepted. If the link manager accepts a connection with a maximum possible token rate and a service type of guaranteed, then the link manager should try to meet this by refusing all connection requests from remote devices. It could also maximise bandwidth available to the ACL connection by stopping periodic page and inquiry scans (it doesn't want to accept new connections anyway, so there's not a lot of point in scanning for new devices in the area).

Link managers at opposite ends of a link must agree on the QOS they are trying to achieve: It is no good to one link manager successfully transmitting lots of packets if the

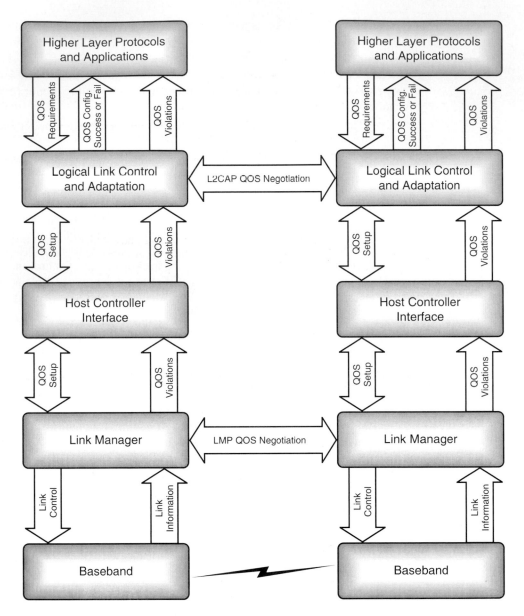

Figure 17–1 Quality of service messaging.

LM at the other end doesn't have the resources to receive them and forward them up the stack. So in addition to controlling the baseband layers, LM performs end to end negotiations of QOS using the LMP. When L2CAP requests a particular QOS configuration, link managers at the opposite ends of a link negotiate. If they agree that they can achieve the requested QOS, the L2CAP which requested it is informed, and it can tell its peer L2CAP that QOS configuration has succeeded; otherwise, QOS configuration fails and L2CAP must decide whether to give up or try again with a different QOS. This decision is actually taken by the application above L2CAP which requested the QOS in the first place.

It should be obvious by now that QOS involves some complex tradeoffs in the management of a device's ACL links. Sometimes the required QOS won't be possible because of interference on the radio link, and sometimes it won't be possible just because the device doesn't have the capacity available. To cope with this, the Bluetooth specification provides a variety of messages at various levels to negotiate acceptable levels in QOS, and to signal when those levels just can't be met.

17.1   REQUESTING QOS

When a link is first set up, there is usually a negotiation phase where the parameters for the link are configured. This is the point where security is usually configured; QOS can be configured at this point too. Just as with security, the QOS can be changed later on if higher layer applications or protocols need to change it. This might be because a new service wants to use the link, or because the radio environment has changed and the requested QOS is no longer realistic. This section explains how the layers of the Bluetooth protocol stack interact to change QOS on a link in response to a QOS request.

17.1.1   QOS Requests from Higher Layers to L2CA

A service, application, or higher level protocol which needs a certain QOS requests it at the time a Logical Link Control and Adaptation Layer (L2CA) connection is set up by sending a configuration request to L2CA. The exact format of exchanges between higher layers and L2CA is implementation-specific, but the Bluetooth specification suggests possible primitives.

L2CA_ConfigReq is used to request configuration of a channel. Among its parameters, this request includes a channel identifier and a flow specification which gives the QOS required on the channel. How L2CA responds to this message depends upon the state of the L2CA channel when the request is sent:

- If the channel is closed, then an L2CA_ConfigRspNeg is returned to the upper layer indicating that the channel cannot be configured.
- If the channel is in configuration state, then L2CA begins QOS negotiation.
- If the channel is open, data transmission on the channel is stopped at a convenient point (say at the end of an L2CAP packet), then L2CA moves the channel to the configuration state and begins QOS negotiation.

To begin QOS negotiations, an L2CAP_ConfigReq Message is sent to the L2CA at the other end of the channel (see Figure 17–1) and an RTX timer is started to check the response time.

17.1.2   L2CAP Peer-to-Peer QOS Request

To configure QOS at the Logical Link Control and Adaptation (L2CA) layer, a configuration packet is sent. The structure of this packet is shown in Figure 17–2. The packet begins with the fields common to all L2CA signalling commands:

- Code—Identifies the type of command. The code 0x04 identifies the configuration command.
- Identifier—This field is changed for each request, and copied into the response, so that responses and requests can be matched up.
- Length—Identifies the overall length in bytes of the data part of the command (this does not include the code, identifier, and length fields).

These are followed by four fields common to all L2CA configuration request commands:

- Destination channel ID—Identifies the endpoint of the channel on the device which is receiving the command.
- Flags—Although this is a 2-byte field, only the least significant byte is used in versions 1.0 and 1.1 of the specification. This is a continuation flag. If this is 1, then

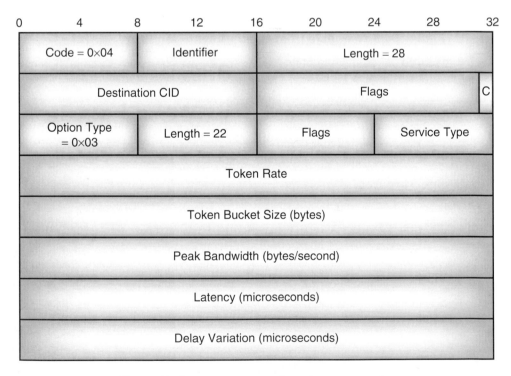

Figure 17–2   L2CA QOS configuration request packet.

more configuration requests will follow; if it is 0, then the channel is configured, and the remote device may enter the open state.

- Option type—Set to 0x03, this indicates the configuration request deals with QOS.
- Option length—The length of the remaining option parameters.

The remaining fields contain the configuration options for QOS.

- Flags—In versions 1.0 and 1.1, this is reserved for future use, and must be set to zero.
- Service type—The level of service; possible values are no service, best effort, or guaranteed. If best effort is chosen, the device receiving the request has three options: it may choose to ignore the rest of the parameters, it may try to satisfy the request but not respond, or it may respond with the settings it believes it can achieve.
- Token rate—The rate at which an application using the channel will be granted credit. It is measured in bytes per second. An application may send data up to the token rate, but shouldn't exceed it. 0xFFFFFFFF is actually a value larger than the maximum capacity of a Bluetooth link, so it has a special meaning: it requests the maximum available rate. 0x00000000 also has a special meaning: rather than indicating zero token rate, it indicates that the requester is not specifying a token rate.
- Token rate bucket size—The size of the token bucket, that is to say the size of buffer which should be made available to receive data. Bursty data needs a large token bucket; continuous data needs a small bucket, or none at all (predictably, if no token bucket is needed, this is indicated by sending a bucket size of 0x00000000). Again the value 0xFFFFFFFF has a special meaning: it means that the largest possible token bucket should be allocated.
- Peak bandwidth—The maximum rate at which applications may send back to back packets. The value 0x00000000 does not say that maximum bandwidth is zero, rather it says that the maximum bandwidth is not known.
- Latency—The maximum delay between sending a bit and it being transmitted for the first time over air. (Note that "for the first time" implies that retransmissions may mean that the real latency is higher than this value.) The value 0xFFFFFFFF has a special meaning: it indicates that the requester doesn't care about latency.
- Delay variation—The difference in microseconds between the longest and shortest delay a packet will experience. This affects the amount of buffer space that will be needed to reassemble a continuous stream of data. The value 0xFFFFFFFF has a special meaning: it indicates that the requester doesn't care about delay variation.

If QOS is not configured, the device should use the following default values:

- Service Type = Best effort.
- Token rate = 0x00000000 (unspecified).
- Token bucket size = 0x00000000 (no bucket needed).
- Peak bandwidth = 0x00000000 (unknown).

- Latency = 0xFFFFFFFF (don't care).
- Delay variation = 0xFFFFFFFF (don't care).

If L2CA only needs the default QOS parameters, then QOS does not need to be configured. If any other parameters are needed, then an L2CAP_ConfigReq is sent, informing the remote L2CA of the parameters the local L2CA wants.

The remote side may disagree, in which case it sends an L2CAP_ConfigRsp with Result = Configuration Failed. The local side must try again with different parameters, or give up on the connection.

The local L2CA keeps trying again with different parameters until the remote L2CA agrees; the local L2CA decides the QOS level achievable is unacceptable.

17.1.3   HCI QOS Setup

For systems with a separate host and Bluetooth module, the HCI provides the means for the Logical Link Control and Adapatation Layer (L2CA) to control the link manager.

The link manager provides QOS capabilities according to the requests from L2CAP. On systems with an HCI, these requests are received via HCI_QOS_Setup commands.

When L2CAP receives an L2CAP_ConfigReq message with new configuration options for QOS, it must find out if the link manager can satisfy the request. On systems with a separate host and Bluetooth module, the sequence of messages shown in Figure 17–3 are triggered by the host requesting a new QOS. The sections below go through these messages in turn.

The first message is an HCI_QoS_Setup. Its parameters reflect the parameters of the L2CAP_ConfigReq received by the L2CA layer (see section 17.1.2); they are:

- Connection_Handle—Identifies an ACL connection. This is the connection carrying the L2CA channel being configured.
- Flags—Reserved.

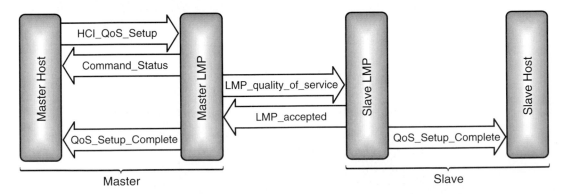

Figure 17–3   Message sequence chart for HCI_QoS_Setup.

- Service_Type—One of: no traffic, best effort, or guaranteed.
- Token_Rate—In bytes per second.
- Peak_Bandwidth—In bytes per second.
- Latency—In microseconds.
- Delay_Variation—In microseconds.

For a Slave, this command triggers an LMP request to the Master to provide the Slave with the specified QOS. For a Master device, this command triggers a request to the Slave to accept the specified QOS.

17.1.4 LMP QOS Negotiation

LMP commands can be used to configure the poll interval and N_{BC}. The poll interval is the maximum interval between packets sent from Master to Slave. N_{BC} is the number of times a broadcast packet will be repeated (because broadcast packets are not acknowledged, they must be repeated to ensure that they have been received).

The LMP QOS request can be used to request a new poll interval and N_{BC}. If the Master sends LMP_quality_of_service, the Slave cannot reject the new QOS so there is no need for an LMP_accepted message. This is shown in Figure 17–4.

In contrast, Figure 17–5 shows an LMP_quality_of_service_req which can be rejected, so this message requires an LMP_accepted (or LMP_not_accepted) response.

17.1.5 QOS Setup Completion

The HCI_QoS_Setup_Complete event is generated when LMP has finished setting up QOS. The HCI_QoS_Setup event contains a status field. If the setup succeeded (an LMP_accepted was received), then this is set to zero to indicate success; if the setup failed (an LMP_not_accepted was received), then the status field will indicate an error. For instance, the value 0x0d indicates that the host at the other end of the link terminated the connection, due to low resources. This could also be used to indicate that the remote host would not accept the QOS parameters requested. (In fact, the host has not completely rejected the connection and LMP can try again with different QOS parameters; while slightly inaccurate, this is the error message that best reflects the situation).

If HCI_QoS_Setup indicates that QOS setup failed, then the L2CA layer must send a L2CAP_ConfigRsp with Result = Configuration Failed. The L2CA which sent

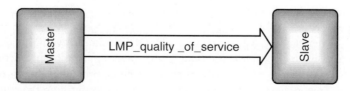

Figure 17–4   LMP message sequence chart for QOS request from Master.

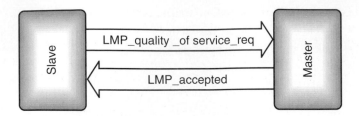

Figure 17–5 LMP message sequence chart for QOS request from Slave.

the original L2CAP_ConfigReq can then signal to the higher layer application which requested the QOS that it is unavailable by sending an L2CA_ConfigRspNeg. The application must then decide whether to try again with a less demanding QOS, or to give up. At this stage, a decision could also be made to shut down some connections or services so that the desired QOS could be achieved. The Bluetooth specification does not specify how the higher layers should handle failure to achieve the desired QOS, this is left up to the implementers of the higher layer applications, services, or protocols.

If HCI_QOS_Setup indicates that QOS setup suceeeded, then the L2CA layer must send a L2CAP_ConfigRsp with Result = Success. The L2CA which sent the original L2CAP_ConfigReq can then signal to the higher layer application which requested the QOS that it is available by sending an L2CA_ConfigRsp. If this was the last configuration request on the L2CA channel, the channel will then move to the open state and be available for transferring data at the desired QOS.

17.2 QOS VIOLATIONS

Once a channel has been configured for a particular QOS, it is possible that interference or system errors may stop that QOS from being achieved. It is important that applications are aware if their QOS is not as requested, as they may wish to shut down the link rather than run it at an inappropriate quality, or the user may wish to shut down other links to improve the quality available on this link.

The link manager attempts to empty its transmit buffers at the rate specified by the QOS parameters to which it has agreed. If the transmit buffers overflow LM reacts by sending a QOS violation event to the L2CA layer. Even if the service type is best effort, unless L2CA said it didn't care about token rate, a QOS violation event should be reported. In systems with an HCI, the QOS violation event is sent as an HCI_QOS_Violation event.

When the L2CA layer receives the QOS violation event, it calls an L2CA_QoSViolationInd callback to indicate to the higher layer application protocol or service using the connection that the requested service is not being provided. This provides an opportunity for the higher layer to decide whether it wants to reconfigure the connection or take some other action.

17.3   FLUSHING AND DELAYS

The link manager will attempt to enforce delay variance by setting the polling interval for each connection. This ensures that packets are transmitted regularly on all connections. However, sometimes a connection is subject to interference and packets just can't get through. Old data will accumulate in the stack, while the baseband tries again and again to transmit the same packet. On systems with an HCI, when the lower layers of the stack run out of buffers, the host will be flow controlled and the lower layers will continue trying to resend the same old data while the host is prevented from sending new data.

This is a good system where it is vital that every packet gets through. For example, if a file is being transferred across an ACL link, it is important for every byte to get through correctly. However, on some types of links, it is more important that fresh data is sent. For example, some video compression systems can handle a missing packet by freezing the picture, and if such a system is being used, it is more important to show up to date information than to make sure that every last byte gets through.

For systems where it is important for data to be fresh and not so important for every byte to get through, the Bluetooth specification provides flush commands at the HCI. If the host sends an HCI_Flush command, all data currently waiting for transmission on a link is thrown away. This might mean that the first part of an L2CAP packet is thrown away, so if data transmission started again immediately after an HCI_Flush, the far end of the link could be sent part of an L2CAP packet. Such a fragment of an L2CAP packet would have to be discarded by the receiving L2CA layer, so there is really no point in sending it. Instead, the host controller just discards any data packets it receives for the flushed link until it sees the start of the next L2CAP packet. Once the start of the next L2CAP packet is seen, data transmission begins again as normal. When the flush has finished, an HCI_Command_Complete is returned to tell the host that data transmission is restarting.

Because each ACL link goes to a different device, it is possible for one link to need flushing, while other links are perfectly okay. So, the HCI_Flush command takes a Connection_Handle, which allows the host to specify which link it wants to flush old data from.

Some applications will want to flush whenever data gets beyond a certain age. On poor links, this could lead to many HCI_Flush commands being sent. To save on the number of messages being sent up and down the stack, the Bluetooth specification provides a facility for automatically flushing data once it gets beyond a preset age. The higher layers decide upon a timeout, which governs how long the baseband will spend trying to send an L2CAP packet. A timer is started when the first fragment of each L2CAP packet is sent. If the whole packet hasn't been sent by the time the timer has expired, then the packet is flushed. The flush timeout is set by the host using the HCI_Write_Automatic_ Flush_Timeout command. Like the HCI_Flush command, this command has a Connection_Handle parameter to specify which ACL link it applies to, and of course, it also has a parameter Flush_Timeout, specifying the length of the timer. The timer is specified in units of $625\mu S$ (the length of a Bluetooth slot). If the timeout is set to zero, this doesn't mean flush a packet before it has been sent, it means don't flush any packets on that link, that is to say, switch off automatic flushing.

The value of the timer can be checked with an HCI_Read_Automatic_Flush_Timeout command.

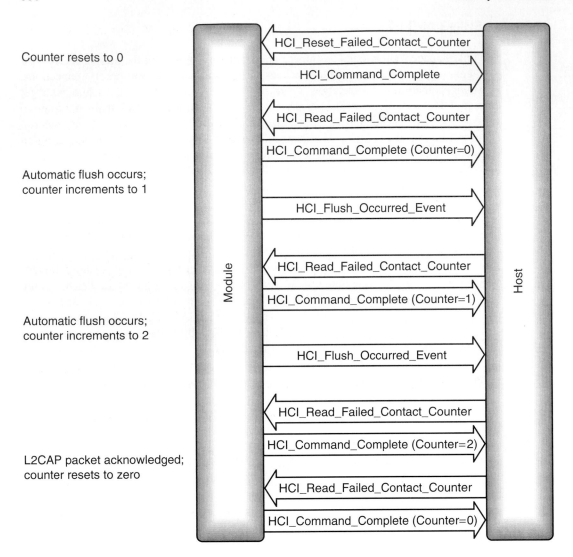

Figure 17–6   Automatic flushing and failed contact counter.

An HCI_Flush_Occurred event is generated each time a flush occurs. This event is generated whether the flush occurred because of an HCI_Flush command, or because of an automatic flush.

17.3.1   Failed Contact Counter

The failed contact counter measures the number of times in a row an automatic flush happens. Although the counter is returned in a 2 byte parameter, only 12 bits of it are used, so its range is from 0 to 0x0FFF. When a host sends an HCI_Read_Failed_Contact_Counter command, the counter's value is returned in an HCI_Command_Complete event.

The failed contact counter increments each time an automatic flush happens. The counter is reset to zero when a new connection is established, and when an L2CAP packet is acknowledged for the connection. The counter can also be reset to zero by the HCI_Reset_Failed_Contact_Counter command. This means that the counter will only be nonzero while a series of automatic flush events are happening.

Figure 17–6 shows how the value of the failed contact counter changes as a series of flush events happens.

17.4 LINK SUPERVISION

If enough flushes occur in a row, it is possible that the link is incapable of use: maybe the device at the other end has moved out of range, or perhaps it has even been switched off. If this happens, a link supervision timer will elapse and allow the link to be shut down, so that its active member address (AM_ADDR) can be reused.

A separate link supervision timer, $T_{supervision}$, is kept for each link. Each link supervision timer is reset whenever a packet which passes its Header Error Check (HEC) and has the correct AM_ADDR is received on a link. The supervision timer begins counting from a value, supervisionTO. The default value is 20 s, but it can be changed using an HCI_Write_Link_Supervision_Timeout command; possible values range from 0.625 s to 40.9 s. The current value of supervisionTO can be checked with the command HCI_Read_Link_Supervision_Timeout. Since the timer can be set differently on each connection, this command takes a Connection_Handle parameter.

The Master determines how often the Slaves will be contacted, so the Master determines the link supervision timeout. It then communicates the timeout to Slaves by sending an LMP_supervision_timeout command to the Slave's link manager as shown in Figure 17–7.

The value of the supervision timeout should be set to be longer than any hold or sniff periods which are in force on the link. Parked Slaves can be unparked and reparked before the timer elapses, or the timer can be switched off.

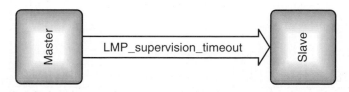

Figure 17–7   Message sequence chart for LMP_supervision_timeout.

17.5 BROADCAST CHANNEL RELIABILITY

When a packet is unicast (sent point to point), the Master transmits and the Slave replies. The Slave's reply carries an Acknowledge (ARQN) bit in the packet's header which lets the Master know whether or not its transmission was received correctly. When a packet is broadcast, it is sent to many Slaves. There is no reply because if all Slaves replied at once, their transmissions would interfere with each other and no data would get through.

Because Slaves cannot acknowledge receipt of broadcast packets, the Master doesn't know when broadcast packets have been received, and when they were wiped out by radio interference, so the Master doesn't know when it needs to retransmit packets. To make the broadcast link reasonably reliable, the Master can transmit each broadcast packet several times. This gives a reasonable chance that one of the broadcast transmissions will get through.

Figure 17–8 shows the difference between broadcast and unicast transmission:

- Packet 1 is a unicast from the Master to Slave 1.
- Packet 2 carries the Slaves reply, including an acknowledge bit to tell the Master the packet got through intact.
- Packet 3 is a SCO packet to Slave 2.

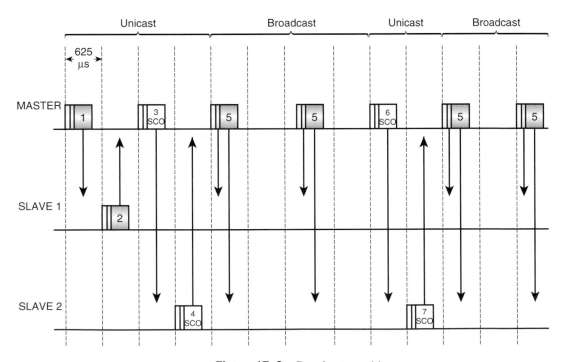

Figure 17–8   Broadcast repetition.

- Packet 4 is the Slave's reply. SCO packets are never retransmitted, so even though they carry the standard header including the ARQN bit, it is not used for retransmission.
- Packet 5 is a broadcast packet sent by the Master to both Slaves. Neither Slave replies, so this packet it re-transmitted several times to make sure it gets through.
- Packets 6 and 7 are SCO packets. Since these must go out regularly in reserved slots, they interrupt the broadcast repetitions.

Because Slaves only transmit on ACL links when they are addressed by the Master, only the Master is allowed to broadcast on an ACL link.

The more times the Master retransmits, the more reliable the broadcast will be. On the other hand, the more times the Master retransmits, the more bandwidth will be used up, so the data rate will go down. The number of broadcast repetitions must be set to give a tradeoff between data rate and reliability.

For systems with an HCI, the HCI_Write_Num_Broadcast_Retransmissions command sets the number of times the Master transmits each broadcast packet to be sent by the host. The command has a single parameter: the number of retransmissions. The default number of retransmissions is one, that is to say each broadcast packet is sent twice (one transmission plus one retransmission). The HCI_Read_Num_Broadcast_Retransmissions command can be used to check the current broadcast retransmission setting.

The number of broadcast retransmissions should be adjusted as the quality of the link can be expected to vary for many reasons: the distance mobile devices can vary affecting signal strength; objects can get in the way of the link and absorb power; and sources of radio interference can reduce the channel quality.

17.5.1   Channel Quality Monitoring

The host should adjust parameters such as broadcast retransmission according to the quality of the link. To do this, it has to get information on the link quality. The HCI provides the HCI_Get_Link_Quality command to aid in monitoring link quality.

The HCI_Get_Link_Quality command retrieves a value of link quality for a specified connection (the connection is identified by a Connection_Handle parameter). The link quality value is a number between 0 and 255; how it is calculated is up to each implementation to decide, though all implementations have higher numbers indicating higher quality links. This value could be used to reflect a Bit Error Rate (BER) on the link.

17.6   DATA RATES AND PACKET TYPES

The Bluetooth specification provides a variety of packets for carrying data. Usually DM and DH packets will be used on ACL links. DM stands for Data Medium rate and DH stands for Data High rate. The DH packets achieve a higher rate by using less error correction in the packet; this leaves more room for data. Naturally, the single-slot packets DM1 and DH1 carry less data than the 3-slot packets DM3 and DH3, and the 5 slot pack-

Table 17–1   DM and DH Packets

Packet Type	Max. Payload (bytes)	FEC	Max Symmetric Data Rate (kb/s)	Asymmetric Data Rate Forward (kb/s)	Asymmetric Data Rate Reverse (kb/s)
DM1	17	2/3	108.8	108.8	108.8
DH1	27	None	172.8	172.8	172.8
DM3	121	2/3	258.1	387.2	54.4
DH3	183	None	390.4	585.6	86.4
DM5	224	2/3	286.7	477.8	36.3
DH5	339	None	433.9	723.2	57.6

ets DM5 and DH5 have the maximum capacity for payload data. Table 17–1 shows the difference in capacity of the different packet types.

Table 17–1 gives figures for symmetric, asymmetric forward, and asymmetric reverse channels. A symmetric channel uses the same packet types in both directions. This channel type would be used when both Master and Slave needed to send data at about the same rate. Often data will need to be transferred faster in one direction than in the other; for example, if a PDA is browsing the Web via a server, there will be a high data rate from the server to the PDA as Web pages are downloaded, but in the reverse direction, only a few bytes of data will need to be transferred to specify the next link to browse. For such situations, Bluetooth provides asymmetric channels: a large packet size is used in the forward (high data rate) direction, and a small packet size is used in the reverse (low data rate) direction. Figure 17–9 shows a symmetric channel with single-slot packets in both directions, an asymmetric channel with the Master sending 3 slot packets, and the Slave sending single slot packets. Asymmetric channels can be configured so that the Master or the Slave transmits at the higher rate.

Asymmetric channels can give higher data rates in the forward direction, but the data rates given in Table 17–1 are for the maximum number of bytes of data which can be transferred on air. When calculating data rates for applications, it should be kept in mind that packet sizes will affect how efficiently packets are transferred. This can mean that asymmetric channels may not be appropriate. Also, higher protocol layers such as L2CAP and RFCOMM will use some of the channel's capacity with headers and framing information.

For example, if we assume that a regular stream of 20 byte packets is sent via RFCOMM, L2CAP, and HCI, this is what will happen:

RFCOMM adds a byte of address, a byte of control, a byte of length indicator, and a byte of Frame Check Sequence (FCS). (See Chapter 10 for more details.) These extra four bytes mean that L2CAP receives a 24 byte packet. (In fact, RFCOMM escapes some characters, so the data rate could be worse, depending on the data patterns sent.)

L2CAP adds two bytes of length and two bytes of channel ID onto the packet. (See Chapter 10 for more details.) These extra four bytes mean that HCI receives a 28 byte packet.

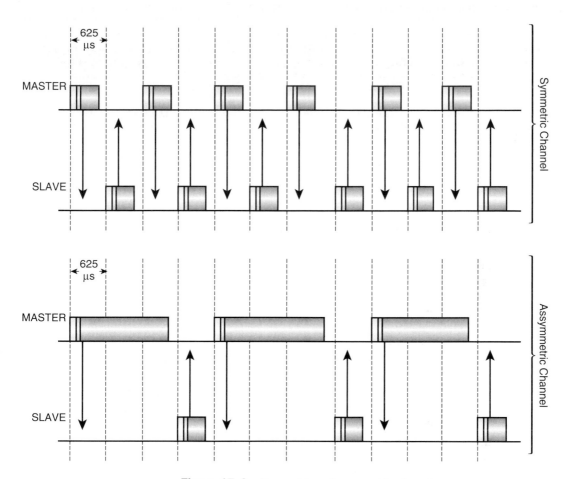

Figure 17–9   Symmetric and asymmetric channels.

If the link is using DH1 packets, the payload is 27 bytes, so the L2CAP packet will have to be split up into two DH1 packets.

A DH1 packet can be transmitted at most once every slot pair, which is once every 1350 µS, so 800 packets can be sent each second. Each packet could carry 27 bytes, giving a maximum data rate of 21.6 Kbyte/s, or 172.8 Kbits/s; but in practice, each pair of packets is carrying 28 bytes, giving a data rate on air of 112.2 Kbyte/s, or 89.6 Kbits/s. The data rate is down by almost half at 52%.

400 packets of 20 bytes each can be sent per second to RFCOMM, so above RFCOMM, the data rate is only 8 Kbyte/s, or 64 Kbit/s. Now the data rate is down by 37% of the maximum on air rate.

If we repeat the calculations and see what transfer rates are achieved above RFCOMM for 20 byte packets, we get the figures in Table 17–2. As the packet sizes in-

Table 17–2   Data Rates for 20 byte Packet into RFCOMM Compared with Maximum Rates on Air

Packet Type	Symmetric Data Rate (Kbit/S)		Asymmetric Forward Data rate (Kbit/S)		Asymmetric Reverse Data Rate (Kbit/S)	
	Max Rate On Air	Rate at RFCOMM with 20-byte Packets	Max Rate On Air	Rate at RFCOMM with 20-byte Packets	Max Rate On Air	Rate at RFCOMM with 20-byte Packets
DM1	108.8	64	108.8	64	108.8	64
DH1	172.8	128	172.8	128	172.8	64
DM3	258.1	42.3	387.2	64	54.4	32
DH3	390.4	42.3	585.6	64	86.6	32
DM5	286.7	25.7	477.8	42.7	36.2	21.3
DH5	433.9	25.7	723.2	42.7	57.6	21.3

crease, they become a less and less efficient way of transporting the small RFCOMM packets, so instead of data rates increasing, they decrease.

The example above was chosen to make a point and the figures are particularly bad, but it should be kept in mind that figures quoted for Bluetooth channel rates in the specification will not translate to the same data rate at the Application Level.

Another consideration when choosing packet types is the likelihood of corruption. If many packets are being retransmitted, then it is better to use short packets, as these are more likely to get through without errors.

In a real system, losses due to retransmission and signalling packets interfering with data flow will also reduce the data rate.

17.6.1   Channel Quality-Driven Data Rate

The host can change the packet types in use on the link using the HCI_Change_Connection_Packet_Type command. This command has two parameters: a Connection_Handle identifying the connection being configured and a Packet_Type parameter that sets the range of packets which may be used for transferring data on the connection. At least one packet type must be specified.

For ACL connections, the packets are chosen from DM1, DH1, DM3, DH3, DM5, and DH5. Note that the AUX packets are used for test, but are not used for transferring data in normal operation, so they are not among the packet types which can be set by the HCI_Change_Connection_Packet_Type command.

For SCO connections, the packets are chosen from HV1, HV2, and HV3. Note that connections cannot be configured to use DV packets. The baseband specification suggests that the device could automatically use DV packets to transfer data on the SCO link, if data is available to be sent to the same destination as the SCO packet.

If a connection is configured to use both high rate and medium rate packets, there is a choice of higher data rate (DH packets) or better error protection (DM packets). The

Bluetooth specification provides a mechanism for devices to automatically switch between DM and DH packet types according to the error rate on the link.

The simplest mechanism would be for each device to monitor the link. If it saw a high BER on the link when it was using DH packets, it could switch to sending DM packets; if it saw a good link when using DM packets, it could switch back to DH packets. However, it is possible for the quality of radio receivers to vary greatly between devices. This could lead to one device seeing few errors on the channel while the other sees a much higher error rate. Therefore, the type of packet transmitted on the link has to be controlled by the quality of the packet at the opposite end of the link, not at the same end; that is to say the Master chooses the Slave's packet types, and the Slave chooses the Master's packet types.

To achieve this control, messages have to be sent across the link. The Link Management Protocol is used to do this. To begin using channel-driven QOS, the LMP_auto_rate message is sent, as shown in Figure 17–10. This signals that the device sending the message is willing to let its peer LM choose packet types on the link. If the link manager at the far end of the link decides that it wants to change the packet type, it sends back an LMP_preferred_rate message, which has a single parameter: the data rate, which can be set to high rate (use DH packets) or medium rate (use DM packets).

Note that the LMP_preferred_rate message is not used to switch between single slot, 3 slot, and 5 slot packets; it merely chooses whether DH packets or DM packets are used.

To make the choice between packet types, the link manager needs information on the quality of the link. The Forward Error Correction (FEC) and Header Error Correction (HEC) are dealt with by the baseband part of the Bluetooth protocol stack. The baseband also takes care of retransmissions. In order for link manager to choose whether or not to switch between high and medium rate packet types, it must be able to access information from the baseband on how many errors the baseband is correcting and how many packets are being retransmitted.

In some environments, the link quality will fluctuate, with periodic bursts of errors caused by interference, objects blocking the link, or devices moving around. If a device is frequently switching between DH and DM packets, it may use more bandwidth on the messages causing the switch than it saves on using DH packets. Under such circumstances, it would make sense to stay using DM packets, or at least require a low bit error rate to be measured for a while before the switch is made.

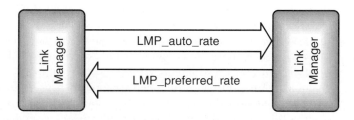

Figure 17–10   Message sequence chart for channel quality-driven packet type change.

The Bluetooth specification does not specify the exact criteria for making the switch between packet types, so it is up to implementers to decide the details of when they will choose to switch rates, both in the data used to make the decision to switch and the levels of errors at which the switch is made.

17.7 SUMMARY

For the Bluetooth specification, getting Quality of Service (QOS) means getting the required data rate, delay variance, and reliability.

The link manager provides QOS capabilities by a variety of means, including choosing packet types, setting polling intervals, allocating buffers, allocating bandwidth to links, and deciding whether to perform scans. Link Managers negotiate peer-to-peer to ensure that QOS is coordinated at both ends of a link.

At the L2CA level, too, QOS is negotiated end-to-end: one L2CA signals its peer to request a QOS; this peer in turn asks its local link manager if it can fulfill the request. On systems with an HCI, this interaction between L2CA and link manager is accomplished through a series of HCI commands and events.

For unicast (point to point), a reliable link is provided by the receiver acknowledging packets. Any packets which are not acknowledged are retransmitted. Broadcast packets are not acknowledged, so to provide a reliable link, a Bluetooth device can be set to retransmit broadcast packets a certain number of times.

Sometimes on point-to-point links, the baseband's attempts to provide a reliable link can result in data being kept in the stack and retransmitted time and time again while the baseband waits for an acknowledgement. For some applications, old data is not worth sending, so a flushing mechanism can be used to override the reliable link and allow the system to throw away data. This can be done directly with a command, or automatically when a timer elapses.

L2CA and the lower layers of the stack do their best to provide the QOS which higher layer applications and protocols request, but as with any wireless system, there are never any real guarantees, so sometimes the QOS requested can't be achieved. In such cases, the lower layers tell the higher layers by sending QOS_violation events, so the higher layers of the stack know the required QOS is not being achieved and can decide what to do about it.

If a link's quality deteriorates, one thing that can be done is changing the packet types in use. These can be set directly through the HCI, or the Link Manager can be set to automatically switch between high-rate packets and medium-rate packets, which have better error protection. If multi-slot packets are in use, then using shorter packets can also help to make a link more reliable, though it should be kept in mind that data rates can suffer if short packets or packets with more error protection are used.

Sometimes a link is lost altogether and no good packets can be received. If this happens a supervision timer will elapse. When this happens, the link is judged to be beyond saving, so it will be reset. Any higher layer applications or services wanting to use the link will have to set it up again from scratch.

18

Managing Bluetooth Devices

The OSI divides management into five functional areas:

- Configuration and Name Management—Controls, identifies, collects data from, and provides data managed objects to assist in interconnection services.
- Performance Management—Evaluates the behaviour of managed objects, and the effectiveness of communication activities.
- Security Management—Provides security management to protect managed objects and services.
- Fault Management—Detects, isolates, and corrects abnormal operation of the OSI system.
- Accounting Management—Enables charging for use of managed objects.

The Bluetooth specification provides for fault management, with many layers of error recovery and recovery from lost links; however, it is silent on how the other OSI management areas should be handled. This is because the Bluetooth specification defines requirements for end to end interoperability; it does not set out to define details of implementation architecture. Most aspects of device management are internal architectural design issues. As such, they do not affect interoperation with other devices, so they do not need to be explicitly specified.

Although the Bluetooth specification does not dictate how implementers should manage their devices, the SIG does have some advice to give about management. The Bluetooth white papers provide some suggestions for possible management schemes; also the Bluetooth specifications gives hints. For instance, L2CAP primitives and HCI commands suggest particular ways things could be done. The final decision, though, is left up to the individual designer.

So what decisions must be made? Most products will not need to cover all the OSI management areas. Bluetooth links use the ISM band, which is freely available, and they are short-range, so they do not require expensive network infrastructure. This means that any charges associated with a Bluetooth device are likely to be levied at the Application or Service Level, rather than being associated with the Bluetooth links. Given that the specification covers fault management, this leaves designers having to decide:

- How to manage discovery and connection to devices?
- How to configure and manage link performance once connected?
- How to manage security?
- How to integrate applications?

The following sections highlight some management issues and make some suggestions. However, because of the wide variety of devices that will incorporate Bluetooth wireless technology, no particular management method can possibly be perfect for every device. So in the area of device management, there is real scope for implementers to come up with good designs to differentiate their products from the rest.

18.1   LINK CONFIGURATION AND MANAGEMENT

Some part of the system must manage the creation and configuration of ACL links. Looking at the functionality of the various parts of the Bluetoooth protocol stack, the L2CA layer looks like a natural candidate for this job for several reasons:

- Data on ACL links is L2CAP data, so L2CA owns the connections which use the ACL links.
- L2CA has a primitive to establish an ACL connection.

However, in the 1.0b and 1.1 specifications, L2CA has no primitive to delete an ACL connection. It makes no sense to have an entity which can create links but not delete them. So either a delete function has to be added to L2CA or ACL link creation should be moved to another part of the stack.

Which option is sensible will depend upon the capabilities of the Bluetooth device. A simple device such as a headset will only ever have to manage one link at a time and will want to put the minimal load on its processor. For such a device, ACL links and L2CAP links can be created and deleted together, and it makes sense to combine the functions.

In more complex devices such as laptops multiple higher layer protocols and services may wish to use one link, each with different QOS requirements. Trading off the QOS requirements may involve complex calculations; these could be more easily handled if separated from the basic L2CA functions. So for complex devices, a separate device management entity makes sense.

The wide range of devices in which Bluetooth wireless technology can be used means that devices will have a range of capabilities. To illustrate the different issues involved in managing devices with different capabilities it is useful to divide devices into four broad categories:

- Personal devices—These are the simplest devices; they will only link to one other preset device, and inquiry is not used.
- Point to point devices—Only supports one link, could be to any device, needs inquiry, and must keep database of devices it has discovered.
- Point to multipoint devices—Must handle QOS balancing between links.
- Scatternet devices—These must be able to maintain information on two (or more) piconets simultaneously, and must handle QOS issues on two time domains.

These four categories of device are illustrated in Figure 18–1.

Note that these are just arbitrary categories chosen as examples to illustrate management issues. They do not cover the complete range of requirements Bluetooth devices might have. (For example, an LAN access point will have to manage multiple links, but it does not have to conduct inquiries.) However, these four categories do provide enough variety to usefully illustrate the issues involved in managing Bluetooth devices.

18.1.1   Personal Devices

A personal device is the simplest possible Bluetooth device to manage. It will only connect to one other preset device. If any other device attempts to connect to a personal device, it refuses the LMP connection request message, LMP_host_connection_req, with an LMP_not_accepted message containing the error code 0x0F, "Host rejected due to remote device is only a personal device".

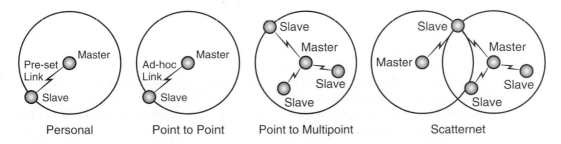

Figure 18–1   Bluetooth devices with different capabilities.

An example of such a device might be a headset sold with a cellular phone. One could imagine a headset with a user interface limited to a single button. The headset could be set up so that holding the button for a second switches the power on or off, but a brief tap on the button would answer an incoming call. Such a headset could automatically connect to its cellular phone and park itself whenever it was switched on, then it would just wait for calls in Park mode.

The cheapest way to make such a headset would be to preset it in the factory to only work with the device it is sold with; thereafter, the headset would be completely useless with any other Bluetooth device. Alternatively, one could avoid having an expensive user interface on the headset by writing a simple proprietary application which could be used to reset the Bluetooth device address of the device the headset would work with. Either way, if the headset only ever had to work with one device at a time, managing its links would be quite simple.

Link management would only have to handle links from one device, and at the L2CAP level, the link could only ever go to SDP or the headset control. A SCO link would only ever be routed to the same destination. A complex management system would be wasted on such a device, so link management could be combined with the implementation of L2CAP.

This is an example of a possible, very simple Bluetooth device. In fact, the Bluetooth headset profile requires headsets to support general inquiry, so such a device would not conform to the headset profile. At the time of writing, the Link Management Protocol supported the messages needed to deal with personal devices, but there were no profiles which supported personal devices. It is important to realise that personal devices would not be able to claim conformance to the profiles released with version 1.0b and 1.1.

18.1.2   Point to Point Devices

A point to point device only supports one ACL (data) link at a time. This link could be to any device, so it needs inquiry and must keep a database of devices it has discovered.

When a Bluetooth device inquires for other devices in the area, it receives FHS packets. These contain all the information required to connect to the devices, including a clock offset. This information will not be valid forever for several reasons.

Bluetooth devices are mobile. A traditional networking environment is static, with few changes in configuration. A Bluetooth networking environment is dynamic, with devices frequently appearing and disappearing. So any information on devices in the area may quickly become out-of-date and useless. Users do not wish to be presented with a choice of devices to connect with, only to find that none are available; therefore, suitable timeouts should be applied to ensure that inquiry information is updated. This will usually be done by setting the period of inquiry.

The clock offsets passed in FHS packets will become invalid as each device maintains its own clock, and the clocks on two devices will slowly drift apart. There is no particular problem with using the wrong clock offset when connecting, though it will just take slightly longer to establish the link.

The inquiry procedure retrieves information on how to connect to a device. There may be other steps before the user decides whether to use a device's services:

- An ACL link may be set up to retrieve the device's friendly name.
- An L2CAP link may be set up to retrieve information on protocols and services from the device's service discovery database.

The inquiry information is dynamic, but this information is likely to be more static. For example, a mobile phone will be carried in and out of an area as its owner walks around, so it will move in and out of range of other devices. However, if it has been labeled with the friendly name "Don's phone," that name is unlikely to change very often. The services offered by a phone, such as connecting to a headset, are even less likely to change.

The user of a Bluetooth device may wish to enter extra information about it; for example, security authorisation PIN codes to be used when connecting. This information is also unlikely to change very often, so some applications will wish to offer the facility to store PIN codes, and the link keys derived from them, for reuse.

So point to point devices will have to manage information about devices they may connect to in the area with long term caches for some information and short term caches for other information. A typical process for a point to point device discovering devices in its area might look like Figure 18–2.

The inquiry procedure allows the user to be told the Bluetooth Device Address (BD_ADDR) and device class of any devices which answer the inquiry. The first time a device is discovered, it must be connected to retrieve its friendly name. This is likely to be more useful to the user. Then an L2CAP link is established to retrieve service discovery information on services and protocols supported by the device. Whether this stage is done and exactly what service discovery information is retrieved will depend on the device. A device which only supports the Bluetooth audio gateway profile would only be interested in retrieving more information from devices in the audio device class, and when it connected to them, it would only retrieve the headset service record. A PC which supported many Bluetooth profiles might retrieve information from a wide variety of devices and would be interested in more services.

The friendly name and service discovery information can be stored. Periodic inquiries are used to check that devices are still in the neighbourhood and available for connection. When a device disappears from view, its information is no longer presented to the user, but the friendly name and service discovery information are still stored. Then when the device again answers an inquiry, there is no need to form a connection; the information on the device can be retrieved from storage.

Service discovery provides a status record which changes whenever a service discovery database changes, so devices may choose to periodically connect to devices in their area to check that their stored service discovery information is up to date by examining the status of their neighbours service discovery records.

Retrieving and storing information on a variety of devices like this uses power for the links and memory for storage. Some devices will follow this way of operating, but for others, limited memory resources and the need to conserve battery power will make it impractical. Such devices may only retrieve information when specifically requested by the

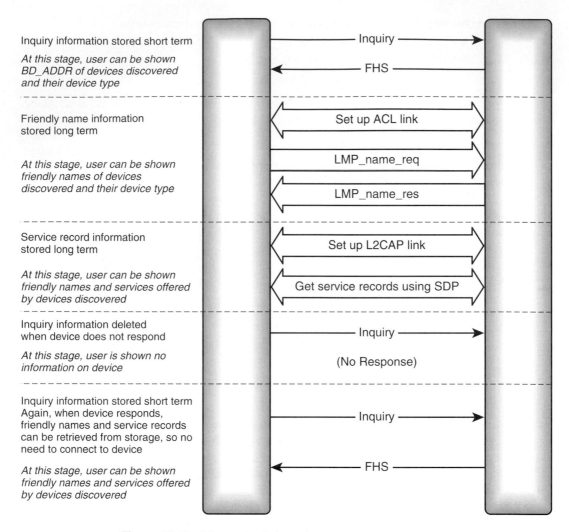

Figure 18–2   Discovering information about devices in the neighbourhood.

user. Applications designers will have to trade off convenience for the user against resource usage in the device.

This section has considered a point to point device which inquires to discover other
devices in the neighbourhood. Of course, devices may also inquiry scan and reply to inquiries, passing on information about themselves. This allows other devices to initiate
connections. When an incoming connection is received, a device might wish to consult its
cached information to see if it can retrieve information on the connecting device, and if it
has no information, it may wish to initiate procedures to build up information such as the
friendly name for the connecting device.

18.1.3 Point to Multipoint Devices

Point to multipoint devices can establish links to several devices at once. Once multiple links are in place, the device must handle QOS balancing between the links. That is to say, it must decide how much bandwidth to allocate to each link.

Higher layer protocols and services will pass down bandwidth requirements, and initially these will be used to allocate bandwidth to the various links. If the radio environment deteriorates, it is possible that the link will have to shift from using high rate data packets which carry little error protection (DH packets), to lower rate data packets which can correct errors (DM packets). This will reduce the overall bandwidth available. Depending upon the source of interference, a change in the local radio propagation environment may affect some links but not others.

When link quality deteriorates to below the QOS which has been granted to higher layers, the lower layers send QOS violation events to the higher layers. If there is a deterioration in link quality which affects all links, there is a choice: the bandwidth split between all links could be kept the same, in which case all higher layer protocols and services are sent QOS violations, or the device could choose to shut down low priority connections preserving the bandwidth for higher priority connections.

Bluetooth does not define a method for prioritising applications for the purposes of allocating bandwidth, so a suitable scheme would have to be designed to suit the needs of an application running on a particular device by its systems designers. One can envision a system where a connection in use by a WAP micro-browser might be given high priority because delays would be very visible to the user, whereas a connection being used to transfer email might be given lower priority because delays would be less visible.

18.1.4 Scatternets

A group of linked piconets joined by common members is called a scatternet. The members linking the piconets can be Slaves on both piconets, or a Master of one piconet and a Slave on another. It is not possible to have a device which is a Master on two different piconets because a piconet is a group of devices hopping on a sequence defined by the clock and Bluetooth device address of the Master. All devices with the same Master must be on the same piconet, and conversely, two different Masters are needed to make two piconets.

Figure 18–3 shows two different scatternets. On the left is a scatternet where one device is a Slave in one piconet and a Master in another. On the right is a scatternet where one device is a Slave in two piconets.

The devices that link the scatternet must maintain two different hop sequences, and must communicate in two different time domains. The devices that are present on more than one piconet do this by time sharing. They spend a few slots on one piconet synchronised to its hopping sequence and timing, then change the hop sequence and timing to match the other piconet and spend a few slots communicating in that time domain.

When switching between timings, there will be some slots which cannot be used. In Figure 18–4, the area above the top line shows the packets transmitted and received by the Master of Piconet 1. The middle line shows packets transmitted and received by one of its Slaves, which is also the Master of a second piconet, 2, and the bottom line shows

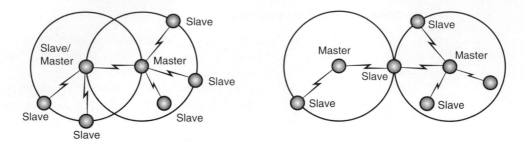

Figure 18–3   Scatternets.

packets transmitted and received by a Slave on Piconet 2. Starting at the left Master 1 transmits and receives to its Slave. The Slave then moves timing onto its own piconet. It wants to transmit to its own Slave, but because of the difference in timing between the two piconets, it doesn't have time to retune its radio and transmit, so it has to leave a slot pair and wait to transmit and receive. Then it can retune again and return to Piconet 1. This time it has more time to retune, so it can use the next free slot pair.

The time spent moving between the timings has meant that during six slot periods, the device which is present on two piconets has only been able to send and receive two packets. Effectively its bandwidth has been reduced by a third. If a higher layer applica-

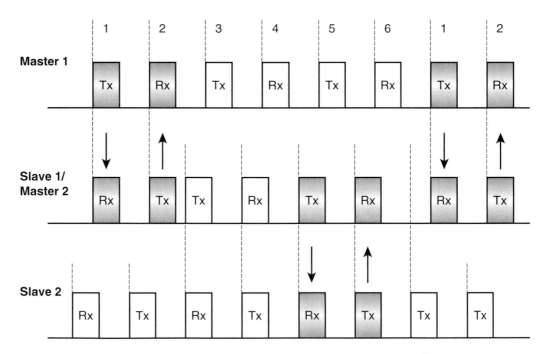

Figure 18–4   Scatternet timing.

tion were using this device to move data between two piconets, it would effectively use six slots to transfer packets between Master 1 and Slave 2, when it would only have needed two slots had they been on the same piconet.

In this example, Slave 1/Master 2 switches timing after each slot pair. This is particularly inefficient (and as we shall see below, practical limitations of negotiating sniff parameters could make such rapid switching awkward). The device could transfer data faster by spending more time on each piconet, but it will still lose bandwidth each time it does a timing switch. The time spent on one piconet will be limited by the need to stop link timers expiring while it is absent from the other piconet.

Because of problems with changing between different slot timings, a device which is present on two piconets will never be able to use the full bandwidth it would have if it were only on one piconet. Each time it changes timing, some slots will be lost, so its available bandwidth will always be lower than a device which is only present on one piconet.

This raises the obvious question: Why not unite the timings, so that the whole scatternet is synchronized? At first thought, this seems like an attractive proposition, but consider the case shown in Figure 18–5.

This figure shows the scatternet on the left being united with the scatternet on the right by the link shown in white. In order for the whole scatternet to be united on one timing sequence, timing information would have to be passed around every device on the new scatternet. Bluetooth does not provide a means to pass this information between devices. Also, as scatternets formed and broke, if timing was shared between members of a scatternet, then every device in an area would tend to end up on the same timing sequence. This would increase the chance of packets in different piconets colliding, as all devices would be transmitting together, and all devices would be retuning their radios to hop frequencies together. By increasing the chance of packets colliding, this mass synchronisation effect would lower the overall bandwidth available to piconets in an area.

Another issue associated with managing devices in scatternets is the time a device is missing from one piconet while participating on another piconet. There are two aspects to this:

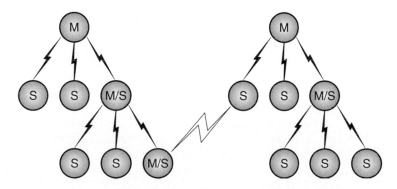

Figure 18–5   Linking scatternets.

- A Master that is missing from a piconet may miss polling Slaves and must ensure that it does not miss beacon slots and sniff slots of its Slaves, or links may time out.
- A Slave that is missing from a piconet could appear to its Master to have gone out of range, or to be in a poor quality link.

Dealing with a Master missing from its piconet is fairly simple. When the Master negotiates link parameters such as sniff slots, beacon slots, and poll intervals, it must ensure that it will be present on the piconet at the points where it needs to transmit to sniffing Slaves and parked Slaves, and it must ensure that it will have enough spare capacity on the piconet to poll all of its Slaves before their link timeouts elapse. As a Master controls a piconet, this is just a matter of doing the arithmetic to ensure that it is not over-committed. The actual timing of sniff slots and beacon parameters is negotiated by link manager, the higher layers merely request intervals. The link manager may have to renegotiate sniff and beacon slots when a Master establishes a link to a second piconet. If the link manager is not intelligent enough to automatically renegotiate the sniff and beacon slot timings, renegotiation could be forced by higher layers requesting that Slaves be removed from Park and Sniff modes, then put in Hold mode while the scatternet link is established. Once the scatternet link is established and the Master knows the time it will spend on the second piconet, its Slaves could be put into Park and Sniff modes again.

For the Slave side, handling presence on two piconets requires the cooperation of the Master. The Master must agree not to communicate with the Slave while it is absent. If this is not done, the Master will try to contact the Slave and will get no response. The Master may keep retransmitting, wasting its power while it tries to contact a Slave who is absent because it is communicating on a different piconet. When the Master fails to contact the Slave, it may conclude that the link is poor quality. This could trigger a switch from high-rate (DH) packets to medium-rate (DM) packets. (The medium-rate packets have less data capacity but more error protection, so they are used on poor-quality links.) If the link is actually good quality but the Slave is just not listening, then the channel quality-driven switch to medium-rate packets will unnecessarily reduce throughput on the link.

To save the Master's power and to avoid misleading the Master on link quality, the Slave could negotiate periods where it is out of communication. The way to arrange this is for the Slave to negotiate Sniff mode with its Master. During the sniff slots, it will be present on the piconet and able to communicate. In between the sniff slots, it can leave and visit the other piconet. The timing of the first sniff slot is determined by the link manager, so the link manager must know when the device will be present on each piconet. Figure 18–6 shows how sniff slots can be used to allow a device to participate in two piconets.

The upper line shows the sniff slots on one piconet, and the lower line shows the sniff slots on the second piconet. If the LM of the device which is present on two piconets can negotiate these sniff slots, then it can move between piconets without a Master deciding its link to the device has deteriorated or failed.

Because a device may not get a perfect transmission in its first sniff slot, it would be wise to negotiate several slots for the sniff attempt. The HCI sets the minimum length of sniff timeout to a single slot, so if Sniff mode is used to manage a device's movement be-

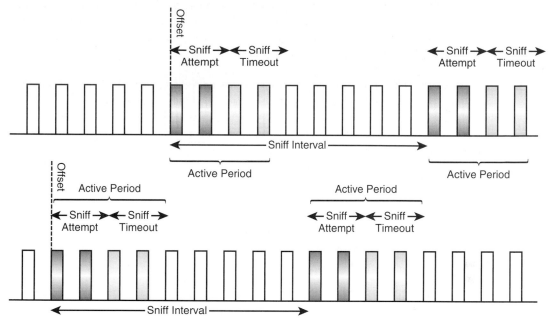

Figure 18–6 Managing scatternet timings with Sniff mode.

tween piconets, there will always be at least one slot in the sniff timeout. This limits the speed with which a sniffing device can switch piconets. However, as explained above, rapidly switching piconets can be a bad idea, as bandwidth is lost on every switch between time domains.

In addition to balancing sniff slots, beacon slots, and poll intervals, a device which is present on two piconets must also handle QOS balancing between the links on the two piconets. Here the issues are similar to balancing QOS between multiple links on one piconet, except that if more bandwidth is to be given to one piconet, then sniff slots have to be renegotiated.

Although the sniff mechanism provides for the possibility of gracefully negotiating absence from a piconet, the Bluetooth specification does not explicitly provide for it to be used in this way, so it is possible that the link managers in many implementations may not be intelligent enough to take into account piconet timing switches when negotiating sniff slots for devices which are present on more than one piconet.

Also, while it is theoretically possible to manage scatternets with Sniff mode in this way, one must question whether it is the best use of available bandwidth. Data rates in the sniffing Slave would be reduced to the point where it might make more sense to manage communications with multiple piconets by alternately using Hold mode on each piconet and communicating in longer bursts.

Figure 18–7 shows how Hold mode might be used to manage presence on two scatternets. The device communicates in bursts on one piconet while it is in Hold mode on the

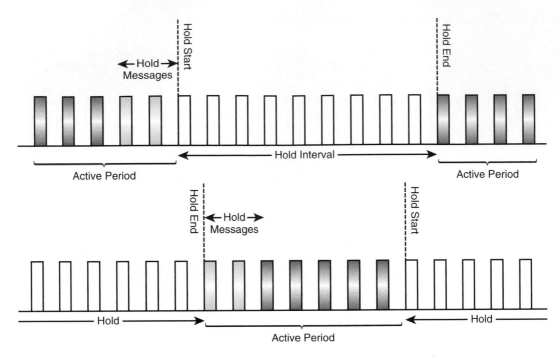

Figure 18–7   Managing scatternet timings with Hold mode.

other piconet. Bandwidth is only lost due to exchange of LMP messages to negotiate the hold, and for some guard slots when moving between the two piconets timings. The example shown here has just two slots lost for hold messaging; obviously a Master which had to put multiple Slaves on hold would require more slots. One possible drawback of using Hold mode to manage scatternets is that Slave devices can not guarantee to negotiate suitable hold intervals with their Master.

It is possible that because of the low bandwidth of scatternet links and the fact that a scatternet device is not present on any piconet continuously, they may prove of little use to most devices. None of the profiles released with version 1.0b and 1.1 required the long-term use of scatternets (although the LAN access profile moves through a phase where a device maintains two sets of timings, this is only done as part of connection setup, and the scatternet configuration is not used for user data transfer).

In summary, there are two main management issues involved in scatternet operation.

- Bandwidth is reduced by the time taken to switch between piconets (though this effect is reduced if the switch is done infrequently).
- Devices are absent from one piconet when present on the other, and this absence should be managed, if maximum efficiency is required.

Managing piconets involves calculation and negotiation of parameters for QOS, and may also involve beacon slots, sniff slots, or hold times.

18.2 DEVICE MANAGER ARCHITECTURE

Section 18.1 looked at some of the issues involved in managing Bluetooth links for devices with different capabilities. The diversity of management needs is an argument for developing a separate device management entity for Bluetooth protocol stacks. If management is handled in a separate functional block, then only that block needs to be tailored to fit different devices; the remainder of the functional blocks can remain identical.

L2CA is the other main candidate for a functional block to handle device management. The L2CAP data transfer features are identical in all profiles and device types, as are its segmentation and reassembly features, and its interfaces to HCI; even the interfaces to higher layers of the protocol stack do not need to differ between devices. If device management is extracted into a separate functional block, then L2CA becomes a device-independent block which can be reused in many implementations. Of course, this is not a consideration for anybody who is only implementing a single device. However, given the effort involved in implementing a Bluetooth protocol stack, it is likely that the implementation will be reused in more than one device.

The device manager can handle configuration and control of the Bluetooth device, including the facilities required by the Generic Access Profile (GAP). Examples of features which could be handled by a device manager are:

- Setup, teardown, and configuration of the baseband links.
- QOS tradeoffs between links and setting of QOS parameters.
- Management of higher layer links.
- Discovering devices in the neighbourhood and caching information on them.

Figure 18–8 shows how a device manager might be placed in a Bluetooth protocol stack.

Because the device manager must control the baseband, it has an interface to HCI. It also interfaces to RFCOMM and L2CA to allow it to track the setup of links at various levels of the protocol stack. If the device manager is aware when higher layer links are set up and torn down, it can tear down the baseband links when there are no longer any higher layer links using them.

The device manager acts as a translator between applications and the functional blocks of the Bluetooth protocol stack. When applications request links, they request them from the device manager. When they wish to discover devices in the neighbourhood, those requests also go through the device manager. Configuration control and information on the neighbourhood passes through the device manager; transfer of raw data does not involve the device manager.

18.2.1 Configuration Application

Some part of the system must handle the initial startup of the system. This is shown in Figure 18–8 as a separate configuration application. On power up, this causes the Blue-

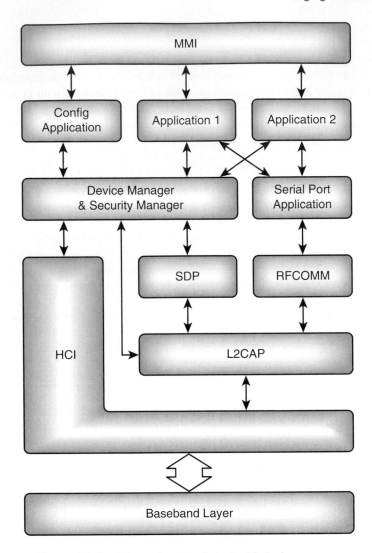

Figure 18–8   Bluetooth protocol stack with device manager.

tooth baseband to be reset. It also sets the device properties: page, inquiry, and scan intervals, user friendly name, and so forth.

The configuration application could be built into the device manager, or it could be part of an application supporting a profile. In a complex device supporting many profiles, it is possible that the device will frequently be reconfigured, and depending upon the mode in which it is being used, it may want to select from several different sets of startup settings. For instance, a laptop could power up a Bluetooth module with different settings depending upon whether it is currently running from mains power or from battery power. If the laptop switches between battery powered and mains powered, the configuration application could be notified and could reconfigure the Bluetooth device to suit the new mode of operation. In such complex devices, it makes sense to split off the management function into a separate functional block to ease software design and maintenance.

In devices such as headsets, there will be far fewer configuration decisions to make, and the configuration application could well be combined with another block in the system, either the headset application or the device manager.

18.2.2   Registering Applications

If applications are to request the facilities of the Bluetooth device through the device manager, then there must be a clearly defined interface between the applications and the device manager.

Applications could register with the device manager. As they register, they could tell the device manager which baseband events are of interest to them, and provide callback functions to be used when baseband events of interest to the application occur.

The level of discrimination in events provided by the device manager is a decision for the implementer. At one extreme, one could imagine a complex device manager offering an application interested in audio devices the ability to be notified whenever an inquiry discovers a new audio device. At the other extreme, a simple device manager might just pass up information on all devices discovered regardless of whether they have been seen before, and regardless of their device type.

Figure 18–9 shows an example message sequence chart for applications registering with a device manager. If there is a separate configuration application, it must register before the other applications can use the device manager's facilities.

Once applications have registered with the device manager, they receive a ready indication to confirm that the baseband is configured and ready for use. Then they can ask the device manager for connections. The device manager will set up and tear down links as needed. Potentially, a device manager could handle several link types:

- ACL links for use by L2CAP and SCO links.
- L2CAP links for use by SDP and RFCOMM.
- SDP and RFCOMM links for use by applications.

Several applications may share a link, so the device manager maintains a database of applications which are using links and what QOS requirements each application has placed on the link. When applications stop using the link, they signal to the device manager to free the link, and the device manager deletes that application from its database for the link. When the last application using a link frees the link, the device manager can free the link.

Some links may be set up and torn down frequently under this system, so system designers may wish to implement a timeout before the link is shut down.

An example sequence for a system incorporating a device manager could be:

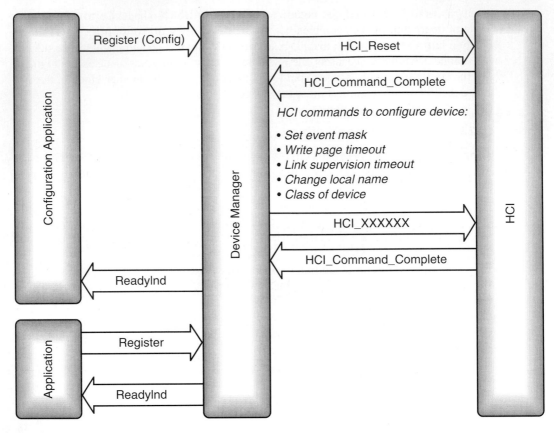

Figure 18–9 Device configuration.

- The configuration application registers, and the device manager configures the baseband.
- A profile application registers.
- The profile application requests SDP information.
- The device manager performs an inquiry via HCI.
- The inquiry result returns information on a remote device.
- The device manager establishes an ACL link to the remote device via HCI.
- The device manager establishes an L2CAP link to the remote device.
- The device manager gets SDP information via SDP (which uses the L2CAP link).
- The device manager passes SDP information to the requesting application.
- If there are no more SDP requests after a timeout, the device manager shuts down links.

This example illustrates how the complexity of Bluetooth management can be abstracted into a device manager. Obviously, if there are many applications in a system it is easier for them to implement a simple interface to the device manager than a complex interface to L2CAP, HCI, and SDP.

18.3 SECURITY MANAGEMENT

Section 18.2 covered how links can be set up and configured, but it is worth considering security configuration separately from general link configuration.

When one application using a link requests security, all traffic on that ACL link is encrypted. A central security manager can turn on encryption when the first application requests it; the other applications will be unaware that this has happened. The security manager could turn off encryption when no application is left using the link which has requested security. To be able to do this, the security manager maintains a database of security requirements.

In the same way that applications register with the device manager, applications wishing to use security services register with the security manager. Each service can register its security level, which is stored in the security database, so there is no need to repeatedly query the application on security. Legacy applications may not understand Bluetooth security requirements, in which case, their requirements could be preregistered in the database. Security services would then be implemented on their behalf by the security manager, without the application ever needing to understand or even be aware of Bluetooth security.

Device-level security settings such as security mode and pairing mode can also be stored in the security database.

The service and device settings for a security profile are modified via user interaction. Although in normal operation the user would be unaware of security procedures; a user could choose to be involved in some security procedures; for instance:

- Access requests—When remote devices request access to local services.
- Security checks such as authentication and pairing are applied as defined by the profile.
- Security checks can be initiated by user interaction.

Most users would not wish to be directly involved in security procedures, so the security manager could also implement bonding. As explained in Chapter 15, bonding allows a user to set up paired relationships before access to facilities is required. Then later on, services can be accessed automatically using the paired relationship, without the user having to get involved and re-entering PINs.

As Figure 18–10 shows, the security manager and device manager have similar interfaces to applications. They also have similar database requirements. They could be implemented as one combined entity.

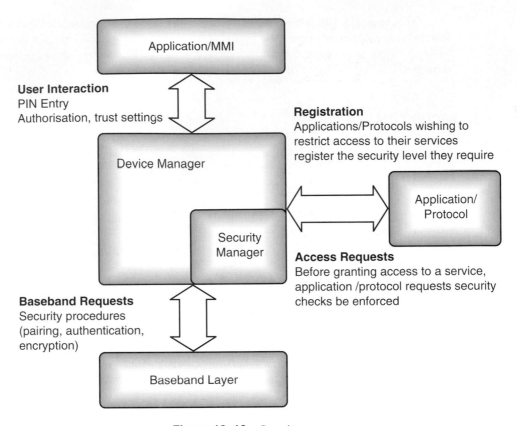

Figure 18–10   Security manager.

18.4   INTEGRATING APPLICATIONS

Applications implement the functionality of the Bluetooth profiles. A Bluetooth application could be a complete solution designed specifically for use in a Bluetooth device. This is likely to be the case for a headset. Alternatively, it could be an existing legacy system which has to be integrated with Bluetooth. This is likely to be the case for dial up networking (modems), where there is a great deal of investment in providing the required functionality from scratch, and far less effort required to integrate an existing system.

The rule when integrating applications with the Bluetooth protocol stack should be to keep the interface to applications as clean and simple as possible. As discussed above, a device manager can be used to simplify the interface to the core Bluetooth control, and a security manager can be used to simplify access control. A configuration application can also be used to simplify startup procedures.

Not only do simple interfaces ease the integration of applications, but they can also help with the process of Bluetooth qualification. Parts of a complete Bluetooth system can be prequalified. If these parts are unchanged in the final system, they do not have to be put through the full qualification process again. Only elements of the system which have changed have to be qualified. For manufacturers with several products to put through qualification, or for those who are buying in prequalified designs, a simple, clean application interface can make the process of deciding which parts to requalify simpler.

Continuing on this theme, it is also worth considering a separate MMI (Man Machine Interface). Because the Bluetooth standard defines the basic functionality of a profile to ensure interoperability, there is limited scope for differentiation in features. One key area for product differentiation is in the user interface. A manufacturer could choose to use a standard Bluetooth solution, but customize the MMI. This allows a range of differentiated products to share the same core.

A reusable core with a variable MMI allows the user interface to be updated without impacting the core (for instance, a new display type might be installed in an upgraded product, or a keypad might be replaced with voice recognition). This minimises development risk and time to market. It also minimises requalification required.

There are several ways to separate the MMI from a core protocol stack:

- Use generic functions for user output and to communicate messages and alerts. The MMI decides whether these are displayed by LEDs, LCD display, audio output, etc.
- Use generic functions for user input to control the stack. These could be tied to switches, buttons, keypad, voice control, etc.
- Use a registration and callback interface. This allows different MMI systems to connect with the same core.
- Have software systems which interface via macros, so that any customizing can be confined to a thin macro layer.

Generally, when integrating applications, the goal should be to keep interfaces as simple as possible, and wherever possible to hide the complexity of Bluetooth within the core protocol stack, so that applications designers can concentrate on providing application functionality rather than having to deal with Bluetooth system management.

18.5   ACCOUNTING MANAGEMENT

Accounting management covers the billing of services. Because Bluetooth devices are cheap and they use the ISM band, which is freely available, there are unlikely to ever be any charges for using a Bluetooth link. This is in contrast to mobile telephones, for instance, where the link is usually charged for.

Just because the ISM band links are free does not mean that there are no billing issues at all in Bluetooth systems. As an example, consider a LAN access point in a public place which users may connect with. The LAN access point is providing a useful service which could be charged to the user, but to charge for a service, its use must be restricted to those who pay, and how it is used must be tracked somehow.

PINs can be used to restrict access to services over Bluetooth links. It would be possible to give each user a separate PIN. Users could then pay per hour, and once their time was used up, the LAN access point could be reconfigured via network to not accept connection with the expired PIN.

Paying per megabyte would be more difficult as management and overhead traffic is transferred on a Bluetooth link. Users do not want to pay for system administration traffic. Anyway, Bluetooth does not provide any standardised way to monitor quantities of data transferred on a link. So to charge by traffic usage, this would have to happen at a higher level in the protocol stack.

PIN-restricted access time is certainly the simplest system for controlling access to Bluetooth links. Other systems are technically feasible, but are not provided for in the standard and might require a specially modified L2CAP layer.

18.6   CAPACITY

The Bluetooth specification provides QOS features for managing link capacity. A Bluetooth device manager could participate in the process of managing link capacity. This would be done by choosing packet types on links, juggling QOS requirements between links, refusing connections when QOS can't be met, handling QOS violations, and setting the policy on when to abandon a link with poor quality service characteristics.

As more Bluetooth devices are switched on in an area, they will eventually start to interfere with one another, and link quality will inevitably deteriorate. Because Bluetooth implements a random frequency hopping sequence, collisions will be random, and deterioration of the radio propagation environment due to interference will be gradual. Bluetooth is a robust protocol which is tolerant of errors, thanks to many levels of error correction and the ability to retransmit. So as link quality deteriorates, this will not be seen as errors on the link; rather, it will appear as reduced throughput.

Applications such as file transfers may request high bandwidth, but they can tolerate slow and bursty data rates. Such applications can usefully be kept running even in very poor link conditions.

Isochronous applications, that is to say those which are transmitting time bounded information, cannot tolerate variable delays. Variable delays will appear in crowded environments where there are frequent random collisions between Bluetooth piconets, causing frequent retransmissions. A device management function could shut down isochronous applications when link quality deteriorates in this way.

18.7   USER INTERFACE DESIGN

The processes involved in managing Bluetooth devices can be quite complex. If Bluetooth is to succeed, it is vital that this complexity is hidden from the end user. If two Bluetooth products are brought into close proximity, the user should be able to establish a connection between them with as little thought as joining them with wires. It is useful to consider an example of how a pair of Bluetooth-enabled devices might connect and how this might appear to the user.

Consider a cellular mobile phone handset which is switched on in the same area as a Bluetooth headset and a Bluetooth enabled printer. The phone could automatically send an inquiry. Devices within reach, including the headset and a printer, answer with FHS packets. The phone knows from the device classes carried in the FHS packet what types of devices have answered. It also knows that it cannot use the services of a printer, so it ignores this device.

The headset looks more interesting, so the phone connects to it and requests its user friendly name, then establishes an L2CAP connection and sends a service discovery request to see if it supports the headset profile. The phone then displays the headset as an icon with its user friendly name beneath it. The user can select the icon to establish a connection. All the user sees is a device pop up on the screen; all the complexity of inquiring, connecting, and retrieving information is hidden.

One drawback to this procedure is that establishing connections to every device in an area could take some time, and the user may get impatient with the wait. So alternatively, the user interface could display interesting devices with an icon representing their device class when they are first discovered. Then, as more information becomes available, it could be added to the display. Some sort of progress bar could be used to indicate how far the device had progressed through the process of retrieving information.

Yet another possibility is to avoid having automatic device discovery and put the user in control of the whole process. For devices with very stringent battery requirements, it could be useful for the user to be able to completely power down the Bluetooth module in a product when it is not needed. In this case, the user would have to initiate the discovery process. This could be done in a variety of ways—for instance, by selecting from a menu, pressing a button, or clicking on an icon. Only when the user did this would the Bluetooth module begin to discover other devices in its neighbourhood. In this way, battery life would be extended.

Designers of user interfaces must also consider how much of the underlying nature of Bluetooth is exposed to the user. As discussed earlier in Chapter 2 the placing and orientation of an antenna will affect signal strength, and this in turn will affect the quality of the Bluetooth link. It is common for cellular phones to display signal strength indicators on the user interface. These allow users to move to areas of better reception. Similarly, Bluetooth user interfaces could display signal strength obtained from the HCI_Read_RSSI command. This would allow users to site devices in the best positions for a reliable link. However, such displays move Bluetooth away from direct cable replacement, so some device designers may choose not to expose the user to this sort of information.

For battery-operated devices, battery charge indicators will also be useful, although for many devices, such as laptops and cellular phones, these will already be incorporated into the user interface.

Because presenting extra information to the user requires better display capabilities and the exchange of more informational messages, system and application designers will have to trade off the simplest interface for the user against the requirements to produce cheap devices with long battery life.

18.8 SUMMARY

Bluetooth system designers have many issues to deal with in managing Bluetooth links. Because they are radio links, quality is variable, and devices move in an out of radio coverage, giving a highly dynamic networking environment quite unlike more traditional networks.

This poses management challenges for the Bluetooth system designer. There are no standard solutions to these management issues. Because they do not affect interoperability, they are not covered by the Bluetooth specification. There are also no standard answers because the architecture of Bluetooth systems will vary. The architecture will depend upon the complexity of the device. What is appropriate for a complex device such as a PC implementing several profiles will not be appropriate for a simple device such as a Bluetooth headset.

One possibility is abstracting link management, device management, security, and configuration into separate device manager and security manager functional blocks. This allows reuse of standard elements of the core protocol stack, while preserving flexibility in system management.

However management of a Bluetooth device is accomplished, it is vital that it be unobtrusive. A user should find linking devices with Bluetooth wireless technology as easy as joining devices with a cable. Application designers should bear in mind that if the user is exposed to complex configuration and management, then Bluetooth will have failed in its aim to be easy to use.

APPLICATIONS—THE BLUETOOH PROFILES

19

Foundation Profiles

The purpose of a profile is to provide a clear description of how a full specification of a standard system should be used to implement a given end-user function. If everyone deploys a particular communications standard in the same way, then each product so created should be able to interoperate. This notion of profiles originated from the International Organisation for Standardisation (ISO/IEC TR10000).

ISO defines the notion of a profile in a more rigorous way as follows:

- Implementation options are reduced so that applications share the same features.
- Parameters are defined so that applications operate in similar ways.
- Standard mechanisms for combining different standards are defined.
- User interface guidelines are defined.

Bluetooth profiles work in just the same way: they ensure interoperability by providing a well defined set of higher layer procedures and uniform ways of using the lower layers of Bluetooth. By doing this, the Bluetooth profiles provide a way for Bluetooth technology to slot into different devices and applications, yet still work in standardised ways. For example, a Bluetooth headset purchased from Manufacturer A will interwork with a Bluetooth enabled cellular phone purchased from Manufacturer B.

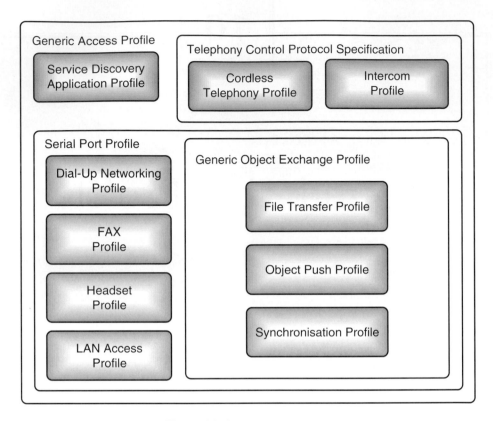

Figure 19–1   Bluetooth profiles.

Figure 19–1 shows how the Bluetooth foundation profiles are organised into groups, with each profile building upon the one beneath and inheriting features from below. Other, additional features are drawn in from the standard as required. For developers, this means that key features of one Bluetooth solution can be recycled in other solutions, bringing down development costs and speeding up the development cycle. The resulting standardisation also means that users of one Bluetooth device will instantly recognise the look and feel of other Bluetooth devices, thus reducing the learning curve and increasing market acceptance of new devices.

Profiles are a powerful tool for ad hoc networking. Profiles mean that devices from different manufacturers that have never worked together before can always rely on a set of standard features working in predictable ways. If manufacturers started implementing their own proprietary ways of communicating, then the whole concept of ad hoc connectivity would break down. In order to avoid this, the Bluetooth SIG continues to support the development of new profiles to cover the most popular ways of using Bluetooth. Companies with a new use for Bluetooth which is not yet covered by a profile are encouraged to contact the Bluetooth SIG in order to form a new profile working group.

This chapter covers the foundation profiles which were released with version 1.0b of the Bluetooth specification, when version 1.1 was released these were still the only profiles incorporated in the specification. However, many Bluetooth SIG working groups have recently released new profiles. The next three chapters will look at some of the new profiles which are emerging from the Bluetooth SIG's working groups.

19.1 STRUCTURE OF PROFILES

Anyone browsing through the Bluetooth profiles will quickly realise that they all share the same structure:

- A single paragraph stating what the profile defines.
- A contents list.
- An indication of any dependencies which the profile has on other profiles.
- Symbols and conventions used in the profile.
- Which parts of the Bluetooth protocol stack the profile uses together with any additional entities it might require.
- User requirements and scenarios (essentially, how a user will view the profile).
- The body of the profile, covering how it uses the protocol stack layer by layer, including a service record for service discovery, if relevant.
- Appendices, if appropriate.
- Textual references, if appropriate.

A template is available to facilitate the definition of new profiles. Anyone wanting to define a new profile should use this template and follow the common structure. This is not just a matter of following rules, it is also common sense. The structure helps to ensure that no elements essential to interoperability are missed and aids understanding of new profiles by familiarity with the existing profiles' structure.

19.2 THE GENERIC ACCESS PROFILE

The Generic Access Profile (GAP) is the most basic Bluetooth profile; all other profiles are built upon it and use its facilities.

The purpose of the Generic Access Profile is to make sure that all devices can successfully establish a baseband link. To do this, the Generic Access profile defines:

- Requirements for features which *must* be implemented in all devices.
- Generic procedures for discovering Bluetooth devices.
- Link management facilities for connecting to Bluetooth devices.
- Procedures related to the use of different security levels.

- Common format requirements for device parameters accessible on the user interface level (naming conventions).

19.2.1   Terminology

The Generic Access Profile defines the terminology to be used in the user interface. In some cases, this does not match the terminology used in the rest of the Bluetooth specification. For example, the core specification calls the security information entered by a user the PIN (Personal Identification Number), but the Generic Access Profile calls it the Bluetooth passkey.

The Generic Access Profile defines the following areas of general terminology:

- Connection-related (link, channel...).
- Device-related (trusted device, silent device...).
- Procedure-related (service discovery, name discovery...).
- Security-related (pairing, bonding, trusting).

Specific user interface terminology is also defined, such as device address, device name, passkey, class of device.

By standardising the naming conventions at the user interface, the Generic Access Profile ensures that users will recognise Bluetooth functionality across different user interface designs.

19.2.2   Modes of Operation

The Generic Access Profile describes modes of operation for Bluetooth devices, defining which ones are compulsory and which are optional. The modes described are:

- Discoverability—Governs the use of inquiry scan and whether other devices can discover a Bluetooth device when it comes within their area of radio coverage.
- Connectability—Governs the use of page scan and whether other devices can connect to a Bluetooth device when it comes within their area of radio coverage.
- Pairability—Governs the use of the link manager's pairing facilities, which are used to create link keys for use on encrypted links.
- Security—Governs when and how encryption is initiated on a link.

There are three different discoverability modes: nondiscoverable, limited discoverable, and general discoverable. The discoverability modes relate to the baseband inquiry scan procedures as follows:

- A nondiscoverable device will not perform inquiry scans and cannot be found by an inquiring device.
- A limited discoverability device inquiry scans using the Limited Inquiry Access Code (LIAC) and can only be discovered by devices inquiring with this code.

- A general discoverable device inquiry scans using the General Inquiry Access Code (GIAC) and can only be discovered by devices inquiring with this code.

Either limited or general discovery mode must be supported, and if limited discoverable mode is supported, then nondiscoverable must also be supported.

There are two connectability modes: connectable and nonconnectable. A connectable device periodically page scans to allow other devices to connect with it. A device in nonconnectable mode does not periodically page scan, so a nonconnectable device will only enter into links by paging other devices itself, that is to say, it must initiate the link. Connectable mode is mandatory; nonconnectable mode is optional.

There are two pairability modes: pairable, which is capable of setting up a link key with another device, and nonpairable, which cannot. Bonding is where a trusted relationship is established between devices at higher levels using the pairing facilities of the link manager. If the bonding feature is supported, then pairable mode is mandatory, and either general or limited inquiry modes must also be supported.

There are three security modes which are further discussed in the chapter on security:

- Mode 1 (nonsecure)—Security is never initiated.
- Mode 2 (service level enforced security)—Security is not initiated until an L2CAP channel is established, then it is established according to the requirements of services.
- Mode 3 (link level enforced security)—Security is initiated when the baseband ACL link is established.

Authentication is optional for devices which only support Mode 1. However, authentication is required for devices which support either of the other two security modes.

19.3 THE SERIAL PORT PROFILE

The serial port profile provides RS-232 serial cable emulation for Bluetooth devices. In this way, legacy applications do not have to be modified to use Bluetooth; they can simply treat a Bluetooth link as a serial cable link. The serial port profile is not just for legacy applications, though; it provides a simple, standard way for applications to interoperate.

The serial port profile is based on the GSM standard TS 07.10, which allows multiplexing of numerous serial connections over one serial link. It supports two device types: a communication endpoint (such as a laptop) and intermediate devices, which form part of a communications link (such as modems). Type 1 devices, which emulate serial ports, enable Bluetooth to support legacy serial port-based applications. Type 2 devices forming part of a communications link enable Bluetooth to replace serial cables which link devices to modems or other intermediate devices. The protocol stacks for the two device types are shown in Figure 19–2.

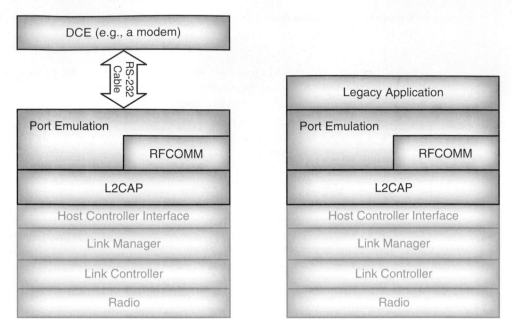

Figure 19–2   Type 1 and Type 2 RFCOMM protocol stacks.

As described earlier, the serial port profile builds on the Generic Access Profile. However, eight further foundation profiles are built up on the serial port profile:

- Dial Up Networking (DUN).
- FAX.
- Headset.
- LAN access.
- Generic object exchange.
- File transfer.
- Object push.
- Synchronisation.

The serial port profile uses RFCOMM to provide serial port emulation. The device which sets up the RFCOMM connection is called the initiator, while the other is referred to as the responder.

Since a number of steps are required to set up the virtual serial port and establish a connection, some type of device management function is required to set up the virtual serial port and connection.

The first step in setting up a virtual serial cable is to find the Bluetooth device address of the device at the other end of the connection. There are several ways to do this:

- Inquire to discover the devices in the neighbourhood. The user then picks a device from the list.
- The user enters the Bluetooth device address directly.
- Personal devices could be pre-paired, so they only connect to one other device and do not need to inquire.

The next step is paging the chosen device to create a baseband ACL connection.

An L2CAP channel is then created to the SDP server. SDP retrieves the RFCOMM server channel number of the serial port service. At this stage, the user can be given the service name information retrieved by SDP to verify that the correct service has been chosen.

An L2CAP channel is created to RFCOMM in the responder. An RFCOMM multiplexer session is then started across the L2CAP channel.

If parameters of the RFCOMM data link connection have to be negotiated, this is done now, before requesting the RFCOMM data link connection. In version 1.0b parameter negotiation was optional, but it became mandatory in version 1.1. This was done to facilitate negotiation of credit based flow control.

Support for security is mandatory in the serial port profile, but security does not have to be used. At this stage, either device may request bonding; this requires the use of a shared secret PIN. The PIN can be preconfigured or may need to be entered via a user interface. If the devices do not already share a PIN, users will have to exchange a PIN by means other than Bluetooth (e.g., by simply passing a paper note). Either side can then request the baseband link to be encrypted.

Application software can now communicate across the virtual serial port using UIH (Unnumbered Information with Header) frames on the RFCOMM channel.

19.4   DIAL UP NETWORKING

The Dial Up Networking (DUN) profile provides a dialup data connection. This allows a computing device (such as a laptop) to access a telephone network using the services of a communication device (such as a cellular phone or modem). Two types of connection are possible: One uses Remote Access Server (RAS) technology, the other connects via a cordless modem.

Figure 19–3 shows two examples of devices using the dialup networking profile. In the upper example, a laptop links via a cellular phone to the mobile network. In the lower example, a laptop links via a modem to the PSTN. The device which is at the end of the link (in these cases, a laptop) is known as the data terminal. The communications devices forming the link to a telephone network are known as gateways (in these cases, the cellular phone and modem are acting as gateways).

Figure 19–4 shows the protocol stack for the dialup networking profile. The dialing and control layer defines commands and procedures for automatic dialing and control over the asynchronous serial link provided by the lower layers. The modem emulation layer emulates the modem, and the modem driver is the driver software in the data terminal.

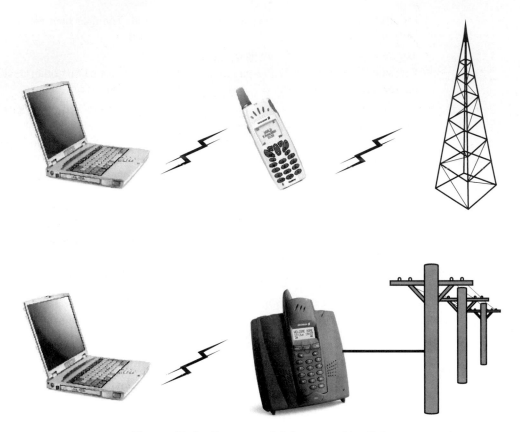

Figure 19–3   Two types of dialup networking link.

19.4.1   Establishing a Dialup Networking Connection

Figure 19–5 illustrates the stages in setting up a dialup networking connection between a data terminal and a gateway. In this case, the data terminal is a laptop and the gateway is a cellular phone.

First, a baseband link must be established by paging (there may have been a stage before this where the devices discovered one another by inquiring and inquiry scanning, or they could have been configured to connect to one another via the user interface). Once the baseband link is in place and following any LM configuration of the baseband link, an L2CAP connection can be set up. Service discovery information related to the profile can be retrieved across this L2CAP connection. Once this is done, the L2CAP connection may be used to query about other services, or it may be dropped. The L2CAP channel established at this stage cannot be used to actually access the service, because it is set up with a protocol service multiplexer value which is dedicated to service discovery.

A second L2CAP channel must be set up to access the service. This channel is set up with the protocol service multiplexer number reserved for RFCOMM (Bluetooth serial

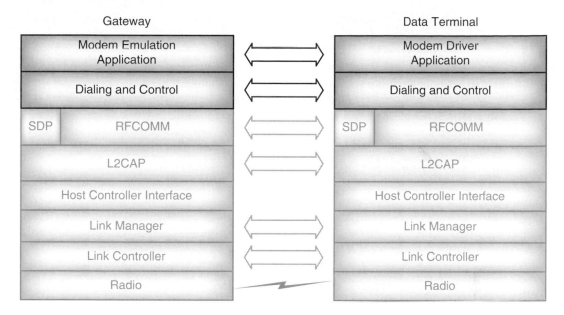

Figure 19–4   Dial Up Networking protocol stack.

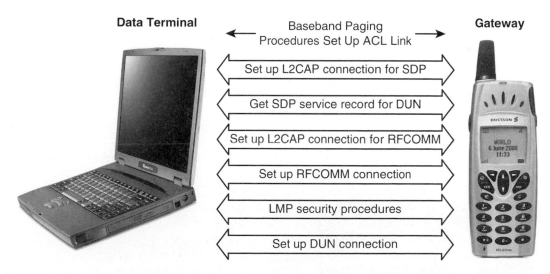

Figure 19–5   Steps in establishing a dialup networking connection.

port emulation layer). An RFCOMM connection is set up across this channel, and finally, a dialup networking connection may be established across the RFCOMM connection.

The connection is controlled by AT commands. The profile lists the commands which the gateway must support. These allow for dialing, answering, echo, hook control, volume control, circuit monitoring and control pulse or tone dialing, and command line editing.

During setup of the link across the PSTN, the gateway and data terminal can optionally provide audio feedback to the user (the audio feedback is the series of tones heard when a modem is trying to connect). If this is to be done, then a separate SCO channel is established when the communication equipment at the far end of the phone link picks up the call. This SCO link is then used to carry the audio feedback.

To the application on the data terminal using dialup networking the line should appear the same as if the device were connected to the gateway by a cable.

19.5 FAX PROFILE

The FAX profile defines procedures for sending and receiving FAXes without wires. The FAX profile is very similar to the dialup networking profile in that a data terminal connects via a gateway device. Again, the gateway device is used to provide access to the PSTN. The gateway could be a cellular phone, cordless phone, or a modem.

The FAX profile protocol stack is basically the same as the dialup networking profile's protocol stack as shown in Figure 19–6. As for the dialup networking profile, the di-

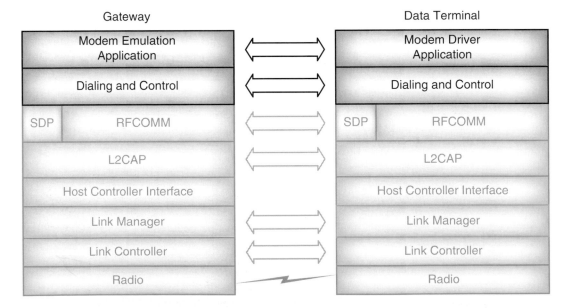

Figure 19–6 FAX profile protocol stack.

aling and control layer defines commands and procedures for automatic dialing and control over the asynchronous serial link provided by the lower layers.

The modem emulation layer emulates the modem; the modem driver is the driver software in the data terminal. The procedures for setting up links are the same as are used in the dialup networking profile. The FAX link is established over a phone link which is controlled using AT commands, again as is the case with the dialup networking profile.

One difference between the two profiles is that security is mandatory in the FAX profile, but optional in dialup networking. And of course, rather than transferring data calls, the information transferred across the phone link is a FAX. The profile provides for up to three classes of FAX to be supported:

- FAX Class 1 TIA-578-A and ITU T.31.
- FAX Class 2.0 TIA-592-A and ITU T.32.
- FAX Service Class 2 (this is manufacturer specific, rather than industry standard).

The profile does not require support for a particular class of FAX, so the AT command AT+FCLASS may be used to find out which class of FAX a particular implementation supports.

19.6   HEADSET PROFILE

The headset profile defines the facilities required to make and receive hands-free voice calls from a headset to a cellular phone handset. Of course, it can also be used to transfer voice calls between other Bluetooth devices. Bluetooth headsets can be driven via buttons on the headset, but voice-activated command and control provides a more elegant interface and should be popular for consumer headsets. The specification only assumes that there is some way for the user to initiate an action and doesn't specify how that will be done.

The Bluetooth headset profile defines two roles:

- Audio Gateway (**AG**)—This is the device that is the gateway of the audio, both for input and output (e.g., cellular phone, personal computer).
- Headset (**HS**)—This is the device acting as the remote audio input and output mechanism.

Figure 19–7 shows the protocol stack used by the Bluetooth headset profile. The audio port emulation layer is the entity emulating the audio port. This layer could reside on a cellular phone or PC. The audio driver is the driver software in the headset.

19.6.1   Establishing a Call to a Bluetooth Headset

Figure 19–8 shows how an Audio Gateway establishes a call to a Bluetooth headset. Usually, the Audio Gateway will initiate the connection to the headset because it has received an incoming call. For example, the Audio Gateway could be in a cellular phone handset. When the phone receives a phone call, it activates a Bluetooth connection and passes the

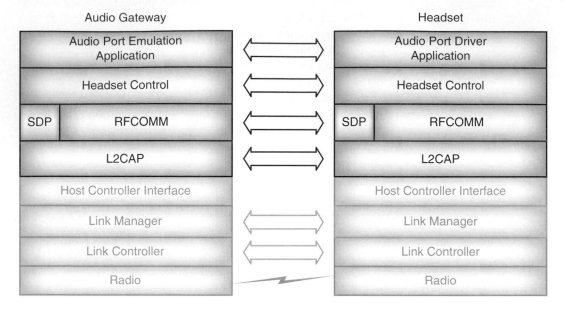

Figure 19–7   Headset profile protocol stack.

call to the headset. It is possible that some internal event could also cause the gateway to call the headset; for example, an application running on a PDA might send an alarm call with a prerecorded message, warning the headset's wearer of an appointment.

The first step of the Audio Gateway establishing a call is to set up an ACL connection. This could be done by paging, or it could be done by unparking if the headset were previously parked for power saving. A parked device is already synchronised to its Master's clock, so unparking would be faster than paging. For more details on parking and unparking, see Chapter 17.

Once the ACL link is established, it can be used to send a ring tone. The ring tone is sent using an AT RING command as defined in ITU-T Recommendations V.250.

In version 1.0b this AT RING command was mandatory, in version 1.1 it became optional. Instead of the AT RING command, a ring tone can be sent on a SCO link, or, in systems which are only handling data calls, there might be no need for a ring signal at all, so optionally the sequence can completely omit any form of ring signal.

The example in Figure 19–8 uses a ring signal on the ACL link to signal a call. The example in Figure 19–9 shows the SCO link being set up earlier and the ring signal being sent on the SCO link.

The audio quality provided by Bluetooth SCO links is equivalent to that provided by a mobile cellular phone. As such, the headset profile does not allow hi-fi quality audio communication. Although technically feasible to use ACL links for higher quality audio, the set of profiles released with 1.0 of the Bluetooth specification do not cover such a device.

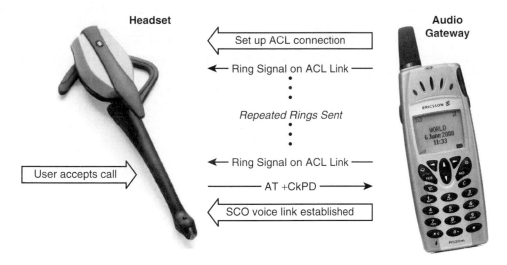

Figure 19–8   Establishing a call to a Bluetooth headset.

19.7   LAN ACCESS PROFILE

The LAN access profile allows a Bluetooth enabled device to access a fixed network via a Bluetooth link to a LAN Access Point (LAP). Such a device could be used in many scenarios: as a personal work area access point, replacing the network cable and allowing mobility within range of the access point; as a shared access point in a meeting room,

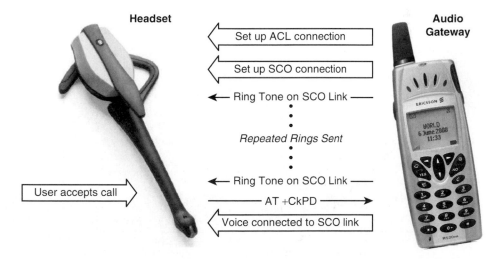

Figure 19–9   Establishing a call to a Bluetooth headset using in-band ring tone.

allowing fast establishment of network connections; or as a public access point, allowing easy access to information and services, for example, at airport check-ins.

LAN Access is secured by the use of PINs. Version 1.0b of the LAN access profile specifies a zero length PIN as the default for nonsecure links. However, since the HCI does not permit a host to send a Bluetooth module a PIN with a length of less than one byte, version 1.1 changed the default PIN to a single byte set to zero.

The LAN Access profile specifies using PPP over RFCOMM to link an IP stack to the Bluetooth stack. The resultant configuration is shown in Figure 19–10.

The figure shows a LAN access point acting as an intermediary between a Bluetooth device and a server resident on a LAN. However, the LAN access profile simply specifies how to layer an IP stack on top of a Bluetooth stack, so it could also be used to provide a TCP/IP link between a pair of PCs or to provide a network between a group of local PCs and a LAN access point.

19.7.1   Connecting to a LAN Access Point

To reduce connection times, the LAN access point's address can be pre-entered into connecting devices. The LAN access point periodically holds its links and page scans, allow-

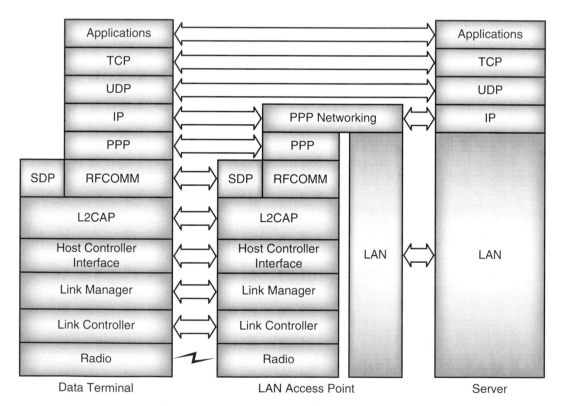

Figure 19–10   Protocol stack for LAN access profile.

Piconet 1: Access Point Is Master

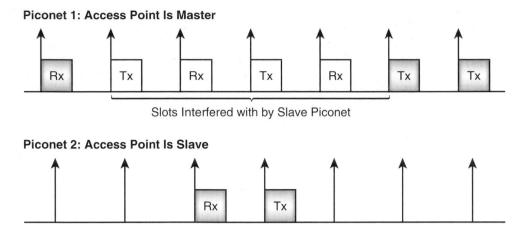

Slots Interfered with by Slave Piconet

Piconet 2: Access Point Is Slave

Figure 19–11   Timing of multiple piconets.

ing connecting devices to simply page the access point and conduct a Master/Slave switch to hand over control of the link to the LAN access point.

Figure 19–11 illustrates why it is necessary for the connecting device and LAN access point to do a Master/Slave switch, giving the LAN access point control of the link timing. If the connecting device were allowed to continue to run as master of the link, it would be running on a different clock from other links to the access point. One slot pair from the new Slave would overlap with two slot pairs on the LAN access point's native timing, so the connecting device would be using the bandwidth of the LAN access point inefficiently. Furthermore, if the connecting device remained as master of the link, it would decide when to transmit, so the LAN access point would lose control over its own bandwidth, potentially preventing it from meeting quality of service commitments.

The steps in connecting to a LAN access point are shown in Figure 19–12. First, the data terminal must find a LAN access point. It does this by inquiring and finding devices with the LAN access point device type. For LAN access points, the minor device type tells the data terminal how fully utilised a LAN access point is. This allows the data terminal to ignore LAN Access Points that are 100% utilised. If the data terminal has a choice of LAN access points to connect with, the information in the minor device type allows it to choose the least utilised one, as it is likely to deliver a better bandwidth on the link.

When the data terminal pages the LAN access point, the link will only be accepted if the data terminal is willing to do a Master/Slave switch, allowing the LAN access point to become master of the link.

Once a baseband link is established, an L2CAP connection is set up and the data terminal queries the service records with service class LANAccessUsingPPP. This gives the parameters needed to connect to the LAN access point.

The L2CAP link used for service discovery can be dropped, and a separate L2CAP link is set up for LAN access. RFCOMM and PPP connections are established across this L2CAP link. The data terminal must then negotiate an IP address with the LAN access point using

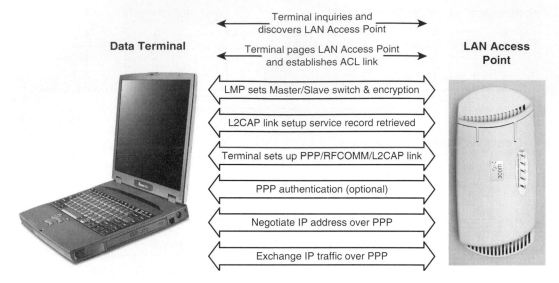

Figure 19–12   Establishing a connection to a LAN access point.

PPP. Once the data terminal has obtained an IP address, it can begin accessing the LAN. All PPP traffic is exchanged on an encrypted link, but authentication at the PPP level is optional.

19.8   GENERIC OBJECT EXCHANGE PROFILE

Three profiles rely on the generic object exchange profile:

- File transfer.
- Object push.
- Synchronisation.

The generic object exchange profile uses IrDA's OBEX layer and defines how it is used within Bluetooth. It also defines how the Link Layer sets up client/server communications. It does not, however, define the Application Layer; this is done in the file transfer, object exchange, and synchronisation profiles.

The generic object exchange profile defines two roles: the server device to and from which objects are pushed and pulled, and the client device, which can push and/or pull data objects to and from the server. Figure 19–13 shows the Protocol stacks for generic object exchange client and server applications.

The generic object exchange profile requires the use of the following OBEX operations: connect, disconnect put, get, and setpath. For more details of how these operations are used, refer to Chapter 13.

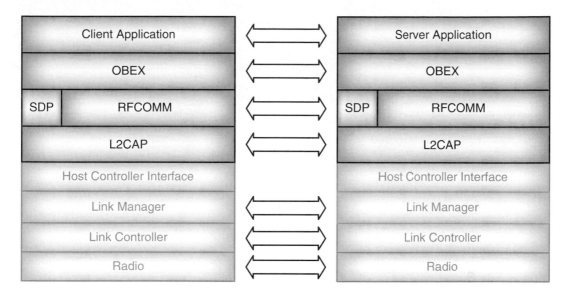

Figure 19–13   Generic object exchange profile protocol stack.

Information is transferred by OBEX using a variety of headers, many of which are optional. To aid in interoperability, the generic object exchange profile defines which headers should be used. These are: count, name, type, length, time, description, target, http, body, end of body, who, connection ID, authentication challenge, authentication response, application parameters, and object class.

Note that although authentication challenge and authentication response are specified in the set of headers, support of authentication is not mandatory. If authentication is supported, then authentication should take place before the first OBEX connection is set up. Authentication requires an OBEX password. This could be the same as the Bluetooth passkey to avoid the user having to enter two sets of security information for one link.

Refer to Chapter 13 for details of how to set up an OBEX connection across a Bluetooth link, and for details of how to push and pull data across a link.

19.9   OBJECT PUSH PROFILE

The object push profile provides facilities for exchanging business cards between client and server, for pulling business cards from a server, and for pushing a limited range of objects onto a server. As with all OBEX transactions, it is the client side that initiates operations.

An object has one of a defined set of content formats; for example, a virtual business card which fits the vCard object format. Although the use of defined content formats limits what can be done with object exchange, it does facilitate interoperability. For exchange of freely formatted data, other profiles should be used.

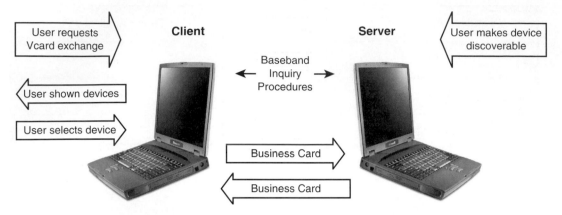

Figure 19–14   Exchanging vCards.

To provide the option of protecting the user's data, all devices supporting the object push profile must be capable of supporting authentication and encryption on the Bluetooth baseband links (though it is up to the application or the user whether these security features are actually used). The object push profile does not use OBEX authentication.

The user must initiate all operations carried out by the object push profile. Figure 19–14 shows an example of this. Two laptops exchange business cards, but only after the user on the client side has requested the exchange to happen. This example also illustrates that the server must be discoverable before the exchange can happen. The client device will inquire for devices in the area, find which ones support the object push profile by using service discovery procedures, then offer the user a choice of devices with which to exchange cards.

The same rules apply for business card pull and object exchange. The client user must initiate the action, the server must be discoverable, and the user selects from a list of discoverable devices with which to interact.

19.10   FILE TRANSFER PROFILE

The file transfer profile provides wireless data transfer between a variety of devices; for example, laptops, PDAs, and digital cameras. A typical application of the file transfer profile would be a PC to PC direct link for small meetings, providing convenient, cable-free connectivity.

Like the object push profile, the file transfer profile rests on the capabilities provided by OBEX as specified in the generic object exchange profile. This in turn rests on the generic access, serial port, and object exchange profiles.

The object push profile only provides for pushing and pulling a very limited range of objects. The file transfer profile provides richer features for dealing with files and fold-

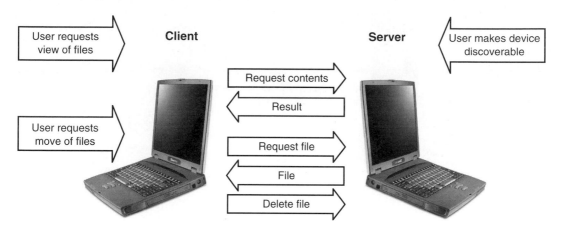

Figure 19–15   Using file transfer facilities to move a file.

ers: folders can be browsed, created, or transferred from one device to another; files can be browsed, pulled, pushed, and deleted.

Figure 19–15 shows some of the operations which can be performed using the file transfer profile. Here the contents of a folder are requested and a file is selected from the folder and moved from the server to the client. The move is a two-part operation: first a copy of the file is requested, then the original file is deleted. Supporting delete is not mandatory, and many servers may choose not to support it for security reasons.

In addition to pushing, pulling, and deleting files and folders, the file transfer profile provides for browsing capabilities using the OBEX SetPath operation. Each server provides a default browse root; this does not necessarily have to be the root of the server's native file system, as the server may choose not to expose all its files to devices using the file transfer profile. After the initial OBEX connect operation, the client will be placed in the browse root directory. The client can then navigate from that directory by listing contents of folders and using SetPath to move to a chosen folder.

Files and folders can also be created on the server using the OBEX put operation. For more details on how OBEX operations are used, refer to Chapter 13.

19.11   SYNCHRONISATION PROFILE

The synchronisation profile provides a standard way to synchronise personal data between Bluetooth enabled devices. For example, the synchronisation profile could be used to ensure that appointments entered into a calendar application on a laptop were kept up-to-date with a version managed on a PDA.

Synchronisation can be triggered when devices come within range of one another and can happen automatically without user intervention. This ability of applications to act without user input has been referred to as "hidden computing" or "unconscious com-

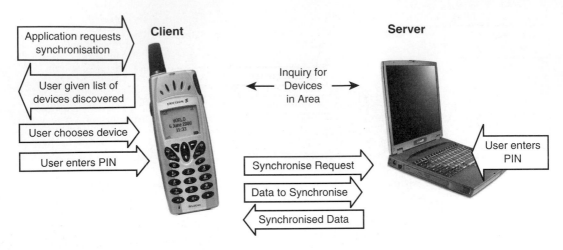

Figure 19–16   Synchronising devices.

puting," and is one of the means by which Bluetooth can potentially make applications far easier and more convenient to use than the cabled, connected versions it replaces.

Figure 19–16 shows how the synchronisation profile could be used. A user has a phone with new entries in its address book, which need to be downloaded onto a laptop. The user selects synchronise on the phone. The phone searches for devices in the area and presents them to the user, who selects the laptop for synchronisation. At this stage, PIN codes are entered to authorise the operation. Then the synchronisation is processed.

Once PINs have been entered, devices are bonded, and the next time a synchronisation happens, the authentication sequence may be skipped. Devices could even be set to periodically inquire for other devices they are bonded with and perform synchronisation automatically. For example, if a user knew that at 11:00 every day his or her phone was likely to be on the desk next to his or her laptop, the laptop could be set to request synchronisation with the phone at that time. In this way, devices may be synchronised "unconsciously"—true hidden computing!

19.12   INTERCOM PROFILE

The intercom profile supports direct point to point voice connections between Bluetooth handsets and is most appropriate when combined with the +20 dBm radios which provide operation in the 50–100m range.

TCS provides call control facilities for the intercom links. The signalling is carried across ACL links, which are routed to the TCS stack through L2CAP. For details of TCS operation, see Chapter 14. The intercom speech links are carried on SCO links.

Figure 19–17 shows the stages in establishing a direct intercom connection between two Bluetooth enabled handsets. The handsets may well support other connections; they

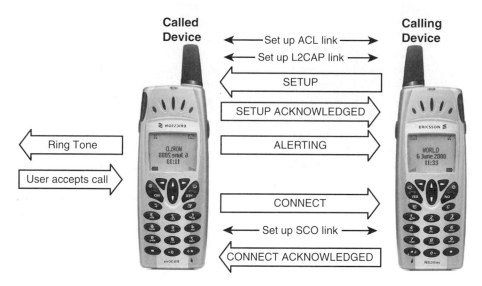

Figure 19–17   Establishing an intercom connection.

could be cellular phones for instance, or they could be dedicated Bluetooth intercom devices.

    The calling device must first set up a baseband ACL link to the device it wishes to call. It then sets up an L2CAP link; this is used to carry the TCS signalling. The first signal is SETUP, which is acknowledged by the called device. The SETUP command causes the called device to begin alerting the user, usually by a ring tone. The called device notifies the caller that it is alerting the user, then when the user accepts the call, sends a CONNECT message. In version 1.0b the CONNECT message causes the calling device to set up a SCO link to carry voice traffic; in version 1.1 this was corrected so the receiving device sets up the SCO link. After all, it is the receiving side which decides whether to accept the call, so it makes sense that it is the receiver which establishes the audio channel. Once the SCO link is in place, a CONNECT ACKNOWLEDGED signal is sent and the intercoms can be used to hold a conversation.

    Bluetooth does not define any call handover facilities, and the only connection provided is direct handset-to-handset, so the Bluetooth intercom profile does not at present represent serious competition for systems such as DECT. However, it is possible that future versions of Bluetooth may provide handover facilities.

19.13 THE CORDLESS TELEPHONY PROFILE

The Bluetooth cordless telephony profile enables a Bluetooth handset to connect to a variety of telephony base stations. At home, the handset could connect to a wall mounted device which connects into the PSTN; in the office, the same handset could connect to an internal telephone network; and on the move, it could connect to a cellular mobile phone carried in a briefcase or bag.

The cordless telephony profile defines two roles for Bluetooth devices: a gateway which connects to an external network and receives incoming calls, and a terminal which receives the calls from the gateway and provides speech and/or data links to the user. The gateway is the master of a piconet, so one gateway can connect to up to seven terminals at a time, though of course, due to the limitations on SCO capacity, only three active voice links can be supported simultaneously.

The gateway can pass calls to the terminals, or the terminals can initiate calls and route them through the gateway. This allows Bluetooth devices which do not have telephony links to access telephone networks through the gateway. For example, a Bluetooth enabled laptop could be used as a speaker phone connecting to a mobile network using a cellular mobile phone as a gateway, or alternatively a mobile phone could be used to link to a company's internal telephone network using a wall mounted access point as a gateway.

The cordless telephony profile also supports intercom-like calls between two devices in the network, and allows usage of all TCS facilities such as DTMF tones and register recall. For more details on TCS, refer to Chapter 14.

TCS provides call control and group management across L2CAP's connection-oriented and connectionless channels, carried on encrypted ACL links. The speech links are carried on SCO links.

Terminals which are out of range of a gateway periodically try to connect by paging the gateway. Gateways, in their turn, page scan as often as they can to allow roaming devices to connect. Once a terminal has connected to a gateway, it performs a Master/Slave switch. This is carried out for the same reasons as when connecting to a LAN access point and returns control of the piconet to the gateway, allowing the master to allocate bandwidth efficiently.

The terminal then optionally goes into Park mode; this allows it to save power, but it can still be reached by broadcasting in beacon slots. This allows the gateway to distribute configuration information around parked devices in beacon slots. The beacon slots should be spaced so that when incoming calls arrive, the terminal can be unparked fast enough to answer the call.

In version 1.0b support of Park Mode for devices implementing the Cordless Telephony Profile was mandatory. Because this was the only profile which made park mode support mandatory, it was felt to be too restrictive, so in version 1.1 park mode support became optional. Still, it is advisory to implement it, as it greatly extends battery life on mobile devices.

Connections between terminal devices use the group management facilities of TCS to locate devices and find the information needed to connect with them (see Chapter 14). Links are set up in the same way as intercom connections (see Section 19.12 above).

A connection between the gateway and a terminal device is illustrated in Figure 19–18. The TCS signalling for the call is identical to the signalling used during the setup of an intercom call. The difference is that here, ACL and L2CAP links do not

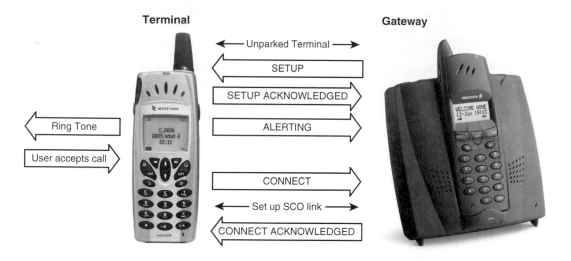

Figure 19–18   A cordless telephony gateway establishing a call to a terminal.

have to be established. The gateway establishes an L2CAP link to each terminal device before it is parked. These connections are kept when the devices are parked and do not have to be established again when an incoming call triggers the gateway to unpark a device. In this way, parked devices can respond more rapidly to calls arriving from the gateway.

19.14   BENEFITS OF PROFILES

For users, the profiles provide a way for technology to be used in many devices and applications, but with a common look and feel provided by the Generic Access Profile. For developers, the profiles provide a common reusable set of building blocks, obviating the need for separate solutions to similar problems. Once one of the profiles built upon the serial port profile has been implemented, for example, much of the solution can be reused to implement other profiles layered on the serial port profile.

Use of profiles ensures that different implementations of Bluetooth are standardised, enabling implementations from various manufacturers to interwork reliably and increasing the overall market confidence in Bluetooth as a robust standard system.

For marketers, the common look and feel provided by the profiles should ease adoption of Bluetooth by breaking down the barriers which lack of familiarity presents. Products must clearly identify the profiles which they support, and to this end, a series of names have been defined to use in marketing purposes which do not correspond exactly with the profile names in all cases. Table 19–1 lists these names, alongside those used in the Bluetooth specification.

To avoid confusion for consumers, as new profiles are defined, product literature should specify which other products have been shown to interoperate with the product.

Table 19–1   Marketing Names for Bluetooth Profiles

Name in Profile Specification	Name to Be Used in Marketing
Generic Access	Generic Access
Service Discovery	Service Discovery
Cordless Telephony	Cordless Telephony
Intercom	Local Telephony
Headset	Headset
Dial Up Networking	Modem
FAX	FAX
LAN Access	Network Access Point
Serial Port	Serial Port
Generic Object Exchange	Object Exchange
Object Push	Object Push
File Transfer/Data Sharing	Data Sharing
Synchronisation	Synchronisation

19.15 SUMMARY

Profiles describe how the Bluetooth specification should be used in applications, and by doing this, they help to ensure that applications from different manufacturers will interoperate reliably and in a familiar way.

The profiles implemented by Bluetooth version 1.0 and 1.1 are:

- Generic Access—This defines the basic rules for using the protocol stack and is the foundation for all the other profiles.
- Serial Port—How RFCOMM's serial port emulation capabilities are to be used in Bluetooth products.
- Dialup networking—A Bluetooth link to a modem.
- FAX—How to transfer a FAX over Bluetooth.
- Headset—A duplex link to a headset, controlled by an audio gateway, such as a cellular mobile phone.
- LAN Access Point—A link to a LAN via Bluetooth.
- Generic Object exchange—A set of rules for using OBEX, which supports file transfer, object push, and synchronisation profiles.
- File transfer—Transferring files between Bluetooth devices.
- Object push—Pushing objects from a Bluetooth enabled server to a client.
- Synchronisation—Synchronising objects between Bluetooth devices.

- Cordless telephony—Forwarding telephone calls to Bluetooth devices.
- Intercom—Short range voice connections between Bluetooth devices.

The profiles are arranged in a hierarchy with some profiles depending on others. The Generic Access Profile defines basic baseband link functionality, such as device discovery and link setup, and so all other profiles rely on it.

More profiles are being defined by a series of Bluetooth SIG working groups. The next chapter will examine the first few of these new profiles to be released.

20

Draft Post–Foundation Profiles

When version 1.1 of the Bluetooth specification was released, it contained the same thirteen profiles which were released with version 1.0. These are sometimes called the foundation profiles, and whilst they provided a good start for product manufacturers, they could not cover all possible uses for Bluetooth devices.

To expand the range of profiles available, the Bluetooth SIG has a series of working groups which are developing new profiles. Profiles go through a series of drafts before they are finally adopted into the Bluetooth specification. When profiles reach draft version 0.9, they are released for viewing by all Bluetooth adopters. By this stage the profiles have already undergone extensive review by the Bluetooth Architectural Review Board, Bluetooth Associates, and the Bluetooth Test and Interoperability workgroup, so they are unlikely to change in any significant ways before release.

This chapter covers draft profiles which have been released to adopters, but are not yet formally adopted into the Bluetooth specification. At the time of writing six draft profiles were on release to adopters:

- HID—Human interface devices such as a mouse or keyboard.
- CAR—Hands free phone use.
- Basic Imaging—Basic image transfer.
- Hard Copy Cable Replacement—Replacement of a printer cable with a Bluetooth link.

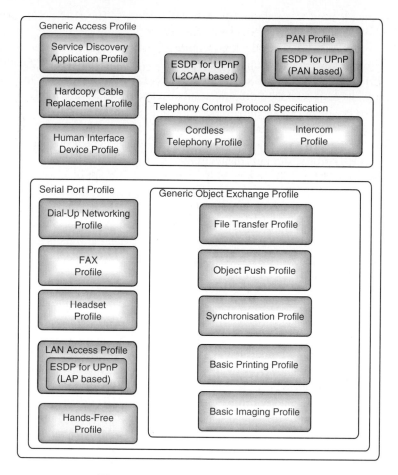

Figure 20–1   The new Bluetooth profiles.

- Basic Printing—Sending text and XML formatted documents to printers, and printer control.
- PAN—IP over Bluetooth.

Many more profiles are on the way, for details see Chapter 28.

Figure 20–1 shows how the new draft profiles fit within the overall structure of Bluetooth profiles.

20.1   THE HUMAN INTERFACE DEVICE PROFILE

The Human Interface Device (HID) Profile allows devices such as a computer mouse, keyboard, or tracker ball to communicate using a Bluetooth link. The profile uses the HID protocol which is used to communicate with HID devices. The HID protocol originates from the Universal Serial Bus (USB) specification.

Because human interface devices require a fast response, the HID profile is designed to provide low latency communications. This is done using L2CAP Quality of Service (QOS) settings. Many Bluetooth devices do not implement the full QOS functionality, so designers should be aware that response times are likely to suffer if a HID is a slave in a piconet containing other Bluetooth slave devices.

The profile provides a means for the device to describe itself. Some HIDs may require output to the user; for example, a display or force feedback joystick both require output, so the HID profile supports data output as well as input.

Because the HID profile can be used in so many different types of device, it is not possible to say exactly which layers of the Bluetooth protocol stack will be present. Figure 20–2 shows two example stacks. On the left is the type of configuration that might be found on a Host such as a desktop PC with a separate Host Processor and Bluetooth module, so this example includes a Host Controller Interface. On the right is an example from a Human Interface Device; because such devices have limited functionality, all processing can be done within a Bluetooth device's own processor, so there is no need for a Host Controller Interface.

Figure 20–2 also illustrates the two roles defined by the HID profile: the HID itself and the host which uses the services of the HID. Usually, the host would be the master, but this is not mandatory.

It is likely that many hosts, such as PCs, will already have USB HID drivers. These can be used with Bluetooth devices by the addition of an adapter driver, sometimes called a miniport driver. The adapter driver handles the Bluetooth specific connection management and passes HID protocol information up to the USB HID driver.

The HID profile aims to allow devices to run for three months on three AAA or two AA alkaline batteries. To achieve this the host should allow HIDs to initiate sniff and park

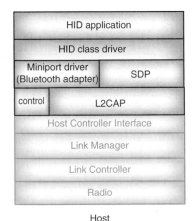

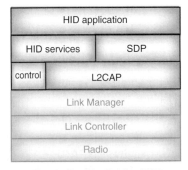

Host   Human Interface Device (HID)

Figure 20–2   Example HID protocol stacks.

modes, although hold mode is optional. If the host wants to send data to a parked or sniffing slave, it simply sends an unsniff or unpark request. Designers should be aware that putting a device in park or sniff mode will add a delay to communications as the unpark or unsniff request goes out in one beacon, then the response comes back in the next beacon, then data can be transferred on the next host poll.

20.1.1   HID Descriptors

Information about a HID is stored in descriptors. These are just records held in segments of memory. (In production devices the descriptors would usually be stored in ROM because it is a very cheap form of memory.) The HID profile uses four types of descriptor:

- Interface Descriptor—Identifies the class, or type, of the device. The class is used to identify the correct HID class driver which can communicate with the HID.
- Device Descriptor—Gives the types and sizes of descriptors other than the interface descriptor.
- Report Descriptor—Defines items which describe an output such as a position or button state. The report descriptor tells the HID class driver about the size and composition of data reports from a particular item.
- Physical Descriptor—Optional information on parts of the human body used to activate the controls on a HID.

20.1.2   L2CAP Interrupt and Control Channels

There are two different types of reports: HID reports carrying input or output data on user interactions requiring a fast response and feature reports carrying background control information which are not so time critical. HID reports and feature reports are carried on different L2CAP channels, each with its own QOS and each identified by its own protocol service multiplexor (PSM).

HID reports can be input reports carrying data from HID to host, or output reports carrying data from host to HID. One example of an input report is a key press report from a keyboard; an example of an output report is a report to trigger force feedback effects in a joystick. To achieve the best response time, HID reports should be carried on an L2CAP channel which can be set to guaranteed quality of service, this is called the interrupt channel or HID_Interrupt. There is no point using a guaranteed channel if there is no data to transfer, and it is possible that a HID will only send data in one direction. If the HID doesn't declare any data input reports, then the input direction has QOS set to No Traffic. Similarly, if the HID declares no output reports, then the output direction has QOS set to No Traffic. If a device declares data input reports and data output reports, then they are both carried on the same L2CAP channel HID_Interrupt, in this case the latency specified in the L2CA_ConfigReq primitive will affect data flow in both directions, so it should be set to satisfy the direction needing the lowest latency.

Feature reports carry initialisation information and control data for the application. For example, they might carry information on device options or device state or coordinate scaling parameters. The background control data carried in feature reports does not require fast responses. In order to allow HID reports to take priority over feature reports, the feature reports are carried on an L2CAP channel with best effort quality of service. The channel used for feature reports is called the Control channel or HID_Control.

It is possible that one HID might implement more than one function, for instance, a combination keypad and joystick. Such multifunction devices appear to be two different HIDs both on the same Bluetooth link. The two HIDs can share the same control and Interrupt channels because the HID protocol uses report IDs to sort out which HID a particular report is coming from.

20.1.3   Configuring an HID Device

A cabled HID is configured across its wired connection, but for Bluetooth HIDs the device must be discovered and configured across the Bluetooth link. The HID profile recommends that HIDs should use limited discoverable mode. The HID would enter discoverable mode by human interaction. This is needed for two reasons: first, HIDs are likely to be battery powered and constant inquiry scans would drain their batteries; second, entering discoverable mode only at the push of a button helps to make the HID more secure by hiding it from inquiries most of the time.

Once the HID is in discoverable mode the host can find it, establish a link, and the HID passes its HID descriptors to the host. The HID profile defines the same default PIN code as the LAN Access Profile: a single byte set to zero.

There is a curious problem when initiating an authenticated link with a Bluetooth keyboard: the host hasn't got a keyboard to enter the PIN on! The solution is for the host to generate a random PIN and display it. The number displayed is then entered on the keyboard, in this way both ends of the link get the same PIN and authentication can proceed.

The profile recommends that authentication and encryption are used with HIDs, but neither is mandatory.

The HID_Control channel is established first, then the HID_Interrupt channel, but because L2CAP configuration can take a while, both channels may be being configured at the same time.

It is usual for PC hosts to need keyboard interaction as the system is booting, so keyboard support has to be built into the BIOS. The HID profile suggests that for PC hosts which do not have BIOS support, the keyboard could be provided with a USB/PS2 adapter which would allow the keyboard to be used as a wired device whilst the PC was booting.

20.1.4   Virtual Cables—Reconnecting to HIDs

When a HID has been connected with a host, if both sides want to keep a one to one link, then they have the option of marking both sides of the link as virtually cabled. HIDs which want to use virtual cables set HIDVirtualCable to TRUE in their Service Discovery Records. A virtual cable can only connect one HID to one host. For example, a virtually cabled remote control can't be used to switch two devices simultaneously (as could be done with an infrared remote control). If another host tries to connect to a virtually cabled HID, the second host will be refused.

If a virtually cabled connection is dropped, automatic reconnection will be attempted. Since HID and host have to agree on which side will do the paging, the HID device has a HIDReconnectInitiate service record. If this is true, the HID will initiate reconnection by paging; if it is false the HID will page scan and wait for the host to initiate reconnection. If the HID initiates the connection to the host, a master/slave switch is used to avoid the HID remaining as the master of the link.

A HID connection might be lost for many reasons: HID and host move out of one another's radio range, either device is reset, or perhaps there is a prolonged burst of interference. The host will try to reconnect for 30 seconds, after this time it is allowed to time out, though of course the user can always restart the connection process.

Virtually cabled devices store information to allow reconnection. To disconnect the virtual cable and connect the HID to another host the user must intervene. For instance, the user could press a button on the HID before it is connected to another host. The HID would then try to inform its virtually cabled host that the virtual cable was being unplugged.

20.1.5 HID Protocol

The HID profile provides a Bluetooth HID (BT-HID) protocol for communications between host and HID. This protocol defines a set of services and provides support for transferring messages belonging to a further two protocols: Boot Protocol and Report protocol.

One obvious question is why BT-HID implements both report and boot protocol: is this just unnecessary complication? The reason is that devices such as PCs may need to communicate with mice and keyboards during bootup. Having a simpler boot protocol makes it easier to implement a simple HID driver at the BIOS level, allowing input from HIDs during bootup. However, because the boot protocol is simple, it only allows limited input reports: in the case of keyboards, 103 keys as provided on PC-AT keyboards, and in the case of mice a simple three button mouse with movement in two directions.

Report Protocol uses a parser to interpret the Report Descriptor which is stored in the HID's SDP service record. This allows more complex information to be sent, allowing extended functionality in HIDs. The Report protocol parser is too complex for most manufacturers to want to implement it at BIOS level.

Both protocols use transactions: a transaction consists of a request from the host to the HID followed by a data or handshake payload from the HID to the host. Some messages are just used by boot protocol, some by report protocol, and some are used by both. The sections on boot and report protocol below describe how and when the messages are used.

In order to distinguish between the different HID message types, all HID messages begin with a single byte header called the BT-HID Transaction Header (THdr). Figure 20–3 illustrates the format of the header: just four bits to identify the type of transaction and four bits of parameter. The meaning of the parameter bits depends upon the Transaction Type. The possible values of the Transaction Type are:

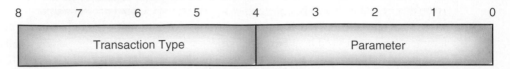

Figure 20–3 BT-HID Transaction Header.

- 0x0 - HANDSHAKE—Acknowledges a request when no data needs to be sent.
- 0x1 - HID_CONTROL—Requests a major state change.
- 0x2 - 0x3—Reserved.
- 0x4 - GET_REPORT—Gets report data.
- 0x5 - SET_REPORT—Sets report data.
- 0x6 - GET_PROTOCOL—Retrieves the current protocol being used.
- 0x7 - SET_PROTOCOL—Sets the protocol to use.
- 0x8 - GET_IDLE—Retrieves idle rate of a device.
- 0x9 - SET_IDLE—Sets preferred idle rate of a device.
- 0xA - DATA—Carries payload data.
- 0xB - DATC—Carries continuation of data which would not fit in a DATA report.
- 0xC-0xF—Reserved.

If any GET request is received with no errors, the HID replies with a DATA payload. If the data requested doesn't fit in one DATA payload, then data continuation DATC payloads are used until all data has been sent.

If any SET request is received, the device responds with a HANDSHAKE. The HANDSHAKE message is also used to reply to any GET request with an error.

20.1.6   Boot Protocol

Version 0.9 of the HID protocol defines boot protocol support for keyboards and mice. As mentioned above, the boot protocol does not need a parser because it uses predefined Report Descriptors which are defined in the HID specification.

Not all HIDs will support Boot protocol, so Boot protocol support is indicated in the FHS class of device, or using the HIDBootDevice attribute in SDP.

In both boot mode and report mode GET_REPORT is used to poll a device for data, and SET_REPORT is used to send data to a device. If the data does not fit in one payload, data continuation (DATC) messages are used to send remaining data.

A multifunction device might implement both mouse and keyboard functionality—for example, a gamepad might incorporate a joystick which provided directional information and a range of buttons which acted like a keypad. The reports from the mouse function must be separated from the reports from the keyboard function, but both are coming across the same Bluetooth link. The HID profile identifies the type of HID a re-

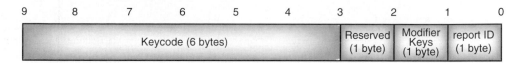

Figure 20–4 BT-HID keyboard input report.

port comes from by starting each report with a single byte Report ID. The Report IDs defined in version 0.9 of the HID specification are:

- 0—Reserved.
- 1—Keyboard. Input report size is 9 bytes as shown in Figure 20–4, output size is 2 bytes as shown in Figure 20–5.
- 2—Mouse. Report size is 4 bytes as shown in Figure 20–6.
- 3–255—Reserved.

A keyboard requires an output report as well as an input report because the keyboard must receive modifier keys. Modifier keys are keys such as CTRL, ALT, SHIFT, which are pressed in combination with another key to change its meaning. Since several modifier keys can be pressed at once, the keyboard output report is a bit field; bits are simply set to one if a key is pressed and zero otherwise.

After the report ID comes a report which uses the format defined in the HID specification. Because of the report ID, the HID reports are 1 byte longer than the standard records, giving a 9 byte keyboard report and 4 byte mouse report.

In report protocol the report ID can be omitted from devices which do not support multiple functions (it is possible to tell from service records whether a device is single function or multifunction). In boot protocol the report ID is always used because it is simpler to implement a fixed format than one with optional elements.

It is possible to add extra data onto the end of the reports. In boot mode the host will ignore the extra data, but it is useful to be able to send it, as it means a HID can send extra data related to functions described in the report mode descriptor. By allowing a HID to do this, the specification allows it to send identical reports in boot mode and report mode, thus allowing the HID design to be simpler.

In addition to sending data reports, all devices which implement boot protocol must support two transactions:

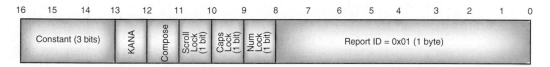

Figure 20–5 BT-HID keyboard output report.

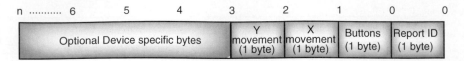

Figure 20–6 BT-HID mouse report.

- GET_PROTOCOL—Gets the current protocol on the HID; the reply is a byte of data set to 0 for report protocol and 1 for boot protocol.
- SET_PROTOCOL—Switches a device between boot protocol and report protocol.

Keyboards must also support two extra transactions to manage idle rate. The idle rate reports how often a keyboard sends key down information to the host. The two messages used to manage idle rate are:

- GET_IDLE—Gets the current state of the HID; the reply is a byte of data giving the idle rate.
- SET_IDLE—Used to change the idle rate in line with user preferences.

A zero idle rate means a keyboard only reports when a key is pressed. Non-zero values give the time between reports in units of 4 milliseconds. Of course, the reports are limited by the QOS of the L2CAP HID_Interrupt channel, so if the idle rate is less than the channel latency, the reports will be generated at the Interrupt channel latency rate.

20.1.7   Report Protocol

Report mode can use more complex formats in its reports, allowing more functionality to be implemented in devices. To do this report mode requires a parser. An extra message: HID_CONTROL is supported to handle more complex functions.

The HID_CONTROL message requests a major state change in a HID. It carries a parameter to identify the new state. Possible values for the parameter are:

- 0x0—No Operation (NOP).
- 0x1—Hard Reset: Restart device including Power On Self Test (POST) reinitialisation and restart normal operation.
- 0x2—Soft Reset: Initialise all variables and restart normal operation.
- 0x3—Suspend: Go to reduced power mode.
- 0x4—Exit Suspend.
- 0x5—0xF—Reserved.

The Suspend command allows a host to inform the HID when reduced response times are acceptable. This might be because the Bluetooth link is being used for high bandwidth data transfer, so normal QOS is not possible, or it might be because inactivity has triggered a low power standby state in the host. This allows the HID to use park or sniff mode; of course, it may also choose to perform other power saving operations, such as switching off LEDs or lowering the key scan frequency.

Low power modes are crucial if HID devices are to achieve the three month battery life target the HID profile sets. Therefore, the host should use the HID_CONTROL message to allow suspend whenever higher latency communications are acceptable.

20.2   THE HANDS-FREE PROFILE

The Hands-Free Profile (HFP) defines functionality which allows a mobile phone to be used with a hands-free device. It differs from the headset profile by providing remote control of the phone as well as a voice connection. The hands-free profile was developed by the Bluetooth SIG's Car working group, so not surprisingly the main usage model mentioned in the profile is using a phone with a hands-free device installed in a car.

As Figure 20–1 shows, the hands-free profile relies upon the Serial Port Profile and the Generic Access Profile. Figure 20–6 shows how the hands-free control relies upon RFCOMM for data transfer. The protocol stack looks similar to the stack used for the headset profile; in fact, the signalling is AT command based, as is the signalling in the headset profile.

The Audio Gateway (AG) is the device which is the gateway for audio coming from a network. A typical Audio Gateway device is a cellular phone. The Hands-Free Unit (HF) acts as a remote audio input and output for the Audio Gateway and also provides some control of the Audio Gateway. An example is a hands-free unit installed in a car.

The Hands-Free Profile supports service level connections, which are RFCOMM connections used for control and status updates. It also supports a single audio connection

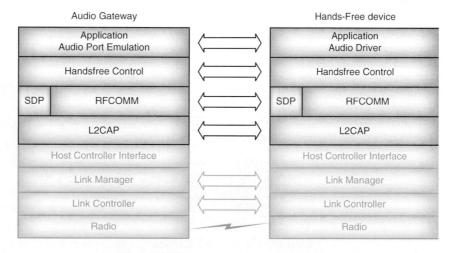

Figure 20–7   Hands-free protocol stack.

which provides bidirectional (duplex) audio across a SCO link using the CVSD codec. CVSD was chosen because it is the most error-tolerant of the codecs supported by the Bluetooth Core specification.

20.2.1   Establishing a Service Level Connection

A service level connection is used to transfer control information between Hands-Free and Audio Gateway. Figure 20–8 shows an example of establishing an audio gateway. In this example the connection is initiated by the user interacting with the Hands-Free device, but it is also possible for the connection to be initiated by user interaction at the Audio Gateway side, or by an automatic internal event in either device.

The first stage is to establish an RFCOMM connection, initialising RFCOMM if necessary. In order to do this, the initiating device may need to establish an SDP session to retrieve service records giving the parameters needed to set up the RFCOMM connection.

The Hands-Free profile passes status information from the Audio Gateway to the Hands-Free as indicators. Two indicators are supported:

- service—Gives service availability: 0=no service, 1 = service is present.
- call—Call status indicator: 0 = no call in progress, 1 = a call is in progress.

The Hands-Free retrieves information on which indicators are supported from the Audio Gateway using an AT+CIND=? command. The gateway replies with a +CIND giving the call indicators and an OK confirming successful completion of the command.

Once the Hands-Free knows which indicators are supported, it can request the current status of the indicators in the Audio Gateway using an AT+CIND? command. The Audio gateway replies with a +CIND giving the status of the indicators and an OK confirming successful completion of the command.

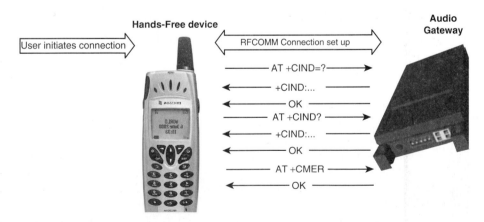

Figure 20–8   Establishing a service level connection.

The Hands-Free requests the Audio Gateway to enable status update using the AT+CMER=... command. This can be used to set indicator events reporting, that is to say reporting when there is an event affecting service availability or whether there is a call in progress. There are only two permitted parameter strings for this command:

- AT+CMER=3,0,0,1 switches on indicator events reporting.
- AT+CMER=3,0,0,0 switches off indicator events reporting.

The Audio gateway replies with OK to confirm successful completion of the command.

Once the indicator events reporting has been set up, the service level connection has been established and the Hands-Free is ready to be used with the Audio Gateway.

If there is no subsequent activity, and if the Hands-Free and Audio Gateway support park mode, the connection is parked. Either side can request park mode. When the connection enters park mode, the L2CAP and RFCOMM data link channels are not released, so that service can be made available as quickly as possible when it is needed. Either side can request an unpark and return the connection to active mode as a result of an internal event (such as a timer expiry) or as a result of user interaction. If park mode is not supported, then the link remains active, as it is required for status updates.

20.2.2   Transferring Status Information

The previous section explained how the AT+CMER command is used to enable or disable indicator events reporting.

Once Indicator events reporting is enabled, the Audio Gateway will send the Hands-Free a +CIEV result code whenever its current call status changes. The Hands-Free uses the information from the +CIEV result code to generate a "call process ongoing" or "no call present" indication for the user.

The CIEV result code is sent whenever a call is answered, terminated, or dialed.

20.2.3   Handling Calls

When the Audio Gateway receives an incoming call from the network, it sends a series of unsolicited RING alerts to the Hand-Free device. Optionally, it may send an in-band ringing tone using the audio connection. The Audio Gateway may also optionally use the CLIP command to send a Calling Line Identification Notification.

The RING alerts are repeated as long as an incoming call is still present and the Hands-Free has neither accepted nor rejected the call. Figure 20–9 shows an incoming call being accepted after two repeats of the RING.

If the user accepts the call, the Hands-Free sends an ATA command, the Audio Gateway replies with OK to confirm successful completion of the command, and the Audio Gateway sends a +CIEV event notification to indicate the call status has changed to call active.

If the user rejects the call, then instead of the +ATA command, the Hand-Free sends an AT+CHUP hangup command. The Audio Gateway still replies with OK to confirm

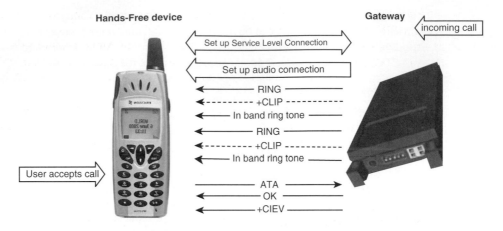

Figure 20–9 Answering an incoming call.

successful completion of the command and still sends a +CIEV to indicate the call status has changed, but this time the new status is "no call".

Figure 20–9 shows a call being answered when there is in band ringing. If in-band ringing is not used, then the setup of the audio connection can be delayed until after the +CIEV event is sent. This avoids setting up an audio connection before it is known whether the call will be accepted or rejected.

Call termination is shown in Figure 20–10. First the user intervenes to terminate the call. This causes the hands-free device to send the same +CHUP command which is used to reject an incoming call. The Audio Gateway drops the call and responds with an OK to

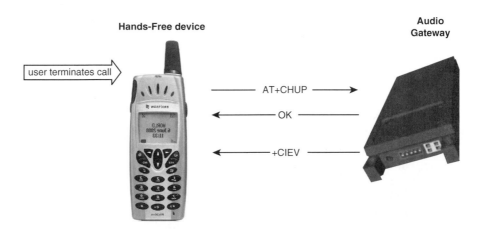

Figure 20–10 Terminating a call.

confirm that the command was successful. Finally, the Audio Gateway sends a +CIEV event to notify the new call status, which is "no call".

It is possible that a call will be terminated from the Audio Gateway end—for instance, if the call is dropped due to network problems. In this case the Audio Gateway simply sends a +CIEV event notification with a call status of "no call". This informs the Hands-Free that the call is no longer present.

The Hands-Free can make an outgoing call simply by providing the audio gateway with the number to call. Figure 20–11 shows how this is done using an ATDdd...dd command. The dd...dd part of the command is the digits of the number to be dialed. The Audio Gateway begins setting up the outgoing call, then sends an OK back to the Hands-Free to confirm that the dial command has been successful. When the call goes through, the Audio Gateway notifies the Hands-Free with a +CIEV event using a call status of "call active". If there isn't already an audio connection between the Hands-Free and the Audio Gateway, then the Audio Gateway sets one up at this point so that it can carry the call.

Similar procedures can be used to dial from the Audio Gateway's memory or to redial the last number called. To dial from memory the ATDdd....dd command is replaced with a ATD>nnn command where nnn identifies the memory location on the Audio Gateway holding the number to dial. The rest of the procedure is the same as when dialing using the ATDdd...dd command.

To redial the last number called, a special extension to the AT command set has been defined by the Hands-Free Profile. This is the AT+BLDN command. The Hands-Free sends AT+BLDN in place of the ATDdd...dd command, and the Audio Gateway retrieves the last number called from memory. The rest of the procedure is the same as when dialing using the ATDdd...dd command.

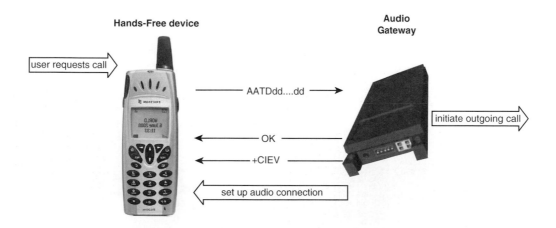

Figure 20–11   Hands-Free makes an outgoing call.

20.2.4   Call Waiting and Call Holding

The Hands-Free Profile supports two types of call information notifications which the Audio Gateway can send to the Hands-Free to give the Hands-Free more information whilst a call is in progress. These are Call waiting and caller line identification.

Notifications must be enabled before they will be used. The Hands-Free sends the AT+CCWA command to enable call waiting notification, the Audio Gateway replies with OK to indicate that call waiting notification has successfully been enabled. Once Call Waiting notification is enabled, the Audio Gateway will send a +CCWA unsolicited result code to the Hands-Free whenever an incoming call is waiting whilst a call is in progress. Some Audio Gateways will only be able to handle one call at a time, and so they will not be able to detect an incoming call whilst another call is active. These Audio Gateways will be unable to support Call Waiting notification.

If the user wants to switch to a call which is waiting, they will have to hold the existing call. When the user requests hold, the Hands-Free sends a AT+CHLD command to the Audio Gateway, the Gateway replies with OK, and switches to the waiting call. The AT+CHLD command can then be used (with different parameters from the first time) to create a three way call. Of course, a three way call can only be established if the Audio Gateway supports this feature. The messages exchanged when a Hands-Free wishes to hold a call and then initiate a multiparty call are shown in Figure 20–12.

20.2.5   Caller Line Identification

The number of an incoming call can be sent from the Audio Gateway to the Hands-Free, so that the user can be informed on which number is calling. To enable this feature the Hands-Free sends an AT+CLIP command to the Audio Gateway, the Audio Gateway replies with OK to confirm that the command has been successful. The next time an in-

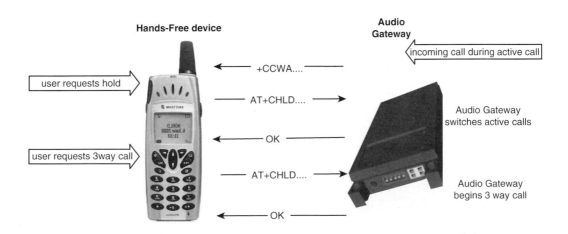

Figure 20–12   Hands-Free holds a call then makes a multiparty call.

coming call is received, the Audio Gateway sends a +CLIP Calling Line Identification notification to the Hands-Free.

The Caller Line Identification feature remains enabled until it is disabled using another +CLIP command from the Hands-Free or until the Service Level Connection between the Audio Gateway and Hands-Free is dropped.

20.2.6 Controlling Audio Functions and DTMF Tones

A variety of commands are available to control the audio functions of the Audio Gateway: the Echo Cancelling and Noise Reduction can be enabled or disabled, the volume can be remotely controlled, and DTMF tones can be generated.

If the Audio Gateway supports Echo Cancelling and Noise Reduction, these features are enabled by default. They can be switched on and off using the AT+NREC command. The settings remain in effect until changed again with the AT+NREC command, or until the service level connection is dropped.

The Audio Gateway can control the Hands-Free's microphone gain by sending a +VGM to the Hands-Free. Similarly, the Audio Gateway can control the speaker gain by sending a +VGS to the Hands-Free. The gains are given on a scale from 0 to 15, so, for instance, +VGS:15 sets maximum volume on the speaker, and +VGM:0 sets minimum gain on the microphone.

The Hands-Free may store volume levels so that they don't have to be set every time a connection is established. If the Hands-Free does this, then when a new connection is established, it tells the Audio Gateway what levels it has retrieved by using AT+VGS and AT+VGM commands.

If the user manually changes the speaker gain, the Hands-Free informs the Audio Gateway with an AT+VGS command, the Audio Gateway replies with the usual OK response. Similarly, if the microphone gain is changed by the user, the Hands-Free sends the Audio Gateway an AT+VGM command, and again receives an OK confirming it has been received.

DTMF tones can only be generated whilst there is an active call. The Hands-Free sends the Audio Gateway an AT+VTS command to generate a DTMF tone. The tone to generate is carried as a parameter following the AT+VTS command.

20.2.7 Voice Recognition

If the Audio Gateway supports voice recognition, it must support the AT+BVRA command. This is an extension to the AT command set defined by the Hands-Free profile and is used to switch voice recognition features on and off. The Audio Gateway confirms success of the command by replying with an OK.

Obviously, for voice recognition to work, there must be an audio link active between the Audio Gateway and the Hands-Free. So if the AT+BVRA command enables voice recognition when there isn't an audio link present, the Audio Gateway sets up an Audio link after sending the OK response.

The AT+BVRA command remains in effect until another AT+BVRA command is sent, the service level connection is dropped, or the LMP link is dropped.

Hands-Free devices which support voice recognition can attach a phone number to a voice tag. This provides much more user-friendly interaction with the Audio Gateway—for instance, the user can say "Fred" instead of reading out Fred's number.

The Audio Gateway stores the last voice tag it recognised in memory. If the Hands-Free wants to access this information, it sends the Audio Gateway an AT+BINP=1 command. This is an extension to the AT command set defined by the Hands-Free profile. The parameter 1 tells the Audio Gateway that the Hands-Free wants the number associated with the last voice tag recognised. The Audio Gateway responds with a +BINP response with a data parameter containing the phone number associated with the voice tag.

20.2.8   Summary of AT Commands

The Hands-Free profile uses AT commands derived from the GSM 07.07 standard. The previous sections have described how these commands are used in the profile, for reference they are also summarised here:

- ATA—Call Answer.
- ATDdddddd...—Place a call (dial) using the supplied digits ddddd for the called number.
- ATD>nnnnn—Place a call (dial) using a number from memory.
- Error—Indicates a syntax, format, or procedure error.
- OK—Acknowledges execution of a command.
- RING—Indicates an incoming call.
- AT+CCWA—Call waiting notification.
- +CCWA—Unsolicited result code for call waiting notification.
- AT+CHLD—Call hold and multiparty management.
- AT+CHUP—Hangup.
- AT+CIND—Indicator update, used to get status information.
- +CLIP—Unsolicited result code for Calling Line Identification Notification.
- AT+CMER—Activate event reporting.
- +CIEV—Unsolicited result code for indicator events reporting.
- AT+VTS—DTMF tone generation.

The Hands-Free profile also defines the following new AT commands:

- AT+BINP—Request specified data from Audio Gateway.
- AT+BLDN—Redial the last number dialed.
- AT+BVRA —Enable or disable voice recognition.
- +BVRA—Unsolicited result code for autonomous voice recognition disable by Audio Gateway.

- AT+NREC—Disable echo cancelling and noise reduction functions.
- AT+VGM—Report microphone gain level.
- +VGM—Unsolicited result code giving microphone gain.
- AT+VGS—Report speaker gain level.
- +VGS—Unsolicited result code giving speaker gain.

The extra commands defined by the Hands-Free profile use the standard GSM 07.07 format and syntax rules.

20.3 THE BASIC IMAGING PROFILE

The Basic Imaging Profile (BIP) defines functionality which allows a device such as a camera to transfer still images in a predefined format across a Bluetooth link.

Of course, images could be transferred as files using the File Transfer Profile, the Basic Image Profile adds the ability to negotiate image size and format. The Basic Imaging Profile was created by the Bluetooth SIG imaging working group.

As Figure 20–1 shows, the Basic Imaging Profile relies upon the Generic Object Exchange Profile and the Generic Access Profile. Figure 20–13 shows how the Basic Imaging Profile relies upon OBEX for data transfer and follows the OBEX client/server architecture with the Imaging initiator acting as the client device and the imaging responder taking the server role. An example of such roles might be a laptop PC acting as an initiator requesting image files from a digital camera which would act as responder. Many of the Bluetooth profiles have ignored much of the control and coordination of the Bluetooth

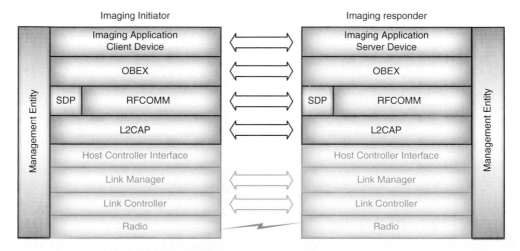

Figure 20–13   Basic Imaging protocol stack.

layers, so it is worth noting that the Basic Imaging Profile explicitly states that there should be a management entity (ME) coordinating initialisation and managing the link state. This entity is shown in Figure 20–13 stretching across all the layers of the protocol stack.

There are no fixed rules as to which device is master and which is slave, although to act as the Imaging Responder, a device must be configured in advance. Configuration as an Imaging Responder is done by entering Bluetooth imaging mode. This sets the imaging responder as connectable and allows it to receive commands from Imaging initiators.

The Basic Imaging Profile recommends that Bluetooth imaging mode should be set by user interaction, though it does not forbid entering the mode automatically.

20.3.1   Features and Capabilities

All devices supporting the Basic Imaging Profile must be able to exchange basic imaging data; this is called Generic Imaging capability. Supporting generic imaging implies supporting either Image Push or Image Pull.

There are three extra optional capabilities. These are only required for particular types of device, so they are not required for all devices supporting the Basic Imaging Profile:

- Bluetooth Controlled Capturing—Controlling the capture of an image.
- Bluetooth Controlled Printing—Controlling the printing of images.
- Bluetooth Controlled Display—Controlling the display of images.

Generic Imaging and the three extra capabilities can be combined to enable the Basic Imaging Profile to support six features:

- Image Push—Push images to a responder.
- Image Pull—Browse images stored in a responder and download images on request.
- Advanced Image Printing—Send print jobs to an imaging responder which is a printer.
- Automatic Archive—Triggers an Imaging responder to download some or all images stored on the imaging initiator.
- Remote Camera—For an imaging responder which allows image capture, such as a digital camera; allows the imaging initiator to monitor thumbnail images from the imaging responder and to trigger the shutter on the imaging responder.
- Remote Display—for an imaging responder with display capability, allows the user to push images for display, and to control the display sequence.

20.3.1   Image Push

The Image Push feature allows an Imaging Initiator to send images to an Imaging Responder. It uses four functions:

- GetCapabilities—This is optional and allows the Imaging Initiator to find out the image encodings and sizes which are supported by the Imaging Responder.
- PutImage—Pushes an image from Imaging Initiator to Imaging Responder.
- PutLinkedThumbnail—This is used by an Imaging Responder immediately after it has pushed an image to the Imaging Initiator; PutLinkedThumbnail pushes a thumbnail version of the image.
- PutLinkedAttachment—This is used by an Imaging Responder immediately after it has pushed an image to the Imaging Initiator, PutLinkedAttachment pushes an attachment related to the image.

Figure 20–14 shows an example sequence of messages exchanged during use of the Image Push feature. The functions are carried in OBEX Get and Put messages.

First the Imaging Initiator establishes a connection to the Image Push service. This will involve using SDP to find the services attributes and establishing all the underlying connections through the layers of the Bluetooth protocol stack shown in Figure 20–13.

The Imaging Initiator optionally sends a GetCapabilities request in an OBEX Get Request. The Imaging Responder replies with a Success Get Response containing its ImagingCapabilities.

The Imaging Initiator then pushes images to the Imaging responder using Put Requests. After each Put Request, the Imaging Responder replies with a PutResponse.

The example shown in Figure 20–14 is based on Annex A of the Basic Imaging Profile. It shows two images being pushed. The ImagingResponder replies to the first PutImage with a Success Response. After the second image has been pushed, the Imaging responder requests extra content by replying with a Put response: Partial Content. The

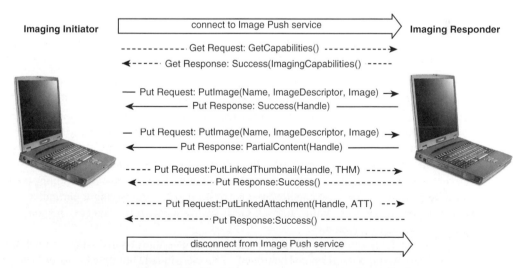

Figure 20–14 Message sequence chart for Image Push.

Imaging Initiator responds by sending extra content associated with the image in two further OBEX Put requests. The first Put request sends a thumbnail using PutLinkedThumbnail. The second Put request sends an attachment using PutLinkedAttachment.

This example shows just two images being transferred; however, the session can continue as long as the Imaging initiator wishes to keep requesting content from the Imaging Responder. Once the Imaging Initiator has finished requesting content it will disconnect from the Image Push Service.

20.3.2   Image Pull

The Image Pull feature allows an Image Initiator to browse images stored in an Image Responder and download images on request.

It uses the same GetCapabilities function as the Image Push feature, but also uses six more functions:

- GetImagesList—Gets a list of handles for images on the Imaging Responder along with file information such as creation and modification dates.
- GetImageProperties—Gets image formats and encodings information which are available for an image.
- GetImage—Gets an image from the Imaging responder in a specified format and encoding.
- GetLinkedThumbnail—Gets a thumbnail sized image from the Imaging responder.
- GetLinkedAttachment—Gets an attachment related to an image from the Imaging Responder.
- DeleteImage—Deletes a specified image from the Imaging Responder.

Figure 20–15 shows an example sequence of messages exchanged during use of the Image Pull feature. As with all Basic Imaging functions, the messages are carried in OBEX Put and Get messages.

First the Imaging Initiator establishes a connection to the Image Pull service. This will involve using SDP to find the services attributes, and establishing all the underlying connections through the layers of the Bluetooth protocol stack shown in Figure 20–13.

The Imaging Initiator sends a GetImageList request in an OBEX Get request. The Imaging Responder replies with a Success Get Response containing handles for images which it has available for retrieval.

The Imaging Initiator can now begin retrieving images. Optionally, it may send a GetImageProperty request for each image to find out what formats and encodings are supported for images. The GetImageRequest carries a Handle identifying a particular image. The Imaging Responder replies to each GetImageRequest with a Success response containing the image's properties.

The Imaging initiator may also optionally retrieve thumbnails using an OBEX Get request containing a GetLinkedThumbnail. The GetLinkedThumbnail carries a Handle identifying a particular image. The Imaging Responder replies with a Success response carrying the thumbnail image.

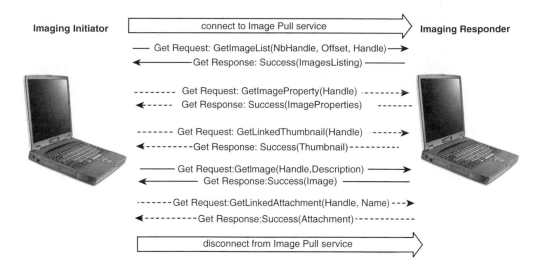

Figure 20–15 Message sequence chart for Image Pull.

To retrieve the images themselves, a GetImage request is sent. This has a Handle identifying the image and an image description specifying the format and encoding to be used. The Imaging Responder sends the image back in a Success response.

Optionally, the Imaging Initiator can retrieve an attachment related to the image. To do this it sends a Get Request containing GetLinkedAttachment. A handle identifies the image the attachment is related to, and a name identifies the file name of the attachment (this enables multiple attachments related to one image to be retrieved).

The example shown in Figure 20–15 is based on Annex A of the Basic Imaging Profile. It shows just one thumbnail, image and attachment being retrieved; however, the Imaging Initiator can retrieve as many images, thumbnails, and attachments as are available. Once the Imaging Initiator has finished retrieving content, it disconnects from the Image Pull Service.

20.3.3   Advanced Image Printing

The Advanced Image Printing feature is used to send print jobs to an Imaging Responder which is a printer. It uses the same GetCapabilities function which is used by other features. In the case of an Image Responder which is a printer, the GetCapabilities function retrieves the printing capabilities. The Advanced Image Printing feature also uses three more functions:

- GetPartial Image—This is used by the Imaging Responder to retrieve images needed for a print job.
- StartPrint—This is used by an Imaging Initiator to request an Imaging Responder to start printing.

• GetStatus—This is used by an Imaging Initiator to monitor a secondary connection which may be used to retrieve information required for a print job.

Figure 20–16 shows an example sequence of messages exchanged during use of the Advanced Image Printing feature. The functions are carried in OBEX Get and Put messages. This figure shows two instances of the Imaging Initiator. These are both the same device, but the Imaging initiator has two roles: as Primary Client and as Secondary Server. To make the message flows to each role easier to distinguish, the same Imaging Initiator has been shown twice on the diagram, once for each role it takes.

First the Imaging Initiator establishes a connection to the Advanced Image Printing service. This will involve using SDP to find the service's attributes and establishing all the underlying connections through the layers of the Bluetooth protocol stack shown in Figure 20–13. The initial connection is made by the Imaging Initiator in its Primary Client role.

Optionally, the Imaging Initiator may send a GetCapabilities Request to find the Capabilities of the Imaging Responder.

The Imaging Initiator will then use an OBEX Put message to send a StartPrint message to the Imaging Responder. If this successfully starts a print job, the Imaging Responder replies with Success.

The print job will include information about images to be printed. To retrieve these images, the Imaging Responder opens a second channel to the Imaging Initiator. This channel connects to the Referenced Objects Service.

Usually the Imaging responder acts as a server, but in order to retrieve the images it needs to print, it must act as a client and request the images from the Imaging Initiator. It does this with OBEX Get requests containing GetPartialImage messages. The Imaging Initiator acts as a client on this secondary connection and supplies the images requested in Success responses.

Whilst images are being retrieved, the Imaging Initiator can check on the status of the job by sending GetStatus messages to the Imaging Responder on the primary channel,

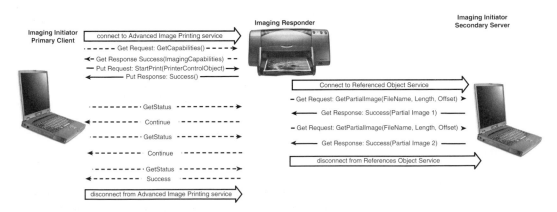

Figure 20–16 Message sequence chart for Advanced Image Printing.

as long as images are being retrieved the Imaging Responder will reply with a Continue response.

When the final image has been retrieved, the Imaging Responder disconnects from the Referenced Objects service. If the Imaging Initiator sends the Imaging Responder a status message after disconnection of the secondary channel, it will get a Success response back. This signals that the job has finished and allows the Imaging Initiator to disconnect from the Advanced Imaging Service.

The example shown in Figure 20–14 is based on Annex A of the Basic Imaging Profile. It shows two GetPartialImage commands being used to retrieve image information from the Imaging Initiator; however, the session can continue as long as the Print job still specifies more images to be printed.

20.3.4 Automatic Archive

The Automatic Archive feature triggers an Imaging Responder to download some or all images stored on the Imaging Initiator.

It uses the same GetCapabilities function which is used by other features. Automatic Archive also uses the GetStatus, DeleteImage, GetLinkedThumbnail, GetLinkedAttachment, GetImage, GetImageProperties, and GetImageList functions used by other features. In addition, the Automatic Archive feature also has a feature-specific function:

- StartArchive—This is used by an Imaging Initiator to request an Imaging responder to start the archiving process.

Figure 20–17 shows an example sequence of messages exchanged during use of the Automatic Archive feature. The functions are carried in OBEX Get and Put messages. This figure shows two instances of the Imaging Initiator. These are both the same device, but the Imaging Initiator has two roles: as Primary Client and as Secondary Server. To make the message flows to each role easier to distinguish, the same Imaging Initiator has been shown twice on the diagram, once for each role it takes.

First the Imaging Initiator establishes a connection to the Automatic Archive service. This will involve using SDP to find the service's attributes and establishing all the underlying connections through the layers of the Bluetooth protocol stack shown in Figure 20–13. The initial connection is made by the Imaging Initiator in its Primary Client role.

The Imaging Initiator triggers the start of the archiving process by sending a StartArchive Message in an OBEX Put request. The Imaging Responder replies with a Success response.

To retrieve the Archive images, the Imaging Responder opens a second channel to the Imaging Initiator. This channel connects to the Archived Objects Service.

Optionally, the Imaging Responder may send a GetCapabilities Request to find the Capabilities of the Imaging Initiator.

Usually the Imaging responder acts as a server, but in order to retrieve the images it needs to archive, it must act as a client and request the images from the Imaging Initiator. First the Imaging responder sends a Get Request containing a GetImageList message; the

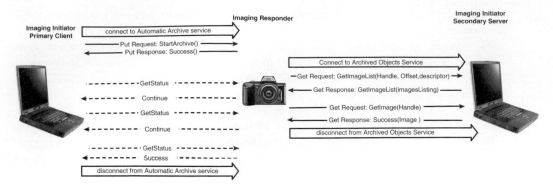

Figure 20–17   Message sequence chart for Automatic Archive.

Imaging Initiator responds with a Get response containing GetImageList with a list of the images to be archived. Once the Imaging responder has a list of images to archive, it retrieves the images using OBEX Get requests containing GetImage messages. The Imaging Initiator acts as a client on this secondary connection and supplies the images requested in Success responses.

Whilst images are being retrieved, the Imaging Initiator can check on the status of the job by sending GetStatus messages to the Imaging Responder on the primary channel, as long as images are being retrieved the Imaging Responder will reply with a Continue response.

When the final image has been retrieved, the Imaging Responder disconnects from the Archived Objects service. If the Imaging Initiator sends the Imaging Responder a status message after disconnection of the secondary channel, then it will get a Success response back. This signals that the job has finished and allows the Imaging Initiator to disconnect from the Automatic Archive Service.

The example shown in Figure 20–17 is based on Annex A of the Basic Imaging Profile. It shows a single GetImage command being used to retrieve image information from the Imaging Initiator; however, the session can continue as long as the list of images sent to the Imaging responder in the GetImageList still specifies more images to be archived.

20.3.5   Remote Camera

For an Imaging Responder which allows image capture, such as a digital camera: the Remote Camera feature allows the Imaging Initiator to monitoring thumbnail images from the imaging responder, and to trigger the shutter on the Imaging Responder.

It uses the same GetImage, GetImageProperties and GetLinkedThumbnail functions as other features, in addition the Remote Camera feature also has a feature specific function:

- GetMonitoringImage_This is used to retrieve a monitoring image from an Imaging Responder which is capable of capturing images. This message can include a Store-

Flag which can be used to indicate whether the Imaging Responder should store the image.

Figure 20–18 shows an example sequence of messages exchanged during use of the Remote Camera feature. As with all Basic Imaging functions, the messages are carried in OBEX Put and Get messages.

First the Imaging Initiator establishes a connection to the Remote Camera service. This will involve using SDP to find the services attributes and establishing all the underlying connections through the layers of the Bluetooth protocol stack shown in Figure 20–13.

The Imaging Initiator monitors images from the Imaging Responder by sending GetMonitoringImage requests in OBEX Get requests. The Imaging Responder replies with a Success Get response containing the current image.

As long as the Imaging Initiator just wishes to monitor images, it continues sending GetMonitoringImage requests with the StoreFlag parameter set to 0x00. When the user of the Imaging Initiator indicates that he or she wants to capture an image, the Imaging Initiator sends a GetMonitoringImage with the StoreFlag set to 0x01. This triggers the Imaging Responder to store the current image. The Imaging Responder then sends the Imaging Initiator a Success response with the Image it just captured and a handle which can be used to retrieve the image from store.

The example shown in Figure 20–18 is based on Annex A of the Basic Imaging Profile. It shows just one image being stored; however, the Imaging Initiator can keep the session going as long as it wants to keep triggering the Imaging Responder to store images. The Imaging Initiator can also retrieve the captured images or thumbnails of the images. Once the Imaging Initiator has finished asking the Imaging Responder to store images, it disconnects from the Remote Camera service.

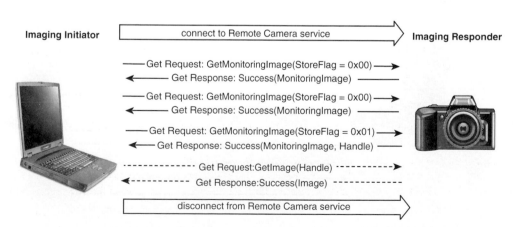

Figure 20–18 Message sequence chart for Remote Camera.

20.3.6   Remote Display

The Remote Display feature is used with an imaging responder that has display capability. It allows the user to push images for display and to control the display sequence.

It uses the same GetCapabilities, GetImagesList, and PutImage functions as other features; in addition, the Remote Delay feature also has two feature specific functions:

- PutLinkedThumbnail—This is used by the Imaging Initiator to send a thumbnail version of an image to the Imaging Responder.
- RemoteDisplay—This is used to control the display of images on the Imaging Responder. It can be used to display a specific Image or to step to the next or previous image.

Figure 20–19 shows an example sequence of messages exchanged during use of the Remote Display feature. As with all Basic Imaging functions, the messages are carried in OBEX Put and Get messages.

First the Imaging Initiator establishes a connection to the Remote Display service. This will involve using SDP to find the services attributes, and establishing all the underlying connections through the layers of the Bluetooth protocol stack shown in Figure 20–13.

The Imaging Initiator optionally sends a GetCapabilities request in an OBEX Get request. The Imaging Responder replies with a Success Get response containing its ImagingCapabilities.

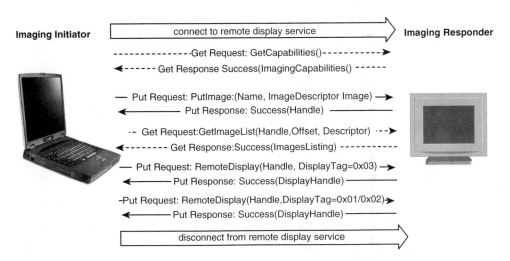

Figure 20–19   Message sequence chart for Remote Display.

The Imaging Initiator then sends images for display to the Imaging Responder by sending PutImage requests in OBEX Get requests. The Imaging Responder stores each image and replies with a Success Get response containing a handle for the image. The image handles are used in the Remote Display message to identify images. The Remote Display message also has a DisplayTag parameter which can have one of four values:

- 0x01—NextImage: Display next image, handle parameter must be empty.
- 0x02—PreviousImage—Display previous image, handle parameter must be empty.
- 0x03—SelectImage—The handle parameter selects the image to display.
- 0x04—CurrentImage—Leave image the same, handle parameter must be empty.

The example shown in Figure 20–18 is based on Annex A of the Basic Imaging profile. It shows just one image being displayed; however, the Imaging Initiator can keep the session going as long as it wants to keep displaying images on the Imaging Responder. The Imaging Initiator can also send thumbnails for display. Once the Imaging Initiator has finished asking the Imaging responder to display images it disconnects from the Remote Display service.

20.3.7   Data Formats

Thumbnails in the Basic Imaging Profile are JPEG images 160x120 pixels. In addition, the Basic Imaging Profile supports JPEG, GIF, WBMP, and PNG formats. Proprietary encodings can be represented using a tag beginning with "USR-". The Basic Imaging Profile makes extensive use of XML to transfer information. For example, the imaging capabilities and Image Descriptors are transferred as XML strings. Attachments are described using MIME content types. UTC time is used to identify creation and modification times.

20.4   THE BASIC PRINTING PROFILE

The Basic Printing Profile (BPP) defines functionality which allows devices to control a Bluetooth enabled printer and send print jobs to it without needing a dedicated driver for that printer. The profile provides plain or formatted text printing for devices with limited processing capability, XML printing which allows more complex formatting, and a reflected user interface feature which allows printer control. For networked devices, it is possible to print information from an Internet or intranet by passing a reference or pointer which identifies the item to be printed.

As Figure 20–1 shows, the Basic Printing Profile relies upon the Generic Object Exchange Profile and the Generic Access Profile. Figure 20–20 shows how the Basic Printing profile relies upon OBEX for data transfer. The profile follows the OBEX client/server architecture with the Sender side acting as the client device and the Printer side taking the server role.

The Printer side supports four modes:

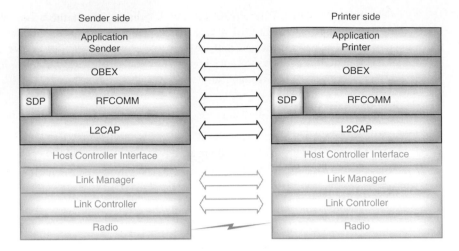

Figure 20–20 Printing protocol stacks.

- Bluetooth off-line mode—The Printer cannot be discovered or connected with.
- Bluetooth bonding mode—The Printer is waiting to be bonded with a sender.
- Bluetooth on-line mode—Printer cannot be discovered, but can be connected with.
- Public on-line mode—Printer can be discovered and can be connected with.

In Bluetooth on-line mode only devices which already know the printer's address will be able to send print jobs to it. In Public on-line mode any device will be able to discover the printer, so devices do not need to know its Bluetooth address in advance to send it print jobs.

All printers must support Bluetooth bonding mode and Public on-line mode; Bluetooth off-line mode and Bluetooth on-line mode are optional.

20.4.1   Simple Push Service

The Simple Push is designed to allow devices with very limited processing capabilities to print text in a very simple way.

The Basic Printing Profile provides different OBEX channels for different services, each of which is identified by its own Universally Unique Identifier (UUID). Chapter 13 explained how the OBEX target header could be used in a connect message to specify the destination for data. For simple FilePush, the sender connects using an OBEX target header set to DPS_UUID (the UUID for Direct Printing Service).

Once the sender has connected to the correct channel he or she simply sends the printer a Put request with a FilePush. The OBEX headers contain the type of the document, which is expressed as a MIME type, the document's data, information on the document, and the document's name.

Figure 20–21 shows a single OBEX Put operation, but if the information is too much to fit in a single Put operation, it may be split across several Put operations.

When using the Simple Push Service, the printer uses its default printer and job attributes to print the job. There are no configuration or monitoring facilities, and the job can't be cancelled once it's been sent to the printer.

20.4.2   Referenced Objects

The Simple Push service also supports a method of passing references to the printer, then having the printer get the referenced object from the sender, as shown in Figure 20–22.

In order to send a reference to the printer, the sender must first connect using an OBEX target header set to PBR_UUID (the UUID for Print By Reference). The sender may then send the Printer a Put request with a SimpleReferencePush. As a minimum the OBEX headers must contain the URL of the reference. Optionally, more information can be sent. Some possibilities are information on how to locate a server which can supply the reference, type information, authentication information, a billing code, and even instructions to the printer to print the object on a new sheet of paper. Figure 20–22 shows the simplest case where just a URL is sent.

The SimpleReferencePush is sent as an OBEX Put command using the following headers:

- Type: Simple Reference, XML Reference, or reference list.
- Body: Contains the URL of the reference.
- Description: A description of the object referenced.

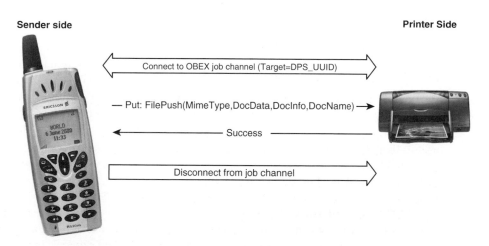

Figure 20–21   Message sequence chart for printing a file using Simple Push.

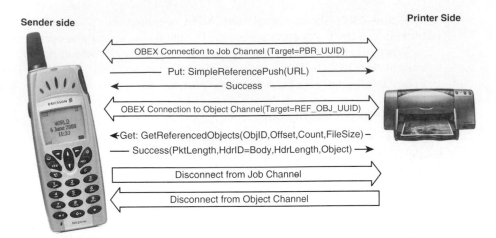

Figure 20–22 Message sequence chart for printing a reference using Simple Push.

- Name: Contains an Object Identifier locally identifying the reference on the Sender.
- HTTP: This can contain authentication credentials if they will be needed to retrieve the reference.

The Printer acknowledges the Push operation with a Success response, then opens a second channel back to the Sender and uses this channel to request the information from the sender. This second channel is connected using a Target Header of REF_OBJ_UUID (the UUID for the Referenced Objects Channel, also called just the object channel). On the object channel the Printer sends an OBEX Get request with a GetReferencedObjects. The OBEX headers contain an ObjectIdentifier, a byte offset, count, and filename.

Why use two channels when the sender could simply collect all information and send it down a single channel? The answer is that the sender may not have enough memory or processing power to download a complete page and transform it into a format the printer can process. By using references the Sender has shifted a lot of the memory and processing requirements onto the printer. As printers are likely to have comparatively large memory and processing reserves, it makes sense that they should do the processing and formatting.

The reference is retrieved using a GetReferencedObjects operation. This is an OBEX Get containing the following parameters:

- ObjectIdentifier—Identifies the referenced object on the Sender.
- Offset—Used when several requests are needed to retrieve a whole object. The offset gives how many bytes into the object retrieval should start.

- Count—Says how may bytes should be sent.
- FileSize—This is ignored in the request, but its presence causes the sender to return the size of the requested object in the response.

The ObjectIdentifier is sent in a Name header. The Offset, Count, and FileSize are all packed into an Application Parameters header.

When the Job channel is disconnected by the sender, the printer disconnects from the Object channel. Because the Object channel closes when the Job channel closes, the sender should allow any referenced objects to be retrieved before closing the Job channel.

20.4.3   Job Based Service

This service can be used to print more complex documents. As with the simple push service, the job based service can be used with referenced objects, or plain documents. The difference is that with the job based service the sender initiates a print session, rather than just using a single push operation. The session allows the sender to use a series of commands to configure and control the printer.

- CreateJob Create—Used to submit job attributes, in return the sender gets a JobID.
- SendDocument—Transfers print content to the printer; used with CreateJob.
- GetJobAttributes—Used to query attributes and status of a job.
- GetPrinterAttributes—Ask for the status and capabilities of the printer.
- CancelJob—Used to cancel a job using the JobID.
- GetReferencedObjects—Used to retrieve referenced objects from a sending device.
- GetEvent—Used to ask for status information during printing.
- CreatePreciseJob—Used for enhanced layout.
- GetMargins—Used for enhanced layout.
- SendReference—Sends a reference for printing.
- GetRUI—Gets a web page which gives a user interface to configure and control the printer.

Figure 20–23 shows a simple example of a print session. First a CreateJob is sent in an OBEX Get message. The CreateJob can be used to specify how the printer should be configured for this job. The example shows JobName and Copies attributes being sent with the CreateJob. These are just two of the possible attributes which can be sent with a CreateJob. The following attributes could be sent:

- JobName—A user friendly name.
- JobOriginatingUserName—Name of user who sent the job.
- DocumentFormat—The MIME type of the document.
- Copies—Number of copies of the document to print.

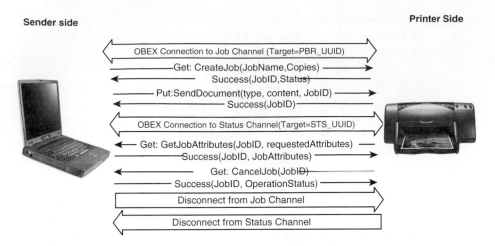

Figure 20–23 Message sequence chart for a simple print job.

- Sides—Single sided, double sided flip on long edge, double sided flip on short edge.
- NumberUp—Number of document pages to print on a single side, options are one per side, two per side or four per side.
- OrientationRequested—Portrait, landscape, reverse-landscape, reverse-portrait.
- MediaSize—Size of paper to print on.
- PrintQuality—Draft, normal, or high.
- MediaType—Type of paper, acetate, etc. to print on.
- CancelOnLostLink—Whether to cancel printing if the Bluetooth link is lost.

These attributes are sent as a Simple Object Access Protocol (SOAP) message. The SOAP message is carried in the body of the OBEX Get message. SOAP is an XML language, so all the attributes are laid out in plain text one attribute per line surrounded by markers explaining what the attribute is. So, for instance, if the JobName was "MyPrintout", the SOAP encoded attribute would be:

<JobName>MyPrintout</JobName>

The Printer must be able to handle all these attributes. That doesn't mean it has to support every single value: for instance, it may only print single sided, but it must understand and react properly to a request for double sided printing.

The Sender does not have to support any of the CreateJob attributes, if any are missed out a default value is used.

The CreateJob Response has just two attributes:

- JobName—A user friendly name.
- JobID—The identifying number the printer has allocated for this job
- OperationStatus—The Status of the job, indicating whether the CreateJob succeeded or failed, if it failed the reason is given with an error code.

Once the job has successfully been created, the document can be sent. Figure 20–23 shows a document being sent with a SendDocument operation carried in an OBEX Put request. The attributes of the SendDocument are the document type, the content of the document itself, and the JobID. PrintByReference can also be used to send content for printing, in the same way as it can be used to send content in the Simple Push Service.

The message exchange could stop at this point, the example shows how more messages can be used to monitor the job, and cancel it.

Figure 20–23 shows a second status channel being opened to monitor and control the job. Having a second channel means that status can be read and commands sent whilst the Job Channel is busy with the document being sent.

The figure shows a GetJobAttributes being sent, a JobID identifies the Job, and a list of attributes is sent so that the printer knows what to report on. The printer replies with the JobID and all of the requested attributes. Possible attributes are:

- JobState—Printing, waiting, stopped, completed, aborted, cancelled, unknown.
- JobName—The user friendly name allocated when the job was created.
- JobMediaSheetsCompleted—Some printers don't count and will always report zero!
- NumberOfInterveningJobs—Place in print queue.
- OperationStatus—Whether the GetJobAtributes operation succeeded.

In our simple example the user successfully gets the response back then decides he or she doesn't want the job after all—perhaps the NumberOfInterveningJobs attribute was quite large and the user doesn't want to wait. The user cancels the job with a CancelJob operation on the Status channel and gets a Success response back with a JobID and status confirming that the Job has been cancelled.

Having cancelled the job, the Sender can disconnect the Job and Status channels.

In Figure 20–23 the job was monitored using a GetJobAttributes. A GetEvent operation can also be sent on the status channel to monitor the job. The GetEvent response always contains the same set of attributes:

- JobID—The ID allocated when the job was created.
- JobState—The user friendly name allocated when the job was created.
- PrinterState—Idle, processing or stopped.
- PrinterStateReasons—Error code to explain PrinterState if it is stopped.
- OperationStatus—Whether the GetEvent operation succeeded.

To further monitor the state of the printer, a GetPrinterAttributes operation can used. This is sent in an OBEX Get request on the status channel. The GetPrinterAttributes operation can request the following attributes:

- PrinterName—The user friendly name of the printer.
- PrinterLocation—A string such as "My Office".
- PrinterState—Idle, processing or stopped.
- PrinterStateReasons—Error code to explain PrinterState if it is stopped.
- DocumentFormatsSupported—An array giving MIME Types of supported formats.
- ColorSupported—Whether printer supports full colour.
- MaxCopiesSupported—Maximum value for Copies parameter in CreateJob.
- SidesSupported—Whether printer supports double sided printing.
- NumberUpSupported—Maximum NumberUp value for NumberUp in CreateJob.
- OrientationRequestedSupported—Whether the printer can print at different orientations.
- MediaSizesSupported—Sizes the supported, these may not be loaded at present.
- MediaTypesSupported—Types of media supported—these may not be loaded at present.
- MediaLoaded—Details, size and type of media loaded, this is an array allowing details of more than one medium to be passed.
- PrintQualitySupported—Possible values for PrintQuality parameter in CreateJob.
- QueuedJobCount—Number of jobs in the printer queue.
- ImageFormatsSupported—The types of image the printer can interpret in an XML document.
- BasicTextPageWidth—Number of characters in a line for default font and paper size.
- BasicTextPageHeight—Number of lines in a page for default font and paper size.
- PrinterGeneralCurrentOperator—Contact information for printer support.
- OperationStatus—Whether the GetEvent operation succeeded.

The GetPrinterAttributes can be sent before CreateJob, as it contains useful information on the printer's capabilities which can be used to decide the parameters for the CreateJob operation.

20.4.4 Enhanced Layout—Formatting Print Jobs

When using the Job Based service the CreatePreciseJob and GetMargins operations can be used to control formatting.

CreatePreciseJob has the same attributes as CreateJob, except that if the printer cannot print the job precisely as the attributes specify, then the document is not printed. If the printer knows in advance that it cannot print as requested, it will return an error immediately and refuse the job. If it discovers during the job that it cannot print (for example, because it cannot retrieve a referenced object), then it will abort the job.

GetMargins is used to find out about margins needed for a particular size and type of medium. The GetMargins request specifies the size and type, the response gives values for Top, Right, Bottom, and Left Margins and an OperationStatus.

The GetMargins request is sent before the CreateJob to find out how the job should be formatted or to help choose an appropriate medium type and size.

20.4.5 Reflected User Interface Service

The previous sections showed how a printer can be controlled using various standard operations. The ReflectedUserInterface can be used to provide a richer user interface which can control the printer in ways not specified above.

The GetRUI operation gets a web page which gives a user interface to configure and control the printer. By following hyperlinks on the page the user can invoke operations particular to that printer.

The sender sends GetRUI in an Obex command, the printer responds with the user interface which is sent as an XML form. At the sender side this form is presented to the user for data entry. The sender then returns form information along with a Job Identifier in another Get OBEX command. The printer may return another form in the response; for example, it could return a status page.

Many control forms may be sent between sender and printer to fully configure and monitor a print job.

20.5 THE HARD COPY CABLE REPLACEMENT PROFILE

The Hard Copy Cable Replacement Profile (HCCP) provides a way of printing using a printer driver on the client device. The profile supports a 1284ID string which can be used to identify a driver. It also provides simple credit based flow control. The profile copes with loss of connection in the middle of a print job. The profile also allows a client to register an interest in certain events—this will cause the server to send an asynchronous notification if the event happens during a job.

Figure 20–24 shows how simple the protocol stack for the hard copy cable replacement profile is. The profile rests directly on L2CAP; there is no need for RFCOMM or OBEX layers. The client side has an application running on the HCRP layer which is usually a printer driver. On the server (printer) side the application is likely to be an interpreter or some other application which can generate a page description format.

The Hard Copy Cable Replacement Profile relies upon having the correct driver for a printer installed, so it provides a command to identify the driver.

The Hardcopy Cable Replacement Profile makes use of three channels:

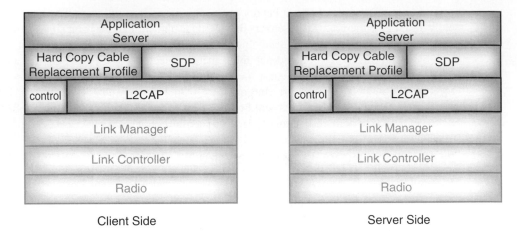

Client Side   Server Side

Figure 20–24 Protocol stacks for Hard Copy Cable Replacement Profile.

- Data—Used to transmit device-specific data including the document to be printed and any control which is specific to the printer driver.
- Control—Used to transmit HCRP control requests.
- Notification—Used by the server to notify the client of asynchronous events. Each event has a different channel, and the notification channel numbers can be obtained via SDP.

The control channel is used to identify the printer driver type, get status information, handle flow control, request notifications, and also handle resets. A separate control channel is provided so that all of the control functions can be used whilst document data is being exchanged. Obviously, if you want to reset a printer because a job is stopped, you don't want to have to wait for the job to finish exchanging data before you can request a reset!

Messages are sent as PDUs in L2CAP, the PDU structure is shown in Figure 20–25. Each message begins with a PDU ID, a Transaction ID, and a Parameter length. The PDU ID identifies the type of message, and the transaction ID is a number used to match requests and replies together. Every time a request is sent, the transaction ID is incremented by one, and replies copy the transaction ID from the request they are responding to. The parameter length simply gives the number of bytes of parameters following.

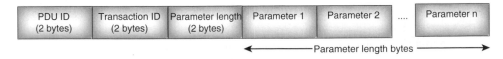

Figure 20–25 PDU structure for Hard Copy Cable Replacement Profile.

A reply PDU always has a 2 byte status code as its first parameter. This status is used to tell whether the request succeeded or failed. It can also indicate reasons for failure.

20.5.2   Control

The control channel is used for sending control specific to the Hard Copy Cable Replacement Profile. Control messages which are generated by the printer device driver are sent on the data channel, (see section 20.5.3).

One of the most important control messages is the CR_Get1284ID, which is used to identify the correct driver for a printer. This is sent by the client to the server, and the server returns a CR_Get1284ID reply which can be used to identify a suitable driver for the printer.

Another useful command is CR_GetLPTStatus which can be used to check on the printer's status including whether it has run out of paper. This command is in addition to any commands provided by the device driver. The printer sends a CR_GetLPTStatus reply with a byte of status bits.

20.5.1   Notifications

The notification channels carry notifications of asynchronous events from the printer to the client. Figure 20–26 shows an example of messages used in the notification process.

Before it can receive notifications, the client has to register an interest with the server. This is done by sending the CR_RegisterNotification command on the Control channel. This command has three parameters:

- register—Whether to register or deregister for notification.
- CallbackContextID_An ID which will be sent back with the notification.
- CallBackTimeout—The time to keep a notification channel alive after sending a request. This is just a request, and the server can choose to shut down a notification channel sooner than the requested timeout.

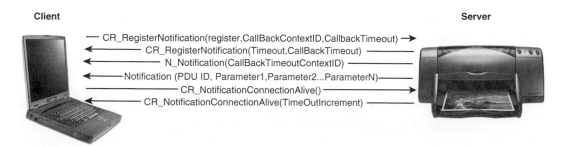

Figure 20–26   Message sequence chart for notifications.

The server replies with a CR_RegisterNotification reply giving a timeout, which is the time before the notification request will expire, and a CallBackTimeout, which gives the time the server will shut down the notification channel after sending a notification.

When the client has registered for notifications, and an event occurs on the server, the server sends a N_Notification on the appropriate notification channel. This tells the client that the server has notification information to deliver. The N_Notification carries the CallbackContextID which has been registered.

How the client reacts to the N_Notification will vary between implementations. The client may have to open a return channel so that it can respond to the notification, or it may just wait to receive more information.

The server then sends a notification PDU which contains a PDU ID identifying the event which has occurred. It may also contain a set of parameters giving more information.

It is assumed that the client has finished processing the notification when the notification channel closes. If the client needs more processing time, it can send a CR_NotificationConnectionAlive request on the control channel to keep the channel open for longer—this request has no parameters. The server adds a value TimeOutIncrement to the CallBackTimeout to keep the notification channel open a little longer and tells the client what the TimeOutIncrement is by sending it back as a parameter in a CR_NotificationConnectionAliveResponse.

There are two commands used to reset a printer: CR_SoftReset and CR_HardReset. If CR_SoftReset is used, the printer remembers whether notifications are registered. If CR_HardReset is used, it will forget all settings and CR_RegisterNotification must be sent again if the client requires notifications.

20.5.3   Flow Control

The Hard Copy Cable Replacement Profile uses a credit based flow control scheme similar to the system used by the version 1.1 of RFCOMM. Each side requests credit from the other and keeps a count of the number of bytes of credit granted. As data is sent the count reduces by the number of bytes sent.

The PDUs used for credit based flow control are:

- CR_DataChannelCreditGrant—Used by the client to grant credit for the data channel to the server.
- CR_DataChannelCreditRequest—Used by the client to request an increase in credit granted to it by the server.
- CR_DataChannelCreditReturn—Used by the client to return credit it will not use. This might be used at the end of a print job.
- CR_DataChannelCreditQuery—Used by the client to tell the server how much credit it has left on the data channel to the server. The server replies with how much credit is has left on the data channel to the client.

Clients should periodically grant credit to the server to ensure that data continues to flow. This is particularly important as the server has no message to request credit from the client.

20.5.4 Data Format

The format for sending data on the data channel is not specified; it will depend upon the printer driver being used. This means that the data channel can be used for sending driver-specific commands as well as the document data itself.

Effectively, the data channel carries the same information that would be sent on the cable the Bluetooth link is replacing.

20.6 SUMMARY

This chapter has examined five draft profiles all of which have reached version 0.9 and are available to adopter members of the Bluetooth SIG to download from the SIG Web site *http://www.Bluetooth.org/member/specifications.htm.*

The Human Interface Profile can be used to control mice, keyboards, and other human interface devices such as joysticks. It has two modes: the boot mode, simple enough to be implemented in a BIOS, allows a keyboard or mouse to be used before an operating system has booted. The report mode is more complex and allows for richer interaction including force feedback effects. The Human Interface Device Profile reuses protocols and data structures from USB human interface devices.

The Hands-Free profile extends on the capabilities of the Headset Profile. The Hands-Free profile allows a hands-free user to control a phone dialing, receiving calling line IDs, and even optionally using voice recognition via a remote user interface. The Hands-Free profile uses AT commands as did the Headset Profile, but the Hands-Free profile defines an extension to the AT command set specifically for Bluetooth devices.

The Basic Imaging profile allows transfer of images, thumbnails, and linked attachments between devices. In addition to transfer of individual images, images can be browsed, an archive feature allows groups of images to be backed up, a remote camera feature allows control of a camera, and a display feature allows groups of images to be viewed on a remote display.

Basic Printing is used to transfer plain text or XML formatted documents to a printer without using a dedicated printer driver. The profile provides a means for a printer to retrieve content via references embedded in a document. To enable more complex functionality the printer can send a reflected user interface. This uses XML forms sent to the user to provide a user interface which can be customised by each printer.

The Hard Copy Cable Replacement Profile allows printing using a dedicated printer driver. A data channel is used to simulate the printer cable and carries raw implementation specific data. A control channel provides profile defined control signals including credit based flow control facilities, and notification features allow the printer to inform the sender of events related to printing.

At the time of writing these new profiles are released to all adopters, but have not yet reached version 1.0. However, they have all reached version 0.9 and changes between 0.9 and 1.0 are usually minor.

21

Personal Area Networking

The first version of the Bluetooth specification relied upon OBEX for file transfer. OBEX is a small, simple lightweight protocol which suits mobile devices well. However, as technology moves, handheld devices such as smart phones are emerging which incorporate Web browsers with complete IP stacks. The availability of compact IP stacks has opened the door for Bluetooth to adopt the protocol suite which drives the Internet, and it is the Personal Area Networking (PAN) profile which lays out the ground rules for doing this.

This chapter begins with the PAN profile itself, then moves on to cover Bluetooth Network Encapsulation Protocol which allows ethernet packets to be carried across Bluetooth links. These two additions to the Bluetooth specification combine to bring the power of IP networking to Bluetooth devices, opening up the possibility of uniting wired and wireless networks.

21.1   THE PAN PROFILE

The PAN Profile lays out the rules for carrying IP traffic across Bluetooth connections. This is done using ethernet packets encapsulated in L2CAP packet payloads using the Bluetooth Network Encapsulation Protocol (BNEP). The PAN profile relies upon the Generic Access Profile, but does not make use of any other profiles.

The profile provides two ways of connecting. Devices can connect to a Network Access Point (NAP) in order to access a remote network. The Network Access Point provides a bridge to the network. The Network can be a fixed or mobile network as shown in Figure 21–1. Alternatively, devices can connect directly to one another using Group ad-hoc Networks (GN) exchanging data with no outside network involvement as shown in Figure 21–2. These two types of connection require three different roles:

- Network Access Point (NAP)—A device acting as a bridge to connect a piconet to an IP network. It forwards packets to and from the network and amongst PAN users.
- Group ad-hoc network (GN)—A device which connects to one or more PAN users, forwarding packets between PAN users when more than one is connected.
- PAN user (PANU)—A client device which uses the Group ad-hoc Network or Network Access Point service.

The two services have different needs, and the PAN Profile provides different architectures to satisfy those needs, but both Network Access Points and Group ad-hoc Networks

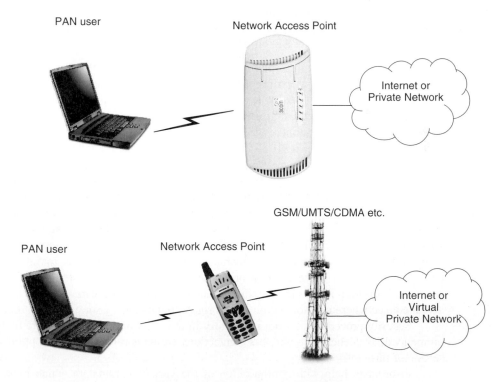

Figure 21–1   Network Access Points.

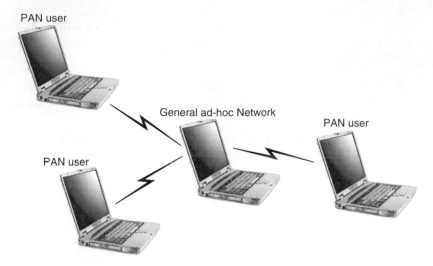

Figure 21–2   Group ad-hoc network.

rely upon the Bluetooth Network Encapsulation Protocol (BNEP) to carry IP traffic in ethernet packets across Bluetooth links.

21.1.1   Initialising PAN Services

Network Access Points and Group ad-hoc Networks rely on SDP to advertise their services to PAN users, so they must register their services in a service discovery database before they can be used. Optionally, PAN users may also register the PANU service, but this is not required. This is because it is possible that PAN users may prefer to always initiate connections, in which case there would be no need for another device to discover details of their services.

When the Network Access Point or Group ad-hoc Network service is initialised, the device must initialise its packet filtering database. This database defines which packet types will be forwarded across the Bluetooth link. If it is initialised empty, then all packets will be forwarded; however, some packet types are unlikely to be of interest to PAN users, so to save bandwidth, and hence save power, it is sensible to have a default set of packet types which will be filtered out.

During initialisation devices which use security will also need to initialise their security database. This will contain information on authorised and trusted devices defining which authorisation mode and encryption modes are to be used with each device. This is also the place where information on access rights to data and various keys is stored.

Security procedures are not mandatory in the PAN profile, but they are highly recommended, as unencrypted wireless connections are vulnerable to eavesdropping and insertion of false information.

In order to help with configuration of the various parameters which must be initialised, Network Access Points may have Management Information Bases (MIBs). A

Management Information Base is simply a database containing useful information and settings which can be used to configure a device. The PAN profile does not specify the full contents of a Network Access Point MIB, but it does suggest a few items which would be useful to include:

- Maximum number of users—The number of PAN users who can connect simultaneously. If this is set to zero, the device is currently disabled.
- Discoverable/Non-Discoverable mode—Whether the device will scan for inquiries.
- Packet Filter Database—A list of packets which will be filtered out; that is, packets which will not be forwarded across Bluetooth links. This is optional.
- Security modes—What security procedures will be used.
- Configurable parameters of the service record.
- Networking, device, and security parameters such as device link keys and access lists.

A Management Information Base is optional. If one is supported, the entries above are recommended but not mandatory, and optionally an implementation can add extra information to the Management Information Base.

21.1.2   Discovering PAN Services

Both Network Access Points and Group ad-hoc Networks begin connections in exactly the same way, as shown in Figure 21–3.

First an ACL (data) link is set up, using inquiry procedures if necessary followed by paging.

Once the ACL link is in place, an LMP_host_connection_req is sent. The example shows this being followed by a Master/Slave switch using LMP_switch_req and LMP_accepted messages. In fact, this switch is only necessary if the device being connected with is configured to accept multiple connections—the PAN profile calls this multiuser mode, If the device receiving the connection is not in multiuser mode, then the master/slave switch is not needed.

Now the two devices set up security. This may involve creating link keys, authenticating, and establishing an encrypted link (see Chapter 15 for more details). Either Link Keys or PIN codes are needed to set up a secure encrypted link; these must be supplied independently to both devices. They could be entered by a user, or they might be provided by software running on the device.

Once the link setup is completed and confirmed by an exchange of LMP_setup_complete messages, a channel can be set up to Service Discovery. The channnel is used to find out about the device's PAN services.

The example shows an LMP_detach after service discovery, but the PAN user could go on immediately to using PAN services.

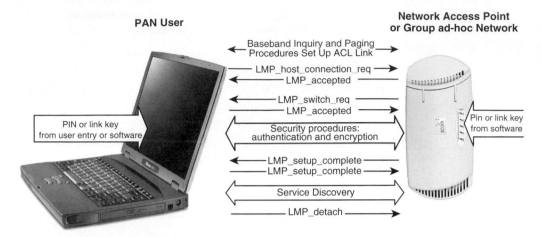

Figure 21–3   PAN initialisation.

21.1.3   Establishing a PAN Service Connection

Once a PAN user has identified a device it wishes to connect with, it creates an ACL connection, going through master/slave switch and security procedures if necessary to connect at host level. A group ad-hoc network can initiate a connection to a device which advertises the PAN user service. The connection procedure is the same, except that no master/slave switch will be required.

PAN provides various different modes which govern the security procedures used when establishing a connection:

- Authorisation Mode—This controls if and when authentication and access rights checks are used. Mode 1 is no authorisation, mode 2 the PAN user is authenticated, mode 3 the PAN user is authenticated and its access rights are verified.
- Security Mode—This controls if and when link keys are required, and when other security procedures are used. Mode 1 is nonsecure, mode 2 is service level enforced security (this happens when the L2CAP channel is established), mode 3 is link-level enforced security (this happens when the ACL link is established as shown in Figure 21–4).
- Secrecy Mode—This controls if and when encryption is switched on. Clear mode means no encryption, encrypted mode means all PAN communications are encrypted. Encryption could be done by the Bluetooth baseband or at BNEP/IP level.

The modes above are the usual Bluetooth security modes (see Chapter15 for more details on security modes). However, if the Security Mode is set to mode 2 (service level enforced security), then PAN service-level enforced security mode is applied. This includes higher layer security (802.1X, IPSEC) as well as Bluetooth security.

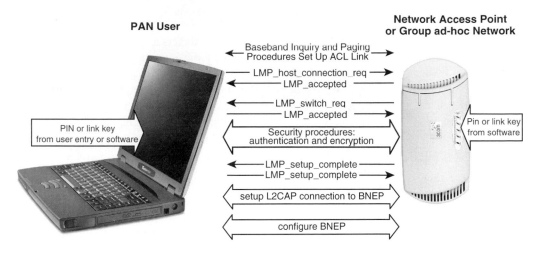

Figure 21–4   Setting up a PAN connection.

It is important to realise that security procedures are applied individually to each link. It is possible that a Group ad-hoc Network or Network Access Point could have connections with different secrecy modes active simultaneously. In that case, data which was sent by a PAN user across a secure link would then be repeated unencrypted across any connections with secrecy mode set to clear. This creates an obvious security risk, though configuring Group ad-hoc Networks and Network Access Points to always require encryption on all links easily eliminates the problem.

Once an ACL link is established and any link level security has been enforced an L2CAP channel is opened for BNEP. The minimum value for the L2CAP MTU (Maximum Transmission Unit) is a value required by BNEP of 1691 bytes. This minimum value is necessary because BNEP takes ethernet packets and puts them into L2CAP payloads. BNEP cannot segment ethernet packets across more than one L2CAP packet. If the L2CAP MTU was set too small, it just wouldn't be possible for ethernet packets to get across the link. Of course, the two devices can negotiate a larger MTU if they wish, but since larger values of MTU make demands on memory, most devices will just use the minimum value set by BNEP.

Only one BNEP connection ever exists between a pair of devices. If there is already an L2CAP connection to BNEP, when a request comes in, the device will refuse the second request to connect an L2CAP channel to BNEP.

Once the L2CAP channel is configured, BNEP control commands are used to initialise the BNEP connection and set up filtering of different network packets. At this point any default packet filters set up during initialisation can be used or new packet filters can be negotiated.

Once BNEP is configured, ethernet traffic can be carried across the PAN link. Each ethernet packet is carried in an L2CAP packet using the Bluetooth Network Encapsulation Protocol (BNEP).

21.1.4   Packet Forwarding

The Network Access Point or Group ad-hoc Network acts as a bridge and forwards packets between PAN users. It performs a subset of the operations specified by the IEEE 802.1D standard for MAC bridges.

Each PAN user is treated as if it was a bridge port, so traffic is forwarded to and from each user. For Network Access Points the Ethernet connection is also treated as a bridge port. Broadcast traffic must be sent to all ports, although devices are allowed to develop their own means of efficiently handling the problem of supporting broadcasts to PAN users in low power modes.

Which packet types are forwarded and which are filtered is decided by the packet filtering database. The 802.1D standard gives the definitive set of rules for filtering and forwarding. It is not as simple as just looking at the type and deciding whether to drop a packet or forward it: as packets are sent, information is learned which affects decisions.

The Network Access Point or Group ad-hoc Network may add its own intelligent algorithms to the rules laid out in 802.11D. For example, Ethernets carry Address Resolution Protocol (ARP) Frames. Address Resolution Protocol is used to translate IP addresses into ethernet addresses. IP and ethernet addresses are allocated completely separately, so to find out which ethernet address corresponds to an IP address, a broadcast ARP request is sent out to every computer on the Ethernet. The ARP request contains an IP address which some device is trying to match up with an IP address. Every computer receives the packet, and the one with the matching IP address replies with a response giving its matching ethernet address.

Now the Network Access Point or Group ad-hoc Network could act as an ARP proxy to avoid having to forward every ARP request it sees. To do this, it learns the IP addresses and ethernet addresses of the PAN users which are connected to it, then, instead of forwarding ARP requests to them, it can simply reply on their behalf with the same response they would have sent. It is not compulsory for devices to implement this sort of functionality, but ones which do will help to cut down unnecessary traffic.

For addressing PAN supports both IP version 4 including dynamic configuration of link-local addresses and IP version 6 including address assignment by IP version 6 autoconfiguration as defined by RFC2462. Because PAN supports both IP version 4 and IP version 6, the technique used by a PAN user to get an IP address and the length of the address will vary.

Since PAN uses Multicast DNS, all devices must comply with the rules for Multicast DNS (at present in an Internet draft, soon to become an RFC). However, some devices such as WAP clients may never need to resolve names into addresses, in which case they do not need to implement any name-to-address functionality.

21.1.5   PAN Phase 2

The Bluetooth SIG's PAN working group is still active and will produce a Phase 2 PAN profile. Phase 2 will use scatternets and will provide support for roaming between access points. For this to be done the capabilities of the Bluetooth core specification will have to be improved, as at present scatternet capabilities are not well defined, and there are no messages allowing handover from one Bluetooth piconet to another.

The Radio working group is extending the core specification to better support scatternets and to provide handover between piconets. The output of this group will be crucial to enabling Phase 2 PAN.

Phase 2 of the PAN Profile will also improve Quality of Service handling. Bluetooth already provides many messages for handling quality of service at L2CAP and LMP levels. A Bluetooth SIG study group is examining how these capabilities can be used and enhanced. Doubtless, the output of this study group will help to enhance the Phase 2 PAN profile's QOS capabilities.

21.2   BLUETOOTH NETWORK ENCAPSULATION PROTOCOL

Bluetooth Network Encapsulation Protocol (BNEP) allows IP packets to be carried in the payload of L2CAP packets. The BNEP layer sits directly above the L2CAP layer, providing an Internet Protocol (IP) transport as shown by Figure 21–5.

The IP layer above BNEP in turn supports a session management layer. This could be Transport Control Protocol (TCP) or User Datagram Protocol (UDP). The two provide very similar services to the application except that UDP is unreliable whilst TCP is reliable.

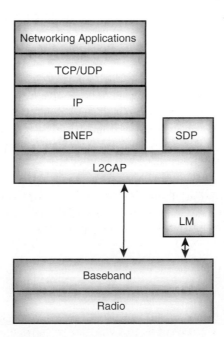

Figure 21–5   The BNEP protocol stack.

It is possible that the device terminating the BNEP link acts purely as a router, just forwarding IP packets onto an ethernet. Packets can be forwarded by the IP layer, never reaching the TCP or UDP layer, so some IP router implementations omit the higher layers. These implementations have protocol stacks which stop at the IP layer and omit the session layer. In BNEP though a session must be established and managed as an L2CAP channel must be set up and a BNEP channel connected to a service, so even if a full UDP or TCP implementation is not required some session management functions will be needed to manage the Bluetooth connections.

21.2.1   BNEP Packet Structure

BNEP uses an L2CAP channel to transport both control and data packets. BNEP has to attach a header to the information so that it is possible to identify what type of packet it is. Figure 21–6 shows the format of a BNEP packet header. The header begins with a 7 bit type field which identifies the type of information carried in the packet.

- 0x00—BNEP_GENERAL_ETHERNET, used to carry ethernet packets to and from Bluetooth devices.
- 0x01—BNEP_CONTROL, used to exchange control information.
- 0x02—BNEP_COMPRESSED_ETHERNET, used to carry ethernet packets to and from Bluetooth devices. No source and destination addresses are needed because the source and destination devices are connected to the L2CAP channel on which the packet is sent.
- 0x03—BNEP_COMPRESSED_ETHERNET_SOURCE_ONLY, used to carry ethernet packets to a device where no destination address is needed because the destination device is the one connected to the L2CAP channel on which the packet is sent.
- 0x04—BNEP_COMPRESSED_ETHERNET_DEST_ONLY, used to carry ethernet packets from a device where no source address is needed because the source device is the one connected to the L2CAP channel on which the packet is sent.
- 0x05 to 0x7E—Reserved for future use.
- 0x7F—Reserved for 802.2 LLC Packets for 802.11 Working Group.

The type field is followed by an extension bit E. If the E bit is set to 0x1, then more extension headers follow. Extension headers are extra BNEP control messages. They are placed after the header, but before any payload data. Extension headers allow filtering information to be piggybacked onto a data packet. This way data can flow uninterrupted at the

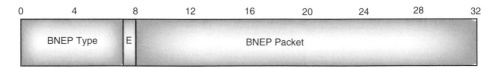

Figure 21–6   The BNEP protocol stack.

same time as control information. If the E bit is zero, then the BNEP payload follows immediately after the header. See section 21.2.3 below for more details on control packets.

21.2.2 Ethernet Encapsulation

Ethernet is an IEEE802.3 standard. Already there are various transport media defined for Ethernet: 10base2 and 10base5 use co-axial cable, 10baseT uses Unshielded Twisted Pair cable (UTP), and 10baseF uses fibre optic cables. BNEP simply replaces the various ethernet cables with wireless links.

Figure 21–7 shows the structure of an ethernet frame, and how BNEP encapsulates the frame into an L2CAP packet. The ethernet frame begins with a preamble for synchronisation and a Start of Frame Delimiter (SFD) which marks the beginning of the packet. L2CAP relies upon the Bluetooth baseband for synchronisation, so the Ethernet preamble and start of frame delimiter are not needed and are simply discarded.

Next in the ethernet frame comes the ethernet header. This contains a 6 byte destination address, a 6 byte source address, and a single byte length field. The source and destination addresses are MAC addresses allocated by the IEEE to manufacturers of ethernet cards adapters and motherboards. Bluetooth device addresses are also 6 byte addresses allocated by the IEEE, so they can safely be used as source and destination addresses in ethernet frames.

In Ethernets all packets are broadcast on the same cable, so all devices receive them, meaning every frame must have a source and destination address. BNEP uses connection oriented L2CAP channels which give point to point links. This means that it is not always necessary to put source and destination addresses on every single packet. Addresses take up bandwidth; if they are not required, it makes sense to miss them out. BNEP provides four different packet types to allow source and destination addresses which aren't needed to be omitted.

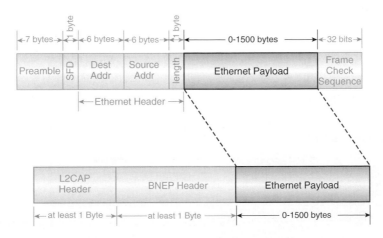

Figure 21–7   Ethernet payload encapsulation.

Figure 21–8 shows how the headers for the four BNEP packets are used to carry ethernet payloads. The BNEP_GENERAL_ETHERNET packet at the top of the figure carries all addressing information. The figure shows how the other three packet types have shorter headers because they omit Source or Destination Addresses belonging to devices connected to the L2CAP channel the packet is sent on. Figure 21–8 shows the simplest packets with the Extension Bit set to zero so there are no extension headers and the payload immediately follows the Networking protocol Type. If the E bit was set to 1, this would mean that extension headers were included before the payload.

The Networking Protocol Type field identifies the type of networking protocol contained in the payload. Possible values include:

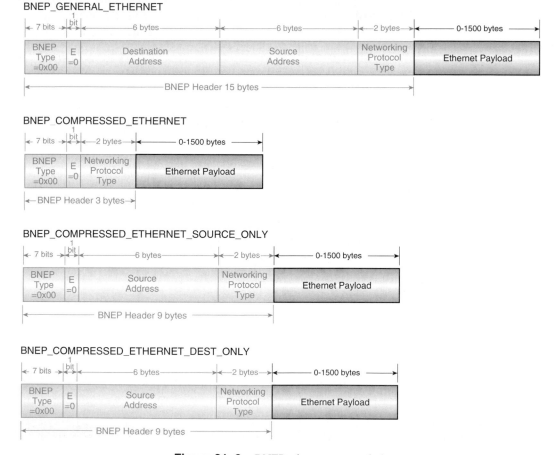

Figure 21–8   BNEP ethernet encapsulation.

- 0x0800—Network Protocol Type Internet IP (IPv4).
- 0x8100—IEEE 802.1p Header.
- 0x86DD—Network Protocol Type Internet IP (IPv6).

Once the BNEP header has been constructed, the ethernet payload is copied into the rest of the L2CAP packet. The ethernet payload contains up to 1500 bytes of data. If necessary, the data is padded to make an integral number of bytes. In ethernet frames the data is followed by a 32 bit Frame Check Sequence (FCS). This is not mentioned in the BNEP specification; however, the specification does give the maximum Ethernet payload length as 1500 bytes. If the Frame Check Sequence were included, the maximum length would be 1504 bytes. This implies that the 4 byte Frame Check Sequence is not regarded as part of the payload and is not copied into the L2CAP packet. This means that Network Access Points must regenerate the 32 bit Frame Check Sequence from received payload data before forwarding packets onto an ethernet.

21.2.3 BNEP Control

Section 21.2.1 has already explained how setting the type field in a BNEP header to 0x01 makes the packet type BNEP_CONTROL and allows control information to be carried in a packet. However, one type of control packet would not be enough to pass all the control information which is needed to manage BNEP links.

To provide more packet types a single byte Control Type field is used to identify the type of control message being sent, this follows the E bit as shown in Figure 21–9. Possible values for Control Type are:

- 0x00—BNEP_.CONTROL_COMMAND_NOT_UNDERSTOOD.
- 0x01—BNEP_SETUP_CONNECTION_REQUEST_MSG.
- 0x02—BNEP_SETUP_CONNECTION_RESPONSE_MSG.
- 0x03—BNEP_FILTER_NET_TYPE_SET_MSG.
- 0x04—BNEP_FILTER_NET_TYPE_RESPONSE_MSG.
- 0x05—BNEP_FILTER_MULTI_ADDR_SET_MSG.
- 0x06—BNEP_FILTER_MULTI_ADDR_RESPONSE_MSG.
- 0x07 to 0xFF—Reserved for future use.

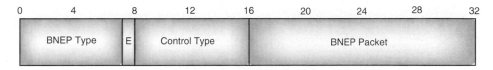

Figure 21–9 Position of BNEP Control Type field.

The BNEP_CONTROL_COMMAND_NOT_UNDERSTOOD is sent whenever a control message is received with a type which is not recognised. This means that if the BNEP control messages are expanded in the future, there will still be a way for devices to acknowledge messages even if they cannot recognise and process them.

The BNEP_SETUP_CONNECTION_REQUEST_MSG is used to request a device to open a BNEP channel and connect it to a service. Three parameters following the Control Type are used to identify the services to be connected to the BNEP channel:

- UUID Size—A single byte field giving the size of the UUIDs which follow. Because there is only one size field for both UUIDS, both Destination and Source UUIDs must be the same size.
- Destination Service UUID—A 2 to 16 byte SDP UUID identifying the service which the source device wants the BNEP channel to be connecting to at the destination end.
- Source Service UUID—A 2 to 16 byte SDP UUID identifying the service which the source device is connecting to the BNEP channel.

As shown in Figure 21–10, the destination device replies with a BNEP_SETUP_CON-NECTION_RESPONSE_MSG. This has a single Response Message parameter which indicates whether the setup operation was successful or failed. The setup operation will fail if any of the UUIDs sent are not valid, or if the connection is not allowed. The connection might not be allowed for security reasons, or possibly because the device has insufficient resources to support the channel.

The remaining BNEP control types deal with filtering and will be explained in the next section.

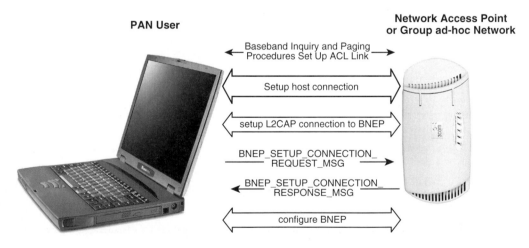

PAN User   **Network Access Point or Group ad-hoc Network**

Baseband Inquiry and Paging Procedures Set Up ACL Link

Setup host connection

setup L2CAP connection to BNEP

BNEP_SETUP_CONNECTION_ REQUEST_MSG

BNEP_SETUP_CONNECTION_ RESPONSE_MSG

configure BNEP

Figure 21–10   Setting up a BNEP channel.

21.2.4   BNEP Filtering

BNEP provides filtering capabilities so that Network Access Points and Group ad-hoc Networks do not have to indiscriminately forward all packets to every connected PAN user. Filtering can be set on packet types or on multicast addresses.

Four control messages allow packet filtering information to be sent across BNEP links, collectively these are called BNEP_FILTER_CONTROL messages. Each message affecting filter settings must be acknowledged with a response before another message affecting filter settings can be sent. A timeout is started when a message affecting filter settings is sent, and if no response is received when the timeout elapses, the message is assumed to have been lost and can be retransmitted.

The BNEP_FILTER_NET_TYPE_SET_MSG is used to filter network protocol types. Its parameters begin with a list length, giving the number of bytes of protocol information which follows, then there is a list of Network Protocol Type ranges which will not be filtered out. Each range has a 2 byte start of range and a 2 byte end of range. Figure 21–11 shows the structure of the message which would be used to filter out everything except IPv6 messages. In this case, since just one message type is being received, the start and end of the Network Protocol range are both the same.

The BNEP_FILTER_NET_TYPE_SET_MSG must be acknowledged with a BNEP_FILTER_NET_TYPE_RESPONSE_MSG. This has a single 2 byte Response Message parameter after the Control Type field. The Response Message parameter indicates whether the operation to set filtering succeeded or failed. The operation could fail because the device does not support filtering, because the Networking Protocol Range is invalid, because the device has reached its maximum number of Network Protocol Type filter settings, or because the filters settings cannot be changed for security reasons. Obviously, filter settings are only changed when the Response message is set to Operation Successful.

The BNEP_FILTER_MULTI_ADDR_SET_MSG is used to filter out multicast messages by their multicast destination address. Its structure is similar to the BNEP_FILTER_NET_TYPE_SET_MSG: its parameters begin with a list length, giving the number

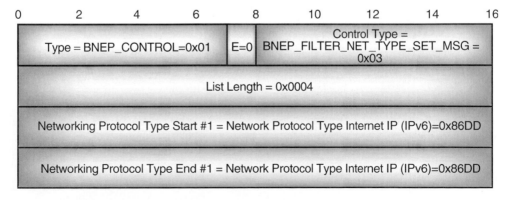

Figure 21–11   Structure of BNEP_FILTER_NET_TYPE_SET_MSG.

of bytes of multicast address information which follows, then there is a list of multicast address ranges to be received. As destination addresses are 6 bytes long, each range has a 6 byte start of range and a 6 byte end of range. Figure 21–12 shows the structure of the message which would be used to set a filter to only enable IPv5 neighbour discovery multicast addresses (0x333300000000 to 0x3333FFFFFFFF).

   The BNEP_FILTER_MULTI_ADDR_SET_MSG must be acknowledged with a BNEP_FILTER_MULTI_ADDR_RESPONSE_MSG. This has a single 2 byte Response Message parameter after the Control Type field. The Response Message parameter indicated whether the operation to set filtering succeeded or failed. The operation could fail because the device does not support filtering, because the Multicast Address Range is invalid, because the device has reached its maximum number of Multicast filter settings, or because the filters settings cannot be changed for security reasons. Obviously, filter settings are only changed when the Response message is set to Operation Successful.

21.2.5   Prioritisation Tags

The IEEE 802.1p specification defines a way to prioritise frames by including tags at the beginning of the payload. If the Networking Protocol type is 0x8100, then an IEEE 802.1p header is placed immediately before the start of the payload data.

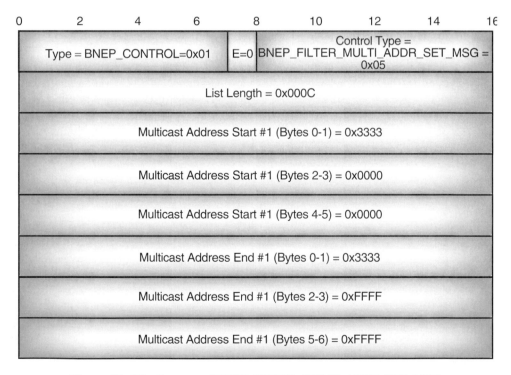

Figure 21–12   Structure of BNEP_FILTER_MULTI_ADDR_SET_MSG.

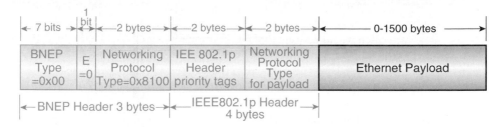

Figure 21–13   Structure of a packet with an 802.1p header.

Figure 21–13 gives shows the structure of a BNEP_COMPRESSED_ETHERNET packet which includes an IEEE 802.1p header. The IEEE 802.1p header is 4 bytes long. The first 2 bytes hold the prioritisation information. The next 2 bytes give the Networking Protocol Type of the payload which follows. This is needed because the first Networking Protocol Type field was used to indicate the presence of the IEEE 802.1p header. This means that BNEP devices must be able to interpret IEEE 802.1p headers correctly in order to guarantee that they can correctly identify the networking protocol type which is in use.

Prioritisation provides a powerful tool for ensuring that time critical information gets handled as quickly as possible on low bandwidth links, so IEEE 802.1p prioritisation tags are a useful addition to BNEP's capabilities.

21.3 SUMMARY

The Personal Area Networking (PAN) profile uses BNEP to enable ad-hoc IP networks. A series of PAN users can connect to a Network Access Point (NAP) which acts as a bridge forwarding packets to and from an ethernet. Alternatively, PAN users can connect to a Group ad-hoc Network. In this case there is no outside network connection, the Group ad-hoc network device simply forwards packets between all of its connected PAN users. So the PAN profile can provide the ability for slaves to communicate with an outside network, or with one another.

Bluetooth Network Encapsulation (BNEP) provides a way for IP packets to be routed to and from Bluetooth devices. IP networks can carry a lot of multicast traffic which could overwhelm low bandwidth Bluetooth links, so BNEP provides filtering capabilities which help to cut unnecessary traffic to a minimum.

PAN and BNEP combine to greatly increase the power of ad-hoc networks. Previous profiles concentrated on masters and slaves communicating on point to point links, but did not allow slaves to communicate directly with one another. PAN provides peer to peer communication not just slave to slave, but also with networked devices opening the way for Bluetooth devices to interface with IP networked devices.

22

ESDP for UPnP

Extended Service Discovery Protocol for Universal Plug and Play (ESDP for UPnP) is the first extension to the service discovery capabilities of Bluetooth; more extensions to SDP are likely to be released in the future.

ESDP for UPnP brings Universal Plug and Play features to Bluetooth, making it easier than ever before to connect without cables! However, UPnP does not stop at merely discovering device capabilities, it also allows devices to be controlled, allows state change information to be sent out to interested devices, and provides tools for presenting information about a device's services.

ESDP for UPnP provides three ways to use UPnP with Bluetooth: directly on top of L2CAP, with the LAN Access profile, or with the new PAN profile. This chapter begins with a look at the UPnP device architecture, then goes on to examine how ESDP for UPnP functions in the three different Bluetooth stack configurations.

22.1 UNIVERSAL PLUG AND PLAY DEVICE ARCHITECTURE

Universal Plug and Play is an architecture for peer to peer IP based networking designed to support intelligent appliances, wireless devices, and PCs. It is designed to support ad-hoc networking without the need for any configuration. Devices join networks, get IP addresses, advertise their services, find other devices nearby, and learn about their capabilities. Instead of using device drivers to communicate, devices share a common set of protocols including IP, TCP, UDP, HTTP, and XML. The UPnP Forum is an industry initiative with working committees creating UPnP standards for individual services. For instance, there is a playCD service template to facilitate use of CD players as a UPnP service. There is a logo program, but manufacturers are also free to build devices using the UPnP device architecture without going through a formal standards procedure.

The Universal Plug and Play architecture defines the protocols for communicating between control points and devices. A control point is simply a device which is using the services of another device.

Figure 22–1 shows part of the protocol stack used by a UPnP device connected to an IP network. In Bluetooth devices which do not implement IP networking, the UDP/TCP and IP layers may be replaced by the L2CAP transport as shown in Figure 22–2.

Stage 1 of UPnP uses the UPnP service discovery protocol. This is used both to advertise their services on the network, and to search for devices of interest on the network. Devices advertise their type, identifier, and a URL which provides a pointer to more detailed information. UPnP Service discovery uses Simple Service Discovery Protocol (SSDP).

Stage 2 is to retrieve a description from any devices which look interesting. The UPnP description for a device is written in XML. A device may contain other logical devices, as well as services. The XML description of a device includes a list of any embedded devices or services, as well as URLs for control, eventing, and presentation. Each service has a list of actions which can be used to control it, and each action in turn has arguements or parameters. Each service also has a list of state variables.

Stage 3 is to control a device's service by sending it actions. Actions are sent in control messages which use SOAP (Simple Object Access Protocol). Actions are sent to the service's control URL. The control URL is given in the service's description. The ser-

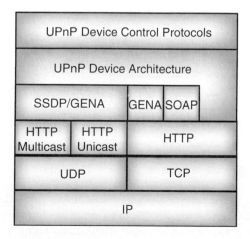

Figure 22–1   Universal Plug and Play protocol stack.

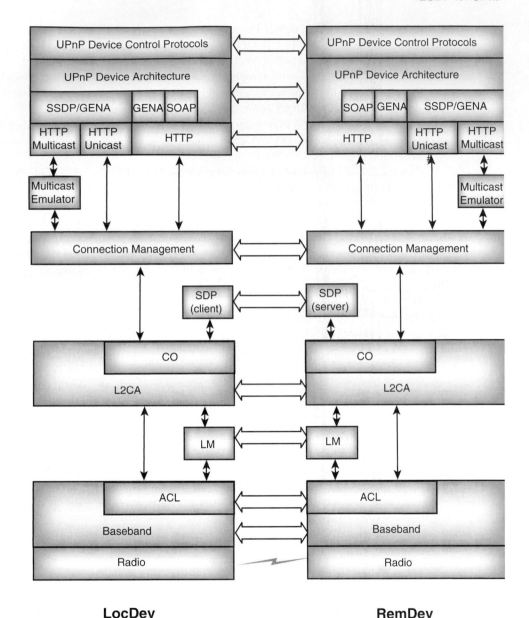

Figure 22–2 Universal Plug and Play using and L2CAP based solution.

vice responds to the control message by returning any values generated as a result of the action. The action may result in changes to the service's state variables.

Stage 4 is eventing. The state variables in a UPnP's device description may change as a result of actions the service is responding to. Control points which are interacting with the service can ask to be notified when the service's state variables change, this is called subscribing for events. The service will then inform the control point of state changes by sending event messages. Event messages use XML and are formatted using the General Event Notification Architecture (GENA). When a control point first subscribes, it is sent an initial event message containing the names and current values of every variable which will be covered by event messages. After this initial message, messages are sent to all subscribed control points whenever a state variable changes, whether it changed as a result of an action by that particular control point.

Stage 5 is presentation. Not all devices have URLs for presentation, but those devices which do provide pages which control points can load using a URL published in the device's description. Pages may just allow control points to view status, or they may allow a user to control the device.

22.2   L2CAP BASED SOLUTIONS

Figure 22–2 shows how the upper part of the UPnP protocol stack is connected to the L2CAP transport in Bluetooth devices which do not implement IP networking.

There are two roles: the local device (LocDev) and the remote device (RemDev). The local device may be either a UPnP Control Point or a UPnP device providing a service.

L2CAP based solutions use peer to peer connections, but the peer device may act as a bridge and proxy the services of a device on the other side of the bridge.

Initially, service discovery is performed using SDP; however, SDP may discover devices with the UPnP capability, in which case Simple Service Discovery Protocol (SSDP) and the General Event Notification Architecture (GENA) may then be used.

GENA relies upon HTTP multicast (HTTPMU) to send notifications to several devices which have registered for event notifications. A multicast emulator is used to translate the multicast request into multiple unicast requests. These are then sent point to point across connection oriented L2CAP links. The multicast emulator gathers information about UPnP devices within radio range so that it can request the Connection Management layer to establish connections with them providing a capability to multicast to all UPnP devices in radio range.

22.2.1   Connection Management

A connection management layer transfers messages from the multicast layer and from HTTP unicast (HTTPU) onto L2CAP links. This layer is responsible for setting up and managing point to point L2CAP links as and when they are needed. Only one L2CAP connection is used between any two devices for UPnP traffic. If two devices simultaneously open up L2CAP connections to each other so that there are two connections between them, the connection initiated by the device with the lower BD_ADDR is rejected or terminated.

Once an L2CAP connection is established, the connection management layer transmits information and control in PDUs with 3 byte headers as shown in Figure 22–3. The packet starts with a 4 bit type field. This can take four values:

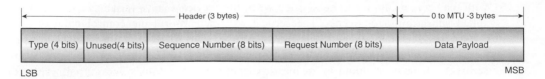

Figure 22–3   Data PDU.

- 0x0—Data
- 0x1—Data Acknowledgement
- 0x2—Window Size Control
- 0x3—Window Size Control Acknowledgement

The Sequence number is a modulo 256 number which is incremented by one every time a data packet is sent. A return data packet can be used to acknowledge data by filling in the Request Number field with the number of the next packet expected. Usually, this would increment every time a packet is received, but if a packet is lost, or a packet is received with errors, then the Request number is set to one more than the last error free in sequence packet received.

If the receiving device has no data to send, it uses a Data Acknowledgement packet to acknowledge receipt of packets.

Several packets can be sent before an acknowledgement is received. The number of packets which can be sent without acknowledgement is called the window size. Because packets are not individually acknowledged the transmitting device must be able to buffer the number of packets that fit in the window size so that they can be retransmitted if it turns out that they were not received correctly.

The window size starts off at 2, but a Window Size Control PDU can be sent to change the window size. The window size is sent as a single byte in the Data Payload of the PDU. The Window Size Control PDUs have their own sequence number which increments modulo 256 with every Window Size Control. The Window Size Control PDU is acknowledged with a Window Size Control Acknowledgement which has no payload. In the same way as the data PDUs the Window Size Control Acknowledgement carries the sequence number of the next Window Size Control PDU expected in its Request Number field. The acknowledgement PDU should be received with a Request Number set to 1 higher than the Sequence Number sent in the Window Size Control. If the request number in the acknowledgement is wrong, the Window Size Control PDU is retransmitted. The Windows Size Control PDU is also retransmitted if a timeout elapses before an acknowledgement has been received.

A busy device, or a device with a full receive buffer, advertises a window size of zero. In this way Window Size Control messages can be used to flow control an L2CAP channel.

A device with large receive buffers can advertise a larger window. This can lead to wasted bandwidth: a device only stops transmitting when it reaches the end of its window, so a lot of data may have to be retransmitted if errors occurred or packets were lost at the start of a large window.

A system which relies on infrequent acknowledgements is obviously vulnerable to acknowledgements getting lost. This problem is solved by using timeouts. If an expected acknowledgement isn't received after a timeout expires, then all unacknowledged data is retransmitted.

The connection management layer also provides segmentation and reassembly services to cope with payloads which would exceed the L2CAP maximum transmission unit (MTU). Data is segmented into the L2CAP MTU minus 3 bytes to allow for the 3 byte data PDU header. On reception data is sent to higher layers in the order received.

22.2.2   URLs

UPnP makes extensive use of URLs, so some method is needed to map URLs onto Bluetooth piconets. This is done by using the Bluetooth device address as part of the URL, followed by .bt.local to indicate that this is a Bluetooth device address. For example the following URLs are for HTTP and HTTPU addressing a device with BD_ADDR 0x00025BFF40F7:

> HTTP://00025BFF40F7.bt.local/
> HTTPU://00025BFF40F7.bt.local/

To send a multicast to all UPnP devices within radio range, a multicast address is used with an all Fs address, this is combined with HTTPMU addressing format to give:

> HTTPMU://FFFFFFFFFFFF.bt.local

By providing connection management, multicast support, HTTP encapsulation, and URL addressing EDSP for UPnP allows UPnP services to be used across L2CAP. This means that Bluetooth devices that do not support IP networking can take advantage of UPnP networking.

22.3   IP BASED SOLUTIONS

Bluetooth devices can implement IP transport via the LAN Access Profile (LAP), or the Personal Area Networking Profile (PAN), so EDSP for UPnP messages may be carried using IP with devices implementing either of those profiles.

In order to use IP to transport UPnP messages, devices must first have an IP address. UPnP is designed for ad-hoc networks, so it does not use preallocated IP addresses. UPnP devices obtain IP addresses using Dynamic Host Configuration Protocol (DHCP) clients. These clients search for DHCP servers when first connected to a network. If a DHCP client finds a DHCP server, the client obtains an IP address from the server. If a DHCP client fails to find a DHCP server, the client device uses Auto IP to choose an IP address from a reserved set of addresses. In this way UPnP devices can obtain IP addresses whether they are connected to a managed network.

Bluetooth devices can access IP networks using two profiles: the LAN Access Profile or the PAN profile. Each uses a slightly different protocol stack to implement UPnP functions. The following sections look at PAN and LAN Access Point based solutions in turn.

22.3.1   PAN Based Solutions

Devices using the PAN profile establish a peer to peer IP connection and use UPnP services across the IP link. This gives rise to the protocol stack in Figure 22–4. If this figure is compared with Figure 22–1, it can be seen that the PAN profile provides the UDP/TCP and IP layers which transport IP traffic for the upper UPnP layers.

UPnP can be combined with the PAN profile to control services of other UPnP devices on the network in three ways: first, a control point can use UPnP services of a de-

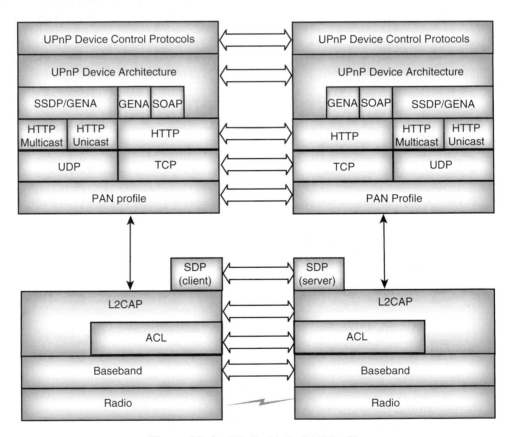

Figure 22–4   UPnP with the PAN Profile.

vice across a direct peer to peer connection; second, a control point can use UPnP services of a device which is connected to the same IP network via a Group Ad-hoc Network or Network Access Point; and third, services can be accessed via a bridge device which acts as a proxy for the UPnP device forwarding messages to and from a service on the other side of the bridge.

So the UPnP services do not have to come from the device which is connected directly to the control point. Indeed, the device which is at the other end of the direct connection may not even support UPnP. For example, a PAN Network Access Point can provide connectivity to a UPnP service provided by a device connected to the same network. The Network Access Point does not have to understand UPnP itself.

22.3.2 LAN Access Point Based Solutions

Devices using the LAN Access profile establish a peer to peer IP connection, across an underlying PPP connection as shown in Figure 22–5. UPnP sits above the TCP layer using the IP transport in the same way as any other application layered on the LAN Access Point Profile.

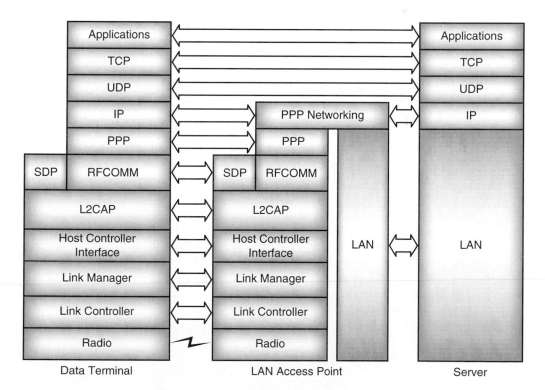

Figure 22–5   UPnP with the LAN Access Profile.

Once an IP link is established, devices using UPnP with the LAN Access Profile function similarly to devices using UPnP with the PAN profile. So a device which is connected to a LAN Access Point may use UPnP services of the LAN Access Point itself, but is more likely to use services of other devices connected to the same IP network across a LAN.

Figure 22–5 shows how the LAN Access Point can just implement layers of the protocol stack up to PPP. It is not necessary for it to implement higher layers if it is just acting as a bridge forwarding packet onto UPnP devices connected to the LAN.

The Bluetooth device connected to the LAN Access Point can act as a control point for any UPnP devices attached to the same IP network, but equally it is possible for the Bluetooth device to act as a UPnP device providing services for UPnP Control Points on the LAN.

23.4 SUMMARY

Extended Service Discovery Protocol for Universal Plug and Play (EDSP for UPnP) is the first of a series of extensions to the Bluetooth Service Discovery Protocol to be released. It can be used in three ways: across L2CAP connections, with the LAN Access Profile (LAP), or with the new Personal Area Networking (PAN) profile.

UPnP does not just provide service discovery capabilities, its capabilities include:

- The means for devices to discover other UPnP devices.
- Ways to learn about services using standard XMl based transactions.
- The ability to control the actions of a service.
- Registration for event notifications which provide updates whenever the status of a service changes.
- Presentation of control or state information via XML pages.

UPnP provides all these capabilities without device drivers by relying on a common set of protocols based on http and XML.

ESDP for UPnP greatly increases the power of ad-hoc networks by providing ways of using services with zero configuration. Because it uses standard protocols, even device types which have not been encountered before can be monitored and controlled via UPnP.

TEST AND QUALIFICATION

23

Test Mode

Qualification tests are carried out on samples of a product. To ensure that the radio performance of real products meets the same standards as the samples used for regulatory and qualification testing, Bluetooth provides a test mode, which is used in production line testing.

Figure 23–1 shows the interfaces used by test mode. The unit under test is put into test mode by a local connection. The unit under test is controlled and configured using LMP commands from the tester.

23.1 ACTIVATING TEST MODE

The test mode has to be activated locally. If a device could be put into test mode just through LMP commands, then devices in normal use could accidentally be put into test mode by an LMP packet with errors. Not only would this be inconvenient for the users, but devices in test mode can violate government regulations for using the ISM band because they can switch off frequency hopping. Local activation of test mode ensures that devices should never accidentally enter this mode.

For devices with an HCI, the Device Under Test (DUT) can be put into test mode using the HCI_Enable_Device_Under_Test_Mode command. Special test software could be used to issue this command, or a special password might be required to activate a test mode. However it is handled, there should be some step taken to ensure that a device in

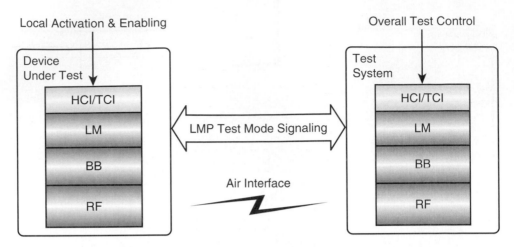

Figure 23–1   Test mode for production radio testing.

normal use will never enter test mode. There is no HCI_Disable_ Test_Mode command; rather, the device is just sent an HCI_Reset to locally disable test mode. After reset, the device will return to normal operation, and test mode cannot be used without being locally reactivated.

For devices that do not have an HCI, the test mode will still need to have the radios tested, so these devices will need some other method of activating the test mode. Since testing is done as the devices are produced, it is possible to add a couple of test points to a product's circuit board. A tester can short-circuit these points or apply a voltage to them. When the device's microprocessor detects that the test points are being used, it puts the device into test mode. In this way, it is possible to locally activate test mode without having to add the whole HCI to products which don't need it for any other purpose. Of course, when the product is finished, its case will hide the test points, so there is no danger of test mode being activated accidentally.

Once test mode has been activated locally, the tester's LM can control testing through LMP. Of course, to send LMP messages, the tester must have established an ACL link to the unit under test. Figure 23–2 shows a possible sequence of messages which could be used by a tester to enter test mode:

- Test mode is activated locally, by using test points or sending an HCI_Enable_Device_Under_Test_Mode.
- The tester pages the device under test and establishes a baseband link.
- The tester sends LMP messages to establish an ACL link at link management level.
- The tester sends an LMP_test_activate message, telling the device under test to enter test mode. At this point, the device under test switches off data whitening on its radio.
- The tester and the device under test go through the test sequences, exchanging LMP messages and test packets.

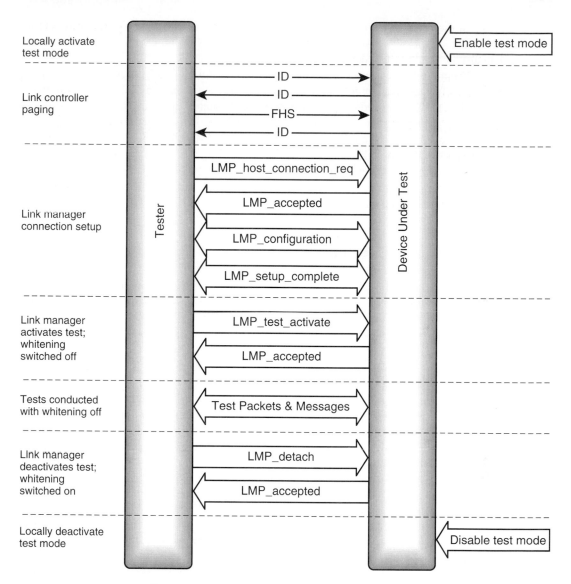

Figure 23–2   Message sequence chart for activating test mode.

- When the tester has finished the test, it sends an LMP_detach message. This shuts down the ACL link and also causes the device under test to exit test mode. At this point, the device under test switches data whitening on its radio again.
- The test mode is deactivated locally by stopping using test points or by sending an HCI_Reset command.

In the example above, the device under test leaves test mode because it is sent an LMP_detach message. An LMP_test_control message with an exit test mode parameter can also be used to tell a device to leave test mode.

From the sequence above, it can be seen that throughout test mode, data whitening is turned off. Data whitening is used to scramble the data in packets. The reason for this is that if data with a long sequence of ones or zeroes is sent, it can cause the radio to drift off frequency. Whitening data ensures that long sequences of ones or zeroes are never sent, so the radio stays on the correct frequency. Some of the test scenarios use a test sequence of all ones or all zeroes. These may be useful for testing baseband transmitter characteristics across wired links, but because of the frequency drift they cause in radios, they cause problems in radio testing. For this reason, the all ones and all zeroes patterns have not been used in the Bluetooth radio qualification test suite.

23.2   CONTROLLING TEST MODE

The tester's LM controls the test process by sending LMP messages to the device under test. As discussed above, an LMP_test_activate message is used to tell a device which has test mode locally activated that it should enter test mode.

Test mode must be activated both locally and via the LMP_test_activate command. If either step is missed, then LMP_test_control messages will be rejected as shown in Figure 23–3. Naturally, if test mode is locally deactivated during a test, then LMP_test_control messages will also be rejected.

The LMP_test_control message is used to activate the various different production tests required to check each Bluetooth product. Its structure is shown in Figure 23–4.

The LMP_test_control message begins like any other LMP message with a transaction identifier and an OpCode. The transaction identifier is zero if a Master initiated the

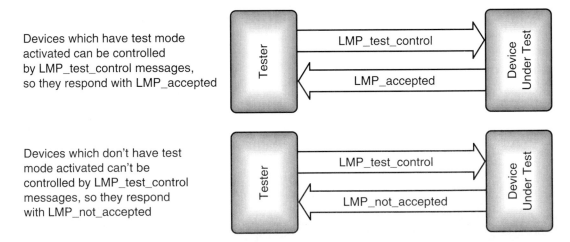

Figure 23–3   LMP message sequence charts for LMP_test_control.

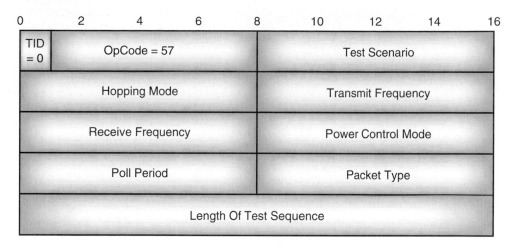

Figure 23–4   Structure of an LMP_test_control message.

transaction (see Chapter 7). The tester is always a Master, and the LMP_test_control message is only ever issued by a tester, so the transaction ID is always zero in this message. This is followed by the 7 bit Operation Code (OpCode), which identifies the type of LMP message being sent; for LMP_test_control, the OpCode is 57.

The message has eight parameters as follows:

- Test scenario—This determines the test to be performed; see below for more details.
- Hopping mode—This parameter can be used to switch hopping off altogether, to select a reduced hopping sequence used especially for testing, or to select one of the various national hopping sequences.
- Transmit frequency for device under test to use—Used when frequency hopping is switched off, this is an offset in MHz from 2402 MHz. The offset's value can be from 0 to 93.
- Receive frequency for device under test to use—Used when frequency hopping is switched off, this is an offset in MHz from 2402 MHz. The offset's value can be from 0 to 93.
- Power control mode—This chooses from a fixed output power, or adaptive power control.
- Poll period—This is set in units of 1.25 microseconds.
- Packet type—Sets the packet type to be used during the next test.
- Length of test sequence—An unsigned integer giving the number of bytes in the user data part of the test packets. The length of test sequence is obviously limited by the maximum payload size of the packet type chosen.

The test scenario chooses which test will be performed; it is chosen from:

- Transmitter test using a test data pattern of all 0's.
- Transmitter test using a test data pattern of all 1's.
- Transmitter test using a test data pattern of 101010.
- Transmitter test using a test data pattern of 11110000.
- Transmitter test using a pseudo-random bit sequence for the test data pattern.
- Closed loopback test of ACL packets.
- Closed loopback test of SCO packets.
- ACL packets with no data whitening.
- SCO packets with no data whitening.

In addition to the LMP_test_control messages, other LMP messages may be used in test mode. For instance, if active power control is selected, the LMP_incr_power_req and LMP_decr_power_req messages will be used to control power in the same way they are used in normal operation (see Chapter 7).

23.3 RADIO TRANSMITTER TEST

Because there are government regulations on how wireless devices can use the ISM band, it is vital that all Bluetooth products have radios which do not transmit too much power. For Bluetooth devices to work reliably, their radios must be capable of accurately hopping to the correct frequencies and at the right time. The radio transmitter test is used to check that the radios in Bluetooth products are performing correctly.

The radio transmitter test covers:

- Exercising extremes of frequency band.
- Testing that drift through a packet is within tolerance.
- Verifying that jitter is within tolerance.
- Testing power control.

23.3.1 Timing of Transmitter Test

During the transmitter test, the tester sends poll packets to the device under test. Because the tester is acting as a Master, it transmits in even slots. The Slave replies with a burst of test data; the pattern of the data is defined by the test scenario in the LMP_test_control message.

The interval between poll packets is defined in the LMP_test_control message. The first poll packet must be sent to start the transmitter test, but once the test has started, because the device under test knows when the poll packet is due to arrive, it can transmit its test data even if it didn't receive a poll. This situation is shown at the right of Figure 23–5. This figure also shows what happens if the length of the test sequence is longer than will fit into a single slot: The tester's poll packets are timed to fit in the next available even

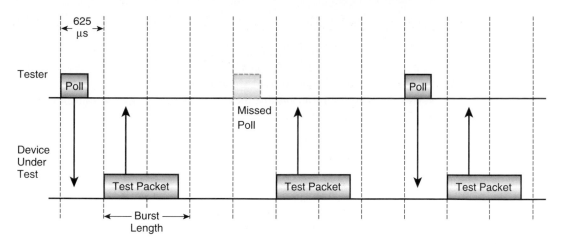

Figure 23–5   Timing of radio transmitter test.

slot, and the device under test begins its transmissions in the odd slots following the slots in which polls are due.

23.3.2   Test Packets

The structure of test packets is the same as the structure of normal packets, except that the payload data is replaced by a test sequence. Figure 23–6 shows how the payload varies according to the packet type. SCO packets just carry the test sequence in the payload. AUX packets add a payload header, but have no error correction, so SCO and AUX pack-

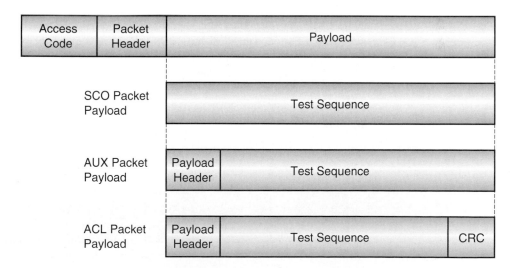

Figure 23–6   Structure of test packets.

ets can both be used to measure Bit Error Rates on a link. ACL packets have a payload header and CRC (Cyclic Redundancy Checksum).

SCO packets may be used in the loopback test, but are not used in the transmitter test. During the transmitter test, error rates on the link may be measured, so packets with Forward Error Correction should not be used, otherwise the baseband will correct errors before they can be measured. This means that the only packets suitable for transmitter test are HV3, DH1, DH3, DH5, and AUX.

23.3.3   Test Hopping Sequence

To test a radio, it should be exercised over its complete operational range of frequencies, but the standard channel hopping sequence has a very long repeat length, and could take a long time to cover the complete range of frequencies. To make testing easier, a reduced hopping sequence has been specified. The reduced hopping sequence uses just five frequencies. As Figure 23–7 shows, the device hops based on CLK, the value of the Master's Bluetooth clock. Bit zero of the clock changes every half slot; this bit is not used, which means that in test mode, the device hops once per slot.

The usual hopping sequence covers channels zero to seventyeight. The test mode hopping sequence extends from zero to ninetythree. The reason for this is that early versions of the Bluetooth specification had limited hopping sequences which extended into these channels, so they had to be tested. Although these hopping sequences are no longer recommended, test mode has retained their channels as this is simpler for implementers than changing test mode.

It is also possible to switch frequency hopping off altogether in test mode. If this is done, the LMP_test_control command parameters determine the fixed receive and transmit frequencies used by the device under test.

When the hop sequence is changed by an LMP_test_control command, the change takes effect after the LMP_accepted message has been transmitted back by the device under test. This means that the exchanges of messages to control the test takes place on the old hopping sequence, and the test takes place on the new hopping sequence. The switch has to be done in this way because if the tester moves to the new frequency immediately, but the device under test rejects the LMP_test_control message, then the device under test remains on the same hop sequence as before, and the tester misses its LMP_not_accepted response.

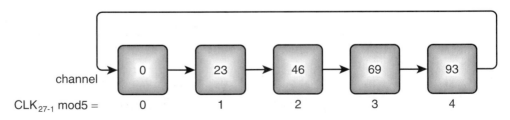

Figure 23–7   Reduced hopping sequence for test.

23.3.4   Power Control

Not all Bluetooth devices will implement power control. For those that do, it is important to check that the power control steps are correct. To do this, the tester uses the same LMP messages that are used to control power in normal operation (see Chapter 7).

The device under test begins transmitting at maximum power. It is sent LMP_decr_power messages to check its complete range of power transmission, one step at a time.

23.4   LOOPBACK TEST

In a loopback test, the device under test is sent normal packets. It receives and decodes the contents, then returns the data to the tester in the same sort of packet.

Figure 23–8 shows the two ways in which the device under test can return the packet to the tester. The packet is either returned in the next slot, or delayed and returned as a response to the tester's next transmission.

If the device is in test mode when the loopback test is conducted, then whitening will be switched off. A loopback test can be conducted when the device is not in test mode, in which case, whitening will be switched on.

If the device under test does not detect the synchword, it will not be aware that a packet was transmitted to it, so it will not generate a reply. This is unlike the transmitter test, when

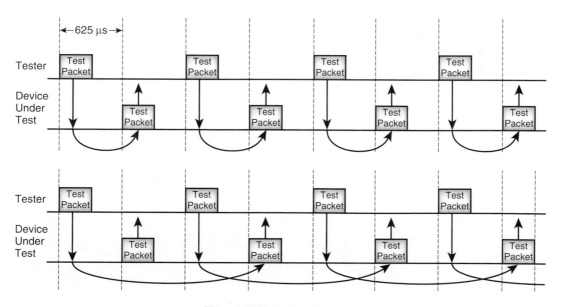

Figure 23–8   Loopback test.

the device under test can generate a response whether it detects a transmission from the tester, but clearly since the device under test is returning data it has received from the tester, it cannot possibly generate a reply if it has not received any data to return.

LMP packets relating to test mode are executed, but are not looped back, though the ACK or NACK is returned as usual.

To test the HEC, if the Device Under Test receives a packet which fails its header error check, it has a choice: it can either ignore the packet generating no response, or it can return a NULL packet with the ARQN bit set to NAK, i.e., a Negative Acknowledgement.

To test the CRC, the CRC on the data is decoded. If the packet fails the CRC, the packet is returned with a NAK. The number of bytes indicated in the payload header are looped back with a freshly calculated CRC.

To test FEC handling, the FEC is decoded when the packet's data is decoded. The FEC is then regenerated when the packet is regenerated for transmission.

By deliberately generating packets with various errors and analyzing the responses, a tester can exercise the FEC, CRC, HEC, ACK, and NAK behaviour of the device under test.

For devices with an HCI, the device can be put into loopback mode locally using the HCI command HCI_Write_Loopback_Mode command. The loopback mode can be checked with the HCI_Read_Loopback_Mode command. For devices without an HCI, loopback mode could be implemented via test points on the device's circuit board.

23.5 SUMMARY

Once samples of a product have passed through the Bluetooth qualification process, and through regulatory testing, they can go into production and be sold. A test mode is available which can be used for production line testing to ensure that the radio performance of real products match the samples which were put through qualification and regulatory test.

Because devices in test mode can violate regulations on the ISM band, it is important that devices cannot be accidentally put into test mode. Therefore, test mode must be activated both locally and by LMP commands over the air interface.

Transmitter tests can test the characteristics of the Bluetooth radio. Loopback tests can be used to check FEC, HEC, CRC, ACL, and NAK behaviour.

24

Qualification
and Type Approval

The Bluetooth qualification process ensures conformance to the Bluetooth specification. Only products passing the qualification process are permitted to use the Bluetooth brand. This will mean that consumers know that devices carrying the brand can be relied upon to work correctly.

The Bluetooth promoters (Ericsson in particular) have key patents on Bluetooth technology. License to use these patents is granted free to manufacturers whose products pass Bluetooth qualification procedures.

Because the core promoters own patents essential to implementing Bluetooth technology, and the Bluetooth SIG owns the Bluetooth trademark, it is possible for the Bluetooth promoters group to prosecute anybody labeling a product as Bluetooth without passing through qualification.

There are three levels of Bluetooth qualification testing:

- Qualification testing to ensure conformance to the Bluetooth core specification.
- Interoperability testing to ensure that devices work with one another at the profile level.
- Checking documentation to ensure it conforms to the Bluetooth brand book.

In addition, Bluetooth products will need regulatory type approval to ensure that their radios meet government regulations for devices using the Industrial, Scientific, and Medical (ISM) band.

This chapter begins by looking at the Bluetooth qualification process. It then goes on to briefly look at government regulatory testing.

24.1 BLUETOOTH QUALIFICATION

The Bluetooth qualification process ensures that products comply with the Bluetooth specification. Only products which pass the Bluetooth qualification process are entitled to use the free license to the patents required to implement Bluetooth wireless technology and to use the Bluetooth brand. By ensuring that products comply with the specification, the qualification process helps to ensure that Bluetooth products will work reliably and that they will work with other Bluetooth products.

The requirements for qualification are split into four categories:

- Bluetooth radio link requirements.
- Bluetooth protocol requirements.
- Bluetooth profile requirements.
- Bluetooth information requirements.

Passing the qualification tests does not excuse a product from regulatory type approval for the radio. Manufacturers must make sure that the radio is also put through the testing required by government regulations in the countries where it will be sold.

24.1.1 Organisational Structure

The SIG Regulatory Working Group TF2/TF1 defines the qualification process. This working group has defined a structure of organisations which administer Bluetooth qualification as shown in Figure 24–1.

Each of the different entities in Figure 24–1 fulfills a different function. These are as follows:

- SIG Regulatory Working Group TF2/TF1—Defines the qualification process.
- Bluetooth Qualification Review Board (BQRB)—Manages/reviews/improves the qualification process. Can give compliance waiver.
- Bluetooth Qualification Administrator (BQA)—Administers qualification program, approves testers, keeps records of approved products.
- Bluetooth Qualification Test Facility (BQTF)—Recognised test facility, delivers test plan and test reports, may be test house or manufacturer's in-house facility.
- Bluetooth Qualification Body (BQB)—Checks declarations and reviews test reports; may be test house or manufacturer's in-house facility.
- Bluetooth Technical Advisory Board (BTAB)—Forum for test/qualification problems and information exchange.

Between them, these entities carry out the Bluetooth qualification process and feed back information from testing and adopters, which enables the testing process to be continuously improved.

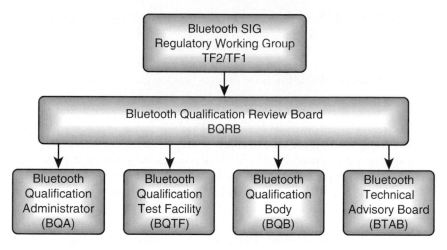

Figure 24–1   Bluetooth qualification bodies.

24.1.2   Qualification Process

Only Bluetooth adopters can get the Bluetooth license, so the first step in the qualification process is to become a Bluetooth adopter. This is just a matter of signing an adopter's agreement, which is available from *http://www.Bluetooth.com,* the Bluetooth Web site. Adopters can download the parts of the Bluetooth specification from the Web site, along with qualification program documents, which detail the tests that products will be put through during the Bluetooth qualification process.

Having become a Bluetooth adopter, a manufacturer then produces sample Bluetooth products, either by developing them in-house or by using bought in solutions. The sample products will be put through the Bluetooth qualification process.

The manufacturer must also produce an Implementation Conformance Statement (ICS). Basically, this is a document describing the features of the Bluetooth specification which the device supports. The Bluetooth Web site has template ICS documents for the various different Bluetooth profiles, so these just need to be filled in.

The manufacturer delivers the ICS and sample products to a Bluetooth Qualification Test Facility (BQTF). The test facility is an organisation which is capable of running the test suites to check that the product conforms to the Bluetooth specification. It could be an in-house facility, or it could be an external test house. Cetecom and 7 Layers were amongst the first test houses to become involved in the Bluetooth qualification program; more are joining the program. A list of Bluetooth Qualification Test Facilities is issued by the Bluetooth Qualification Review Board (BQRB).

If the BQTF is an external test facility, the manufacturer will have to provide documentation and may have to provide the test facility with additional products to enable the Bluetooth product to be tested. For example, a PCMCIA card would need to be installed in a computer, a LAP point would need to be attached to LAN equipment, and a GSM phone would need to be attached to GSM test facilities. Many test houses will be able to provide these additional test systems. But, ensuring that the test facilities have appropriate equipment is one of the criteria for choosing a BQTF.

The implementation conformance statement declares the features a product supports, so the BQTF tests these facilities against the latest test specifications. The BQTF then prepares a test report. If the product fails the tests, the manufacturer can fix problems and retest.

When the product passes the tests, the manufacturer can send an application to the Bluetooth Qualification Body (BQB). The BQB is a person authorized by the Bluetooth Qualification Review Board to check test reports and documentation. The manufacturer's application contains a description of the product and a signed statement declaring that the product complies with the Bluetooth specification. This declaration covers not just the core specification of Bluetooth wireless technology, but also the usage of the Bluetooth brand book.

When the Bluetooth Qualification Body approves the application, they give the manufacturer a qualified product notice, and list the product in the qualified product database.

Figure 24–2 summarises the process of getting a product through the Bluetooth qualification process.

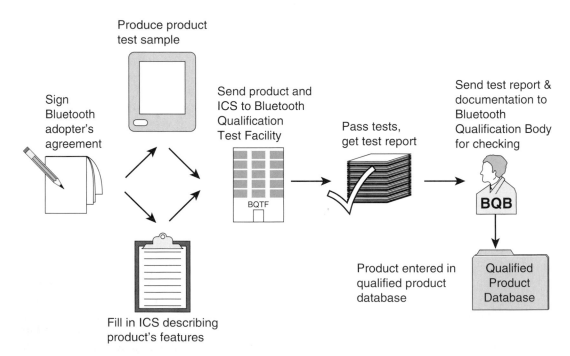

Figure 24–2   Process of getting a product into the qualified product database.

24.1.3 Waivers

Many Bluetooth products were in development as the specifications and test processes were still being written, so some early products deviated from the final specification slightly. To allow manufacturers to release these products without undergoing substantial redevelopment, the SIG introduced compliance waivers which allowed temporary deviation from the specification. These waivers ceased being granted in 2001, waivers which were granted are only valid for a limited period, so eventually all devices on sale will be fully compliant in all ways.

Development systems and demonstration systems are exempt from testing by a BQTF. This is because they will not be sold to consumers, so they will not adversely affect the Bluetooth brand by causing interoperability problems. In addition, it is recognized that development systems by their very nature may not have the same features as final products. This particularly applies to the early development systems which were being produced as the Bluetooth specification was being written. Such systems should still comply with the rules of the Bluetooth brand book, and it should be made clear when they are sold or demonstrated that they have not undergone qualification testing for compliance with the Bluetooth specification.

Although there is no requirement for full qualification testing, adopters with demonstration or development systems must file an application for Bluetooth product qualification. This application will be handled differently from a full product application: instead of qualification involving BQTF test reports, it is just based upon the adopter's declaration of compliance with the specification and brand book.

24.1.4 Test Documentation

Bluetooth adopters may download all the documentation relating to Bluetooth qualification from the Bluetooth Web site, *http://www.bluetooth.com.*

The first documents to consider are, of course, the parts of the Bluetooth specification. This is made up of three parts:

- Specification of the Bluetooth System Volume 1 core.
- Specification of the Bluetooth System Volume 2 profiles.
- The Bluetooth brand book.

A product must comply with all the relevant parts of the Bluetooth specification. The profiles clearly explain which parts of the core specification are relevant for each profile.

The Bluetooth brand book covers how the Bluetooth brand should be applied to products. This applies to marketing literature, identifying marks on products, packaging, and documentation. (This is why when a product has passed through qualification and its implementation of Bluetooth wireless technology has passed the qualification tests, its documentation must be submitted to the BQB along with the test reports.)

In addition to the Bluetooth specification, a range of documents relevant to Bluetooth qualification can be downloaded from the Bluetooth Web site:

- Bluetooth Qualification Program Reference Document—Describes the qualification process.
- Bluetooth test case reference list—Summary list of all tests.
- Bluetooth test specifications—These cover core specification and profiles.
- Implementation Conformance Statement (ICS)—Pro formas to fill in.
- IXIT proforma—A form to fill out for extra information needed to run tests on a particular product.
- BQTF checklist—List of things required to become a BQTF.
- BQTF application form—Form to submit to become a BQTF.
- BQB checklist—List of things required to become a BQB.
- BQB application form—Form to submit to become a BQB.
- Bluetooth Qualification Test Report (BQTR)—Template for report submitted to BQB.

The Bluetooth Qualification Program Reference Document describes the qualification process in detail. This document is reissued periodically as the qualification process matures.

The Bluetooth test case reference list is a reference document which contains a summary of all the test cases contained in the various Bluetooth test suites.

The Implementation Conformance Statement (ICS) is the statement which a manufacturer fills out to say that its product complies with the Bluetooth specification. A series of pro forma (template) Implementation Conformance Statements are available; these cover the different profiles and the different parts of the core specification. A manufacturer simply takes these and fills in the ones that are relevant to a product. There is also a summary ICS with check boxes to say which of the other ICS documents apply to a particular product.

IXIT stands for Implementation Extra Information for Testing. The IXIT details the parameters to be used in testing a Bluetooth IUT (Implementation Under Test) and the behaviour that can be triggered and observed. The IXIT is used with the ICS to make a test plan. IXITs come in two types: PIXITs, which are protocol IXITs, and profile IXITs. Both are needed to fully describe a product. The purpose of IXITs is to provide information about products in a standardized manner, so the SIG provides a standard pro forma (a form to be filled in), along with instructions on how to fill it in. An IXIT pro forma becomes an IXIT when it has been filled in correctly.

The Bluetooth test specifications detail the actual test cases that are carried out during the process of qualification. There are a series of test specifications, with different documents for the various parts of the core specifications and for each of the profiles. A BQTF uses the ICS to decide which of the test specifications should be run for a particular product. In addition to detailing tests to be run, the test specification documents explain the purposes of the tests.

The Bluetooth test specifications come in two formats. Informal test specifications are readable by humans and they include descriptions of tests and message sequence charts. A set of Test Vectors provide the formal test specifications and are intended for automating tests.

The Test Vectors are written in a language developed by ETSI called TTCN (Tree Tabular Combined Notation). TTCN is an ISO/ITU standard (ISO/IEC 964-3 and X.292).

TTCN uses ASN1 (Abstract Syntax Notation 1) to describe data structures such as the data trees found within SDP ASN.1 is an ISO/IEC standard: ISO/IEC 8824:1994. TTCN was designed to allow "black box" testing of communication protocols and services, so it is ideal for testing the Bluetooth protocol stack. The Bluetooth test vectors define test configurations, and points in the protocol stack where signals are injected and observed to test system behaviour.

The TTCN and ASN.1 are used to create Abstract Test Suites (ATSs). An ATS has the following parts:

- Overview—This contains indices for test groups, cases, suites, defaults, and exports. The overview also contains a test suite structure.
- Declarations—These are given in TTCN or ASN.1.
- Constraints—The values which any variables in the test may take, e.g., PDU values.
- Dynamic Part—These are the actual test cases, steps, and defaults. This part contains the core TTCN code, which is used to drive the tests.

The formal test specification ATSs may be used to automate testing of Bluetooth devices, and because TTCN is a standardised language, the same set of TTCN vectors can be used on several different test platforms.

There is a danger in adopting a set of automated test vectors to run on many different test systems: any errors in TTCN test vectors could cause serious delays in qualification, as the errors would affect all test systems at once. Because of this danger before release the test vectors themselves must be tested! To do this a test validation group runs new test vectors on more than one test platform and tests more than one implementation of the Bluetooth Protocol stack. Only if the test vector performs correctly on these systems does it become part of the formal qualification process.

The BQTF checklist is filled out by any organisation wishing to register as a Bluetooth Qualification Test Facility. It then submits a BQTF application form to the Bluetooth Qualification Administrator (BQA). If the application is successful, the BQA lists the new BQTF. The list of all BQTFs is available to Bluetooth adopters.

The BQB checklist is filled out by any person wishing to register as a Bluetooth Qualification Body. He or she then submits a BQB application form to the Bluetooth Qualification Administrator (BQA). If the application is successful, the BQA lists the new BQB. The list of all BQBs is available to Bluetooth adopters. Bluetooth Qualification Bodies on the BQA list are provided with information necessary to carry out their duties.

The Bluetooth Qualification Test Report (BQTR) is a pro forma for the report produced by the Bluetooth Qualification Test Facility (BQTF) after testing a product. Using a standardized form makes it easier for the BQTFs to produce test reports, and it also makes it easier for the BQBs to process test reports, thus speeding up the process of qualification.

In many ways, the core specification is ambiguous. The test documents are far more rigorous, and it is the test documents which determine whether a product will qualify to use the Bluetooth wireless technology and carry the Bluetooth brand. Therefore, anyone planning on producing a Bluetooth product should familiarise him- or herself with the Bluetooth qualification process and the Bluetooth test specifications, as well as the core specification.

24.1.5   Test Case Categories

There are four different test case categories which govern who can conduct a test and what evidence is required:

- Category A tests have to be conducted by a Bluetooth Qualified Test Facility (BQTF).
- Category B are tested by the manufacturer, who must submit evidence to a BQB that they have passed the test.
- Category C tests are self-certified by manufacturers, no evidence is required.
- Category D are informative, these may be new tests due to be introduced in full later on, or may be tests which have been found to have problems, which have been downgraded to category D whilst they are being corrected.

There are several requirements before a test case can become category A. First, a validated test system must be available. Validation involves a test house preparing a report on the system and a validation group considering whether the system adequately fulfills the requirements for testing. The test case itself must also be validated to ensure that it matches the specification. There must be more than one commercially available BQTF ready to offer the test. This requirement is to prevent one BQTF from gaining a monopoly. It means that there must be two BQTFs with validated test systems. Finally, the test must be approved by the BQRB. All of these requirements are to ensure that products are not asked to pass tests which are faulty in some way.

As a further safeguard, there are delays built into the system which slow down movement of tests between categories. For instance a new test must wait six months before it can be raised to category A (where BQTF testing is required), but a test which is in category B or C can be raised to category A with three months notice. This notice period ensures that a product doesn't get half way through testing and then suddenly has to pass new tests without notice. A full list of the notice periods required to move tests between categories is given in the Program Reference Document.

24.1.6   Samples for Testing

Testing is carried out on samples provided by the manufacturer. These samples may need to be special versions of the product produced especially for test purposes, so production of test systems should be planned into product development.

At least two samples are needed for conformance testing, and at least two samples are needed for radio regulatory testing. Generally, it is a good idea to have more samples available, as samples may be needed for debugging. If a product has different forms, then samples of each different implementation will be needed.

Special test versions of products may be needed because the testing process uses test interfaces to drive the system. Systems which do not have an HCI in the final product will need a Test Control Interface (TCI). The TCI is essentially the same as the HCI. A second Test Control Interface is used to drive the system at L2CAP level, and the air interface uses a wired antenna replacement, so a connector for this will be required.

Figure 24–3 illustrates how special interfaces may be needed. The extra test elements in the device under test at the right have lighter shading. Although the MMI is shown as connected to the tester, this will be driven by a test operator rather than by a piece of test equipment.

During testing of the various protocol layers, the DUT is connected to a tester, both by the wire replacing the air interface and by the HCI/TCI interfaces.

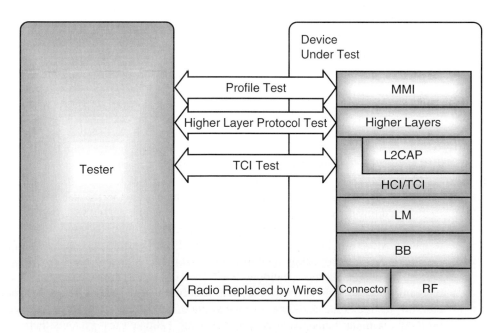

Figure 24–3   Test interfaces.

The higher layer protocol interface shown may be used when testing systems such as LAPs, where the device will need to be driven with data from a higher layer sitting above L2CAP.

The requirement for the various test interfaces means special development boards provided with the appropriate test hooks will have to be used as test samples. If the test samples are different from the final product, then the manufacturer will have to guarantee that the baseband, LM, and Logical Link Control and Adaptation are the same as the final product. If the product includes an HCI, then the manufacturer must also guarantee that it is the same as the final product.

Testing against a validated test system is the only way to verify conformance to the specification. Examples of test systems are Rhode & Schwarz's PTW60, or Cetecom's Byte. At the time of writing no test systems were fully validated, so interim test methods were in use. More test equipment is under development.

24.1.7   Component Qualification

Bluetooth components such as baseband ASICs, radio chips, and Bluetooth modules can be put through Bluetooth qualification. The components are built into an evaluation board, which provides suitable test interfaces and qualification tests appropriate to the component being tested.

Once the component is qualified, systems using that component would not need all tests rerun, but only those tests whose results might have been affected by the way the system was being used. So, for example, a single chip Bluetooth baseband implementing all functions below HCI would have to have tests above HCI rerun, and because radio performance varies with antenna siting, some radio tests would have to be rerun. Regulatory tests, such as FCC tests, would also have to be rerun on each new complete system.

Once a product has been Bluetooth-qualified, the qualification applies to a particular version of hardware and software. After qualification, all changes to a product must be recorded and reviewed by the BQB that issued its qualification certificate to check that it still qualifies. The BQB decides whether additional testing is required before the new version of the product is granted qualification.

24.2   BLUETOOTH INTEROPERABILITY TESTING

In addition to testing the protocol stack, the implementation of the Bluetooth profiles has to be tested to ensure that products implementing the same profile will interoperate.

The Generic Access Profile is mandatory for all Bluetooth devices, so this must be tested. In addition, all other profiles implemented will be tested.

Ericsson is producing reference implementations of Bluetooth known as "blue units". These are effectively calibrated reference Ericsson Bluetooth developer's kits. The blue units are available to test houses that qualify as BQTFs and will be used for interoperability testing. Blue units are an intermediate step towards full testing. Once the full protocol stack can be tested at category A using validated test systems there will be no need for Blue Unit testing.

Profile testing is done against other devices supporting the same profile(s). Designated Profile Interoperability Testers (DPITS) can be proposed to form standard devices which can be used for testing. At the time of writing there are no registered DPITS and testing of profiles is mostly carried out at unplugfests (see below), although some test houses maintain stocks of devices for informal interoperability testing.

Once interoperability testing has been peformed, products may be sold with a statement on the box saying which profiles are supported and which devices interoperation tests have been carried out with. It is expected that certain devices will emerge as standards for interoperation tests.

Early products are being prepared for release before the full Bluetooth qualification process is in place, so the SIG has organised a series of events where manufacturers can gather and test early versions of products to ensure they will interoperate. Similar events have been organised for other new communications protocols; for example, the ATM forum had plugfests where early ATM switches were tested against one another. Because Bluetooth devices do not need wired connections, the interoperability events for Bluetooth are known as unplugfests, or unplug parties.

Testing at unplugfests can be done at several levels:

- Radio-level interoperability.
- Protocol-level interoperability.
- Profile-level interoperability.

Test documents are provided for unplugfests. These specify what features are required to attend and how features will be tested. There have been criticisms of these as artificial—that they introduce special service records for test purposes. This entails extra work for the participants as test service records will not be present in the final products and are not necessary for qualification. However, they do have advantages, because otherwise each profile would have its own different service record, and testing would be more difficult.

Because many manufacturers are sensitive about exposing early prototypes of products, the unplug fests happen behind closed doors, and all details of the results are confidential.

24.3   REGULATORY-TYPE APPROVAL

Because Bluetooth devices have radios that operate in the ISM band, they must pass the regulatory tests of the countries in which they are sold. There are different national and international regulations, each with its own set of tests, which ones have to be passed will depend upon where a product is going to be sold. It is illegal to use radio devices which have not passed the relevant regulatory tests.

Regulatory-type approval is a complex business. Various companies called test houses exist which will help manufacturers to get through type approval for the countries in which they plan to sell their products. Cetecom and 7 Layers were two of the first test houses to offer Bluetooth qualification testing. Both also help manufacturers to get through government regulatory testing.

In some countries, it may not be possible to get regulatory-type approval for Bluetooth devices. For instance, at the time of writing, it was not clear as to whether Egypt and Israel were going to allow Bluetooth devices to be used.

Bluetooth radios operating in the ISM band for Europe and America will need testing to ETS 300-328, ETS 300-826, and FCC§15. Different countries may have other regulatory tests.

24.3.1   Costs

Every test house will have its own scale of charges, and differences between products will mean that different products will cost different amounts to put through testing. Regulatory-type approval testing to ETS 300-328, ETS 300-826, and FCC§15 will probably take around three days assuming that everything goes to plan. Obviously, if problems are found with the radio, then rework and retest will add to time and expense.

Most test houses will charge for Bluetooth conformance testing of early products at an hourly rate. The radio and baseband layer will take at least two days to test, and protocol testing at least another two days. Once fully automated test systems are available testing should speed up.

Bluetooth interoperability testing will depend upon the number of profiles being tested, and the number of devices interoperated with. It will probably take at least two hours per profile, per device. Once again, when automated testing is in place, testing times should diminish, but many devices will require manual intervention at the Man Machine Interface which will prevent complete automation of tests.

Experience suggests that the main cost in qualification and type approval is not the test itself, but the need for rework and retest as the test processes uncover problems with the product which were not detected during development.

24.4   SUMMARY

The Bluetooth qualification program checks that products conform to the Bluetooth specification.

To use the Bluetooth brand, and to take advantage of a free license to the patents needed to implement Bluetooth wireless technology, adopters' products must first pass through the Bluetooth qualification program.

Interoperability tests must also be carried out to check that Bluetooth devices correctly implement the Bluetooth profiles and can interwork with other devices implementing the same profiles. Devices can then be sold with a statement of which profiles they support so that it is perfectly clear to consumers which products will work together.

To legally use ISM band radios, Bluetooth products must also pass regulatory tests, which check that their radios meet government regulations. Different countries may have different regulatory tests for radios.

PART 5

BLUETOOTH
IN CONTEXT

25

Implementation

25.1 INTRODUCTION

This chapter will consider the various issues related to implementing the Bluetooth specification in real products. There are many conflicting design issues, tradeoffs, and the usual cost vs. performance vs. time to market problems which face any product development exercise. However, Bluetooth seems to face a larger and more bewildering array of such issues than most new technologies. This is due—in part—to the sudden explosion in interest from both suppliers and users of the technology and also to the technology itself and the overriding need for low cost and "out of the box experience," which Bluetooth savvy people like to refer to. That is, Bluetooth-enabled products absolutely have to work reliably and seamlessly with no special configuration straight out of the box.

We start by considering the partitioning between hardware and software, and the types of engines which might be used to run software—i.e., microcontroller, DSP, RISC, or CISC. We then look at the various system design choices—i.e., one silicon device or two silicon devices and some key technical considerations—i.e., clock frequencies and silicon processes. We consider the radio design issues and finally the option of purchasing Bluetooth technology as an Intellectual Property (IP) core to add to an existing product development.

Although originally thought by many to be a relatively straightforward and simple system to implement, Bluetooth has proved to be more complex, especially if one wishes to realise a full implementation of the specification in an optimal way. Many developers have been working on Bluetooth solutions since 1998 with sizable teams of hardware and software engineers. The Bluetooth protocol stack is a complex multithreaded and multi-layered piece of real time software, while the lower layer hardware component requires carefully designed autonomous state control and timebase management with a keen focus on power and cost optimisation.

Bluetooth is clearly not a simple system to implement. Though it is fair to say that if one only requires a point-to-point, low bandwidth link, perhaps suitable for a data synchronisation application, then a greatly reduced Bluetooth implementation can be much more straightforward. However, since the majority of applications end up requiring most Bluetooth features, the task soon scales upward.

The key tradeoffs to be addressed in successful Bluetooth system design are summarised below, and in common with most tradeoffs, there is neither a right nor a wrong answer. In this chapter, we aim to highlight these issues and illustrate the different trade-offs one can make:

- Software vs. hardware partitioning.
- Single-chip vs. digital part + RF part.
- Software partitioning between embedded MCU and the host.
- Which profiles to support.

We also discuss how it is possible through the right design choices to meet the commonly highlighted target parameters for a Bluetooth-enabled product:

- $5 additional cost to the Bill Of Materials (BOM).
- Length of autonomy—many days on one charge: 10s µA Standby, 10s mA Active.
- Form factor—space for only one or two silicon packages.
- Seamless and easy Out Of Box Experience (OOBE).

25.2   SYSTEM PARTITIONING

There are a great many ways of incorporating Bluetooth technology into a product. Early Bluetooth solutions adopted a simple add-on strategy using bought-in modules connecting to an existing product. The cellular handset market is an obvious example of this, and three common options are depicted in Figure 25–1. The first diagram shows the ubiquitous Bluetooth dongle, requiring no special support in the handset; the second shows a Bluetooth-enabled battery module requiring some handset support; and the third example depicts the most sustainable option for anything other than a quick market entry demonstrator, the snap-in or slide-in card.

This strategy is the lowest risk and shortest time to market, but of course, it has the highest cost, largest form factor and is the least integrated and seamless. An evolutionary path exists, where the module may be decomposed and absorbed into the product, and this

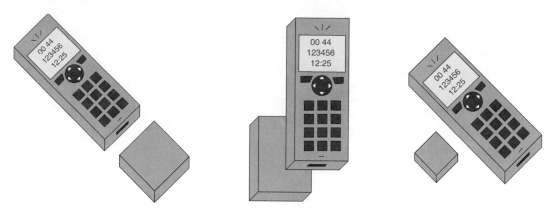

Figure 25–1   Handset add-on options.

is the likely scenario for handsets in particular. First, a complete module may be integrated onto the PCB. For major cost savings, the components themselves may be integrated onto the PCB using, for example, an RF module and separate baseband ASIC, followed by integration of the RF device and associated circuitry. At this point, there are several choices: absorb the Bluetooth digital part (baseband and MCU) into the system ASIC and add a simple RF device, or integrate the RF and digital parts together.

It is interesting to note that as the Bluetooth market takes off at the time of this second edition, we are seeing a distinct move away from the dongle or plug-in module solutions in favour of PCB level integration. As the volumes rise, this is inevitable in order to reduce the cost to consumer levels.

25.2.1   Software vs. Hardware

The block diagram in Figure 25–2 shows once again the familiar protocol stack diagram. This time we are particularly interested in the interfaces between the various parts of the stack. To investigate the optimum partition between hardware and software, we must understand the requirements of each of the constituent parts.

The radio is, of course, unlikely to be implemented in anything other than hardware for some time yet. The baseband will need an element of hardware to at least control the basic on-air symbol timing and radio-enable strobes (RxOn, TxOn, SynthOn, etc.). However, many of the baseband operations such as bit stream processing, encryption, and frequency hop calculation are quite suitable for implementation on a Digital Signal Processor (DSP), if not on a MicroController Unit (MCU). Although modern MCUs such as the ARM7 are reasonably well-equipped in this area, taken as a whole, the Baseband Layer represents a sizable task if implemented on a processor, requiring a large number of "processor MIPS".

The most interesting area for partitioning is between the Baseband Layer and link control level. This requires a lot of decision making and context switching between links, but it is extremely time critical to get the right information programmed into the radio in time to be active on the next slot. We saw in the earlier link control chapter how the LC state machine had to switch context many times and often in a very short space of time.

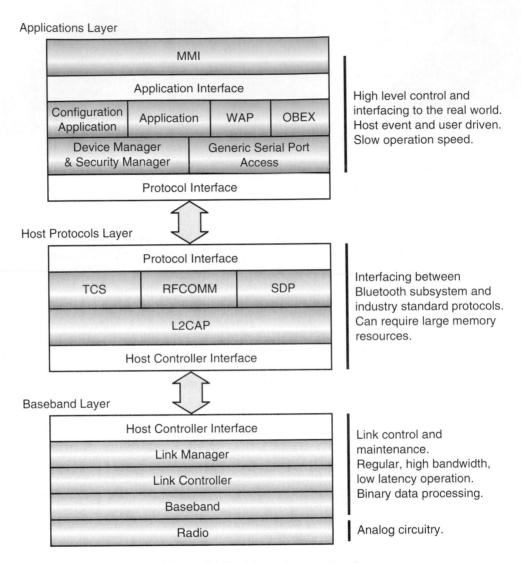

Figure 25–2 Bluetooth protocol stack.

The next layer up the stack, the LM, is relatively time independent, with most LMP operations being self-timed and carried out across several time slots. The HCI is a well-defined part of the specification and therefore a sensible place to make a natural break in the stack. HCI commands are available for link establishment and clearing down and controlling the various aspects of Bluetooth, such as audio and encryption. The defined HCI transports provide a standard way of physically interconnecting two devices with an HCI interface, and indeed, the specification has been written with this split between the Bluetooth module and the host device in mind.

The diagram attaches some arbitrary but useful names to the separate parts of the stack. The Baseband Layer is the part which exhibits time criticality, requiring knowledge of Bluetooth slot timing and is very bit-operation intensive. As such, it is typically part of the embedded Bluetooth entity which would reside in a Bluetooth module. The Host Protocols Layer is so called as it would most commonly reside on a host, such as a PC or handset. This provides an interface between Bluetooth HCI to a higher layer standard, together with data segmentation and re-assembly. This layer is not time critical, but can have large buffering requirements and be very memory intensive if dealing with large host data packets. As such, it may not really sit well alongside the lower layers in a single, embedded CPU. The Applications Layer consists of the high-level management entities and user interface, which interface closely with the Host Protocols Layer.

25.2.1.1 Software Considerations.   It is useful to provide an indication of the magnitude of the baseband layer task. Assuming a full software implementation of LC, LM and HCI running on a RISC MCU, then a fully occupied system (multiple slaves, SCO links, Scan and scatternet operation) would require around 10 to 15 RISC MIPS.[1] This means that at worst case system loading, an embedded RISC MCU such as the ARM7 running at 20 MHz will be fully occupied running the baseband layer protocols. Placing some or all of the LC state control in hardware will greatly ease the burden on the processor, but at the expense of increased risk and decreased flexibility.

The complexity of the stack makes use of a high-level language such as C and some kind of Real-Time Operating System (RTOS) essential to provide the necessary interprocess communication, resource scheduling, and debug facilities. As explained below, latency is so critical for Bluetooth, as is footprint (i.e., memory usage, etc.), that the choice of RTOS is another critical factor. Increasing processor speed and performance cannot unfortunately be relied upon to ease the situation. As for most Bluetooth applications, ultra-low power operation and low cost are paramount. These are also strong reasons why a DSP implementation is not generally attractive, others being that most of the stack requires operating system support, context switching, and large address range operation, all of which are not generally available from a DSP.

The timing diagram in Figure 25–3 shows how critical a task the link controller is. The diagram shows the end of a receive packet protruding into the current slot. The worst case figure given is that for an ID packet received in the second half of the slot ($312 + 72$ μs). This is, of course, a specific case during page, inquiry, or unparking. However, in an ordinary connection, the worst case packet end is only slightly better at 376 μs for a DM3. The transmission itself could be offset by up to 10 μs and still be successful due to the uncertainty window. Following reception, the baseband must notify the LC (typically via an interrupt), which must then examine the relevant status information to ascertain what to do in the next slot. Among the various decisions to be taken are:

---

[1]Millions of Instructions Per Second, where each instruction is a simple operation such as is typical in a Reduced Instruction Set Computer-type MCU.

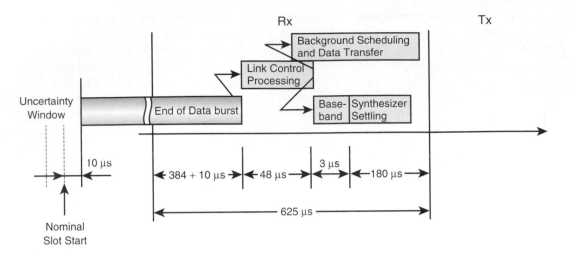

Figure 25–3 Link controller time criticality.

- Was the previous Tx successful and can new data be transferred to the Tx buffer?
- More importantly, was the packet just received something unexpected—an LMP control message overriding what should perhaps have been an SCO slot?

This latter example will most definitely alter what the device now does in the very next slot. The LC processing must complete and program the baseband and radio in enough time to allow the radio to be ready for the next slot. Since the frequency hop will depend directly on the baseband state, and this will depend on the previous packet received, the LC has only $625 - 180 - 384 - 10 = 51$ μs to do this—a very short space of time, especially if it is operating as an Interrupt Service Routine (ISR) on an MCU also running a RTOS.

The diagram allocates a further 3 μs to the baseband to allow for any setup or pre-clocking required, such as buffer switching or synthesizer data serialization and 180 μs to the channel synthesizer for frequency settling. Clearly, reducing the synthesizer's settling time can increase the LC time. However, commercial solutions are in the range 150 to 200 μs, and 180 μs is fairly typical, so there is a limited degree of flexibility here. A faster processor will "cram in" more processing within this critical window, although another constraint exists: the lower priority background task of scheduling the other links, other LC tasks, and transferring data into and out of the baseband. This task is difficult to speed up as it is only driven by the end of the Rx or Tx burst and will probably be active for most of the slot. Again, it must complete before the next Tx or Rx begins.

25.2.1.2 Hardware Considerations. Figure 25–4 shows an example baseband system block diagram. Although similar to the diagram in the baseband chapter, it includes an interface to the MCU, which executes the protocol stack software. This would typically comprise a register set, interrupt control logic, and probably a Direct Memory

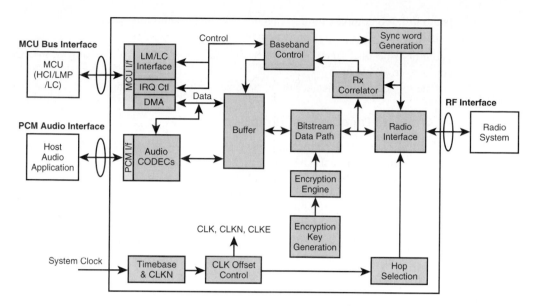

Figure 25–4   Typical baseband block diagram.

Access (DMA) engine to provide faster[2] memory transfers to and from the buffer memory. The buffer memory itself is shown as one block since this is more area efficient and thus cost efficient in silicon terms.

The "Baseband Control" block is so named because this may contain some or all of the link control protocol and state machine. In some implementations, this consists of a basic state machine driven by a software link control task. The advantage of this is lower risk, less complex hardware, and more flexibility, at the expense of a heavily occupied MCU. At the other extreme, some implementations place most or all of the link control task in this control block. This has the advantage of using much less of the MCU, which is running the remainder of the stack; however, at the expense of a very large silicon area and with much greater risk and less flexibility.

Several of the blocks shown may be implemented in software, particularly if the MCU is actually a DSP device. The prime candidates would be the audio CODECs, bitstream processing, and hop selection, although the on-air data rate would need to be maintained and/or additional FIFO buffering might be required.

Some of the questions to address in getting the software/hardware partition right are listed below:

- Is the task too fast to be carried out by software?
- Is the task very bit-intensive and not byte/word-oriented?

---

[2]Most processors will take more than several cycles to first read a memory location, then write to another, increment a counter and loop. This all makes the time criticality worse, whereas a DMA engine will typically transfer a complete word in one or maybe two cycles.

- Is the task too complex to make a hardware implementation efficient?
  —In silicon area or in power consumption?
- Is the task too ill-defined or complex such that the risk of "hard-wiring" it into silicon is excessively high?
  —Due to the risk of mistakes or of the specification itself changing?

25.2.2   Where to Run the Host Protocols

As discussed already, if we implement the LC protocol in software and require a full Bluetooth system, we may not have much processing bandwidth left for the higher layers if we are using a small, low-power, embedded processor, such as the ARM7, Hitachi H8, embedded Power PC, or Motorola Dragonball, to name but a few. We could adopt a much higher performance MCU such as the ARM9, Hitachi SH, or similar, but these do not *currently*[3] fit the target low-power or cost parameters we listed above.

The following numbers are just lower and upper bounds gleaned from an overview of the various solutions and partitions currently on the market and serve to illustrate the issues driving the question of partitioning. The actual point in the range, especially the baseband end, depends on the exact partitioning used. For example, the Baseband CPU can also be handling some of the low level Baseband control and Bitstream data processing in order to reduce associated hardware gate count. It is also important to note that although easy to grasp, such MIPS estimates can be dangerous, as they give no indication of latency or instantaneous peak load requirements.

Baseband Layer (Some Baseband functions, LC, LM and HCI):   8 - 12 MIPS

Host Protocols Layer (HCI, L2CAP, RFCOMM, SDP):   1 - 2 MIPS

The Applications Layer requirements are very difficult to quantify, as they depend largely on the other protocols and/or services defined by the relevant profile. A headset, for example, will impose a minor additional processor load, while a LAN access point with IP routing and large Segmentation and Reassembly (SAR) requirements will exhibit significant additional processor loading.

As each of the embedded low-power processors listed above provides around 10 to 30 MIPS with acceptable power consumption, the stack may just be squeezed into one such CPU running at its maximum performance level. However, it is unlikely that any resource will be left to run any interesting applications in. The latency issues alone make integration of any other real-time system (especially a cellular telephony standard like GSM) a very difficult exercise requiring much more than just the sum of the respective MIPS!

One solution to this is to run different parts of the stack on different processors. Figure 25–5 shows three different ways of splitting the stack for different applications with different requirements.

---

[3]But naturally, this will change. Over the next few years, CPU performance and power efficiency will increase dramatically, facilitating a complete solution in one processor, though there are other reasons for optimising the partitioning as described here.

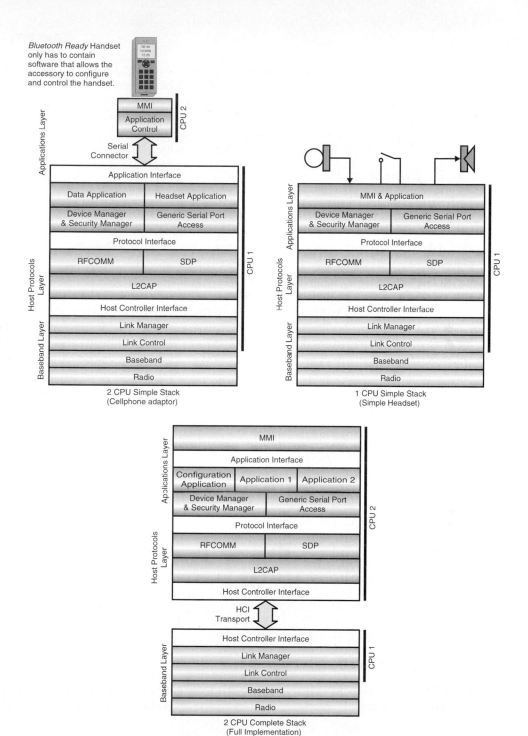

Figure 25–5 Different stack splits.

The first is the classic handset add-on solution. A complete Bluetooth subsystem is implemented in the add-on; however, since only the headset and dialup profiles with point to point connectivity are required, the entire stack up to the application level can be run on one CPU. The L2CAP task, which requires much buffering for Segmentation And Reassembly (SAR), is greatly simplified in this case, and the data bandwidth required is quite low (14.4 kb/s for GSM). The host processor in the phone, however, will require some MMI and control application to interface with the Bluetooth stack. This is relatively straightforward and easily implemented alongside the GSM stack since it has no real-time components.

The second example is a typical headset with only a microphone and switch as inputs and a speaker as output. Since the L2CAP, SDP, and RFCOMM components are minimal for such a simple profile, they are easily implemented all together in one CPU. Only one link is likely and, quite probably, multislot packets will not be required. In fact, for an optimal solution, the entire Host Protocols and Applications Layers may be integrated into one "headset" application program.

Finally, the third example is of a complete, fully featured stack where the Baseband Layer resides in one embedded CPU, but since this does not have sufficient spare resource, the Host and Application Layers are run on the host CPU. This represents the case in a PC where the HCI USB transport might be used to provide a clean industry-standard interface to many other devices and systems and is the reason for the natural break in the stack at the HCI. The upper layers are then run on the PC, PDA, or Smartphone, where they happily reside alongside the myriad of other software tasks running on a relatively high-performance CPU.

25.3 HARDWARE INTEGRATION OPTIONS

Having decided on where to split the software tasks, we must still decide on the physical partitioning of the system. We need an MCU and associated memory to run the higher layers, a baseband logic core, and a radio system. Typically, we will embed the MCU and memory within the same silicon Application-Specific Integrated Circuit (ASIC), Figure 25–6, to create a baseband to the HCI core with an embedded CPU running the stack up to the HCI and add a separate RF transceiver device. However, we may instead wish to use an existing host MCU.[4] Figure 25–7 shows such a partition where the baseband core sits alongside the radio system as a Bluetooth transceiver device with a standard processor bus interface. However, this latter example is difficult to realise due to RF/digital integration issues, which we will look at in the section on the single-chip solution.

25.3.1 Two-Chip Solution

At present, commercially available two-chip solutions revolve around separation of the RF from the baseband, since the RF function is typically implemented in BiCMOS

---

[4]Providing one is available with enough residual resource and performance, or perhaps we have implemented much of the critical LC protocol in the baseband logic core.

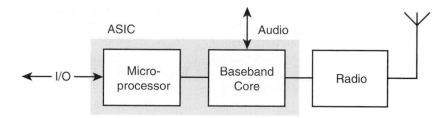

Figure 25–6   Two-chip solution: baseband to HCI + radio transceiver.

(slightly larger area and more expensive, but easily realises the required RF performance) and the digital part in CMOS (smaller, cheaper, lower power, but without the performance necessary for RF). The interface to the digital part is then direct PCM and HCI via a high speed UART and / or USB transport.

The BlueRF initiative is of major importance here since a standardised interface between the baseband / LC device and RF device will drive the market for such parts immensely due to the multiple sourcing flexibility it provides. Many RF device manufacturers are claiming BlueRF support, and the SIG looks set to adopt this as the industry standard Bluetooth RF interface. This allows different solutions to be easily used from various suppliers featuring different performance/cost tradeoffs and features with a standard interface. Furthermore, one product can be specified with several different radio options, as required.

25.3.2   Single-Chip Solution

The holy grail of Bluetooth implementations is the so-called single-chip solution, which is illustrated in Figure 25–8. Here the digital baseband to HCI part and radio are all integrated into one device. This device may also feature support for applications, such as headset circuitry and the entire stack required for that profile as depicted in Figure 25–5.

Figure 25–9 shows an example of how a single-chip device could be laid out. The key issue is the integration of RF onto the same die as the digital circuitry. Two problems must be overcome:

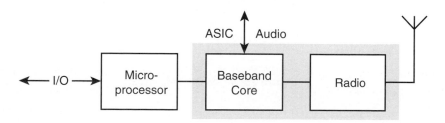

Figure 25–7   Two-chip solution: micro + baseband and radio transceiver.

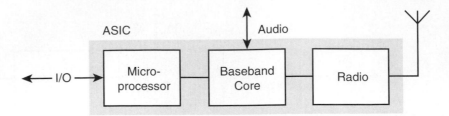

Figure 25–8   Single-chip solution.

- CMOS is the only cost effective option for the baseband (a large digital system). The standard CMOS process must be improved to provide the necessary low noise and high Ft[5] (Transition Frequency) required for RF circuitry. Also, additional silicon processing (typically only one further polysilicon layer) must be added to facilitate the construction of passive components such as capacitors.
- Interference and noise injection from the digital circuitry into the RF via the silicon substrate must be prevented.

The advantages of a single-chip solution are reduced cost, smallest footprint, and an "off the shelf" solution with less knowledge or design-in of RF circuitry required. Manufacturers provide reference designs, following these gives the simplest route to a qualified

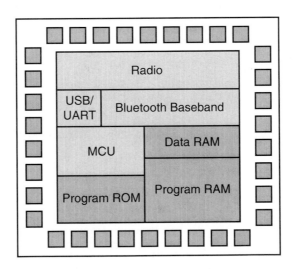

Figure 25–9   Single-chip layout.

[5]Transition Frequency (Ft) is the linear bandwidth of operation provided by the transistors. It defines the frequency performance of a process. For a 2.5GHz RF transceiver, a minimum Ft of 25GHz is necessary.

Figure 25–10   Single-chip device (Courtesy of CSR).

product. (Implementers who lack in depth radio experience should take great care when using reference designs, as even changing the source of a component to substitute one which is apparently equivalent can subtly alter characteristics so that system behaviour changes.)

There are some disadvantages of single chip solutions. Less RF flexibility is possible, although it is possible to add an external PA for +20 dBm operation. There are limited possibilities to gain access to the processor, although chips such as the one illustrated in Figure 25–10 can have user applications added, the memory and interfaces available are limited. Finally, no further integration into a system ASIC is possible.

Optimised RF processes, such as BiCMOS, are not far behind digital CMOS processes in size and cost; especially RF capable CMOS. So, assuming similar volumes for RF only devices and integrated single-chip devices, an RF only device may allow a lower footprint and cost implementation where integration of the digital baseband circuitry into a larger scale System On Chip (SOC) ASIC is possible, along with other system blocks, as shown in Figure 25–11.

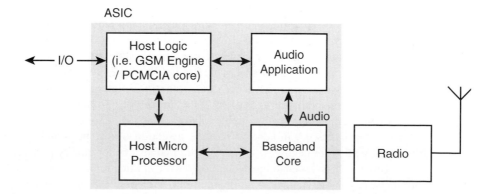

Figure 25–11   Fully embedded solution: SOC ASIC + radio transceiver.

25.3.3   Fully Embedded Solution

This approach is ideal for complex products such as digital cameras, cellular handsets, PDAs, game pads, etc. where a large-scale ASIC is used to integrate the system-level block functions together. The addition of a small RF transceiver is all that is required on the PCB, together with a handful of passive devices. This of course also provides us with the same RF advantages of the two-chip solution and allows Bluetooth to be added as a PCB option in manufacture (albeit with some overhead in the SOC ASIC).

With time, the risks and additional cost associated with integrating the RF part will be reduced. However, there will always be advantages attached to the separate radio transceiver solution for certain applications such as the opportunity to integrate digital circuitry into an SOC ASIC, the flexibility of RF supply, and the possibility of higher performance RF on better silicon processes than is possible with the single-chip solution. As is usually the case, there is no one right answer!

25.4   BLUETOOTH AS AN IP CORE

We now consider an extension to the SOC solution presented above, that is, inclusion of a third-party-supplied Bluetooth core. The opportunity to be in at the beginning and the sheer size of market predictions for Bluetooth have attracted a number of companies into the field of Intellectual Property (IP) design and licensing. As described at the beginning of this chapter, the development effort, and in particular, the elapsed time demanded to produce a Bluetooth solution are sufficient to make the cost and time to market issues related to licensing a Bluetooth IP solution a very attractive proposition indeed.

There are several suppliers of such products, each with a different background, product partitioning, feature set, and business model. Indeed, the size of the potential market seems to encourage discussion and to some extent cooperation among what is likely to become a very competitive sector of the marketplace.

25.4.1   Why IP?

The advantages of adopting an IP solution for any new technology development are reduced time to market, higher levels of integration through SOC design, and a very low Bill Of Materials (BOM) as the cost is reduced to the additional silicon area only. It is important, however, to recognize that some form of license fee will be payable.

The IP supplier should warrant the core to the Bluetooth specification, and through some form of maintenance agreement, maintain the design and supply updates and improvements both as the specification evolves and as the supplier improves its product. In addition, the licensee will benefit from the detection of any bugs and inconsistencies in the core by all other licensees, so they should realise a better quality product over time.

Bluetooth is an enabling technology with applications across a whole variety of products. A great advantage of an IP solution is the possibility to reuse the one core many times, realising new product solutions quickly and easily. Maintenance of the core technology is centralised, with minor variants to the central design easily made and then usually only involving the external interfaces. The increased volume of several product lines combined also facilitates amortisation of the license fees across what is now a very large volume of units.

25.4.2   What Are the Issues?

There are some risks attached to such a solution. Any "bought in" design must be integrated within the design team, the tool environment, and the company methodologies. Dealing with another organisation as an IP supplier adds management and logistical issues. The question of quality and functionality of the supplied core is also important, as is how problems or bugs get dealt with and fixed.

Any IP core must—just like Bluetooth itself—be "Plug & Play". The supplied core must be complete and ready to use. Design transfer, support and training, and documentation are important. The use of generic or easily redesignable interfaces is also important, as each system's requirements are different. The core must be capable of integrating into the SOC with a minimum of effort to deliver the promised fast time to market and low risk.

Confidence factor is another key issue, as licensees need to be convinced of success. This will probably be provided by demonstrator kits, reference designs, and ultimately, design-win examples.

If an organisation is going to buy source code, they have the right to expect a quality product in both form and function, so the quality of coding style and documentation is arguably even more important than for an internal development. After all, someone else is going to have to pick up the code and work with it. Some kind of warranty will be expected, and in most cases, suppliers guarantee conformance to the latest version of the Bluetooth specification.

The design itself must be able to cater to all possible requirements of the various customers who will use it while meeting the cost needs of the lower specified products, so a full implementation is probably important. This is a major area where suppliers must work hard to differentiate themselves—providing services and/or solutions to meet the *exact* needs of each customer.

25.4.3   Source Code Supply

A complete solution is essential. This should comprise a full design hierarchy of well-documented code following a consistent style guide, a full documentation suite at both the module and system level, and a full set of compile and (for hardware) synthesis scripts, including reference constraints for specific processes. The design should also be supplied with a set of module-level test benches where appropriate and a suite of system verification test benches with accompanying reference data to validate the major areas of functionality, such as inquiry, paging, and all packet types used in connection, etc.

The baseband is most likely to be supplied as Register Transfer Level (RTL) VHDL, or Verilog code, and the protocol stack software as portable ANSI C code. Both of these are industry-standard, portable design formats.

25.4.3.1 Baseband Core. The design must be "tool-friendly" and well structured. Automatic Test Pattern Generation (ATPG) tools and synthesis tools require that certain design rules have been followed to deliver good results. A modular design approach provides easy redesign for specific interface requirements and resizing of the memory requirements and silicon area if certain features are not required, such as encryption, for example. This might include porting of the design to support a different MCU, radio, or audio subsystem.

Subsidiary functions may be useful if included, such as MCU peripherals, audio circuitry, and LPO control circuitry to remove the need for additional components, i.e., "just add MCU and memory!" If the supplier is a "one-stop shop", also supplying the complete software stack, then different protocol software/baseband partitioning may be possible, allowing MCU resource vs. performance to be traded for specific implementations.

25.4.3.2 Protocol Stack Software. Again, modular and well-structured code is important. The choice of RTOS is also very important, particularly as in most cases, the licensee will be looking to add their own code and so they will either wish to reuse their existing choice of RTOS or will be adopting the IP vendor's choice. For these reasons, it is advantageous if the software IP is written to use a Generic Kernel Interface (GKI), as shown in Figure 25–12. This itself is a difficult exercise to get right as we now have an RTOS and a thin API layer above it, which risks increasing the software load and latency issues. However, if implemented well, there are many benefits, such as:

- Portability to different RTOSs by porting only the GKI and simply recompiling the stack.

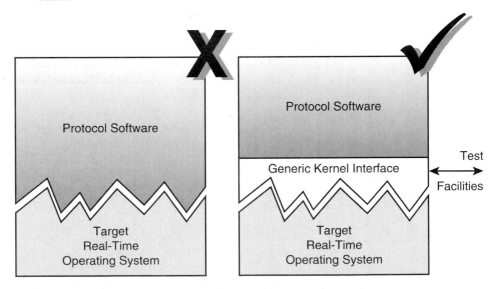

Figure 25–12   Generic kernel interface (Courtesy of TTP Communications).

- A common and reusable API presented to the stack (and any application) software.
- Integrated test features built into the GKI, which aid third-party integration and testing.

25.4.4   The Radio

A generic solution must support or be easily configurable to support all interfaces required by the various licensees. The radio is where this is most manifest as there are a number of different ways of interfacing to the radio and a number of different radio solutions available. Everyone has their own preferred radio solution based on different requirements and commercial pressures. Given the plethora of choices and interface options, a clean generic interface that easily facilitates redesign is the most flexible solution. A "soft" or reprogrammable interface will support some options, but there really are too many emerging to make this generally viable. Since Bluetooth RF requirements are not onerous with a binary digital interface and simple channel synthesiser programming, a simple interface can be easily retargeted with an optimal implementation each time.

The BlueRF initiative will have a strong positive influence on the use of IP solutions in the same way as described in section 25.3.1. Having procured an IP baseband and protocol stack solution, the remaining part of the puzzle—the RF—which is not easily integrated onto the same silicon anyway, will be available from many different suppliers with a standard interface to the supplied IP core.

25.4.5   Reference Designs

Turning the supplied IP into a real product is where the challenge lies. If the IP option is to prove advantageous in the long run, then the route to a product has to be rapid, easy, and low in risk. A key way for an IP vendor to enable this is to provide a "worked example" of the IP in the form of a reference design. Of course, a specific implementation will not be appropriate for all system solutions, but a good, well-thought out reference design or family of reference designs should be useful as a basis for the licensee's system design, and should greatly speed the product development cycle.

The reference design should be well proven, and indeed, will probably double as a technology proving platform and a sales and demonstrator tool. A well-designed and fully functional demonstrator will build immense confidence and will allow preconformance testing on the IP core itself, leading to possible precertification.

However, to be useful, it must not impose artificial constraints on a customer's product design, such as locking a designer into using a specific interface device or MCU simply because that's what the reference design uses and the IP solution has been designed to work with. A further risk is that adopting the reference design limits the possibility of product differentiation, although this may be provided by the MMI or application software design. In any case, a tradeoff may usefully be made here between product differentiation and time to market.

Figure 25–13 shows a typical Bluetooth reference platform. This uses a standalone ARM7-based MCU, a Xilinx Virtex high-performance FPGA containing the baseband IP

Figure 25–13   Bluetooth evaluation board (Courtesy of TTP Communications).

core, and FLASH ROM containing the protocol stack software IP. This particular board also incorporates an MMI control board for standalone use.

25.4.6   Design Services

Major reasons for adopting an IP solution are time to market, resource shortages, and risk reduction. It is therefore valid to ask, "Why not outsource the whole Bluetooth subsystem, including modifications to the IP?" Indeed, the best people to modify the code and work with it are those that designed it in the first place. A common scenario is that a company wishes to absorb the technology themselves over time, but at least the first generation products need to be brought to market quickly and risk free, even if they are less differentiated and more costly. It is, therefore, quite common that an IP vendor will be asked to supply services to go with the IP. In fact, some suppliers only supply the IP as part of an overall design services package.

These services are likely to include modifications to the core (especially to the system interfaces), porting of the software to a different MCU, baseband synthesis to the customer's chosen ASIC library including production test and ATPG generation, and assistance with production test and verification, or working sample approval. Finally, when ready, the vendor must supply sufficient training and design transfer support to ensure that customers are able to modify and maintain the code themselves when or if they wish to.

It is an interesting paradox that often the licensee wants to own the solution but does not want to modify and maintain it. The reassurance of knowing that the designer is on hand as required is very valuable indeed!

25.5   ASIC PROTOTYPING AND FPGAs

It is most likely that the final implementation of the baseband core is likely to be in silicon as a custom or semi-custom ASIC. However, it is highly desirable to validate the hardware and software together as a system before "tape out" of the costly silicon design, and as with most real time systems, this is very difficult to do in any meaningful way without some kind of hardware prototype being built.

Field Programmable Gate Arrays (FPGAs) have been around for some time, but they have tended to be very slow in performance terms and difficult to fit any complex design into due to their lack of internal resource. Furthermore, they have always required the adoption of specific design rules, which really do not follow good ASIC design practice. However, this has changed dramatically in recent years. Due to orders of magnitude, increases in performance, and greatly improved architectural design, the latest state of the art devices such as the Virtex series from Xilinx or the Apex series from Altera offer true SOC capabilities. Performance is on a par with ASIC processes of only a couple of generations ago and no specific design rules have to be adopted other than just good ASIC design practice. For a technology such as Bluetooth, which is not terribly demanding of current ASIC technology, a good FPGA implementation is very feasible.

Most Bluetooth IP suppliers at present have demonstration systems that utilise high performance FPGAs, and these are able to promote confidence in the IP, prove the technology, and provide better coverage of bugs and system testing. Of course, there are some "porting" issues to be addressed when moving to an ASIC implementation such as embedding what was an external MCU and moving from the internal FPGA RAM to an embedded ASIC RAM block. It is particularly important to ensure that enough validation is carried out on the ASIC design itself and not just to rely on the lab bench verification of the FPGA-based system.

Although FPGAs are expensive, due to their low risk, fast turnaround time, and flexible nature, they can provide a viable product route in themselves and make a pragmatic solution for low-volume, high-value products.

25.6   MAKING THE RIGHT DESIGN CHOICES

25.6.1   Profiles Support

Specific applications require support of a particular Bluetooth profile or set of profiles, and each profile in turn will demand a certain set of protocols and features. For example, OBEX is not required for the headset profile, whereas the telephony profile requires the addition of the whole TCS stack.

All profiles are layered on the Generic Access Profile, shown in Figure 25–14, which includes requirements for certain parts of the specification such as Master and Slave operation, ACL and SCO link support, and encryption support. Other profiles add their own requirements on top of the Generic Access Profile.

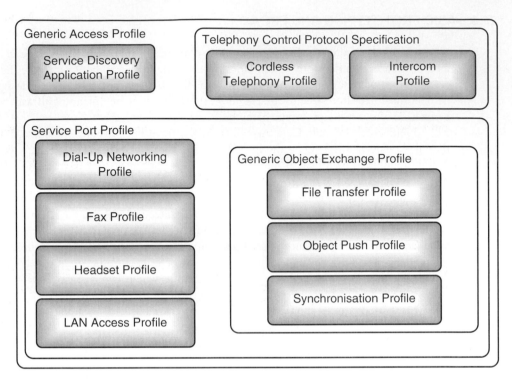

Figure 25–14   Layering of profiles.

This makes it very important to be precise about what functionality is required in any implementation; adding support for another profile could suddenly bring a whole lot of baggage with it. The whole topic of profiles is a complex one. However, the SIG is planning to enable Bluetooth developers to create their own tailored profiles, which will enable specific optimal designs to include only the parts of the specification required for that specific application.

25.6.2   Memory Requirements

For any optimal solution in cost, size, and power consumption terms, memory usage must be reduced to the absolute minimum. RAM is more expensive in all these respects than ROM, and the data buffering requirements of Bluetooth can be quite large. We have already seen that L2CAP can become very memory-intense when supporting multiple high-bandwidth links driven by a networking application with a large packet size.

Currently, manufacturers are nervous about committing to a specific software code set in a masked ROM, and so most implementations—even current single-chip solutions—use FLASH. Since ASIC processes on 0.25 μm and better have recently added FLASH cores as a standard library component, this is not such an issue. But, of course, it isn't free.

The range of memory requirements exhibited by different implementations is quite diverse and driven mostly by the hardware / software tradeoff. However, other factors are also important, such as coding method and specific processor architecture. As an example, a design based on a large operating system might require 256 kB of ROM and 128 kB RAM, whereas a carefully hand-coded system using a small RTOS may use 128 kB ROM and 32 kB RAM. By reducing the segmentation and reassembly load on L2CAP, the RAM figure will drop noticeably further.

Although the LMP specification makes reference to the use of Nonvolatile RAM (NVRAM), it is desirable (and indeed the SIG has worked to avoid the need for it) to not require nonvolatile data storage. Real-time FLASH reprogramming is not straightforward and the presence of FLASH cannot be relied upon anyway. Other NVRAM technologies are not readily integrated on silicon and will add cost if implemented on the PCB. Therefore, it is highly preferable to avoid the requirement for NVRAM at all. This imposes restrictions on the high-level functionality of a device, as it may need to pass important information to the host for storage, or always require reconfiguration after a power down, for example.

25.6.3   Clock Requirements and Low Power Considerations

The choice of system clock has important ramifications. In cellular applications, 13 MHz is a common frequency; in office equipment, 10 MHz is common. Computing equipment such as PDAs, laptops, etc. use clock frequencies such as 33 MHz, 50 MHz, 66 MHz, or more. Since extra crystal oscillators add PCB area and cost, it is desirable to use the same system clock reference for the MCU, baseband processing, and the 1 MHz symbol timing; however, this requires that it must be accurate to ±20 ppm as defined in the specification. Running a system at a high clock rate increases power consumption, and so unless the clock to parts of the system can be turned off when they are inactive, multiple divided down clock domains may be required. This complicates the design and so has to be balanced against the power savings if the reference clock is large, say above 50 MHz.

The low-power modes defined in the link control protocol allow the system to lie dormant for a period of time, but still require the Bluetooth clock counter, CLKN, to be maintained with a 32 kHz reference, which is specified to be tolerant to ± 250 ppm. It is crucial that this crystal stays within this accuracy during its life or is calibrated in some way to maintain robust operation. It is also important when in low-power mode that everything on the PCB that can be turned off is turned off so as to maximise power conservation.

As process voltages drop and battery technology improves, design techniques have to be more rigorous to deal with the lower operating voltages which result. In addition, below 2.7 v, the range of different operating voltages becomes larger and different devices require level shifting and DC-DC conversion to work together, both of which add cost and power consumption. Battery technology has always evolved slowly, but in the next few years, lithium ion will become commonplace, even for cheap consumer products, while new technologies like lithium poly will become available for longer autonomy in higher end products.

25.7   RADIO IMPLEMENTATION

Existing RF architectures for general purpose ISM or DECT applications are relatively easy to bring to market quickly in support of Bluetooth. However, due to various factors,

Bluetooth specific RF designs can be made smaller, cheaper, and lower in power. In some ways, they need to be more complex to deal with certain Bluetooth specific issues such as the very short DC-free preamble. DC thresholding is much easier in DECT, as this uses 16 bits with an uncertainty window of ± 10 bits. Bluetooth's 4 bit preamble, however, demands a new mechanism for both DC thresholding and receive clock recovery. The Philips UAA3558 part is an example of a DECT-based RF device which has been optimised to create a Bluetooth transceiver. By contrast, the Philsar 2401 is a clean sheet design that was targeted at Bluetooth from the start and has been designed on SiGe to offer robust operation in a fairly hostile environment.

Suppliers of radio devices are optimising their products to meet the cost and performance needs of Bluetooth with new architectures and techniques being developed to create optimal solutions in the following areas:

- Robustness—Advanced dynamic gain control, distributed gain stages, and fast DC thresholding
- System performance—Fractional N synthesiser design
- Lower power—Removing the need for mixer stages, increasing sensitivity, and lowering noise.

BiCMOS is the most popular choice for radio devices due to its low cost, which is almost as low as a digital CMOS process. However, some implementations use other processes; the Philsar device is based on SiGe, which gives lower power operation with lower noise and better sensitivity. CMOS has already been mentioned as an RF process in the section on single-chip solutions, where the issues of RF signal performance were discussed. However, as CMOS process voltages drop to conserve power, it becomes harder to maintain the low noise and high enough Ft for RF operation on the same silicon.

Figure 25–15 shows how increasing receiver sensitivity gives longer range operation. Two points are plotted: the Bluetooth-specific -70 dBm figure, which gives 10 m op-

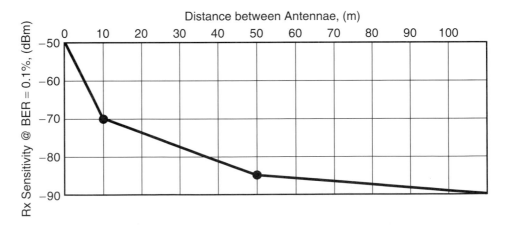

Figure 25–15   Receiver sensitivity vs. operation range.

eration, and the higher value of -85 dBm, which some suppliers are specifying and which leads to claims of a huge increase in ranges up to 50 m. Moving to a more power hungry +20 dBm transmitter is not the only way to increase range. Clearly, in either case, both devices must share higher sensitivity or Tx power if a long range link is to be realised.

Bluetooth's RF requirements are not overdemanding of modern radio design and process technology with their simple binary digital interface and channel synthesiser programming; however, there are some issues to be kept in mind, such as the DC thresholding, receive clock, and data recovery and fast synthesiser settling requirements. Furthermore, more than other communication systems, the radio link must be as robust as possible to cope with the many interference sources present, the low link budget, and the low modulation index. In addition to all these factors, it must still maintain the user's "quality experience".

25.8 SUMMARY

We have looked at a range of issues concerning the realisation of a functional and optimal Bluetooth-enabled solution for a variety of applications. The choices and tradeoffs are myriad, and competing solutions aimed at addressing them are numerous. However, there are some definite conclusions one can make:

- The quality of "user experience" is very important and must be designed in.
- The target application must be well understood and specified.
- Any commercially successful implementation must be tightly optimised for cost and performance.
- SOC ASIC design should not be shied away from. There are very good sources of IP for Bluetooth, but they are not free and must come with a complete package of services and support.
- Standardisation of interfaces will make Bluetooth system design and implementation easier and the market larger.
- Bluetooth needs to be very high volume and thus has to be very low cost.

26

Related Standards and Technologies

26.1 INTRODUCTION

In this chapter, we will consider the different wireless communications systems which overlap with Bluetooth either in technology terms or market segments, explaining the various strengths and weaknesses in each case. In some cases, they may appear to compete directly with Bluetooth; in others, they may appear to be orthogonal. However, what makes the wireless networking business so interesting is exactly how all these different technologies and initiatives do interact and impact one another, and—for the most part—they all do!

26.2 WHAT ARE THE REQUIREMENTS?

Figure 26–1 gives some idea of the various applications for wireless connectivity and breaks these down depending on the required range and bandwidth. At one extreme is the home AV setup, where one might transfer video from a digital camcorder to a home video entertainment centre or VCR. This would typically only require a range of a few tens of centimetres, but the data rates could be very high. At the other extreme, cordless headphones or a remote controller would need only modest data rates, but the range could be tens of metres to work in the home environment. In between, we have office productivity

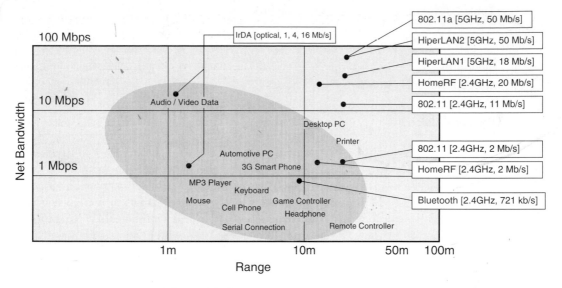

Figure 26–1　Wireless applications and requirements.

devices such as printers and PCs; indeed, the classic Wireless LAN (WLAN) where both high data rate and reasonable range are important.

Recently, the rise of voice over IP (VOIP) systems has complicated the picture. As yet there are few commercial installations, but if voice over IP becomes popular, it will put an unprecedented load onto networks previously used only for data. Voice traffic is extremely sensitive to delays and places entirely different Quality of Service requirements on a network than data, so this is an area which many infrastructure providers are watching with interest.

The diagram also shows where each of the technologies we will discuss here fit in and how it is unlikely—for now at least—that any one standard can cover all the possible applications.

26.3　INFRARED DATA ASSOCIATION (IrDA)

The IrDA created a communications system based on infrared light. As such, IrDA is limited to line of sight and cannot penetrate furniture or walls as a radio-based system can. While this places limitations on device placement, proponents of IrDA point out that it does provide controlled and private data exchange.

The IrDA suite of standards were published in late 1993 and include the Serial Infrared (SIR) link specification, Link Access Protocol (IrLAP) specification, and Link Management Protocol (IrLMP) specification. In 1995, IrDA released extensions to the SIR standard for 4Mb/s operation, and since then has expanded the standard to include high-speed extensions for 1.152 Mb/s, 4.0 Mb/s, and 16 Mb/s operations using Pulse Position Modulation (PPM).

Table 26–1   IrDA and Bluetooth Compared

Parameter	IrDA	Bluetooth
Medium	Optical / Directional	RF / Omni-directional
Gross Data Rate (Mb/s)	1.152, 4, 16	1[1]
Max Range	20cm / 1.2m	10m / 100m
Data and Voice?	Data only	Data and Voice

Bluetooth and IrDA are both short-range technologies, but Bluetooth has a much more complete networking architecture. However, there are several interworking aspects. Bluetooth's common OBEX support enables the same applications to use either access medium and there is some application commonality (IrMC) with standard content format, such as vCard and vCalendar. Table 26–1 compares IrDA with Bluetooth.

26.4   DIGITAL ENHANCED CORDLESS TELECOMMUNICATIONS (DECT)

The DECT standard was developed during 1992 within ETSI as ETS 300 175 and 300 176 as a successor to the CT2 and CT3 digital cordless telephone systems in Europe. Today, DECT has a major share of the cordless telephone market worldwide and is also being rolled out as a Wireless Local Loop (WLL) solution in rural areas and the developing world. Dual-mode DECT/GSM systems are also becoming available, such as the One-Phone product from BT Cellnet in the UK, an integrated GSM cellular phone which switches to cordless operation when in the home using the cheaper, more convenient PSTN. Although slow to materialize, data applications using DECT are also now becoming apparent.

Based on a multi-carrier TDMA TDD scheme (see Figure 26–2), DECT uses ten frequency carriers in the range 1.88 to 1.9 GHz. Each time frame lasts 10 ms and the specified 24 time slots are split into two TDD halves: 12 slots for the downlink and 12 for the uplink, with each slot typically containing 32kb/s ADPCM[2]—coded voice data. This provides for up to twelve simultaneous full-duplex voice links. Due to the flexibility of the specification, these multiple channels can be combined into a single bearer of n x 24 kb/s (net data rate after error protection) for a maximum of 552 kb/s for data applications.

A DECT system comprises one or more DECT Fixed Parts (FPs), or base stations, and one or more DECT Portable Parts (PPs). There is no limit to the size of the infrastructure as far as the number of base stations or cordless terminals is concerned.

---

[1]This chapter refers to Gross Data Rates (symbol rate); application data rates are lower, see section 18.6.
[2]Adaptive Differential Pulse Code Modulation (ADPCM) is a high-quality speech coding scheme that exploits the human auditory function to realize a high level of speech compression.

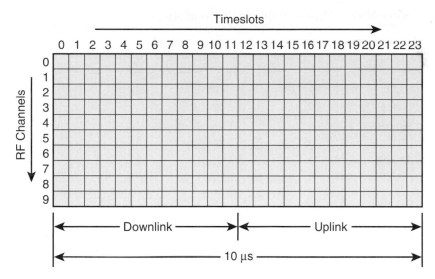

Figure 26–2   DECT frame structure.

   The base standard only covers the interface between a fixed part and a portable part. It provides a toolbox with protocols and messages from which selections can be made (similar to the way in which Bluetooth profiles work) to access any specific type of network. DECT profiles have been defined for Radio in the Local Loop applications (RAP), ISDN Interworking (IAP), and GSM Interworking (GIP).

   A DECT base station transmits continuously on at least one channel, providing a beacon function for portables to lock onto. The station's beacon transmission carries broadcast information—in a multiframe, multiplexed structure—on base station identity, system capabilities, base station status, and paging information for incoming call setup. Portables locked on to a beacon transmission will analyse the broadcast information to determine whether the portable has access rights to the base station, whether the system capabilities match the services required by the portable, and whether the base station has free capacity to establish a radio link with the portable.

   Dynamic channel selection and allocation and a seamless handover capability mean that portables can escape an interfered radio connection by establishing a second radio link—on a newly selected channel—to either the same base station or another base station. The two links are maintained in parallel, with identical speech information being carried while link quality is analysed. The base station then determines which link has the best quality and releases the other link.

   Another aspect of this "handover" process is that as the portable moves out of range of a base station, it may hand over to another nearer base station, and this allows the effective range to be increased by adding more fixed parts to the system, something which version 1.0 and 1.1 of Bluetooth cannot do.

   Without handover, Bluetooth cannot offer the features or the range of a DECT cordless installation, which make DECT so valuable as a scalable cordless telephony system.

Table 26–2   DECT and Bluetooth Compared

Parameter	DECT	Bluetooth
Frequency Band (GHz)	1.88–1.9	2.4
Gross Data Rate (Mb/s)	1.152	1
Max Range	300 m	10 m / 50 m
Handover?	Inter-cell and intra-cell handover	Handover between piconets not supported
Max Full-duplex Voice Links	12	3

If Bluetooth were to define a handover mechanism, it could threaten DECT. On the other hand, DECT's dedicated spectrum is a major advantage. If Bluetooth becomes all pervasive, it may guarantee DECT's longevity due to its not being in the band dominated by Bluetooth's fast hopping interference. Table 26–2 compares DECT with Bluetooth.

26.5   IEEE 802.11

The 802.11 working group of the IEEE standards body in the United States is responsible for defining and maintaining the Wireless Local Area Networks (WLANs) specification and standardisation. The original IEEE Standard 802.11-1997 specification defined three Physical (PHY) Layer specifications and one common Medium Access Control (MAC) specification. However, since then, further work has been carried out to extend the initial PHY specifications to provide higher data rates. This has led to Standards 802.11a and 802.11b. The current published specifications are IEEE 802.11-1999, IEEE 802.11a-1999, and IEEE 802.11b-1999.

We shall first consider the common MAC and the original PHYs before discussing the two enhanced data rate versions.

The MAC works with two network configurations:

- Independent configuration—Stations communicate directly to each other with no infrastructure support (so-called ad-hoc networking), which although easy to operate, provides a limited coverage area.
- Infrastructure configuration—Stations communicate via access points, which are part of a wider area distribution system, allowing access to an extended coverage area.

The MAC provides a basic access mechanism with clear channel assessment, channel synchronisation, and collision avoidance using the Carrier Sense Multiple Access (CSMA)[3]

---

[3]A device listens to the channel before transmitting and only transmits if the channel is unused; this is also referred to as "Collision Avoidance" or CSMA/CA.

scheme. It also provides service scanning (similar to Bluetooth inquiry and scan), link setup, data fragmentation, authentication, encryption, power management, and roaming facilities.

The 802.11 specification defines three associated PHYs:

- Frequency Hop Spread Spectrum (FHSS)
  2.4 GHz ISM band, 1 and 2 Mb/s
  2-level GFSK[4] and 4-level GFSK modulation
  Hopping at 50 hops/s over 79 channels
- Direct Sequence Spread Spectrum (DSSS)
  2.4 GHz ISM band, 1 and 2 Mb/s
  DBPSK[5] and DQPSK[6] modulation
  11-chip Barker sequence for spreading
- Baseband IR
  Diffuse infrared
  1 and 2 Mb/s transmission
  16 PPM[7] and 4 PPM modulation

The FHSS PHY is similar to Bluetooth but with a much slower hopping rate, and this has made it easier to implement 802.11 radio technology. With the current state of the art, however, the speed demanded by Bluetooth hopping is not really an issue any more. By using deeper modulation such as 4 level GFSK, the 802.11 data rate is easily increased. However, as the data rate is increased, so is noise sensitivity. With careful radio design, this can be tolerated, as is evidenced by the number of 802.11 FH-based PC WLAN cards now available on the market.

The DSSS PHY continuously spreads the data across the frequency spectrum rather than hopping in discrete time sequence.

26.5.1   IEEE 802.11b

Harris and Lucent Technologies proposed the chosen modulation scheme for 802.11b. This extends the 802.11 DSSS PHY to provide 5.5 and 11 Mb/s, in addition to the 1 and 2 Mb/s data by using 8-chip Complementary Code Keying (CCK) as the modulation scheme. The chipping rate is still 11 MHz, as for the standard DSSS system, and so the channel bandwidth occupied remains the same. The new PHY is referred to as High-Rate Direct Sequence Spread Spectrum (HR/DSSS). Since the same preamble and header are used, both the 802.11 DSSS and 802.11b HR/DSSS PHYs can coexist in the same network.

---

[3]A device listens to the channel before transmitting and only transmits if the channel is unused; this is also referred to as "Collision Avoidance" or CSMA/CA.
[4]Gaussian Frequency Shift Keying.
[5]Differential Binary Phase Shift Keying.
[6]Differential Quadrature Phase Shift Keying.
[7]Pulse Position Modulation.

The adoption of the HR PHY has been a challenging task for the various manufacturers of 802.11-based WLAN products (mostly U.S.-based). However, 5.5 and 11 Mb/s products are now available from various suppliers, though these products are not in the same low cost arena as Bluetooth.

26.5.2   IEEE 802.11.a

The 802.11a PHY was proposed by NTT and Lucent Technologies and is very close to that specified for the HIPERLAN Type 2 standard (H/2) to facilitate common PHY silicon. We consider H/2 in the section below on HIPERLAN. Clearly, the ability to separate PHY and MAC is an attractive feature of the 802.11 architecture, and it is a testament to the designers that they were able to adopt a state of the art PHY to plug into their existing MAC.

The 802.11 family of standards is well entrenched in the world, particularly in the United States Proprietary products were available before 802.11 was finalised, and indeed, much of the impetus behind 802.11 was the concern that lack of interoperability between proprietary WLAN solutions could stifle the market. Right now, remaining proprietary solutions are being migrated toward 802.11 (the HR variant usually), and it looks as though it's here to stay.

There are some questions as to whether bandwidth can be maintained at the high end, although reports indicate that rate back-off allows sustained data rates of well in excess of 5 Mb/s. A more crucial point is the overuse of the ISM 2.4 GHz spectrum—already crowded and now with two flavours of 802.11 and Bluetooth about to join the fray. Bluetooth's fast frequency hopping should ensure that it does not become hindered; however, its impact on the slower hopping WLAN schemes is a topic of some discussion and research. The Bluetooth SIG has formed a "Coexistence/Interoperability with ISM devices" working group which is addressing issues of coexistence between Bluetooth and other equipment sharing the ISM band. This group has three main activities: quantifying the effect of interference on performance, developing methods of Bluetooth operation which can be used to improve coexistence, and coordinating with working groups which are producing future versions of the Bluetooth specification to evaluate coexistence issues in proposed new radio designs. Many commercial and standards organisations are also investigating the effects of coexistence in the ISM band, and several white papers have been published looking at effects of 802.11 and Bluetooth coexistence. The results are too complex to summarise here, but in brief the two technologies coexist, but suffer from reduced data rates as one would expect. Since both technologies implement power control grouping devices using one technology close together allows low power to be used and reduced the effects of interference. Similarly the more seperation between Bluetooth piconets and 802.11 networks the less the effect of interference.

In terms of cost, at present, 802.11-based products start at $99 and may cost as much as $200 for the HR version. This must be compared to tens of dollars for commercial Bluetooth products.

Because Bluetooth and 802.11 are in similar but not identical niches, there is a demand for devices equipped with both technologies. Some companies are working on combined devices which can exist on both a Bluetooth piconet and an 802.11 network at the same time.

26.6　THE HOMERF™ WORKING GROUP (HRFWG)

The HRFWG was formed in March 1998 to create an open industry specification for wireless digital communication between PCs and consumer electronic devices anywhere in and around the home and to act as a forum for the encouragement and support of home wireless networking.

The group now has more than 90 members including Intel, IBM, Compaq, and Microsoft. Drawn from the PC, consumer electronics, peripherals, communications, software, and semiconductor industries, many products are now available from various sources.

The HRFWG recognised that wired technologies make roaming with portable devices difficult, and in particular, the high cost and impracticality of adding new wires in-home will inhibit the widespread adoption of home networking technologies. To address these issues, they developed a specification for wireless communications in the home called the Shared Wireless Access Protocol (SWAP) to combine voice telephony with data distribution in the home environment.

Three subcommittees exist within the HRFWG. The HRFWG-Japan sub-committee is responsible for ensuring that the SWAP specification complies with Japanese regulations, while the others are planning future versions of SWAP to address wireless multimedia (20 Mb/s) and lower cost applications.

26.6.1　Shared Wireless Access Protocol (SWAP)

SWAP is designed to carry both voice and data traffic by combining DECT and 802.11 FHSS. It supports both a Time Division Multiple Access (TDMA) service to provide delivery of isochronous services, such as interactive voice, and a high-speed packet data service using the 802.11 CSMA/CA scheme (see Figure 26–3). The frames are 20 ms in duration,

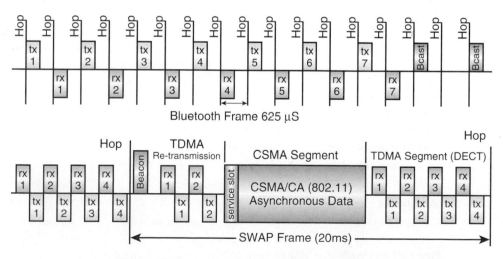

Figure 26–3　SWAP and Bluetooth frame structures.

with voice retransmission at the beginning, voice traffic at the end, and interleaved asynchronous data packets on multiple links in between. The DECT beacon transmission signifies the start of the frame and is provided by the connection point network manager node.

SWAP was designed to be low cost by using a more relaxed radio specification than 802.11 (PHY) but maintaining the same hopping scheme. Also, by eliminating the complex parts of the protocol (PCF and CTS/RTS), cost has been kept down. However, 802.11 TCP/IP support is included. The voice segment uses DECT with retransmission and employs the DECT calling stack and A/B fields. The voice-coding scheme used is the usual 32kb/s ADPCM.

A SWAP system can operate either as an ad-hoc network or as a managed network under the control of a connection point. The latter case is required for isochronous communications such as voice where the connection point provides the gateway to the PSTN. Each node can operate as one of the following:

- A connection point supporting both voice and data services.
- A voice terminal that only uses the TDMA service to communicate with a base station.
- A data node that uses the CSMA/CA service to communicate with a base station and other data nodes.
- A voice and data node using both types of services.

The HRWG has lobbied the FCC to change the FCC Part 15 regulations to allow channels up to 5 MHz, so-called Wideband Frequency Hopping (WBFH). Some suppliers of existing 1 MHz-based WLAN products have contested this, but the FCC is sympathetic to the request, which would allow HomeRF to migrate to a higher bit rate while maintaining the same FH PHY. There is also much interest in supporting multimedia applications at around 20 Mb/s, and this initiative is referred to as HomeRF/MM.

Table 26–3 lists the main features of SWAP and compares them with Bluetooth.

Table 26–3   SWAP and Bluetooth Compared

Parameter	SWAP	Bluetooth
Frequency (hops/second)	50	1600
Transmit power (mW)	100	10 / 100
Gross data rate (Mb/s)	1 (2FSK mod)	
	2 (4FSK mod)	1 (2FSK mod only)
Max Range	50m	10m / 50m / 100m
Max No. of Nodes	127 devices per network	8 per piconet; many more via scatternet or parking
Max Full-duplex Voice Links	6	3
Security Algorithm	Blowfish	SAFER+

SWAP and the HomeRF concept may appear to be a direct competitor to Bluetooth. The HomeRF position is that while Bluetooth provides the Personal Area Network (PAN) connectivity, SWAP provides the Home Area Network (HAN) connectivity. This point of view has some merit, although Bluetooth does look set to evolve in terms of range and data rate and the cost of a Bluetooth subsystem is going to be much lower than a combined 802.11 / DECT subsystem. However, as noted above, at present DECT is far superior to Bluetooth for cordless telephony, and 802.11 is an accomplished WLAN standard. Although Bluetooth started out as a short-range wireless replacement technology, it is fast becoming many things to many people. Though this in itself can be dangerous, if controlled, Bluetooth could soon "mop up" the HomeRF concept along the way, offering as it does a lower cost solution and through evolution, similar range and data rates with improved cordless telephony support.

26.7   IEEE 802.15 AND THE WIRELESS PERSONAL AREA NETWORK (WPAN)

The 802.15 group was created shortly after the public release of the Bluetooth standard in the summer of 1999 to create an IEEE-based PAN standard to complement the work of 802.11. The term "PAN" defines a new usage scenario in WLANs, where the key factors are lower power consumption, lower cost, and superior ease of use.[8] Shorter range and lower bit rate are less important for this range of applications.

In agreement with the Bluetooth SIG, the group decided to adopt the Bluetooth v1.0b standard as the basis for its work and was tasked with reworking the standard to fit with the IEEE networking model. Figure 26–4 shows the portions of the Bluetooth stack which 802.15.1 has adopted. These are shaded on the right; on the left is the IEE standard layers, showing how the IEEE MAC and PHY layers encompass the functionality of the Bluetooth stack from the radio up to L2CAP level.

In January 2000, the IEEE approved a second task group, 802.15.2, to examine coexistence and interoperability between 802.15 WPANs and 802.11 WLANs. The group is expected to produce recommended practices for coexistence and to suggest modifications to other 802.15 or 802.11 standards to enhance coexistence with other specified wireless devices operating in unlicensed frequency bands.

In March 2000, at the suggestion of Cisco, Eastman Kodak, and Motorola, the IEEE approved a third task group, 802.15.3, to create a high-rate WPAN standard. The group is tasked with creating the PHY and MAC specifications for high data rate wireless connectivity between fixed, portable, and moving devices within or entering a Personal Operating Space (POS).[9] The eventual standard is intended to achieve a level of interoperability or coexistence with 802.15.1 and through the efforts of 802.15.2 other wireless devices. The data rate is intended to be high enough—20 Mb/s or more—to satisfy consumer mul-

---

[8]Sometimes referred to as pervasive or hidden networking. The user does not need to even consider that he and all his belongings are networked.

[9]The space about a person or object that typically extends up to 10 meters in all directions and envelops the person/object whether stationary or in motion.

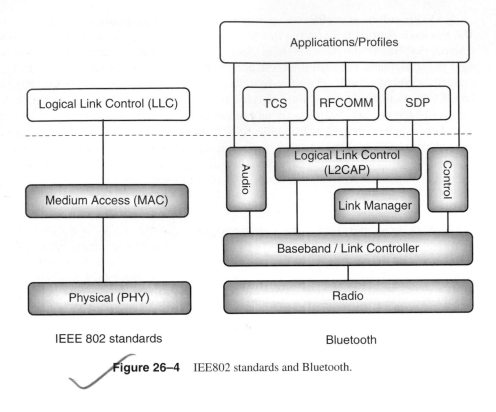

Figure 26–4   IEE802 standards and Bluetooth.

timedia industry needs for Wireless Pan (WPAN) communications, and the work is also expected to address the Quality of Service (QOS) capabilities required to support multimedia data types such as digital imaging and video applications.

26.8 HIPERLAN

The High Performance Radio Local Area Network (HIPERLAN) standard was developed within the European Telecommunications Standards Institute (ETSI) during the period 1991 to 1996. The HIPERLAN work group concluded that shared spectrum such as the ISM band did not facilitate the high data rates and guaranteed QOS they considered necessary for advanced multimedia-based wireless networking, and so both HIPERLAN Type 1 (H/1) and HIPERLAN Type 2 (H/2) use dedicated spectrum at 5 GHz. H/1 was completed in late 1997 as ETSI standard ETS 300 652.

Whereas H/1 is very much like a modern wireless Ethernet, there was a requirement for a follow-on development more akin to a wireless version of ATM, which led to the development of H/2. As work got underway on H/2, other related initiatives with common requirements were united within ETSI to form a new project, which was termed the Broadband Radio Access Network project, or BRAN.

The ongoing global industry debate between the IP camp and the ATM camp as to which is to be *the* future all-pervasive wired networking standard is well known to most people and we are sure that readers have their own views. However, the same debate now rages about H/1 and H/2. Although their respective PHYs are very different with H/2 promising much higher future data rates, H/1 can easily be improved to compete. In fact, they offer similar solutions but in different ways, and therefore suit different applications, depending on whether a centralized or ad-hoc network architecture is required.

The complete suite of H/2 specifications offers options for bit rates of 54, 36, 16, and 6 Mb/s. The PHY adopts an OFDM multiple carrier scheme using 48 carrier frequencies per OFDM symbol. Each carrier may then be modulated using BPSK, QPSK, 16-QAM, or 64-QAM to provide different data rates. The modulation schemes chosen for the higher bit rates will make practical implementations very challenging, and there may need to be further development to achieve throughput in the range 30–50 Mb/s.

Table 26–4 summarizes the features of both H/1 and H/2. Clearly they have some strong similarities and some marked differences. Several companies in the United States have already announced H/1 products, and components are under development by other companies. H/2 provides a different, more centralised protocol stack and higher data rates, but at the expense of a more complex system design, and products are unlikely to be around for a while. Several companies are reputed to be working on chipsets which support the lower layers for H/2, IEEE 802.11a, and MMAC.

Although all members of the Wireless LAN fraternity, HIPERLAN and 802.11a are really quite different from Bluetooth in terms of cost, performance, and application. H/1 and H/2 provide high-rate, medium-range multimedia distribution with video QOS, reserved spectrum, and good in-building propagation. H/1 uses an advanced channel equalizer to deal with intersymbol interference and signal multipath, while H/2 avoids these by using OFDM and a frequency transform function. These complex modulation/demodula-

Table 26–4   HIPERLAN Type 1 and HIPERLAN Type 2 Compared

Parameter	HIPERLAN Type 1	HIPERLAN Type 2
Application	Wireless Ethernet LAN	Wireless ATM
Gross Data Rate (Mb/s)	23.5	6, 16, 36, 54
Net Data Rate (Mb/s)	> 18	50 (max)
Transmit Power (mW)	10 / 100 / 1000	10 / 100 / 1000
Max Range	50m	50m
Services	Time-bounded and asynchronous	Time-bounded and asynchronous
Channel Access	Dynamic, priority-driven	Reserved
Modulation	Gaussian Minimum Shift Keying (GMSK)	Orthogonal Frequency Division Multiplexing (OFDM) + BPSK, QPSK, and QAM carrier modulation

tion schemes and their 5 GHz operation make them both expensive. Bluetooth, on the other hand, is at least an order of magnitude slower and does not yet provide the same capabilities for multimedia distribution, range, or propagation.

26.9 MMAC

Multimedia Mobile Access Communication Systems (MMAC) is an initiative under the Japanese Association of Radio Industries and Businesses (ARIB) to produce an ultra high speed, high quality multimedia communications standard. Set for a launch date of 2002, the system aims to provide a four-tier scheme as follows:

- High-speed wireless access (outdoor, indoor)
  e.g., mobile video telephony
  30 Mb/s in the range 3–60 GHz
- Ultra high-speed wireless LAN (indoor)
  e.g., high quality televisual applications
  Up to 156 Mb/s in the range 30–300 GHz
- 5 GHz band mobile access (outdoor, indoor)
  e.g., ATM access and Ethernet LAN applications
  20–25 Mb/s in the 5 GHz band
- Wireless home-link (indoor)
  e.g., home PC and audiovisual equipment networking
  Up to 100 Mb/s in the range 3–60 GHz

Essentially, it is a parallel development to the H/2 / 802.11a work and is the subject of some liaison between both ARIB and ETSI. Currently, the 5 GHZ PHY specs are aligned to allow common silicon.

26.10 THE FUTURE

Home-wired networking is happening right now based on the IEEE 1394[10] standard. ETSI BRAN has been quick to realise this and is now working on IEEE 1394/H/2 convergence. Ericsson is involved in BRAN and the H/2 work, so it is not impossible to imagine Bluetooth (high-rate) evolving in a similar direction to H/2. Indeed, the SIG has announced that medium and high rate Bluetooth devices will preserve backwards compatibility with earlier Bluetooth devices. This implies that the faster devices will support multiple modulation schemes as HIPERLAN/2 devices.

---

[10]A high speed serial communication standard for linking home and computer equipment, typically audio/video.

There has been some discussion between IEEE 802 and ETSI on unifying 802.11 and HIPERLAN; however, this is not well-supported in BRAN to date since the IEEE 802.11a MAC is very different from that of H/2. The two physical layer specifications are, however, broadly similar and harmonised to facilitate silicon device reuse.

The emergence of the home area network (HAN) and the personal area network (PAN) have made the picture much more complex. The traditional wireless computing system network, the WLAN, now has at least three different incarnations—in the office, home, and personal space. Bluetooth is targeted directly at the new PAN scenario and is set to succeed incredibly well there. However, will it evolve to provide the functionality of a HAN? HomeRF has a very good story to tell, but it has to fight against dropping costs of separate WLAN and DECT products and the possibility that Bluetooth will become a viable cordless telephony technology. DECT itself has a large installed base and this itself may prevent Bluetooth from commanding that market. Then again, Bluetooth is just starting out, and DECT has been around for some time now.

One of the key areas for the evolution of the Bluetooth specification past 1.1 will be increasing the data rate, and this could make a big difference to the way that the PAN / HAN story plays out. The main attraction right now of HAN is the desire to distribute video around the home for integrated AV entertainment connectivity without the need for wires, in particular to distribute broadband multimedia services inside the home once delivered to the kerb side.

This is where the work in BRAN has most recently been focused. Table 26–5 lists the most important data rates involved. The consumer DV gross data rate of 32 Mb/s is the value which the home environment group within BRAN has set as the minimum data rate for the BRAN H/2 standard to support for home applications.

There has been much discussion in the industry on the minimum bit rates appropriate for the distribution of real time MPEG-encoded video services around the home, but the general consensus seems to be that a fixed bit rate coding scheme should require at least 5 Mb/s and a statistically multiplexed bit rate scheme between 4.5 and 8 Mb/s. The Digital Television Group (DTG) in the UK has adopted a minimum figure of 5 Mb/s and a peak of 9 Mb/s per channel for demanding material.

Table 26–5   Video Data Rates

Format	Digital Video (DV) Consumer	Digital Video (DV) Professional	Digital Versatile Disc (DVD)
Application	Digital video cameras and camcorders	Broadcast television	Video playback and PC use
Data rate (Mb/s)	24.96 32 (via IEEE 1394)	50	10.08 (gross) 8.5 (net peak) 3.6 (net average)

26.11 SUMMARY

Clearly, the current version of Bluetooth does not provide suitable data rates for the complete home network; however, it can provide a part of that environment as a PAN or evolve through Bluetooth version 2.0 to support the higher data rates necessary. Even then, there is still a requirement for different networking paradigms for different purposes, i.e., voice based cordless telephony.

IEEE 802.11 is an established WLAN standard, and products are shipping. The family of specifications provides a complete wireless networking system which Bluetooth, as it stands, is not capable of offering. However, Bluetooth offers service discovery capabilities which enable ad-hoc net.

DECT is also an established product and doing well as a cordless telephony system. The development of data based DECT is underway, but looks unlikely to succeed now as there are already many attractive solutions available. Thus, while Bluetooth does not support the range and handover capabilities of DECT, DECT should survive. It is also unhindered by the crowding in the ISM band, operating as it does just outside in its own dedicated spectrum.

The most interesting comparison is that to be drawn between Bluetooth and HomeRF, where there is a window of opportunity for SWAP to establish itself just above Bluetooth as the HAN while Bluetooth becomes the Personal Area Network (PAN). However, one feels that Bluetooth is likely to evolve to compete directly with HomeRF, unless higher data rate versions arrive to create added value. But, then again, H/1 and H/2 already have that base covered.

A very interesting development is the establishment of IEEE 802.15, and in particular, the high rate work in 802.15.3. The authors are unaware of what liaison is going on—if any—between 802.15.3 and the Bluetooth version 2.0 working groups. However, either way, with a target of 20 Mb/s for high rate PANs, one can expect the picture to only get more complex.

IrDA has now fixed many of its earlier issues related to interoperability and incompatible devices. In the early days, the standard was mostly unregulated, and though IrDA became a standard fit in most portable computer equipment (largely due to the me-too factor), it never became an industry or cross-industry standard.

This was because it proved frustrating to users as it was difficult to configure, required having an exact setup with appropriate system information, and devices had to be aimed—in particular, placed close together because misalignment caused problems. At the Application Level, it was not standardised and it never made it to desktop machines, so cables were still required to get data back to the desktop. Although in the short term, getting built in wins sales and makes the technology look promising. If it's not being used, then it won't command a price premium and will die out in the longer term. By contrast, a major selling point for Bluetooth is ease of use and its work-first-time "out of the box experience" (OOBE).

26.12   USEFUL WEB ADDRESSES

IrDA:	*http://www.irda.org*
DECT:	*http://www.dectweb.com*
IEEE 802.11:	*http://grouper.ieee.org/groups/802/11*
IEEE 802.15:	*http://grouper.ieee.org/groups/802/15*
HomeRF:	*http://www.homerf.org*
H/1:	*http://www.HIPERLAN.com*
H/2:	*http://www.H/2.com*
ETSI BRAN:	*http://www.etsi.org/bran*
MMAC:	*http://www.arib.or.jp/mmac*

27

The Bluetooth Market

27.1 INTRODUCTION

We are told by many people that the Bluetooth market is going to be huge. Forecasts suggest that we can expect to see half a billion Bluetooth-enabled devices by 2004, with a total market for Bluetooth components worth $2 billion in the same year. In this chapter, we will attempt to understand the truth behind these bold claims and try to explain the hype surrounding one of the most talked about technologies of the decade.

First of all, we will look more closely at what is going on in the consumer electronics industry what the consumers' requirements (market pull) are, and indeed what the latest technology developments (technology push) have been.

27.2 MARKET PULL AND TECHNOLOGY PUSH

In the last several years, the penetration of mobile cellular telephony has risen exponentially around the globe. The consumer has now reached a point where voice communications anywhere at any time are the norm. If one wants to ask a friend or colleague a minor question, perhaps "Did you book that holiday yet?," then there's no need to wait, just call them up right now. This exemplifies the "on-demand" nature of today's society. The other major technological impact on today's society is the recent Internet explosion; we now have vast amounts of information on-tap, hence the often coined expression "the information society". E-commerce is all around us, and although it is only just now rolling out, the pace at which new services and Internet products are becoming available is incredible. These services and the Internet in general are maturing at an incredible rate with secure payment services, online shopping, and banking available from all the big name corporations.

As this book goes to print, we are poised on the edge of the mobile information revolution. In the next several years, the telephony on-demand scenario will give way to information on-demand. Instead of calling one's friend to ask about the holiday, just surf the Web to the travel agent's Web site, check out the streaming video, and book the holiday, paying for it by e-cash. This is already possible. Very soon, not only will we be *able* to do this while sitting in a field waiting for the next bus home using a shirt-pocket-sized smart phone or Personal Digital Assistant (PDA), we will *expect* to; it will be the norm.

The major cellular operators are rolling out the first enhanced rate packet data services such as GPRS[1] and EDGE[2] (so called 2.5 generation cellular), and the long awaited third generation cellular UMTS[3] services are on the way. No longer will there be a dialup delay, and the data rates (144 kb/s to 2 Mb/s) will support full multimedia Internet traffic. Current estimates suggest that 30% of all Internet traffic will be mobile by 2005.

Enabling the "last meter" of connectivity from the cellular terminal to the handheld PDA is not the only application for Bluetooth, but it is going to be an important one. Bluetooth in its simplest guise just removes the need for connecting cables. However, that simple concept has major repercussions. The effort required to find the mobile phone data cable, the cost of purchase, and even reading the manual to work out how to enable it are all obstacles to using the data capabilities of a mobile phone, or for that matter, of plugging a PDA into a laptop to synchronise it. By removing the cables, Bluetooth allows all these things to occur without the user needing to know. In fact, the success of Bluetooth will be measured more by the number of people who don't know of its existence than by those who do!

A logical extension of this is to take a look at an existing cellular phone handset and ask some fundamental questions regarding its use. Many people already carry some form of information appliance such as a PDA or organiser, which has a more superior screen than the cellular phone and is more intelligent. So why carry two devices which are necessarily large enough to fit the human form factor, i.e., keypad, display, earpiece/mouthpiece? Figure 27–1 shows how Bluetooth would allow the familiar cellular phone to be broken up into its constituent parts. We are left with the smallest possible cellular "access node" that would fit neatly on a belt clip, a large screen, but small form factor touchpad PDA, an earpiece/earring, and a clip-on microphone with a call action button. This concept is sometimes referred to as wearable technology! Already wristwatch sized display driven by wireless links exist. The technology is here, mass market products will follow.

---

[1]General Packet Radio Services combine timeslots to provide higher data rates for GSM and adopt packet data for asynchronous communication, with no dial-up requirement.
[2]Enhanced data rates for GSM use deeper modulation to increase the basic data rate over GSM.
[3]Universal Mobile Telephony System is the next generation of high data rate cellular WAN for voice and data.

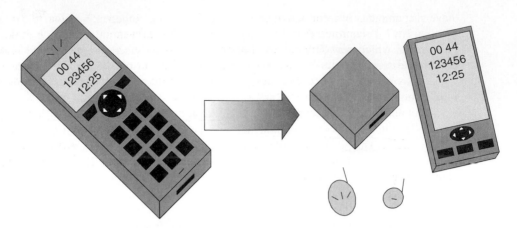

Figure 27–1   Breaking up the cellular phone.

The alternative viewpoint is that the cellular phone itself becomes the information appliance, the so-called smartphone. This is also a valid supposition—already we see devices such as the Sony Z5 and Nokia communicator offering browsing capabilities and blurring the lines between phone and PDA. We will see both scenarios, with different consumers opting for whatever suits them best. In this case, the central information appliance will still need to communicate with other devices around it like the headset, PC, camera, camcorder, and printer.

Figure 27–2   Personal Area Network (PAN).

These scenarios lead us to the situation depicted in Figure 27–2, where the user is surrounded by electronic devices which either require data input or provide data output (data sink or data source) in the personal space, or indeed, even on the user's person. This is now commonly referred to as the Personal Area Network (PAN).

Increasingly, we are interacting with more information appliances and becoming more connected to the Internet. Bluetooth enables us to be permanently connected with all these devices and the Internet without even knowing it. The effort factor will be virtually zero when we see something on the television and decide to pick up our PDA to select the "more info" tick box. When we wish to put our holiday pictures on our laptop and email them, we will not need to plug anything in; we won't even need to *find* the camera. As long as it's in range, we will just wirelessly connect to it.

27.3 MARKET SEGMENTS

Mobile cellular handsets are currently the largest consumer electronics market. With the proliferation of wired headsets now in use, this market sector is fairly well-assured. Other applications listed below will evolve over time as the technology becomes known and trusted through early adopters such as the mobile professional. Then, mainstream customers such as business users will move into the market, causing volumes to increase greatly and driving prices down. As prices drop, the technology becomes viable for new areas and opportunities as exemplified by the wireless home. Table 27–1 describes these segments while Table 27–2 lists the various application areas.

Ultimately, the home area networking (HAN) and personal area networking (PAN) paradigms can be realised as the technology becomes all-pervasive (Figure 27–3), but only if the key performance metrics of cost, autonomy, and ease of use are first met.

Table 27–2 describes the various areas of the market where Bluetooth promises to deliver. Cable replacement is the classic first target for Bluetooth as we described above.

Data and voice access points are a logical development, enabling connectivity between the Bluetooth-enabled device and the office LAN, private networks, and the Internet. The development of Bluetooth as a wireless voice telephony system, however, is dependent on a number of factors, as was noted in the chapter on related technologies. The emergence of Voice Over IP (VOIP) for low-cost long-distance calls via the Internet or LAN-based in-building telephony may catalyse this.

Table 27–1 Market Segmentation

Market Segment	Characteristics
Mobile professionals	Early adopters. Will pay premium price for convenience and novelty factor.
Business users	Reliability and functionality essential. Business needs will enjoy true benefit from the technology.
Home users	Low cost and ease of use essential. New usage paradigm required.

Table 27–2   Product Categories and Applications

Cable Replacement

The wireless desktop:

    PCs and peripherals: mouse, keyboard, printers, scanners, fax, digital camera

    Laptop-to-laptop file transfer

    PDA synchronisation

Wireless audio headset:

    MP3 player / Walkman / cellular phone / radio / TV

Audiovisual home networking

Mobile handset and headset

Wireless speakers and display panel / Web pad

In-building cable replacement for lighting or air conditioning

Remote control devices

Data and Voice Access Points

LAN access:

    Web and email

    E-commerce

    Virtual Private Networks (VPNs)

DECT replacement

Voice Over IP (VOIP)

Ad-hoc Networking

Data exchange:

    Business card presentation/Document exchange

Multi-player electronic games or toys

Peer-to-peer WLAN using TCP/IP

Vending/ATM/airport check in / ticket collection/cashless transactions

Public LAN access: lounge / lamp-post access

Home networking:

    refrigerator/freezer/TV/Internet access point

Tracking: Short-range, in-building location services

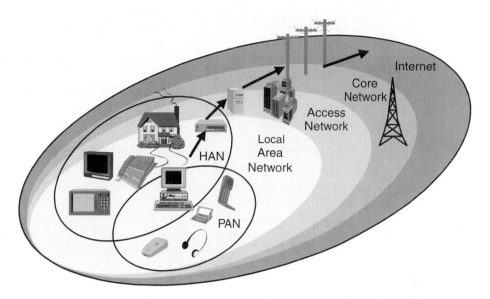

Figure 27–3   How PAN fits into the overall network.

Finally, ad-hoc networking based on existing wireless LAN technologies like IEEE 802.11 has been around for a little while now. Bluetooth professes to offer similar capabilities, although with certain limitations. However, its low cost, small form factor, and ease of use will make possible a whole plethora of applications and services all based on the notion of ad-hoc connectivity and interactivity, such as multiplayer games, automated vending, and transparent data exchange.

27.4   SUCCESS IN THE MARKETPLACE

Bluetooth absolutely must be easy to use straight out of the box with little or no configuration required; indeed, it should not need to ship with an instruction book! Power consumption must be sufficiently low that a Bluetooth enabled device does not need to be left to charge significantly longer than a nonenabled device. The MMI must be highly intuitive, i.e. "Do you want to connect to: Dave's PDA, the laser printer, the fridge?"

Interoperability is the most important issue of all. There will be many different Bluetooth solutions from different suppliers built in to a whole plethora of different devices. This in itself is very positive, since the consumer demands choice and multiple availability; one solution, form factor, or colour will never suit everyone. However, this makes the job of guaranteeing interoperability an onerous task. All devices in the public domain must work together seamlessly and transparently, avoiding the pitfalls which IrDA experienced in its early days.

At the time of this second edition, the level of interoperability between Bluetooth products is very good indeed. At the first unplugfest event, in mid 1999 when the technology was still very young, fifteen organisations showed up and, although the level of interoperability was not high, there was a basic level of information exchange and discussion. At the second event in early 2000, 250 organisations made it, and this time, only working products with a basic level of interoperation with Ericsson's development kits were admitted. Overall, the success rate was around 70%. Since then, during 2000 and 2001, there have been four more such events with many more products and participants and the results have only got better. These events will continue and are particularly invaluable in identifying application level issues between different ways of managing and configuring the Bluetooth stack. They also play their part in maintaining the high level of interoperability now attained through the evolution of the Bluetooth specification.

The whole question of partitioning between—even the emergence of—the PAN/HAN and how that impacts or not on the classic Wireless LAN one might expect to find in the office environment is undecided right now. Bluetooth may occupy a very useful niche as the PAN and as such the volumes will be huge as we have already described. However, if, as described in the chapter on related technologies, Bluetooth evolves upwards, it might well become the integrated PAN and HAN and even give the established WLAN incumbents a run for their money.

During 2001 there has been much discussion regarding the interaction of IEEE 802.11b and Bluetooth both in the same radio spectrum and in the same market. The spectrum coexistence question is being addressed both in proprietary solutions and in the standardisation world with IEEE802.15.2 and efforts within the SIG. The market coexistence is, however, more hotly debated. Essentially, 802.11b represents a true WLAN suitable for high speed peer to peer networking but represents a high power consumption and higher cost system, where interoperability is not guaranteed and product qualification is not available.

Bluetooth does not compete head-on with WLANs, but if it has the right price point and meets consumer needs, then perhaps small clustered office piconets will facilitate the entire printer and disc sharing required in small offices. A Bluetooth LAN access point might then provide a connection to the backbone or wider area WLAN.

As another example, a traveller in a public space, such as an airport, might use a PDA or smartphone via Bluetooth and associated access points to access flight details, book tickets, and browse sales offers, but then sit down to use his or her 802.11enabled laptop computer to surf the Web and view video-mails via other WLAN access points. The point is that a smartphone or PDA type of device will not bear the cost and power consumption requirements of a true WLAN subsystem, but will likely already include Bluetooth for its PAN needs.

Both of these examples show how Bluetooth and 802.11 may overlap with each other but offer specifically different costs and benefits. Indeed, there is sufficient benefit from both technologies that some manufacturers are already looking at combining both technologies in dual-mode devices.

Already there are a large number of Bluetooth components available, including single chip devices, two chip devices, and integrated modules. Sites such as BlueUnplugged.com retail Bluetooth connectivity products. Many products are already commercially available, including:

- PCMCIA Cards from IBM, Toshiba, Xircom, Brain Boxes Fujitsu, and TDK.
- Compact Flash Cards from AnyCom, Fujitsu, and Sunderland.
- USB and RS232 adapters from AnyCom, Sunderland, and TDK.
- Cellphones from Ericsson and Nokia.
- Headsets from Ericsson and Plantronics.
- Printer dongles from Anycom.
- Access points from Red-M, Axis, Widcomm, Anycom PicoBlue, and Ericsson.
- Add ons for PDAs from Red-M, TDK, and AnyCom.
- Laptops with embedded Bluetooth from Toshiba, IBM, Compaq, Sony, and Fujitsu.

More products are emerging onto the market. These are backed up by developers tools with ever-increasing functionality, such as CSR's Bluelab which lets you develop software to build embedded applications running on a single chip Bluetooth system. Development kits are also available from many companies well known in the Bluetooth world such as Ericsson, Widcomm, and Silicon Wave. IP suppliers such as TTPCom and Tality also provide development tools and evaluation boards to ease integration of Bluetooth IP into products. The wide choice of sophisticated development tools combined with new profiles is fueling developments in next generation Bluetooth enabled products.

27.5   ENABLING TECHNOLOGIES AND COMPONENTS

As we discussed in the chapter on implementation, there are various ways of creating a Bluetooth solution. Single-chip solutions facilitate simple, quick, and low cost deployment, and most importantly, the inclusion of Bluetooth in high-volume products which would not typically incorporate such advanced[4] technology. Products such as toys or in-building electrical controls, for example, are in this category.

Two-chip solutions (RF + digital link control/baseband) will facilitate choice and flexibility of RF source, providing for more powerful or higher quality radio systems suitable for WLAN applications, for example. Embedding the Bluetooth specific technology inside an existing ASIC for SOC levels of integration will become crucial in the longer term to enable some of the more exciting applications of Bluetooth, such as Bluetooth enabled multiplayer game pads, ultralow cost headsets, or even Bluetooth headset earrings and other wearable wireless jewellery!

The key to successful product development for Bluetooth has to be cost. For many applications, Bluetooth is replacing a piece of wire which costs a few cents. Of course, it adds some additional value, but until the market is won, this is a hard sell to the consumer. There is much talk of the $5 Bill Of Materials (BOM) cost adder, which basically

---

[4]And difficult to implement in a low-technology product where RF PCB techniques are not readily available.

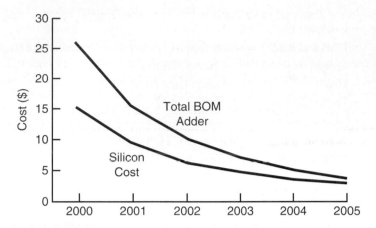

Figure 27–4   Projected silicon and BOM costs for Bluetooth.

results from the belief that a consumer might pay $39 retail for a Bluetooth headset as opposed to $29 for a wired headset, assuming a 200% markup between BOM and retail price. The graph in Figure 27–4 gives some indication of the likely drop in cost both for silicon and the total added BOM cost due to extra components like antenna and passives. Most people agree that $5 is achievable.

At the time of publication, many companies had announced products or development/licensing partnerships. Broadly speaking, there are silicon components available in the shape of single or dual chip solutions, IP solutions available for license, and development kits and radio test or protocol analysis equipment available. Modules are available to speed integration into new products. The number and range of consumer products under development is truly bewildering, with each exploiting the various component solutions in different ways to add value to the product.

27.6   CONSUMER PRODUCTS

The first devices to appear on the market were external add-on modules. For cellular phones, these were add-on "dongles," which plugged into the bottom of the phone, or "smart batteries," which added Bluetooth functionality inside the battery pack. For PDAs, there are compact flash devices and Bluetooth enabled cradles; for laptops and some palmtop devices PCMCIA cards are available.

Already these add-ons have been followed by laptops and phones with built in Bluetooth, and amongst headset manufacturers the emphasis has moved from overcoming technical difficulties to getting the best styling.

As the Bluetooth data rate evolves upwards, it will become suitable for other applications such as the AV/multimedia applications discussed in the related technologies chapter. These and other applications are driving new profiles being defined within the Bluetooth SIG.

It was already mentioned in the introduction that GPRS and UMTS will have a major effect on Bluetooth, and vice versa. The timeline in Figure 27–5 gives projected dates for these service rollouts and an indication of how Bluetooth will itself roll out over the next few years. If this pace is kept up, we are likely to see the kinds of product volumes which many people have bullishly been talking about for some time now, as shown in Figure 27–6. With reports of Bluetooth chip volumes reaching millions per month, the predictions are already beginning to be realised.

27.7   THE BLUETOOTH BRAND

It is well known that a brand portrays a powerful message in the marketplace. Already the Bluetooth name has become well known and understood to relate to wireless connectivity and freedom. By developing the name into a brand and providing a Bluetooth brand book with guidance on the use of the mark and logo, the SIG has tried very hard to give Bluetooth a consumer brand image which will guarantee its success in the marketplace.

The brand book forms part of the Bluetooth specification and describes how the brand should be used. It is available from the Bluetooth Web site at *http://www.Bluetooth.com,* and manufacturers producing Bluetooth devices must comply with the rules which it describes in just the same way that they must comply with the rest of the Bluetooth specification.

The Bluetooth combination mark is shown in Figure 27–7, it consists of the figure mark and the word mark. In addition to the marks there is also a tagline and jingles.

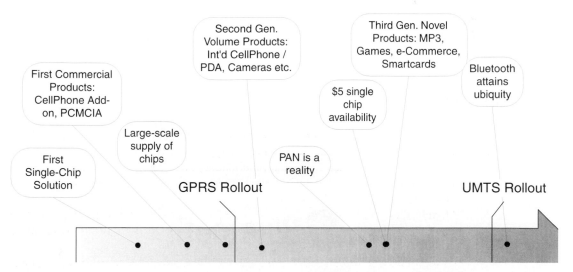

Figure 27–5   Timeline for Bluetooth technology rollout.

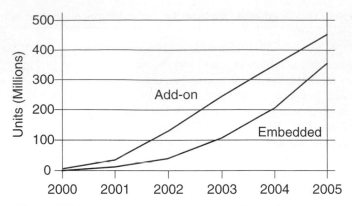

Figure 27–6   Projected volumes of Bluetooth-enabled devices.

27.7.1   Legality

By tying in use of the brand with the qualification procedure which itself is essential for obtaining free rights to essential Bluetooth IP, only quality devices which correctly implement the standard may be marked with the name Bluetooth. Conversely, if something is not so marked, it is not qualified and is thus in breach of the essential IP licensing arrangements. So, the brand may only be applied to approved, tested devices and the mark effectively has legal significance and can be used to facilitate prosecution of pirates.

27.7.2   Consumer's View

The brand reinforces the presence of Bluetooth technology in the market, making it clear that there is widespread availability of compatible devices. Through conformance testing, the brand is associated with the Bluetooth profiles and indicates that a product has been through testing, serving as a quality mark and effectively providing a badge of interoperability. The brand is designed to be used so as to make it clear that Bluetooth is not proprietary, but has many adopters.

Figure 27–7   Two forms of the Bluetooth wordmark.

Table 27–3   Bluetooth Features and Limitations

Features	Limitations
Point to point and point to multipoint links	8 devices per piconet with limited extension via scatternet
Voice and data links	Short-range
Compact form factor	No handover facility
Low power	Max data rate of 723.2 Kb/s
Low cost	Occupies the crowded ISM band
Robust frequency hopping, error correction	Slow connection setup
Profiles ensure Application Level interoperability	
High level of security through frequency hopping, encryption, and authentication	
Nondirectional	
Unlicensed ISM band	

27.7.3   Manufacturer's View

The Bluetooth brand adds value to a product, adding the overall Bluetooth marketing message for the product in question and indicating that the product has enhanced functionality. The compatibility guarantee associated with the brand widens potential markets, i.e., the consumer *knows* that one headset will work with many different handsets. This interoperability is vital for Bluetooth technology to deliver on its ad-hoc networking promise.

27.8   SUMMARY

There are a great many opportunities for Bluetooth-enabled products that exploit the various features of the technology as described in Table 27–3 to add value. However, there are many factors which could work against it. Potentially competing technologies, such as HomeRF and to a lesser extent 802.11, or even IrDA, could cause consumer confusion and at worst push Bluetooth into a niche corner. However, both HomeRF and 802.11 have said they are working to form a cooperative harmonisation between the technologies, though how that will work out remains to be seen.

For manufacturers, the cost of the technology is paramount. For Bluetooth to become ubiquitous, it must be built into mass market products, not just the high-end models.

For consumers, poor interoperability and/or poor user experience could be a major problem for Bluetooth and cause it to falter. The well-discussed "Out Of Box Experience" (OOBE) has to be seamless and simple.

Whatever happens, one thing is sure. Bluetooth will be big, spectacularly big—either as a consumer flop, or as a massive success. We think it most likely the latter.

28

Future Developments

When the Bluetooth SIG was originally formed, its aim was simply to produce version 1.0 of the Bluetooth specification. The plan was to dissolve the SIG at that point. As time went by, it became obvious that more could be done with Bluetooth in many ways:

- Version 1.0 was produced in a hurry and still needed corrections and clarifications.
- The list of profiles did not cover important areas, so there was scope for more profiles.
- There were proposals for enhancing Bluetooth to produce a version 2.0.

The Bluetooth SIG promoters announced that the SIG would continue in operation as long as Bluetooth devices were being made. The SIG reformed into a version 1.2 SIG, and members of the original SIG. Unlike the original SIG, the new version is incorporated as a U.S. not-for-profit organisation. The original SIG is now obsolete and its members have been asked to join the new SIG by signing up on-line at *http://www.bluetooth.org*.

To take the Bluetooth specification forward, the promoters also put in place working groups to continue enhancing and developing the Bluetooth specification.

28.1 WORKING GROUPS AND NEW BLUETOOTH PROFILES

A series of working groups continue the process of producing and refining the Bluetooth specification. An errata group considers corrections and clarifications to the specifications and includes reviewers who consider whether changes should be recommended. At present there is also an errata process group working under a BARB errata program manager; this group is formalising the errata process. Members of the Bluetooth SIG can submit and view errata at *http://www.bluetooth.org/member/errata.htm.*

At the time of publication, the remaining working groups were working on new profiles. The current list of profile working groups is as follows:

- AV, Audio/Video—CD quality audio, video suitable for conferencing.
- Ca—Produced the Hands-Free Profile (see Draft Post 1.1 Profiles chapter); the same group also has within its scope looking at diagnostics and positioning for cars.
- Coexist—Coexistence working group: working on coexistence of Bluetooth and other ISM band technologies.
- ESDP—Extended Service Discovery protocol: working on support for more discovery protocols such as Jini.
- HCI—This group is looking at extending the HCI part of the core specification.
- HID—Produced the Human Interface Device Profile (see Draft Post 1.1 profiles chapter).
- Imaging, Still Image—considers image exchange for storage display or forwarding. This group has produced the Basic Image Profile (see Draft Post 1.1 Profiles chapter).
- ISDN—Interoperability with ISDN services and applications.
- LP—Local positioning: aims to provide locationing information on Bluetooth devices to augment GPS services for indoor, underground, or builtup areas.
- PAN, Personal Area Networking—This group has produced the PAN profile and BNEP specification allowing Bluetooth to act as a bearer for IP based services (see PAN and BNEP chapter).
- Printing—Text document and image printing, this group has produced the Basic Printing Profile and Hardcopy Cable Replacement Profile (see Draft Post 1.1 profiles chapter).
- Radio—This group is looking at future versions of the Bluetooth specification aiming at best throughput for cost effective handhelds. It is split into two groups, one of which is looking at medium rate (Mb/s) and one at high rate (10 Mb/s).
- UDI—Unrestricted Digital Information protocol or UDI is a data system used in Japanese handsets. This group looks at interfacing Bluetooth to UDI systems.
- Security—This group is looking at improving and extending Bluetooth security procedures.

Additional groups will be formed as and when the need for new Bluetooth profiles emerges. Members of the Bluetooth SIG who are working on new products having usage models not covered by the current profiles are invited to submit ideas for new profiles.

28.2   PROFILE WORKING GROUPS

All Bluetooth profile working groups have some work in common. Every working group must consider:

- Issues of security, pairing, etc.
- Which features will be mandatory at various levels (LC, LM, etc.).
- How to define a service record for the profile.
- How to provide a royalty free specification wherever possible.
- How profiles will be tested.
- How to reuse existing work where possible.

In addition, each working group will address issues specific to the profile they are specifying.

The following sections look in more detail at the activities of some of the working groups.

28.2.1   Audio/Visual Profile

As Chapter 6 illustrated, the audio quality provided by Bluetooth SCO channels is inadequate for carrying music. However, the Bluetooth data links have a much higher bandwidth and could be used for carrying music, although the limited data rates of Bluetooth 1.0 and 1.1 mean that some form of compression technique is necessary to achieve transfer of video and high-quality audio.

As early as the first quarter of 2000 at CeBIT (the premier European consumer electronics showcase), there were several demonstrations of compressed video carried over Bluetooth. Although the bandwidth does not allow cinematic quality video, it is sufficient for many monitoring applications.

An audio/visual work group has been formed within the Bluetooth SIG to address issues involved in digital audio and sound distribution over Bluetooth's data (ACL) links. The group is chaired by Philips and includes members from Ericsson, Nokia, Sony, and Toshiba.

The audio/visual work group aims to define formats and mechanisms for distributing video and high-quality audio over Bluetooth, reusing existing audio/visual standards wherever possible. The group aims to create the following profiles:

- Generic Distribution Profile—Mono and stereo CD-quality sound distribution.
- Advanced Audio Distribution Profile—Surround sound distribution.

- Remote Control Profile
- Video Conferencing Profile—video suitable for business use, this profile is not intended to provide video distribution for entertainment use.

The audio/visual profiles will be built upon L2CAP. They will include a security layer, which will aid with copy protection of material distributed over Bluetooth. Naturally with such high bandwidth applications, the profiles will use Bluetooth's QOS facilities.

For displays, the work group may produce two sets of specifications: one which relies upon the data rates provided by Bluetooth 1.0, with display sizes limited to Z\v VGA, and one using Bluetooth 2.0 radio data rates, which allow full VGA display.

To support their profiles, the Audio Video Group is working on two transports: the Distribution Transport protocol, and the Control Transport protocol.

28.2.2 Car Working Group Profiles

The Car working group has already produced the Hands-Free Profile which allows a Bluetooth enabled phone to work with a Hands-Free device such as might be used in a car. See Chapter 20 for more details of this Profile. A Phone Access Profile which adds extra functionality not provided in the Hands-Free Profile is currently being developed, as is a SIM Access Profile to govern communications with a Subscriber Identity Module (SIM).

The Car working group scope also covers other aspects of Bluetooth in the automotive environment. The applications for Bluetooth in cars are many and various. Within a car, Bluetooth devices can connect to one another and access services provided by the car.

The car can also communicate with the surrounding environment. Bluetooth 1.0 connection speeds do not allow a fast moving car to drive past a toll point, establish a connection, and transfer data before it is out of range, but there are many possible uses for a more static connection to a car. Car parking could be paid for over a Bluetooth link. Car diagnostics could be transferred to a unit in a garage or held by a mechanic. Tourist information points could transfer information to car navigation systems over Bluetooth. Fleet managers could extract information from vehicles using Bluetooth links. The list of applications goes on and on.

Even in advance of output from the Car working group, Bluetooth has received widespread interest from car manufacturers. BMW, SAAB, Ford, and Volvo are among the notable names from the automotive industry who have joined the Bluetooth SIG. A Car profile standardising the usage of Bluetooth in cars can only increase interest among manufacturers.

28.2.3 Extended Service Discovery Profile

The extended service discovery profile working group is looking at interoperability between the Bluetooth Service Discovery Protocol (SDP) and other service discovery protocols. The first specification being considered is UPnP (Universal Plug and Play). More information on UPnP can be found at *http://www.upnp.org*. Other service discovery profiles will be produced as and when a need for them is identified. Other profiles may be mapped to UPnP as part of the mapping effort.

28.2.4   Local Positioning Profile

The local positioning profile work group is examining how Bluetooth can be used to enable users to accurately find their position indoors and outdoors in builtup environments. The location information could be passed up the stack for use and display by applications. In particular, the information could be used with Web based applications.

Such capabilities could be useful in environments where GPS or cellular positioning systems do not perform well: inside buildings, underground, and in heavily builtup areas.

The working group will need to produce a descriptor, which can hold positioning information for passing to applications in a standardised format. This could be a new development or could reuse existing work from other specifications. Wherever possible, existing work will be reused.

Because locationing information is propagated between devices which may not be able to precisely identify one another's location, it will need to incorporate some information on how much uncertainty there is in the location.

28.2.5   UDI—Bluetooth in Japanese 3G Handsets/UDI

Japan has different cellular phones from Europe and America, and the Japanese market often places different demands on the capabilities of handsets. Because of this, there is always a danger that specifications which meet with widespread acceptance in Europe and America will stumble in Japan. Therefore, a working group has been set up to explicitly consider issues related to using Bluetooth in Japanese third Generation (3G) handsets. This group will consider how to transport video over the Japanese 3G network and to generally resolve issues with incorporating Bluetooth into Japanese 3G handsets.

28.2.5   Further Profiles

The process of defining new profiles is open to any adopter company. The first step of course is to see if there is a real need for a new profile. Profiles are intended to aid interoperation between products, so if an existing profile could be made to serve an application, then it makes more sense to use that profile than to invent a new one. This way, more devices will be available which support the profile and interoperability between devices will be higher. (There is of course the common sense argument of why invent something new if what you've got serves the purpose!)

If an application is not served by any existing profile, the next step is to ask if there is a sufficiently strong market to justify a new profile. In the cases where the profile would only serve a small specialised market, it may make more sense to implement a proprietary solution. Profiles are appropriate when there is a need for different manufacturers' devices to interoperate. If it is a case where the market is so small that there will never be more than one manufacturer interested in serving it, interoperation is not a benefit.

When an application is identified which justifies a new profile, then a proposal for a new profile can be drawn up using the standard format followed by the other profiles. This is submitted to the core promoters group, and if it is seen as a useful and valid contribution to the Bluetooth specification, a working group is drawn up to consider the profile. The advantage of working groups is that many different companies have the opportunity to contribute their viewpoints. A profile drawn up by just one organisation may miss useful elements just because they are not useful to that particular group's applications. A working group is likely to produce a more rounded, and more generally useful, profile.

At various stages during profile development the profile is reviewed by groups within the Bluetooth SIG to ensure that it fits in with other developments in Bluetooth and to ensure that it is testable. Finally, the work group outputs the finished profile it undergoes a legal review to ensure that it does not infringe intellectual property rights, and it can be incorporated into the Bluetooth specification after approval by the Bluetooth SIG Board of Directors.

28.3 FUTURE BLUETOOTH CORE SPECIFICATIONS

In addition to the profile working groups the SIG has working groups which are looking at improving and extending the core specification.

28.3.1   HCI Working Group

The HCI Working group formed in 2001 to look at extending the HCI part of the core specification. The group includes three subgroups: PCI, SD, and UART, each of which is considering a different transport. The UART group is looking at an alternative transport for serial lines: the existing UART protocol was intended for communication between chips on the same circuit board and has deficiencies when used with serial cables. For instance, it cannot correct for the bit errors occasionally encountered in a long serial cable. This group also helps to review HCI errata.

28.3.2 Coexistence Working Group

The coexistence working group (Coexist) is considering how Bluetooth can coexist with other wireless LAN standards in the ISM band. Bluetooth is not the only wireless telecommunications specification using the ISM band for communications, and it is possible that users may wish to use two ISM band protocols in the same device. For example, a user might want to install an 802.11b PCMCIA device in a notebook which already contains a Bluetooth module.

Already manufacturers and developers are investigating the development of baseband and radio devices that can work with more than one ISM band communications protocol. This, combined with hosts linked to more than one ISM band module, opens up the possibility of bridging devices which could link Bluetooth to 2.4 GHz WANs.

The working group considering coexistence with other ISM band devices will develop and recommend usage models for the ISM environment. To aid in this, they will work on interoperability issues in cross-industry groups and may suggest improvements to Bluetooth for incorporation in future specifications.

28.3.3   Radio Working Group

The radio working group is looking at an optional extension to the Bluetooth 1.0 radio. There will be two extensions: medium and high rate. The medium rate will be capable of data rates of around 2.0 Mb/s, the high rate offers around 10 Mb/s. The attractions are obvious; such high data rates would allow Bluetooth to carry hi-fi quality audio or even video and would align Bluetooth with 3G cellular systems.

The radio working group has been charged with maintaining the global availability of Bluetooth. This is likely to lead to the radio remaining confined to the ISM band. The constraints of the ISM band mean that the radio would have to use a more complex modulation scheme. The cost target is less than around $10 (USD), which will make complex modulation challenging for developers to implement.

Bluetooth 2.0 devices should preserve backwards compatibility with version 1.0 devices. This could mean having devices capable of handling two modulation schemes. The Radio 2.0 group is also looking at changing the inquiry mechanism to speed up the process of discovering Bluetooth devices. Finally, the Radio 2.0 group is also considering introducing an option for handover of Bluetooth voice and data calls. This will be particularly challenging, as established systems which implement handover between local groups of communicating devices use a backbone network to coordinate handover.

The very concept of handing over a call implies that there must be some backbone network taking the call. Handing over synchronisation of one cellular phone and PDA address book to synchronise with another's address book makes no sense, but handing over a connection with one LAN access point to another LAN access point feeding into the same LAN makes perfect sense. The difference is that the PDA and cell phone were a self-sufficient piconet, but the LAN access points both feed into the same wider network, in this case a LAN, so somehow the roaming Bluetooth device must be coordinated with different access points supporting connection to the same wider area service.

Because Bluetooth connections are short range and involve mobile devices, it is possible to roam between piconets faster than the rate of cell switching normally expected on systems such as GSM. Fast acquisition of connections will be a requirement for handing over calls when devices are rapidly roaming between piconets. So the Radio 2.0 working group's work on speeding up inquiry mechanisms could tie in with the work on handing over calls.

Some manufacturers have implemented scatternet capability, but up to version 1.1 it was not well supported by the specification, the radio group is investigating ways of better defining scatternet in the core specification.

Devices implementing future versions of the specification should be compatible with Bluetooth 1.0 and 1.1 devices. One proposal for achieving this is to have all devices connect in 1.0 mode, then negotiate a move to higher rate modes if all devices involved adhere to a higher rate specification.

28.4 SUMMARY

The SIG has created a series of new working groups that are continuing development of the Bluetooth specification. The development is ongoing in three key areas: correction and clarification of the version 1.0 specification, the development of further profiles, and the development of an enhanced radio and baseband, which will lead to a new version 2.0 core specification.

The SIG has also provided a mechanism for Bluetooth adopter companies to propose further profiles.

APPENDIX

Bluetooth 1.1 Updates

WHY BLUETOOTH 1.1?

A lot of questions have been posed about why version 1.1 of the Bluetooth specification was brought out and exactly what the changes were between that and version 1.0b. For all the fine details, the best place to look will always be the Bluetooth adopter's Web site, *http://www.bluetooth.org,* where Bluetooth adopters can find the specification itself and all the errata that led to the changes. However, it can be a slow process wading through errata, and if you're not very familiar with the specification, sometimes it's not obvious why and where changes have been made. This appendix looks at the differences between version 1.0b and version 1.1 and attempts to offer some explanations for the changes.

WHY CHANGE AT ALL?

A prime objective for Bluetooth technology is interoperability. Any pair of devices carrying the Bluetooth brand should be capable of working together at a basic level. Any pair of devices supporting compatible Bluetooth profiles should be capable of connecting and using one another's services. This means that users can mix and match devices from any manufacturers, and the Bluetooth brand guarantees that they will work.

Well, that's the theory anyway, but to be able to do that, everybody has to interpret the specification the same way. Any areas of ambiguity could ruin interoperability. The working groups that wrote the Bluetooth specification thought they'd made it unambiguous, but it turned out that manufacturers were interpreting the specification in different ways. That meant that devices couldn't always work together. Worse still, it turned out that some features couldn't even be relied on to work reliably between two devices from the same manufacturer. Something had to be done!

The Bluetooth Special Interest Group (SIG) has an errata process for fixing problems with the Bluetooth specifications. Any SIG member can submit errata through a Web page. Then an errata working group considers errata and votes on whether to accept them. By the summer of 2000, it was becoming obvious that there were so many errata on version 1.0b of the specification that it was worth going to a whole new version. However, there were concerns that the specification still might not be right. How could the SIG reassure everyone that the next version would be any better than the last?

The Bluetooth SIG organizes testing events called unplugfests, where many manufacturers get together and test their devices against one another. They decided to identify the errata that were most critical for interoperability and then ask everyone to test them at unplugfest 4, held in November 2000. If version 1.0b plus the critical errata had no serious interoperability problems, then this could be used as the foundation of version 1.1. As it turned out, the unplugfest was a great success, so the SIG went ahead and produced a draft version of 1.1. After a few months, this was slightly modified, and version 1.1 was formally adopted.

WHAT CHANGED?

Many changes took place throughout the Bluetooth specification. This section looks in detail at each of the changes and gives some background on why the changes were required.

Radio

When the Bluetooth specification began, Spain, France, and Japan used restricted portions of the ISM band. Spain and Japan have now opened up the full band, and France has a change scheduled to take place in 2003. This all means that the original frequency allocation table is no longer valid. The Bluetooth SIG is lobbying to get the whole world to adopt the complete ISM band, so, rather than continuing to show France in the table, Erratum 1044 moved it to a footnote to emphasize that limited-frequency bands are the exception not the rule. (By removing Spain from the list of exceptions, this erratum coincidentally removed an error in the table: The guard band for Spain had been too large.)

Baseband

Interoperability testing during unplugfests showed that the description of a master-slave switch was ambiguous. Erratum 1067 completely rewrote Section 10.9.3 of the baseband specification to make the description of master-slave switch clearer.

The Bluetooth security procedures begin with units generating an initialization key that is derived from a PIN code and a Bluetooth device address. This key is used to secure data used to generate link keys. The link keys, in turn, are used to generate encryption keys for encrypting data on the link. In version 1.0b, the initialization keys were authenticated. The initialization keys are discarded as soon as the link keys have been generated, and the link keys are authenticated before the encryption keys are generated. There is really no need to authenticate both link keys and initialization keys, so Erratum 1071 changed the text to make authentication happen after link key exchange. Sometimes authentication is used to verify the identity of a unit, but the units don't go on to encrypt traffic, so the same errata marked generation of an encryption key as optional.

Version 1.0b of the specification was unclear on the order of bits from the CVSD encoder, which caused some interoperability problems. Erratum 1077 clarified that CVSD bits should be sent over the air in the same order that they are generated by the CVSD encoder.

In version 1.0b of the specification, ARQN numbers, which are used to acknowledge data transfer, were frozen throughout hold and sniff modes. Data can be transferred during sniff mode, and freezing the ARQN numbers made the sniff-mode data transfer unreliable. In hold mode, no data can be transferred, so there's no point in specifying that ARQN numbers don't change. Erratum 1079 removed the text that stopped ARQN numbers from changing during hold and sniff modes, thus giving sniff mode the capability to transfer data reliably.

The baseband and Link Manager sections described the parameters used in sniff mode inconsistently. Erratum 1081 fixed this by bringing the baseband in line with the Link Manager.

Link Manager

With 25 critical errata, the Link Manager attracted more changes than any other section of the 1.0b Bluetooth specification. Because there were so many changes to the Link Manager, this section is split up into the different areas of Link Management behavior that were affected.

Security.   In version 1.0b, there was no clearly defined way for the slave to stop encryption. Erratum 1092 specified that any unit wanting to stop encryption could send an LMP_encryption_mode_req with the encryption-mode parameter set to no encryption (zero). If the other device responds with LMP_accepted, the master sends an LMP_stop_encryption_req message. The same erratum specified that encryption had to be stopped before an encryption key could be changed.

Erratum 1095 corresponded with Erratum 1071 from the baseband: It removed the redundant authentication on link keys and specified that mutual authentication should happen every time link keys are changed.

Version 1.0b allowed link keys to be changed at any time. For the semipermanent keys used on point to point links, this makes sense, but temporary keys are in use only for one session, so they don't need to be changed. Errata 1098 and 1099 changed the specification so that temporary link keys could not be changed. Erratum 1098 also removed some text that specified that the semipermanent link keys should be stored in nonvolatile memory; in version 1.1, it just says that they should be stored—where they go is up to the implementer. Errata 1098 and 1099 also specified that after changing link keys, mutual authentication had to take place. Previously, this was required by the baseband part of the specification, but it had been forgotten in the Link Manager specification.

When link keys are changed, encryption is stopped and restarted, but in version 1.0b, the Link Manager specification did not say how it should be restarted. Some implementers thought that it automatically restarted without signaling, while others thought that LMP messages were needed to restart encryption. By adding a reference to the procedures used to restart encryption, Erratum 1100 got rid of the ambiguity and made it clear that LMP_encryption_mode_req should be used to restart encryption.

Data transmission must be stopped when encryption mode changes; otherwise, data could be sent when the encryption mode is indeterminate, which would lead to data being corrupted or lost. To avoid this, data transmission is stopped before any encryption change. Version 1.0b of the specification said that data traffic had to be temporarily stopped, but there was some disagreement among implementers as to when to stop it: Should it stop immediately, at the end of an ACL packet, or at the end of an L2CAP packet? Erratum 1114 clarified that data transmission should stop at the end of the current ACL packet with L2CAP data.

As a side effect of a successful authentication procedure, a parameter called the Authenticated Ciphering Offset (ACO) is calculated and then used to generate the ciphering keys, which are then used to encrypt data. If a master and a slave initiated authentication together, they could end up with two different ACOs, so they would not be capable of decrypting one another's encrypted data. To keep this from happening, Erratum 1203 introduced a new rule that Link Managers must reply to any outstanding LMP_au_rand authentication request signals with LMP_sres secure response signals before sending their own LMP_au_rand authentication request signals. It is still possible for LMP_au_rand messages to cross, however. If this happens and the master receives a reponse to its own LMP_au_rand, it is allowed to respond with LMP_not_accepted with the error code "LMP Error Transaction Collision". In this way, Link Managers should be capable of ensuring that only one authentication is in progress at any time, thus also avoiding mismatching ACOs.

Allowed and Disallowed Messages.   During unplugfests and other interoperability testing, it was found that many implementations had problems with LMP messages sent before the LMP_host_connection_req. Erratum 1093 clarified exactly which LMP messages could be sent in the interval between paging and the LMP_host _connection_req. The list allowed for version 1.1 is: clock offset request, LMP version, supported features, name request, and detach.

Erratum 1109 clarified how the Link Manager should handle PDUs that are disallowed on a link. Some Link Managers had been taking drastic action and disconnecting if they saw a disallowed PDU. This seemed like an overreaction to others, who simply ignored the PDUs. Even ignoring them caused problems because some Link Managers hung waiting for a response that never came, and then they timed out. To solve all these problems, version 1.1 now says that if the disallowed PDU is one that expects a response, then an LMP_not_accepted with a reason code "PDU not allowed" should be sent as a response; otherwise, the PDU should be ignored.

Transactions.   During unplugfests and other interoperability testing, a lot of confusion arose about transaction IDs, in particular the IDs to be sent on the LMP_setup_complete messages. Several implementers gave up checking the transaction IDs altogether as the only way to achieve interoperability! Erratum 1097 clarified the situation by simply stating, "The transaction ID shall be 0 if LMP_setup_complete is sent from the master, and 1 if it is sent from the slave."

LMP uses transaction IDs to identify whether a transaction was started by the master or the slave, but in version 1.0b it was unclear exactly what a transaction was. Erratum 1185 made it clear that a transaction could extend across several LMP exchanges. For instance, it said that all the security sequences in Section 3.3, including mutual authentication after link key creation, form a single transaction. Therefore, all use the transaction ID from the first LMP_in_rand. The erratum added several more examples to make it clear exactly what was defined as a single transaction.

Master-Slave Switch.   The description of a master-slave switch in version 1.0b was ambiguous, which led to many interoperability problems. Version 1.1 greatly improved the descriptions of how it should work. Erratum 1094 was part of this improvement: In version 1.0b, there was no description of how to do a master-slave switch during connection setup and no specification of exactly when the switch messages should be sent. Erratum 1094 clarified when LMP_setup_complete should be sent and when non-LMP traffic can start.

Another part of the master-slave switch ambiguity in version 1.0b was that how to calculate the slot offset between master and slave clocks was not clearly defined. Erratum 1194 clarified this. The message contains a BD_ADDR and a slot offset. The BD_ADDR is the slave that will become master in a switch. To calculate the slot offset, you work out the value in microseconds of the start of a TX slot as if the slave were master of a piconet. Then you subtract the value in microseconds of the start of the current master's transmit slot. You then do a modulo 1250 operation to get a value between 0 and 1249. So, if the time that a transmit slot starts on the current piconet is TXstart $_{\text{slave's clock}}$ and the time that a transmit slot would start if the slave were master is TXstart $_{\text{master's clock}}$, then the offset is given by this equation:

$$\text{offset} = (\text{TXstart}_{\text{slave's clock}} - \text{TXstart}_{\text{master's clock}}) \bmod 250$$

A third problem with the master-slave switch was that the instant to make the switch was not defined. Erratum 1190 added a switch instant parameter to the LMP_switch_req to indicate when the switch should happen. Procedures such as stopping traffic before the switch and determining the exact sequence of messages were also defined in this erratum. Some implementations had trouble reacting fast enough to a master-slave switch request, so this erratum also said that the switch instant should be set at least $2*T_{poll}$ or 32 slots (whichever is greater) after the LMP_switch_req.

Low-Power Modes. Erratum 1101 covered the LMP_unpark_PM_ADDR message. This message contains an AM_ADDR. In version 1.0b, 4 bits were allocated for the AM_ADDR, but only 3 are needed. This confused implementers, who did not know whether they should use the high bits or low bits. Version 1.1 specifies just 3 bits for the AM_ADDR, so there can be no confusion on where to store it.

In version 1.0b, the sniff parameters sniff attempt and sniff timeout were counted in slots. Some implementers counted transmit and receive slots, and some just counted receive slots. This obviously caused interoperability problems because some implementers made the sniff attempt and sniff timeout twice as long as the others did. Erratum 1102 added the description "number of receive slots" to these two parameters to ensure that everybody interprets them in the same way.

Erratum 1106 removed a section that allowed a master to force sniff mode. This proved to be an impractical feature because the master could not tell whether the slave could support the sniff settings that it supported. Masters can still request slaves to enter sniff mode, so removing the capability to force sniff mode does not make any great change in functionality.

Because the link control level packet delivery is unreliable, there were potential problems with hold mode. For example, a master could ask a slave to hold, and the slave would send a response that then got lost. The master would then continue trying to hold the slave, while the slave was inactive. If the link supervision timeout didn't elapse, the master would still be trying to hold the slave when it came back out of hold mode, so the slave would exit hold mode only to go straight back in again. Obviously, this sort of thing can waste a lot of bandwidth, so the LMP_hold message was changed by Erratum 1188 to add a hold instant parameter specifying exactly when the hold should happen. That way, if the Link Controller did keep trying to send a stale LMP_hold message, the device that received it could tell that the message was out-of-date because the hold instant would be in the past. To give the message a chance to work its way through from one Link Manager to the other, the hold instant must be set to at least $6*T_{poll}$ slots in the future.

Erratum 1189 attempted to clear up a problem with entering park mode. It had been possible for a master to park a slave: The slave replied with LMP_accepted and parked, but the master didn't see the LMP_accepted and thus didn't know the slave was parked. As a result, the master kept trying to park the slave. Alternatively, the master might assume that it had missed an LMP_accepted and believe a slave to be parked when, in fact, the LMP_park message had been lost. This could lead to the master reusing the AM_ADDR for a slave that was still active. To mitigate this problem, some timers were introduced into version 1.1. The slave must now try to send the LMP_accepted message until it gets a baseband acknowledgement or until $6*T_{poll}$ slots have passed, whichever is sooner. The master is not allowed to reuse the parked slave's AM_ADDR until $6*T_{poll}$ slots after it has received LMP_accepted. If it doesn't receive LMP_accepted, then a link supervision timeout happens and the slave is detached. These procedures aren't perfect, but it seems that there is no perfect way to guarantee to park a slave using messages across an unreliable radio link. These procedures are at least a lot more reliable than the 1.0b procedures for parking.

Erratum 1189 also removed the forced park mode because there was no way to guarantee that the slave could handle the beacon parameters that were being forced upon it.

Multislot Packets.   In version 1.0b, the master could control whether the slave used multislot packets, but the slave had no such control over the master. This was a problem for slaves with limited capabilities, for example, because they were trying to meet tight time constraints in scatternets. Erratum 1096 made the default for any new connection single-slot packets. This included connections formed by slaves returning from park mode or formed by a master-slave switch. In version 1.1, multislot packets cannot be used until they have been negotiated with LMP_max_slot and LMP_max_slot_req.

Detach.   When a slave has been detached (disconnected), the master can reuse the AM_ADDR that it used to identify the slave. This is the procedure that Erratum 1187 defined: first, the LM initiating detach finishes sending the current ACL packet with L2CAP information and stops sending L2CAP data. Obviously, it makes no sense to detach from a device and still try to send it data! Next an LMP_detach message is queued for transmission, and the Link Manager starts a timer of $6*T_{poll}$ slots (where T_{poll} is the poll interval for the connection). If this timer expires before a baseband acknowledgement is received, then the link is dropped and a link supervision timer is started. When that timer has elapsed, the AM_ADDR for the dropped link can be reused. If a baseband-level acknowledgement for the LMP_detach is received before the $6*T_{poll}$ timer expires, the detached link's AM_ADDR can be reused after $3*T_{poll}$ slots. On the receiving side, a timer is also used. A master starts a timer of $6*T_{poll}$ slots when it receives an LMP_detach, and a slave uses a timer of $3*T_{poll}$. When this timer expires, the link can be dropped and the AM_ADDR can be reused. If the LMP_detach message is lost due to interference, then a link supervision timeout will occur and the link will be detached eventually anyway. These procedures might seem complicated, but they avoid using the same address for two devices at the same time.

Timing.   Erratum 1191 added an explanation of interaction between the Link Manager and the Link Controller. The erratum explains that the Link Controller guarantees to communicate only once every T_{poll} slots. So, for instance, if a Link Manager issues a detach or park, it can't immediately reuse the AM_ADDR because it has not yet received a Link Controller level acknowledgement indicating that the old connection is inactive. The erratum also points out that Link Managers must be aware of Link Controller level timings during a master-slave switch and when starting hold mode because Link Managers must read the baseband clock to synchronize these actions.

Erratum 1193 also dealt with timings, but this time it was Link Management level timing. LMP defines a 30-second timeout between an LMP PDU and its response. Erratum 1193 said that this timeout should also apply between a Link Control level connection being established and a LMP_host_connection_req being sent. It also said that the

LMP_setup_complete should be sent before the LMP response timeout from the preceding transaction had timed out. This change was made because some implementations were hanging up during connection setup, and there was no real mechanism to allow a Link Manager to escape from that situation: it was just stuck waiting with no reason to go on and no reason to disconnect.

Flow Control Lag.   When a baseband receives a packet with its flow bit set to 0, it should stop transmitting L2CAP data. However, delays in processing the flow bit can mean that there is a lag between receiving the 0 flow bit and acting on it. This lag can result in data being received for a while after the flow off bit has been set. For maximum efficiency, it is useful to know what the likely lag at the other end of a link is. That way, a flow bit can be set to 0 when there are still enough buffers left to accommodate data sent during the flow lag period. To allow for this information to be passed, Erratum 1305 added a 3-bit field into the features parameter to give the total amount of L2CAP data that can be sent following the receipt of a valid payload header with the payload header flow bit set to 0. The unit for flow lag is 256 bytes (so, for example, 0b010 gives a flow lag of 512 bytes).

Host Controller Interface

There were no critical errata raised against the Host Controller Interface for version 1.0b, but a change in functionality was made as a result of Erratum 1142 (this was not listed as critical). In version 1.0b, an HCI reset command left a Bluetooth device in standby mode and caused it to lose its current operational state. Because the device lost all state after the reset was performed, it had no way to tell if it had been reset or just powered up; the command complete was returned before the reset was performed instead of afterward.

In Erratum 1142, the reset caused a device to lose operational state below HCI, so in version 1.1, connections are dropped and parameters that are not stored (such as inquiry window) return to default values. The HCI interface itself did not reset: This means that USB devices do not need to re-enumerate, saving a good deal of time for them. Because the HCI interface does not reset, it is possible to tell the difference between a reset and a power-on, so in version 1.1, the command complete event for a reset is sent after the reset is executed. Some implementers have criticized the new reset because it prevents them from resetting on-chip processors. Not being able to do a complete chip reset also means that problems such as memory leaks may persist through an HCI reset. However, the new reset scheme is better for the higher layers because they now know when a reset has completed and can rely on HCI transport to function seamlessly across a reset (although the upper layers aren't allowed to send commands during the reset itself).

Logical Link Control

L2CAP has a response timer, RTX, that is used to keep track of the time it takes to get a response to a signaling message. Version 1.0b stated that when the timer expired, the channel should be disconnected, but it wasn't clear exactly how this should happen. The normal procedure for disconnecting an L2CAP channel is to send an L2CAP_DisconnectReq, but if the RTX timer has expired, that implies that the peer L2CAP isn't listening to signaling requests. It seems rather pointless to send another signaling request! Erratum 1000 clarified that when the RTX timer expires, the channel goes straight to the closed state, with no extra signaling messages required.

L2CAP uses channel IDs to identify which channel a particular request affects. Usually, if an invalid channel ID is received in an L2CAP signal, a command reject is sent back. For configuration requests, however, the 1.0b specification required a configuration response to be sent. This made it impossible to reject configuration on an invalid channel ID. Erratum 1002 corrected this by allowing a command reject to be sent in response to a configuration request when an error condition made a reject appropriate.

RFCOMM

RFCOMM is based on GSM TS07.10, so unless RFCOMM specifically overrides the GSM standards, the rules of GSM TS07.10 are used. This means that RFCOMM could send several multiplexer control messages in one frame. RFCOMM is used in the headset profile, which is likely to be implemented in devices with very little memory or processing power, so keeping it simple is a good idea. In the interests of simplifying this protocol layer, Erratum 1047 limited RFCOMM to sending only one multiplexer control message per frame.

The Modem Status Command (MSC) was the flow-control mechanism for individual channels in version 1.0b. Erratum 1050 clarified which bits were used for flow control. The draft version of 1.1 also introduced credit-based flow control to RFCOMM. With credit-based flow control, units grant credits to one another. Then each time a packet is sent, one credit is used up. Before the introduction of credit-based flow control, RFCOMM channels used FCON and FCOFF messages for flow control on individual channels. Because Bluetooth channels are unreliable, these messages could require several retransmissions to switch off the flow of packets. This could lead to RFCOMM layer buffers overflowing and data being lost.

RFCOMM uses a new frame type for credit-based flow control with the CL1-CL4 field redefined. In GSM TS07.10, this field gives the convergence layer to use. In RFCOMM versions up to 1.0B, this field was forced to 0. In version 1.1, this field is used to indicate whether the frame carries credit-based flow-control messages.

RFCOMM uses a Parameter Negotiation (PN) command to negotiate various parameters, including frame size and flow-control method. Use of the PN command was optional in the draft version of 1.1, but it was made mandatory in the final version because, otherwise, the responding device could miss the chance of ever negotiating the parameters on its channel. Because credit-based flow control must be negotiated without mandatory parameter negotiation, units could not rely on being able to use credit-based flow control. The k1-k3 field is used to indicate the initial number of credits issued to a peer; there are 3 bits, so the initial credit value can range from 0 to 7. If credit-based flow control is not used, the k1-k3 bits stay as 0.

Erratum 1048 said that units must support the default RFCOMM frame length because they couldn't rely on negotiating parameters. In the final 1.1 specification, however, parameter negotiation on connection setup was made mandatory, so this no longer held true. The same erratum also pointed out that units did not have to accept any changes in parameters once an RFCOMM channel was set up.

SDP

Erratum 1159 corrected a simple typo. The value given for the base UUID in the SDP part of the specification was invalid. The correct value was already given in the Bluetooth Assigned Numbers document: 00000000-0000-1000-8000-00805F9B34FB.

Similarly, Erratum 1160 corrected the value given to PublicBrowseRoot to 00001002-0000-1000-8000-00805F9B34FB (UUID16: 0x1002). Again, the correct value came from the Bluetooth Assigned Numbers document.

Erratum 1163 clarified the meaning of MaximumAttributeByteCount. Some implementers had thought that it specified the maximum number of attributes that could be returned in all responses to a request. In fact, it specified the maximum number of attributes that could be returned in a single response packet, but the response could be split over several packets.

Cordless Telephony Profile

Version 1.0b of the Cordless Telephony Profile has a service record with service class Generic Telephony followed by service class Cordless Telephony. The rules for service class UUIDs in profiles state that the most specific class comes first, with more generic classes coming later. Erratum 1195 reversed the order of the service classes to make Cordless Telephony come before Generic Telephony.

Erratum 1306 made park mode optional for the Cordless Telephony Profile. This was done because the Cordless Telephony Profile was the only profile that had park mode as mandatory, and LMP changes had made 1.0b park mode incompatible with version 1.1. By making park optional, the profile allowed devices implementing the Cordless Telephony Profile to be backward compatible with version 1.0b.

Intercom Profile

Erratum 1220 was similar to Erratum 1195 from the Cordless Telephony Profile: The service classes Intercom and Generic Telephony had been wrong in the service records, so they were reversed to put Intercom (the most specific class) first.

Erratum 1238 corrected an error in Figure 10.1, which had an SCO link being established by the outgoing side rather than the incoming side.

Headset Profile

Erratum 1204 simply corrected a typing error: The ServiceClass0 which had been "Headset" was corrected to read "HeadsetAudioGateway."

Erratum 1211 changed the type of the headset gain value from an unsigned octet to a decimal numeric constant. This change was made because, if an unsigned octet was used, some possible values could match the codes used for command termination and response formatting.

Erratum 1215 made the RING signal before connecting a headset call optional. This was done because the Headset Profile might be used for data calls, and, in this case, no RING signal is needed. The same erratum also clarified that in-band (audio) ring tones could be sent instead of the RING signal. Due to a clerical error this critical erratum was not incorporated in version 1.1 and will be incorporated as an addendum to the specification.

Erratum 1217 finished a correction that was made between versions 1.0a and 1.0b, when pairing was made optional for the Headset Profile. The change had been made to pairing, but bonding was left as mandatory, which made no sense, so both were made optional.

Dialup Networking Profile

Erratum 1198 was also similar to Erratum 1195 from the Cordless Telephony Profile: The service classes Dialup Networking and Generic Networking had been wrong in the service records, so they were reversed to put Dialup Networking (the most specific class) first.

Erratum 1282 was a minor change bringing the Dialup Networking Profile in line with the Generic Access Profile. Version 1.0b had required devices supporting limited discoverable mode to also support general discoverable mode. This was changed to allow a device to support just limited discoverable mode (because a device in limited discoverable mode will respond to general inquiries anyway).

Fax Profile

Erratum 1206 made nondiscoverable and nonpairable modes optional. Previously they had been mandatory, but this requirement was removed because it did not contribute to interoperability, which, after all, is the goal of the profile's requirements.

Erratum 1207 was also similar to Erratum 1195 from the Cordless Telephony Profile: The service classes Fax and Generic Telephony had been wrong in the service records, so they were reversed to put Fax (the most specific class) first.

LAN Access Profile

Erratum 1055 changed the default PIN for a LAN access point. It had been set to a zero-length PIN, but the rules of the HCI interface did not allow a zero-length PIN to be set. Instead, the default was set to a single byte with all bits set to 0.

Assigned Numbers

Erratum 1113 wasn't really an erratum; it just created a new version number in the assigned numbers so that the LMP_version_req and LMP_version_res messages have a value assigned for version 1.1. This erratum was originally raised on the Link Management part of the specification because the Link Management protocol needed the parameter, but the change was made in the Bluetooth assigned numbers.

In version 1.1, the assigned numbers were split off from the rest of the core specification. This was done because the assigned numbers are likely to change often, for instance, as new profiles are released or as new manufacturers are assigned company IDs. Separating the assigned numbers avoids having to keep re-releasing the whole core specification every time a new number is added.

WHAT EFFECTS WILL USERS SEE?

From the users' point of view, all the detailed changes between version 1.0b and version 1.1 add up to just two things: reliability and interoperability. The good news is that version 1.1 implementations will interoperate with one another and will work much more reliably than under version 1.0b. In particular, low-power modes (hold, park, and sniff), security procedures, and the master-slave switch will work much more reliably. The bad news is that low-power modes, security procedures, and the master-slave switch are incompatible between version 1.0b and 1.1. Basic connections will work between version 1.0b and 1.1 implementations, so they are capable of connecting and transferring voice and data, but don't expect to use security, low-power modes, or the master-slave switch if you have incompatible versions.

This means that some profiles are likely to work as long as security isn't switched on. For instance, the Headset Profile or the Generic Object Exchange group of profiles (object push, file transfer, and synchronization) are compatible. However, the LAN Access Profile relies upon the master-slave switch, so it will not be possible to connect several 1.0b devices to a 1.1 LAN access point.

Overall, the increased reliability and much improved interoperability of version 1.1 is good news for Bluetooth devices. The specification also is now much clearer, which is good news for anybody starting out to implement Bluetooth.

Glossary

This glossary includes some acronyms which have not been used in this book, but which may be encountered when reading the Bluetooth standards and other literature relating to Bluetooth.

Term	Definition
802.11	The working group within IEEE responsible for definition and maintenance of wireless LAN standards.
D_B	Spacing of beacon slots in the beacon train.
ABM	Asynchronous Balanced Mode: the mode used by RFCOMM when connected.
ACK	ACKnowledge: a bit used in Bluetooth baseband packets to acknowledge that the last packet was received correctly.
ACL	Asynchronous ConnectionLess: the links used by Bluetooth to send data. These links are also important to voice systems because SCO (voice) links can only be set up after an ACL (data) link has been set up between two devices to allow them to exchange control and configuration data.
ADPCM	Adaptive Differential Pulse Code Modulation: an audio compression encoding scheme.

Term	Definition
AG	Audio Gateway: a device that transmits audio to a headset supporting the Bluetooth headset profile.
AM_ADDR	Active Member ADDRess: an address allocated by the master to each active slave in a piconet. The address is used to identify the particular slave a packet is intended for.
ANSI	American National Standards Institute: standards body with home page at *http://www.ansi.org*. ANSI administers and coordinates the private sector voluntary standardization system in the United States ANSI does not develop standards itself, but facilitates their development by private-sector organisations.
AR_ADDR	Access Request ADDRess: the address used by parked slaves to request unparking.
ARIB	Association of Radio Industries and Businesses: a Japanese industry association.
ARP	Address Resolution Protocol: allows a device to build a table of MAC addresses of devices connected to a network along with their corresponding to IP addresses.
ARQ	Automatic Repeat reQuest: a bit in a Bluetooth baseband packet which is used to request a retransmission of any packets received with errors.
ARQN	An acknowledgement bit used in ACL packets to let the device at the other end of the link know whether the last packet was received correctly.
ASIC	Application Specific Integrated Circuit: silicon device designed to carry out a specific function.
AT	ATtention: a command set commonly used to control modems, and also used in Headset and Hands-Free Profiles.
ATM	Asynchronous Transfer Mode: a networking protocol.
ATS	Abstract Test Suite: a method of describing tests which can be read by machines. It facilitates automated testing.
AUDIO GATEWAY	A device that connects to a Bluetooth headset and sends it a stream of audio information.
AUTHENTICATION	A security procedure. During authentication, two Bluetooth devices exchange link management packets to verify that they both have the same secret key.
AUTHORISATION	A security procedure whereby a device is given permission to access a particular service.
BASEBAND	The part of a device which controls the radio.
BB	BaseBand: the part of a protocol stack that controls the radio.

Term	Definition
BCD	Binary Coded Decimal: a way of representing numbers where each decimal digit is represented by four binary digits.
BC FLAG	BroadCast flag: identifies data in HCI packets as broadcast or point to point.
BCH	Bose, Chaudhuri, Hocquenghem: a family of cyclic parity codes which when added to data before transmission allows the receiver to detect and correct errors. BCH codes improve the autocorrelation properties in the Bluetooth synchronisation word.
BD_ADDR	Bluetooth Device ADDRess: a unique number used to identify a Bluetooth device. The Bluetooth device address is also used in encryption and in generation of frequency hop sequences.
BER	Bit Error Rate: used to measure the quality of a link.
BIP	Basic Imaging Pofile: allows images to be transferred between devices in various formats and encodings.
BLUE UNIT	A reference implementation of Bluetooth used as a standard during Bluetooth qualification testing.
BLUETOOTH	A short-range wireless communication technology that communicates via a frequency hopping transceiver in the ISM band.
BNEP	Bluetooth Network Encapsulation Protocol: allows ethernet frames with IPv4 or IPv6 traffic to be carried across Bluetooth L2CAP connections.
BOM	Bill Of Materials: component part list and costing for a product.
BONDING	A high level security procedure for establishing a trusted relationship between two devices. Once bonded, devices can exchange information on an encrypted link.
BPP	Basic Printing Profile: defines functionality which allows documents to be sent across a Bluetooth link and printed without using a printer-specific driver.
BPSK	Binary Phase Shift Keying: A data bit (1 or 0) is signalled by two possible phase values.
BQA	Bluetooth Qualification Administrator: administers the qualification program, approves testers, and keeps records of approved products.
BQB	Bluetooth Qualification Body: checks declarations, reviews test reports, and may be test house or manufacturer's in-house facility.
BQRB	Bluetooth Qualification Review Board: manages/reviews/improves qualification process; can give compliance waiver.

Term	Definition
BQTF	Bluetooth Qualified Test Facility: recognised test facility that delivers test plan and test reports; may be test house or manufacturer's in-house facility.
BRAN	Broadband Radio Access to the Network: a working group within ETSI focused on the issue of high-speed wireless access to core networks.
BT	BlueTooth: a short-range wireless communication technology. Originally developed for mobile devices.
BTAB	Bluetooth Technical Advisory Board: forum for test/qualification problems and information exchange.
CAC	Channel Access Code: derived from the Master's Bluetooth device address, this is used at the beginning of packets to identify their piconet.
CC	Call Control: the part of TCS which allows voice and data calls between Bluetooth devices to be set up and cleared down.
CCITT	Comite Consultatif Internationale de Telegraphique et Telephonique, or Consultative Committee on International Telephone and Telegraphy: an ITU standardization committee for telecommunications. Since February 1993, the CCITT has been replaced by the ITU-T.
CCK	Complementary Code Keying
C.ɪ	Conditional: used when specifying which Bluetooth features a profile should support.
CID	Channel Identifier: used in L2CAP packets to identify which higher layer entity is using the channel.
CL	ConnectionLess: a broadcast connection from a Master to a number of Slaves.
CLIENT	A device that wishes to use the services of another device (the server). Generally, clients send requests, and servers respond to clients' requests.
CLK	The Master clock that defines the timing on a Bluetooth piconet.
CLKE	An estimate of another device's clock.
CLKN	The native clock of a Bluetooth device, a Slave device must add an offset to its own CLKN to synchronise with CLK, the Master's clock.
Cnf	Confirm: a suffix used on signals from lower layers to higher layers when responding to higher layer requests. See also Pnd.

Term	Definition
COBS	Consistent Overhead Byte Stuffing: used in RS232 to allow 0x7E to delimit frames. Zeroes are eliminated from the data stream, then 0x7E in the data is replaced with 0x00.
CoD	Class of Device: a field in an FHS packet which identifies the class of Bluetooth device sending the packet.
CODEC	COder DECoder: a circuit for processing voice signals.
COMAR	IEEE U.S. Committee On Man And Radiation.
CONNECTABLE	A device is connectable if it will respond to paging, so it is possible for another device to connect with it.
CONNECTIONLESS	Not tied to one particular device. For instance, a broadcast link is a connectionless link because it is not directed at a single device.
CONVERGENCE	The process by which computers and communications devices, which used to be completely separate, are merging in devices such as smart phones. By providing cheap, short range links which enable various devices which could not communicate to link up and use one another's services, including accessing long distance links through other devices, Bluetooth is part of the convergence process.
CORRELATOR	A circuit that scans incoming data looking for a particular pattern. The correlator "triggers" and generates a signal when it sees the pattern it is searching for.
CR	A Carriage Return character.
CRC	Cyclic Redundancy Checksum: a checksum generated by a polynomial which allows data integrity to be verified.
CRC-CCITT	Used in RS232 transport layer: a CCITT scheme using a 16 bit checksum attached at the end of each packet before an ending delimiter of 0x7E.
CRLF	A Carriage Return character followed by a Line Feed.
CSMA	Carrier Sense Multiple Access: a device listens to the channel before transmitting and only transmits if the channel is unused. This is also referred to as "Collision Avoidance."
CTP	Cordless Telephony Profile: a Bluetooth specification for how to support cordless telephony across Bluetooth links.
CTS	Clear To Send: used on RS232 and UART links.

Term	Definition
CVSD	Continuous Variable Slope Delta modulation: a voice CODEC which is particularly good at handling errors, and thus suitable for Bluetooth use.
DAC	Device Access Code: a code which identifies a particular device. This code is derived from the device's Bluetooth device address and is used when paging the device.
D_{ACCESS}	Time from beacon instant to first access slot.
D_B	Timing of the first beacon slot (used for master to transmit to parked slaves).
dBm	deciBel Metres: a power rating used to describe the signal strength of Bluetooth radios.
DBPSK	Differential Binary Phase Shift Keying: As BPSK, but it is the phase change which is significant.
D_{BSLEEP}	Timing of first beacon slave at which the slave wakes.
DC	Direct Current
DCE	Data Circuit terminating Equipment: equipment at the end of a communications link which converts signals from the data terminal equipment and communications line.
DCI	Default Check Initialisation: a zero value used to initialise header error check generator for FHS packets sent in inquiry response states (usually the Master's UAP is used, but for an inquiry response, there may be no available Master from which to derive a UAP).
DECT	Digital Enhanced Cordless Telephony (formerly Digital European Cordless Telephony): a standard for cordless telephony.
DEVICE NAME	A test device name which can easily be read by a human. For instance, "Don's PC" is easier to read than hexadecimal digits of a Bluetooth device address. Also known as the user-friendly name, or friendly name.
DH	Data High rate: a category of Bluetooth packets which achieves high data rates by using reduced error checking.
DHCP	Dynamic Host Configuration Protocol: a protocol which allows client devices without pre-allocated IP addresses to dynamically obtain IP addresses from a DHCP server connected to the same IP network.

Term	Definition
DIAC	Dedicated Inquiry Access Code (another term for LIAC): this is sent in ID packets by devices wanting to discover other Bluetooth devices in the area which have previously been set to search for the DIAC.
DISC	DISConnect: one of the low-level RFCOMM command frames used to terminate an RFCOMM connection.
DISCOVERABLE	A Bluetooth device is discoverable if it will respond to inquiries so other Bluetooth devices in the area can discover its presence.
DLC	Data Link Connection: an RFCOMM channel.
DLCI	Data Link Connection Identifier: an RFCOMM channel number.
DM	Disconnect Mode: one of the low-level RFCOMM command frames.
DM	Data Medium rate: a category of Bluetooth packets that achieves high reliability by adding error checking. Reliability is achieved at the expense of a lower data rate.
DNS	Domain Name Server: provides mapping between test names of hosts and their numeric IP addresses.
DPS	Direct Printing Service: the simplest service of the Basic Printing profile which uses a FilePush to send a document to a printer.
DQPSK	Differential Quadrature Phase Shift Keying: similar to QPSK, but now two data bits (00, 01, 10, 11) are signalled by phase change or the phase change between one of the remaining three possible values.
DSP	Digital Signal Processor: a simple microprocessor dedicated to real-time signal processing.
DSS	Digital Subscriber Signaling system: an ITU recommendation for signaling controlling calls on ISDN systems.
DSSS	Direct Sequence Spread Spectrum: a modulation technique which spreads data across the entire transmission spectrum using a spreading code.
DT	Data Terminal: a device acting as a source and sink of data at the end of a communications link, e.g., a PC.
DTE	Data Terminal Equipment: a device at the end of a communications link, e.g., a computer, acts as a source and sink of data.
DTMF	Dual Tone Multiple Freqency: control tones used in telephony systems.

Term	Definition
DUN	Dial-Up Networking: a profile defining how Bluetooth can be used to access a network via a device which can provide a dialup connection (e.g., a modem or cell phone).
DUT	Device Under Test (see also IUT)
DV	Data Voice: a type of Bluetooth packet sent on SCO (voice) links, which can carry data as well as voice traffic.
EBDK	Ericsson Bluetooth Developers Kit.
ETSI	European Telecommunications Standards Institute: the European standards organisation which defined the GSM and DECT specifications.
EDGE	Enhanced Data Rates for GSM: a specification for increased data rates over GSM by using a deeper modulation scheme.
ESDP	Extended Service Discovery: rules for using service discovery facilities across Bluetooth in addition to the core SDP capabilities.
F	Final bit: bit 5 in the RFCOMM command field for frames carrying a response (see also P/F). Identifies whether a response to the frame is expected.
FCC	Federal Communications Commission: U.S. regulatory body which sets regulations for type approval of radios.
FCS	Frame Check Sequence: used to check for errors in a packet.
FDM	Frequency Division Multiplexing: dividing up a radio channel between users by allowing each user a different radio frequency.
FEC	Forward Error Correction: an error correction code used to protect data on some Bluetooth packets.
FCON	RFCOMM command used to switch on flow control.
FCOFF	RFCOMM command used to switch off flow control.
FCS	Frame Check Sequence: a parity check at the end of a frame used to detect errors in the frame.
FHS	Frequency Hop Synchronisation: the packet used to pass the information needed to allow one Bluetooth device to synchronise with the hop sequence of another Bluetooth device.
FHSS	Frequency Hop Spread Spectrum: a modulation technique which spreads data across the entire transmission spectrum by transmitting successive data on different channels, or "hopping".

Term	Definition
FIFO	First In First Out: buffers used to transfer SCO data.
FRIENDLY NAME	A test device name which can easily be read by a human. For instance, "Don's PC" is easier to read than the hexadecimal digits of a Bluetooth device address.
FSK	Frequency Shift Keying: a type of modulation where values are represented by a change in frequency.
FW	FirmWare: programs which are stored in a chip, such as boot PROMS or programs in flash memory.
GAP	Generic Access Profile: defines a basic set of procedures that all Bluetooth devices use both in handling connections (e.g., timers) and at the user interface level (e.g., naming conventions).
GATEWAY	A device that acts as an intermediary, allowing otherwise incompatible systems to communicate.
GENA	General Event Notification Architecture: a system used by UPnP to multicast information on service state changes to control points which have registered an interest.
GFSK	Gaussian Frequency Shift Keying: a modulation technique that represents a data bit by a shift in frequency.
GIAC	General Inquiry Access Code: a fixed standard code used to inquire for devices; its value is 0x9E8B33.
GM	Group Management: the part of TCS used to organize devices into groups which share information, allowing them to connect quickly to one another.
GN	Group ad-hoc Network: a device which can connect to one or more PAN users and forward IP traffic between them.
GOEP	Generic Object Exchange Profile: the part of the Bluetooth specification which describes how products will implement Object Exchange (OBEX).
GPRS	General Packet Radio Service: a specification for providing packet data services over the GSM system.
GPSK	Gaussian Phase Shift Keying: a modulation technique that represents a data bit by a shift in phase.
GSM	Global System for Mobile communications: a digital cellular phone standard.
GSM07.10	A standard for emulating multiple serial cables used in GSM systems.
GW	GateWay: a device that acts as an intermediary. Devices that cannot communicate directly with one another can communicate through a gateway.

Term	Definition
HA	Host Application: software running on a Bluetooth host on top of the Bluetooth protocol stack.
HAN	Home Area Network: a wireless network linking together electronic devices in the home.
HCI	Host Controller Interface: the interface which links a Bluetooth host to a Bluetooth module. Data, commands, and events pass across this interface.
HCRP	Hardcopy Cable Replacement Profile: defines functionality which allows a Bluetooth link to replace a printer cable allowing standard printer drivers to be adapted to use Bluetooth links.
HDLC	High-level Data Link Control procedures: the HDLC layer ensures that data passed to higher layers has been received exactly as it was transmitted with no errors, no lost data, and no changes in the order of the data. It also looks after flow control.
HEC	Header Error Check: a short code used by the receiving device to work out whether there are any errors in a received packet's header.
HF	Hands-Free device: a device which provides remote audio input and output along with simple remote control for an Audio Gateway.
HFP	Hands-Free Profile: defines functionality which allows a mobile phone to be used with a hands-free device.
HI	Header ID: used in OBEX headers, this identifies the type of data being carried in a header.
HID	Human Interface Device: for example, a PC mouse, keyboard, or remote control.
HIDP	Human Interface Device Profile: defines functionality which allows a Human Interface to be connected over a Bluetooth link.
HOLD	A mode where a Bluetooth link is deactivated for a short period.
HOP SEQUENCE	Bluetooth devices retune their radios onto a new frequency in a pseudo-random sequence called a hop sequence or frequency hop sequence. In an active piconet, the hop sequence is set by the clock and Bluetooth device address of the piconet's master. There are separate hop sequences used for inquiry, paging, inquiry scanning, page scanning, and test mode.
HOST	A device implementing Bluetooth higher layers which controls a separate module providing the Bluetooth lower layers. For example, if a PC has a Bluetooth card inserted, the PC is the host and the Bluetooth card is the module.

Term	Definition
HRFWG	HomeRF Working Group: organisation which defines HomeRF standards.
HS	HeadSet: Bluetooth supports a headset profile which defines how two-way speech can be sent across Bluetooth links to a headset product with earpiece and microphone.
HTML	HyperText Markup Language: a language used to define pages on the World Wide Web.
HTTP	HyperText Transfer Protocol: the protocol used to transfer Web pages written in HTML. This protocol is used to follow links from one Web page to another.
HV	Header Value: the part of OBEX headers containing information.
HV	High quality Voice: packets used to carry voice on Bluetooth audio (SCO) links. Actually, this could be viewed as a bit of a misnomer because Bluetooth HV packets only offer the sort of quality you'd get from a mobile phone, and some could argue that this is not high quality! There are three types of HV packets: HV1, HV2, and HV3. These are set every slot pair, every second slot pair, and every third slot pair, respectively.
HW	HardWare: the physical parts of a system such as electronics, as opposed to software (programs).
I	Irrelevant: used when specifying which Bluetooth features a profile should support.
IA5	International Alphabet number 5: defined by CCITT.
IAC	Inquiry Access Code: this is sent in ID packets by devices wanting to discover other Bluetooth devices in the area.
ICS	Implementation Conformance Statement: a statement of the capabilities of a Bluetooth device and profiles which the device supports. This statement is used as part of the Bluetooth qualification testing process. It provides a reference to identify the tests required, and provides an overview of the implementation.
IEC	International Electrotechnical Commission: the international standards and conformity assessment body for electrotechnology (electricity, electronics, and related technologies). There are many IEC/ISO standards created by the IEC in association with the ISO (International Standards Organisation).
IEEE	Institute of Electronic and Electrical Engineers: organisation that promotes electrical engineering worldwide. IEEE has fostered many standards, including the IEEE 802.11 standard for wireless LANs.
IETF	Internet Engineering Task Force: the standards body that defines the specifications used on the Internet.

Term	Definition
Ind	Indication: a suffix used on signals from lower layers to higher layers when notifying higher layers of events happening in lower layers.
INQUIRY	A bluetooth device transmits inquiry messages to find out about other devices within range of its radio. Devices scanning for inquiries reply with the information needed to connect to them.
IP	Internet Protocol: a Protocol that provides addressing, routing, segmentation, and reassembly.
IP	Intellectual Property: ideas, designs, and patents. This usually refers to intellectual property which is licensed or sold between companies.
IPR	Intellectual Property Rights: the legal rights of a company to intellectual property (ideas, designs, and patents). IPR is often traded (licensed or sold outright) between companies.
IrCOMM	Provides COM (serial and parallel) port emulation on connections using IrDA protocols.
IrDA	Infrared Data Association: an organisation that defines the infrared communications protocol used by many laptops and mobile cellular phones to exchange data at short ranges.
IrDAIAS	IrLMP hint bit assignments and known IAS definitions.
IrLAN	IrDA specifications for Infrared Local Area Network: an IrDA-defined protocol for accessing Local Area Networks (LANs) across infrared links.
IrLAP	serial Infrared Link Access Protocol: IrDA-defined protocol which provides reliable, ordered data transfer between devices; also provides device discovery procedures.
IrLMP	IrDA specification for Infrared Link Management Protocol.
IrMC	IrDA specifications for Infrared Mobile Communications: specifies how mobile telephony and communication devices can exchange data, including phone books, calendars, and messages.
IrOBEX	IrDA specifications for Infrared OBject EXchange: provides the abilty to exchange data objects between devices; also abbreviated further to OBEX. Can be used on protocols other than IrDA and is used with the Bluetooth protocol stack.
IRPA	International Radiation Protection Association
IRQ	Interrrupt: a signal that stops a processor from running one software task and causes it to run an Interrupt Service Routine (ISR) instead. After the ISR has dealt with whatever caused the interrupt signal, the processor is usually returned to running the task it was on before the interrupt.

Term	Definition
IrTRANP	Infrared TRANsport Protocol: an image exchange protocol defined by IrDA; used in digital cameras.
ISDN	Integrated Services Digital Network: high bandwidth combined digital data and voice telephony service.
ISM	Industrial, Scientific, and Medical: a name for the frequency band Bluetooth uses.
ISOCHRONOUS	Information which must be transferred within a fixed time; for instance, compressed video is isochronous, because its quality is affected if it is delayed by varying amounts.
ISR	Interrupt Service Routine: software routine to handle a special signal called an interrupt. An interrupt signal causes an ISR to interrupt whatever other software a processor was running when the signal arrived.
ITU	International Telecommunication Union: an international organization made up of governments and private sector companies which coordinates global telecommunication networks and services.
ITU-T	Telecommunication standardization sector of ITU: a standards organisation that facilitates cooperative standards for telecommunications. Located in Geneva, Switzerland, it was previously known as the CCITT.
IUT	Implementation Under Test: an implementation of one or more parts of the Bluetooth protocol stack which is being tested to become an approved component or product (see also DUT).
IXIT	Implementation eXtra Information for Testing: a questionnaire that details the parameters to be used in testing a Bluetooth IUT (Implementation Under Test), and the behaviour which can be triggered and observed. The IXIT is used with the ICS to make a test plan.
KNOWN DEVICE	A device which has been contacted previously and information stored about it (at least its Bluetooth device address must be stored).
L	Line status bits in an RFCOMM RLS command: used to signal overrun, parity, and framing errors on an RFCOMM channel.
L_CH	Logical Channel: a pair of bits in Bluetooth baseband packets used to identify whether an ACL (data) packet contains the start of an L2CAP packet, a continuing fragment of an L2CAP packet, or an LMP packet.
LAN	Local Area Network
LAP	Lower Address Part: 24 least-significant bits of a Bluetooth device address
LAP	LAN Access Point: one of the Bluetooth profiles used to define how products can be made which allow devices to use Bluetooth links to access a LAN.

Term	Definition
L2CA	Logical Link Control and Adaptation: the layer of the Bluetooth stack which implements L2CAP. This provides segmentation and reassembly services to allow large packets to pass across Bluetooth links; also provides multiplexing for higher layer protocols and services.
L2CAP	Logical Link Control and Adaptation Protocol (see L2CA above).
LC	Link Controller: the part of a Bluetooth module which controls ACL and SCO links, deciding what packet is going to be sent next.
LCP	Link Control Protocol: this name is sometimes used for the procedures which Link Controllers (LCs) use to exchange information. There are no packets used directly to signal between LCs, rather bits such as ARQN (Acknowledgement) and SEQN (Sequence) LCs are sent in the header of every packet. The link controllers use these bit fields to exchange information. The term "LCP" is used in the TCI (Test Control Interface) definition.
LF	Line Feed
LFSR	Linear Feedback Shift Register: a shift register that has feedback paths which take bits being shifted out of the register and feed them back into locations earlier in the shift, usually with an Exclusive OR (XOR) combination. LFSRs are used extensively in the Bluetooth baseband, e.g., they are used for encryption, pseudorandom noise generation, and header error check generation.
LIAC	Limited Inquiry Access Code: an inquiry access code that devices may agree to use for a short period in place of the usual General Inquiry Access Code (GIAC). The LIAC is defined as 0x9E8B00.
LIMITED DISCOVERABLE	A device is limited discoverable if it will respond to inquiries using the Limited Inquiry Access Code (LIAC), but will not respond to inquiries using the General Inquiry Access Code (GIAC).
LINK KEY	A key used to encrypt data on a Bluetooth baseband link.
LM	Link Manager: the layer which implements LMP, this handles configuration and control of the Bluetooth baseband links.
LMP	Link Management Protocol (see LM above).
LocDev	Local Device: the device at the near end of a Bluetooth link. This term is used in documents dealing with service discovery.
LOGICAL CHANNEL	Different types of channels which can be carried across a physical baseband link.
LP	Lower Protocol: often used as a generic label for lower layers when an upper layer can be interfaced to more than one lower layer.

Term	Definition
LSB	Least-Significant Bit: the bit in a binary representation of a number that represents the lowest value.
M	Master: the device that controls and coordinates a group of Bluetooth devices (the controlled devices are called slaves). The master sets the frequency hop sequence, and decides when each slave will be allowed to transmit.
M	Mandatory: used when specifying which Bluetooth features a profile should support.
MAC	Medium Access Control: a protocol used to regulate access to a physical link (this term is commonly used to refer to the Data Link Layer of the Ethernet LAN system).
MAPI	Messaging Application Procedure Interface: a standard set of C functions placed into a code library known as a Dynamic Link Library (DLL). MAPI standardises the way applications interface. It was originally written by Microsoft, but has been taken up by other companies.
MASTER	The device which controls a group of Bluetooth devices, the master sets the timing, frequency hopping sequence and decides when other devices have permission to transmit.
M_{ACCESS}	Number of repetitions of the access window. To increase reliability when messages are sent to parked slaves in beacon slots, they can be repeated a number of times in successive access windows. So if M_{access} has a high value, the parked slaves are more likely to get a message; but of course, more bandwidth will be needed to send the message.
ME	Management Entity: the part of a Bluetooth device which initiates and manages its links.
MIB	Management Information Base: a block or database of information containing data needed to manage a device's participation in a network.
MIME	Multipurpose Internet Mail Extension: an Internet standard, MIME extends the format of Internet mail to allow non-ASCII text messages, nontext messages, multipart messages, and non-ASCII information in message headers. MIME types are also used to distinguish WAP content from nonWAP content in WAP servers and WAP gateways.
MIPS	Mega-Instructions Per Second: a measure of processor speed.
MODULE	A unit which implements the lower layers of the Bluetooth stack up to the Host Controller Interface (HCI). To make a complete Bluetooth device, a module would need to be controlled by a host.
MMAC	Multimedia Mobile Access Communication systems: a Japanese initiative to produce an ultra-high-speed, high-quality multimedia communications standard.

Term	Definition
MMI	Man Machine Interface: this is made up of all the parts of a machine which let a human interact with it; for example, the physical part of a PC's MMI usually consists of a screen, mouse, keypad, maybe some speakers, a microphone, and a joystick. The MMI also consists of the way the PC presents data to the user and takes input from the user, so if you change keyboard mappings to make the keys do different things, you change the MMI. MMI design is an important part of making machines easy to use.
MS	Mobile Station: commonly used in networks to describe a mobile device. For example, in the GSM standard, a GSM cellular phone handset is an example of a mobile station.
MS	Multiplexing Sublayer: part of a protocol stack which splits up one data stream to allow several higher layer protocols or services to use a single link.
MSB	Most Significant Bit: the bit in a binary representation of a number that represents the highest value.
MSC	Message Sequence Chart: a chart showing messages exchanged between devices or between entities in a protocol stack.
MTU	Maximum Transmission Unit: the largest size packet payload which a particular layer can handle. Used when referring to layers such as HCI and L2CAP, which can be implemented with different maximum packet sizes.
MUX	MUltipleXing sublayer: part of a protocol stack which splits up one data stream to allow several higher layer protocols or services to use a single link.
$N_{ACC-SLOTS}$	Number of slave to master access slots.
NACK	Negative ACKnowledgement: bit used to signal when a packet has been received with errors, or when a packet was expected and not received.
NAK	Negative AcKnowledgement (see NACK above).
NAP	Nonsignificant Address Part (of a Bluetooth device address): 16 bits of Bluetooth device address taken from the middle, between the LAP and UAP.
NAP	Network Access Point: a device which provides some ethernet bridge facilities across Bluetooth links including forwarding IP packets. The NAP service is defined in the Personal Area Networking (PAN) profile.
N_B	Number of beacon slots within one beacon train.
NCRP	National Council on Radiation Protection and measurements
N_{POLL}	Number of slots after the access window that a slave listens after requesting unpark.

Term	Definition
N$_{Bsleep}$	Number of beacon train at which slave wakes (it sleeps N$_{Bsleep}$-1 beacon trains).
NRE	Non-Recurring Engineering: initial costs in developing a product.
NSC	Non-Supported Command: a response used by RFCOMM to indicate that it has received a command it does not support.
NT	Network Terminal: the terminal at the end of a communications network which allows data to be entered or retrieved.
O	Optional: used when specifying which Bluetooth features a profile should support.
OBEX	OBject EXchange protocol (defined by IrDA): allows devices to exchange arbitrary data objects.
OCF	OpCode Command Field: identifies an HCI command within a group of commands.
OFDM	Orthogonal Frequency Division Multiplexing: a modulation technique that transmits data across many carriers for high data rates at lower symbol rates.
OGF	OpCode Group Field: identifies a group of HCI commands.
O.I	qualified Optional: used when specifying which Bluetooth features a profile should support when options are mutually exclusive or selectable. In these cases, an integer is used to identify a related group of options.
OOBE	Out Of the Box Experience
OpCode	Operation Code: code used in signals to identify the type of information being carried in a message.
OS	Operating System: the software which provides basic system facilities. At its most basic, an OS provides facilities for scheduling tasks and accessing memory and device I/O (Input/Output). A more complex OS provides file handling, user interface, and applications interfaces.
OSI	Open Systems Interconnect: the goal of OSI is to provide standards which allow hosts to interoperate regardless of hardware and underlying operating systems.
P	Poll bit: bit 5 in the RFCOMM command field for frames carrying a command (see also P/F).
P/F	Poll/Final bit: bit 5 in the RFCOMM command field, which identifies whether a message needs a response.
PABX	Private Automatic Branch EXchange: a local telephone exchange.

Term	Definition
PACKET	A structured package of data transferred as one unit. For instance, Bluetooth uses packets with header information to transfer data across the baseband links.
PAGING	To transmit the ID of another device to establish a connection to it.
PAGE SCAN	To listen for its own ID. If the page scanning device receives its ID, then it connects to the device which sent it.
PAIRING	A security procedure involving exchanging link management packets to establish a link key for use between two Bluetooth devices.
PAN	Personal Area Network: a term describing the small, ad-hoc networks facilitated by Bluetooth, which join together a group of personal devices.
PANU	PAN user: a device which is using a service defined by the Personal Area Networking (PAN) profile.
PARK	A mode where a slave Bluetooth device is only active on a link during periodic beacon slots. During those beacon slots, it can request to be unparked and return to normal activity, or the master can order it to unpark.
PASSKEY	Another name for PIN (Personal Identification Number): a number entered by a user, or built into a device, which is used for security checks.
PB FLAG	Packet Boundary flag: identifies start and continuing L2CAP data in HCI packets.
PBR	Print By Reference: used in the basic printing profile, instead of sending data to a printer a reference to a file is sent, the file is then retrieved by the printer using a seperate channel.
PCB	Printed Circuit Board
PCM	Pulse Coded Modulation: a commonly used way of encoding speech.
PDA	Personal Digital Assistant: a small handheld computing device such as a Palm Pilot or Psion organizer.
PDU	Protocol Data Unit: a packet of data used to exchange information in the format specified by a communications protocol.
PFD	Packet Filter Database: a list of filters kept by a bridge or router to decide which packets to forward and which to discard.
PHY	PHYsical layer: the lowest layer of the OSI seven-layer model.
PHYSICAL LINK	The lowest level connection between devices. In Bluetooth wireless technology, the physical link is a radio link.

Term	Definition
PICONET	A group of Bluetooth devices joined together into a short-range network by Bluetooth links. The group is synchronised to the timing and hopping sequence of one device (the device which sets the timing and hopping sequence for the rest of the piconet is called the Master).
PICS	Protocol Implementation Conformance Statement: used by the WAP forum members to say that their devices conform to the WAP specification (see also ICS).
PID	Physical Interface Device: a class of Human Interface Devices (HID) which provides physical output in addition to receiving human input; for example, Force Feedback Joysticks.
PIFA	Planar Inverted F Antenna: a cheap, compact antenna suitable for Bluetooth frequencies which looks like an F on its side.
PIN	Personal Identification Number: a number entered by a user, or built into a device, which is used for security checks.
PIXIT	Protocol EXtra Information for Testing (see IXIT): information about a Bluetooth product which is being supplied for testing. The PIXIT provides extra information needed by the test house over and above the information supplied in the ICS (Implementation Conformance Statement). For example, a PIXIT could describe commands needed at the user interface to drive the device.
PM_ADDR	Parked Member ADDRess: slaves, when entering the low power Park mode, exchange their Active Member ADDRess (AM_ADDR) for a Parked Member ADDRess (PM_ADDR). The PM_ADDR is then used by the master when it wants to unpark the slave.
PN	Port Negotiation: RFCOMM command used to configure a data link connection.
PN	Pseudorandom Noise: a series of numbers which appear random, but actually repeat over a very long sequence.
Pnd	Pending: a suffix used on signals from lower layers to higher layers when responding to higher layer requests; indicates that the lower layer has more processing to do.
PNP	Plug and Play: Plug and Play matches up physical devices with software by automatically telling device drivers where to find hardware such as Bluetooth cards. Plug and Play allocates I/O addresses, IRQs, DMA channels, and memory regions.
POTS	Plain Old Telephone System: a telephone system which can only carry circuit-switched voice and does not have sophisticated signaling systems or data capabilities beyond those offered by analog modes.
PPM	Parts Per Million

Term	Definition
PPM	Pulse Position Modulation: a modulation technique where data is represented by the relative position of a pulse in a time frame.
PPP	Point to Point Protocol: an Internet protocol which provides a standard way of transporting datagrams from many other protocols over point to point links.
PRBS	Pseudo Random Bit Sequence: a sequence of bits which appears random because it has a very long repetition period.
PRNG	Pseudo Random Noise Generation: the generation of a sequence of numbers which are not random, but which are in such a long sequence that they appear to be random.
PROFILE	A set of rules for how to use the Bluetooth protocol stack in a device. Different profiles are defined for different types of devices. The aim of the profiles is to ensure that different device types will be able to interoperate.
PROMOTER	One of a group of companies that run the Bluetooth specification process. The original promoters group was: Ericsson Mobile Communications AB, Intel Corp., IBM Corp., Toshiba Corp., and Nokia Mobile Phones. In December 1999, Microsoft, Lucent, Motorola, and 3Com joined the promoters group.
PROTOCOL	A set of rules for behaviour. A communications protocol is a set of rules for how devices should behave towards one another when communicating. It is essential for devices to follow the same protocol if they are to communicate well.
PROTOCOL STACK	A layered set of functional units which between them implement a protocol. Each layer in a protocol stack has clearly defined duties and responsibilities, and also has clearly defined interfaces to adjacent layers in the protocol stack.
PROXY	A device which acts as an intermediary, allowing otherwise incompatible systems to communicate. A proxy may represent the device it is translating for, so that devices speaking to the proxy are unaware that it is present and believe that they are communicating directly to the device which is communicating through the proxy.
PSK	Phase Shift Keying: a modulation technique that represents a bit by a shift in phase.
PSM	Protocol/Service Multiplexer: used by L2CAP to identify the type of higher layer entity using an L2CAP connection, e.g., RFCOMM always has PSM = 0x0003.
PSTN	Public Switched Telephony Network
Q.931	ITU-T standard for signaling system used for call control.
qualification	A process of testing to ensure that a device meets the Bluetooth specification.

Term	Definition
QPSK	Quadrature Phase Shift Keying: a modulation scheme which uses four phase values to encode two data bits per modulated symbol.
QoS	Quality of Service: defines the bandwidth and latency a device can expect on a connection.
QAM	Quadrature Amplitude Modulation: a modulation technique which uses amplitude as well as phase for encoding data for higher data rates.
RAND	RANDom Number
REMDEV	Remote Device: the device at the far end of a Bluetooth link. This term is used in documents dealing with service discovery.
Req	Request: a suffix used on signals passing commands from higher layers to lower layers.
RF	Radio Frequency
RFC	Request For Comments: the standards which define the working of the Internet are issued as RFCs to allow people to give feedback on the documents. Each RFC is given a number, for example, HyperText Transfer Protocol (HTTP) is RFC2068.
RFCOMM	Protocol for RS-232 serial cable emulation.
RLS	Remote Line Status: RFCOMM command used to communicate errors on a data link connection.
RPN	Remote Port Negotiation: RFCOMM command used to configure communication settings at the far end of a link.
RSSI	Receive Signal Strength Indication: used to decide whether power at the far end of a radio link should be turned up or down.
Rsp	Response: a suffix used on signals from higher layers responding to indications from lower layers.
RTOS	Real-Time Operating System: the software which provides basic system facilities. An RTOS provides facilities for scheduling tasks and accessing memory and device I/O (Input/Output).
RTS	Ready To Send: used on RS-232 and UART links.
RUI	Reflected User Interface: uses OBEX channels to provide a remote user interface to control a device.

Term	Definition
RX	Receive or Receiver
RXD	Receive Data: used on RS232 and UART links.
S	Slave: a device linked to a master, the slave follows the master's frequency hop sequence and timing and may only transmit when permitted to by the master.
SABM	Set Asynchronous UnBalanced Mode: low-level command packet used by RFCOMM to start up a link.
SAP	Service Access Point: a term from the OSI reference model for the interface points between layers, which are used by adjacent layers to communicate. A SAP consists of a data structure and an identifier for a buffer area in system memory used as the interface.
SAPI	Service Access Point Identifier: a number identifying the protocol supported by a Service Access Point (SAP), e.g., SAP 0x42 = IEE 802.11, SAP 0x06 = IP.
SAR	Specific Absorption Rate: rate of energy absorption averaged for mass and time; this is used to set safety standards for radio power.
SAR	Segmentation And Reassembly: a service which allows large higher layer packets to pass across lower Bluetooth layers (SAR is one of the functions of L2CAP).
SCATTERNET	A group of Bluetooth piconets joined together by devices that are in more than one piconet.
SCO	Synchronous Connection-Oriented: the links used by Bluetooth to send voice, these links use reserved time slots.
SDAP	Service Discovery Application Profile: the Bluetooth specification for how a service discovery application should be supported in Bluetooth products.
SDDB	Service Discovery DataBase: information about services supported by a Bluetooth device.
SDL	Functional Specification and Description Language: a high level formal language for describing systems.
SDP	Service Discovery Protocol: a Bluetooth protocol which allows a client to discover the devices offered by a server.
SEQN	A sequence bit, this helps a Bluetooth device receiving packets to work out if any packets were lost due to radio interference or fading of the radio signal.
SERVER	A device offering services which may be used by another device (the client). Generally, clients send requests, and servers respond to clients' requests.
SERVICE DISCOVERY	The process of discovering the capabilities and services offered by other devices.

Term	Definition
SERVICE RECORD	Information about a service which is needed to connect to and use the service. The Service Discovery Protocol (SDP) is used to access service records.
SFD	Start of Frame Delimiter: a code word set to 10101000 used to mark the start of an ethernet frame.
SIG	Special Interest Group: the Bluetooth SIG is a group of all companies who have registered an interest in Bluetooth via the SIG Web site at *http://www.Bluetooth.org*.
SIM	Subscriber Identity Module: the chip in a cellular phone which holds the subscriber's information.
SMS	Short Message Service: a facility to transfer short text message between mobile phones.
SNIFF	A low-power mode where a device is only active on its Bluetooth link during periodic slots called sniff slots.
SOAP	Simple Object Access Protocol: an XML based language used to access services.
SOC	System On Chip: a complete system in a single ASIC, usually including a microprocessor, memory, external interfaces, and specific system functional blocks.
SPP	Serial Port Profile: a Bluetooth specification for how serial ports should be emulated in Bluetooth products.
SS	Supplementary Services: extra services provided in telephony systems such as SMS (Short Message Service).
SSDP	Simple Service Discovery Protocol: a service Discovery Protocol used by UPnP.
SSI	Signal Strength Indication: used to measure power on a link.
SSL	Secure Sockets Layer: the part of the Internet Protocol (IP) stack which provides security.
SUT	System Under Test: a system containing an Implementation Under Test (IUT), that is to say a system containing a component or product which is undergoing Bluetooth qualification testing.
SW	SoftWare
SWAP	Shared Wireless Access Protocol: the air interface protocol used by the HomeRF system.
TA	Terminal Adaptor: the piece of equipment that replaces a modem in ISDN systems.

Term	Definition
T_{ACCESS}	Width of access window used by parked slaves to request unparking.
TAE	Terminal Adaptor Equipment: a piece of equipment that interfaces a terminal to a digital communications system (such as an ISDN line).
T_B	Interval between beacon trains.
TBD	To Be Defined, Decided, or Determined.
TC	Test Control: an interface used to control a device during testing.
TCI	Test Control Interface: a special variant of the HCI (Host Controller Interface) used to control a device during the Bluetooth qualification process.
TCP	Transport Control Protocol: part of the Internet protocol suite which provides reliable data transfer.
TCP/IP	Transport Control Protocol/Internet Protocol: part of the Internet protocol suite which provides reliable data transfer.
TCS	Telephony Control protocol Specification: part of the Bluetooth core specification which defines a signaling scheme for connecting voice and data calls.
TCS-BIN	Telephony Control protocol Specification—BINary: part of the Bluetooth standard dealing with control of telephone calls.
TDD	Time Division Duplex: sharing a channel in two directions by letting each direction transmit in turn.
TDM	Time Division Multiplexing: splitting up a communications channel among several users by allowing one user to use it, then another, then another, so it is divided up into slots of time.
TH_{DR}	Transaction Header: a header used in the HID profile to identify the type of message being sent.
TID	Terminal IDentifier: a unique part of the Service Profile IDentifier (SPID) that identifies the device or terminal currently in use. This term is commonly used in ISDN systems.
Tiny TP	Tiny Transport Protocol: an IrDA protocol which provides flow control, segmentation, and reassembly.
TL	Terminal: A device at the end of a network, which allows data to be entered or retrieved.
TLS	Transport Layer Security: a layer providing security services such as the Secure Sockets Layer (SSL) in IP or WTLS in WAP.

Term	Definition
TRUSTED DEVICE	A device which is paired (shares a link key) with the local device and also explicitly marked as trusted in a security database.
TTP	Tiny Transport Protocol: a layer between OBEX and UDP.
TX	Transmit or Transmitter
TXD	Transmit Data: used on RS232 and UART links.
UA	User Asynchronous: the logical channel used by the Bluetooth baseband to carry L2CAP packets. Identified by L_CH bits in the ACL packet; set to 10 or 01.
UAP	Upper Address Part (of a Bluetooth device address): 8 most-significant bits of a Bluetooth device address.
UART	Universal Asynchronous Receiver Transmitter: a chip used for transmitting and receiving on serial interfaces.
UC	User Control
UDP	User Datagram Protocol: a packet-based, unreliable, connectionless transport protocol which works over Internet Protocol (IP).
UDP/IP	Universal Datagram Protocol/Internet Protocol: an unreliable datagram transport protocol.
UI	User Isochronous: essentially the same as User Asynchronous (UA). A logical channel used by the Bluetooth baseband to carry L2CAP packets.
UI	Unnumbered Information: an optional GSM07.10 frame type used to send data on emulated serial links.
UI	User Interface: the application which a user interacts with; also called MMI, or Man Machine Interface.
UIAC	Unlimited Inquiry Access Code: another name for GIAC.
UIH	Unnumbered Information with Header error check: an RFCOMM data frame.
UNIT KEY	A key built into a unit which is used as part of the process of producing the link key used to encrypt data on a Bluetooth baseband link.
UPnP	Universal Plug and Play: a standard of the UPnP forum which allows services of intelligent appliances, wireless devices and PCs to be discovered, and controlled with zero configuration. UPnP is designed for ad-hoc IP networks.
URI	Uniform Resource Identifier

Term	Definition
URL	Uniform Resource Locator: defined by RFC1738, this is a standard way of writing addresses on the Internet; for example, *http://www.bluetooth.com* is a URL.
URN	Uniform Resource Name
US	User Synchronous: a logical channel used by Bluetooth to carry synchronous data. This maps onto the SCO (Synchronous Connection-Oriented) baseband links.
USB	Universal Serial Bus: a high-speed connection standard widely used to connect devices to PCs. USB allows devices to describe themselves and allows groups of related devices to be driven by the same generic device driver.
USER-FRIENDLY NAME	A test device name which can easily be read by a human. For instance, "Don's PC" is easier to read than the hexadecimal digits of a Bluetooth device address.
UUID	Universally Unique IDentifier: a 128-bit number derived by a method which guarantees it will be unique.
VIRTUAL CABLE	The one to one association between a Human Interface Device (HID) and its host used in the HID profile.
VSWR	Voltage Standing Wave Ration: a measure of relative radio signal strengths.
W3C	World Wide Web Consortium: a standards body that produces standards for the World Wide Web (e.g., XML). The home page is *http://www.w3.org*.
WAE	Wireless Application Environment: the Application Layer of the WAP specification.
WAP	Wireless Application Protocol: a communications protocol which aims to give mobile devices access to the Internet and other advanced data services.
WBFH	WideBand Frequency Hopping: same as FHSS, but wider channels allow more data to be carried in each hopping channel using multiple carriers.
WLAN	Wireless Local Area Network
WLL	Wireless Local Loop: a fixed local area network but using a wireless carrier (usually telephony based in this context).
WDP	Wireless Datagram Protocol: an unreliable packet-based protocol defined in the WAP specification (equivalent to UDP in the Internet protocol suite).
WML	Wireless Markup Language: a language defined in the WAP specification which is used to define WAP Web pages in the same way that HTML is used to define "ordinary" pages on the World Wide Web.
WSP	Wireless Session Protocol: the session layer of the WAP specification.

Term	Definition
WTA	Wireless Telephony Application: a telephony application that is part of the WAP specification.
WTLS	Wireless Transport Layer Security: the part of the WAP specification supporting secure links.
WTP	Wireless Transaction Protocol: part of the WAP specification providing reliable links over lower, unreliable transport layers.
WUG	Wireless User Group: a group of devices supporting TCS with a Master that sends device information to all devices, enabling them to make fast connections to one another.
WWW	World Wide Web
X	eXcluded: used to identify prohibited features when specifying which Bluetooth features a profile should support.
XML	eXtensible Markup Language: a generic markup language which is a W3C recommendation (see *http://www.w3org/XML/*).
XOR	eXclusive OR

References

Telefonaktiebolaget LM Ericsson, International Business Machines Corporation, Intel Corporation, Nokia Corporation, Toshiba Corporation, "Specification of the Bluetooth System, Specification Volume 1, Core", Version 1.0b, December 1999.

Telefonaktiebolaget LM Ericsson, International Business Machines Corporation, Intel Corporation, Nokia Corporation, Toshiba Corporation, "Specification of the Bluetooth System, Specification Volume 2, Profiles", Version 1.0b, December 1999.

Ericsson Mobile Communications AB, "Bluetooth Brand Book", Version 1.0, 2000.

H. Andersson, R. Bidari, P. Canero, K. Kosonen, P. Lee, J. Moidel, K. Rantala, F. Truntzer, T. Will, and C. Zechlin, "Bluetooth UnPlugFest-2, Interoperability Testing Plan", V3.0, March 2000.

The ITU Telecommunication Standardization Sector (ITU-T), "Q.931, Digital Subscriber Signalling System No. 1(DSS 1) – ISDN User-Network interface Layer 3 Specification for Basic Call Control", March 1993.

P. J. Leach et al., UUIDs and GUIDs, *http://www.ietf.org/internet-drafts/draft-leach-uuids-guids-01.txt,* February 1998.

European Telecommunications Standards Institute (ETSI), "Digital cellular telecommunications system (Phase 2+); Terminal Equipment to Mobile Station (TE-MS) multiplexer protocol (GSM 07.10 version 6.3.0)", 1999.

"Qualification Program Reference Document", Bluetooth Special Interest Group, Revision 0.66 draft, Bluetooth SIG, Telefonaktiebolaget LM Ericsson, 1998.

T. Müller, "Bluetooth Security Architecture", A Bluetooth SIG White Paper, Revision 1.0, July 1999.

J. Haartsen and S. Zürbes, "Bluetooth voice and data performance in 802.11 DS WLAN environment", A Bluetooth SIG White Paper, Revision C, May 1999.

Riku Mettälä, "Bluetooth Protocol Architecture", A Bluetooth SIG White Paper, Revision 0.95, July 1999.

S. Kambhatla, "Bluetooth PC Software Architecture", A Bluetooth SIG White Paper, Intel Corporation, Version 0.30, October 1998.

J. Carlson, S. Cheshire, and M. Baker, draft-ietf-pppext-cobs-00, "PPP Consistent Overhead Byte Stuffing (COBS)", November 1997.

Infrared Data Association, "IrMC (Ir Mobile Communications) Specification", Version 1.1, February 1999.

P. Megowan, D. Suvak, and D. Kogan, "Infrared Data Association, IrDA Object Exchange Protocol (IrOBEX)", Version 1.2, April 1999.

The Internet Mail Consortium, "vCard - The Electronic Business Card Exchange Format", Version 2.1, September 1996.

The Internet Mail Consortium, "vCalendar - The Electronic Calendaring and Scheduling Exchange Format", Version 1.0, September 1996.

Simpson, W., Editor, "The Point-to-Point Protocol (PPP)", STD 50, RFC 1661, Daydreamer, July 1994.

Simpson, W., Editor, "PPP in HDLC Framing", STD 51, RFC 1662, Daydreamer, July 1994.

Wireless Application Protocol Forum, "Wireless Application Protocol", Version 1.0, 1998.

Wireless Application Protocol Forum, "WAP Conformance", Draft version 27, May 1998.

Radio Equipment and Systems (RES), "Wideband transmission systems: Technical characteristics and test conditions for data transmission equipment operating in the 2,4 GHz ISM band and using spread spectrum modulation techniques", ETSI ETS 300 328, November 1996.

International Telecommunications Union (ITU-T) Recommendations G.711, November 1988.

J. A. Greefkes and K. Riemens, "Code Modulation with Digitally Controlled Companding for Speech Transmission", Philips Technical Review, pp. 335–353, 1970.

CML Semiconductor Products, Continuously Variable Slope Delta Modulation (CVSD) - A Tutorial, AN/G-Purp/CVSD_1, November 1997.

Prof. J. L. Massey, Prof. G. H. Khachatrian, and Dr. M. K. Kuregian, SAFER+ Candidate algorithm for AES - Submission document, Cylink Corp., June 1998.

John Kelsey, Bruce Schneier, and David Wagner, Key Schedule Weaknesses in SAFER+, Submission to AES Candidate Testing Conference, 1999.

DECT Specification, ETSI ETS 300 175-1, Edition 2, 1996.

802.11 Architecture presentation, (Ref: IEEE P802.11-96/49B), IEEE Std 802.11-1997, IEEE 802.11-1999, IEEE 802.11a-1999 and IEEE 802.11b-1999, March 1996. (All available from *http://grouper.ieee.org/groups/802/11*)

802.15 TG1 Draft Standard Overview, March 2000.

802.15 TG3 Proposal, January 2000. (Both available from: http://grouper.ieee.org/groups/802/15)

HomeRF Working Group, Home Networking Technologies, Comdex, November 1999.

Technical Summary of the SWAP Specification (Available from *http://www. homerf.org*), March 1998.

HIPERLAN Type 1 Standard, ETSI ETS 300 652, WA2, December 1997.

L. Taylor, HIPERLAN Type 1 White Paper. (Available from *http://www.hiperlan.com),* Rev 0.9, June 1999.

Broadband Radio Access Networks (BRAN), HIPERLAN Type 2 Technical Specification, Physical (PHY) Layer, DTS/BRAN 0023003, 1999.

"Enabling Effortless Connectivity between Devices", Proceedings of the IIR Conference, Geneva, April 2000.

K. W. Lee, Prospect of Bluetooth Solution in Consumer Electronics, Samsung Electronics, Presentation at IIR Conference, Geneva, April 2000.

J. G. Proakis, Digital Communications, 3rd edition, McGraw-Hill, 1995.

USB Implementers' Forum, *http://www.usb.org,* Universal Serial Bus Device Class Definition for Human Interface Devices (HID), version 1.11, 27th June 2001.

USB Implementers' Forum, *http://www.usb.org,* Universal Serial Bus Specification, version 1.1, September 23, 1998.

USB Implementers' Forum, *http://www.usb.org,* Universal Serial Bus HID Usage Tables, 27th June 2001.

UPnP Forum, *http://www/upnp.org,* "Universal Plug and Play Device Architecture", version 1.0, June 100.

Internet Engineering Task Force, *http://www.ietf.org,* IETF Directory List of RFCs.

European Telecommunications Standards Institute (ETSI), ETS300 916, "Digital Cellular Communications systems (Phase 2+); AT command set for GSM Mobile Equipment (ME) (GSM 07.07 version 6.3.0)" July 1999.

W3C,http://www.w3.org/TR/SOAP/ "Simple Object Access Protocol (SOAP) 1.1", W3C Note 08 May 2000.

Bluetooth Special Interest Group "Bluetooth Network Encapsulation Protocol (BNEP) Specification", Specification of the Bluetooth System, version 0.95, June 12, 2001.

Bluetooth Special Interest Group "Human Interface Device Profile" version 0.90b, 30th July 2001.

Bluetooth Special Interest Group "Hands Free Profile" version 0.9, 14 August 2001.

Bluetooth Special Interest Group "Personal Area Networking Profile" version 0.95a, June 26, 2001.

Bluetooth Special Interest Group "Basic Printing Profile, Interoperability Specification" version 0.9, 25 May 2001.

Bluetooth Special Interest Group "Basic Imaging Profile Interoperability Specification" version 0.9 28th June 2001.

Bluetooth Special Interest Group "Bluetooth EDSP for UPnP", version 0.95b, 15 March 2001.

Bluetooth Special Interest Group "Specification Volume 1, Specification of the Bluetooth System, Core" version 1.1, February 22 2001.

Bluetooth Special Interest Group "Specification Volume 1, Specification of the Bluetooth System, Profiles" version 1.1, February 22 2001.

Bluetooth Special Interest Group "Bluetooth Assigned Numbers" Version 2.1, September, 19th 2001 (latest version is at *http://www.bluetooth.org/assigned-numbers/*).

Bluetooth Special Interest Group, "Bluetooth Brand Book 2" Version 1.0, March 2001.

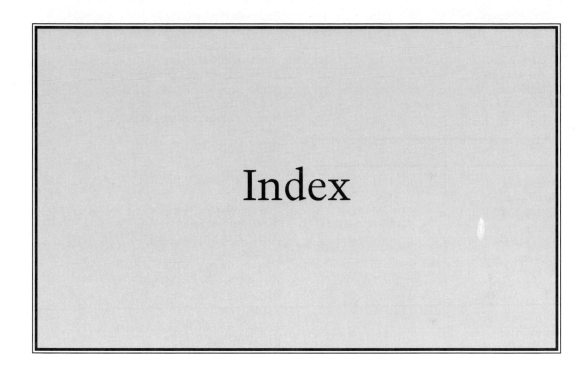

Index

D

I

Q

R

X

About the Authors

Jennifer Bray has a bachelor's in Physics with Microcomputer Electronics, a master's in Satellite Communications Engineering, and a doctorate in the field of wireless communications. More recently, she gained a distinction in the Open University's Management of Technology course. Her decade of experience in communications product development includes working on Nortel and 3Com's first ATM systems, as well as wireless ATM, the first secure ethernet repeater, ADSL to ATM gateways, FDDI, CDMA, and GSM. In addition to her communications development work, she has worked on cutting edge control and monitoring systems for FormulaONE and Indy cars, and acted as an ISO 9001 and CMM auditor, advising blue-chip companies on how to improve their development and support processes.

Jennifer has written and delivered technology training courses (naturally including Bluetooth), and is a frequent speaker at conferences. She is a consultant at Cambridge Silicon Radio (CSR).

In contrast to her high-tech work, Jennifer's hobbies include early medieval re-enactment, spinning, weaving, and motorcycling.

Charles Sturman has spent more than 10 years working in the electronics industry, first at Acorn Computers—the forerunner to Advanced Risc Machines (ARM)—and then at TTP Communications, a supplier of digital wireless Intellectual Property solutions.

Charles obtained a bachelor's degree in Electronic Engineering and a master's in Information Engineering from Southampton University before joining Acorn Computers in 1990. His responsibilities ranged from processor bus and graphics sub-system design to the management of several European collaborative research projects, which contributed to Acorn's portable information appliance the NewsPAD and the flagship multi-ARM-based RiscPC.

In 1994, Charles joined TTP Communications, where he worked on system design and architecture of GSM cellular silicon products, and then business development and consultancy in both Digital Audio Broadcast (DAB) and Hiperlan. After the completion of a Hiperlan development, Charles became interested in the emergence of Bluetooth. He has found the last two years to be the most challenging time yet in his career, as he first grappled with the specification, pulled together a team, defined a system architecture, and then implemented a complete Bluetooth Baseband design from scratch in a very short space of time. Currently, Charles is responsible for the ongoing business and roadmap development of TTPCom's Bluetooth silicon programme.

When not working, Charles likes to divide his time between his partner, Heather, the garden, and the odd skiing trip. Time permitting, photography is his favourite pastime, as illustrated by the front cover of "Connect".